# COMPARATIVE SOCIALIST SYSTEMS

# COMPARATIVE SOCIALIST SYSTEMS: ESSAYS ON POLITICS AND ECONOMICS

CARMELO MESA-LAGO
and CARL BECK
Editors

University of Pittsburgh Center for International Studies
Pittsburgh
1975

International Standard Book Number 0-916002-01-2
Printed in the United States of America

Additional copies are available from:
UCIS/Publications
G-6 Mervis Hall
University of Pittsburgh
Pittsburgh, PA 15260
(Discounts available for orders in bulk)

# CONTENTS

## IV. *SUMMARY*

# LIST OF FIGURES

*Chapter 7*



*Chapter 9*



*Chapter 11*

# LIST OF TABLES

*Chapter 13*



*Chapter 14*



Appendix

# PREFACE

Until the 1960s we lacked comparative studies of socialist (communist) systems because the field was basically dominated by the study of the Soviet Union. This was determined by the uniformity of the Soviet "model" throughout the socialist world. With Stalin's death, and the Yugoslav and Chinese splits, multiplicity made its appearance and the monopoly began to crack. The trend towards diversity accelerated in the 1960s as a result of Eastern European economic reforms and the establishment of socialism in Cuba. At the same time there was an increase of the information available and of specialists from various disciplines (mostly political scientists, economists, sociologists) trained in specific socialist countries. These events resulted in a proportional decline of studies dealing with the USSR in a global sense and in a parallel increase of specialized monographs of specific aspects of the Soviet system. More significantly, a rising number of studies which were increasingly sophisticated dealt with other socialist countries or compared two or more socialist systems.

The first truly comparative studies of socialist systems attempting to combine various disciplines and develop the methodology for comparison appeared in the late 1960s and early 1970s. However, these studies still relied heavily on one discipline (e.g., political science, economics), and dealt mostly with theoretical comparisons and, in the majority of cases, concentrated on Eastern Europe.

This volume attempts to advance the methodology to compare socialist systems by combining both theoretical approaches and empirical comparisons in a multidisciplinary and systematic fashion. In addition, an effort is made to include most socialist countries in the various studies. This is not to say, however, that Soviet predominance has been overcome. Out of the sixteen contributions to the volume, all but two include the USSR; all of them also refer to Eastern Europe, but in four cases exclude Albania and Yugoslavia. Only six contributions include China in the comparison, and five include Cuba. None of the contributions deal with North Vietnam, North Korea, or Mongolia. In spite of these omissions we feel that this volume has achieved a true comparative perspective and broken new ground in the field.

The book is divided into four major sections. The first deals with abstract-theoretical comparisons by using classification schemes, typoligies, taxonomies, or spectra. It opens with Shoup's research inventory and analysis of indicators of social and political development generated in the USSR and Eastern Europe which provide a solid basis for future comparisons. Next is Montias' universal classification of socialist economic systems and Welsh's socio-political-economic classification of Soviet and Eastern European systems. The first section closes with Mesa-Lago's attempt to both substitute a continuum model for types and a multidisciplinary approach for a unidisciplinary comparison.

The second section is devoted to comparisons of the political system. Beck discusses a diversity in the contemporary political systems of Eastern Europe. Dunn develops a conceptual framework for comparing organizations in socialist systems (applying it to China, Cuba, and Yugoslavia) and analyzes interrelations between organizational, socio-political, and technological variables. Korbonski measures the level of liberalization in Czechoslovakia, Poland, and Hungary by ranking three major variables and develops a liberalization paradigm. Cocks reviews three categories of control used by socialist regimes —ethics, rationality, and terror—in light of the Soviet experience, but also in a comparative context within Eastern Europe and with China. Triska and Johnson apply to the USSR and all Eastern Europe both cross-national "political development" and "political change" analyses and evaluate the usefulness of both approaches. Closing this section, Fleron explores the relationship between technological change and the communist culture-transforming process touching on the Soviet, Chinese, and Cuban cases.

The third section concentrates on the economic angle of socialist systems. Gomulka and Wiles address themselves to the problem of realism of five-year plans in socialist countries and design a methodology to test and apply them to the USSR and Poland. Pryor compares in a quantitative fashion, primarily in Eastern Europe, a number of features of the socialist industrial organization at three levels: local enterprises and agencies, intermediate with excellence the professional copy editing. rights, managerial powers, and incentives in socialist economies, drawing examples from the USSR, Eastern Europe, China, and Cuba. Marer examines foreign trade statistics of the seven countries that belonged to CEMA in 1960-72 and focuses on three major problems: reconciliation between Eastern and Western trade data, bilateralism versus multilateralism in East-West trade, and the use of surpluses generated by CEMA-developed countries from LDCs for financing imports from the West. To conclude the section, Wilczynski evaluates the level of development achieved in cybernation and automation by the European CEMA countries and examines the extent to which such developments can contribute to the evolution from socialism to communism.

In the fourth and final section, Hollander provides a summary and integration of the major findings of the volume and explores the future of both socialist systems and the field.

The book is one product of the Comparative Communism Program of Pittsburgh whose chairman is Professor Beck. In 1967, the five major institutions of higher learning of the city (Carlow College, Carnegie-Mellon University, Chatham College, Duquesne University, and the University of Pittsburgh) combined their resources to establish a consortium for teaching, lectures, and research on comparative socialist systems. Grants from the Pittsburgh Foundation and the Carnegie Corporation of New York helped establish and expand the program, which has sponsored several seminars and public lecture series, among them: "Comparative Communist Political Leadership" (1967-71); "Comparative Communist Economic Systems" (1968-70); and "Particularism and Universalism in Communist Development" (1968-70).

In 1972-73, the Comparative Communism Program sponsored its fourth public lecture series, organized by Professor Mesa-Lago, on "Methodological Comparison of Socialist Systems." Two dozen specialists from North America, Western and Eastern Europe, and Oceania presented or wrote original papers for the series. Previous commitments precluded four of the participants (Professors Morris, Borstein, Branko Horvat, Frank Parkin, and Jan Szczepanski) from making their papers available for this volume. The end product of the series is the sixteen essays of this book. Practically all of them are published here for the first time with a few in a substantially modified and improved format.

The editors want to express their gratitude to the Pittsburgh Foundation whose financial support made this enterprise possible. The following people from the University of Pittsburgh provided significant help to the project in its various stages: Rose Mary Pease arranged most administrative and social aspects of the lecture series assisted by Carol Zinsser; June Belkin and Stella Saurer handled respectively part of the publicity and correspondence of the series; Shirley Kregar, Gertrude Whitman, and Carolyn Wilson handled the copious correspondence dealing with the book; and Professors Zdenek Suda and Thomas McKechnie respectively helped in the invitation of some speakers and in the organization of the lecture series.

C.B. C.M.L.

PART ONE

# INDICATORS, TYPES AND MODELS FOR COMPARISON

# 1

# Indicators of Socio–Politico–Economic Development

Paul S. Shoup

The purpose of this paper is to discuss literature appearing in Eastern Europe and the Soviet Union which bears on the measurement of social and political phenomena. Our focus is on those studies which provide basic data on levels of development, the standard of living, and regional differences within countries of the area, and on political research which contains empirical data relevant to the problem of political development or change.

There are a number of limitations to the scope of this discussion, of which the reader should be aware. First, of the many studies which have appeared in Eastern Europe and the Soviet Union on the topic of social change, only those which are felt to be most relevant to the question of making comparisons of levels of development are cited here. The vast "information explosion" which has taken place in Eastern Europe and the Soviet Union in the field of the social sciences is, therefore, only partially recorded here.

Secondly, the works of Western authors who have dealt with the problem of comparing levels of development of these systems, while they are brought into the analysis at various points, are not stressed. This permits us to focus on Eastern European and Soviet materials. Comparative data from Western and United Nations sources will be used mainly to give the reader a better picture of the overall availability and compatibility of statistics dealing with social and political development in the area than could be gotten from Soviet and Eastern European data alone.

Finally, we have chosen to reproduce certain statistical tables and brief observations on the data. (The reader is invited to make comparisons among the tables in order to judge for himself the extent to which there is agreement among various sources on degrees of change and levels of development in Eastern Europe and the Soviet Union.) But our discussion will focus on the sources of the data, the comparability of statistics in the various areas with which we are dealing, and the problem of relating social and political measurement in research on Eastern Europe and the Soviet Union.

Several general observations are called for on the nature of the problem to which we are addressing ourselves, prior to an examination of the Eastern European and Soviet materials. We may note first the difficulties that arise in attempting to quantify social and political phenomena, and then establish a relationship between them. These difficulties have several sources: the imbalance that exists in respect to the amount and precision of data that can be gathered on political, as contrasted to social, phenomena; the danger that political development will be seen primarily as the product of social change, in part because the data on the latter subject are more plentiful and more precise; and the temptation to focus on certain aspects of social and political development just because they are quantifiable, without considering the relevance of these data to the underlying forces shaping the social and political systems under investigation. The last mentioned difficulty, it should be noted, is particularly evident in respect to the measurement of political phenomena. We are already in possession of a not inconsiderable amount of quantitative data on the political systems of Eastern Europe and the Soviet Union whose exact relevance for political development is still open to challenge.[1]

We must also explain briefly the meaning of social and political change as discussed here. This account will refer frequently to social and economic "development." What this implies in respect to the political system will be discussed below. Development, in the context of social change, is normally taken to mean economic growth, and we shall follow this usual practice in referring to development in the pages to follow, noting sources in Eastern European and Soviet literature which have been concerned with problems of national income analysis, standards of living, and related problems. At the same time, it is clear that social development means something far broader and more complex than economic growth alone. For one thing, the term "development," as used in the literature on the subject published by the UN and other international agencies, refers to that stage of economic and social change in which societies begin to lift themselves out of a condition of backwardness. We shall have occasion to note, in the account that follows, that the measurement of social change in Eastern Europe and the Soviet Union has focused primarily on recording changes of this nature—that is, of the gains made in escaping backwardness. The development of a social system need not be limited to indices of progress of this type, however. Social change, and therefore social development, may be considered in its broadest sense as the natural pattern of evolution which a society follows, resulting from factors such as changes in the pattern of social stratification, demographic trends, the alteration of cultural values, and so forth. A complex model of measuring social change would wish to take all these factors into account. This would seem especially pertinent in the case of social systems which, like those of Eastern Europe and the Soviet Union, have passed through a revolutionary phase; one might anticipate that patterns of social change and development would reflect this experience over a longer period of time, perhaps hastening patterns of change set in motion by the process of modernization, but also working in ways contrary to the modernization experience.

Unfortunately, the very complexity of the phenomena to which we are referring forces us to limit our discussion to the investigation of the process of development in the narrower sense utilized by economists and international agencies—that is, to changes in indices of progress, as well as to some structural indices of development.[2] There is a need to work with these indices so that they may become more comparable, and so that our analysis of political development will be based on truly comparative data. Thus there is every justification for limiting the discussion in the fashion we are doing here. At the same time it must be borne in mind that the problems that arise in relating social and political development are not confined to this one area alone. Indeed, our account will seek to emphasize the importance of moving beyond the measurement of development *per se* if relationships between social and political phenomena are to be understood.

Any account which deals with data from Eastern Europe and the Soviet Union faces the task of warning the unwary reader against the use of deceptive statistics, and at the same time overcoming the credibility gap that has given rise to the belief that statistical reporting in the area is deeply suspect and basically unsound. The truth is that through the work of individual scholars, and as a result of the desire of governments to make basic statistics available for planning purposes, a fund of reliable data has been created in a very short time on which it is possible to draw for the purpose of making comparisons, at least as far as the majority of the Eastern European nations are concerned.

There are, however, important exceptions to this rule, which we shall mention briefly. First, of course, is the difference that exists between the quality of statistics in most countries of Eastern Europe and in the Soviet Union. The Soviet Union lags far behind most of the Eastern European states in respect to the quantity and quality of data published. This gap is to some extent made up by the publications of individual scholars in the Soviet Union whose works are cited below, and thanks to whom data otherwise not available find the light of day. It should be borne in mind, nevertheless, that these are not *official* data (although presumably they are based on some official source). Thus figures published by one individual need not correspond to those given by another. This differs from the situation in most Eastern European countries, where official sources of data are cited in a routine fashion by scholars and where such sources may be checked by the reader with relative ease. (This is not true, however, in respect to political data. Not infrequently this type of information, when published by Eastern European scholars, comes from sources with limited circulation.)

Among Eastern European materials, those in the Polish, Czech, and Yugoslav languages predominate. The lack of reference to Hungarian sources in this paper is a gap of which the reader should be aware; some English-language materials dealing with Hungary are cited, but they only scratch the surface. Rumanian materials are also left out of the discussion, but here the omission is less important. Statistical studies originating in Rumania have not been as comprehensive or informative as those from the other Eastern European countries discussed here.

It should be kept in mind throughout that the discussion is designed only to introduce a complex and very broad subject (as well as one not studied in a methodical way up until now). No claim for comprehensiveness is made. Data are given to illustrate the nature of the difficulties that arise when making comparisons, and the kind of approach taken toward these problems in Eastern European and Soviet materials, rather than with the purpose of establishing a set of indices on which definitive measurements of social and political development can be based. This latter task remains to be undertaken and—as will become quickly apparent—faces many obstacles before it can be carried through to completion.

We also wish to remind the reader of the broader context in which this largely methodological discussion takes place. Eastern Europe and the Soviet Union have passed through a period of unprecedented economic, social, and political change in the course of the past two decades. The significance of this experience has been the subject of intense debate in these countries. Some see the industrialization and social transformation of the post-war years as a step toward creating a society freed of the restraints of backwardness and poverty, in which the goal of the revolution—to build a society around the working class—can finally be realized. Others interpret the changes of the past two decades as a sign that Eastern Europe and the Soviet Union are passing through a period similar to the early stages of industrialization in the West. Such persons tend to assume that the ultimate outcome of political and social development will be the modification of both the political and social systems of the countries in the area to accommodate a more complex stage of development, characterized by greater political freedoms, the free play of interest groups, and the like. There is also a vein of pessimism in the writings of some Eastern Europeans. These feelings originate with persons who have in one form or another expressed the fear that the societies of Eastern Europe are not losing their conservative bureaucratic and parochial traits *fast enough*, or that they are demonstrating a high degree of vulnerability to centrifugal pressures and may become (if not already) "conflict societies."

All of these theories bear directly on the question of social and political development in Eastern Europe, and invite the use of data and comparative techniques. We have avoided the temptation to become involved in these discussions in order to focus on the sources of the data. Still, it is interest in these larger political questions which provides the ultimate justification for gathering and comparing data, and which in many instances has prompted the undertaking of empirical research. Thus, although the issues raised by the great debate over the future development of Eastern Europe and the Soviet Union are not directly mentioned here, they form the ever-present and inescapable backdrop against which our discussion takes place.

We may now turn to the discussion of social and political development indices, focusing initially on the former of these two categories. As indicated above, a choice arises between developmental indicators, and those of a structural character. We shall concern ourselves with two types of developmental indicators and two of a structural nature. In the first category we include measurements of national income and the standard of living; in the second, changes in the composition of the labor force and the analysis of regional differences. In the study of regional differences we are concerned with literature in which problems of income, the size of the labor force, and, broadly speaking, economic development, play a part—that is, with problems which are already examined at the national level in connection with other topics.

All of these indices, it should be noted, serve multiple purposes. They are for the most part indicators of economic development, and therefore the domain of the economist. At the same time, they are measures of systemic change, and therefore provide the baseline against which other dimensions of change can be measured—and for this reason are of special interest to us. For the economist, there will be a number of special considerations related specifically to the problems of economic analysis which will determine his reaction to and his use of such indicators. For those interested in the broader problem of social change and in the comparative analysis of social and political development, a number of factors—not purely economic in nature— will be of importance. Thus, one will wish to ask: how well does a given indicator reflect the essence of the quality of change being measured? How well does it correlate with other indicators? What function does it best serve: to distinguish among levels of development, or to suggest structural changes taking place in a society? Last, but certainly not least, there is the question, can it be compared?

Among the indices chosen here, national income is among the most important and most widely discussed. It provides a synthetic indicator which allows countries to be scaled according to levels of economic development, and thus, in a very crude way, by levels of "development" generally. If not measured by per capita, but simply in gross terms, it also provides a measure of economic power. Kuznets and others have, on occasion, pointed to the importance of this measure for the non-economist. On the other hand, national income is not necessarily well correlated with other indicators of social change at early stages of the development process,[3] and is a poor indicator of the structure of social systems, or of changes therein. (This point is frequently brought up in connection with discussions of the standard of living, as we shall see shortly.) Finally, there seems to be some disagreement among the Eastern European and Soviet scholars themselves over the question of whether indicators of national income tend to exaggerate, or to lessen, differences among nations or among regions as compared to other types of indicators. We shall return to this problem again in the course of the discussion.

The difficulties that arise when one uses national income as a comparative index of development in respect to Eastern Europe and the Soviet Union are two fold, disregarding for the moment the broader problem of whether national income is the best measure of systemic change in a society. These difficulties may be characterized as conceptual and structural. The conceptual problem arises because national income is defined as encompassing only the "productive" sector of the economy; the structural problem from the lack of a system of meaningful prices which would permit the national income of one country to be compared with the national income of another. Both of these issues have been thoroughly discussed in Western literature, and have now been quite extensively examined in the works of Eastern European and Soviet economists (the reader is referred to works cited below). The use of the material product concept has been criticized on a number of occasions by Eastern European and Soviet economists,[4] and is now, in the words of Abram Bergson, "in the process of erosion."[5]

There are also certain difficulties in respect to the terminology employed in discussing national income. While these pose no problem to the economist, they may be a source of confusion to the political scientist or sociologist interested in utilizing data from Eastern European or Soviet sources. Net Material Product (NMP) is used by Western economists when describing what appears in Eastern European and Soviet statistics under the designation "national income." Western data, on the other hand, are generally given in terms of GNP–Gross National Product. In contradistinction to NMP, GNP includes services as part of national income. UN data, which we also cite as a useful guide to levels of development in Eastern Europe and the Soviet Union, often refer to GDP–Gross Domestic Product, or to GNP net of the balance of exports over imports. The non-economist will also find it helpful to keep in mind that NMP is a measure of national income *after* depreciation has been removed from the value of output. Eastern European and Soviet data also include figures for Gross Social Product and, in certain cases, "social product." Both differ from "national income" by virtue of the fact that they include depreciation costs. The former figure is not much used, and inflates national income by counting the total value of output at every stage of the manufacturing process.[6]

Subject to certain reservations given below, the use of NMP as a means of rank-ordering countries by level of development does not seem to produce results greatly different from those obtained when GNP is employed. At the same time, it must be borne in mind that rank-ordering—examples of which are given in the tables, and will be discussed shortly—is a rather crude exercise which may allow for a good deal of margin of error in respect to the kind of data being compared, and that great difficulties accompany *any* effort to compare absolute levels of GNP in Eastern Europe and the Soviet Union due to the pricing problems mentioned earlier. Also, differences exist among Eastern European countries, and between them and the Soviet Union, over what properly belongs within the "material," or "productive," sphere. These differences are of more than passing interest, even for the individual not concerned with the technical aspects of comparing national income data, because they re-appear in other types of data (for example, those dealing with the labor force), and reveal certain national biases. Thus, for example, Yugoslavia includes the hotel industry as part of the productive sector, undoubtedly because of the importance of her tourist industry, while other Eastern European countries and the Soviet Union do not.[7]

Soviet and Eastern European literature on the problem of how to utilize national income data is now extensive, and may be consulted with profit by the non-economist interested in understanding not only the methodological issues that arise in this area, but the assumptions that lie behind the measurement of national income, the evaluation of its utility as a measure of development (as contrasted, for example, to measures of the standard of living), and the significance of national income differences in the context of the overall development of the region.[8]

Data on absolute levels of national income given in Western European and Eastern European/Soviet sources can be found in Tables1 through 4, which also show how different sources, and the choice of different years, can influence the rank-ordering of the countries of the area when national income is used as a guide. The data are in agreement with the fact that the Soviet Union improved her position *vis-à-vis* the countries of Eastern Europe in the 1960s in terms of per capita national income. The Soviet figures (see Table 1) show a dramatic change in the position of Bulgaria—from next to last in 1950 to a position above that of Poland and Rumania in 1969—which is startling and at odds with Western sources. It should be emphasized that the comparison made in Table 1 is in *Soviet* prices, which may account for the discrepancies with Western measures.

Table 1

*Zhelev Data: National Income (NMP) Per Capita, 1950 and 1959*
(Index Numbers. USSR = 100. Calculated in Soviet Prices)

| | *1950* | | | *1969* | | |
|---|---|---|---|---|---|---|
| | National Income | Industrial Production | Agricultural Production | National Income | Industrial Production | Agricultural Production |
| Czechoslovkia | 157 | 151 | 110 | 113 | 123 | 76 |
| GDR | 112 | 131 | 99 | 135 | 167 | 138 |
| Hungary | 114 | 77 | 138 | 82 | 74 | 110 |
| USSR | 100 | 100 | 100 | 100 | 100 | 100 |
| Poland | 103 | 185 | 185 | 76 | 79 | 113 |
| Bulgaria | 66 | 97 | 97 | 85 | 80 | 161 |
| Rumania | 56 | 77 | 77 | 69 | 52 | 98 |

Source: G. E. Zhelev, *Problemy vosproizvodstva i mezhdunarodnogo razdeleniya truda v stranakh-chlenakh SEV* (Moscow, 1971), p. 145.

Table 2

*Ernst Data: GNP Per Capita, 1964 and 1967*
(in Dollars)

| | *1964* | *1967* |
|---|---|---|
| Czechoslovakia | 1,280 | 1,600 |
| GDR | 1,220 | 1,480 |
| Hungary | 880 | 1,080 |
| Poland | 770 | 920 |
| Bulgaria | 600 | 870 |
| Rumania | 590 | 840 |

Source: Joint Economic Committee, U.S. Congress, *New Directions in the Soviet Economy*, Part IV, p. 877. For 1967, see Joint Economic Committee, *Economic Developments in Countries of Eastern Europe*, p. 49.

We shall not attempt to pass judgment on these data as a measure of development of the nations of Eastern Europe and the Soviet Union at this time, except to point out that, in contradistinction to data on industrial output utilized in the past by the countries of Eastern Europe and the Soviet Union (and presented in Table 1) and data on the standard of living (to be discussed below), per capita national income "exaggerates" differences while at the same time showing a large industrial nation such as the Soviet Union in a relatively favorable light. On the other hand, national income remains the only synthetic indicator of development which provides a way of measuring absolute differences among the countries of the area.

Table 3

*UN Data: 1963 "Average" Prices, Per Capita GDP*
(Index Numbers. USSR =100)

| | *1950* | *1967* | *1965* |
|---|---|---|---|
| Czechoslovakia | 698 | 1,421 | 136 |
| GDR | 553 | 1,476 | 136 |
| Hungary | 475 | 984 | 96 |
| Poland | 449 | 961 | 94 |
| USSR | 417 | 1,104 | 100 |
| Bulgaria | 312 | 917 | 83 |
| Rumania | 243 | 723 | 66 |
| Yugoslavia | – | – | 66 |

Source: Economic Commission for Europe, *Economic Survey of Europe in 1969*, Part I, p. 9. For 1965 data, p. 144.

Table 4

*Pryor Data: GNP, 1956 and 1962*
(USA in 1956 = 100)

| | *1956* | *1962* |
|---|---|---|
| USA | 100 | 107 |
| GDR | 50 | 67 |
| Czechoslovakia | 50 | 67 |
| USSR | 38 | 50 |
| Italy | 36 | 51 |
| Hungary | 35 | 47 |
| Poland | 32 | 40 |
| Rumania | 22 | 34 |
| Bulgaria | 21 | 33 |
| Yugoslavia | 18 | 27 |

Source: Frederick Pryor, *Public Expenditures in Communist and Capitalist Nations*, p. 401.

Great difficulties arise in making comparative assessments of the standard of living in Eastern Europe and the Soviet Union. The problems are well known, and result from differing approaches to the way in which personal income is calculated, the impossibility of measuring qualitative differences of goods made available to the consumer, and the problems that arise in measuring overall levels of income or consumption in comparable prices. In addition, it can be noted that the discussion of the standard of living involves a great deal of subjective judgment concerning those qualities which make for a better life. In debates in international organizations it has proven extremely difficult to gain agreement over what should be included in indices of living "levels." In the course of these debates, differences have emerged between the Soviet and Eastern European position and that of the Western countries over the emphasis that should be placed on international comparisons. The Soviet position, supported by most Eastern European countries, has stressed the importance of measuring differences within societies as a way of determining living standards, rather than what they term "averages" contained in international statistics.[9]

Notwithstanding these difficulties, the subject of living standards has a great fascination for scholars (and for the popular press) in Eastern Europe and the Soviet Union. Comparative studies of living standards in Poland and Austria and in Hungary and Great Britain have been carried out, providing the basic methodology for comparative analysis of the problem of living standards within the area.[10] Comecon has also been active in initiating studies within Eastern Europe, although the results are disappointing in terms of published data.[11] For quite some time it has been the practice in Eastern Europe to publish figures comparing countries with respect to the stock of consumer goods, the amount of housing, the quality of diets, and so forth. These data, despite their shortcomings, give a picture of changing consumption habits in the region, and to a certain extent enable one to judge not only relative standards of living, but degrees of difference among the Eastern European states, and between them and the Soviet Union. (Most national statistical handbooks have international sections containing figures of this kind; the Comecon statistical handbook is also an excellent source for such data.)

There is also a growing body of methodological literature of high quality in which the theoretical problems encountered in making comparisions of living standards are examined. The reader is referred in this connection to the works of Mód, Nedorezova, Manz, and Kreczkowska,[12] as well to studies of the standard of living in individual countries by Berislav Šefer and others.[13]

If one wishes to compare the countries of Eastern Europe and the Soviet Union in terms of absolute differences in the standard of living, there is less material from which to choose. This is partly because of the inherent difficulties of the task and partly, it seems, because national governments are reluctant to see such comparisons published. One common approach, utilized both for comparisons of living standards among the countries of the area as well as at the regional level, is to measure the value of trade carried on by retail outlets.[14] This measure correlates fairly well with other indicators of development at the regional level in the Soviet Union, and in international comparisons carried out among the Eastern European countries,[15] but does pose the danger of double counting,[16] and is usually not considered *in isolation* as a reliable indicator of the standard of living when making comparisons. A second method, that of comparing the material consumption funds[17] of each of the Comecon countries, was attempted in the mid-1960s. The results, given in Table 5, reflect an attempt to make corrections for the different price systems of the countries of the area through an exchange rate derived from the cost of a "market basket" selection of consumer goods (in this case in Poland and the Soviet Union). These may be compared to the estimates of Ernst (Table 6), also for the 1950s and the mid-1960s. Both sources exclude Yugoslavia while Ernst deals only with Czechoslovakia, the German Democratic Republic, Hungary, and Poland. As we have remarked, the Soviet Union appears less advanced on the basis of these data than when the standard of national income per capita is employed; differences among the Eastern European nations, and between the Eastern European nations and the Soviet Union, also appear less. Table 7 gives total consumption per capita, and includes Yugoslavia. This concept of consumption, in contrast to that just used above, includes expenditures for administration and defense and is therefore not an accurate measure of the standard of living. It does, however, give another rough estimate of the income at the disposal of the country net of investments, and may be used for purposes of rank-ordering as is done here.

We have noted that in the theoretical literature, and in debates in the United Nations, the Eastern European and Soviet position has stressed the need to take into consideration differences within countries, as well as "average" living standards. This same literature also distinguishes between levels of living and "living conditions" (usloviya zhizni; "Lebenslage"), including in the latter such factors as levels of unemployment. In actual practice, neither of these concepts seems to have been applied to any great extent in measuring living standards in Eastern Europe and the Soviet Union. The problem of class differences in respect to living standards is in fact treated with a great deal of caution in the literature. (It is not uncommon, however, to find discussions of differences in living standards between the rural and urban population.) Although it is not directly utilizable for purposes of comparing levels of development, the reader is referred to a growing body of literature in Eastern Europe which deals, directly or indirectly, with differences of levels of living within the population ((regional differences will be discussed below).[18]

Changes in the composition of the labor force constitute what we have referred to earlier as a "structural" measure of social change, one which is closely associated with the development process but is not in itself a direct measure of the welfare of the population. Two aspects of changes of this type may be singled out for discussion here: the shift from agricultural to non-agricultural pursuits, and the increase of persons employed in tertiary sectors of economic activity at a more advanced stage of development.

### Table 5

*Kotkovskii Index: Per Capita Material Consumption, 1963*
(USSR = 100)

| | |
|---|---|
| GDR | 150 |
| Czechoslovakia | 138 |
| Hungary | 110 |
| Poland | 106 |
| USSR | 100 |
| Bulgaria | 99 |

Source: Kotkovskii, *Sopostavlenie urovney ekonomicheskogo razvitiya sotsialisticheskikh stran* (Moscow, 1965), p. 207.

### Table 6

*Ernst Index: Per Capita Personal Consumption, 1950, 1955, 1960 and 1964*
(Federal Republic of Germany = 100)

| | *1950* | *1955* | *1960* | *1964* |
|---|---|---|---|---|
| West Germany | 100 | 100 | 100 | 100 |
| Austria | 100 | 79 | 78 | 79 |
| Czechoslovakia | 100 | 71 | 63 | 57 |
| Hungary | 69 | 52 | 49 | 48 |
| Poland | 60 | 48 | 42 | 40 |
| GDR | 54 | 68 | 68 | 60 |

Source: *New Directions in the Soviet Economy,* op. cit., p. 887.

### Table 7

*Total Consumption Per Capita, Calculated from Estimates of GDP, 1965*

| | |
|---|---|
| GDR | 146 |
| Czechoslovakia | 143 |
| Hungary | 109 |
| Soviet Union | 100 |
| Poland | 99 |
| Bulgaria | 87 |
| Yugoslavia | 73 |
| Rumania | 71 |

Source: *Economic Survey of Europe,* op. cit., p. 344.

The shift of the labor force from agricultural to non-agricultural occupations is a change associated with the early stages of development. Research on development indicators in non-communist countries suggests that the decline in the labor force employed in agriculture correlates highly—in fact, more so than any other indicator—with other indices of development, both social and economic.[19] By the same token a country which still retains a sizable proportion of its population in the agricultural sector is commonly considered to fall into the category of "lesser-developed."

These facts are recognized by the Eastern Europeans, and changes in the size of the agricultural population in these countries are considered an important indicator of social change and economic development (often this will be expressed as a ratio of the agricultural population to the population engaged in industry). Comparisons of the percent of the population employed in agriculture in two countries in Eastern Europe (for example, Poland and Czechoslovakia) are not uncommon. There are far fewer data in Eastern European sources in which a number of countries—or the area as a whole—are compared, however. There are several possible explanations for this: Soviet practice, followed in a number of the East European states, is to give data on the *rural* population, and to make international comparisons using this standard. Also, it is difficult to determine which part of the economically active population belongs to the agricultural labor force in those countries with collectivized agriculture because not all collective farmers are in agriculture, and not all those who engage in agricultural activity are members of the collective farms. In Yugoslavia and Poland, on the other hand, accurate information on the size of the agricultural population can be gained only from census data. Although census results can be used for determining the size of the agricultural population, corrections must be made in order to account for differences in definitions of the agricultural labor force, both among the Eastern European countries, and in the same country over time.

These problems make the calculations of the agricultural population of Eastern Europe and the Soviet Union in comparable terms a difficult task, but not an impossible one. If such data exist in Eastern European and Soviet sources, however, they are not readily available. Discussions of the labor force in Eastern Europe do not, to the best of this writer's knowledge, contain comparable data of this type based on Eastern European or Soviet calculations in which all the necessary corrections have been made to take into account private agriculture, different approaches to counting the agricultural labor force in Eastern European and Soviet statistics, and so forth.

In Table 8 we have, therefore, presented Western statistics on the agricultural labor force in Eastern Europe and the Soviet Union. It will be noted that the ranking of the countries of the area by this means gives results basically the same as those cited earlier. The Soviet Union, which shows the greatest tendency to shift position according to the measure being employed, in this case falls into a category which includes Poland and Hungary—the middle group of Eastern European nations.

### Table 8

*Percent of the Economically Active Population in Agriculture, 1950, 1967 and 1968*

| | JEC Estimates | | UN Estimates | |
|---|---|---|---|---|
| | *1950* | *1968* | *1950* | *1967* |
| GDR | 24.4 | 14.9 | 21.8 | 15.3 |
| Czechoslovakia | 37.7 | 19.7 | 38.6 | 19.9 |
| Hungary | 48.4 | 29.2 | 50.1 | 30.0 |
| Poland | 55.9 | 38.2 | 56.5 | 41.7 |
| Rumania | 71.2 | 55.6 | 73.5 | 54.6 |
| Bulgaria | 72.5 | 42.0 | 69.7 | 41.0 |
| USSR | – | – | 48.8 | 30.5 |

Source: *Economic Developments in the Countries of Eastern Europe,* op. cit., p. 216; Economic Commission for Europe, op. cit., p. 18.

Eastern European social scientists have on several occasions shown greatest interest in the theory that the tertiary sector of the economy tends to predominate in mature industrial societies. Antoni Rajkiewicz, a leading Polish labor economist, has investigated this trend in respect to Poland in the early 1960s;[20] Radovan Richta and other Czech social scientists stressed the importance of this development in works devoted to the future development of the Czech economy and society written in the mid-1960s.[21] Rajkiewicz called this anticipated transformation of the economy the stage of "servicization" (*serwicyzacja*); the Richta group alluded to the emergence in Czechoslovakia of a "tertiary civilization," or "services civilization."

These discussions have helped lay the groundwork for the comparative study of changes in the structure of the labor force of Eastern Europe utilizing the concepts of primary, secondary, and tertiary activities employed in the West. A number of Eastern European countries now follow international standards in reporting labor force data, permitting the analyst to make comparisons along the lines under consideration here.[22]

At the same time the *principal* method of distinguishing among sectors of the labor force in Eastern Europe and the Soviet Union remains, as in the past, the concept of the material, or productive, sectors and the non-material, or service, sectors of the economy. Labor force data presented in this fashion differ from that given in the West in several ways: they do not distinguish a "primary" sector (as noted above, difficulties in connection with the presentation of statistics on the size of the agricultural labor force in Eastern Europe and the Soviet Union make it hard to isolate this sector from other material sectors of the economy); they follow an "activity" concept in classifying the labor force, which entails placing certain groups in the sphere of non-material production even though they are employed by industries or enterprises engaged in agricultural or industrial activity; they do not, finally, make the same distinction between services and industry used in Western statistics (the labor force in transport and commerce, in Eastern European and Soviet practice, is generally considered part of the productive, or material, sector; in labor force statistics of the International Labor Organization and generally in the West these two types of activity are included in the tertiary, or services, sector).

Dogmatic resistance to classifying sectors of the economy in any way other than that just described is weakening. Soviet writers now accept the fact that as their society advances into a more mature stage of industrialization, the service sector of the economy can be expected to grow more rapidly than the industrial sector. Soviet writers who have discussed the problem, such as A. D. Kuznetsov,[23] are nevertheless clearly opposed to the notion that the working class will one day be transformed totally or in part into white collar employees engaged in service-type activities. Nor do these authors attempt to compare changes in the structure of the labor force in any way other than that based on the distinction between the productive and non-productive sectors of the economy.

Regional comparisons of changes in the structure of the labor force in Eastern European and Soviet sources leave a great deal to be desired. The studies of Rajkiewicz, Richta, and Bošnjović (to cite three examples), although they urge adoption of the three-fold division of the labor force developed in the West, present only fragmentary data on the Eastern European countries in which this approach is utilized; for this reason we have not reproduced any of their comparisons here. For purposes of comparing trends in the material and non-material sectors of the economy we present, in Table 9, UN data (compiled, of course, from East European and Soviet statistics). In Table 10, we give statistics on primary, secondary, and tertiary labor force distribution for selected Eastern European countries in the 1960s based on census data reported to the ILO. Although it is not our intention to comment on the tables at great length, it may be noted that the breakdown according to the material and non-material sectors, while it does show a growth of the latter category, does not discriminate very successfully between levels of development in Eastern Europe and the Soviet Union, and in at least one case (that of Hungary) shows a trend which is the reverse of that which might be normally expected—that is, an increase of the labor force in the productive sector. In general, the data on the labor force classified by Western methods show that while the tertiary sector has grown rapidly, the distinguishing feature of the period of the 1950s and 1960s in Eastern Europe has been the expansion of the industrial working force. Census data from Hungary for 1960 and 1970 suggest that this remained true throughout the 1960s—i.e., that the anticipated shift from the industrial and agricultural labor force into the services sector has not yet taken place in *major* proportions.

Table 9

*UN Data on Distribution of Employment by Material and Non-Material Sectors, 1950 and 1967*

| | *1950* | *1967* |
|---|---|---|
| Bulgaria | | |
| Material Sectors | 91.1 | 86.9 |
| Non-material Sectors | 8.9 | 13.1 |
| Czechoslovakia | | |
| Material Sectors | 88.7 | 81.8 |
| Non-material Sectors | 11.3 | 18.2 |
| GDR | | |
| Material Sectors | 86.8 | 81.6 |
| Non-material Sectors | 13.2 | 18.4 |
| Hungary | | |
| Material Sectors | 83.4 | 82.6 |
| Non-material Sectors | 16.6 | 17.4 |
| Poland | | |
| Material Sectors | 89.4 | 85.6 |
| Non-material Sectors | 10.6 | 14.4 |
| Rumania | | |
| Material Sectors | 93.6 | 89.8 |
| Non-material Sectors | 6.4 | 10.2 |
| USSR | | |
| Material Sectors | 87.8 | 82.4 |
| Non-material Sectors | 12.2 | 17.6 |

Source: *Economic Commission for Europe*, op. cit., Part I, p. 18.

Table 10

*ILO Data on Percentage Distribution of Economically Active Population by Primary, Secondary, and Tertiary Activities*

| | *Primary in %* | *Secondary in %* | *Tertiary in %* |
|---|---|---|---|
| Bulgaria (1965) | 44.1 | 33.7 | 22.2* |
| Czechoslovakia (1961) | 24.9 | 47.1 | 28.0* |
| Hungary | | | |
| 1960 | 38.4 | 35.0 | 26.6* |
| 1970 | 24.6 | 45.1 | 30.3* |

Source: ILO, *Yearbook of Labor Statistics, 1971.*
*Includes non-classifiable groups.

The comparison of regions within the countries of Eastern Europe and the Soviet Union is the last area we shall consider in this account of developmental data. As we have noted earlier, comparisons of this type embrace all aspects of the developmental problem treated so far in addition to involving certain special problems not present in international comparisons.

The material available in respect to regional problems in Eastern Europe and the Soviet Union is extensive,[24] and the comparisons that are made at this level reveal a great deal about the overall stage of development of the countries in question, as well as giving valuable information on the problems of backwardness characteristic of the more underdeveloped regions. The work of Kosta Mihailović on underdeveloped regions in Eastern Europe and Yugoslavia,[25] the comparisons of economic growth and social change in Slovakia and the Czech lands by Radoslav Selucký and Pavel Turčan,[26] and the studies of the Polish provinces by Barbara Prandecka and others provide a wealth of data for comparative analysis.[27] There is also a growing body of the literature in this field in the Soviet Union, of which two recent works by L. N. Telepko and G. V. Mil'ner deserve special mention.[28]

Working with data at the regional level has certain advantages over the analysis of materials gathered for the purpose of making international comparisons, the most obvious being the compatibility of most types of data. On the other hand, regional boundaries can change, thus limiting comparisons over time to national republics or regions whose boundaries tend to remain stable. (The seventeen Polish provinces, whose boundaries up until now have not been changed, also fall into this category.) The reader should also be aware that the analysis and comparison of regional data on national income pose special problems. At least three deficiencies in Eastern European and Soviet national income data account for this fact: (a) the inclusion of the turnover tax in calculations of output; (b) the failure when giving regional data on national income to calculate only that income actually created within the boundaries of the region itself; and (c) the exclusion of the non-material sectors of the economy from calculations of national income. Each of these procedures works to distort comparisons of levels of income at the regional level, where differences in the structure of the economy are pronounced.

The degree to which regional data on national income have been adjusted to take into account one or more of these problems must therefore be considered. Yugoslav national income figures are calculated by the method of final use, and figures for national income for the republics have been adjusted to reflect value added within the republic only.[29] Regional data on national income in Yugoslavia nevertheless do not measure the contribution of the non-material sectors of the economy to total output. Subsidies and taxes also distort regional comparisons of national income in Yugoslavia, probably increasing the differences among levels of national income. Soviet national income figures for the republics attempt to make some corrections in respect to the turnover tax, but the method employed has been questioned by Soviet economists.[30] Czech data have not, in the past, made allowance for the problems of imports and exports out of regions and for this reason have been sharply criticized by Selucký.[31] Information on the Polish system of calculating national income levels within the provinces and districts of the country may be found in a work by Barbara Prandecka.[32]

It may also be noted that differences of opinion (reflecting to a certain degree the different circumstances prevailing in each of the individual countries of the area) exist in respect to the effect of various indices in magnifying or diminishing the measurement of regional differences. Telepko, in the work cited earlier, argues for the use of national income data in measuring regional levels of economic development in the Soviet Union in preference to the great number of physical indicators employed in the past. Mihailović, apparently expressing a view shared by a number of other Eastern European regional specialists, questions the use of national income statistics on the grounds that they tend to exaggerate differences between regions, and argues that measures of the living standard are the only real grounds on which to judge levels of regional development. (We reproduce in Table 12 data originally presented by Kuklinski and then reprinted by Mihailović in order to prove this point. In it, national income data, and data on the standard of living, are compared for the Polish provinces.) Mihailović's preference for using the standard of living as the basis for measuring regional development is shared by the contributors to the Mil'ner volume, and by Zbigniew Gontarski, in his discussion of the problems of doing research on regional differences on living standards in Poland.[33]

Other measures of regional differences include estimates of the real wages and income of the population, the percent of the population in agricultural pursuits and, of course, a variety of indicators relating to health, education, and the like. All of these present certain problems when they are placed in a comparative context, even those which seem most straightforward.[34] Tables 10 through 14 are limited to data showing regional differences in the Soviet Union, Yugoslavia, and Poland by national income. Soviet data are based on NMP, Yugoslav data on social product, and Polish data on GNP. The reader may observe here the effect of calculating national income in the Soviet Union by "value added" (keeping in mind that the methods employed are those of Telepko, and that others might calculate this amount in a different way), as well as by republic, with and without turnover taxes. It will be quickly seen that the difference between the economic regions is greater when the "value added" method is used (54.7 index points in the first case; 89 index points in the second). Correcting for the effect of the turnover tax on republic national income, as Vedeshchev has done, seems to make less difference in terms of extremes of per capita national income, although the figures for individual republics do change a good deal. Polish data in "GNP" are somewhat suspect, but provide a means of comparing national income measurements of regional differences with other methods. Yugoslav data are given in a way to make them roughly comparable to Soviet figures; it will be seen that if Kosovo is eliminated from the Yugoslav table, regional differences in Yugoslavia are not that much greater than those in the USSR.

### Table 11

*"National Income" Per Capita and "Additional Product" of Main Economic Regions of the USSR, 1968*
(USSR = 100)

| | *National Income Per Capita** | | *Additional Product Created (in Regions)** | |
|---|---|---|---|---|
| | Rubles | Index | Rubles | Index |
| USSR | 2134 | 100.0 | 1198 | 100.0 |
| Central | 2669 | 124.8 | 1716 | 143.0 |
| Northwest | 2609 | 122.4 | 1481 | 123.4 |
| Volga-Vyatka | 2585 | 121.3 | 1685 | 140.4 |
| Urals | 2341 | 109.9 | 1277 | 106.4 |
| Baltic | 2288 | 107.4 | 1283 | 106.9 |
| Donets Pridneprov | 2284 | 107.2 | 1229 | 102.4 |
| Western Regions | 2212 | 103.8 | 1290 | 107.5 |
| West Siberia | 2176 | 102.1 | 1143 | 95.2 |
| White Russia | 2135 | 100.2 | 1338 | 111.5 |
| South | 2079 | 97.6 | 1200 | 100.0 |
| Far East | 2018 | 94.7 | 648 | 54.0 |
| North Caucasus | 1969 | 92.4 | 1064 | 88.6 |
| Central Black Earth | 1961 | 92.0 | 1115 | 92.9 |
| Southwest | 1945 | 91.3 | 1208 | 100.6 |
| Povolzhskii | 1943 | 91.2 | 1013 | 84.3 |
| East Siberia | 1895 | 88.9 | 765 | 63.7 |
| Eastern Regions | 1870 | 87.7 | 880 | 73.3 |
| Moldavia | 1792 | 83.9 | 1065 | 88.7 |
| Kazakh | 1690 | 79.4 | 748 | 62.3 |
| Central Asia | 1680 | 78.8 | 924 | 77.0 |
| Transcaucasus | 1495 | 70.1 | 793 | 66.1 |

*Working Age Population
Source: Telepko, op. cit., p. 93.

Table 12

*Vedeshchev Data: National Income Per Capita by Republics, With and Without Turnover Tax*
(Index Number. USSR = 100)

| | *With Turnover Tax* | *Without Turnover Tax* |
|---|---|---|
| USSR | 100.00 | 100.00 |
| Latvian SSR | 142.45 | 140.27 |
| Estonian SSR | 138.71 | 144.75 |
| RSFSR | 111.33 | 111.17 |
| Lithuanian SSR | 109.68 | 101.82 |
| Ukranian SSR | 101.30 | 101.30 |
| Moldavian SSR | 85.72 | 87.00 |
| White Russian | 78.91 | 81.20 |
| Armenian SSR | 75.35 | 73.46 |
| Georgian SSR | 69.34 | 69.20 |
| Azerbaidzan SSR | 67.61 | 59.78 |
| Turkmen SSR | 64.05 | 58.10 |
| Kirghiz SSR | 64.03 | 62.73 |
| Kazakh SSR | 63.97 | 70.47 |
| Uzbek SSR | 62.72 | 61.94 |
| Tadzhik SSR | 55.18 | 54.98 |
| Maximum Indicator | 142.40 | 144.70 |
| Minimum Indicator | 55.20 | 54.30 |

Source: A. A. Ivanchenko, *Ekonomicheskie problemi razmeshcheniya proizvoditel'nikh sil,* p. 82.

This brief account of materials dealing with indices of development raises several questions. The first concerns the problem of comparative materials. Clearly, the comparing of data is developing more slowly than one might expect on the basis of the interest that exists in problems of development, the fact that many methodological discussions have been devoted to the issue of making comparisons, and the level of sophistication of national statistics in most East European countries. This conclusion may require qualification insofar as there exist Comecon-sponsored studies which are available to the social scientists of Eastern Europe and the Soviet Union on a limited circulation basis. It is also a fact—to which we have alluded—that comparative statistics are frequently cited in the newspapers, and in scholarly articles as well. But in the area situated between the presumably detailed but unpublished comparative studies of Comecon, and the popular but often unreliable data appearing in newspapers and even scholarly journals, a gap exists which up until now has been filled by calculations made by Western scholars or with data published by the United Nations.

Second, there arises the question of what the data can tell us. Our account, focusing as it does on certain select aspects of the development process, does not pretend to give an answer to that question. We have presented certain data relevant to the problem of rank-ordering the states of Eastern Europe, since this is a relatively straightforward type of exercise bearing on the question of which nation is more advanced, which less so. Most speculation concerning political development relates in one way or another to this issue. On the other hand, we have said nothing here about *rates* of development, or *why* one nation

**Table 13**

*Index of Regional Differences in Poland, 1961*
(Per Capita)

| *Province* | *GNP* | *GNP Created in Industry* | *GNP Created in Agriculture* | *Net Output in Agriculture, Per Capita of Agricultural Population* | *Personal Consumption* |
|---|---|---|---|---|---|
| Katowice | 138.0 | 209.3 | 28.5 | 111 | 119.5 |
| Opole | 111.8 | 108.5 | 128.8 | 135 | 103.4 |
| Lodz | 111.3 | 139.2 | 82.4 | 86 | 96.9 |
| Wroclaw | 108.5 | 117.8 | 95.1 | 141 | 105.4 |
| Krakow | 107.3 | 125.8 | 77.7 | 75 | 96.3 |
| Gdansk | 102.9 | 99.8 | 73.5 | 124 | 111.8 |
| Poznan | 102.1 | 88.0 | 136.3 | 141 | 107.1 |
| Szczecin | 101.2 | 73.5 | 109.3 | 130 | 110.0 |
| Warszawa | 101.0 | 90.8 | 81.4 | 86 | 106.8 |
| Bydgoszcz | 95.0 | 76.6 | 138.8 | 140 | 99.7 |
| Zielona Gora | 94.6 | 77.1 | 114.8 | 122 | 96.7 |
| Rzeszow | 81.8 | 64.4 | 123.9 | 81 | 83.6 |
| Olsztyn | 74.7 | 30.8 | 129.9 | 98 | 86.9 |
| Lublin | 74.5 | 35.8 | 157.9 | 91 | 86.7 |
| Koszalin | 74.5 | 31.2 | 130.3 | 110 | 98.2 |
| Kielce | 74.4 | 61.9 | 109.1 | 73 | 78.7 |
| Bialystok | 65.5 | 30.7 | 130.5 | 80 | 80.1 |
| Average for Poland | 100.0 | 100.0 | 100.0 | 100 | 100.0 |

Source: Mihailović, *Regionalni razvoj*, op. cit., p. 200.

### Table 14

*Yugoslav Republics: Social Product* Per Capita*
(In 1968 current prices)

| | |
|---|---|
| Yugoslavia | 100 |
| Slovenia | 180 |
| Croatia | 125 |
| Vojvodina | 107 |
| Lesser Serbia | 104 |
| Macedonia | 67 |
| Montenegro | 67 |
| Bosnia Hercegovina | 62 |
| Kosovo | 33 |

*Social Product: NMP before removing depreciation. Measuring national income by republic gives similar proportions to those shown here.

Source: *Jugoslovenski Pregled,* op. cit., p. 55.

is "behind" another. Nor do the kinds of data given here necessarily make it possible to identify stages through which these countries are passing (although data on the labor force, to cite an obvious example, do contribute to this end). The problem of providing answers to these questions is also faced by Eastern European and Soviet analysts, and accounts in part for the differences that do arise among them over the nature of development indices, whether one or many indices should be utilized, the desirability of using physical indices rather than those of a synthetic kind, and so forth.

In the Eastern European and Soviet literature there does seem to be a growing tendency to search for synthetic indicators, rather than trying to measure development with the aid of a vast arsenal of quantitative data, as apparently was the case during the period when the Soviet Union and Comecon first became interested in making international comparisons.[35] There is also, we would suggest, a tendency to focus less on indices dealing with the modern sector and its growth (steel output, the consumption of electrical energy, and the like), and more on those aspects of society which still show signs of backwardness, or in some way exhibit disproportions in their development. This is evident, for example, in respect to studies concerned with differences at the regional level. Initially, the emphasis was almost entirely on the speed with which the backward areas were catching up with the rest of the country. Now, to a much greater extent, the discussion is concerned with underlying structural differences between the developed and less developed regions. This is evident in the work of Mihailovič, who has made the study of underdeveloped areas in Eastern

## Table 15

*Yugoslav Republics: Development Indicators*

| | *Per Capita Income US $, 1966* | *Non-Agricultural Population– Share in Total Pop., 1961* | *Share of Industry in Total Social Product, 1966* | *% Literacy of Total Population Over 10 Years of Age, 1961* |
|---|---|---|---|---|
| Yugoslavia | 612 | 50.3% | 44.3% | 80.3 |
| Slovenia | 1,138 | 68.5 | 52.1 | 98.2 |
| Croatia | 743 | 56.1 | 46.8 | 87.9 |
| Vojvodina | 656 | 48.1 | 34.4 | 89.4 |
| Serbia (Lesser) | 601 | 43.8 | 41.5 | 77.0 |
| Serbia (all) | 563 | 43.9 | 39.2 | 78.1 |
| Macedonia | 471 | 48.5 | 40.3 | 75.5 |
| Montenegro | 459 | 53.1 | 43.2 | 78.3 |
| Bosnia Hercegovina | 431 | 49.9 | 46.8 | 67.5 |
| Kosovo | 256 | 35.9 | 37.6 | 58.9 |

Source: Ekonomski Institut Zagreb, *Problemi provodjenja društveno-ekonomske reforme*, p. 170.

Europe his specialty. It can be seen in the discussion of Telepko and the volume edited by Mil'ner, as well as in the publications of the new school of rural sociology in the Soviet Union.[36] The study of Czech society under the direction of Pavel Machonin—in those parts dealing with differences between Slovakia and the Czech lands—also stresses the importance of underlying differences in the social structure of the two Czechoslovak republics.[37]

Measuring political change in Eastern Europe[38] poses a special set of problems, and our treatment of research in this area necessarily must be somewhat different than the discussion of indices of development. First, we shall briefly indicate some of the methodological problems that are encountered in this kind of measurement and analysis. Then we shall turn to the literature which has appeared in Eastern Europe dealing with one aspect or another of political development. Rather than presenting data in the form of tables, as we have done up until now, we shall summarize the main conclusions of these studies, and examine some of the problems these works raise for the study of political and social development in the area.

It should be pointed out that the problem of how to measure political development has never been fully resolved, either in Western research or in that carried out in Eastern Europe. Several ways exist by which such change can be measured. One can attempt to develop indices of political mobilization. Elite change can be measured (through identifying the social composition, education, and other attributes of elites). Finally, one can focus on institutional and structural changes within the political system, utilizing broad criteria of effectiveness and responsiveness as criteria of development. (Changes in the party system may also be considered as a measure of the development of the political system, but there are even fewer guides in this area than in others concerning what is a truly "developmental" change.)

Unlike changes in the social system during periods of rapid economic growth, political changes do not have to show a high degree of correlation. At certain times, they may work at odds with one another —for example, when rapid social and political mobilization under the auspices of a revolutionary regime reduce the ability of the political system to develop a flexible and responsive decision-making structure. In other circumstances political development may be marked by a degree of correlation of these indicators (an example would be the emergence of a two-party system in which political mobilization was accompanied by institutional change in the direction of greater flexibility and responsiveness). In short, the direction of change of political institutions will be influenced by a multitude of often contradictory developments, none of which can be predicted with confidence beforehand. This situation is attributable not to our lack of knowledge or our inability to make precise measurements of political phenomena, but to the very nature of political systems themselves.

Indices of political development are also difficult to quantify. Of the three areas we have identified as being associated with political development, only elite change has an easily quantifiable dimension, but even in this case there is no clear-cut answer to the question of whether those aspects of elite change which are being measured (social background, education, and the like) bear a demonstrable relationship to concrete types of political change.[39] While social mobilization can be quantified through the use of certain indices—newspaper circulation, for example—political mobilization is more difficult to measure. In Eastern Europe attempts to identify a quantifiable dimension to political mobilization have taken two forms: that of measuring party membership and participation in party meetings, and through the device of determining the degree of information on political problems displayed by various groups in the population. Each of these techniques has its drawbacks, however, and the question of what constitutes a measure of political mobilization may be said to remain open for further examination and analysis.[40] Finally, it may be possible, in some rough fashion, to develop an index of "responsiveness." There are precedents for such an approach in research on developing countries, utilizing data on the degree to which the population of various regions of a country is supplied with government services and other benefits by the central authorities.[41] Dennis Pirage devised a measure of this type for the purpose of comparing degrees of political responsiveness to regional needs in Poland.[42] Measures of responsiveness such as these are valid only where it is possible to make regional comparisons, however, and do not really answer the question of how responsiveness in a political sense can be measured.

Notwithstanding these difficulties, it may be possible to develop scales which measure certain aspects of the operation of a political system and, through factor analysis or other techniques, relate such differences to developmental indices or other measures of social change. Case studies may reveal that the structure of power or political attitudes at the local level are related to levels of economic and social development, thus providing insights into the relationship between the social and political system. A great deal of evidence can be gathered indirectly about relations between social and political change, for example in the study of elites, where it can be shown that political systems have often failed to incorporate rising elite groups associated with the modernization process into the power structure. Under exceptionally favorable circumstances, it may be possible to undertake an in-depth study of two regions at different stages of development, and relate differences in the social structure, the standard of living, and the values of the society to the nature of political power and the operation of the political system. This was attempted in the Machonin study alluded to earlier. Finally, there remains the element of international comparison. Here one encounters the problem that the number of

Eastern European states for which measurements can be made is small, while global studies of a cross-national kind for a variety of reasons usually do not include the Eastern European countries and the Soviet Union.[43] Nevertheless, it is possible to compare many aspects of the relationship between the political system and social change through an examination of case studies. The ruling parties can also be compared– a subject to which we shall return shortly.

The study of regional differences also offers another approach to the analysis of relationships between social and political development. Two studies now exist which attempt to use factor analysis to explore relationships between social and political variables at the regional level in Poland. First, there is the work of the American political scientist Pirage, to which we have already referred. Secondly, there is the study of the Polish sociologists Krzysztof Ostrowski and Adam Przeworski.[44] Both studies use factor analysis to test relationships between social and political variables in the Polish provinces. Each has certain disadvantages. The Pirage study lacks a broad variety of political variables. The research carried on by Przeworski and Ostrowski utilizes a good deal of political data but within narrow limits, namely, that of political change and modernization in the Polish countryside. While the conclusions of the Pirage study will not concern us here, the Przeworski and Ostrowski work suggests the importance of a "modernization" and "mobilization" component in respect to the changes which were taking place in the Polish countryside in the early 1960s. Their findings tend to support the argument that political mobilization does have attributes which *under certain conditions* can be isolated and measured. The study also makes a case for the proposition that the strength of the party in the countryside is linked to a more primitive, not a more advanced, system of agriculture, an observation which is not unfamiliar to students of social and political change in Eastern Europe and the Soviet Union.

As yet, no systematic comparative study of social and political development in the Yugoslav republics has appeared, either in Yugoslavia or in the West.[45]

The principal Eastern European sources to which one must turn for materials on political development are not comparative (either regional or international), but encompass studies of party membership, on the one hand, and local power elites and groups in the enterprise, on the other. We shall briefly comment on each of these types of studies and their findings in the remainder of the discussion.

Research on problems of party membership has been carried out by Sadowski, Wiatr, and Ostrowski in Poland,[46] by Mažibrada and others in Yugoslavia,[47] and by Lubomir Brokl, in connection with the study of Czech society carried out by Machonin.[48] Omitting for the moment works dealing with local power elites and the role of the party in the enterprise, the data gathered in this area are surprisingly small.

Sadowski has attempted to ascertain the size of certain social groups in the Polish population, and then relate this to party statistics on the social class of party members. From this he has derived certain conclusions on the problem of the degree to which social and occupational groups in Poland are party members. Brokl and Mažibrada have provided concrete information which ties together social factors (education, family background) and the vertical mobility of the individual party member within the power structure. Their findings relate closely to those which have emerged from studies of local power elites, and will be discussed in that context.

These studies must be considered only a beginning. A great deal of data on the Yugoslav party await analysis, and Sadowski's work still does not provide a *precise* description of how data on the Polish party are broken down into occupational and social categories—the first step for a documented and comparable set of statistics in which party penetration of (or control by) various social groups in Polish society could be shown. On the basis of statistics available on a limited circulation basis, it is presently possible to extend the work of regional comparison begun by Przeworski and Ostrowski to include trends in party membership in both rural and urban areas. This work has not been undertaken, however, of if completed, its results have not been published.

In lieu of such studies by either Eastern European or Western social scientists, we present, in Table 16, data showing the social background of party members in the Yugoslav republics for the year 1964, which permit the reader to compare levels of development (Tables 14 and 15) with the social structure of the party (data on social and occupation status are for *current* situation or position, not that at the time of entering the party). It will be noticed that the social composition of the party does not appear to be closely tied to development: the highest percentage of workers (by a very marginal amount) is to be found in the least developed republic (Bosnia-Hercegovina). If one groups together those party members in the "modern" sector (engineers, those in health and education, lawyers and economists, and those with a higher education), Slovenia ranks first with 21 percent, followed by Macedonia (one of the lesser developed republics) with 18.5 percent. Croatia is in last place with 15.1 percent. On the other hand, the percentage of peasants in the republic parties correlates well with the level of development measured by national income as given in Table 14.

It should be borne in mind that cross-regional analysis of this type will not give results similar to those of trend analysis, but would show a close relationship between changes in the social structure of the party and economic development. Since, however, there is clearly a time factor operating in trend analysis—that is, a shift of the social structure of the party is related to the passage of time without economic development ever taking place—we cannot be sure of existence of a link

## Table 16

*Yugoslav League of Communists, Social Composition, 1964*
(In Percent)

| | *Yugoslavia* | *Bosnia Hercegovina* | *Montenegro* | *Croatia* | *Macedonia* | *Slovenia* | *Serbia* |
|---|---|---|---|---|---|---|---|
| Workers | 36.2 | 39.8 | 33.1 | 39.7 | 36.2 | 36.2 | 37.7 |
| Peasants | 7.9 | 8.2 | 15.2 | 5.7 | 9.8 | 1.3 | 10.0 |
| Engineers & Technicians | 4.8 | 5.3 | 4.0 | 4.1 | 4.8 | 8.0 | 4.7 |
| Health Workers | 1.2 | 1.3 | 1.1 | 0.9 | 1.8 | 1.3 | 1.4 |
| Educational Workers | 5.6 | 6.2 | 6.9 | 5.4 | 6.9 | 6.3 | 5.9 |
| Lawyers & Economists | 2.3 | 2.1 | 2.4 | 1.8 | 3.3 | 2.2 | 2.8 |
| Remainder with Higher Education | 2.2 | 2.3 | 2.1 | 2.9 | 1.7 | 3.2 | 2.1 |
| Remainder with Middle Education | 8.0 | 7.7 | 7.9 | 9.0 | 8.0 | 10.2 | 8.3 |
| Remainder with Lower Education | 14.3 | 15.6 | 12.3 | 14.6 | 19.0 | 16.0 | 15.2 |
| Students & Pupils | 3.5 | 3.6 | 1.3 | 4.7 | 3.8 | 3.6 | 3.6 |
| Permanent Members of the Army | 5.6 | — | — | — | — | — | — |
| Others | 8.4 | 8.0 | 13.7 | 11.2 | 4.7 | 11.7 | 8.3 |

Data give current social position. The earlier category of "official" covers all those except worker, peasant, and members of the army.

between social and political development, even in this context.

The analysis of the local power structure and the role of the party in the factory have been areas favored by empirical research.[49] Rather than trying to summarize the results of the numerous case studies that have been made in this field, we shall make several general observations concerning their findings.

On the one hand, this research lends support to the view that the party is an instrument of modernization. The best educated groups have a high degree of party membership. The demands of industrialization have, in the findings of a number of these studies, led to changes in the type of party member given positions of responsibility. Educated and technically skilled cadre have come to replace poorly educated party members recruited during the revolutionary seizure of power.

On the other hand, there is a great deal of evidence in these works which points to the existence of centers of power with great influence at the local level; a shortage of adequately trained managerial personnel; and the crystallization, *within the party itself*, of a new elite, based on those who have had access to a university education.[50] These facts suggest, if not the presence of a "new class" hostile to change, the existence of certain contradictions which have arisen in the course of political development in these countries, and seem more in accord with the actual state of politics than those findings which stress the role of the political system as an agent of modernization.

These findings may not be in conflict with one another. One can suggest that it is the very nature of any developing system to exhibit elements of bureaucracy and resistance to change, and at the same time to contain vigorous, modernizing groups. There remains, nevertheless, much that is ambiguous and unresolved in this type of research. Broad questions arise in respect to the problem of where resistance to change can be found in these societies, and the ways in which democratic or authoritarian values associate themselves with social classes, interests, or even national groups. It is almost axiomatic in theoretical discussions of the problem of social development and political change that the more advanced a society, the greater its democratic tendencies. This argument is supported by the results of the Machonin study, which found a correlation between the more advanced economic level and egalitarian society of Czechoslovakia and the broader base of power and authority, in contrast to the situation in Slovakia. This finding, nevertheless, reflects well known prejudices of Czechs (and some Slovaks) on the political traditions of the two regions. While the Machonin study itself is an admirable work, its conclusions concerning political behavior must be approached with some caution.

Also, there is some evidence in Western research—specifically that of Pirage—that the more advanced, industrialized regions of Poland tend to have a less flexible attitude toward politics, while those regions in the course of modernization show a more adaptable set of political values. Pirage suggests that in certain cases, the party in a more industrialized region may therefore be more conservative (that is, more doctrinaire) in its political attitudes than party organizations in "developing" areas. Some indirect support for this conclusion is supplied by Jerovšek, who reported finding more elements of an authoritarian power structure in the industrially *more developed* communes in Yugoslavia.[51]

None of these findings are persuasive, however. It would seem that what is required is that *all* techniques of research into political development be brought to bear on certain selected problems, and that this be reinforced by comparative studies and by the careful use of data on social change, in order to test general hypotheses of the kind just mentioned.

Perhaps a deliberate effort at developing comparative studies offers an opportunity for broadening research in this fashion. A change of attitudes may also be required to further this end. Eastern European social scientists may wish to reconsider the possibility that in addition to what they can learn by studying Western countries and the Soviet Union, there is much to be gained from studying one another.

If comparative studies offers a hope for furthering research in the realm of social and political development, one must not disregard the importance of studies of national societies which, in the 1960s, have laid the groundwork for future study. A great step forward has been taken in developing tools of research and making basic data available. One also feels that the nature of Eastern European society (and to a lesser extent, that of the Soviet Union) in the 1960s was such as to make analysis difficult. These were systems in a stage of transition between revolutionary politics and more normal forms of change. Showing the interplay of these factors, and relating them to social and economic transformations accompanying industrialization, is a tremendously difficult task, one with which we are still only beginning to come to terms.

## NOTES

1. Note William Welsh's comments to the effect that while it is assumed that changes in social and economic structures will lead to changes in elite structures, the evidence at present in our possession does not prove such a link. Carl Beck, ed., *Comparative Communist Political Leadership*, (New York, 1973), p. 31.

2. A distinction made by the United Nations Research Institute for Social Development in its studies on problems of social change. See the publication of the Institute, *Contents and Measurements of Socio-Economic Development* (Geneva, 1970), p. 10. What we call progress indicators are referred to by the Institute publication as "development" indicators, and include such aspects as growth in education, health standards, income, and the like. Structural indicators are those

whose change does not automatically bring any direct benefits to society, but are nevertheless associated with the process of development: demographic changes, urbanization, and the like.

3. *Ibid*., p. 10.

4. Wlodzimierz Brus, "To Count or Not to Count," *Eastern European Economics* 1, no. 1 (Fall 1962):41-48.

5. Vladimir G. Treml and John P. Hardt, eds., *Soviet Economic Statistics* (Durham, N. C., 1972), p. 148.

6. Data do sometimes appear on "social product." This is especially true in the case of Yugoslavia (for an example, see Appendix 5). "Social product" in the Yugoslav data is not greatly different from "national income" and seems to give the same general results in terms of levels of development of the republics, and so forth.

7. See Kudrova, Table 1, *infra*.

8. E. S. Kudrova, *Statistika natsional'nogo dokhoda evropeiskhikh sotsialisticheskikh stran* (Moscow, 1969) provides a useful guide to differences in national income accounting methods of the Eastern European members of Comecon. See especially Table 1, p. 9, where what is included, and what excluded, from the material sector in each country, is shown. For a more general treatment in a Soviet source to the problem of comparing economic indicators, the reader is referred to O. K. Rybakov, *Metodologiya sravneniya ekonomicheskikh pokazateley stran sotsializma* (Moscow, 1968), and to other sources cited in this account, especially those dealing with the problem of making regional comparisons of national income. The reader of Polish will find Eugenia Krzeczkowska a useful review, not only of the problem of national income, but of all aspects of the problem of development indicators: "Wybrane zagadnienia porownan miedzynarodowych," *Wiadomosći statystyczne* 14, no. 1 (Jan. 1969):3-6. For a discussion of the Yugoslav approach to calculating national income, see Gojko Grdić *et al., Statistika za ekonomiste* (Belgrade, 1969). The measurement of physical indicators has played an important role in attempts by Eastern European economists to circumvent the problem of artificial prices when making international comparisons of national income. The method has been pioneered by Hungarian economists and utilized in some of the UN comparisons of national income which we shall cite below. The non-economist can also gain by consulting this literature. See especially the work of Eva Ehrlich, "Dynamic International Comparisons of National Incomes Expressed in Terms of Physical Indicators," *Osteuropa Wirtschaft* 14, no. 1 (March 1969):1-25.

9. United Nations Economic and Social Council, Statistical Commission, 9th Session, *Comments of Governments on the Report on International Definition and Measurement of Standards and Levels of Living* (Jan. 20, 1956).

10. United Nations Statistical Commission and Economic Commission for Europe, *Comparison of Levels of Consumption in Austria and Poland* (New York, 1969); Gyula Varga, "Changes in the Peasant Living Standard," *The New Hungarian Quarterly* 7, no. 21 (Spring 1966):86-101, gives a description of the findings of the Hungarian-British study carried out in 1959.

11. Comparative studies of living standards among several of the Comecon countries were undertaken in the late 1950s and early 1960s, but their results were not published.

12. M. Mód *et al.*, *The Standard of Living: Some Problems of Analysis and International Comparison* (Budapest, 1962); T. I. Nedorezova, "Metodologicheskie voprosy issledovaniya urovnya zhizni pri sotsializme," *Vestnik Moskovskogo Universiteta*, Series 7, *Ekonomika* no. 24:40-48; Gunter Manz, ed., *Beitrage zur Lebensstandardforschung* (Berlin, 1967); Krzeczkowska; Juraj Červeň, "O jednej metóde merania a modelovania životnej urovne," *Statistika* (Prague), no. 11-12 (1969):473-79.

13. Berislav Šefer, *Socijalni razvoj u samoupravnom društvu* (Belgrade, 1971); Krystyna Jacek and Wanda Pieniążek, "Zmiany w strukturze spożycia w Polsce Ludowej," *Wiadomości statystyczne* 15, no. 6 (June 1970):11-14; Jiří Večerník, "Problémy příjmu a životni úrovně v sociální diferenciaci," in Pavel Machonin, *Československá společnost*, pp. 295-321; L. Rendoš, *Osobná spotreba je obrazom rozvoja človeka a spoločnosti* (Bratislava, 1969).

14. The measure is also used by Pirage and by Ostrowski and Przeworkski in factor analysis of social and political indicators in the Polish provinces. See our discussion of political literature below.

15. Gertrude Schroeder, "Regional Differences in Incomes and Levels of Living in the USSR," soon to be published, contains a rank order of a number of indicators of levels of living of the Soviet republics, in which retail sales and services per capita correlate quite closely with certain other indices measuring the standard of living. Further reference to these data will be made below. For use of this measure in comparisons of Yugoslav, Bulgarian, and Rumanian standards of living, Kosta Mihailović, *Regionalni razvoj socijalističkih zemalja* (Belgrade, 1972), p. 89. Joint Economic Committee, *Economic Developments in Countries of Eastern Europe* (Washington, D. C., 1970), p. 302, reproduces data on per capita retail sales of four Comecon countries–Czechoslovakia, Hungary, Poland, and the USSR–taken from Kotkovskii, *infra*. Maria-Elisabeth Ruban, *Die Entwicklung des Lebensstandards in der Sowjetunion* (Berlin, 1965), pp. 89-90, also contains comparisons of Soviet and West German living standards calculated on this basis.

16. Arising from the fact that a portion of the retail trade recorded in Soviet statistics is actually sold to wholesale outlets, then sold once again to the population. See Marshall Goldman's remarks concerning the *melkii opt* network in the Soviet Union in Treml and Hardt, *Soviet Economic Statistics*, p. 335.

17. The manner in which this statistic is calculated in Eastern European national income accounts is well described in Economic Commission for Europe, *Incomes in Postwar Europe* (Geneva, 1967), p. 23.

18. Soviet scholars are now speaking out with more directness about differences within society, and especially about the gap that still separates rural and urban classes in respect to the standard of living. See Yu. V. Arutyunyan, *Sotsial'naya strukktura sel'skogo naseleniya SSSR* (Moscow, 1971), which deals with this problem. A convenient source which reviews the problem of income distribution in Hungary is Rezso Nyers, "Problems of Profitability and Income Distribution," *The New Hungarian Quarterly* 11, no. 40 (Winter 1970):11-29. A more ambitious and important study of standards of living of groups in Yugoslav society is the work of Josip Stahan, *Strukturne promjene i razvojne tendencije osobne potrošnje u Jugoslaviji* (Zagreb, 1970). Income distribution in Poland is discussed by Zygmunt

Zekonski and Irena Zukowska, "Analiza koncentracji plac, dochodow i wydatkow," *Gospodarka planowa*, 23, no. 9 (1968):8-14.

19. U.N. Research Institute for Social Development, *Socio-Economic Development*, p. 10.

20. *Zatrudnienie w Polsce Ludowej w latach 1950-1970* (Warsaw, 1965).

21. *Civilization at the Crossroads* (1969). See also J. Kosta, "Strukturálni změny společenské pracovni síly ve světle mezinárodního srovnáni," *Politická Ekonomie* no. 1 (1967) and T. Frejka, *Rozbor odvětvoré Struktury pracovni síly* (Prague, 1965).

22. In Yugoslavia there is also interest in analyzing the growth of the tertiary sector in the belief that this may provide a way of alleviating unemployment in underdeveloped regions. See Ilijas Bošnjović, *Tercijarne djelatnosti na nedovoljno razvijenom području* (Sarajevo, 1971). Other Yugoslav sources on the labor force, in which the distinction among primary, secondary, and tertiary sectors is employed, include Miloš Macura, *Stanovništvo kao činilac privrednog razvoja Jugoslavije* (Belgrade, 1958); "Employment, 1952-1966," *Yugoslav Survey* 8, no. 4 (Nov. 1967):49-62.

23. *Razvitie proizvodstvennoĭ i neproizvodstvennoĭ sfer v SSSR* (Moscow, 1964).

24. Several Eastern Europeans have contributed articles to the volume of E. A. G. Robinson, *Backward Areas in Advanced Countries* (New York, 1969). The work is a useful introduction to problems of regional development in the area.

25. *Regionalni razvoj socijalističkih zemalja* (Belgrade, 1972), and Kosta Mihailović and Eva Berković, *Razvoj i životni standard regiona Jugoslavije* (Belgrade, 1970). For additional data, see "Neki indikatori nivoa razvijenosti republika i pokrajina 1964-1968," *Jugoslovenski Pregled* 14, no. 4 (April 1970):157-162. For a discussion of the definition of underdeveloped regions in Yugoslavia, see Ekonomski Institut Zagreb, *Problemi provodjenja društveno-ekonomske reforme* (Zagreb, 1969), pp. 163-172.

26. Radoslav Selucký, *Ekonomické vyrovnávání slovenska s českými kraji* (Prague, 1960); Pavel Turčan and Viktor Pavlenda, *Le Dévelopement economique de la Slovaquie au sein de la Tchécoslovaquie socialiste* (Bratislava, 1963); Viktor Pavlenda, *Ekonomické základy socialistické riešenia narodnostnej otkázky v Československu* (Bratislava, 1968); Selucký, "The Economic Equalization of Slovakia with the Czech Lands," *Czechoslovak Economic Papers* 1964, no. 3:42-59.

27. *Wzrost gospodarczy polski w układzie przestrezennym* (Warsaw, 1969); Jan Dangel, *Przekształcenia sieci miejskie j w Polsce pod wpływem rozwoju ludności i porzemysłowienia kraju w okresie 1946-1960* (Warsaw, 1968). Zbigniew Gontarski, "Warunki bytowe ludności w badaniach regionalnych," *Wiadomości statystyczne* 15, no. 7 (July 1970):9-10; Zygmunt Sprycha, "Terenowy przekrój wzrostu dochodów ludności w latach 1961-1967," *Gospodarka planowa* 23, no. 9 (September, 1968):1-8. Note should be made that the Committee on Space Problems of the Polish Academy of Sciences (Komitet Przestrzennego zagospodarowania kraju) publishes many works devoted to this problem.

28. L. N. Telepko, *Urovni ekonomicheskogo razvitiya raionov SSSR* (Moscow, 1971); G. V. Mil'ner, ed., *Territorial'nie problemi dokhodov i potrebleniya*

*trudyashchikhsya* (Moscow, 1966). A. I. Vedeshchev, "Soizmerenie urovneĭ khozyaǐstvennogo razvitiya ekonomicheskhikh raionov SSSR," in A. A. Ivanchenko, ed., *Ekonomicheskie problemi razmeshcheniya proizvoditel'nikh sil SSSR* (Moscow, 1969), pp. 53-95.

29. Data on regional incomes in Yugoslavia were compiled by the federal statistical office in the mid 1960s. The basic source from which all such comparisons are derived in Yugoslav discussions of regional differences of national income is Savezni zavod za statistiku, "Kretanje drustvenog proizvoda i narodnog dohotka Jugoslavije 1952-1968 godine," *Analize i Prikazi* no. 45 (Belgrade, 1969).

30. Telepko, *Urovni ekonomicheskogo*, pp. 58-59.

31. Selucký, *Ekonomické vyrovnávání slovenska s českými kraji.*

32. *Analiza tworzenia i podziału dochodu narodowego Polski w układzie regionalnym*, Komitet Przestrzennego zagospodarowanie kraju PAN, Studia Vol. 9 (Warsaw, 1965).

33. See references cited in footnotes 27 and 28.

34. One variable often overlooked is the age structure of the population, which must be taken into account when making comparisons in the areas of education and health. Differences in the cost of living are also an important consideration when comparing wages and incomes of the population. The lack of data on the size of the agricultural population hampers regional comparisons and also makes it difficult to compare productivity figures in agriculture: Soviet practice is to give agricultural output in terms of per capita figures for the population of the entire region. See Vedeshchev, "Soizmerenie," p. 66. The reader may see for himself how misleading such data can be by examining the figures in Appendix 1 given by Zhelev for agricultural output per capita for the members of Comecon.

35. Telepko, *Urovni ekonomicheskago*, p. 18, notes that some *260* indicators were developed for the purpose of comparing the Soviet Union with Western nations.

36. Arutyunyan, *Sotsial'naya struktura.*

37. Pavel Machonin, ed., *Československa společnost* (Bratislava, 1969).

38. The discussion is restricted to Eastern Europe. Soviet studies of this type do not exist.

39. Rather, political changes seem to shape the elite structure. See Carl Beck, "Career Characteristics of Eastern European Leadership," in R. Barry Farrell, ed., *Political Leadership in Eastern Europe and the Soviet Union*, (Chicago: Aldine, 1970), pp. 157-194.

40. The latter of these two methods was used by Dean Frease in his study of attitudes in Yugoslav society. See "Demografski faktori u masovnoj politizaciji," *Sociologija* (Belgrade) 12, no. 1 (1970):83-95. (Frease is an American sociologist.) The problem in this case concerns those who were politically alienated in Yugoslav society. The approach taken by Frease excludes them from the politically mobilized because of their lack of information on current political events. Dennis Pirage has addressed himself to the same problem in Poland. He explores the assumption that "politicization" is a unidimensional concept reflected in a number of indices (an interest in foreign affairs, readership of political journals, and the like) but finds

little or no correlation among these factors in the data at his disposal. See his *Modernization and Political Tension Management* (New York, 1972), p. 183. Przeworski and Ostrowski, in a study to be cited below, measured political mobilization in the Polish countryside along several dimensions, including party membership (more precisely, the ratio of PUWP members to the size of the labor force employed in agriculture), and degree of activity in party organizations. The former measure correlated with changes taking place in the Polish countryside associated with modernization; the latter did not. With this kind of political mobilization, there are obvious limitations to the use of this type of index outside areas which are undergoing political mobilization for the first time, which seems to have been the case here.

41. See Ronald D. Brunner and Garry D. Brewer, *Organized Complexity* (New York, 1971).

42. He proposes such measures as the supply of social services, increases in wages, the size of the retail trade network. His final set of indices includes wage increases, per capita educational investments, turnover in the retail trade network of consumer goods. Pirage, *Modernization*, pp. 179-181.

43. Exceptions include Phillips Cutright, "National Political Development," *American Sociological Review* 28, no. 2 (April 1963):253-264, which uses data on Eastern Europe; Phillip M. Gregg and Arthur S. Banks, "Dimensions of Political Systems: Factor Analysis of a Cross Polity Survey," *American Political Science Review* 59, no. 3 (Sept. 1965):602-14.

44. "Local Leadership in Poland," *The Polish Sociological Review* no. 2 (1967):53-71.

45. The work of Zaninovich nevertheless suggests the importance of differences between the outlook of those in the northern republics, and the attitudes and values of those in the south. This difference, Zaninovich shows, originates in differences in cultural values, not levels of development, and has a discernable influence on the political attitudes of persons in these two parts of the country. See George Zaninovich, "Party and Non-Party Attitudes on Societal Change," in Farrell, *Political Leadership*, pp. 294-334.

46. Michael Sadowski, "Przemiany społezcne a partie polityczne PRL," *Studia socjologiczne* no. 3 (1968):89-113; Sadowski, *Przemiany społeczne a system partyjny PRL* (Warsaw, 1969). Jerzy Wiatr and Krzysztof Ostrowski, "Political Leadership: What Kind of Professionalism," *Studies in Polish Political System* (Warsaw, 1967).

47. Dušan Mažibrada, "Društvene pokretlivost članova Saveza komunista na području Dalmacije," *Sociologija* 13 (1971):21-39; Krsto S. Kilibarda, *Samoupravljanje i Savez komunista* (Belgrade, 1966); pp. 746-788 of Miloš Nikolić, ed., *Saveza komunista u uslovima samoupravljanja* (Belgrade, 1967).

48. Lubomir Brokl, "Power and Social Stratification," *International Journal of Sociology* 1, no. 3 (Fall 1971).

49. Zygmunt Bauman, "Economic Growth, Social Structure, Elite Formation: The Case of Poland," *International Social Science Journal* 16, no. 2 (1964):205-216; Bauman, "Social Structure of the Party Organization in Industrial Works," *Studies in Polish Political System*, pp. 156-178; W. Narojek, *System*

*wladzy w miescie* (Warsaw, 1967); Stanislaw Widerszpil, *Sklad polskiej klasy robotniczej* (Warsaw, 1965). These should be consulted in connection with the recent volume edited by David Lane, *Social Groups in Polish Society* (New York, 1973). Among Yugoslav works, note especially J. Jerovšek, "Neformalne strukture odlučanje na nivoj opčine," *Sodobnost* no. 12 (1964):1183-94. Jerovšek, "Neki aspekti odnosa izmedju narodnih odbora opština i preduzeća," *Studijski projekat sociološko istraživanje jugoslovensko komune, Bilten*, no. 3 (May 1963):116-21; Stane Možina, "Učešće rukovodećih i stručnih kadrova u radničkom samoupravljanju," *Gledišta* no. 3 (1966):355-361.

50. This finding comes out strongly in the study of social mobility in the Yugoslav League of Communists by Mažibrada, and appears as a theme in Brokl's discussion of the Czech party. The tendency of which we speak has not grown to the point where the old revolutionaries have been removed from positions of power at the top, however. This fits in with a pattern in which the effect of modernization, and the influence on the power structure of the revolution, exist side by side.

51. Jerovšek, "Neki aspekti odnosi izmedju narodnih odbora."

# 2

# A Classification of Communist Economic Systems

John M. Montias

In a paper written in the late 1960s[1] I suggested a classification of "communist economic systems" based on three principles: (1) the system's degree of "mobilization"; (2) the extent of markets; and (3) the centralization or decentralization of decision-making. I argued essentially that the presence of other system traits in observed (past and present) communist economies was so highly correlated with these economies' position along one or more of the three dimensions that there would be no point to using these subsidiary traits as independent classificatory variables. Hence every observed "communist" system could be classified in one of a very small number of ideal types. Four such types turned out to be sufficient for the purpose: (1) mobilization systems; (2) centralized- and (3) decentralized-administered systems; and (4) market socialism. The chief exercise of the paper consisted in noting the relative importance or the specific character of seventeen system traits in these four basic types of socialist systems. The table summarizing this information is reproduced in Table 1 of this chapter.

Since that time my broadening interest in the description and comparison of systems had led me to ask some "prior questions" about purposes and correct methods of classification.[2] In retrospect, I am inclined to feel that my earlier effort was excessively concerned with traditional preoccupations in the sovietological field.

Why, then, should we wish to classify systems? And if classification of systems qualifies as a respectable intellectual activity, on what principles should it be carried out? A subsidiary question can also be asked about "socialist economies," once such a subset of the world's economies has been properly identified: Do they require separate classification, or is it more illuminating to classify them as we would any other economies according to universal criteria?

## Table 1

*System Traits for Four Basic Types of Socialized Economies*

| | *Administered Systems* | | | |
|---|---|---|---|---|
| | *Mobilization* | *Centralized* | *Decentralized* | *Market Socialism* |
| *Organization* | Hierarchical, functional, and/or regional | Hierarchical, functional, or regional | Hierarchical, functional | Polycentric or regional |
| *Mobilization of peasants and workers by low-level party cadres* | High | Low | Low | Low |
| *Reliance on hierarchically transmitted commands* | High | High | Low | Low |
| *Incentives* | "Moral" | Material | Material | Material |
| *Distribution of producer goods* | By rationing on basis of priority | By rationing according to plan | Insufficient evidence | Through markets or by informal rationing |
| *Prices of producer goods* | Centrally set, arbitrary | Centrally set, at average cost | Partly decentralized, set at "full cost" | Market, subject to central and local controls |
| *Consumer goods* | Rationed | Sold at approximately market-clearing prices set by center | Sold at market-clearing prices, some of which set by enterprise | Sold at market-clearing prices |
| *Type of planning (participation of enterprise in planning process)* | "From below," counter-planning | "From above" | "From below" | Insufficient evidence |

| | | | | |
|---|---|---|---|---|
| *Coordination of short-term allocation decisions* | Through priority system | Through central yearly and quarterly plans | Through central plans and informal contacts among producers and their organizations | Through market and informal contacts among producers and their organizations |
| *Development strategy* | Teleological | Genetic | Genetic | Genetic |
| *Managerial latitude* | Medium | Low | Medium | High |
| *Tranquility of enterprise* | Low | Medium | Insufficient evidence | High |
| *Financial relationship of enterprise to state* | Budget relation | *Khozrashchet* with state as residual claimant | Pays taxes to state | Pays taxes to state |
| *Tolerance for remnants of private enterprise in agriculture, retail trade, etc.* | Low | Medium | Medium to high | Medium to high |
| *Macroeconomic policy* | Passive (inflationary in effect) | Budget-active, credits-passive, macroeconomic stability | Active, especially via banking system | Active, especially via banking system |
| *Effect on system on innovations* | Diffusion of foreign technology, occasional adoption of "crank ideas" | Diffusion of foreign technology plus innovation in favored sectors | Insufficient evidence | Insufficient evidence |
| *Organization of factory workers* | Shock workers' battalions and emulation drives | Stakhanovism | Insufficient evidence | Insufficient evidence |
| *Reliance on "volunteer" (unpaid) workers in harvesting, reconstruction, etc.* | Frequent | Rare | Absent | Absent |

Source: John M. Montias, "Types of Communist Economic Systems," in *Change in Communist Systems*, ed. Chalmers Johnson (Stanford, Calif.: Stanford University Press, 1970), pp. 117-134. Reproduced with permission of both the author and Stanford University Press.

If there is a rational purpose to classifying economies according to their salient system traits, I suppose it lies in our attempts to explain or to predict the behavior of decision-makers in each system, given their preferences and the policies they wish to pursue and the environment in which they operate. To make this clear requires us to sharpen our definitions and to introduce a paradigm that will help us get at the impact of system traits on economic outcomes.

An economy in a given period may be represented, in schematic fashion, with the aid of four finite sets: (1) a set of individuals, each with his preferences over the economy's possible outcomes; (2) a set of the possible actions these individuals may undertake; (3) a set of the possible outcomes of these actions; (4) a set of the possible environments that may occur in the period.

Given these sets we may, by analogy with the kind of system analysis used in engineering, define a system as a subset of all the possible action-outcome pairs. If, to each action, there corresponds only one outcome, such a system is said to be *functional*.[3] If a given action results in one outcome when state x occurs and another outcome when y occurs and if x and y both have a positive probability of occurrence, the system cannot be functional. Another way of putting this point is to assert that an economic system can only be functional, in the engineering sense of the word, under a controlled environment.

According to a plausible model of rational behavior, the choice of each individual's actions in an economic system is determined by his preferences regarding their possible outcomes and by the (subjective) probabilities he attaches to the states of the environment that might influence the outcomes.[4] When a decision-maker chooses ahead of time among the actions that he may undertake over several periods under varying environment conditions, we may call such a choice a *strategy*. If the strategy involves the repetition of the same action each time a given state of the environment occurs, it may be termed a *policy*.

Certain actions or policies, which may be called *illegitimate*, will not be undertaken either because they are, by their very nature, rated low in most individuals' preference orderings, or because they are thought to be likely to trigger off secondary outcomes (arrest, fine, social disapproval, or dismissal from an organization) that are too vexatious for the individuals concerned to warrant their taking a chance on them. These (social) constraints on individuals' actions constitute what I propose to call the *structure* of the system. The rules in the system structure may be formal (laws and regulations) or informal (customs, taboos, and so forth). The system's structure, along with individual's preferences and the states of the environment that actually occur, will determine which subset of the possible action-outcome pairs will be observed in a particular period (and, if there are lags in the generation of the outcomes, in subsequent periods as well).[5] A trait of the system structure is then a rule or law constraining the economic behavior of participants in the system.

Only a few individuals have influence over the structure of the system in which they operate. Foremost among these are high-rank individuals in governmental and economic organizations. Their preferences are especially important because, directly or via the rules they impose, they tend to have a strong impact on the choice of actions and policies by all participants in the system. When we select among the numerous outcomes of a system those that "really matter," we usually mean that these powerful individuals place either a very high positive or a very low negative value on these outcomes. If they are highly valued in most of these decision-makers' preferences, outcomes may be called system-specific *desiderata*; if they are deemed highly undesirable they may be termed system-specific *odiosa*. The most commonly encountered (aggregated) desiderata are: (1) a high average level of consumption; (2) rapid growth of aggregate output; (3) stability; (4) equity; and (5) national economic strength. The list of odiosa normally include pollution of the environment and excessive congestion of towns and recreational facilities.[6]

System traits, it should be stressed, may be valued by system participants irrespective of their contribution to other outcomes: decision-makers may value decentralized decision-making for its own sake or for the preservation of a democratic society; others may have a preference for centralized decision-making, again for its own sake, or for the preservation of the "dictatorship of the proletariat." In such cases, there may be a difference between the way system rules really operate and these individuals' perception of how they operate. A system may seem highly centralized because all power nominally cascades down from the summit of a unique all-encompassing hierarchy; but, in fact, because superordinates do not have the means to ensure compliance with their rules and orders, the system may be *de facto* decentralized, in the sense that subordinates may enjoy considerable operational autonomy.

Who or what organizations may set what kind of rules constraining economic decision-making is determined by the political-legal structure of a country. In this sense the structure of the economic system is "embedded," to use Karl Polanyi's favorite expression, in the political system. The "meta-rules" of the latter, incidentally, may also be codified or informal. The extent to which they are codified is itself an important system trait affecting the stability of decision-makers' expectations, their "horizon," and the way in which they compare the utility of present and future outcomes. There is a substantial difference in the character of decision-making in a post revolutionary system where government officials and functionaries of a ruling party are empowered by "revolutionary legality" to take any measures they please (subject to their superiors' approval) and a similar system where the power of officials and functionaries is precisely demarcated and restricted by explicit rules.

A complete inventory of the formal and informal rules governing economic life in any country would fill volumes. The analyst wishing to describe and compare systems must somehow aggregate these myriad rules into a manipulable set of system traits. In so doing, he should be guided by the principle that those distinct rules aggregating into a given trait should be expected to have more or less the same impact on outcomes under a given environment. This is easier said than done, but it is better to strive to adhere to this principle than to amalgamate rules arbitrarily. The following list of aggregated rules or categories of rules represents a crude attempt to classify system traits with the ultimate objective of comparing their effects on outcomes under comparable environments.

1. Rules permitting or rules forbidding individuals to own privately assets yielding monetary returns;[7]

2. Rules permitting certain individuals to issue orders to other individuals who have not consented to this coercion[8] (e.g., the informal rules that permit Communist Party cadres to conscript people for "voluntary labor"; the assignment of school graduates to particular jobs);

3. Rules that oblige economic decision-makers to comply with the provisions of a document called *plan* elaborated and approved by governmental authorities some time before the operational decisions envisaged in the plan are scheduled to be made;

4. Rules determining the structure of organizations (e.g., "who will be subordinate to whom for what");

5. Rules setting the conditions under which goods and factors of production may be exchanged among individuals and among organizations;

6. Rules governing the formation and dissolution of organizations;

7. Rules stipulating how organizations may earn their payoff (e.g., from profits, bonuses, tax farming, etc.);

8. Rules regulating the distribution of an organization's payoff among its members;

9. Rules protecting individuals and organizations from (uncompensated) damages due to negligent or malevolent actions on the part of other entities;

10. Rules regulating the movement of goods and factors out

of and into the country where the system is established.

No two countries in the world, whether "communist" or "capitalist," can be said to have the same system traits along all ten dimensions. Even the Bulgarian system, which in most ways resembles the Soviet, differs from it in the rules for distributing the payoff accruing to economic organizations ("incentive systems") and in the rules governing foreign trade. Nevertheless, socialist countries under the aegis of Marxist-Leninist parties do share at least one common trait: all of them have very strict rules prohibiting the private ownership of almost all assets yielding monetary returns. Such rules have a presumed effect on the distribution of incomes, where incomes include returns on owned assets. If the system-specific desideratum associated with equity is tied to monetary incomes exclusively, then equity is favored by this rule. If, on the other hand, the equity desideratum depends also on the equality of non-monetary privileges and power, then the rules on ownership may have not so clear an impact on the achievement of that goal. Few economists would agree on the effect of ownership rules on consumption and growth (or on the derived desideratum of efficiency), although both the extreme advocates of such rules and their adversaries would look for some such effects—perhaps in opposite directions.

Socialist countries are generally alike in their prohibitory rules on ownership, but they do not all agree on the non-private organizations in which property rights should be vested. In particular, the relative importance of cooperatives and state enterprises differs from country to country. Nothing can be said about the equity or efficiency implications of these basic types of ownership until the rules of organization (who can order whom for what), the rules for distributing payoffs, and the rules regulating exchange (price formation and restraints on trade and markets) are specified. Leading individuals in both "socialist" and "capitalist" countries attach value to ownership rules, often for political or other extra-economic reasons.

Much less attention is paid to custody than to ownership, even though the former may have deeper implications for efficiency than the latter. It does not matter very much, for instance, whether Chinese peasants ultimately own or do not own the communal land they cultivate. The operational question is whether a team of peasants belonging to the same village will have regular custody for, and regularly take care of, a relatively manageable tract of productive land or whether they will be shifted around from one field to the other over the entire area of the commune and therefore have no long-run responsibility for any portion of it. During the Great Leap Forward in China, the authorities of the commune, which embraced tens of villages and averaged a population of some 25,000 inhabitants, had been empowered to mobilize manpower, cattle, and implements to carry out tasks wherever any of these factors of production might be needed on the massive land holdings of the commune.[9] This policy led to a decline in the interest and responsibility of commune members for the proper utilization of the lands that had formerly belonged to them privately or to the cooperatives of which they had been members (before cooperatives were amalgamated into communes). The "three-fix-campaign" of the early 1960s vested custody for manpower, implements, and land in production teams, which cultivated approximately the same lands as were formerly owned by households belonging to the team members' village. This profound operational reform, however, did not undermine the principle of communal ownership, which was upheld as vigorously as ever in the official ideology.

We should be hard put to find any rules other than those governing ownership rights that the socialist states have in common and that other, non-socialist states do not possess. Needless to say, rules permitting coercion are neither common to all socialist states nor unique to them. The mobilization of farmers to carry out certain tasks (including work on building dams), of students to help bring in the harvest, and of citizens at large to enter the labor force and take on certain jobs is indeed fairly prevalent in early post-revolutionary periods, in what has been called the "mobilization phase" of communist regimes. But coercion along these lines plays a virtually negligible role in countries like Hungary or Poland, which are farther down the road of socialist development. Moreover, coercion is frequently sanctioned in wartime "capitalist" economies—viz. the more or less binding decisions of labor exchanges in wartime England—and in many underdeveloped countries as well. In the Central African Republic, for instance, individual farmers cultivating their own land are forced in certain regions to cultivate at least an acre of cotton. (If they don't, they may get beaten up or put in jail, or otherwise be harassed by government agents.) Since the terms of exchange—the prices of output and of commercial inputs—are set by governmental institutions, the position of these captive peasants bears some resemblance to that of producers in the early stages of Soviet industrialization. One crucial difference, however, is that in mobilization regimes the unique party deploys considerably more effort than in the post-colonial states to changing both the beliefs and the preferences of citizens in such a way as to make them more responsive to commands and more enthusiastic about furthering party objectives. This is a distinctive trait of communist policies, however, not of the system structure.

Plans that are nominally binding on the decisions of government officials are not unique to socialist economies either. In many non-socialist developing countries this binding character is in the laws; but the institution that is often missing in these countries—without which plans cannot have real "teeth"—is a complex of rewards for compliance with the plan's provisions and of penalties for failure to comply. Rewards and penalties, of course, are set by rules governing the distribution of organizations' payoffs. We have here two sets of rules—on plan implementation and on the distribution of payoffs—that complement each other: the first set may not be viable without the second.

In Soviet ideology, the hierarchic management of the socialized economy, based on operational orders handed down the line of command, is generally confused with "socialist planning." Yet national economic plans can be implemented without the dispatcher-like apparatus of a command system and, conversely, such a system requires no plans to sustain it. In the Soviet Union of the early 1930s, national economic plans were hardly operational at all. What really counted was the day-to-day decisions on investments and on the allocation of inputs taken by the central dispatchers. In more recent years, both in the Soviet Union and in Eastern Europe, as the plans became better balanced—more "genetic" and less "teleological"—the *ad hoc* decisions of the central dispatchers diminished in importance.

One of the outcomes of interest to comparers of systems as well as to decision-makers within them is "stability"—not just of consumption, growth, and other output variables but more generally of the system itself. Certain constellations of system traits may be *viable* in certain environments and not in others. While we have taken the system structure so far as a datum capable of explaining, in conjunction with information about the environment, the occurrence of certain outcomes, what we learn about the viability of a particular structure in particular environments may shed light on why we observe certain traits and not others in the economies we wish to compare.

To make this point clear, we need to be more specific about policies and states of the environment, the other co-determinants of outcomes. Individuals' actions and their policies are motivated by their preferences, which, as we have seen, are included in the description of an economy's initial environment. We know much too little about people's tastes and about their subjective expectations regarding future states of their environment to predict what their actions will be under given circumstances. From the observation of their repeated actions, we may have a good idea, however, of the policies followed by influential decision-makers. It may be useful in comparing systems to take the policies of these selected individuals or groups as one of the basic sets of variables co-determining outcomes. The policies adopted by the government with respect to the achievement of rapid economic growth, industrialization, income redistribution, and other such goals are evidently crucial, although their inclusion as *explanatory variables* may have to be supplemented by specification of the policies of other groups, including the heads of labor unions, the leaders of the armed forces, and influential members of contending political parties in pluralistic societies.[10]

It is manifest that the set of possible states of an economy's environment is virtually infinite. But it can be partitioned into a finite—indeed, a reasonably small—set of "environmental conditions" that may be thought to have more or less the same impact on system outcomes under a given system structure and policies. Besides the initial preferences of the system's participants, three broad groups of environmental conditions may be distinguished: (1) variables describing the level of development and the complexity of the economy at the beginning of a period of comparison; (2) variables specifying the extent of contact of a given system with its external environment; and (3) indicators of the variability of the external-environment conditions.

A variable belonging to the first group might be the level of national income per head attained in a country just prior to a period of comparison. For certain types of analysis, this indicator may serve as an adequate proxy for the value of capital per employed person, the education and skills of the labor force, and other developmental variables belonging to the initial environment. Alternatively, if the interaction of the system structure with environmental variables were sufficiently complex (and if adequate data were on hand), it might be necessary to break down the initial-environment conditions into several subgroups of variables (including, say, the average level of education achieved by active individuals in each occupational group). A representative variable for the second group may be the share of the combined value of imports and exports in national income. We might wish to include in the third group the coefficient of variation of world prices of a country's main import and export goods, as well possibly as the variance in the rainfall, the temperature range, the incidence of floods, and similar measures of the risk and uncertainty faced by individuals in the system.

The claim that a system trait may be "unviable" under a given environment, should not be taken to mean that the trait in question will not be observed in this particular environment or even that it will not endure, but that it can only continue to be present as long as the "system directors," to use Abram Bergson's phrase, are willing to give up aggregate consumption, growth, or other economic desiderata for the sake of preserving the institution.

At this point some examples are in order. It may be conjectured that the constellation of system rules (1) prohibiting or severely restricting exchanges of goods and services on mutually satisfactory terms, (2) structuring the administration of the economy along strict hierarchic lines geared to command decisions from the top, (3) narrowly limiting the access of decision-makers in the system to foreign goods and techniques and to foreign markets, may be unviable in economies with a high per capita income and a large share (more than 50 percent) of imports and exports in their national income, irrespective of the development policies followed by government leaders. That such centralized, hierarchic system structures which provide little or no scope for free markets may still endure for years under these conditions (e.g., Bulgaria in the 1950s, Hungary in the period 1957-1963) only testifies to the strength of the political factors militating against the removal of these restrictive rules.

"Hydraulic societies" afford another classical example of interdependence between system structure and environment. In these highly centralized systems, farmers and artisans may be mobilized at the will of the rulers to construct or repair dams, to dig canals, or to cope with natural emergencies threatening the survival of the population.[11] The conjecture here is that the system structure gradually evolved toward coercive centralization to mitigate the effect of unpredictable extremes in the environment—which may be construed as an adaptation of the system to high-risk conditions.

The high correlation observed among certain traits of "communist mobilization systems" may also be traced to environmental factors. These systems, as we have already seen, tend to flourish either during, or soon after, periods of great social upheaval and to be accompanied by rapid transformation of the economic structure (as in the Soviet Union in the early 1930s or in Eastern Europe in 1949-1952). It is not surprising to find that a dispatcher-type system of centralized economic management is accompanied by the widespread use of "moral incentives" in such conditions. Given this uncertain environment, the top-level decision-makers know too little about the availability of factors and their productivity in any forthcoming period to construct balanced plans capable of serving as operational blueprints for field decisions. Moreover, supply conditions at the factory level are too chaotic and the vagaries of command decisions leave management too little tranquility to permit the proper operation of material-incentives systems. Such systems, if they are to stimulate the intelligently directed efforts of participants, require that the functionaries who dole out rewards and penalties be able to distinguish the adverse effects on outcomes of lack of effort or discipline from the adverse effects of poor coordination and other causes beyond the control of the subordinates whose work has to be assessed. This is frequently impossible under the highly uncertain conditions in which factories operate.

These speculations on the viability of system rules under different environments may help move us away from "static" toward "dynamic" principles of classification, insofar as they may reveal which constellations of system traits are likely to be stable over time and which not.[12]

The methodological approach suggested in this paper rests on the notion that it is more fruitful to classify system traits, policies, environments, and outcomes than to corset economies into a limited number of ideal types. The intelligent choice of the categories in which system traits, policies, environments, and outcomes may be catalogued should then help to pave the way to an explanatory and predictive theory of systems.

If I may conclude this brief essay on a mildly anti-climactic note, I think that the four-way classification of socialist economic systems in my earlier paper may still have been useful. Each type, after all, corresponds to a fairly clear constellation of system rules and policies operating under similar environments. Moreover, the acid test of a good classification was met, to the extent that it helped to explain or predict some of the more salient system outcomes. It is no wonder, for example, that the rate of economic growth in mobilization systems should be high but extremely uneven or that such systems should be beset by inflation. It is also evident that growth should be less chaotic and that inflation should be less of a problem in "administered systems," whether centralized or decentralized, if only because plans play more of a coordinating role and fewer *ad hoc* allocation decisions are made on a priority basis in such systems than in the mobilization type. What was missing, then, was a methodological framework for analyzing the separate effects of environment policies, and system rules on all the important system outcomes. The identification of a limited number of configurations of system traits was only a first step toward this goal.

## NOTES

1. J. M. Montias, "Types of Communist Economic Systems," in *Change in Communist Systems*, ed. Chalmers Johnson (Stanford, Calif.: Stanford University Press, 1970). For a comparable approach, see also Carmelo Mesa-Lago's contribution in this volume.

2. The ideas in this paper are in part an elaboration of the basic themes in T. C. Koopmans and J. M. Montias, "On the Description and Comparison of Economic Systems," in *Comparison of Economic Systems: Theoretical and Methodological Approaches*, ed. A. Eckstein (Berkeley, Los Angeles and London: University of California Press, 1971), pp. 27-78.

3. Let A be the set of actions (inputs) and O the set of possible outcomes (outputs). The set of all possible action-outcome pairs is the cartesian product of A and O or A x O. The system is a subset s of A x O. If the system is functional, for any action a, the pairs (a, o') only belong to s in case o and o' are identical (i.e., to any action belonging to a pair in s there corresponds only one outcome). For details and examples, see M. D. Mesarovic, D. Macko, and Y. Takahara, *Theory of Hierarchical Mutlilevel Systems* (New York and London: Academic Press, 1970), pp. 69-71.

4. This should not be taken to imply that individuals necessarily maximize their expected utility. They may "satisfice" (choose arbitrarily among various actions yielding them some satisfactory level of expected satisfaction). The satisficing hypothesis also may be invoked to explain routine or habitual behavior.

5. By the above definitions we should include specific orders by members of an organization to their subordinates among the constraints of the social structure. If a sequence of periods is considered, however, it may be more useful to include in the system structure only constraints with a stable character (laws, regulations, bylaws of organizations, etc.).

6. For a more detailed list, see Koopmans and Montias, "On the Description and Comparison of Economic Systems," pp. 42-48.

7. Prohibition against ownership of assets yielding only non-monetary returns, such as owner-occupied housing or a piano, is a rarely encountered system trait.

8. Note that an individual consents to his own (temporary) coercion when he voluntarily accepts employment entailing subordination.

9. T. J. Hughes and D. E. T. Luard, *The Economic Development of Communist China 1949-1958* (New York, London, and Toronto: Oxford University Press, 1959).

10. See Etienne Kirschens and L. Morrissen, "The Objectives and Instruments of Economic Policy," in *Quantitative Planning of Economic Policy*, ed. B. G. Hickman (Washington, D.C.: The Brookings Institution, 1965).

11. Karl A. Wittfogel, *Oriental Despotism: A Comparative Study of Total Power* (New Haven, Conn. and London: Yale University Press, 1957), chapters 1 and 2.

12. Compare the criticism by Nicolas Spulber of what he calls "static typologies" (including my own), which "do not yield explanations of why a particular society comes to rest in a particular category at a given moment, or why and how it comes to combine market, planning and its characteristic form of administration." ("On Some Issues in the Theory of the Socialist Economy," *Kyklos* 25, no. 6 [1972]:729). Note, however, that a number of economists and political scientists have speculated on the changes in system structure accompanying economic development. In particular, see A. Eckstein, "Economic Development and Political Change in Communist Systems," in *World Politics* 22 (July 1970):475-495.

# 3

# Towards an Empirical Typology of Socialist Systems

William A. Welsh

The purpose of this essay is to develop a typology, or classification scheme, for the socialist systems of Eastern Europe, including the Soviet Union. The character of this essay, therefore, is taxonomic, as opposed to explanatory, although substantial data analysis is involved. The data analysis is directed toward identifying patterns of differences between systems which appear to be salient for an understanding of relationships between socioeconomic factors, on the one hand, and political factors, on the other hand, in these socialist polities.

The reader is entirely justified in wondering whether yet another essay in taxonomic distinction-drawing really is called for. He is also entitled to some response beyond the conventional, but somewhat facile, notion that efforts at causal explanation in every branch of science have been preceded by overlapping, and often repetitive, efforts at classification. The argument that biology was essentially a taxonomic enterprise for centuries, or that game theory is still almost wholly classificatory, may not be especially reassuring in a field of study in which it can reasonably be said that there have been many "first steps" toward systematization, but only modest theoretical progress.

But good reasons abound for at least one more excursion into typology development. Most of these reasons have to do with the importance for systematic comparative inquiry of having carefully devised classification schemes for our units of analysis. There are several specific senses in which careful typologizing is crucial to systematic comparison. In the first place, the act of classifying political systems into a limited set of categories constitutes a judgment about the salience of different dimensions of those systems. Typologies, after all, must be based on selected dimensions of the phenomena being classified. In any classification system, the observations included in each category will be more similar to one another on some dimensions than on other dimensions. Implicitly, at least, placing observations into a classification scheme amounts to emphasizing the salience of those dimensions or variables on which within-category variance is smallest and on which between-category variance is greatest.

Second, and relatedly, classification schemes provide the basis for our efforts at *ex post facto* control in cross-national research designs. Regardless of whether one chooses to use a "most-similar-systems design" or a "most-different-systems design,"[1] the bases on which systems are determined to be "similar" or "different" are critical for the selection of units to be compared. Although it is possible in the abstract to examine cases dimension-by-dimension, as a practical matter, it seems clear that students of comparative politics tend to think in terms of clusters of dimensions. That is, we tend to view differences between systems in terms of broad, amalgam sets of dimensions, for example, broad categories of social structure, economic development, or political structure. Prevailing typologies—all too many of which are loosely devised, highly judgmental, and sometimes largely implicit—exert a great deal of influence on the design of cross-national comparative research.

Third, classification schemes may be viewed as definitions of the contexts in which behavioral developments take place. The classification of socialist systems in terms of the degree of centralization of political and economic decision-making is, in effect, a statement that centralization of decision-making is a salient structural feature of these systems, and that individual behaviors may be expected to be influenced by varying degrees of centralization. Another way to view this same point is to say that classification schemes tend to emphasize certain independent or intervening variables which are thought to characterize especially important structural aspects of the environment in which behavior takes place. We then attempt to explain cross-national differences in patterns of within-system behavior in terms of those structural variables which are assumed to define the behavioral context.

Finally, careful attention to issues of typology construction may lead us to raise questions about the utility of some broad, amorphous system-type categories, and perhaps to identify subtypes which might help us to clarify processes of change taking place within broader classes of systems. Of course, one may question the usefulness of efforts to break down the general class of "socialist" systems into distinct subtypes. Would it not be preferable simply to accept the label "socialist" as being broadly descriptive of a category of systems, useful at least for comparison at a very general level, and then to use whatever cross-cutting classifications might seem appropriate for specific research projects—dimensions such as level of national economic development or structure of the party system?

In the view presented here, there is reason to look more carefully within the "socialist" category. Among other things, it is worth investigating the extent to which socialist systems vary among themselves. We should be interested in defining as precisely as possible the *range* of social, economic, and political phenomena that are commonly subsumed under the label "socialist." Relatedly, it is worth asking whether the dimensions which empirically define the greatest similarities among "socialist" systems are dimensions central to socialism as a mode of social and political organization. Our evaluation of the usefulness of "socialism" as a classifying concept should be very much influenced by the extent to which the empirical commonalities which link socialist systems seem congruent with the structural and processual features usually associated deductively with socialism as a descriptive category. It may well be, for example, that the East European socialist systems are more similar to one another on dimensions that seem to have little to do with socialism than they are similar on aspects of socialist societal organization.

There is also some inherent virtue in challenging conventional wisdom, especially when that wisdom has only a modest inductive component. An examination of the recent literature on East European socialism suggests that there are few scholars indeed who would challenge the notion that Yugoslavia is a social, economic, and political "maverick," when viewed alongside other socialist systems. Yet, as the data analyses presented later in this essay suggest, there are good reasons for viewing Yugoslavia as *prototypic* of the processes of social, economic, and political change taking place throughout Eastern Europe.

*The Categorization of European Socialist Systems: Some Preliminary Thoughts*

At the considerable risk of oversimplifying the several explicit, and more often implicit, typologies of socialist systems in Eastern Europe, it can be suggested that there are three prevailing modes of classification. The first focuses on the closely related aspects of ideological "orthodoxy," or requisiteness, and the extent of party hegemony or monocracy. From this perspective, the nine East European socialist systems usually are divided into three groups. The majority fall into the category of ideologically orthodox and monocratic: Albania, the USSR, Romania, Bulgaria, and East Germany. The second grouping, characterized by some political factionalism and a modest amount of ideological controversy, consists of Czechoslovakia, Poland, and Hungary. The third category presently includes only Yugoslavia, although Czechoslovakia would have appeared briefly in this category during the first eight months of 1968; in this category, political factionalism and ideological controversy are continuing and perhaps institutionalized elements of political life.

A second prevailing mode of classification focuses on foreign policy orthodoxy, usually measured from a baseline of pro-Soviet inclinations. Three groupings again are identifiable. The first, which is high on this measure of orthodoxy, includes the Soviet Union itself, Bulgaria, East Germany, and probably Poland. The second grouping consists of Hungary and Czechoslovakia, which are thought to be somewhat more independent in foreign policy, but still operating clearly within circumscribed parameters defined largely by the Soviet Union. The third category is somewhat amorphous in that the directions of "deviation" are different, even though the extent of deviation may seem roughly similar, at least in two of the cases. This category would include Yugoslavia, Albania, and Romania. These are, for substantially different reasons in each case, the foreign policy "mavericks" within the East European context.

The third prevailing mode of classification focuses on the degree of economic "centralization," and sometimes on presumably accompanying political centralization. There are a number of slight variants on this classification theme, perhaps because our more rigorous colleagues in economics have had a greater degree of influence on this mode of classification. The classification categories used by Wilczynski[2] provide a serviceable example of this approach, with some slight modifications added from the work of Gregory[3] and Pryor.[4] This scheme would have six categories, in one of which there currently is not an empirical case. Category I, according to Wilczynski, is the "bureaucratic centralist" model, in which only Albania now fits. Category II is the "planometric centralist" model, toward which East Germany may be leaning, but of which we currently have no acceptably close example. Category III consists of economies which have been "selectively decentralized," but only sporadically and to a limited degree: the two cases in Category III are Romania and the Soviet Union. Category IV is selective decentralization, with at least moderate decentralization occurring in several sectors; included in this category are Poland, East Germany, and Bulgaria. Category V is selective decentralization, but with very substantial impact in several sectors of the economy; here the cases are Hungary and Czechoslovakia. Category VI is referred to by Wilczynski as the "supplemented market" model, and includes only Yugoslavia among the East European socialist systems.

While there are some distinct common threads running through these three modes of classification, collectively these approaches present some difficulties for anyone interested in an overall classification scheme for these nine systems. Hungary and Czechoslovakia, and perhaps Poland, might somehow seem to "fit together" as an identifiable subset. From there, however, things are not all that clear. The Soviet Union and East Germany may be thought to share broadly a number of political and economic characteristics. Still, there are significant divergences between these two countries, particularly in terms of consumption-related economic indicators, and the direction and extent of recent economic reforms. Perhaps Bulgaria might be clustered with the Soviet Union and East Germany, and yet Bulgaria differs from the other two both in terms of a significantly lower base level of economic development, and, conversely, a substantially higher rate of industrial growth. And for those with a broader historical perspective, placing a less-developed Balkan, Slavic-speaking country such as Bulgaria within the same classificatory category as a segment of the German state might seem anomalous, indeed. Romania is domestically "orthodox," but a foreign policy "maverick." Albania is less developed than any of the others, and is developing less. It has avoided any meaningful degree of economic reform or decentralization, and seems to have effectively forestalled political fractionalization. Besides, it adheres to a different axis within the "international communist movement"—if that latter phrase any longer has communicative utility. And what should one do with Yugoslavia, which often seems to necessitate its own classificatory category, or at least to be the odd man out, or perhaps the bridge between "socialist" and "capitalist" social and economic systems? (It is worth noting that Pryor's *Public Expenditures in Communist and Capitalist Nations* includes Yugoslavia as a capitalist country for purposes of comparison between the two types of systems.)

Again, perhaps the implication of this apparent confusion might be that we should not attempt to devise a single, overarching classification scheme for these East European socialist systems. Perhaps we should merely be content with the use of a variety of classification schemes, depending upon the specific purpose of any given piece of research. But if past behavior provides any linking of likely future practices, it seems unlikely that students of socialist systems will be willing to abandon broad classification schemes. Further, to do so would beg the important question of how cases should be selected on the basis of similarity or difference for studies which include a large number of social, economic, and political variables to be interrelated. Single-dimensional classifications of whole systems are not particularly satisfactory for research designs which focus on multi-dimensional within-system relationships. So, for some purposes at least, overarching, multi-dimensional classifications will continue to have importance.

### *Some Reservations about Prevailing Perspectives*

If we look more closely at the bases of these prevailing modes of classification of East European socialist systems it is not surprising that they are not wholly satisfactory for purposes of comparative research design. There are at least a half dozen respects in which these classifications need to be extended or refined. First, they generally reflect a largely cross-sectional perspective—or, at best, a limited time frame. Inadequate attention has been given to the development of typologies which would reflect longer-range processes of economic, social, and political change. This absence of attention to time series data can be troublesome, especially where processes of change differ substantially among cases. A given system may move from category to category within a classification scheme within a relatively short period of time. Whenever we wish to make statements about the extent to which certain salient structural features (i.e., the dimensions upon which classificatory categories are based) have affected within-system relationships over time, the fluctuating membership of the respective categories of the classification scheme presents problems of longitudinal comparability. And not only is it the case that the membership of corresponding categories in cross-sectional classification schemes may change over time; further, categories which were relevant to the cases under study at $T_1$ may not be relevant at $T_2$—and thus may include no cases. It would be much more desirable if we could devise a scheme which simultaneously would take into consideration not only cross-sectional "distances" between systems, but also differences in the longitudinal patterns of change.

A second, and related, problem is that prevailing cross-sectional modes of classification are overly sensitive to what Spiro[5] would call "circumstantial" (event-related) influences. For example, the "Prague spring" of 1968 seemed to alter the classification of Czechoslovakia on most, if not all, of the prevailing dimensions of classification. On the one hand, it may be argued that this simply reflects the real importance of signal events in the political and economic history of any country. On the other hand, as we have suggested, longitudinal problems of comparability arise when event-specific circumstances alter the membership of classification categories. Further, it is often difficult to assess the probable permanence, or degree of lasting impact, of even the most dramatic events. Relatedly, from the point of view of operational social theory, it is difficult to know how best to attempt to relate singular events (as opposed to classes of recurrent events) to more stable time series data.

Third, existing classification schemes, even ones which do not overtly focus on ideological criteria, do seem to be influenced by an implicit ideological overlay. Thus, Yugoslavia, *as a social system*, is generally thought to be significantly different from other East European socialist systems, probably because there are highly visible politico-ideological differences between Yugoslavia and most of the other East European countries. There has been a great deal said about the difficulty of extracting ourselves from the ideological influences of the Cold War period. These influences unfortunately seem to linger, not so much in the form of improperly imputed "totalitarianism" or ideological "orthodoxy," but rather in the form of a tendency to infer an untenably broad set of operating social principles and behaviors from an impressionistic reading of the ideological postures of dominant elites.

In short, we seem to have difficulty rejecting the notion that apparent ideological differences should necessarily be reflected in parallel differences along other social, economic, and political dimensions. These ideological considerations may distract our attention from what are perhaps more basic issues of social and political stability and change. This argument certainly is not to say that politico-ideological, politico-structural, or foreign-policy-based typologies are not useful. But, it does seem important to attempt to look beyond these considerations to basic processes of domestic change. It may well be that the most salient social dimensions for understanding future political behavior in these systems may have little to do with the ideological and related political structure features which have received so much attention in the past.

A fourth characteristic of existing typologies of socialist systems which may need to be refined is the prevailing tendency to think in terms of descriptive (nonrelational) attributes, usually conceptualized at the whole-system level. Much more attention is given to whole-system characteristics than to cross-national differences in within-system attributes, or to different *patterns of relationships* among variables at within-system levels. Fifth, and related to this question, prevailing classifications tend to be deductive and highly judgmental. There has been little inductive, empirical work done in attempting to map cross-national differences among the socialist systems of Eastern Europe. Most of the recent empirical work has dealt with regional integration,[6] and thus has focused on inter-nation linkages, not on cross-national differences in whole-system or within-system characteristics.

Sixth, despite the fact that all typologies necessarily rest implicitly on some notion of functional distance, existing classifications—probably largely because they are not empirically derived—give little attention to distances between classificatory categories. This is important, especially since the inclusion of a given set of cases in a category implies that the within-category functional distances between cases are smaller than the functional distances between members of the category and cases not included in that category. At a minimum, ordinal-level judgments are involved in any grouping of phenomena; it must be possible to say that those observations grouped together are more similar to one another than is any one of them to any other category or grouping. Ideally, we should be seeking quantitative measurement of functional distances, rather than qualitative scaling (ordinal measurement).

Indeed, one might reasonably suspect that forcing ourselves to think more formally about the relationship between within-category and between-category functional distances might yield genuine reservations about some widely used classifications of political systems. This is especially the case when multi-dimensional classification schemes are being used. When one or a small number of dimensions provide the basis for classification, it is sometimes not too difficult to make and combine the necessary ordinal-level judgments about between-system functional distances. But when a relatively large number of dimensions are involved in the classification procedure, ordinal-level judgments may not be good enough; similarly, the results of combining a large number of dimensions into a single classification scheme may not be as intuitively obvious as is the case when a small number of dimensions are used.

*Toward A Classification Strategy For East European Socialist Systems*

What we have said so far suggests that a classification scheme for East European socialist systems should meet at least four basic desiderata, which may be summarized as follows:

1. The classification scheme should reflect processes of change over time, as well as cross-sectional differences between systems at given points in time. It should not be necessary for us to use one classification approach to assess different patterns of change, and a separate classification scheme to place nations in one category or another at a given point in time.
2. The classification scheme should give attention to within-system relationships, as well as to system-level attributes. More specifically, a classification scheme should reflect not only unidimensional differences in the characteristics of systems, but also differences in patterns of relationships among relevant variables within each system. For example, we should be interested not only in cross-national differences in levels of political stability, but also in the relationships between political stability and various social and economic indicators. The extent to which such patterns of relationships differ between systems is at least as important for purposes of classifying those systems as would be the unidimensional differences between them.
3. A classification scheme should provide a basis for determining functional distances between systems, both within and between categories of classification. Ideally, such a system should be based on interval-level measurement, so that we are not faced with the often perplexing problems of combining ordinally scaled variables. Thus our classification scheme should provide a systematic and reasonably objective basis for classifying the systems under study.
4. Our classification scheme should illuminate not only "clusters" of systems, but also *modal* and *peripheral* cases. It should be possible to identify the prototypic case for any given social, economic, or political dimension, or for any set of such dimensions. It also should be possible to measure the functional distances between the modal or peripheral case and all other cases. The ability to identify

modal, or prototypic, cases should add precision to the basic nature of the parent classification (i.e., "socialist" systems). Identifying the peripheral cases should clarify the classification's *boundaries* (i.e., the range of phenomena included within the parent classification). Thus, the examination of peripheral cases should dramatize the functional distances over which the classification "socialist" is being used.

These are ideal characteristics of a classification scheme, and we probably should expect to do no better than an approximation thereof. At the same time, the procedural, or methodological, requirements that we are suggesting are not, in themselves, difficult to achieve. Typically, especially for the study of socialist systems in Eastern Europe, the difficulties encountered are likely to be a product largely of the kinds of data which are available with consistency over time and across systems. The shortcomings of the typology which will be suggested below are primarily a product of problems in the availability of data, rather than difficulties in handling the data in ways consistent with the classification desiderata listed above.

*Pattern Analysis as a Classification Method*

The procedure used in this essay to develop an empirical typology of East European socialist systems is pattern analysis. Specifically, we shall make use of the version of pattern analysis first advanced by Zaninovich[7] and used heretofore in studies of communication content in the international political system,[8] and in studies of regional integration in Eastern Europe.[9] This version of pattern analysis is a remarkably flexible technique, the core of which is the measurement of functional distances between time series. The method involves the calculation of mean vertical distances (MVD), which reflect the magnitude of difference between the values of pairs of variables at a given point in time, and mean transitional distances (MTD), which assess the extent to which two time series are moving in the same direction between adjacent points in time. Thus the technique reflects both cross-sectional and longitudinal differences between time series. The MTD and MVD are summed to yield an index value called a "functional distance" by Zaninovich. This functional distance thus reflects differences between time series on the two dimensions, cross-sectional and longitudinal.

One of the important virtues of pattern analysis for our purposes is that it does not make restrictive assumptions about the nature of the data being used. As long as two time series are measured on a standardized scale, the two time series can be compared. The functional distance measure is, obviously, neither an inferential statistic nor a correlational technique. Autocorrelation of a time series does not affect the calculation of the measure, and is not relevant to its interpretation. Equally important, there are no restraints on the ratio between the number of variables and the number of cases. Such a constraint limits the applicability of factor analysis, or other techniques based on correlation, to research situations such as ours. Specifically, we wish to use a relatively large number of variables, but we have a small number of cases. This situation leads to overdetermination of models based on correlational methods. But with pattern analysis, we can compare an infinite number of time series on a pair-wise basis, and then calculate mean functional distances, either among a series of variables within a given country, or for corresponding variables across an infinite set of countries.

In the application reported here, three basic sets of measures are used. First, average cross-national functional distances are calculated for a series of socio-economic variables. For example, we look at energy consumption per capita in each of the nine systems under study, and calculate the functional distance between the time series for energy consumption per capita for each pair of nations. We do the same for a number of other socio-economic variables, giving us as many cross-national functional distances between each pair of nations as we have variables. The distances between each pair of nations can then be averaged, providing us a single mean cross-national socio-economic distance for each pair of nations. We could, in fact, make cross-national comparisons on the basis of a single variable, or any given subset of socio-economic indicators, or for all of the socio-economic measures, viewed collectively. In this essay, comparisons are based on mean cross-national functional distances for all socio-economic variables, and not for any subsets thereof.

The second measure used is a set of average cross-national functional distances for indicators of government control activity, and of political stability. Again, the same procedure is used. For example, a political violence index has been constructed for each of the nine systems, and the functional distances between the political violence time series are calculated for each pair of countries. The same is done for four other political measures, and mean political distances are calculated for each pair of countries.

Finally, we examine cross-national deviations from mean within-system functional distances between socio-economic and political variables. Here the procedure is slightly different. For each country (i.e., *within* each country), we calculate functional distances between standardized time series. On the one hand, we have a series of socio-economic indicators; on the other hand, a group of indicators of political activity. We pair each socio-economic variable with each political variable. One such measure, for example, is the functional distance between the time series for energy consumption per capita and the time series for political violence. It is then possible to calculate a mean functional distance for each country showing the average distance between socio-economic time series on one hand, and political time series, on the other hand. This is viewed as a characterization of the extent to which within-system socio-economic change is similar to within-system political change. Then, on the basis of these within-system values, we calculate a mean functional distance between socio-economic and political variables for the entire set of nine nations. The measure we ultimately wish to use is the extent to which a country deviates from the within-system functional distance. We may view these deviations from the mean as representing cross-national functional distances with respect to a particular kind of within-system relationship, i.e., the relationship between socio-economic change and political change.

The use of pattern analysis, and these three basic sets of measures derived from the basic pattern analysis model, permit the clustering of these nine Eastern European socialist nations on four bases. First, we can cluster nations in terms of a simple criterion of similarity/dissimilarity. Specifically, we can cluster on the basis of maximum within-category similarity (that is, minimum within-category cross-national functional distances) on the three basic sets of measures described above. Those nations having the smallest average cross-national functional distances for these three sets of measures would be grouped together. Formally, the criterion for inclusion of a nation in a cluster would be whether the inclusion of that nation increased the difference between the mean cross-national functional distance within the category, on the one hand, and the mean functional distance between members of the category and all other cases in the population, on the other hand. For example, let us suppose that we had determined that Hungary and Poland were quite close to one another on each of our three measures. We might believe that Czechoslovakia should also be included in this clustering. We would calculate the mean functional distance for each of our sets of measures between Hungary and Poland; this would give us a mean within-category functional distance. Then we would determine the mean functional distance between Hungary and Poland on one hand, and all other countries, on the other hand. The greater the difference between these two mean values (i.e., between the mean within-category distance and the mean without-category distance), the more "cohesive" the cluster. We would then make the same calculations, including Czechoslovakia in the cluster with Hungary and Poland. If the difference between the mean within-cluster functional distance and the mean without-cluster functional distance *increased* with the inclusion of Czechoslovakia, we would include Czechoslovakia in that cluster. If, on the other hand, the mean functional distance *decreased*, such that the cohesiveness of the cluster was diminished by the inclusion of Czechoslovakia, we would not make that inclusion.

A second basis for clustering of these systems would be the mean functional distance of each system from the "focal," or modal, system for each set of measures. Using Zaninovich's pattern analysis technique, it is possible to identify the focal system for each of our three basic sets of measures. The focal system is the one whose average functional distance from other nations is the smallest. To presage some of our subsequent data analysis, we discover that the focal country with respect to socio-economic development in Eastern Europe is Romania. It is then possible, using cross-national functional distances, to define the distance between Romania and each other East European socialist system. These systems then could be clustered in terms of their distance from the focal case—Romania for socio-economic variables, and, perhaps surprisingly, Yugoslavia for political variables.

A third basis for clustering the nine systems would be the deviation of each system from the mean functional distance for all nations on each of the three measures. In this case, rather than taking the modal system as a base line, we would use the system whose functional distance from other systems was the closest to the *mean functional distance* between all pairs of systems. For example, while Romania is the focal case for socio-economic change (having the smallest average functional distance from all other countries), the country closest to the mean functional socio-economic distance is Bulgaria. Romania has the *smallest* average functional distance; Bulgaria is quite close to the *mean* functional distance among the nine countries. We could then construct clusters in terms of cross-national similarities in deviations from mean functional distances.

Finally, we ultimately seek an overall classificatory pattern, taking into account the three complementary procedures outlined above. That is, it is worth attempting to amalgamate these three clustering strategies to see if we could develop an overarching classification scheme which would permit us to cluster these nine East European socialist systems into a small number of meaningful subsets for purposes of analysis and research design.

*Mode of Data Analysis*

Clearly, some kind of standardization of measures is necessary, especially when we propose to make comparisons both across a substantial number of social, economic, and political variables, and also between countries. The strategy used here is to transform all measures into ten-point scales. Specifically, for each time series (i.e., for each variable, considering all time points for all nine countries) the lowest observed value is given a value of one, and the highest observed value is set equal to ten. All other values are arranged proportionately between one and ten. Through this procedure, all variables are rendered in a standardized scale which permits comparison across variables, and across countries.[10]

This procedure is simple—in fact, it may strike some as being entirely too simple. Some of the implications of having proceeded in this way should be examined. First, the basis of "standardization" is, of course, the set of nine East European socialist countries with which we are dealing. The result of defining our relevant population as consisting only of the nine countries under study is to highlight variance among them. That is, if "global" standardization were used (i.e., if the scale value of one corresponded to the smallest value observed anywhere in the world on that variable, and a scale value of ten, the highest observed anywhere), cross-national variance for the subset of East European systems would have been much less. This would have made it more difficult to identify meaningful differences among them. The socialist countries of Eastern Europe do not represent as substantial a range of variation on these measures as would be represented by all of the independent entities in the world on which such data are available. Our strategy seems appropriate, since we are interested in identifying subsets of East European socialist systems and, therefore, wish to have available to us the most sensitive reading of variation possible.

It may reasonably be asked why *z*-scores, or some other commonly used standardized measurement or logarithmic transformation, have not been used. There is an equally reasonable response: *z*-scores and other such standardized measures are based on the assumption of a normal distribution of values for each of the measures in question. When we deal with time series, many of which exhibit reasonably consistent upward or downward trend, the assumption of a normal distribution of values seems wholly inappropriate. Relatedly, since *z*-scores simply express standard deviation units, the imposition of the normal curve model onto these data could radically distort the longitudinal functional distances between systems. Consequently, it seems much more appropriate simply to transform each of our measurements into a one-to-ten scale, such that within-system measurement differences (e.g., differences in the measurement units between politically violent acts and energy consumption per capita) are washed out, as are cross-national measurement differences (e.g., the use of nonstandard monetary units).

The data analysis for most of this essay is based on the comparison of eleven socio-economic variables, and five political variables, for each of the nine socialist systems in Eastern Europe. For four of the systems (Bulgaria, Czechoslovakia, Hungary, and Poland), more detailed analysis is possible because of a considerably greater range of available reliable data on both socio-economic and political variables. Specifically, it is possible to use twenty-three socio-economic variables and nine political variables in determining functional distances among these four countries. However, in order to maintain a comparable base for all functional distance measures, most of the data analysis reported is based on the use of the eleven core socio-economic measures, and the five measures of political system stability and government control activity.

It was decided to make use simultaneously of some continuous time series, and some discontinuous time series. There are both theoretical and practical reasons for having done so. For many of the socio-economic measures, we use 1950, 1955, 1960, and 1965 data, which constitute discrete time points at five-year intervals. This is done where serial autocorrelation is high (e.g., many economic time series data exhibit a high level of serial autocorrelation), and where, therefore, the addition of more annual observations adds virtually no new information. In addition to this theoretical justification, there is the practical problem that some of these data are reliably available only for the years in question.[11] In some cases, we use continuous time series data, and insert for each of the four time points the average of the five years surrounding that time point. This is done where serial autocorrelation is low, i.e., where episodic and event influences on any given annual value might be great (e.g., political instability scores, which are assumed to vary substantially with episodic or singular societal disruptions). Ultimately, however, the analysis is based on the comparison of time series values for four points in time. In some cases, these values are in fact annual and discrete observations; in other cases, primarily for the political variables, the observations represent averages around the indicated time point.

The data used in this study were taken largely from three machine-readable data bases containing information on the countries of Eastern Europe: The World Handbook II,[12] The Cross Polity Time Series,[13] and the East European Data Bank of the Laboratory for Political Research at the University of Iowa.[14] The Iowa collection is based on material contained in statistical yearbooks and other materials published in Eastern Europe. For most of the analysis, eleven socio-economic indicators and five political variables were included. These indicators are summarized in Table 1.

Generally, the socio-economic variables tap dimensions of social development and modernization, population well-being, and several aspects of system capability and performance—perhaps especially including what Almond and Powell might call the extractive and responsive capabilities of the system.[15] The political variables include three indicators of political system stability and two indicators of regulative system capacity, or government control activity. The system stability indicators include the Feierabend, Feierabend, and Nesvold political instability score,[16] a government instability index constructed from data in the World Handbook II, and a political violence index, constructed from data in the World Handbook II and the Cross Polity Time Series. Indicators of regulative system capacity are security forces as a proportion of the working population, and an index of government control activity constructed from data in the World Handbook II and the Cross Polity Time Series.

It should be emphasized that the government control index does not purport to measure the *extent* of control by authorities over the

Table 1

*Indicators of Socio-economic and Political Change in Eastern Europe*

*SOCIO-ECONOMIC INDICATORS*

| *Basic Set* | *Additions in Extended Set* |
|---|---|
| ***Social Development*** | |
| Literacy rate | Urban population (% in cities 20,000 or more) |
| Enrollment in higher education | |
| ***Population Well-Being*** | |
| Energy consumption/capita (Kilograms) | Passenger cars/capita |
| Energy consumption growth rate | Consumer price index |
| Physicians/capita | Retail trade volume |
| | Earnings (average hourly in manufacturing) |
| | Marriage rate |
| ***System Capabilities and Performance*** | |
| Energy production/capita | GDP/capita from industry |
| Radios/capita | Steel consumption growth rate |
| Newspaper circulation/capita | Domestic capital formation/GNP |
| Proportion of world trade | Employment in manufacturing/labor force |
| Exports/capita | Agricultural production |
| Imports/capita | Telegrams/capita |

*POLITICAL INDICATORS*

*Political Control*

Security forces/working population

Government control activity index (sanctions, amnesty)

| *Political Stability* | *Elite Attributes* |
|---|---|
| Political instability score (Feierabend. Feierabend, & Nesvold) | Attribute change rate (average variability for 37 attributes) |
| Government instability index (government crises, purges) | "Revolutionary" type (Beck) |
| Political violence index (assassinations, riots, other violence) | "Career government official" type (Beck) |
| | "Central political official" type (Beck) |

citizenry, but rather the amount of overt *control-related activity* taking place in the system. It is not necessarily to be assumed that government control is greatest where control activity is highest. In fact, quite the opposite might be the case. The government control index includes the number of government sanctions and other acts of repression. It also includes acts of amnesty and rehabilitation. One may interpret either of these measures as implying either greater or lesser control by authorities over the citizenry. Amnesty may imply a relaxation of controls, or it may imply such a substantial level of control over the population that it is possible to release persons previously thought to be potentially dangerous to regime stability. Similarly, sanctions and other acts of repression may indicate either a high regulative capacity, or substantial uncertainty among political authorities as to the extent of their control. The point to be made is that such quantitative measures can reasonably be thought of as activity in the general area of political control, but it is very difficult to determine whether such indicators imply a greater or lesser degree of political control in the system.

For four of the countries (Bulgaria, Czechoslovakia, Hungary, and Poland), considerably larger numbers of variables, both socio-economic and political, are available. In particular, it is possible to examine four aggregate measures of political elite characteristics for these four countries, and thereby to extend the breadth of our measurement of between-system political differences. These four political elite characteristics are based on measures developed by Beck.[17] Three of these measures describe salient career types (the political revolutionary, the career governmental official, the central political official) which were identified through canonical correlation analysis of the backgrounds and careers of four successive sets of Party Central Committee members in each country. The fourth measure indicates the rate at which background and career characteristics in each of the four central committees changed over time. That is, the measure is an indicator of the average variability between time points for each of the thirty-seven background and career attributes examined by Beck. These four measures provide a basis for assessing the overall process of change in the characteristics of political leaders in these four countries. These indicators are especially useful, and it is unfortunate that they are not available for the other five East European socialist systems under study. Because these elite measures are available for only four countries, they are used here primarily to show that findings based on the five political stability and control measures for those four countries are not materially affected when the data analysis is extended to the elite variables.

It is worth making explicit some of the kinds of indicators which are *not* included in this study, but which can contribute importantly to our understanding of differences among East European socialist systems. First, the data do not include any dyadic inter-nation interaction measures. Indicators of import and export volume, and of overall level of trade activity, are examined, but bilateral trade interactions, for example, are not included. Such data are available, and their exclusion here was based on a conscious decision to emphasize within-nation characteristics, rather than international interactions, since the latter have received much more attention in recent years from scholars writing on Eastern Europe. Second, for the same sort of reasons we have excluded any judgmental data on ideological orthodoxy, or ideological requisiteness, in these systems. There are no indicators which purport to measure the ideological "flavor" of the political system. Third, although our data do seem to get at extractive, regulative, and perhaps responsive capacities of these systems, they inadequately tap the distributive system capability.[18] The measures which might have been used for this concept are not available with sufficient cross-national or longitudinal consistency for the East European socialist countries to warrant their inclusion in this analysis. Finally, we do not include indicators of administrative decentralization, or more generally, the nature of relationships between central and constituent governmental units. Pryor does present such data for most—but unfortunately not all—of the East European socialist systems.[19] At such time as these data may be available for all nine of these systems it would seem especially appropriate to include them in such an analysis, since relations between central and constituent governmental units may be especially important in distinguishing these systems from one another.

*Analysis of Functional Distances: Socio-economic Distances*

Table 2 summarizes the results of the analysis of cross-national distances for eleven socio-economic variables. Perhaps surprisingly, Romania emerges as the focal, or modal, country; its average functional distance from other countries was the smallest. Thus we may conclude that the process of socio-economic change in Romania has been the most "typical" for the nine-nation set. The second most typical, or focal, country is Poland. Hungary, Yugoslavia, and Bulgaria are at a modest distance from the focal case, while the distances for the other four (East Germany, the Soviet Union, Czechoslovakia, and Albania) are rather substantial. Albania is the peripheral case in terms of cross-national socio-economic distances; it has the highest average functional distance from the other nations.

It should not be difficult to understand why Romania and Poland should emerge as focal cases on the socio-economic dimension. These two countries started at relatively low levels of social and economic development, but not at the lowest levels within the nine-nation set, since Yugoslavia and Albania, and on some indicators, Bulgaria, started at lower levels. An examination of the individual time series for social and economic indicators for Poland and Romania shows that they have a substantially similar pattern of relatively slow acceleration during the first half of the period, but considerably more rapid economic growth during the second half of the fifteen-year time span embraced by our data. They remain below the mean in terms of levels of social and economic development, but their rates of growth in recent years are somewhat above the mean. And on several of the socio-economic time series, Romania and Poland occupy a middle ground.

Table 2

*Cross-national Socio-economic Functional Distances*
*Mean Socio-Economic Distances From All Other Countries*

| *Country* | *FDs Based on 11 Variables* | *FDs Based on 23 Variables* | *Deviation from Grand Mean FD* |
|---|---|---|---|
| Romania | 2.2975 | | -.5642 |
| Poland | 2.4085 | 2.3441 | -.4532 |
| Hungary | 2.6184 | 2.3915 | -.2433 |
| Yugoslavia | 2.7546 | | -.1071 |
| Bulgaria | 2.8827 | 2.7152 | +.0210 |
| German Democratic Republic | 3.0261 | | +.1644 |
| USSR | 3.0784 | | +.2167 |
| Czechoslovakia | 3.3188 | 3.0257 | +.4571 |
| Albania | 3.3704 | | +.5087 |
| Grand Mean = | 2.8617 | | |

The peripheral case, Albania, is distinguished by the lowest base point for nearly all of the social and economic measures, and by a substantially more inconsistent pattern of growth than was exhibited by any of the other socialist systems. The mean transitional distances (it will be recalled that functional distances consist of both vertical and transitional distances) for Albania are uniformly high, suggesting that Albania experienced stagnation, even relative decline, on a number of indicators when almost all other East European countries were achieving noticeable growth.

But what is perhaps more surprising than the peripheral position of Albania is the fact that Czechoslovakia was very nearly as socio-economically peripheral as was Albania. Obviously, Czechoslovakia is peripheral in a different direction, at least with respect to levels of social and economic development. On many of the indicators, Czechoslovakia started at the highest level of any East European country. Partly for that reason, the rates of socio-economic growth in Czechoslovakia have been somewhat lower than those for other East European countries.

That is not, however, the whole story. There seems little disagreement among students of Eastern European economics that Czechoslovak economic growth might have been a great deal greater than it has been since 1948. The pattern of Czechoslovak economic progress during this period has been shown by Gregory[20] and Pryor[21] to be quite unusual in the East European context. In the first place, while most East European countries have experienced both significant expansion of domestic demand for industrial products, and substantial increase in the export of finished manufactures, Czechoslovakia has faced an export demand contraction, and a domestic demand curve that has moved only sporadically and modestly upward. For Czechoslovakia, import substitution has been the primary source of industrial expansion. The manufacturing sector has grown 18 percent in its share of gross national product in the post-war period; about 82 percent of that increase can be accounted for by import substitution.[22] Most of the effect of the modest domestic demand expansion was cancelled by export demand contraction. That is, the export sector of the Czechoslovak economy fell substantially below its pre-war levels for a number of years, and is only now beginning to recover. In other East European countries, by contrast, domestic demand has expanded rather more rapidly than in Czechoslovakia, and there was not the offsetting factor of export demand contraction.

There is a second factor, more difficult to explain, but perhaps equally significant in accounting for the unusually slow pace of social and economic growth in Czechoslovakia during the post-war period. Total consumption expenditures in Czechoslovakia are significantly below that predicted by a regression model based on the analysis of data from a cross-section of European nations. Gregory[23] shows, for example, that Czechoslovak consumption expenditures (including both personal consumption and communal consumption) were 19 percentage points below "normal" by 1956, and had dropped to 21 percentage points below "normal" by 1964. (This essentially means that total consumption expenditures were about one-fifth lower than would be expected in a nation with the per capita income level of Czechoslovakia.) East Germany recorded similar figures for those years, but has shown a substantially more impressive recovery in the last 10 years. It must be recognized that the consumption expenditure ratios for all East European socialist nations were negative through the 1950s, but the situation has been rather more pronounced, and more lasting, in Czechoslovakia.

Thus the factors of modest domestic demand expansion, substantial export contraction, and lagging consumption expenditures, both private and governmental, seem to combine to explain the disappointing degree of social and economic growth in Czechoslovakia since 1948.

Czechoslovakia is therefore "peripheral" with respect to socio-economic change, both because it began at a higher level than the other nations of Eastern Europe, and also because its degree of progress has been slight, even less impressive than would have been predicted simply on the basis of its higher starting point.

Table 2 has presented average cross-national functional distances for socio-economic variables. A slightly different way to examine the same data is presented in Table 3. Here we take the focal case, Romania, as a base point, and define clusters of nations in terms of their respective distances from the focal nation. This procedure yields clusters in Table 3 which differ slightly from those in Table 2. This is because the functional distance values in Table 2 are based on the average distance for each country from *all other* countries in the set. In Table 3, we examine only the distance of each country from the focal case, which is Romania.

**Table 3**

*Socio-economic Functional Distances from the Focal Case*

*(Focal Case = Romania)*

| | |
|---|---|
| Yugoslavia | 1.51 |
| Poland | 1.89 |
| Albania | 2.00 |
| Hungary | 2.12 |
| Bulgaria | 2.20 |
| USSR | 2.43 |
| German Democratic Republic | 2.85 |
| Czechoslovakia | 3.33 |

Table 3 shows that Yugoslavia is closest to the focal country. A group of four nations seems to cluster together at a slightly greater distance from the focal case; this cluster consists of Poland, Albania, Hungary, and Bulgaria. The Soviet Union, East Germany, and Czechoslovakia are found at considerably greater distances from Romania. Thus if Romania is to be considered prototypic of the process of socio-economic change, we can say that Yugoslavia's socio-economic change process has also been close to "typical" and that Czechoslovakia deviates furthest from the empirical modal case.

Broadly, the two substantial differences between Tables 2 and 3 are that both Yugoslavia and Albania emerge as closer to "typical" in Table 3, where they are measured only in terms of their distance from the focal case, rather than in terms of their average distances from all of the other East European socialist countries. The change in the position of Albania between Tables 2 and 3 is especially noticeable, and simply reflects the facts that Albania is socio-economically more similar to Yugoslavia and Romania than to any other country, and that Romania happens to be focal with respect to the process of socio-economic change. (Figures 1 through 18 in the Appendix to this paper present, in bar graph form, the average functional distances for each country from all other countries. An examination of the Appendix should clarify how it is possible for Albania to be peripheral in terms of its overall average cross-national distance, but still close to the focal case, Romania. That is, Albania is close to Romania, and also to Yugoslavia, but it is substantially distant from most of the other systems.) Otherwise, Tables 2 and 3 suggest similar patterns of likenesses, especially that the Soviet Union, East Germany, and Czechoslovakia would be clustered together as substantially "deviant" socio-economic cases.

*Cross-National Functional Distances: Political Distances*

Table 4 displays the average cross-national political distances for each country. It should be kept in mind that the five political variables which provide the basis for these calculations refer to government control activity and to indicators of governmental and political system stability. It may seem surprising that Yugoslavia emerges clearly as the focal case, followed by Romania. The average cross-national functional political distances for Yugoslavia and Romania with the other socialist systems of Eastern Europe are the smallest. Further, the gap between Yugoslavia and Romania, and the remainder of the countries, is great. Only Bulgaria also has a relatively modest average political distance from the other socialist systems; the remainder of the countries are strung out with considerably greater average political distances from one another. Poland has a particularly high average political distance from the others.

Lest we suspect that the five political variables being used, because of their focus on political control and stability dimensions, might distort the picture of functional political distances, we should give attention to the average functional distances for the four countries for which political elite measures are also available. It should be noted that the functional distances among Bulgaria, Czechoslovakia, Hungary, and Poland are not substantially changed by the inclusion of the political elite indicators. The average functional distance for Bulgaria goes up slightly; for Czechoslovakia and Hungary there is a slight decrease; and for Poland, a somewhat greater decline. Still, even the use of nine political variables rather than five results in placing Poland in a clearly peripheral position in terms of cross-national political distance.

That one of the most "deviant" countries in terms of ideology, political structure, and foreign policy should emerge as politically focal in terms of control activity and political stability may seem striking.

**Table 4**

*Cross-national Political Functional Distances*

| | *Mean Political Distances From All Other Countries* | | |
|---|---|---|---|
| *Country* | *FDs Based on 5 Variables* | *FDs Based on 9 Variables* | *Deviation from Grand Mean FD* |
| Yugoslavia | 2.7315 | | -.7463 |
| Romania | 2.9272 | | -.5506 |
| Bulgaria | 3.2276 | 3.3868 | -.2502 |
| German Democratic Republic | 3.4740 | | -.0038 |
| USSR | 3.5846 | | +.1068 |
| Czechoslovakia | 3.6576 | 3.5388 | +.1798 |
| Albania | 3.7057 | | +.2279 |
| Hungary | 3.7715 | 3.6248 | +.2937 |
| Poland | 4.2205 | 3.9338 | +.7427 |
| Grand Mean= | 3.4778 | | |

The Yugoslav pattern has been one of moderate and only slightly fluctuating levels of political control and instability. And that is indeed the modal situation for the socialist countries of Eastern Europe, with the distinct exceptions of the trio of Czechoslovakia, Hungary, and Poland, which have experienced substantially greater political unrest and upheaval. Not surprisingly, these three countries constitute three of the four most peripheral countries in terms of average cross-national political distances. The other country which is politically highly distant from the others is Albania, and this should not seem surprising. Albania has been characterized by an unusual combination of domestic political circumstances. In the Albanian case, there has been very little governmental or political instability, but nevertheless, a persistent level of acts of control and repression by the political authorities. Consequently, the Albanian pattern is "deviant" in that the relationship between the magnitude of control activity and measures of political instability is considerably less consistent than is the case for the other East European countries.

Table 5 presents the data on cross-national political distances from our second perspective, namely, the distance of each country from the focal case, which here is Yugoslavia. Table 5 departs almost not at all from the implications of Table 4. It does not seem to matter whether we array the systems of Eastern Europe in terms of their average functional political distances from one another, or in terms of the distance of each from the focal case, Yugoslavia. The clusters are essentially stable: Yugoslavia and Romania cluster together, with East Germany and Bulgaria the closest to them. Czechoslovakia does appear less peripheral from the perspective of Table 5, but the remainder of the systems are arrayed in essentially the same way. Poland is, again, most peripheral.

**Table 5**

*Political Functional Distances from the Focal Case*
*(Focal Case = Yugoslavia)*

| | |
|---|---|
| Romania | 2.03 |
| German Democratic Republic | 2.07 |
| | |
| Bulgaria | 2.660 |
| Czechoslovakia | 2.667 |
| USSR | 2.70 |
| | |
| Albania | 3.00 |
| Hungary | 3.33 |
| Poland | 3.36 |

We cannot stress too strongly the major implication of this analysis of functional political distances. At least with respect to the important indicators of governmental control activity and political stability, two of the countries thought of on some dimensions as the most "deviant" in the region are, in fact, the *most prototypic* of the socialist systems in Eastern Europe. This analysis certainly does not purport to challenge the accepted notion that Yugoslavia and Romania are "peripheral" in their foreign policies, but it does suggest that our sense of their foreign policy peripherality should not obscure the apparently "main-stream" character of the change processes in their domestic spheres of political control and stability.

*Cross-National Differences in Within-System Relationships*

A third set of measures which permits us to identify distances among East European socialist systems is based on functional distances between socio-economic variables and political variables within each country. Here we focus on the degree to which socio-economic trends and political trends exhibit the same basic characteristics. To this point, we have looked at cross-national differences in the time series for each of sixteen variables. Now the focus shifts to within-country functional distances between socio-economic variables, on the one hand, and political variables, on the other hand. We calculate the functional distances between each pair of socio-economic and political variables, and then determine the mean within-system functional distance for each country. Then the mean value for the nine nations for these socio-economic political distances is calculated, and the deviation of each country from the group mean is used to cluster systems.

Table 6 shows the average within-country functional distance between socio-economic and political time series for each country, as well as the deviation for each country from the grand mean. The smallest socio-economic/political "gap" is exhibited by Yugoslavia. That is, socio-economic variables and political variables are more similar in their respective basic trend characteristics in Yugoslavia than in any other East European country. Albania and Romania are also well below the grand mean in these within-country functional distances. Three countries–East Germany, the Soviet Union, and Bulgaria–cluster near the grand mean. Well above the grand mean are Czechoslovakia, Poland, and Hungary. In general, then, socio-economic and political indicators move most closely together in Yugoslavia, Romania, and Albania, and exhibit the greatest disjuncture in Czechoslovakia, Poland, and Hungary. (It is possible to view the average within-country functional distance between socio-economic and political variables as a kind of composite measure of societal instability, in the sense that countries scoring high on this measure appear to be experiencing political change which is "out of pattern" with socio-economic change–or vice-versa.)

**Table 6**

*Within-country Functional Distances*
*(Distances Between Socio-economic and Political Variables)*

| *Country* | *Mean FD* | *Deviation from Grand Mean FD* |
|---|---|---|
| Yugoslavia | 3.2215 | - 1.0661 |
| Romania | 3.4972 | - .7904 |
| Albania | 3.5831 | - .7045 |
| | | |
| USSR | 4.1478 | - .1398 |
| German Democratic Republic | 4.3680 | + .0804 |
| Bulgaria | 4.4567 | + .1691 |
| | | |
| Hungary | 4.8719 | + .5843 |
| Poland | 5.0295 | + .7419 |
| Czechoslovakia | 5.4124 | + 1.1248 |

Grand Mean = 4.2876

What is most interesting about the findings reported in Table 6 is that the clusters of countries are quite similar to the clusters generated by the cross-national socio-economic and cross-national political analyses. Yugoslavia, Romania, and (to a lesser extent) Albania are in several respects similar to one another in their processes of social, economic, and political change. Czechoslovakia, Poland, and Hungary seem to cluster together with some consistency, and to exhibit characteristics which are substantially different from those of the first group. And East Germany, the Soviet Union, and Bulgaria are once again clustered together. Further, the clusters suggested in Table 6 have a good deal of face validity. The countries below the mean in within-country functional distances are less-developed, "southern tier" countries which have exhibited substantively different but noteworthy degrees of political "deviance" from the prevailing "orthodoxies" of East European socialism. Czechoslovakia, Poland, and Hungary are "northern tier" countries, somewhat more highly developed economically, and have experienced substantial political disruptions and upheavals in common. East Germany, the Soviet Union, and Bulgaria exhibit the commonalities of substantial political stability and impressive levels of economic growth and achievement in recent years.

*Toward a Synthesis: Basic Distinctions among East European Socialist Systems*

Since each of the three basic measures reported to this point is based on a series of standardized scale scores, and on a common method of calculating functional distances, it is possible to combine these scores into one synthetic measure of between-system difference. For each pair of countries, an average functional distance score is derived by averaging the between-nation socio-economic distance, the between-nation political distance, and the between-nation difference in degree of deviation from the grand mean within-country functional distance. Clusters are formed on the basis of the inclusion criterion previously used, that is, whether the inclusion of a given country in a cluster increases the cohesiveness of that cluster (i.e., increases the difference between the average functional distance within the cluster, and the average functional distance between members of the cluster and all other systems'.

The results of this overall analysis are presented in Table 7. By far the most cohesive cluster, or pattern, is the grouping of Yugoslavia, Romania, and Albania. The average within-cluster cross-national functional distance is barely more than half the average distance between each of these countries and the six systems not included in this cluster. (It might be emphasized parenthetically that the inclusion of Albania *does* increase the net cohesiveness of the first cluster. Including only Romania and Yugoslavia in the cluster yields a net functional distance difference of .9939; with the inclusion of Albania, the net functional distance difference rises to 1.655. This is true despite the peripheral position of Albania on the measure of cross-national political distances. The explanation for the "fit" of Albania into this overall category with Yugoslavia and Romania is simply that Albania is very close to the other two countries on the cross-national socio-economic measure, and on the within-system distance measure.) The second most cohesive pattern consists of Hungary and Poland. (The difference between the mean within-cluster functional distance and the mean without-cluster functional distance for the second cluster is .9312.)

**Table 7**

*Clusters of East European Socialist Systems*

| | Mean Within-cluster Functional Distance | Mean Without-cluster Functional Distance | Index of Cohesion [a] | Mean FD between Czechoslovakia and Each Cluster |
|---|---|---|---|---|
| *Cluster 1* | | | | |
| Romania | | | | |
| Yugoslavia | | | | |
| Albania | 1.4401 | 2.6056 | 1.1655 | 3.0302 |
| *Cluster 2* | | | | |
| Hungary | | | | |
| Poland | 1.6425 | 2.5737 | .9312 | 2.7939 |
| *Cluster 3* | | | | |
| Bulgaria | | | | |
| German Democratic Republic | | | | |
| USSR | 2.2886 | 2.3900 | .1014 | 2.5016 |
| *"Out of Pattern"* | | | | |
| Czechoslovakia | | | | |

[a]Index of Cohesion = Mean without-cluster FD minus mean within-cluster FD

The third cluster, or pattern, is substantially less cohesive than the first two and, in fact, has an average within-cluster functional distance which is nearly as high as the average without-cluster functional distance. That is, this cluster is barely a cluster by the criterion we are using. This grouping consists of Bulgaria, East Germany, and the Soviet Union.

One of the most interesting findings presented in Table 7 is the fact that Czechoslovakia does not meet our criterion for inclusion in any of the clusters. The inclusion of Czechoslovakia would substantially decrease the cohesiveness of any cluster. Table 7 displays the average functional distance between the members of each of the clusters, on the one hand, and Czechoslovakia, on the other hand. Czechoslovakia is closest—perhaps surprisingly—to the countries of cluster 3, slightly more distant from Hungary and Poland (cluster 2), and furthest, as might have been expected, from the countries of cluster 1. However, the inclusion of Czechoslovakia in cluster 3 would have decreased the already-small difference between within-cluster and without-cluster distances from .1014 to .0074. That is, if Czechoslovakia were included in cluster 3, that cluster essentially would become a residual category.

Several other important interpretations are suggested from an examination of Table 7. First, the three countries most frequently thought of as "mavericks" in socialist East Europe are more similar to one another than might have been imagined and, further, are considerably more prototypic of processes of social, economic, and political change in Eastern Europe than is commonly thought. When we divorce ourselves momentarily from the more visible ideological and foreign policy aspects of the functioning of these systems, and concentrate instead on basic processes of domestic change, these "deviant" cases in fact become focal, or modal, especially Yugoslavia and Romania.

Second, Czechoslovakia emerges from these analyses as, in many respects, the most domestically "deviant" or peripheral case among the socialist systems of Eastern Europe. It is fundamentally unlike any of the other socialist nations in terms of domestic socio-economic and political change. Third, the striking combination of political stability and impressive economic growth exhibited by Bulgaria, especially after the early 1950s, has projected it into a pattern with East Germany and the Soviet Union, despite the significantly lower economic base from which Bulgaria began, and despite the geographic and, to a lesser extent, cultural differences which would seem to place Bulgaria apart from the two larger and more advanced systems of East Germany and the USSR.

The findings reported here do not necessarily call for the rejection of conventional classifications of East European socialist systems; rather, these analyses argue for a broadening of our perspectives, both substantive and methodological. It is obviously important to examine issues of foreign policy, related concerns of inter-nation interaction and regional integration, and information about the ideological content and character of a social system. What has been suggested here is that focusing on these more visible aspects of political activity may sometimes obscure modest but meaningful differences where similarity has been thought to be characteristic and, conversely, may obscure substantial similarities and prototypic patterns where divergence or deviance has been assumed to be characteristic. Ideological and foreign policy stands of the moment should not be permitted to obscure broader pictures of basic social, economic, and political change. It is reasonable to contemplate that these fundamental processes of domestic social change may be more salient in the long run for determining the basic character of these societies than are the more visible, but perhaps more ephemeral, issues of political controversy. Further, the pattern analyses reported here should suggest caution in selecting the bases on which East European socialist systems are determined to be similar to, or different from, one another for purposes of the design of comparative research. These analyses hopefully make a case for more systematic quantitative research as a basis for typology construction in comparative social research.

## Appendix

Figure 1. Albania–Socio-economic Distances

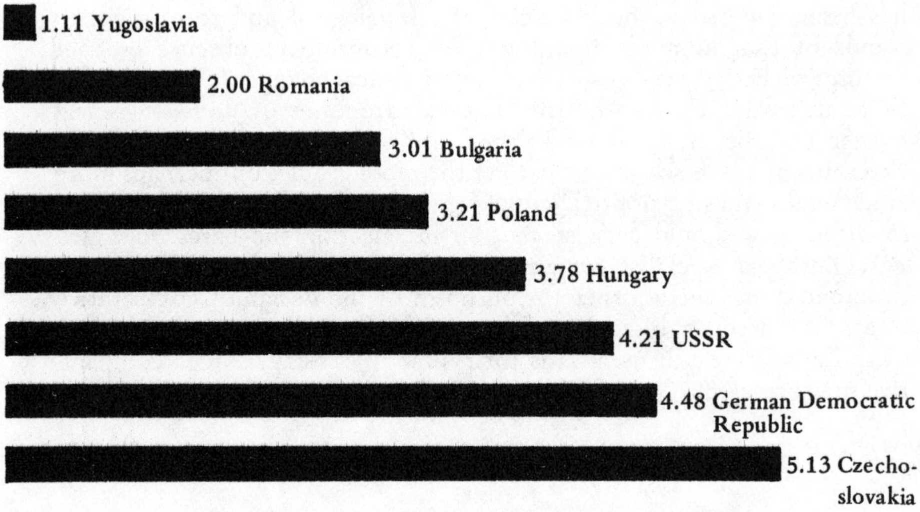


Figure 2. Albania-Political Distances

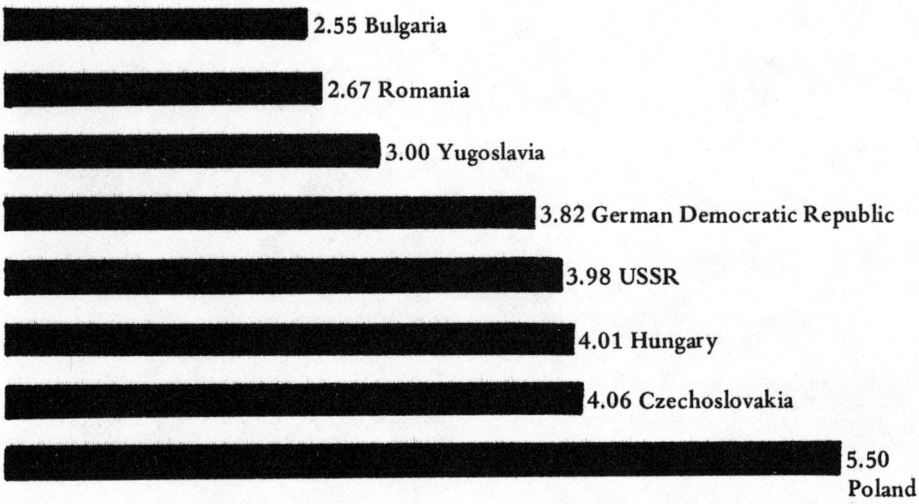

Figure 3. Bulgaria–Socio-economic Distances

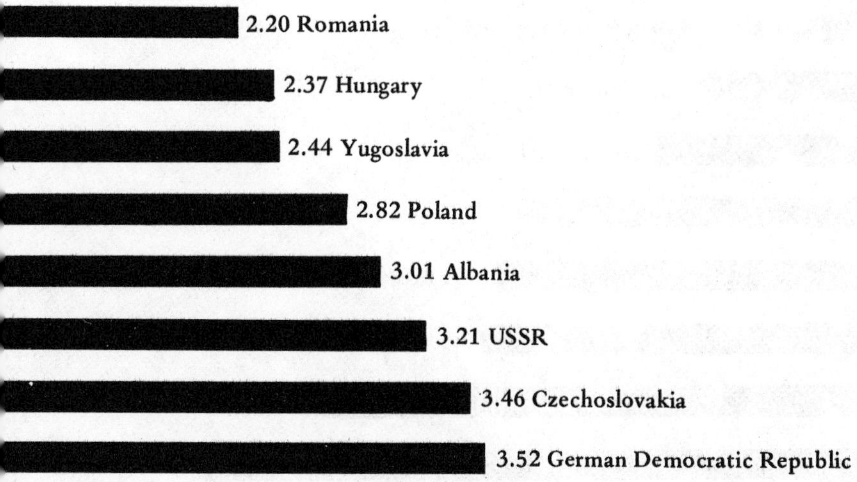


Figure 4. Bulgaria–Political Distances

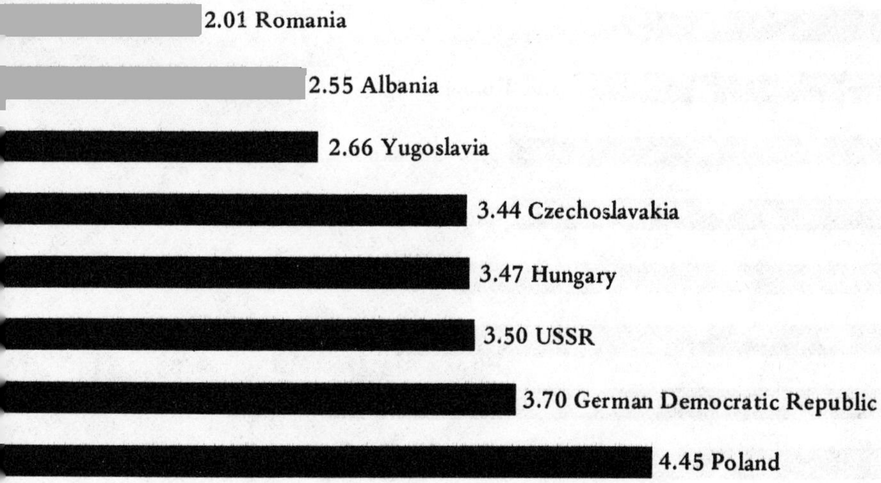

Figure 5. Czechoslovakia–Socio-economic Distances

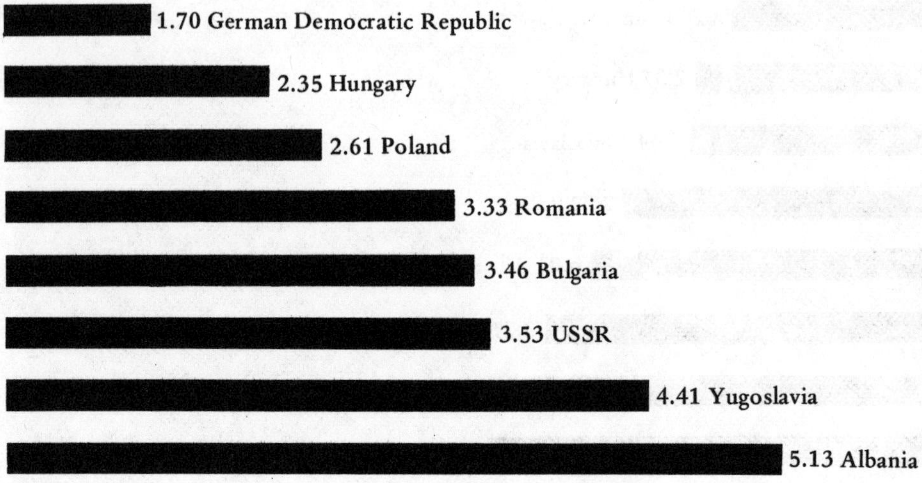


Figure 6. Czechoslovakia–Political Distances

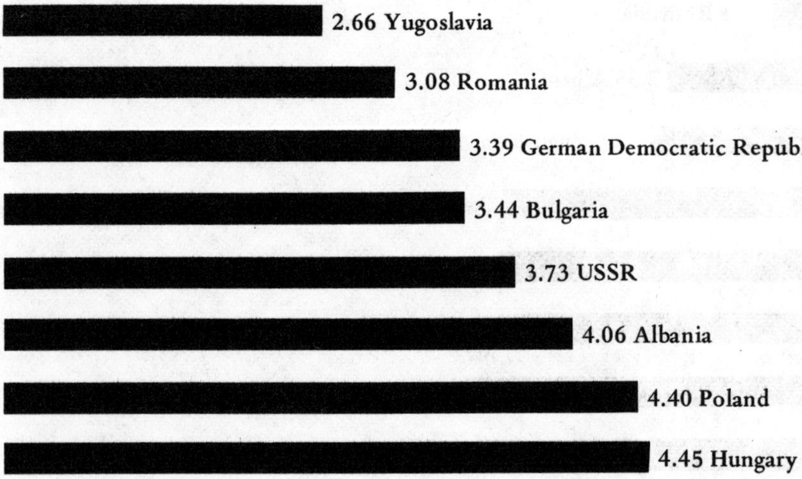

Figure 7. German Democratic Republic–Socio-economic Distances

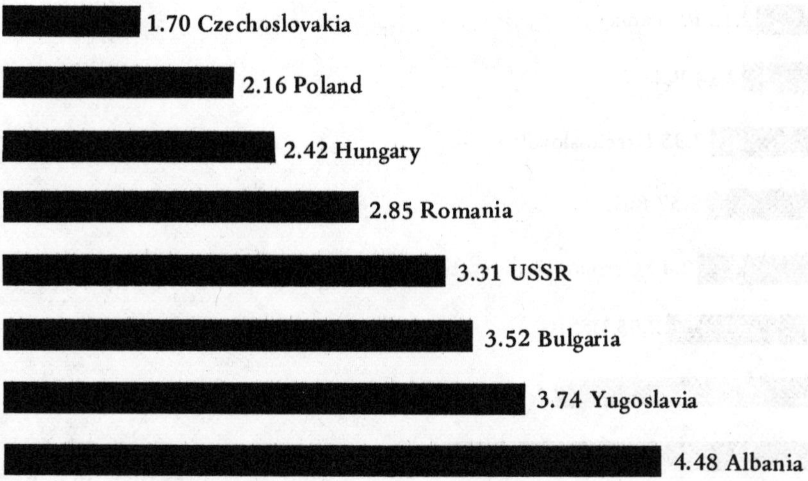


Figure 8. German Democratic Republic–Political Distances

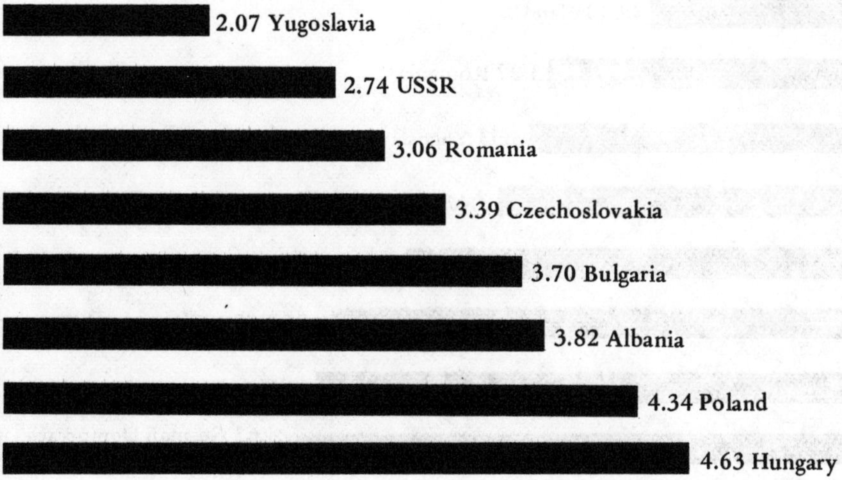

Figure 9. Hungary–Socio-economic Distances

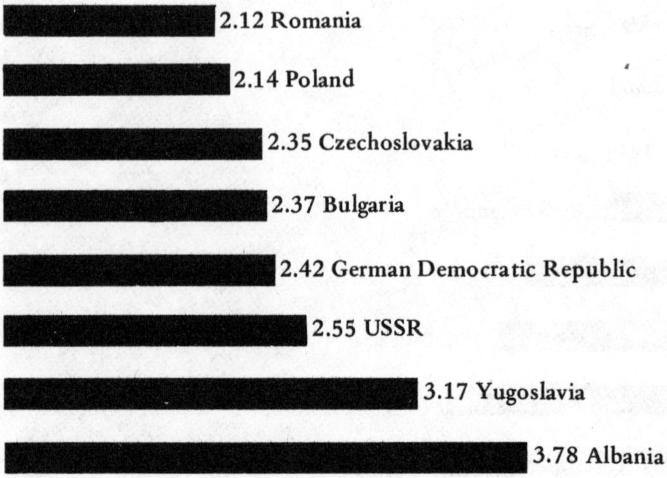


Figure 10. Hungary–Political Distances

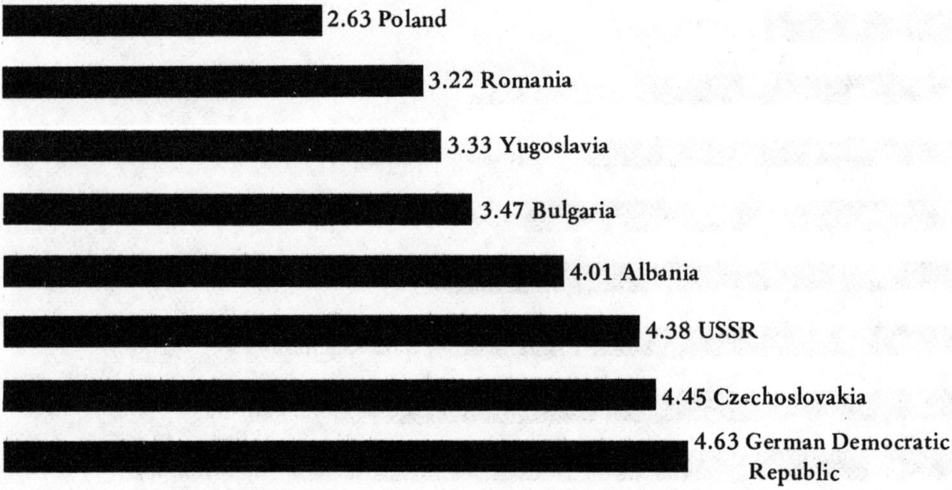

Figure 11. Poland–Socio-economic Distances

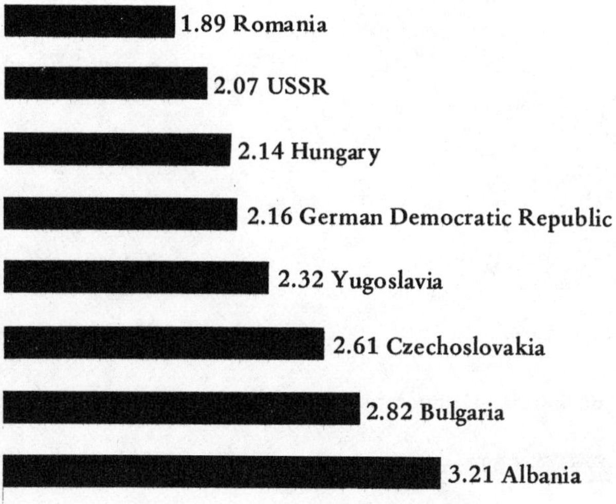


Figure 12. Poland–Political Distances

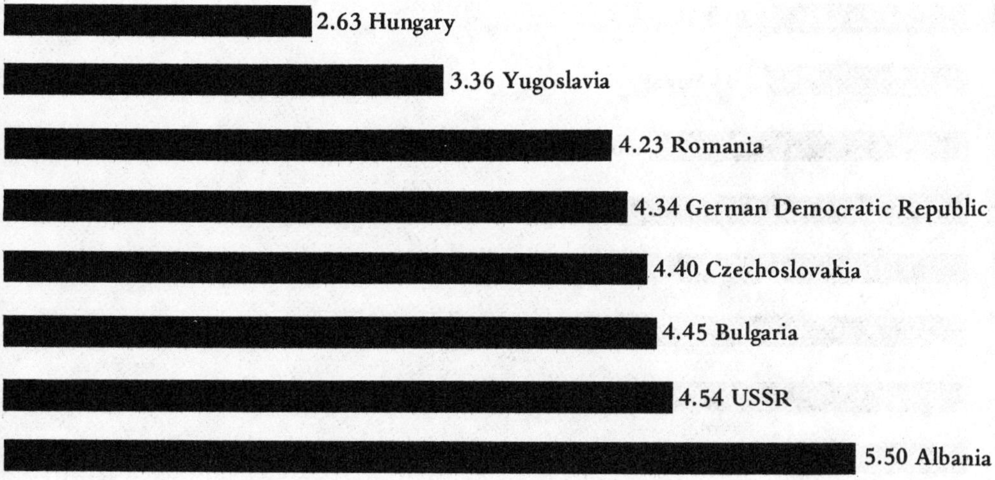

Figure 13. Romania–Socio-economic Distances

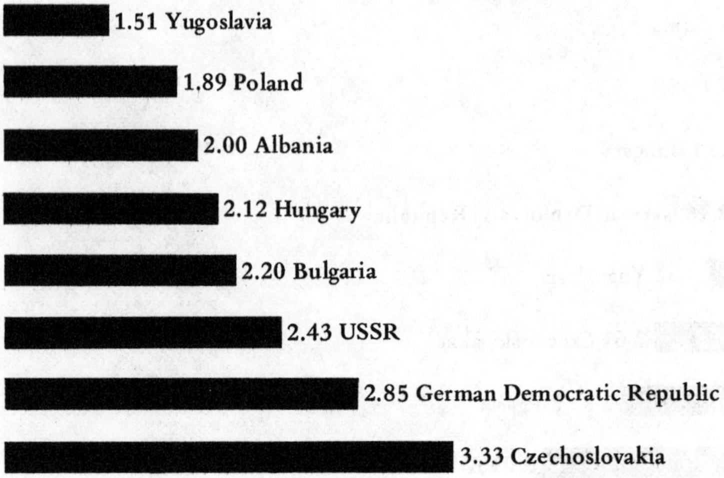


Figure 14. Romania–Political Distances

Figure 15. USSR–Socio-economic Distances

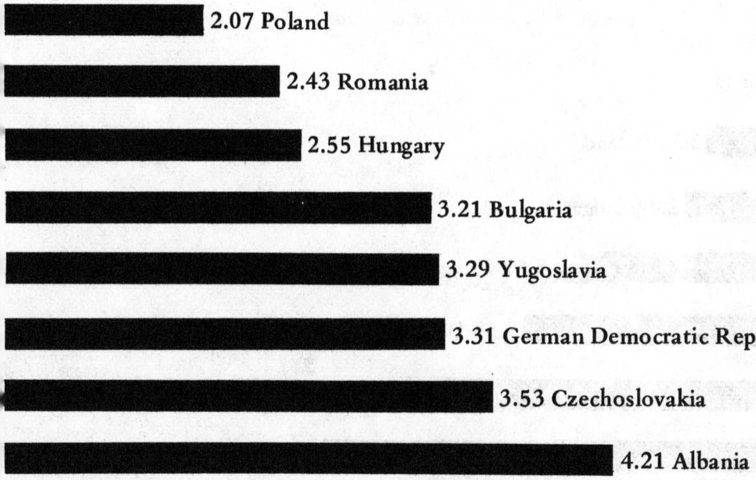


Figure 16. USSR–Political Distances

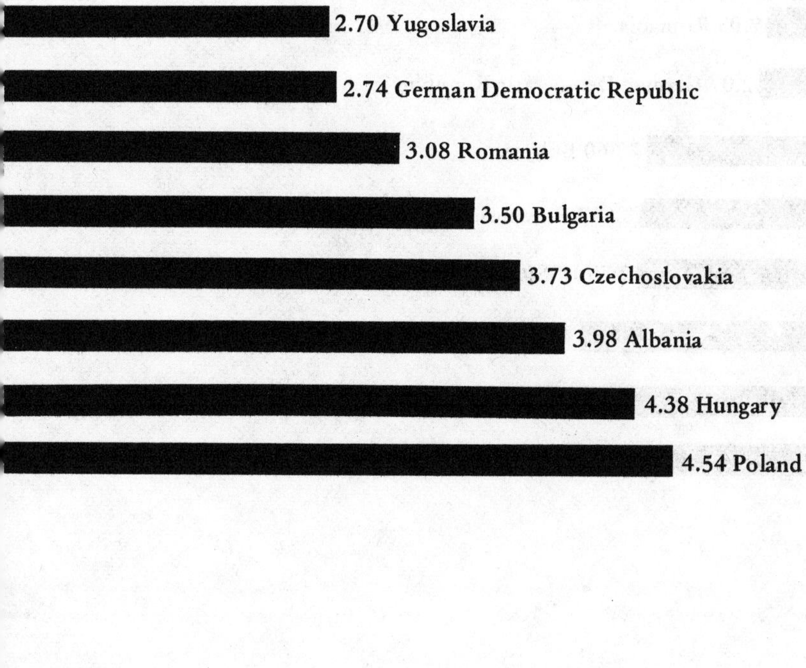

Figure 17. Yugoslavia–Socio-economic Distances

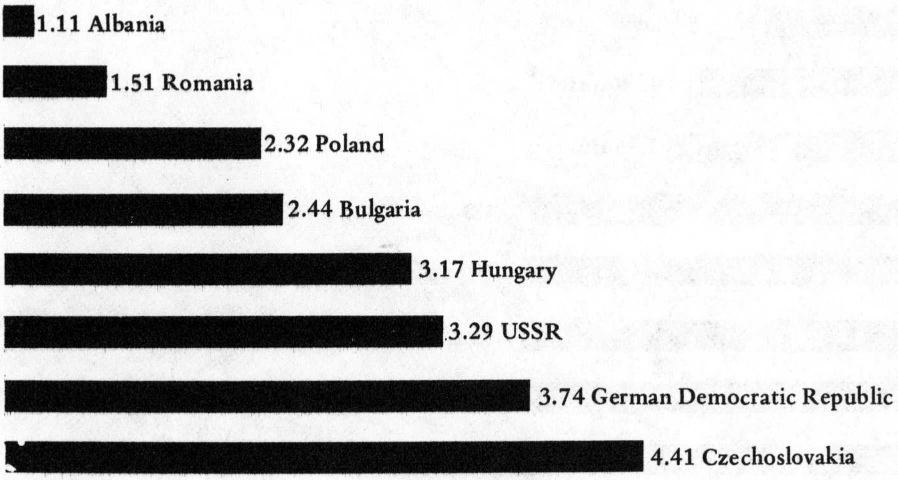


Figure 18. Yugoslavia–Political Distances

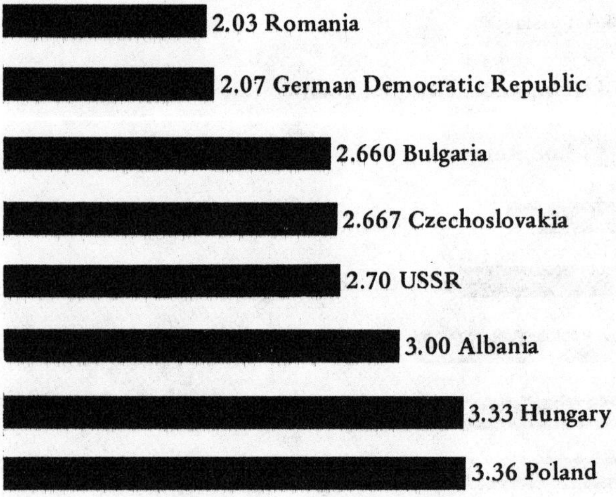

## NOTES

1. This research has benefited a great deal from the assistance of Marjorie Mowlam and Barclay Ward, graduate research assistants in political science; Chia-Hsing Lu, chief programmer in the Laboratory for Political Research; and Barbara A. Gilbert, of the Comparative Legislative Research Center, all of the University of Iowa. Ms. Mowlam and Mr. Ward spent many concentrated hours in data preparation and analysis. Mr. Lu wrote two computer programs used in transforming and analyzing the data. Ms. Gilbert assisted in data analysis, and prepared the manuscript. Computer time was supported by the Graduate College, University of Iowa. Some of the data were provided through the Inter-University Consortium for Political Research.

2. See Adam Przeworski and Henry Teune, *The Logic of Comparative Social Inquiry* (New York: Wiley, 1970). Also relevant to issues having to do with case-selection is David W. Willer, "Conditional Universals and Scope Sampling," in *Scientific Sociology*, ed. David Willer (Englewood Cliffs, N.J.: Prentice-Hall, 1967), pp. 97-115.

3. J. Wilczynski, *The Economics of Socialism* (Chicago: Aldine, 1970), pp. 23-25. A similar, but implicit, typology is suggested from a reading of Michael Gamarnikow, *Economic Reforms in Eastern Europe* (Detroit, Mich.: Wayne State University Press, 1968).

4. Paul Gregory, *Socialist and Nonsocialist Industrialization Patterns: A Comparative Appraisal* (New York: Praeger, 1970).

5. Frederic L. Pryor, *Public Expenditures in Communist and Capitalist Nations* (Homewood, Ill.: Irwin, 1968).

6. See Herbert J. Spiro, "Comparative Politics: A Comprehensive Approach," *American Political Science Review* 56, no. 3 (September 1962): 577-595.

7. For a sampling of recent empirical work on East European integration, see Cal Clark, "Foreign Trade as an Indicator of Political Integration in the Soviet Bloc," *International Studies Quarterly* 15 (1970):259-295; David D. Finley, "Integration among the Communist Party-States: Comparative Case Studies," in *Communist Party-States: Comparative and International Studies*, ed. Jan Triska (Indianapolis, Ind.: Bobbs-Merrill, 1969); Michael Gehlen, "The Integrative Process in East Europe: A Theoretical Framework," *Journal of Politics* 30 (1968):90-113; Barry Hughes and Thomas Volgy, "Distance in Foreign Policy Behavior: A Comparative Study of Eastern Europe," *Midwest* (now *American*) *Journal of Political Science* 14, no. 3 (August 1970):459-492, and the discussion of this research by Kenneth S. Hempel, and by Hughes and Volgy, in the *American Journal of Political Science* 17, no. 2 (May 1973):367-406; Andrzej Korbonski, "Theory and Practice of Regional Integration: The Case of COMECON," *International Organization* 24, no. 4 (Autumn 1970):954-957; Paul Marer, *Soviet and East European Foreign Trade, 1946-1969* (Bloomington, Ind.: Indiana University Press, 1972); two papers presented at a conference on Trends in Integration of the East European Community, University of South Carolina, 1972- –David Pfotenhauer and William A. Welsh, "The Economic Dimension of Integration in Eastern Europe," and Welsh, "Content Analysis and the Study of Integration in Eastern Europe"; also Welsh, "Economic

Change, Economic Reform, and East European Postures Toward Regional Integration," paper, Conference on Inter-Bloc Relations, Virginia Polytechnic Institute and State University, 1972. Copies of the last three papers are available from the Laboratory for Political Research, University of Iowa.

8. Patterns are defined in terms of functional distances (FD). FDs are sums of mean vertical distances (MVD) and mean transitional distances (MTD) between curves, or time series. The formulae for calculation of MVD and MTD are as follows:

$$MVD = \frac{1}{n} \sum_{i=1}^{n} |x_i - y_i|$$

where n=the number of time points in each time series, and where x and y designate the respective variables (time series).

$$MTD = \frac{1}{2n} \sum_{i=1}^{n} |d_i - \Delta_i|$$

where n=the number of between-point intervals in each time series, and where $d_i$ and $\Delta_i$ represent differences between adjacent time points in the respective time series (i.e., for each variable).

9. M. George Zaninovich, "Pattern Analysis of Variables within the International System: the Sino-Soviet Example," *Journal of Conflict Resolution* 6, no. 3 (September 1962):253-268.

10. William A. Welsh, "Economic Change, Economic Reform, and East European Postures Toward Regional Integration," paper, Conference on Inter-Bloc Relations, Virginia Polytechnic Institute and State University, Blacksburg, Virginia, December 8-9, 1972.

11. The computer program which was used to standardize these scores, SCALE, was written for the IBM 360/65 by Chia-Hsing Lu of the Laboratory for Political Research, University of Iowa. The program is available from the Laboratory.

12. This is especially the case for the socio-economic indicators taken from the *World Handbook of Political and Social Indicators, II*, edited by Charles Lewis Taylor and Michael C. Hudson (New Haven, Conn.: Yale University Press, 1970). Most aggregate data in the *World Handbook II* are recorded for 1950, 1955, 1960, and 1965. The data set was made available through the Inter-University Consortium for Political Research.

13. *Ibid.*

14. See Arthur S. Banks, *Cross-Polity Time Series Data* (Cambridge, Mass.: MIT Press, 1971). The data set was made available through the Inter-University Consortium for Political Research.

15. The Iowa collection on Eastern Europe is stored in a Numeric Information Retrieval System (NIRS), programming for which was done by Chia-Hsing Lu.

16. See Gabriel Almond and G. Bingham Powell, *Comparative Politics: A Developmental Approach* (Boston, Mass.: Little, Brown, 1966), chapter 8.

17. Some of the research done by Ivo K. Feierabend, Rosalind L. Feierabend, and Betty A. Nesvold is contained in two research anthologies: John V. Gillespie and Nesvold, eds., *Macro-Quantitative Analysis: Conflict, Development, and Democratization* (Beverly Hills, Calif.: Sage, 1971); and Feierabend, Feierabend, and Ted Robert Gurr, eds., *Anger, Violence, and Politics: Theories and Research* (Englewood Cliffs, N.J.: Prentice Hall, 1972). The data were made available through the Inter-University Consortium for Political Research.

18. See Carl Beck, "Leadership Attributes in Eastern Europe: The Effect of Country and Time," in C. Beck, F. J. Fleron, Jr., M. Lodge, D. J. Waller, W. A. Welsh, and M. G. Zaninovich, *Comparative Communist Political Leadership* (New York: David McKay, 1973), pp. 86-153.

19. See Almond and Powell, *Comparative Politics,* chapter 8. The extent to which there is "redistribution" of resources in socialist systems is debated, and the varying conclusions seem to parallel distinctly different notions of what "redistribution" means in the context of a public-ownership economy. Indeed, the notion of distributive capability, as used by Almond and Powell, may not be applicable to socialist systems.

20. Pryor, *Public Expenditures*; see especially Appendix A.

21. Gregory, *Socialist and Nonsocialist Integration*, pp. 137, 153-156.

22. Pryor, *Public Expenditures*, especially chapters 4-6.

23. Gregory, *Socialist and Nonsocialist Integration*, p. 137.

# 4

# A Continuum Model for Global Comparison*

Carmelo Mesa–Lago

For almost four decades, the study of socialist systems was a "Soviet monopoly," as Peter Wiles has wittily indicated, fundamentally because the Stalinist system reigned uncontested in a "monolithic" socialist world.[1] But with Stalin's death, the Yugoslav and Chinese schisms in the 1950s, Cuba's entrance into the socialist world, the Eastern European reforms, and the Chinese, Yugoslav, and Czech experiments in the 1960s, there has been increasing pluralism in the field. Parallel to these events, two important trends can be registered: more data (both in quantity and quality) have become available, and more scholars from several disciplines have been trained and specialized in a particular socialist country.

Therefore it is not surprising to find, within the last fifteen or twenty years, a significant transformation in the literature of the field.[2] In the second half of the 1950s, "Sovietology" was dominant with only a few case studies done on Yugoslavia and China and no serious attempt for comparison among socialist systems. During the first half of the 1960s, the USSR lost its monopoly but still retained the attention of the majority of experts who mainly wrote global and historical works. There was, however, a noticeable increase in specialization by discipline and by specific aspects within one discipline, e.g., planning within economics, bureaucracy within political science. The quantity of case studies on other socialist countries increased significantly, but most were of a general nature. The first comparative socialist studies and attempts to build models were published in this period.

---

* This chapter is a substantially expanded and thoroughly revised version of a previous paper by the author: "A Continuum Model to Compare Socialist Systems Globally," *Economic Development and Cultural Change* 21 (July 1973): 573-590 (Copyright 1973 by The University of Chicago Press). Materials from the original paper are reproduced here with the proper permission.

In the second half of the 1960s, global treatises on the USSR sharply declined while sectorial monographs increased dramatically. The majority of studies became devoted to other socialist countries, especially China, Cuba, Czechoslovakia, and Yugoslavia. The number and sophistication of comparative studies and theoretical models augmented also. In the early 1970s new advances were made in various aspects of comparative socialist systems: conceptualization and categorization of the subjects of study; standardization and comparison of the data available; refinement of the methodology; and setting the bases for prediction.[3]

In spite of the remarkable progress summarized above, the study of comparative socialist systems remains unidisciplinary and compartmentalized in the sense that it concentrates on a particular discipline and aspect of socialist society, such as the political structure and functions, the organization of the economy, or the system of values. And yet, as Oleg Zinam has stressed, in a socialist system "political, economic, and ideological elements are so inextricably intertwined that. . .to get meaningful results one must either analyze the whole package or give up the effort."[4] Another problem is that the methods available to compare socialist systems are usually typologies that abstract the main features of one or more actual systems, reducing all of them to a small number of types, thus sacrificing divergence among systems for the sake of simplicity. Finally, the less-developed, less-known socialist countries (e.g., Albania, Bulgaria, Cuba, Mongolia, North Korea, North Vietnam) are usually excluded from the comparisons.

In this chapter I propose to go a step further in matters of approach and methodology, comparing socialist systems globally and interdisciplinarily by using a combination of socio-politico-economic variables integrated in a continuum, bipolar model. Diversity is relevant here, hence similar features or variables for all systems, for example, collectivization of industry, are excluded from the model. All distinctive variables of a system cannot be included in the model; thus a selection has been made of those most significant for the comparison.

Even limiting the analysis to a small group of strategic variables in various fields, the task ahead is immense. To properly undertake it would require the work of a team of specialists in various socialist countries and trained in several disciplines—economics, education, philosophy, political science, sociology. A single scholar trained in one or two countries risks the danger of projecting bias both in the selection of variables and in the process of induction-generalization. To somewhat reduce this possibility, I circulated an earlier version of this paper among several specialists and have incorporated many of their suggestions.[5]

This chapter can still be criticized as schematic and/or audacious. Nevertheless, I am exposing this admittedly embryonic model to the academic community because of its potential heuristic value: it identifies and interrelates the fundamental features of socialist systems providing a general framework for their orderly comparison. I advance also various hypotheses whose validity cannot be tested at the present level of the investigation. These pertain to the relative cohesiveness of systems, the deviation of variables from system cohesiveness and the costs of such deviation, and the short- and long-run tendencies of system gravitation and their causes. The main utility of this chapter may be the stimulation of further discussion and interdisciplinary research.

*Problems Faced in Developing the Model*

Besides the general problems discussed above, the development of the model has faced three serious difficulties: (1) the poor availability and reliability of the data needed for measurement of variables; (2) the traditional tendency to use types and categories; and (3) the period of time chosen for the comparison.

1. The difficulties in obtaining information from some socialist countries (e.g., China, Mongolia, North Vietnam) are well known. Such difficulties increase when a socialist country goes into a period of turmoil and isolation, as in the case of China under the Great Leap Forward or the Great Proletarian Cultural Revolution. There are also "sensitive" topics (because they affect internal security or doctrinal principles) on which data are almost impossible to collect regardless of the country, for instance, the power of the armed forces *vis-á-vis* the party, the magnitude of frictional unemployment and underemployment. Generally, statistics in the less-industrialized socialist countries are scarce and present serious problems of accuracy (e.g., Albania, Bulgaria, Cuba, Rumania). Both the availability and the reliability of statistics seem to increase as the socialist country develops.[6] The possibility of conducting objective surveys (e.g., on freedom in party elections, the use of coercive techniques, change in values, extension of the black market) in socialist countries by foreign scholars is almost nil with the exception of Yugoslavia.

Due to these problems, I have at this time limited the use of the model to five countries (China, Cuba, Czechoslovakia, the USSR, and Yugoslavia), but the open model allows future application to the remaining socialist countries. Variables in the model have been qualitatively evaluated (based on published information on the five countries) rather than quantitatively measured.[7] I have indicated, however, potential indices for future measurement of the variables.

2. In order to reduce wide divergence among fourteen socialist countries into manageable dimensions, some scholars have developed types that define and classify one or a group of socialist countries. Each type is commonly identified with one important country or named by

one particular feature of the system. Thus one is identified with the Soviet Union (also East Germany) and/or named "command," "statist" (from the French *étatisme*), "administrative," "bureaucratic," or "centrally planned." A second type is identified with China (and more recently with Cuba) and/or labeled "mobilization," "communal," "leftist," or "orthodox." A third type is identified with Yugoslavia and/or called "market socialist," "rightist," "reformist," or "decentralized." (Also "managerial socialism," "socialist liberalism," "market syndicalism," etc.) As divergence among socialist countries noticeably increases other types are added; for instance, a fourth one is now being identified with Hungary and called "administrative decentralized" or "selectively decentralized."

The typology technique has several defects. First, in trying to reduce increasingly divergent systems into a set of rigid boxes, important features of the systems of the less-known countries are often neglected. As Morris Bornstein has said, "intragroup differences are frequently so great that prototypes are not or cannot be representative."[8]

A second problem is that most of the names or terms selected to identify the types are not comprehensive of the multiple features of a system, but emphasize a particular aspect of the system in question. Thus the terms "centralized" and "command" as opposed to "decentralized" and "market socialist" primarily refer to the planning apparatus and managerial organization of the system.[9] The terms "mobilization" and "syndicalist" opposed to "bureaucratic" and "administrative" refer to the politico-administrative apparatus in charge of goal implementation (e.g., transformation of political culture, economic development) or to the process of routinization or institutionalization of the system.[10] The terms "rightist," "conservative," and "orthodox" as opposed to "leftist," "liberal" (or "radical"), and "reformist" (or "revisionist") are principally connected with ideology, that is, how well the system in question does or does not fit in the "dogma." These are the most general terms but also the most misleading because of their vagueness and relativeness. The use of these terms depends on the stand taken by each socialist country (or by the Western scholar) in classifying its counterparts, as well as in each country's interpretation of the rather loose Marxist-Leninist dogma or in its definition of status quo and change. Aware of this flaw, some scholars have resorted to composite names which are becoming increasingly long and complex, such as "fully state-administered, centrally-directed" (the USSR) or "labor-controlled, market-directed" (Yugoslavia).

Another inconvenience of the typology is its inner difficulty for quantification, particularly for comparative and ranking purposes. Finally, types tend to concentrate on abstract conceptualization and description and do not explain why a country evolves into a specific system and what is its concrete performance at a given time in history.[11]

In trying to avoid some of the problems discussed above, I have developed a continuum of socialist systems placed between two opposite "poles." (See Table 1). Each of the poles represents an ideal, pure or perfect system, that is an abstraction from reality, and its features are described by sixteen variables.

Pole X is mainly (but not exclusively) characterized by emphasis on ideological development (the goal of a New Man, classless society, egalitarianism, etc.), a mobilization regime, and anti-market tendencies. It is theoretically based on an agglomeration of ideas from the "Young Marx," Trotsky, Mao, Guevara, and Castro. It is represented by several unsuccessful attempts made in the socialist world (by the USSR,[12] China, and Cuba) to skip the socialist, transitional stage of development (or at least to go rapidly through it) and enter directly into a communist society.[13]

Pole Y is mainly (but not exclusively) characterized by emphasis on economic development (pragmatic goal as opposed to idealistic goal), institutionalization of politico-administrative processes, and market-oriented tendencies. It is theoretically based on ideas from Marx, Lenin (during National Economic Policy years), Taylor, Lange, Lerner, Sik, Horvat, and others. It is represented by the socialist countries (chiefly Yugoslavia) that have pragmatically accepted the need for a transitional stage of development and temporarily postponed the ultimate goal of the perfect society.[14]

By using the continuum technique, each country is described according to its own peculiarities, and similarities and differences among countries are more clearly shown. (More will be said later on the possibilities of the model for quantitative comparison and ranking, and for the determination of causes in the shaping of a system and measurement of its performances.)

3. The third serious difficulty to overcome in the comparison was the selection of a time period. In their evolution some socialist countries have moved in a linear direction while others have evolved in a cyclical or spiral manner.[15] In Table 2 the periods in the evolution of the five selected socialist countries are summarized. The USSR seems to be a case of quasi-cyclical evolution, China and Cuba of cyclical evolution, and Yugoslavia and Czechoslovakia (until mid-1968) of linear evolution (however, see below).

Lowenthal has cautioned against use of the word "cycle" because of the lack of regularity or the divergent length of each period.[16] This caution is especially true in the case of the Soviet Union in which the Stalinist era could hardly be equated with a cycle. (Actually within the Stalinist era two stages could be distinguished: the first, 1929-1940, being more dogmatic than the second, 1941-1952.) During this period Stalin implemented his system of development, a compromise between dogma and pragmatism, mixing characteristics of the two opposite poles. Thus he routinized a highly centralized system of planning and

## Table 1

*Continuum Static Model of Socialist Systems: Mid-1968*

| Predominance of: | POLE X | China | Cuba | CENTER | USSR | Czechoslovakia | Yugoslavia | POLE Y |
|---|---|---|---|---|---|---|---|---|
| 1. equality over stratification | 2 | 2 | 1 | 0 | –1 | –1 | –2 | –2 |
| 2. moral over material incentives | 2 | 2 | 2 | 0 | –1 | –2 | –2 | –2 |
| 3. permanent revolution over institutionalization | 2 | 2 | 1 | 0 | –2 | –1 | –1 | –2 |
| 4. personal dictatorship over collegiate leadership | 2 | 2 | 2 | 0 | –1 | –2 | –1 | –2 |
| 5. military over party power | 2 | 2 | 2 | 0 | –1 | –2 | –2 | –2 |
| 6. arbitrary coercive over normative-persuasive control | 2 | 2 | 1 | 0 | 0 | –2 | –2 | –2 |
| 7. rigidity over flexibility in cultural expression | 2 | 2 | 0 | 0 | 1 | –2 | –2 | –2 |
| 8. centralized over decentralized planning | 2 | –1 | 2 | 0 | 1 | –1 | –2 | –2 |
| 9. state-administrator over self-management | 2 | –1 | 2 | 0 | 1 | 0 | –2 | –2 |
| 10. loyalty over expertise in manager selection | 2 | 2 | 1 | 0 | 0 | –1 | –1 | –2 |
| 11. budgetary finance over self finance | 2 | 0 | 2 | 0 | 0 | –1 | –2 | –2 |
| 12. capital accumulation over consumption | 2 | 2 | 2 | 0 | 1 | 0 | –1 | –2 |
| 13. state-collective over private ownership of agriculture and services | 2 | 2 | 1 | 0 | 0 | 0 | –2 | –2 |
| 14. full employment over high labor productivity | 2 | 2 | 2 | 0 | 1 | –1 | –2 | –2 |
| 15. isolation over integration with outside world | 2 | 2 | 1 | 0 | –1 | –1 | –2 | –2 |
| 16. commitment to world revolution over coexistence | 2 | 2 | 1 | 0 | 0 | –2 | –2 | –2 |
| TOTALS | 32 | 24 | 23 | 0 | –2 | –19 | –28 | –32 |

**Table 2**

*Cyclical and Linear Evolution of Five Socialist Systems*

Quasi-Cycles in the USSR

| | |
|---|---|
| 1918-1920 | War Communism (movement to pole X) |
| 1921-1928 | New Economic Policy (movement to pole Y) |
| 1929-1953 | Stalinist era (movement to center) |
| 1953-1967 | Economic reform (movement to pole Y) |
| 1968 on | Softening in the application of the reform |

Cycles in China

| | |
|---|---|
| 1953-1957 | Application of Stalinist system |
| 1958-1960 | Great Leap Forward (movement to pole X) |
| 1961-1965 | Return to moderation (movement to center) |
| 1966-1968 | Great Proletarian Cultural Revolution (movement to pole X) |
| 1969 on | Signs of moderation (movement to center) |

Cycles in Cuba

| | |
|---|---|
| 1961-1963 | Application of Stalinist system |
| 1963-1966 | Testing some economic reforms (movement to pole Y) |
| 1966-1968 | Revolutionary Offensive (movement to pole X) |
| 1969 on | Signs of moderation (movement to center) |

Linear Evolution in Yugoslavia

| | |
|---|---|
| 1947-1949 | Application of Stalinist system |
| 1950-1953 | First economic reform (movement to pole Y) |
| 1953-1961 | Implementation |
| 1961-1965 | New changes and discussion |
| 1965 on | Second economic reform (acceleration toward pole Y) |

Quasi-Linear Evolution in Czechoslovakia

| | |
|---|---|
| 1948-1956 | Application of Stalinist system |
| 1956-1961 | Mild economic reform (movement to pole Y) |
| 1962-1966 | Political liberalization, discussion of reform (further movement to Y) |
| 1966-1968 | New Economic Model (approaching pole Y) |
| 1968 on | Soviet invasion (movement to the center) |

decision-making based on almost total collectivization of the means of production but with moderate use of material incentives. After Stalin's death, there was increasing liberalization. A reform movement took momentum in the first half of the 1960s under Krushchev and climaxed in 1965 with Breshnev-Kosygin's legal structuration of the reform. It is a matter of discussion whether the year 1965 or 1968 is the turning point for a softening in the implementation of Soviet reform.

In other countries, however, the cycles are fairly regular, e.g., two to three years in China and Cuba. China, the most typical example of a cyclical evolution, has alternated in successive stages between exalted idealism (or the pursuit of ideological development through mass mobilization techniques) and pragmatic moderation. The cycles of moderation have been accompanied by relative prosperity while those of ideological radicalization have ended with political clashes, economic deterioration, and, eventually, the reestablishment of the former moderate policies.[17]

In Cuba, there was a brief (1961-63) and softened application of the Stalinist system mostly in economics, but with continuous use of mobilization campaigns. After the failure of this system, the Cubans experimented with the type of economic reforms that were being tested in the USSR but, at the same time, mobilization continued and there were also experiments with moral incentives. In mid-1966 a stage of idealism and confrontation with the USSR began, climaxing in early 1968 with the Revolutionary Offensive which had certain features of the Chinese Cultural Revolution. Cuba's endorsement of the Soviet invasion of Czechoslovakia was rapidly followed by *rapprochement* with the USSR and later by increasing moderation in economics and foreign policy.

In Yugoslavia, after a slightly modified and briefly applied Stalinist system, there was a total rejection of it, and a period of discussion of alternative systems followed. In the early 1950s workers' councils and market mechanisms were introduced and a new constitution enacted. Then came a transitional period of semi-implementation of the reform. With the economic recession of the early 1960s, another round of discussions took place. These culminated in 1965 with a new political constitution and more profound economic reforms in favor of decentralization and liberalization.

In Czechoslovakia, the Stalinist system was more rigidly applied and for a longer period of time. The mild economic reforms of the second half of the 1950s were obstructed by the entrenched political orthodoxy. When in the 1960s this barrier was removed, the door opened for more profound economic reforms oriented toward the market. This evolution lasted until 1968 when it was halted and reversed by the USSR. The Czech regression (lasting four years by mid-1972) and that of Hungary (1956-60) suggest that these countries do not have a "pure" linear, but quasi-linear, evolution. I reject calling these setbacks "cycles" because they apparently are unique events caused by external interference and hence do not recur regularly and (at least in the Hungarian case) do not impede the long-run evolution of the country in a linear manner.

Table 2 suggests that after an unsuccessful application of the Stalinist system (with more or less rigidity) and for a period ranging from three to eight years, socialist countries began to experiment with other techniques, moving towards one pole or its opposite in the socialist continuum. The table also manifests the difficulties in referring to "a system" in any of these five countries. The Soviet system of War Communism, for instance, is different from the Stalinist system and from the 1965 economic-reform system. On the other hand, the Chinese, Cuban, Czech, and Yugoslav systems during the early years of the first long-range plans in all of these countries were fairly similar to the Stalinist system. The Cuban system of the Revolutionary Offensive shows strong similarity to the Chinese system of the Great Leap Forward and the Great Proletarian Cultural Revolution.

The year 1968 has been selected for the comparison since, by the middle of that year, several countries had reached a peak in the evolution of a stage or cycle, thereafter changing the direction or velocity of the movement. Thus in August 1968 the economic reform in Czechoslovakia was curtailed by the Soviet invasion; signs of reversing policies appeared in Cuba and China by the second half of 1968 or by early 1969; there was a slowdown in Soviet economic reforms; and in Yugoslavia the student strike possibly resulted in some reconsideration of the pace of change.

### *A Model for Comparison*

Table 1 compares five socialist systems at a given point in history (in mid-1968) by ranking them according to sixteen distinctive features or variables. The table requires further refinement and hence should be regarded cautiously. As I have said, variable evaluation has been made qualitatively instead of quantitatively. The generation of quantitative data through statistics, field surveys, etc., could result, therefore, in a modified ranking of variables, the elimination of non-relevant variables, and/or the addition of new significant variables. A better balance of sociological, political, and economic factors may result in the reshuffling of variables. The comparison is static and in order to have a dynamic one historical data will have to be gathered. This will be discussed in greater detail.

The sixteen variables in the table evaluate the polarization of each system in relation to pole X. Evaluation is made according to the actual implementation of a variable and not in view of the rhetorical position that a country may have concerning that variable. The assigned points should read as follows: 2 = very strong; 1 = strong; 0 = medium; -1 =

weak; and -2 = very weak. The total score of a system places it in an approximate position in the ordinal scale or continuum. A ranking of sixteen 'very strong" (a sum of 32 points) would mean a pure or ideal type, summarized above in terms of idealism, mobilization, and anti-market tendencies. In practice, this ideal type does not exist but the Chinese system is close to it. Conversely a ranking of sixteen "very weak" (a sum of -32) would mean a pure or ideal type summarized above in terms of pragmatism, institutionalization, and market-oriented tendencies. The Yugoslav system approximates such an ideal type. A situation is characterized as "medium" when none of the opposite variables is strong enough to constitute a predominant feature of the system. A ranking of sixteen "medium" (a total of zero) would describe the perfect center position. The Soviet system stands toward the center of the continuum, but closer to pole Y. This is a result of the mild reforms introduced in the USSR by the mid-1960s.

The remaining socialist countries could be placed between China and the USSR, or between the latter and Yugoslavia, gravitating towards the corresponding pole but often restrained in their movement by Soviet centripetal forces.[18] Cuba and Czechoslovakia were selected because, by mid-1968, these two countries were very rapidly approximating pole X and pole Y respectively, but through Soviet pressure and force their natural movement was later reversed (in different degrees) back to the center. If Cuba and Czechoslovakia had been allowed to continue in the same direction for several more months, they might have superseded China and Yugoslavia respectively, converting themselves to the closest systems of the ideal type. (Or they might have moderated their pace by themselves, regardless of the USSR, based on an internal realization that they had gone too far in their evolution.)

*Description of the Variables and Indices for Future Measurement*

The sixteen variables in Table 1 embrace the most distinctive features of a socialist system. They could be clustered in four subsystems: (a) sociological, 1 and 2; (b) politico-administrative, 3 through 7; (c) managerial economic, 8 through 14; and (d) foreign relations, 15 and 16. The inclusion of a variable in a subsystem means that the former is mainly related to the latter, but most variables are related with various subsystems, for example, variable 2 is related to subsystems a and c, variable 7 with subsystems a and b, etc. The clustering shows the proportions that various subsystems have in the model. In this section each variable is described, and potential indices for its quantitative measurement suggested.

The first variable evaluates the degree of egalitarianism achieved in the system. One index related to income (or to individual and collective consumption) could be measured with statistics on wage differentials, income distribution, and the scope of free social services (education, medical care, housing). Another index related to social mobility could be measured by the social extraction of students in higher education (i.e., proportion that comes from manual worker families), professionals and executives in top jobs, and members of the party. A third index related to societal hierarchicalization could be measured by direct observation and field surveys. Important aspects to check would be accessibility of the public to high officials; the terms used by the masses in addressing high officials (e.g., comrade, companion *vis-à-vis* minister, president[19]); the existence (or absence) of privileges granted to top officials (e.g., special rationing coupons; preference in housing; free cars and chauffeurs); the consciousness of inequality among the masses, etc.[20]

The second variable–moral over material incentives–refers to the ambitious attempt of China and Cuba to rapidly develop a "New Man," characterized by asceticism, collective spirit, self-discipline, and selflessness. It could be measured by the weight given to moral rewards such as pennants, flags, medals, honorary titles ("Vanguard Worker," "Hero of Labor") won in socialist competition, over material rewards (wages, bonuses, overtime pay, etc.). In a more sophisticated measurement, the use of individual *vis-à-vis* collective incentives (e.g., wage increases vs. free medicine for all, or medals for individuals vs. pennants for a whole factory,) could be checked.

The third variable presents the dichotomy between a "permanent revolution" regime characterized by constant change, instability, and centralized mass mobilization (as in China and Cuba), and an institutionalized regime characterized by routinization, stability, and an administrative bureaucracy or technocracy (as in the USSR). It could be measured by the length of time in which a consistent government policy is followed, the number of people involved in and frequency of mass (and labor) mobilizations, etc.

The fourth variable indicates whether most political institutions and functions are under the control of a dictator and his inner circle ("personality cult") as in the case of Castro in Cuba and, to a certain extent, Mao in China, or whether power is shared and functions distributed among various personalities. News media could provide the basis for measuring this variable, e.g., how many times his name appears in the newspapers *vis-à-vis* that of other leaders, etc.

The fifth variable shows the importance of the armed forces in Cuba and China, as opposed to the party in the USSR.[21] In the former two countries, the armed forces supply loyal personnel for key posts in administration and in the party; they are also a source of support for the charismatic leader or dictator. An index for measuring this variable would be the number of army personnel *vis-à-vis* party officials holding key posts.

The sixth variable suggests that as a socialist country moves toward modernization and development, the primitive techniques of violence and coercion are gradually substituted by less stringent methods of control such as societal presssures, education, etc. Furthermore, governmental arbitrary (extra-legal) actions gradually yield to legal behavior. The use of violence could be quantified by indices such as the proportion of people killed, put in jail, sent to labor camps, or simply ostracized in relation to the total population. A field survey (or, using Inkeles' approach, a survey among exiles) could determine whether the population has internalized a new set of values and patterns of behavior that negate the need of violent techniques. Illegal actions could be detected by contrasting government's compliance with law; the enactment of retroactive laws; the establishment of exceptional tribunals to judge political crimes; the proportion of decrees and orders enacted *vis-à-vis* laws; the frequency with which instrumental policies (or policy changes) are introduced without the corresponding juridical framework, etc.

The seventh variable weighs the importance given to political indoctrination over technical education, and the degree of state control over artistic expression. Some measuring indices could be: composition of curricula; state control of the forms of artistic expression (e.g., in favor of "socialist realism" and against abstract painting); and state emphasis on establishing "politics" as an objective of art (e.g., painting must be useful in depicting revolutionary behavior, working masses, etc.).

The eighth variable characterizes central planning by a system of commands from above, physical-central allocation of the essential resources (e.g., capital, land, oil, steel), but also in extreme cases even of consumer goods (through rationing), central fixing of wages and output quotas, etc. Conversely, decentralized planning is characterized by allocation of resources made at a regional or local level either by administrative bodies or by market mechanisms (prices, profit, rent, interest rate) and managerial decision-making done at the enterprise (or commune) level under a broad national plan which is a general guideline for the economy. In measuring this variable, several indices could be used: e.g., number of central economic ministries; degree of compulsion of planned targets and work quotas (are there penalties for non-fulfillment?); number of capital goods centrally allocated and of consumer goods rationed; powers entrusted to enterprises (or regional or local bodies) to hire employees, fix wages, and conduct foreign trade independently from the center; greater role of scarcity prices, profit, interest, and rent, etc.[22]

The ninth variable refers to the participation of lower echelons of the power structure in the process of economic decision-making at the enterprise level, through workers' councils *à la* Yugoslavia, communes *à la* China, or other devices. In measuring this variable we will have to check the degree of influence that factory workers, commune members, state-farm workers, and collective farmers (private farmers in Cuba) have in the fixing of output targets or procurement quotas, the percentage of profit to be reinvested or distributed, etc., *vis-à-vis* the influence of the manager or administrator. Another important point would be whether managers are appointed from above or selected from below (workers, commune members, etc.).

The tenth variable presents the traditional controversy of "red versus expert," accentuated in the Sino-Cuban model by the guerrilla leaders' distrust of and distaste for bureaucrats, technicians, and academicians. This frequently has resulted in placing inexperienced laymen, but loyal revolutionaries in charge of important specialized jobs. Compromising but more rational approaches are to appoint an expert to the job and put him under the political supervision of a loyal revolutionary (*commisar*), or to appoint the latter to the job and assign him the former as a technical advisor. Studies on the antecedents or background of important officials could be used in quantifying this variable. (We might evaluate here, or in an additional variable, the dichotomy of multi-faceted over specialized labor, that is, the Sino-Cuban emphasis in making workers knowledgeable in several trades.

In the eleventh variable the budgetary finance system is characterized by capital allocation through the central budget, by the use of nonreturnable capital gifts that are exempted from interest charges, and by a transfer of profits to the state. The self-financed enterprise, on the other hand, is based on repayable loans and interest charges, and the enterprise is allowed to keep most of its profits for reinvestment and/or distribution among its members. In 1968 in Yugoslavia, self-financing was applied throughout the economy; Chinese communes were encouraged to be self-sufficient; part of Soviet industry and transportation was under self-financing and collective farms were self-sufficient; Czechoslovakia was rapidly expanding self-financing; and Cuba expanded the budgetary system to practically all enterprises except for one-third of agriculture organized as small private farms.

The twelfth variable indicates the distribution of GNP (actually GMP) between consumption and gross investment, and the allocation of the latter between the "productive" and "non-productive" sectors. Although all socialist countries emphasize capital accumulation and investment in the productive sector, some (Yugoslavia) are willing to compromise a relatively low investment coefficient and relatively large investment in the non-productive sector to improve the standard of living of the present generation. Official national account statistics (except for China) could provide the basis for measurement of this variable.

The thirteenth variable evaluates the scope of state-owned agricultural land and personal services. (Differences in the degree of collectivization of industry, public utilities, banking, etc., are nil.) Official statistics (except for China) often give the scope of state ownership in agriculture and occasionally in services.

The fourteenth variable presents the controversy between the goal of full employment and efficiency. The rigid application of the Marxist law of socialist full employment has led some socialist countries such as the USSR, China (in radicalization periods), and Cuba to transform overt unemployment into underemployment or disguised unemployment. The price has been the waste of resources and very low labor productivity. But since the early 1950s (and particularly in the 1960s), there has been a relatively high rate of overt unemployment in Yugoslavia resulting from the government's emphasis on avoiding waste and increasing productivity. Doctrinal reasons make this variable difficult to measure. Yugoslavia is the only socialist country that publishes unemployment statistics. I have discussed elsewhere alternative techniques to measure unemployment and underemployment in other socialist countries.[23]

The fifteenth variable evaluates the system's openness to the outside world. Three levels of increasing openness could be distinguished: the first with the socialist camp, the second with third-world countries, and the third with developed capitalist states. In mid-1968 China's isolation (even within the socialist camp) reached a peak while Czechoslovakia almost completely opened its doors to foreign visitors (even from the U.S.) and for natives who wanted to travel abroad. In 1972 a reversal was obvious in both countries. Some measuring indices of this variable are: number of foreign countries with which diplomatic relations and trade are established; participation in international or regional agencies; facilities for natives to travel abroad and for foreigners to enter the country and travel within it; foreign exchange of publications, students, and technicians; influence of foreign ideas in art, literature, and music; facilities for natives to publish abroad, etc.

The sixteenth variable evaluates actual (not rhetorical) commitment to the exportation of the socialist revolution versus nonalignment in blocs. This dichotomy is closely related to the controversy of whether the world establishment of socialism is a prerequisite for full development of socialism in one single country. In measuring this variable a record could be made of public evidence on: sponsored armed expedition or creation of guerrilla *foco* in foreign capitalist countries to subvert their regimes; direct armed intervention of one socialist country in another to stop revolt or deviation from the intervenor's official line; participation in a war between a socialist and a non-socialist nation by sending troops, etc.

### *Variable Relationship and System Cohesiveness*

Neither of the two poles in the model duplicates Marx's ideal schema for "the superior stage of communism." As has been stated many times, Marx did not elaborate a detailed blueprint for full communism, but his ideas were rather diffused and vague. He predicted that socialism (or "the first stage of communism") would occur in fully developed capitalist countries and in several of them at once. Thus the features in his ideal schema were mutually reinforcing; for instance, there would not be an urge to rapidly build up the "material base" (productive forces) because it would be fully developed already; nor would there be an isolated socialist country threatened by capitalist forces but a brotherhood of socialist nations. The revolution would be organized and led by a highly conscious proletariat and the means of production would be concentrated in a few hands so it would be easy to collectivize them. But the socialist revolution took place in backward societies, with productive forces in the initial stage of development, a relatively small proletariat, and the means of production scattered among hundreds of thousands of owners. Thus, in reality, all goals in Marx's schema cannot be pursued at once. Furthermore, some goals seem to be mutually exclusive from others; for instance, the substitution of plan for the market *vis-à-vis* the withering away of the state, or egalitarianism *vis-à-vis* efficiency. The conflicts did not become apparent until socialist leaders in different countries tried to implement Marx's schema and faced a choice of priorities among goals.[24]

In theory, all socialist nations proclaim that they are struggling to fully implement the Marxian schema in their societies. In practice, they have stressed some goals of the schema and ignored or played down others. The Soviets, for example, chose full collectivization, centralized planning, state management, and moderate use of material incentives to foster the rapid development of the material base. The Yugoslavs argued that excessive state control over property, allocation, and management induced the inception of a bureaucratic elite, state capitalism, and a cumbersome economy. These, in turn, impeded the progress of socialism. Thus they gave priority to decentralization and workers' participation in management and decided to partially decollectivize and to use market mechanisms.[25] The Czechs, using a more economic-managerial rather than politico-administrative rationale, alleged that centralized planning was necessary in the first stage of socialist development but became dysfunctional in a mature, complex stage, hence favoring decentralization and market techniques. This argument was partially accepted by the Soviets in the mid-1960s. The Chinese and the Cubans complained that the use of material incentives and market mechanisms was a regressive step in the path towards communism and the development of a New Man, thus supporting moral incentives and egalitarianism. The Cubans have attempted to implement this goal with a centralized system, while the Chinese have tried administrative decentralization in some stages.

None of these countries have officially renounced the future implementation (in full communism) of those Marx goals which are being played down in the current transitional stage. Thus the Soviets allege that, once the society of abundance is achieved, the shaping of a

New Man will be easier. The Yugoslavs, in turn, put the development of a democratic, "associational" society in which the state plays a minor role as a prerequisite for the New Man and abundance. The Chinese and Cubans maintain that a radical change in values and egalitarianism are *sine qua non* conditions to the future democratic society. Each of these socialist countries asserts that its path is the correct one and that its partners, by choosing the wrong path, are moving into a kind of society different from the one envisaged by Marx.[26]

In my model, each of the opposing ideal systems at the poles of the continuum has internal cohesiveness. Pole X is representative of Marx's ideal schema in its goals of collectivization, selflessness, egalitarianism, and full employment, but is opposite to it in other areas, such as excessive centralization (in contradiction to the expected "withering away of the state") and lack of efficiency. Conversely, pole Y follows Marx's schema in its goals of rationality and elimination of state-imposed control but opposes it by expanding market mechanisms, the significant role of the private sector, and the existence of unemployment.

My contention is that in a real system there tends to be an optimal mixture of variables coherent with those goals from Marx's schema that have received priority. Variables in a real system have relative cohesiveness; that is, they tend to reinforce each other and to move in the same direction. This is not to say, however, that all variables in a system are mutually dependent in a rigid manner and in the short run. Often the leadership in a socialist country has chosen a variable mix which is considerably less cohesive than the optimal mix. This could be the result of a compromise to satisfy conflicting interests (e.g., politician-centralizers versus technocrats-managers), thus paying some costs to avoid a potentially more harmful situation. But if the contradictions in the "compromise mix" are acute, some readjustment would have to be done sooner or later to correct their negative effects.[27] An illustrative example of lack of cohesiveness of a mix is China in which variables eight, nine, and eleven (Table 1) seem to be incoherent with the rest of the variables. And yet the history of socialist China suggests that deviations from system cohesiveness are temporary and have been made at certain costs. I will return to this point later.

In order to test the hypotheses of relative cohesiveness of systems, costs for deviation from cohesiveness, and movement of variables in the same direction, further refining of the model is necessary. The first step will be to improve the composition of the matrix. Currently, the managerial-economic subsystem is predominant in the model. Multidisciplinary work may result in the addition of new sociological, politico-administrative, and foreign-relation variables or in disaggregation of one of the present variables into a set of better-defined and more concrete variables. Next there is the need to quantify the variables following the indices suggested in this paper and/or others. Once this task is accomplished, percentages or deciles could substitute for the current five-point evaluative score, thus allowing more precise distinctions among variables, subsystems, and systems. Third is the need to assign different weights to variables according to their significance.[28] As the model stands, a system could have the same score with two divergent profiles. Furthermore, a change in one single variable could be more significant (and influential) than changes in a series of other variables, e.g., a shift from party to military control. Once these refinements are introduced, it would be possible to measure the relationship of variables in a system and their degree of cohesiveness by using factor analysis, factorial discriminant analysis, cluster analysis, or similar techniques. Let me now discuss the point of system gravitation or movement of variables.

*Tendencies in the Gravitation of Systems*

History shows that some socialist countries gravitate toward pole X and others toward pole Y. A country which gravitates toward pole X often emphasizes equality, moral incentives, full employment, total collectivization of the means of production, and rapid elimination of the market. This is presented as a prerequisite to eradicate alienation, selfishness, conflicts, and inequalities. With the substantial curtailment of the market forces, the necessity for central planning, budgetary finance and mobilization techniques becomes apparent. Since the development of a New Man can hardly take place in a short period of time, coercive techniques and militarization of society eventually substitute for economic incentives. Under these circumstances, a dictatorship (usually charismatic) concentrating most power and politico-economic functions appears as more operative than a complex system of checks and balances. The dictator in many cases relies on an inner circle for performing most political functions and on loyal managers for handling the economy. In order to resist pernicious foreign influences (for example, the lure of consumer goods, the demonstration effect of movies), isolationist tendencies tend to grow. This external movement is usually parallel to an internal movement to exert tight control over ideology, education, and culture. The isolated country then reasserts its belief that in order to achieve its ideological goal it is necessary to change the exterior world first, hence the exportation of the revolution becomes a crucial target for the system.

On the other hand, a country which gravitates toward pole Y often emphasizes efficiency techniques, material incentives, and increase in production. In its pursuit of higher productivity and output, such a country often tests market mechanisms (self-financed enterprise, profit, interest, rational prices, rent, etc.) and decentralization becomes necessary. Decollectivization of part of agriculture or decrease in procurement quotas and the rise of prices to collective farmers follow in most cases. The system increasingly demands better qualified technicians as managers and party cadres, and frequently rewards them highly. Producers' associations, workers' councils, or other types of participatory bodies in decision-making may evolve. There are fewer possibilities of achieving a more equal income distribution and even development among regions, and probably unemployment appears. With gradual relaxation of central control and depolitization of the economy, rigidity of dogma could recede and liberal tendencies take place in education and culture. The system thus becomes increasingly institutionalized and liberalized. Communication with the outside world, particularly with non-socialist countries, usually expands and the country accepts peaceful coexistence of different socio-politico-economic systems.

What are the causes which determine the gravitation of a socialist system toward one pole or its opposite? It seems that a combination of factors operating in divergent degree in each country at different times are responsible for its gravitation. Most of these factors are internal: (a) physical characteristics, endowment, or environment; (b) stage of development; (c) ideology and culture; and (d) personality of the leaders. There is an external factor: (e) the politico-economic dependence upon (or independence from) a big power. Finally, (f) random events, both of an internal and external nature.[29]

The role of the endowment (country size, location, topography, natural resources, climate, population) in shaping some features of specific socialist countries has been a subject of study. Thus China's large territory (together with its regionalism) have been pointed out to explain the decentralization of its economy, while overpopulation has been connected with mass mobilization of underemployed rural workers. Conversely the physical characteristics of Cuba, a small island with no serious topographical obstacles (together with a common language, a good communication system, and a tradition of centralism in politics and economics) are alleged reasons for the introduction of a highly centralized organization of the economy and decision-making. Continental socialist countries which contain the basic natural resources (such as the USSR and China) can afford isolation for long periods, but not small socialist countries such as Cuba.

There is increasing literature and concern (particularly within the socialist world) on the relationship between the stage of development and certain features of a system. In the late 1950s, both China and Czechoslovakia tried the Stalinist system but soon discovered that it was inadequate for their respective developmental levels. China was more backward, rural, and poor in 1949 than the USSR twenty years earlier; thus, the Stalinist system was too advanced for it. Conversely, Czechoslovakia in 1948 was more technologically developed than the Soviets at the same time, making the Stalinist system obsolete from the start. Thus the Czechs moved in the direction of pole Y while China turned towards pole X.

Differences in ideology are significant also, although often ideas serve as a facade to hide other motivations. The Chinese and Cubans apparently believe (or at least have believed in certain stages) that subjective conditions are more important than objective conditions and that it is possible to change the superstructure (e.g., set of values, consciousness) first to facilitate the transformation of the structure (i.e., mode of production or material base). Also in both countries a "guerrilla spirit" (asceticism, willingness, egalitarianism, improvisation, solidarity, military life) developed during both the Yenan and Sierra Maestra struggles. After the seizing of power, these ideological factors probably influenced the decision in favor of moral incentives, egalitarianism, mobilization, and exportation of the revolution.

Contemporary social scientists are often reluctant to discuss the role of personalities in shaping history because human behavior is largely an unpredictable, nonquantifiable variable, difficult to integrate into sophisticated models. And yet would the USSR be like it is today if Trotsky instead of Stalin had been victorious in the struggle to fill Lenin's post? In the case of China the predominance of Mao Tse-tung *vis-à-vis* more pragmatic leaders such as Liu Shao-chi (or Chou En-lai) is clearly connected with pole X-oriented cycles. If the dogmatic, doctrinaire Guevara instead of the pragmatic, compromising Castro would have been the dominant leader in Cuba, the Cuban endorsement of the Soviet invasion of Czechoslovakia probably would not have occurred. Tito's personality has been basic in establishing socialism in Yugoslavia, challenging the USSR, launching a new socialist system, and holding the multi-national country together for a quarter century. Specialists on Yugoslavia are reluctant to predict what will happen in that country after Tito's death.

The pivotal role of big-power dominance is clear when we think that the Stalinist system was initially established in all socialist countries regardless of when they came to power and their internal differences in endowment, stage of development, ideology, and personalities. The USSR has resorted to all kinds of actions (military intervention, economic embargo, withdrawal of technicians and aid, politico-economic threats, loans, protection *vis-à-vis* other big powers—some successful, others not—in order to influence the internal system of other socialist nations. The dominance of China over other socialist countries seems to be much weaker and hence less significant in molding their systems.

Finally there are unpredictable, random events, such as natural phenomena (e.g., hurricanes and drought in Cuba, floods in China) which can weaken the economy of a country, making it more vulnerable to external influence. Random events of an external nature (e.g., the Vietnam war, the Arab-Israeli war, the election of a President in the U.S.) have often had an unexpected impact in the gravitation of some socialist countries. For instance, the Middle East crisis generated a wave of anti-Semitism in Poland and this strengthened the position of those in favor of the status quo because several leaders of the "liberalization" trend were Jews.

So we know that certain factors have been influential upon a number of features of some socialist countries at a given moment. But we lack a general methodology to determine a cause-and-effect relationship in a particular country, much less in a comparative manner. One possibility would be to use multiple regression analysis treating the explained six causative factors as independent variables (random events and personalities would have to be clustered as a residue), and the sixteen features of each system (Table 1) as dependent variables. There are, of course, many steps to be taken before we can reach this stage.

At this point it may only be said that, according to past historical experience, most Eastern European countries (including the USSR) seem to evolve in a linear or quasi-linear manner, gravitating toward pole Y in the continuum, although at different paces. On the other hand, socialist countries of Asia and Latin America seem to evolve in a cyclical manner gravitating, at least temporarily, toward pole X. We may expect that pole X-oriented countries (particularly if new in the socialist camp) repeat the attempt to implement the idealistic goal of a classless, conflictless, egalitarian, non-market society integrated by selfless human beings. And yet all sporadic attempts to rapidly implement egalitarian communism have not succeeded, and the country in question has returned to a more pragmatic stand. Lowenthal also points out that as a country becomes more modern (and developed), so it becomes more institutionalized and decreases chances for an upheaval of ideological mobilization.[30]

There is also the possibility of the Soviet Union stopping a client state or satellite which is going faster and further toward pole Y than the maximum velocity and limits permitted. In the 1960s it was thought in the West (and probably in the East) that the USSR would not use open armed intervention in another socialist country. The 1960s evolution of Hungary toward pole Y, in spite of prior Soviet intervention, was pointed out as proof that this movement was inevitable. The Soviet invasion of Czechoslovakia, and its aftermath of regression to the center, appears as a blow to such assumptions. But the Yugoslavs, particularly Milovan Djilas, have expressed optimism that in the long run Czechoslovakia will resume the movement toward pole Y.

The temptation to present a hypothesis of universal, long-run movement toward pole Y, interrupted by short-run setbacks and accidents of a domestic or of an external nature is a strong one. It should be resisted, however, because of the possibility of new events capable of changing history. In the same way that two decades ago Yugoslavia opened a new unexpected path, a socialist country may succeed in a steady approximation to pole Y.

A modified continuum model may be used to show how socialist systems evolve. Instead of using the model for a static-multisystem comparison, it can be used for a dynamic-unisystem comparison. In other words, the distinctive profiles of each of the consecutive stages or cycles of evolution in the history of a given socialist country could be described through the variables in the model.[31] This comparison probably would show how, in the first stage, most socialist countries take a center position. In the case of a country that evolves in a linear or quasi-linear manner towards pole Y, its features would become progressively delineated and strong, although there may be a halt in the movement caused by external interference. On the other hand, in a country which moves in a cyclical manner, approximating pole X and then back to the center, the features of its system would show a zigzag movement. In Figure 1 a graphic representation of the hypothetical gravitation of the five socialist countries selected in this chapter is shown.

*Other Potential Uses of the Model*

An attempt might be made to register the performance of the system in each particular stage in terms of economic growth, income distribution, productivity gains, full employment, political stability, national independence, civic freedoms, etc.[32] Furthermore, a similar stage of evolution could be compared among several socialist countries, e.g., Soviet War Communism, Chinese Great Leap Forward, Cuban Revolutionary Offensive. A comparative evaluation of the performance of linear and cyclical systems (and of the effects of one similar stage in various countries) would throw light on the results of both ways of evolution.

If the above-expressed hypothesis of the cohesiveness of systems is supported by further investigation, the effects of strong deviation from a typical feature or set of features of a system also could be analyzed. A practical example would clarify this. China and Cuba are both ranked as "very strong" in five variables, whereas in seven other variables one of the countries is ranked "very strong" and the other as "strong." But there are a few significant differences between the two systems. In China, participation of the lower echelons in economic decision-making (ninth variable), some degree of decentralization (eighth variable), and self-reliance in communes (eleventh variable) were typical of the Great Leap Forward and the Great Proletarian Cultural Revolution. Conversely in Cuba, centralization, state management, and budgetary enterprise have been characteristics throughout socialism, including the period of the Revolutionary Offensive. To this should be added the fact that the power of Mao was substantially eroded in 1961-1965 (when a collegiate leadership was typical) and shared during the Red Guard movement with other personalities, while Castro has been able to keep his autocratic power almost intact since 1959.

Figure 1

*Hypothetical Representation of the Gravitation of Five Socialist Countries in Time*

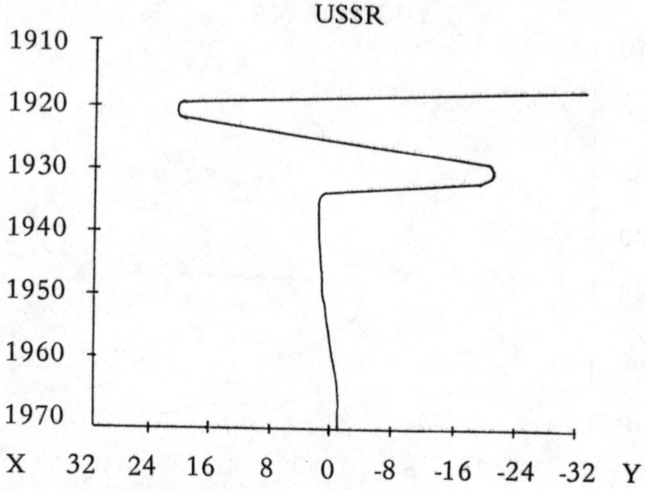


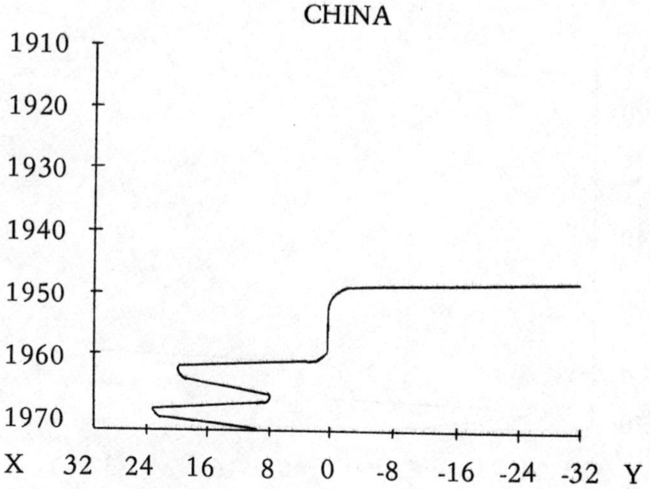

**Figure 1 cont.**

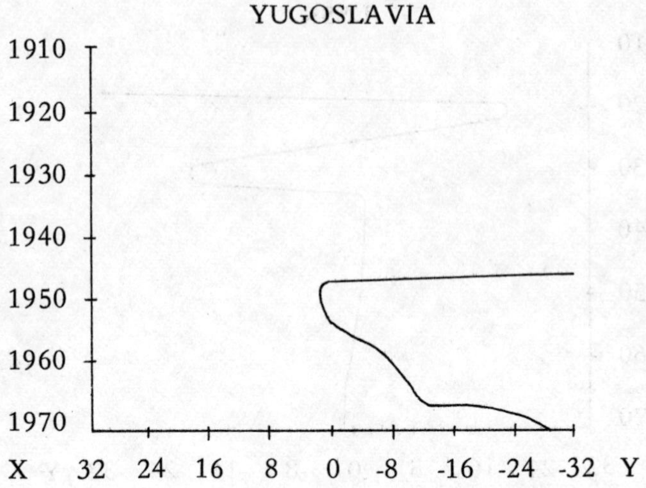


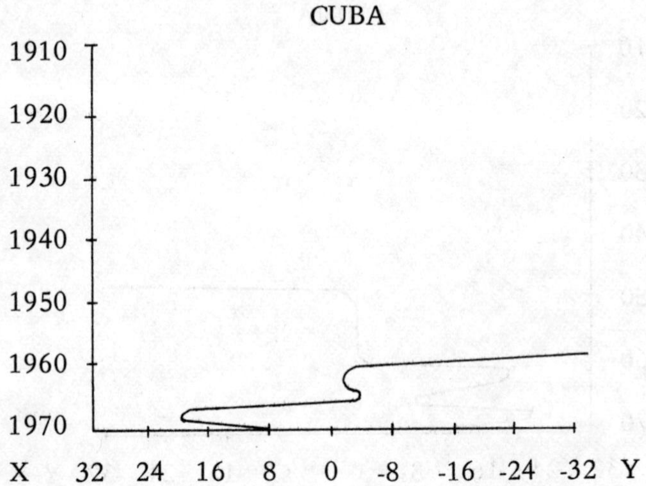

Figure 1. cont.

CZECHOSLOVAKIA

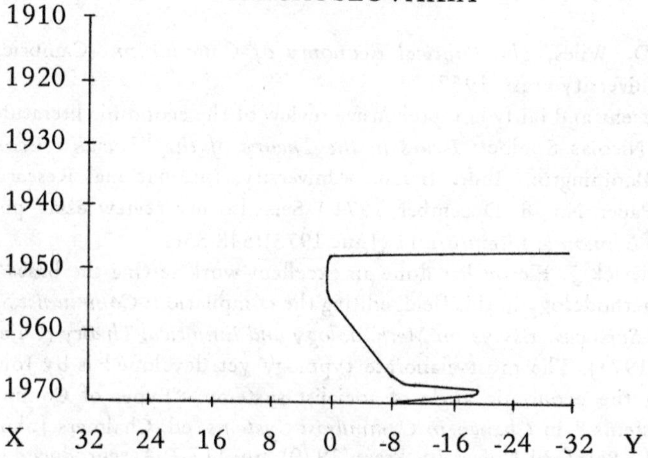


NOTE: These are hypotheses of how these countries have evolved since they began the introduction of their socialist systems. In order to test these hypotheses, quantified dynamic-unisystem models have to be developed.

The effects of the Great Proletarian Cultural Revolution in China and of the Revolutionary Offensive in Cuba have been fairly similar. This seems consistent with the similarity of their systems. For instance, excessive emphasis on mobilization, moral incentives, and egalitarianism on the one hand, and serious negligence of economic incentives, on the other, have induced in both countries a slowdown of labor effort, absenteeism, and declines in output and productivity. The three variables in which China and Cuba show a noticeably divergent performance could have induced different results. Thus economic chaos, labor indiscipline, and factional struggle have been considerably higher in China than in Cuba. This could be partially explained by the prevalence of a strong and united power elite (tightly controlled by Castro) as well as management control and centralization in Cuba, as opposed to erosion of the leader's political control, mass participation in decision-making, and relative decentralization in China.

Finally, the model has the potential for forecasting effects. By establishing a relationship between systems and their results, historically recorded, predictions might be made of what may happen, for instance, in a country that goes into cycle (toward pole X or back to the center) or in one country that follows a linear evolution toward pole Y.

## NOTES

1. P.J.D. Wiles, *The Political Economy of Communism* (Cambridge, Mass.: Harvard University Press, 1962).

2. A recent and fairly comprehensive review of the economic literature has been made by Nicolas Spulber: *Issues in the Theory of the "Socialist Economy": A Survey* (Bloomington, Ind.: Indiana University, International Research Center, Working Paper No. 8, December 1971.) See also my review essay published in *Journal of Economic Literature* 11 (June 1973):548-556.

3. Frederick J. Fleron has done an excellent work setting the bases for advancing the methodology in this field, editing the compilation: *Communist Studies and the Social Sciences: Essays on Methodology and Empirical Theory* (Chicago: Rand McNally, 1971). The most elaborate typology yet developed is by John Montias comparing the economic angle of socialist systems: "Types of Communist Economic Systems," in *Change in Communist Systems*, ed. Chalmers Johnson (Stanford, Calif.: Stanford University Press, 1970), pp. 117-134, reproduced in Montias' contribution to this volume. On standardization of data and prediction, the most comprehensive and sophisticated work is the compilation edited by Wiles: *The Prediction of Communist Economic Performance* (Cambridge, England: Cambridge University Press, 1971).

4. Oleg Zinam, "The Economics of Command Economies," in *Comparative Economic Systems*, ed. Jan S. Prybyla (New York: Appleton-Century-Crofts, 1969), pp. 23, 33. Zinam is probably the first scholar to develop a sophisticated, comparative scheme, based on socio-politico-economic variables. Zinam's scheme was not applied only to socialist economies but to all economic systems and its scope was too wide, losing in concentration and utility.

5. Copies of an earlier draft of this chapter were sent to thirty scholars trained in various disciplines and specializing in the five socialist countries selected to test this model. The scholars were asked to comment on the methodology and ranking of variables. Eighteen of them answered. The listing shows discipline, main country(ies) of specialization, and current academic affiliation: Carl Beck, politics, East Europe, University of Pittsburgh; Roberto Bernardo, economics, Cuba, University of Guelph; Robert Campbell, economics, USSR, Indiana University; William Dunn, politics, Yugoslavia, University of Pittsburgh; Edward Gonzalez, politics, Cuba, University of California–Los Angeles; Gregory Grossman, economics, USSR, University of California–Berkeley; Charles Hoffman, economics, China, State University of New York at Stony Brook; Branko Horvat, economics, Yugoslavia, Institute of Economic Sciences of Yugoslavia; Alex Inkeles, sociology and education, USSR, Stanford University; Bodgan Mieczkowski, economics, East Europe, Ithaca College; John M. Montias, economics, East Europe, Yale University; Jose Moreno, sociology, Cuba, University of Pittsburgh; Paul Novosel, sociology, Yugoslavia, University of Zagreb; Michel Oksenberg, politics, China, Columbia University; Rolland Paulston, education, China-Cuba, University of Pittsburgh; Jan S. Prybyla, economics, China-USSR, Pennsylvania State University; Paul Craig Roberts, ideology, USSR, Hoover Institution, Stanford; and Zdenek Suda, sociology, Czechoslovakia, University of Pittsburgh. I also benefited from comments generated by the presentation of

various drafts of this chapter, especially from: Jan S. Prybyla, Fourteenth Annual Conference of the Southern Economic Association, Atlanta (November 3, 1970); Richard Carson and R. T. McKinnell, Workshop on Developing Countries, Economics Department, Carleton University, Ottawa (November 5, 1971); Heinrich Brunner and his colleagues, discussions at Osteuropa Institute, Freien Universität, Berlin (December 16-18, 1971); John M. Montias and Egon Neuberger, Northeastern Slavic Conference of the AAASS, University of Vermont (April 29, 1972); and several attendants at the Comparative Communist Lecture Series "Methodological Comparison of Socialist Systems," Pittsburgh (May 3, 1972).

6. For a discussion of this problem, see my article, "Availability and Reliability of Statistics in Socialist Cuba," *Latin American Research Review* 4 (Spring 1969):53-54.

7. Basic statistics for the majority of the socialist countries are officially published in statistical yearbooks, although only a few are available in English. A well of data for many socialist countries is Paul Shoup, "Comparing Communist Nations: Prospects for an Empirical Approach," in Fleron, *Communist Studies*, pp. 64-93. Comparative recent statistics on Eastern Europe can be found in Jozef Wilczynski, *The Economics of Socialism* (Chicago: Aldine Publishing Co., 1970). Wiles also includes China in his compilation, *The Prediction*. On Cuba, see note 6 above and C. Paul Roberts, ed., *Cuba 1968* (Los Angeles: Latin American Center, University of California, 1970).

8. Morris Bornstein, "An Integration," in *Comparison of Economic Systems: Theoretical and Methodological Approaches*, ed. Alexander Eckstein (Berkeley, Calif.: University of California Press, 1971), pp. 350-351.

9. The late Rudolf Bićanić distinguished among "monocentric," "oligocentric," and "polycentric" planning types. See *Problems of Planning East and West* (The Hague: Mouton and Co., 1967). Wilczynski, in *The Economics of Socialism* (pp. 23-25), has in turn coined four planning-management types: "bureaucratic centralized," "planometric centralized," "selectively decentralized," and "supplemented market." Nicolas Spulber differentiates between "edict management" and "associational management" in *Socialist Management and Planning: Topics in Comparative Socialist Economics* (Bloomington, Ind.: Indiana University Press, 1971), pp. 72-76.

10. Up to the late 1960s, all socialist systems were classified as "totalitarian" or "authoritarian" with slight colorations such as "conservative" and "radical." More recently, some political scientists have been discussing the evolution of socialist systems through three stages: "pre-totalitarian," "totalitarian," and "post-totalitarian." A scholar still keeping the term "authoritarian" has decided to qualify it by using adjectives such as "quasi," "consultative," "quasi-pluralistic," and "democratizing and pluralistic." See the various papers in Johnson, *Change in Communist Systems*.

11. Independent from his typology (see note 3 above), J. M. Montias has developed with T. C. Koopmans a complex abstract model that interrelates, among other things, causes and performance of comparative economic systems (both socialist and non-socialist). See "On the Description and Comparison of Economic Systems," in Eckstein, *Comparison of Economic Systems*, pp. 27-78. But the two studies have not yet been integrated.

12. Soviet War Communism is often presented as a temporary, emergency policy imposed by war. Another view is that in this period the Bolsheviks made a conscious attempt to implement communism. See Paul Craig Roberts, *Alienation and the Soviet Economy* (Albuquerque, N.M.: University of Mexico Press, 1971).

13. The problem also could be presented as an attempt to build socialism and communism *at the same time*. This is the approach that Fidel Castro took in Cuba in 1966-1970.

14. Yugoslavs commonly insist that they have not given up the goal of societal reconstruction. Professor Horvat argues that Yugoslavs, instead of sacrificing the present generation to achieve the millennium in the very distant future, have preferred to improve the life of the present generation without renouncing their aspirations for a more perfect society. Professor Novosel has presented the difference in terms of patience and flexibility: "The utopians [impatiently] want to press square people into round (utopian) holes immediately, whereas the pragmatists are [patiently] willing to adjust the holes to the people, temporarily."

15. Professor Novosel is in favor of the term "spiral" because "after a spurt these countries never return to the previous state, but to something qualitatively new." This observation seems to be correct in relation to societal change. The term "spiral," however, suggests a steady upward movement which in economics is not supported by empirical evidence.

16. Richard Lowenthal, "Development vs. Utopia in Communist Policy," in Johnson, *Change in Communist Systems*, p. 54.

17. An integral study of cyclical evolution in China is G. William Skinner and Edwin A. Winckler, "Compliance Succession in Rural Communist China: A Cyclical Theory," in *A Sociological Reader on Complex Organizations*, ed. Amitai Etzioni (New York: Holt, Rinehart and Winston, 1969), pp. 410-438. For an economic interpretation see Alexander Eckstein, "Economic Fluctuation in Communist China's Domestic Development," in *China in Crisis*, ed. Ping-ti Ho and Tang Tsou (Chicago: The University of Chicago Press, 1968), vol. 1, book 2, pp. 691-729.

18. In terms of the intensity of economic reform *alone*, Wiles (*The Prediction*, pp. 13-18) and Wilczynski (*The Economics of Socialism*, pp. 25-29) have almost concurred in ranking, from lowest to highest, most socialist countries *circa* 1968 as follows: (Albania), Rumania, USSR, Poland, East Germany, Bulgaria, Czechoslovakia, Hungary, and (Yugoslavia). Countries in parentheses have been ranked by Wilczynski only. Morris Bornstein has arrived at a different ranking: Romania, East Germany, USSR, Bulgaria, Poland, Hungary, and Czechoslovakia. See his "East European Reform and the Convergence of Economic Systems," in *Yearbook of East European Economics* (Munich: Osteuropa Institute, 1970), p. 263.

19. In socialist countries where the language has intimate and formal forms of address (both in the use of pronouns and verb conjugation), egalitarianism could be also measured by the mass use of the intimate form in addressing high officials.

20. See the excellent study by Frank Parkin, *Class Inequality and Political Order: Social Stratification in Capitalist and Communist Societies* (New York: Praeger, 1971), pp. 137-159 and the sources that he uses.

21. Parkin has suggested a third possibility: the intelligentsia. He thinks that in Czechoslovakia in 1968 the technocrats took power over the *apparatchiki* and this

substitution accelerated the depoliticization and decentralization of the economy and the movement towards the market. See his "System Contradiction and Political Transformation," *European Journal of Sociology* 13, no. 1 (1972). Paul M. Sweezy (Sweezy and Charles Bettelheim, *On the Transition to Socialism* [New York: Monthly Review Press, 1971], p. 30) believes that this substitution will eventually occur in the USSR and Eastern Europe, but Parkin has serious doubts about its feasibility. Another alternative is the professionalization of the political cadre together with the party moderate cooptation of the technocrat. See Fleron, "Cooptation as a Mechanism of Adaptation to Change: The Soviet Political Leadership System," in *The Behavioral Revolution and Communist Studies*, ed. Roger Kanet (New York: Free Press, 1971), pp. 125-149.

22. Several of Herbert S. Levine's detailed sets of scales that categorize economic planning for comparative purposes could be used for measuring this variable. See his "On Comparing Planned Economies (A Methodological Inquiry)," in Eckstein, *Comparison of Economic Systems*, pp. 143-150, 159-160.

23. See Carmelo Mesa-Lago, "Unemployment in a Socialist Economy: Yugoslavia," *Industrial and Labor Relation Review* 10 (February 1971):49-69; *The Labor Force, Employment, Unemployment, and Underemployment in Cuba: 1898-1970* (Beverly Hills, Calif.: Sage Professional Papers in International Studies, 1972); and *Unemployment in Socialist Countries: Soviet Union, East Europe, China and Cuba*, Ph.D. dissertation, Cornell University, 1968 (mimeo).

24. See the treatment of these conflicts made by Wiles (*The Political Economy*, pp. 334-349), and Ernest Mandel, "Economics of the Transition Period," *Key Problems of the Transition from Capitalism to Socialism* (New York: Pathfinder Press, 1970), pp. 35-63. Alexander Erlich, failing to list all Marx's goals and to distinguish their interlocking in an ideal situation (full communism) and in reality (transitional stage), suggests that such goals are not in conflict. See " 'Eastern' Approaches to a Comparative Examination of Economic Systems," in Eckstein, *Comparison of Economic Systems*, pp. 301-335.

25. I have discussed this problem in a review essay of Deborah D. Milenkovitch, *Plan and Market in Yugoslav Economic Thought* (New Haven, Conn.: Yale University Press, 1971), published in *Economic Development and Cultural Change* 21 (January 1973):364-370.

26. Western Marxist scholars are not in agreement on which goals should receive priority either. Thus, in 1968, Paul M. Sweezy initiated a long debate with Charles Bettelheim when the former stated that the gradual elimination of the market (substituted by the plan) was the basic condition to build up socialism. Bettelheim argued that in the transitional stage the existence of market forces is inevitable and stated that the basic goal is to keep and expand the "political dominance of the proletariat" (i.e., the direct control by the immediate producers over the means of production and their products) and to create the necessary conditions for the democratic exercise of proletarian power in the future. Interestingly, both scholars criticized the USSR for procreating a "state bourgeoisie" or "class state" and supported China's Cultural Revolution for its anti-bureaucratic, egalitarian features. But while Sweezy hailed Cuba, Bettelheim criticized Castro's autocratism and the lack of workers' power; and while Sweezy criticized Yugoslavia for promoting

capitalism by strengthening the market, Bettelheim kept a diplomatic silence on that country. See Sweezy and Bettelheim, *On the Transition to Socialism*. See also the more complex but less concrete stand taken by Mandel ("Economics of the Transition Period," pp. 35-63) who, in general, seems to be closer to Bettelheim than to Sweezy.

27. The Cuban-Soviet *rapprochement* that began in 1968 has gradually brought the two countries together (as well as Cuba's relations with most Eastern European countries) reaching a peak in 1972 with Cuba's entrance in Comecon. This movement of variable fifteen toward the center has been paralleled, although with less velocity, by a decline in Cuba's exportation of the revolution and an improvement of relations with several Latin American countries (variable sixteen). Still, the emphasis on egalitarianism, moral incentives, mobilization, capital accumulation, and full employment (variables one through three, twelve, fourteen) continued until 1970. The failure of the ten-million-ton sugar harvest and the serious dislocation of the Cuban economy were decisive in a gradual change of all these variables toward the center. It remains to be seen whether the remaining variables will change in the same direction also.

28. The problems involved in measuring a similar scale are discussed by Levine, "On Comparing Planned Economies," pp. 156-158.

29. In Eckstein's compilation *Comparison of Economic Systems* there are several papers that refer to this theme. The most elaborated is the one by Montias and Koopmans (pp. 29-31) who under the term "environment" includes resources, initial technology and preferences, "incomplete interaction," external factors, and random events. Bornstein (pp. 340-344) indicates a series of "forces influencing economic systems": environment (in the strict sense), social and cultural forces, and level of economic development. See also the papers by S. Kuznets on the influence of economic growth, and A. Gerschenkron and A. O. Hirschman on the influence of ideology.

30. Lowenthal, "Development vs. Utopia," p. 54.

31. I have done this, concerning Cuba, in my *Cuba in the 1970s: Pragmatism and Institutionalization* (Albuquerque, N.M.: University of New Mexico Press, 1974), chapter 5.

32. See the sophisticated study of Montias and Koopmans ("Description and Comparison," pp. 41-50) establishing norms or criteria (positive and negative) to evaluate the "outcome" or performance of systems.

# PART TWO

# POLITICS

# 5

# Patterns and Problems of Governance

Carl Beck

Today as much variance exists among the European states that we label as communist as exists between the European states that we label as constitutional democracies. Yet, because the communist states of Europe are all officially engaged in the building of communism and because each political system is dominated by one party, we tend to treat them as if they were alike. The myth of universalism within communist political systems, like most myths, has a foundation in history. All of the communist states of Europe shared a similar homogenizing experience: the period of Stalinism. Since the death of Stalin and the concomitant break-up of the Stalinist empire the universalism that typified Eastern Europe in that period has been pushed aside by particularistic behaviors and structures.

It is the purpose of this paper to explore some of the similarities and differences among the nations of post-Stalinist Eastern Europe—Bulgaria, Czechoslovakia, East Germany, Hungary, Poland, and Romania—for the purpose of identifying emergent types and trends. In this paper aspects of the decision-making structure will serve as the primary focus. There is a broad sweep to this analysis, and unlike the contributions of Mesa-Lago, Montias, and Welsh, less concern with empirically derived comparative findings.

If there is an "ideology" or "orientation" to this analysis, it is that we mask for ourselves the reality of Eastern European politics today if we allow the concepts of the Stalinist period to shape our perceptions of contemporary Eastern Europe. In both the academic and journalistic worlds we search for shorthand labels which allow us to discuss complex phenomena. We search for concepts that capture the major structural characteristics or behaviors of a complex system. We need an idealized language in order to explicate reality and to identify trends, but we always run the risk of misusing such concepts when we begin to conceive of them not as tools useful for analysis but as replications of reality. In the analysis of communist states the concepts of a totalitarian political system and a satellite international system became so analytically enticing[1] and ideologically comfortable that they were often used as a basis for prediction of behavior despite strong empirical evidence that a given country was going in a different direction.[2]

The impetus for universalizing diverse phenomena was present at the beginning of the descriptive and analytic works describing postwar Eastern Europe. Generalization occupied the attention of Western and Soviet scholars alike. Western scholars were interested in identifying patterns that would help to explain the process by which Eastern European countries came under the control of communist parties. Soviet scholars had a vested interest in fitting the East European revolution into a Marxist-Leninist mold—or at least the mold of Marxism-Leninism prevalent at the time.

The search for patterns is, of course, a legitimate and significant social science pursuit, just as is the search for statistical significance. But the significant cases in both historical sociology and statistical analysis are often the deviant cases. They are the ones that help us identify both the strengths and weaknesses of our models and theories and they serve as a basis for comparisons and to identify emergent phenomena.

The search for patterns in the analysis of communist seizure of power contributed to the creation of a series of universal myths about the behaviors of communist parties and ultimately the behavior of communist systems. In the still leading descriptive study of *The East European Revolution*, Professor Seton-Watson plots the course of Eastern Europe revolutions through the analysis of the way in which communist parties entered coalitions, broke them apart, absorbed the other participants, and ultimately ruled unilaterally.[3] This is an apt description of the way in which communist parties came to power in Poland and Hungary, and to a lesser extent in Bulgaria and Czechoslovakia, but it ignores the situational impacts upon this process and the significance of these impacts upon future behavior.

Soviet attempts at universalizing the process were even cruder, as Robert Tucker points out in his study of *The Marxian Revolutionary Idea*.[4] Soviet theorists demonstrated that the communist revolutions of Eastern Europe followed the Soviet revolutionary experience. Granted that a seemingly universal pattern in the environmental conditions in which communist parties came to power—the extensive discrediting of the existing authority structure often energized by conditions of war—there is little else in Eastern Europe that matches the course of the Soviet revolution. Indeed, if there is a major deviant case in communist seizures of power it is the Soviet case. The Russian Revolution is in most ways the unique rather than the idealized revolution. Both the Western and Soviet approaches to analyzing Eastern Europe conditioned us to believe that there was a similarity to all Eastern European countries and that we could ignore the nuances that made each country, and continue to make each country, distinctive.[5]

Communist parties came into power in Eastern Europe by manipulating the existing situation to attain power regardless of what the official interpretation of official ideology would have told them to do. Unlike the communist leaders prior to World War II who were always entangled in their ideological debates and often paralyzed from acting as a result of that entanglement, the communist leaders of Eastern Europe during and after the war were in a situation which required action.[6] The war, in effect, legitimated that action and made weak and discredited parties full participants in the political process. Communist leaders participated with vigor and shrewdness in that process. They also had some help. Richard Burks points out that there were three types of communist seizures of power: direct imposition with the full support and backing of the Soviet Army and party; seizure of power through participation in domestic politics including the use of terror and coercion to achieve political goals (the process which Seton-Watson describes in detail); and seizure of power by nativist movements.[7] The significant point is that the way in which communist parties came into power had direct consequence on how they acted once in power, and how they were perceived by Stalin.

The original period of the Peoples' Democracies was a period of experimentation, of diversity, of bending of dogma, and of multiple strategies for the creation and governance of communist states. It was short-lived.[8] The logic of the system that Stalin wished to create was in conflict with the logic of national roads to socialism. In many ways the shift from the Peoples' Democracies (from revolutionary structures) to Stalinism (to a control system) was as dramatic, ruthless, and brutal as the period of revolution itself.[9]

After the Czechoslovak coup in 1948 the process of universalizing communist politics drew additional strength from events on both the domestic and international scenes. The notion of a Cold War and the attendant notion in international politics of a bifurcated world were strong enough in the period from 1948 on to withstand even the shock of Yugoslavia's explusion from the Cominform. An aspect of the Cold War that reinforced the drive for homogeneity across Eastern Europe was the push by both the Soviet Union and the United States for the creation of alliances. In the case of the communist nations, a sophisticated control system of binational relationships between individual nations and the Soviet Union was created. The Soviet Bloc became marked by a Stalinist interstate system designed to tie each nation directly to the Soviet Union and to minimize interactions among the states composing the bloc and between the bloc and non-bloc countries. The nations of Eastern Europe, with the exception of Yugoslavia, became satellites subject to direct interference from Moscow in domestic and international politics.[10]

*The Stalinist System*

Prior to 1948 communist leaders of Eastern Europe were relatively free to discuss and propose their own roads to socialism. The concept of each nation's own road to socialism was quite strong, particularly among those leaders who had spent the war period active in their own countries. In following these roads the native communist rulers created unique mixes of political structures, and developed non-Soviet-type economic structures as well.[11]

By 1948 it was proclaimed that the Peoples' Democracies were equivalent to the dictatorship of the proletariat. This message meant that the policies and structures of Eastern Europe were to follow the dictates of the Soviet Union. The shift to Stalinism was dramatic. In most countries native communist leaders were replaced with those who had received their training in Moscow and owed their allegiance to Stalin. Nationalized economies became command economies; the class struggle was extended to the countryside, transforming small-holding agricultural systems into ones more amenable to control; and semi-autonomous groups in society such as labor unions, cultural associations, sports associations, and scientific associations were either replaced with more amenable organizations or were transformed into transmission belts. The model that evolved for all to follow was indeed a homogeneous model.

The logic of Stalinism was both all-encompassing and organic. It was also, as later events bore out, synthetic. Seen from our present perspective, the heart of the logic was the establishment of unified political power. The motivations and perceptions of those involved in this process of transformation were more complex than a simple commitment to control, but the political structures and the attendant political behaviors that evolved form a unity when they are assessed in terms of their contribution to a system of control.

All who have explored the system that Stalinism created have noted that primacy of its concern with political control. Centrism and etatism reinforced that primacy, but above all control in a state of transformation rested upon the ability of the system to mobilize.[12] The classic terms of Marxism-Leninism were used to legitimate the system ideologically, but the terms were so redefined as to do violence to their original content. Democratic centralism was reinterpreted to mean not only unquestioning acceptance of what was being done, but unquestioning acceptance of what was being proposed. A once creative philosophy became a reified dogma. Although the process was uneven across the countries of Eastern Europe, the message was quite clear: as soon as possible, a major reshaping of the cultural, social, economic, and political sectors of society was to take place, regardless of the consequences.

The overriding concern with creating a controlled and mobilize-able social system carried with it a distrust and disdain for institutions. Institutionalization carries with it behaviors and norms which disrupt the logic of control. Institutionalization and subsystem autonomy, whether in religious, legal, cultural, or educational institutions, were inimical to what Stalin created and through which he ruled. Even the party was a threat. It rarely met, its leadership and structure were constantly changed, and its relationships with other agencies in society were continually interfered with. The passion to avoid the process of institutionalization made of Stalinism a formless thing. An operational code did exist, but it was always unfolding.[13] At the highest level, the Stalinist system was held together by Stalin's own ability to manipulate what needed to be manipulated in order to enforce his will, which he did with ruthlessness and with seeming satisfaction. Critical to its operation is both the behavior and structures created to link the ruler to the ruled.

### *The Structure of the Elite*

Marxism-Leninism espouses an almost mystical relationship between the rulers and the ruled. The masses become important, particularly in what may be called a period of mobilization, as long as they are led by the revolutionary vanguard. Presumably, the revolutionary vanguard draws sanctity from its mass roots. Marxist theory spells out this relationship with some care and precision. But the theory extends best to revolution, not governance.

In reality, the relationship between the rulers and the ruled has always been difficult in communist political systems. The great disruptions in East Germany, Poland, and Hungary had both a mass pattern and an elite pattern of activity.[14] In these disruptions mass action was important not only for the visibility that it brought with it, but also because of the impact it had upon the structure through which leadership had been exercised. Mass political action, like concerted political action by intermediary groups, is exceedingly difficult for consolidation-of-power-minded communist regimes to absorb.

In an earlier paper, James Malloy and I tried to explicate why this is true in Stalinist type systems.[15] We suggested that four major types of leadership systems could be constructed from the interrelationship of a set of variables germane to the analysis of leadership systems. These four types emerged from a descriptive analysis of the structure and behavioral norms of the elite. We suggested that elite structure and behavior formed patterns which were indicative of the style of politics. In constructing these types, two major variables and two minor variables seemed to us to be of crucial importance. The major variables were leadership structure and leadership behavioral norms. These were effected by and in turn affected the secondary variables: leadership perspectives, and techniques and mechanisms utilized by the leadership for maintaining political control.

Elite structure is viewed as the patterned set of relationships which develop among those individuals and groups which exercise control, and the set of relationships that develop between those individuals and groups which exercise control and those who do not. The behavioral norms are the norms by which leadership-to-leadership interaction and leadership-to-constituent interaction are determined.

When these dimensions are utilized for the analysis of leadership types in communist political systems, particularly in communist political systems of the Stalinist period, certain characteristics stand out. More important, these characteristics seem to create an analytic whole, which then becomes useful for assessing and understanding the difficulties of change within these systems.

The leadership structure that emerges in communist political systems tends to have the following characteristics: The leadership of the political system is the leadership of the party. As a result, there is only one substantive interest that gains continual access to the control structure. It is not just that this single interest controls the decision outputs alone, but that it also controls the process by which problems become articulated, alternative strategies selected, and decisions made and enforced. A coherent leadership group exists at the party apex. The coherence of this leadership group does not exclude competition, but competition takes the form of factionalism. Because institutional competition for control is not legitimated there are no formal mechanisms for the regulation of conflict.[16] The dominant rule of factional struggle is "winner take all." Purge, which seems endemic to this type of structure, becomes both a means for conflict resolution and a means for reinvigoration.[17]

The leadership in this type of system tends to evolve into a core of professionals distinct from the society at large.[18] Although the party assumes the major functions of the social system, the party leadership becomes aloof and distinct from society. In part, this is because mobility into the leadership is circumscribed. Rarely do autonomous power groups exist who can act as a base through which mobility can be achieved. Certainly, such groups do not exist on a permanent basis.

The behavioral norms of the leadership *vis-à-vis* the constituency are shaped by an image of the constituency as object rather than subject. Although a mystical link with the masses exists, there are few empirical ties of accountability or responsibility. The relationship of the leadership to the constituency tends to become total, arbitrary, and unresponsive. There are few intermediary groups, and there is no intermediary group structure that mitigates this dominant relationship on a continual basis.[19]

The technique of control at the leadership level is the purge; the technique of control at the mass level is manipulation. The mechanisms for such control are public organizations, mass constituency organizations, and controlled mass media. There are, of course, inherent restraints upon this system, stemming from the concern with maximizing the scope and intensity of control and concern with mobilization for other than political goals, such as the construction of a modern industrialized economy.[20]

Although the tendency of this leadership structure is towards ossification, there are internal dynamics within this structure. Various types of interests operate, changes occur in the character of political leadership, symbols are manipulated, and, in that manipulation, their contents vary and policies shift. Yet, there is a basic coherence in the system. This coherence is placed in jeopardy under any mix of the following conditions: (a) the death of the leader, (b) sustained mass activity outside the control system, (c) persistent conflict among the leaders, and (d) unique shifts in policy or emphasis by the leadership itself.

The Stalinist leadership system was dependent upon the very personalized rule that kept it together, and was therefore incapable of maintaining itself when the leader died. Soon after the death of Stalin events took place through Eastern Europe which indicated the synthetic and person-bound nature of the Stalinist system. The assault on Stalinism in domestic politics and the break-up of the Stalinist empire had significance to all of the countries of Eastern Europe. The two processes, when taken together, meant that once again domestic forces and domestic considerations would play a dominant role in reshaping political structures and public policies within each country. In most cases domesticism meant some form of decompression. But the process of decompressing a totalistic system is not easy. Any act of decompression ramifies throughout the whole system.

*Break-up of the System: Poland, Hungary, and the DDR*

Within less than four years after the death of Stalin three Eastern European nations of the six under study were to experience traumatic responses to the break-up of the Stalinist system: the German Democratic Republic, the People's Republic of Poland, and the People's Republic of Hungary. Twelve years later in Czechoslovakia an even more extensive revision of the system was to take place. In East Germany the workers' revolt followed a period of decompression in which, in one of the most astonishing documents in the political history of communist regimes, the regime itself announced its own failures, called a halt to the construction of socialism, rewarded everyone but the workers, and then found itself unprepared as the workers protested. The workers' protest was spontaneous. At first it focused entirely on economic issues and therefore bore similarity to a normal labor strike, but soon a *Kulturkampf* was underway as the workers, joined by other groups in society, demanded political as well as economic reforms.[21] It was not until the Soviet Army intervened that order was restored.

Both the Polish October and the Hungarian Revolution were the consequences of the confluence of an elite pattern of politics marked by dissension and factionalism, and a mass pattern of action marked by protests against working conditions, the control apparatus, allegiance to the Soviet Union, and the impacts of the command economy.

In the case of Poland extensive revolution did not take place because the leadership groups were able, for the moment at least, to coalesce around W. Gomulka, who because of his alliance with "domesticism" in an earlier period was acceptable to the reformers and because of his history of party allegiance was at least an acceptable alternative to the hard-liners, particularly when confronted with the unity of all Polish groups including the military. When the Soviet Union acknowledged his claim to leadership the task of party reconstruction could commence. In Hungary no such compromise could be found. The conflict between Rakosi and his vision of a Stalinist Hungary and Nagy and his vision of a reformed Hungary had by then been going on for three years. The Soviet Union and the Hungarian party as well vacillated in their allegiances to either or both. No compromise candidate could be found although a too-late attempt was made when Gero was given a position of major leadership.

All three of these disruptions are significant to an understanding of the difficulty in creating and implementing decompression. The Soviet Union under Malenkov believed that it could undertake some isolated reforms. The DDR believed that it could initiate major ones. The Polish and Hungarian parties, which were in a state of disarray during the Stalinist period, did not know which road to follow.

Although it is possible to find historical currents back in the period of Stalinism which help to explain the East German uprising, the Polish October, and the Hungarian Revolution, the abruptness of the events and the speed with which they took place indicate the synthetic nature of the Stalinist system. They also indicate the difficulty which the Stalinist system had in making any adjustments at all. In those cases where disruption did not take place—Bulgaria, Czechoslovakia, and Romania—none of the leaders ever took the New Course seriously. Some small statements were made in regard to the need for economic reforms, decentralization, etc., but it was quite clear that the policies and codes being promulgated were not a clarion call to reform in any of these cases.

### *The Slow Break-up of a System: Czechoslovakia*

The persistent nature of the unease of any equilibrium in the post-Stalinist period and the search for domestic solutions is dramatically demonstrated by the way in which Dubcek came to power in Czechoslovakia. As in the case of the New Course, the events which brought Dubcek to power affected the two major dimensions of politics in Eastern European communist states that we cited earlier: the relationship of the political leadership to the rest of society and the relationship of political leaders to each other. Although many of the events prior to Dubcek's coming to power can be viewed as discrete and disparate, when taken together they constitute a primary and complete challenge to the existing leadership structure.

The Czechoslovak economy had begun to stagnate in 1962. According to R. V. Burks, the following table is a rough estimate of the statistics on Gross National Product in Czechoslovakia.[22]

**Table 1**

*Gross National Product*

| *Year* | *Percent of* |
|---|---|
| 1961 | 6.8 |
| 1962 | 1.4 |
| 1963 | –2.2 |
| 1964 | 0.0 |
| 1965 | 2.5 |

What is as important as the recession indicated by these figures is the political consequences of the recession. A number of party members came forward with a major program of economic reform. During 1963 extensive discussions by economists had taken place, focusing on the weaknesses of the centralized system. These discussions began to shift from criticism of shortcomings in the system to criticism of the system itself.[23] In January 1964 a special board of the Central Committee Economic Commission was established to study the recommendations of the economists and to submit a report to the Central Committee. The first report, never released in its entirety, was considered to be too revisionist by the Central Committee.[24] By 1966 many of the centrist political leaders, including Novotny, supported some degree of reform and a New Economic Model was proclaimed. The New Economic Model that ultimately emerged from this process decreased the influence of the central planners, increased the autonomy of managers, and, in general, weakened the control of the party apparatus over the economy.

The adoption of a New Economic Model also increased the sense of participation in politics of the managers, technicians, and economists and gave impetus to further reforms. For example, Julius Strinka, a Slovak philosopher, stated that the changes in the structure of socialism should not be limited to the economy alone—there should be greater autonomy in politics as well. Organized opposition within the regime should be created.[25] Zdenek Mlynar, the head of the Central Committee Commission to formulate a political model for Czechoslovakia, stated that a decentralized economy would create interest groups who could then compete in the political process.[26] He welcomed this development.

*The Road to Democratic Socialism* emphasized this point. "For years there were forces within the Communist Party that openly pointed to the fact that a mistaken policy was leading to economic stagnation and drawing the state more and more into a blind alley, . . . , It was absolutely imperative that the centralist model of managing society should be abolished, that administrative and undemocratic interference in all phases of social and cultural life be eliminated, . . . , A system of a wholly uncontrollable concentration of power in the hands of one person had developed within the past years."[27]

The party was unable either to combat the recession or to keep it from becoming a politicized issue. The process by which economic reform developed and the adoption of this model with its attendant consequences threatened the consolidation-of-power motif of Novotny and the apparatus that he constructed. In the debates between September 1968 and January 1969, which culminated in Novotny's fall from power, the New Economic Model occupied a central point of focus.

*De-Stalinization*

*Slovak Nationalism and the Leadership Structure.* At the Twelfth Party Congress in 1962, a commission was established to investigate "violations of party principles that might have been committed in the purges and subsequent trials of 1949-1954."[28] In April 1963, a secret report of this commission led to the expulsion of Bruno Koehler and Vaclav Slavik as members of the Secretariat, and Karel Bacilek as a member of the Presidium and First Secretary of the Slovak Communist Party.

It may well have been the thought of the party leadership that these dismissals would satisfy the critics of the party. When it was announced that the commission had completed its investigation, criticism of the party leadership continued rather than disappeared. Such criticism was most vehement in Slovakia. In May and June of 1963 a number of articles appeared in the Slovak press condemning the party leadership and in particular Viliam Siroky. Miro Hysko, a Slovak journalist, continually criticized the party even after Novotny attacked him publicly in June.[29] In the months that followed it was Novotny rather than Hysko who capitulated. In December, the Central Committee passed a resolution stating that the charges made against the Slovak Communist Party in the purge period were unsubstantiated.[30] The effect of this discussion was twofold: it increased the sense of political strength of Slovak nationalists and brought about changes in the Slovak leadership. The Slovak Communist Party leadership in 1964 did not include anyone who had been in a leadership position ten years before.

Criticism of the party by the Slovaks was limited to the purges. *Kulturny Zivot*, the journal of the Slovak Writers Union, had become a forum for criticism of almost all aspects of socialism in Czechoslovakia. On April 3, 1964, the Central Committee published the "Viewpoint of the Central Committee of the Communist Party of Czechoslovakia on the Mission and State of the Cultural Magazines."[31] This publication expressly criticized the Slovak Writers Union for promoting revisionist views. Following the publication of the "Viewpoint," both the Czechoslovak Writers Union and the Czechoslovak Journalists Union expressed their support for the official party line.[32] But the editors of *Kulturny Zivot*, in a statement signed by "the collective of *Kulturny Zivot*," proclaimed that they could not and would not dissociate themselves from the writers who appeared in their journal.[33]

Support for the Slovak position increased when the twentieth anniversary of the Slovak National Uprising was celebrated. The orthodox interpretation of the uprising, echoed by Novotny during the anniversary celebration, was that the uprising had been instigated by the communists, under the direction of Moscow. The Slovak press in 1964 emphasized that the uprising was undertaken by Slovaks, that the participants included non-communists as well as communists, and that the leadership came from Slovak patriots.[34] The debate demonstrated that political voices espousing alternative lines were not only appearing, but were refusing to be squelched.

A third issue brought the Slovak nationalists into alignment with those who would reform the institutional arrangements of political lives: the constitutional relationship between the Czechs and the Slovaks. Prior to 1967, the official position was that constitutional revision was not desirable. Despite many official pronouncements to this effect, discussion about the need for constitutional revision continued. In November and December 1967, Dubcek indicated that he supported constitutional changes that would strengthen the role of the Slovak National Council, again aligning Slovak nationalists with those who were considered reformists, and dissociating these reformist tendencies from the official pronouncements of the party leadership.[35] The sense of participation and the demand for change in the leadership structure were recurrent in the writings of the Slovak nationalists.

*The Intellectuals and the Leadership Structure.* De-Stalinization helped to support the efforts of two major and disparate groups in Czechoslovakia to change the style of political life: the intellectuals, who demanded concerted changes in the structure as well as the style of politics in the direction of liberalization, participation, and democratization; and the Slovak nationalists, who were more concerned about Slovak identity. The process of de-Stalinization meshed with both of these demands. In the Czechoslovakia of 1966-1968, nationalist aspirations focusing on the issue of greater recognition of Slovakia as a cultural and political entity commingled with the liberal democratic values tentatively emerging in the demands of the intellectuals.

The relationship of the intellectuals to communist political development has always been a matter of ambivalence.[36] Formal Marxism as a structured social theory has an appeal to those interested in changing the system, but revolution requires the talents of those capable of manipulating symbols: the intelligentsia. Once the revolutionary framework was replaced by a framework aimed at consolidating revolutionary power, the intellectuals found it more difficult to become either significant power wielders or even to exert pressure upon the system. For the most part, those organizations in Czechoslovakia that reflected intellectual concerns—the writers union, the journalists union—had been passive until the 1960s. Individuals had, of course, expressed themselves, but they did not have organizational support. The party was able to control these organizations effectively until 1966.

The most dramatic and persistent challenge to the existing leadership structure came from the writers. As early as 1964 the Slovak Writers Union had voiced its criticism. At the June 1967 Congress of the Czechoslovakia Writers Union, a number of participants spoke up against the political and cultural policies of the Novotny regime. Among the outspoken critics were Jan Prochazka, a candidate member of the Central Committee, and Ludvik Vaculik, Milan Kundera, Pavel Kohout, and Ivan Klima, all of whom attacked the regime with vehemence.[37]

In September 1967, the party responded by a counterattack on the writers. Many of the critics were expelled from the writers union and *Literarni noviny* was placed under the control of the Ministry of Culture. Still the polemics continued. The demands for political and cultural freedoms and a dramatic transformation of the political structure, once the mechanisms of control had cracked, spilled over into almost every area. The journalist associations, universities, film producers, and television and radio commentators joined the critics.[38]

The demands for economic reform, the expressions of Slovak nationalism, and the criticism by the intellectuals, all signified a concerted attack upon the structure of the leadership. It was an attack on the way in which leadership constituency relationships were constructed, on the behavioral norms of the leadership, on the perceptions of the leadership, and on the mechanisms that it used to maintain control. This challenge to the leadership structure was supported by changes in the composition of the leadership itself.

*Changes in Leadership.* Although the substance of each of the above sets of events was different, they all came together in terms of their challenge to the existing leadership structure. This challenge might have been met if the composition of the leadership had not changed. This change can be demonstrated by comparing the Czechoslovak Central Committee of 1954 with the Central Committee of 1966, using 36 demographic and career attributes to create 10 empirical career channels into the Central Committee and then using the faces as indices to score each individual member of each Central Committee along each factor. In the calculation of factors the scores are standardized (i.e., scaled to have a mean of 0.00 and a standard deviation of 1.0). Only those persons who scored one standard deviation above the mean on each index are reported in the table below.

**Table 2**

*Comparison of the Two Czechoslovak Central Committees*

| *Factor Number* | *Factor Name* | *1954 (N=83)* | | *1966 (N=123)* | |
|---|---|---|---|---|---|
| | | *N* | *%* | *N* | *%* |
| I | Slovak Party and Government Career | 8 | 9.6% | 18 | 14.6% |
| II | "The Revolutionary" | 19 | 22.9 | 18 | 14.6 |
| III | "The Social Democrat" | 15 | 18.1 | 9 | 7.3 |
| IV | Education | 11 | 13.3 | 26 | 21.1 |
| V | Communist Youth | 11 | 13.3 | 17 | 13.8 |
| VI | Local Party Official | 9 | 10.8 | 25 | 20.3 |
| VII | Central Functionary, Czech Party and Government | 4 | 4.8 | 28 | 22.8 |
| VIII | High-Ranking Czech Party Functionary | 6 | 7.2 | 26 | 21.1 |
| IX | Communist Trade Union Official/Non-Central Government Official | 11 | 13.3 | 23 | 27.7 |
| X | "The Technocrat" | 9 | 10.8 | 23 | 27.7 |

When we compare the two Central Committees in terms of the direction of change in the factors, we note a rather dramatic increase in the "Education" and "Education-Career" factor and the "Technocrat" factor. When we add to this the decrease in the "Revolutionary" factor and the increase in factors that include party and government official and functionary characteristics, we can see that the 1966 Central Committee is not the same as the 1954 Central Committee. The change can best be interpreted as indicating a shift from a concern with revolutionary functions to functions associated with government.

When we add to these data the changes in personnel associated with the Slovak component of the party leadership—for not one of the Slovaks in the 1954 Central Committee was in the 1966 Central Committee—we see a Central Committee that is more amenable to the forces bringing about change in the entire leadership structure. The behavior of the Central Committee in the leadership crisis of December 1967—January 1968 confirms this conclusion.

It would be overly deterministic to argue that these pervasive challenges to the basic characteristics of the leadership structure that existed in Czechoslovakia prior to 1966 ordained the establishment of a Dubcek-type regime. The period from October 1967 when the Central Committee plenum occurred in which Dubcek directly attacked Novotny to his actual achievement of power in January 1968 was marked by many decision points that might have changed the outcome. Among the significant developments of this period were the character of the party leadership split in November and December, the behavior of the Soviet emissaries N. Stephan Chervonenko and Leonid Brezhnev, the character of the open debate of the Central Committee, and the clumsy way in which Novotny attempted to use the military in support of his position. The culmination of these developments was that on January 5, Dubcek received the unanimous vote from both the Presidium and the Central Committee. The experiment in democratic socialism was on its way to being implemented.

The program that evolved under Dubcek called for the democratization of the party, the reconstruction of the state administrative system, the development of a federal system, the end of censorship, the abolition of terror, and increased participation in the government and the party by autonomous groups within the society.[39] This program has been curtailed by the presence of the Soviet Army, which supports the analysis that communist political systems in their past mobilization period have not been able to solve the problem of participation.

The case of Czechoslovakia demonstrates that the leadership structure created for the consolidation of power by communist political movements even without drastic crisis is vulnerable in its reified form as demands for more effective management and increased participation become institutionalized. It is particularly vulnerable when both the scope of these demands and their intensity are extensive. In the Czechoslovak case, democratic socialism, which is one alternative mechanism for confronting this endemic problem, was ruled out, not by the

Czechoslovaks, but by the Soviets. The Soviet invasion of Czechoslovakia indicated to national communist leaders that there are limits to domestic experimentation, but the invasion and the subsequent Brezhnev doctrine[40] did not make clear what those limits really are. Soviet foreign policy in regard to its fraternal brothers as well as the Third World and the West is situationally rather than ideologically determined.

But for the moment the Soviet invasion pushed aside the democratic socialist experiment as one way of coping with the generic conflicts endemic to communist political systems. But, although it ruled out the most liberal and democratic response to these problems, the invasion did not lead to one road to socialism.

*Problems in Governance of Communist Systems*

Despite the Soviet invasion of Czechoslovakia the countries of Eastern Europe have been trying to develop their own solutions to the inherent structural perplexities of contemporary communist systems. The endemic questions that arise include (a) how to reconcile the norms of revolution with the norms of governance, (b) how to balance the need for mobilization with the increasing desires for meaningful participation, (c) how to absorb the differentiated structures and rational behaviors that seem to accompany industrialization and development with one-party rule, and (d) how to accommodate social transformation to distinct environmental conditions. Each of these poses the fundamental question of how indeed should a communist state be governed.

Before discussing the national answers to this major question it is useful to look at the contemporary literature. There is a very strong feeling expressed in many of the writings dealing with contemporary communism, particularly those that focus on the Soviet Union, that there is a fundamental decision that communist states must make once they have become established. They must become pluralistic or they will petrify. The arguments in this regard are thoroughly discussed in a statement by Jerry F. Hough entitled "The Soviet System: Petrification or Pluralism."[41] Hough acknowledges many directions in which the Soviet Union can move and creates an important list of social, political, and economic forces which operate in favor of pluralism, as well as those which assist the system in maintaining its present characteristics. Drawing from the inferences regarding the impact of these forces a number of alternatives ranging from a strong leader to pluralism can be suggested for the future of Soviet politics.

In contemporary Eastern Europe these endemic problems are confronted in each country, and each country has developed its own immediate solution. As with all political systems, the problems raised are probably insolvable and the solutions are always proximate, but it is important to recognize that in contemporary Eastern Europe at least four patterns of governance can be found. We can find examples of pluralism (Dubcek's Czechoslovakia), the integrated regime (the DDR), the hegemonic party (Poland and Hungary), and party rule (in Bulgaria through an institutionalized party) in Romania (through a party leader).

*The Integrated Regime–the DDR*

One structional solution to the ambiguities present in contemporary communist states is what might be called an integrative solution. This is best reflected in the German Democratic Republic. In using the term integrative to describe the DDR today there is a danger that it will be assumed that a coherent unity has been established among all major participants in the development of that society. A major source of conflict in communist political systems is the conflict between those interested in the establishment or presentation of their authority, those interested in the maintenance and extension of the revolutionary vision, and those who have adopted performance criteria as their major reference. At the value level each orientation postulates a different value system and assumes a different perception of the legitimate authority structure for the maintenance of those values. The fascinating aspect of the German Democratic Republic, best set forth in Thomas A. Baylis' recent study *The Technical Intelligence and the East German Elite* is the ability of the East German regime to maintain a monolithic organizational structure and to at the same time pervasively and persuasively extend the ideological component of this organizational idea to most aspects of organized social life.[42] At the leadership level the DDR is a "conservative form of oligarchy by coalition." The technical intelligensia, those who you would expect to hold performance criteria as having high value, are brought into the system with an understanding of the rules of the game. They profit by participation both in material and non-interest ways. All of this becomes reinforced by strict attention to detail in the education of the children, in the provision of welfare services, and in the development of group activities designed to socialize participants into the system.

The DDR has never been a highly personalized regime. Walter Ulbricht chose to rule as an aloof father of his country rather than as a day-to-day manipulator of the system seeking individual glory. He was in many ways the complete bureaucrat.[43] The absence of a succession crisis at Ulbricht's replacement by Hoenecker attests to the degree of success of the system.

The ability of the party to integrate these conflicting norms and perceptions of authority stems, no doubt, from the degree of physical isolation of the DDR and the success of the *Wirtschaftswunder.* There are those who argue that the disciplined nature of the regime is a combination of the organizational weapon coupled with traditional German political culture. Whether or not these are legitimate explanations, there is little doubt of the integrative nature of contemporary East Germany. Whether the regime will be able to continue to absorb new demands and new perspectives is a matter of conjecture.[44]

*Hegemonic Regimes–Poland and Hungary*

In Poland and Hungary a second variant on the contemporary governance in communist countries exists. In both countries the party and the party leader play what one author has called a hegemonic role.[45] In the hegemonic model the party serves to integrate a number of diverse structures at the highest level; in the economy through the plan and in politics through the determination of what semi-autonomous organizations may exist and in what form. Subsystem autonomy can be found in agriculture, in the organization of industry, in local political decision-making units, in institutions of education and research, and in cultural organizations. It is interesting to note that at the most recent meeting of the Central Committee in Hungary economic reform was maintained despite the dismissal of the major designer of the new economic management system, reflecting the decreasing significance of personalized roles in the acceptance of structural arrangements.

The party and the party leader are always in a balancing position in the hegemonic model. They not only must balance structures outside the direct control of the party, but also balance interests within the party which can draw upon and be influenced by external events. The party is probably more dependent upon the rule of the individual leader than is generally recognized, since the potential for factionalism is a function of the desires of some to conform to more traditional communist institutions on the one hand, and the desires of others to extend the decompression process on the other. The fact that an external event, the shipworkers' strike in Poland, led to Edward Gierek's replacing Gomulka indicates the lack of coherence in leadership selection and replacement. The party leader and the party become brokers, but at the same time express a particular interest in the process of brokering. The possibilities for factionalism and isolation of the party from other structures in society are very strong. The dilemma of the hegemonic party is to balance all of these interests without losing sight of party goals and authority. The dependence of this position on economic success is also relatively clear.

*The Party-Centered Solution–Bulgaria and Romania*

One could make the case, and some have, that there is a relationship between the way in which the economic activities of a society are structured and the type of economy that exists, and the way in which communist parties are able to govern. In both party-centered systems the economy is basically agrarian, and the life style is more rural and traditional than urban and modernized. There are two types of party centered regimes in Eastern Europe today: Bulgaria, which has been able to establish an institutionalized party, and Romania where party rule is centered upon one person.

Bulgaria has avoided the extensive ups and downs of the transition from revolution to governance. There was some bending toward a New Course after the death of Stalin, and there have been disputes among the top leaders, but the party has maintained a fairly steadfast course in the construction of a Soviet-type communist system.[45] Although there has been some expansion of new groups into the party Central Committee such as technicians, and although Zhivkov replaced one group of party functionaries (those with central party experience) with another (those with local party leadership), the style and policies of the party and of the party leadership have remained relatively constant.[46] Non-party groups within society, or those groups which have the potential for becoming alternative structures, have been kept under direct supervision and control. In short, Bulgaria has been developing communism in a relatively straightforward manner and in doing so has maintained the centrality of the party as the locus of political, economic, and administrative decision-making.

The Socialist Republic of Romania is ruled more by one person's direct control, Nicolai Ceausescu, than any other communist state in Eastern Europe. The major symbol of his rule has been that of Romanian nationalism and patriotism. Ceausescu did not build this strategy out of whole cloth. As early as 1958 a statement on socialist patriotism and the identification of the Romanian Communist Party with Romanian nationalism had been established by one of Stalin's strongest disciples, Gheorghiu-Dej. It was during 1958 that the Romanians began to explore economic trade with the West and filtered with the Chinese regime. In March 1963 Gheorghiu-Dej formally attacked the policies of the Soviet Union, characterizing them as both economic and political imperialism. Over the ensuing ten years relationships with the Soviet Union have been marked by a strong degree of independence in the Romanian party. Coupled with international behavior quite at variance with the rest of the European communist states, Ceausescu has at home built up a spirit of national unity. He has emphasized the status of the Romanian Communist Party by having its name changed to the Communist Party to indicate its parity with the Communist Party of the Soviet Union. The country has been renamed the Socialist Republic of Romania, a presumptuous title.

In the 1965 constitution many references are made to the independent and sovereign state of Romania. Independent behavior in the international realm has not been coupled with liberalization in Romania itself. The Party bureaucracy dominated by Ceausescu still formulates all public policies, emphasis upon mobilization measures is still fundamental, and the Romanian Communist Party exercises control over all aspects of economic, political, social, and cultural life. Reforms have taken place in some areas of society, but only as they are coupled with the identification of the party with Romanian nationalist and patriotic sentiments. For example, the school system has been extensively revised but these reforms are more nationalist than scientific in motivation.[47]

Some of the more oppressive characteristics of the terrorist control apparatus that existed in the heyday of Gheorghiu-Dej have been abolished, and indeed some of the victims of the earlier purges have been rehabilitated. But the Party dominates all and Ceausescu dominates the party. In this domination much of his power rests upon his ability to merge the symbols of the Communist Party with those of Romanian nationalism and patriotism.

### *Conclusion*

Politics in Eastern Europe since the end of World War II has been shaped by three major thrusts: seizure of power, Stalinism, and the breakup of the Stalinist interstate system. Each of these thrusts has been initiated and accompanied by traumatic events, which reflect the persistent and generic problems in communist systems of governance. These generic problems include: (1) how to reconcile the norms and structures of revolution with those of governance, and (2) how to structure one-party states so that they can effectively operate within existing environmental systems and at the same time transform the environmental system. In this second problem area, one-party states are confronted by the structural conflicts between a participatory system and a mobilization system, and between collegial depersonalized rule and party-centered rule. In short, a persistent crisis of authorities seems to exist within the communist system of government.

None of the existing communist systems of governance have solved these problems. More importantly, no one model has emerged for confronting them. It may be true that all communist states are marching to the same drummer, but it is not clear that they are marching along the same road, or that they even agreed on how the cadence should be interpreted.

Modern theories of development and Marxism have difficulties with this variance. The theories of development suggest that there are certain predictable structural and behavioral consequences of the modernization process. Among these are: the development of differential structures through which a variety of basic political functions are processed in a rational manner; the development of a decision-making process in which the basic political norm is bargaining; and the development of a legal rational authority system. It is an implicit assumption in much of the literature of modernization that the more a political system evolves toward differentiated structures, the more it adapts as a political norm, and the more it assumes legal rationalism, the more viable that political system will be. This often gets translated into a simple choice for contemporary communist regimes: they must move in the direction of pluralism or they will ossify.

Contemporary Eastern Europe is an excellent setting for evaluating theories of modernization and change. But if that evaluation focuses on probabilities of convergence such discussion underplays the dynamism of the area and the contribution that a comparative analysis cna make to political theory.[48] Convergence assumes that under the impact of modernization communist regimes will move toward pluralism for the reasons stated above and pluralistic regimes will move in the direction of increased reliance on planning. At this two-system level of analysis (capitalist or Western systems and communist systems), Eastern Europe is assumed to be homogeneous.

The real potential for using the East European experience for the study of comparative impacts of modernization is lost because of this presumed homogeneity. As this paper has attempted to point out, the reality of Eastern Europe today is the existence of variant structures which confront the generic problems posed by the relationship between communism and modernization. This paper hypothesizes that each of the existing variant types of communist governance is situationally determined and has its own set of dependencies. For example, the hegemonic model is more dependent on economic success than the others, the integrative model more dependent on the effects of a complex socialization process, and the party-centered model on perceptions of the party's legitimacy on the one hand, and the ability of the party leader to successfully manipulate symbols on the other.

In the long run it may be true that the Marxist view of history as an inexorable process is accurate. If so, the most likely alternative system is probably non-Marxist. In the shorter run, we would do better, I believe, by explicating as best we can the impact of situations upon variant types using our theories and hypotheses to identify and discover pressure points on each variant. In brief, the pressing need is for situational analysis. Situational analysis of Eastern Europe will show clearly how distinct these systems really are from each other, and how synthetic was the system of Stalinism despite its logical coherence and brutal dedication to achieving its goals.

## NOTES

1. See for example, the still important study of Daniel Bell, "Ten Theories in Search of Reality," in *World Politics* 10 (April 1958):113-137. Carl J. Friedrich

and Zbigniew K. Brzezinski, *Totalitarian Dictatorship and Autocracy* (Cambridge, Mass.: Harvard University Press, 1956), first published close to 20 years ago is still one of the most referenced works in the study of Contemporary Communist Politics. We have been made aware of the contribution of political science, of the behavior revolution and the post behavior response, but we do not often recognize that descriptive and historical studies of Soviet and East European politics drew upon a range of concepts from anthropology, psychology, and economics which were not usual in political science literature. This non-behavior phenomenon was certainly expansive and perhaps in the long run as significant as the concern with quantification.

2. The literature on Eastern Europe still tends to be ideographic. The major exceptions are Zbigniew K. Brzezinski, *The Soviet Bloc*, Rev. ed. (Cambridge, Mass.: Harvard University Press, 1967); H. Gordon Skilling, *The Government and Politics of East Europe* (New York: Crowell, 1966); and Ghitan Ionescu, *The Politics of the European Communist States* (New York: Praeger, 1967).

3. Hugh Seton-Watson, *The East European Revolution* (New York: Praeger, 1956).

4. Robert C. Tucker, *The Marxian Revolutionary Idea* (New York: Norton, 1969).

5. See for example, Chalmers Johnson, *Peasant Nationalism and Communist Power* (Stanford: Stanford University Press, 1962).

6. For a history of communist parties prior to World War II see Hugh Seton-Watson, *Eastern Europe Between The Wars* (New York: Harper, 1967); George D. Jackson, Jr., *Comintern and Peasant in East Europe 1919-1930* (New York: Columbia University Press, 1966); C. A. Macartney, *October Fifteenth: A History of Modern Hungary, 1929-1945*, 2 vols. (Edinburgh: Edinburgh University Press, 1961); Rudolf L. Tokes, *Bela Kun and the Hungarian Soviet Republic* (New York: Praeger, 1967); Edward Taborsky, *Communism in Czechoslovakia* (Princeton: Princeton University Press, 1961); Joseph Rothschild, *The Communist Party of Bulgaria* (New York: Columbia University Press, 1959); Stephen Fisher-Galati, ed., *Romania* (New York: Praeger, 1957); M. K. Dziewanowski, *The Communist Party of Poland* (Cambridge: Harvard University Press, 1959).

7. R. V. Burks, "Eastern Europe" in Cyril E. Black and Thomas P. Thornton, eds., *Communism and Revolution*, (Princeton: Princeton University Press, 1969) pp. 77-116.

8. Brzezinski, *The Soviet Bloc, op. cit.*; I. P. Trainin, "The Peoples' Democracies" in *Sovetskoe Gosudarstvo I Pravo*, 1 and 3 (1947); Y. M. Shavrov, "The Constitution of the Czechoslovak Republic," *Ibid.*, 8 1956); Jozsef Revai, "The Character of A People's Democracy" in *Foreign Affairs* 28 (October 1949):143-152; H. Gordon Skilling, "People's Democracy in Soviet Theory," in *Soviet Studies* 12 (January 1961):241-262.

9. For a summary see Brzezinski, *The Soviet Bloc*.

10. Gita Ionescu, *The Break-up of the Soviet Empire in Eastern Europe* (Baltimore: Penguin, 1965).

11. There is an intersting perceptual problem in this statement. From the baseline of what had existed prior to World War II the shift in the economy can be

seen as a stage process toward a socialist system. Viewed from the perspective of the Stalinist command economy the economic steps in Eastern Europe prior to Stalinism look very experimental. Compare Doreen Warriner, *Revolution in Eastern Europe* (London: Turnstile, 1950).

12. One of the most accepted dimensions in recent literature for describing and analyzing communist regimes is around the concept of mobilization. See for example, Samuel P. Huntington, *Political Order in Changing Societies* (New Haven and London: Yale University Press, 1968); John Kautsky, *Communism and the Politics of Development* (New York: John Wiley, 1968); Robert C. Tucker, "Towards a Comparative Politics of Movement Regimes" in *American Political Science Review* 55 (June 1961):281-289.

13. Compare Nathan Leites, *The Operational Code of the Politburo* (New York: McGraw-Hill, 1951), with Alexander L. George, "The Operational Code" in *International Studies Quarterly* 13 (June 1969):190-222; J. L. Richardson, "Cold War Revisionism: A Critique," in *World Politics* 24 (July 1972):579-612.

14. Tibor Mera, *That Day in Budapest* (New York: Funk and Wagnalls, 1969); Leslie B. Bain, *The Reluctant Satellites* (New York: MacMillan, 1960); Melvin J. Kasky, ed., *The Hungarian Revolution* (New York: Praeger, 1957); Miklos Molnar, *Budapest 1956* (London: George Allen & Unwin, 1971); Ference A. Vali, *Rift and Revolt in Hungary* (Cambridge: Harvard University Press, 1961); Paul Kecskemeti, *The Unexpected Revolution* (Stanford: Stanford University Press, 1961); Adam Bromke, "Poland's Role in the Loosening of the Communist Bloc," in Kurt London, ed., *Eastern Europe in Transition* (Baltimore: Johns Hopkins Press, 1966) pp. 67-92; Frank Gibney, *The Frozen Revolution* (New York: Farrar, Strauss & Cudahy, 1959); Richard F. Staar, *Poland 1944-1962* (New Orleans: Louisiana State University Press, 1962); Konrad Syrop, *Spring in October* (New York: Praeger, 1957); Hansjakob Stehle, *The Independent Satellite* (New York: Praeger, 1965); Stefan Bryant, *The East German Rising* (New York: 1957); Rainer Hildebrandt, *The Explosion* (New York: Duell, Sloan and Pearce, 1955); Wolfgang Kraus, "Crises and Revolt in a Satellite: The East German Case in Retrospect" in Kurt London, ed., *Eastern Europe in Transition* (Baltimore: Johns Hopkins Press, 1966) pp. 41-65.

15. Carl Beck and James Malloy, *Political Elites: A Mode of Analysis* (Pittsburgh: University Center for International Studies, 1971).

16. Myron Rush, "The Khrushchev Succession Problem" in *World Politics* 24 (January 1962):259-282.

17. Zbigniew K. Brzezinski, *The Permanent Purge: Politics in Soviet Totalitarianism* (Cambridge: Harvard University Press, 1956).

18. M. K. Dziewanowski, *op. cit.*, pp. 252-289.

19. William Kornhauser, *The Politics of Mass Society* (Glencoe: The Free Press, 1959).

20. See for example, Joseph Berliner, *Factory and Manager in the U.S.S.R.* (Cambridge: Harvard University Press, 1957); R. V. Burks, *Technological Innovation and Political Change in Communist Eastern Europe* (Santa Monica: The Rand Corporation Rm. 6051-PR August, 1969); David Granick, *Management of the Industrial Firm in the USSR* (New York: Columbia University Press, 1954).

21. Arnulf M. Baring, *Uprising in East Germany* (Ithaca: Cornell University Press, 1972); Heinz Brandt, *Ein Traum Der Nicht Entführbarist: Meinweg Zwischen Ost Undwest* (Munich, 1967); Fritz Schenk, *Imvorzimmer der Diktatur: Zwölf Jahre Pankow* (Cologne and Berlin, 1962); William E. Griffith, *The European Thaw* (Cambridge, Mass.: MIT Press, 1961).

22. R. V. Burks, "The Decline of Communism in Czechoslovakia," in *Studies in Comparative Communism* 2 (January 1969):21-49.

23. See *Hospodarsye Noviny*, all issues in 1968.

24. *Rude Pravo*, April 6, 1964.

25. *The Road to Democratic Socialism* (Prague: Prago Press, 1968).

26. *Kulturny Zivot*, November 26, 1965.

27. *The Road to Democratic Socialism.*

28. *Rude Pravo*, December 5, 1962.

29. *Ibid.*, April 5, 1963. For a discussion of these events, see Stanley Riveles, "Slovakia: Catalyst of Crisis" in *Problems in Communism* 17 (May 1968):1-9.

30. *Rude Pravo*, May 14, 1963. See in particular the writings of Miro Hysko, *Praca*, May 28, 1973; *Pravada*, June 3, 1962.

31. *Rude Pravo*, April 3, 1964.

32. *Literarni noviny*, April 25, 1964.

33. *Kulturny Zivot*, May 1, 1964.

34. *Riveles*, "Slovakia."

35. *Ibid.* See also H. Gordon Skilling, "Crisis and Change in Czechoslovakia," in *International Journal* 23 (Summer, 1968):456-65.

36. For a general discussion of the relationship of intellectuals to phases of politics, see Harry J. Benda, "Non-Western Intelligentsias as Political Elites" in *Australian Journal of Politics and History* 5 (November 1960):286-94.

37. For a striking discussion of these events, see Ludvik Vaculik, "Culture and Party in Czechoslovakia," reprinted in *East Europe* 16 (September 1967):18-21.

38. Zvi Gitelman, "Revising the Communist Establishment" in *The New Leader* 51 (March 25, 1968):15-17 and Edward Taborsky, "Where is Czechoslovakia Going" in *East Europe* 16 (February 1967):2-12.

39. See H. Gordon Skilling, "Czechoslovakia's Interrupted Revolution" in *Revue Canadienne d'Etude* (Summer, 1968):402-29; Harry Schwartz, *Prague's 200 Days* (New York: Frederick A. Praeger, 1969); Paul Ello, ed., *Czechoslovakia's Blueprint for Freedom* (Washington: Acropolis, 1968).

40. R. J. Mitchell, "The Brezhnev Doctrine and Communist Ideology" in *Review of Politics* 34 (April 1972):190-209.

41. V. N. Dadrian, "Nationalism, Communism, and Soviet Industrialization" in *Sociologia Internationalis* 10 (2, 1972):183-212. Jerry F. Hough, "The Soviet System: Petrification or Pluralism?" in Lenard J. Cohen and Jane P. Shapiro, eds., *Communist Systems in Comparative Perspective* (Garden City: Anchor, 1974):449-486.

42. Thomas A. Baylis, *The Technical Intelligensia and the East German Elite* (Berkeley: University of California Press, 1974); Karl H. Kahrs, "East Germany's New Economic System from the Viewpoint of Cybernetics" in *East European*

*Quarterly* 6 (September 1972):287-300; Peter C. Ludz, *The Changing Party Elite in East Germany* (Cambridge: MIT Press, 1972).

43. Carola Stern, *Ulbricht: A Political Biography* (New York: Praeger, 1965).

44. Myron Rush, *How Communist States Change Their Rulers* (Ithaca: Cornell University Press, 1974); M. Croan, "After Ulbricht: The End of an Era?" in *Survey* 17 (Spring, 1971):74-92.

45. S. M. Lipset and R. B. Dobson, "The Intellectual as Critic and Rebel: with Special Reference to the United States and the Soviet Union" in *Daedalus* 101 (Summer 1972):137-198; Andrzej Korbonski, "Comparing Liberalization Processes in Eastern Europe" in Lenard J. Cohen and Jane P. Shapiro, eds., *Communist Systems in Comparative Perspective* (Garden City: Anchor, 1974) pp. 502-520.

46. Jerzy J. Wiatr, "The Hegemonic Party System in Poland" in Jerzy J. Wiatr, ed., *Studies in Polish Political System* (Warsaw: Ossolineum, 1967):pp. 108-123; F. C. Bruhns, F. Cazzola, and J. Wiatr eds., *Local Politics, Development, and Participation* (Pittsburgh: University Center for International Studies, 1974); D. Granick, "The Hungarian Economic Reform" in *World Politics* 25 (April 1973):414-429.

47. Carl Beck, Gerard A. Johnson, and J. Thomas McKechnie, "Party Careers: A Case Study of Bulgarian Central Committee Members, 1962" in Roger E. Kanet, ed., *The Behavioral Revolution and Communist Studies* (New York: Free Press, 1971).

48. J. F. Brown, "Rumania's Uphill Struggle for an Independent Role" in *World Today* 29 (March 1973):126-133; Kenneth Jowitt, *Revolutionary Break Throughs and National Development: The Case of Romania, 1944-1965* (Berkeley and Los Angeles: University of California Press, 1971).

49. R. M. Mills, "One Theory in Search of Reality: The Development of United States Studies in the Soviet Union" in *Political Science Quarterly* 87 (March 19):63-79.

# 6

# Revolution and Modernization in Economic Organizations*

William N. Dunn

Socialist economic organizations are instruments of social revolution and basic units of societal modernization. The dual character of socialist organizations derives from the concurrent, and sometimes unsuccessful, pursuit of multiple objectives.[1] Objectives of socialist enterprises include the production, exchange, and distribution of goods and services, but also the elimination or mitigation of status differentials and the humanization of work.[2] Socialist economic organizations, to be sure, may be compared with formal, complex, or special-purpose organizations in capitalist countries, at least to the extent that socialist firms purposefully establish sets of roles which are linked with explicit and announced objectives. Nevertheless, to press comparisons further may detract from a recognition that organizational objectives are comprehensive, not limited.[3] For this reason organizational change in systems as diverse as China, Cuba, and Yugoslavia has been guided by dual compliance structures which,themselves reflective of comprehensive multiple objectives, are designed to achieve economic as well as political and socio-cultural goals.

The social, political, and economic consequences of dual organizational compliance structures are not always those anticipated by policymakers. Thus, organizational change in China, Cuba, and Yugoslavia—countries which are representative of somewhat special approaches to the organization of work under socialism—seems often to involve goal displacement, unanticipated negative consequences, and periodic depar-

*Portions of an earlier draft of this paper were presented at the Faculty Seminar on Comparative Communism, Research Institute on Communist Affairs, Columbia University. The author acknowledges the assistance of seminar participants and the Institute's Acting Director, Seweryn Bialer, in offering critical reactions. Helpful critical comments were also provided by colleagues at the University of Pittsburgh, especially Carmelo Mesa-Lago and Frederick Swierczeck.

tures from announced objectives. Ideological doctrines to the contrary notwithstanding, successive periods of incongruence between goals of modernization and goals of revolution are associated with social conflict and patterns of organizational change which fail to conform to any simple or neat representation of mutually reinforcing linear relationships between politics and economics in socialist societies.[4] To come directly to the point: socialist economic organizations embody incongruent and sometimes contradictory relationships between economic activities and the promotion of equality, cooperation, and the humanization of work in organizations.[5]

This paper develops a comparative approach for the analysis of socialist economic organizations, focusing on special cases of organizational change in societies which have departed significantly from conventional patterns of modernization and development in the socialist and non-socialist world alike: China, Cuba, and Yugoslavia. The tasks of this study, which are both methodological and substantive, include: (1) an overview and evaluation of basic approaches and methods employed to compare socialist systems; (2) a summary of major theoretical viewpoints available to explain continuity and change in socialist systems; and (3) the development of a conceptual framework for comparing organizations in socialist systems, including a set of propositions which express interrelationships between organizational, socio-political, and technological variables. In a concluding statement we shall consider practical and theoretical implications of our analysis of dual organizations for understanding problems of revolution and modernization in socialist economic organizations.

*Comparing Socialist Systems: Basic Approaches and Methods*

Organization theory provides a bridge between misplaced abstraction and misplaced concreteness in the analysis of socialist systems. A common methodological property of misplaced abstraction and misplaced concreteness, illustrated best by ideal-type and case-study approaches respectively, is the limitation of opportunities to understand and explain dynamic patterns of organizational change. The comparative analysis of formal, complex, or special-purpose organizations in socialist systems involves explicit and systematic efforts to establish general principles concerning complex variations within and between two or more organizations.[6] Comparative analysis, defined in this way, is as much oriented to generalizations about similarities as it is to general statements about differences.[7] Comparisons yield statements about continuity, stability, and control, as well as those which treat change, conflict, and deviation. The precise character of generalizations depends on what we compare, which may be classified according to four principal strategies in which elements of an organization and/or its setting vary.[8] (See Figure 1.)

**Figure 1.**

*Basic Strategies for Comparison*

| | Same Goals, Structures, Functions | Different Goals, Structures, Functions |
|---|---|---|
| Same Setting | A | B |
| Different Setting | C | D |

A common strategy for comparison involves the analysis of systems believed to be pursuing the same goals, structures, or functions in the same setting. Making assumptions about similarities of social and political setting–including central planning, one-party dominance, and a dogmatic ideology–the comparative productivity of firms employing "moral incentives" might be investigated (Cell A).[9] By holding social setting constant, through such categories as "totalitarian" or "mobilization system," inquiries may be made into the comparative effectiveness of economic organizations with different structures.[10] Here comparisons might include Soviet and Chinese firms in terms of vertical (one-man-management) and horizontal (two participations) authority structures (Cell B). The basis of comparison may be shifted by investigating organizations with similar goals of creating a new socialist man through moral stimulation of work, but doing so in different settings. The effects of "moral incentives" in different socialist systems may be compared in a context of concern with differences in the size of countries, natural resources, and dependence on external sources of capital and technology (Cell C).[11] Comparisons might also focus on different control structures, conceptualized in terms of moral versus material stimulation, and different systems of property rights embedded in social settings which vary considerably in terms of economic centralization, party influence, and social stratification (Cell D).[12] Comparisons of Yugoslav and Cuban industrial organizations might very well follow this latter strategy, depending on the conceptual framework and assumptions of the investigator.

Comparisons within systems sometimes yield greater differences along both dimensions than comparisons between systems. Differences between Cuban export enterprises and those producing for domestic demand appear to be greater than differences between export firms in Cuba and Yugoslavia. Many comparative studies proceed from taxonomies which incorporate references to organizational setting as well as organizational goals, structures, and processes. A characteristic of such taxonomies, however, is their failure to relate variables by providing hypotheses, propositions, or other general principles. Comparisons are often illustrative and yield low potential for explanation and theory-construction. As strategies for comparison of socialist systems move from undifferentiated assumptions (Cell A) to differentiated ones (Cell D), the confidence of observers in results of research tends to decline. Approaches to convergence and modernization, for example, are Cell A strategies which enjoy wide acceptance among students of comparative socialism. Undifferentiated approaches, however, sacrifice specificity, demonstrativeness, and depth for the certitude which comes from believing that one has performed the most exhaustive explanation possible. This must be contrasted with situationally specific comparative strategies which take differences and deviation as the most valuable properties of comparative analysis.[13]

The four basic strategies for comparison represent various ways to ask questions about socialist systems. The questions and their answers vary according to the manner in which research problems have been defined. A classification of strategies for defining problems provides us with a further basis for examining methodological properties of approaches. Strategies for defining problems may reflect two primary interests:[14] (1) discovering relationships between variables applicable to socialist economic organizations; and/or (2) discovering constants shared by socialist economic organizations, including categories (control structure) and attributes (politicization or economic decisions) induced analytically from categories. Answers to questions, or responses to a research problem, may involve (3) exploratory analysis of interrelationships between variables and the formulation of tentative hypotheses; and/or (4) testing of hypotheses which have been deduced from theory or suggested through exploratory analysis (heuristic test). Comparative analysis of socialist economic organizations may be arranged in a cross-classification scheme which expresses six types of research problems (Figure 2).

The variables versus constants dimension provides a demarcation between studies in the field. The majority of comparative studies have been concerned with constants, expressed in terms of categories and attributes associated with ideal-types, global taxonomies, and checklists. This dimension also reflects divergent philosophies of organization, or even of social science itself. The controversy surrounding the relevant maximizing principle of the worker-managed firm in Yugoslavia, for example, is concerned primarily with the discovery of categories and attributes which define essential properties of self-managed socialist firms.[15] Categories such as "collective management" are extracted, from which behavioral attributes of risk-taking, entrepreneurship, collective maximization, and organizational cohesiveness are then induced. In contrast, exploratory studies of workers' management have concentrated on interrelationships between variables. Adizes' comparative study represents a primary interest in exploring variables,[16] as do the works of Mesa-Lago and Bernardo on Cuba,[17] and Hoffman, Andors, and Eckstein on China.[18] Studies by Mesa-Lago and Bernardo are perhaps the best examples of attempts to proceed from the extraction and elaboration of analytic categories (administrative allocation of labor and moral incentives) to an exploratory analysis of interrelationships between variables (moral stimulation and productivity). The latter are then subjected to heuristic tests as tentative hypotheses.

**Figure 2.**

*Research Problems in Comparative Analysis of Socialist Economic Organizations*

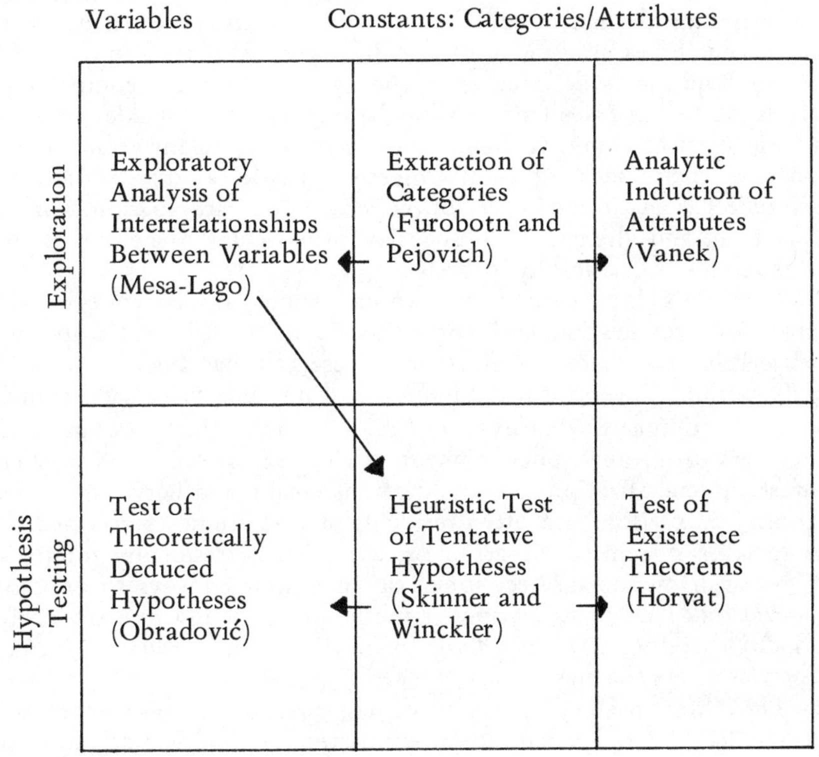

Variables
Constants: Categories/Attributes
Exploration
Hypothesis Testing
Exploratory Analysis of Interrelationships Between Variables (Mesa-Lago)
Extraction of Categories (Furobotn and Pejovich)
Analytic Induction of Attributes (Vanek)
Test of Theoretically Deduced Hypotheses (Obradović)
Heuristic Test of Tentative Hypotheses (Skinner and Winckler)
Test of Existence Theorems (Horvat)

Research problems are analytically distinct, but overlap in research practice. Horvat's interest in extracting categories for use in a general global classification scheme of capitalist, statist, and self-managed economies is supplemented by analytic induction of behavioral attributes, including maximization of collective income through collective preferences for investments in the worker-managed enterprise.[19] Horvat's research also includes the testing of hypotheses, including the finding that an increase in participation in a cross-section of firms was positively related to increased investment.[20] The Ward-Domar axiom of maximization of income per worker was also tested and rejected on analytical grounds.[21]

A major example of the extraction of new categories and attributes is theoretical research on property rights, which marks an advance over reified categories of capitalism, state capitalism, and socialism, each of which tend to be founded on legal criteria.[22] Vanek's theoretical research on labor-managed economies illustrates very well the difficulties of formulating research problems on the basis of attributes derived from categories.[23] It is unclear, for example, whether assumptions about structural and behavioral attributes of the labor-managed firm—including absence of conflicts—have any empirical relevance whatever. Recent hypothesis-testing research suggests that they may not.[24] Tests of hypotheses deduced from theory are rare in the comparative analysis of socialist systems. Although Skinner and Winckler provide heuristic tests of tentative hypotheses concerning organizational compliance in their study of rural Chinese agricultural organizations,[25] Obradović's work on the impact of technology on participation, worker satisfaction, and alienation in Yugoslav firms seems to be one of the few examples of classical hypothesis testing.[26]

The cross-classification of research problems and strategies for comparison provides standards for evaluating methodological properties of research and theory. Comparative research has been developed largely within conventional disciplines, and not as a systematic contribution to comparative analysis *per se.* Research efforts within disciplines vary from an explicit concern with comparisons to an implicit interest in generalizations about variations within and between organizations. Comparisons are often residuals of case studies performed on one socialist system.[27] Nevertheless, explicitly or residually comparative research on socialist economic organizations conveys theories of organization. The identification of methodological and research problems can therefore serve as a basis for outlining and evaluating formal properties of approaches.

The three basic dimensions of comparative analysis presented above—differentiated versus undifferentiated methodological assumptions, emphasis on variables versus constants, exploratory studies versus hypothesis-testing—serve as criteria for evaluating approaches. Without attempting a survey of literature, it seems possible to generalize major characteristics of studies in the field. Comparative research reflects a somewhat pronounced preoccupation with constants and the analytic induction of behavioral and structural attributes from established categories. The use of typological categories for exploratory analysis of interrelationships between variables has not proceeded very far. There is nevertheless more emphasis on analytic induction than analysis of interrelationships between variables, reflected in assumptions about linear evolutionary change most often expressed as some variation of convergence and modernization theses.

Categories for organization analysis continue to come primarily from single disciplines, notably economics. This limits the range of constants and variables considered operative in organizations and their environments. The socialist economy has often been represented in terms of a single-minded concentration on maximizing economic growth and firm-productivity, which is both a problem of misplaced categorization based on assumptions of economics and an unresolved empirical question related to the existence of imputed values. When research manifests an explicit concern with interrelationships among variables—e.g., moral incentives and economic growth—the main categories have been economic ones. Sociocultural and political variables are typically treated as obstacles or constraints on economic growth and efficiency. In the cases of China, Cuba, and even Yugoslavia this *a priori* methodological approach obscures the fact that decisions have sometimes been made to maximize socio-cultural values, subject to economic constraints.[28] A prevalent form of research involves analytic induction of behavioral attributes such as "entrepreneurship" from categories which themselves may be inadequate. Such has been the case with studies of workers' management.[29] Heuristic tests and tests of existence theorems concerning collective behavioral properties would help considerably in reformulating categories and attributes of organizational typologies, from budgetary finance and moral stimulation in Cuba to workers' management in Yugoslavia.[30] Significantly, perhaps, the testing of hypotheses deduced from theory has been oriented toward general organization theory, and not theories of socialist economic organization *per se*. This suggests the need for categories which cut across attributes conventionally assigned to socialist organizations, which may be less "socialist" than originally believed.[31]

An emphasis on predictability, operationalization of concepts and hypotheses, and the utilization of quantitative data in standardized frameworks or checklists evidences a concern with classical hypothesis-testing. This is paradoxical. A preoccupation with data requirements artificially limits opportunities to engage in exploratory analysis of interrelationships between unquantified and perhaps unquantifiable variables, from moral incentives to property rights. The emphasis on predictability, operationalization, and standardization of data—in addition to creating an aura of comparative "objectivity" which can obscure implicit value-assumptions and methodological dilemmas–ignores the fact that the main obstacle to comparative research may not be availability of data, but the state of theory. Theory-construction governs our ability to address a core problem in comparing socialist systems, the explanation of continuity and change.

*Continuity and Change in Socialist Systems: Selected Theoretical Viewpoints*

The capacity to understand and explain continuity and change in socialist economic organizations depends on answers to two kinds of questions:[32] (1) How are organizations *defined* (i.e., according to what variables, categories, or attributes)? (2) How are organizations *explained* (i.e., by what classes of phenomena)? Thus far many comparative studies have been based on undifferentiated methodological assumptions and have emphasized constants. In addition, we can evaluate comparative research in terms of what is explained and how, which provides a classification of theoretical viewpoints available for comparative inquiry into socialist systems. Theoretical viewpoints, which are idealized modes of analysis and not the theories of any individual or school, also enable us to identify the types of empirical observations which certain viewpoints imply. A concern with theoretical viewpoints circumvents problems associated with the social origins of researchers and the assumptions, values, and philosophical antecedents underlying entire conceptual frameworks. Instead, we concentrate on raising problems related to the design, implementation, and interpretation of comparative research.

Comparison depends on how we define organizations, which can take two principal forms: we may choose to emphasize *subjective* characteristics of socialist organizations, or we may stress *objective* behavior relations. The definition of organizations in subjective terms follows the Weberian tradition of treating organizations as systems of continuous purposive activity of a specified kind. Definitions of organizations in primarily objective terms, which has been associated (erroneously) with Marxian sociology, tend to emphasize the primacy of objective interaction. The question of objective versus subjective behavior is a matter of emphasis which may shift over time–as is the well-known case in Marxian theory–or emphasis may be relatively equal. Objectivist approaches are nevertheless associated with an emphasis on structures, including relations between groups and occupants of authority roles. Subjectivist or morphogenetic approaches, while not ignoring roles and group interaction, tend to emphasize social values, motivation, satisfaction, morale, and self-steering and goal-setting characteristics of organizations.[33]

Theoretical viewpoints also focus on particular classes or types of phenomena thought to explain organizations. Emphasis may be placed on conditions *imposed* on organizations via human and non-human environments—from ideological and cultural factors to demographic ones—or via characteristics of organizations themselves. Conditions imposed on organizations via organizations themselves may include factors associated with administrative roles (bureaucracy), group interaction (party domination), or members' attitudes (socialization to conformity through agitation and propaganda). Conversely, stress may be placed on conditions *generated* by organizations themselves which operate via human and non-human environments (social structure and technology) and via organizations themselves (group interaction). Emphasis on generated versus imposed conditions, which is associated with an interest in variables versus constants (Figure 2), tends to reject possibilities for predicting organizational change from knowledge of imposed conditions. Generative models stress the importance of emergent phenomena, including redefined roles, new patterns of group interaction, technological adaptation, and open and flexible relationships between organizations and environing social systems. These two major dimensions are presented in Figure 3. Idealized theoretical viewpoints in each property-space are abstracted from research by Horvat and Vanek on the evolution of worker managed economies; Bernardo's analysis of moral incentives and alienation in Cuba; Adizes' comparative study of leadership and communication in two Yugoslav firms; and from observations on workers' attitudes in Chinese industrial organization by Whyte and Andors.[34]

Theoretical viewpoints may be positioned in a more elaborate classification scheme which includes classes of phenomena and media through which they are imposed on, or generated by, organizations (Figure 4). Socialist economic organizations, defined principally in terms of *objective* behavior relations, may be explained partially or fully by conditions *imposed* on organizations. (1) Ecological factors comprising the non-human environment—including physical endowments, relative sufficiency of natural resources, and the size of a country—promote hierarchical administrative and political structures (ecologism).[35] (2) Demographic changes in the form of overpopulation and labor surplus promote mass mobilization of labor in rural agricultural organizations (demographism).[36] (3) Increasing complexity of economic decision-making within organizations, together with inadequacy of information, promotes global trends toward workers' management and market socialism (evolutionary structuralism).[37] (4) Demands for economic efficiency are facilitated by the cooptation of educated and technically trained individuals within a party representing a modernizing elite (elitism).[38] Lastly, (5) a continuous movement toward more efficient economic organizations is associated with ontological assumptions concerning traits or psychological constants of organizational members. The presence of acquisitive motivation and possessive individualism tends to be a principal assumption of theoreti-

Figure 3.

*Classification of Theoretical Viewpoints in the Analysis of Socialist Economic Organizations*

| *The Principal Phenomena That Explain Organizations Are:* | *The Principal Behavioral Relations That* Define *Organizations Are:* Objective (Materialist) | Subjective (Idealist) |
|---|---|---|
| Imposed on the Organization (Determined) | Workers' Management as an Evolutionary Universal | De-alienation a Function of Labor Allocation and Moral Stimulation |
| Generated by the Organization (Self-steered) | Workers' Management a Function of Leadership Styles and Communication | De-alienation a Function of Role Substitutability and Participation |

cal viewpoints which assert a decline of ideological dogmatism and a trend toward economic and organizational "rationality" (econological psychologism).[39]

Definitions of behavior relations principally in terms of *subjective* characteristics have also been accompanied by explanations based on *imposed* conditions or classes of phenomena. These theoretical viewpoints may be generalized in terms of "cultural imperativism,"[40] which has several principal forms: (a) Dogmatism, denoting a quality of inflexible commitment to socialist values, irrespective of situational variations and constraints, tends to decline over time with economic development, social differentiation, urbanization and technological innovation.[41] (b) Pragmatism renders ideological doctrines more responsive to instrumental values and promotes an orientation to problems that is centered on performance and tangible results.[42] (c) Totalitarianism, which emphasizes the impact of political structures and ideology on the formation of attitudes of submission and acquiescence, contributes to the routinization of coercion through institutionalized expectations that sanctions will be employed in cases of deviation.[43] (d) Modernism, which denotes a process of social differentiation, social mobilization and communication through economic development, indus-

**Figure 4.**

*Organizational Change in Socialist Systems: Selected Theoretical Viewpoints*

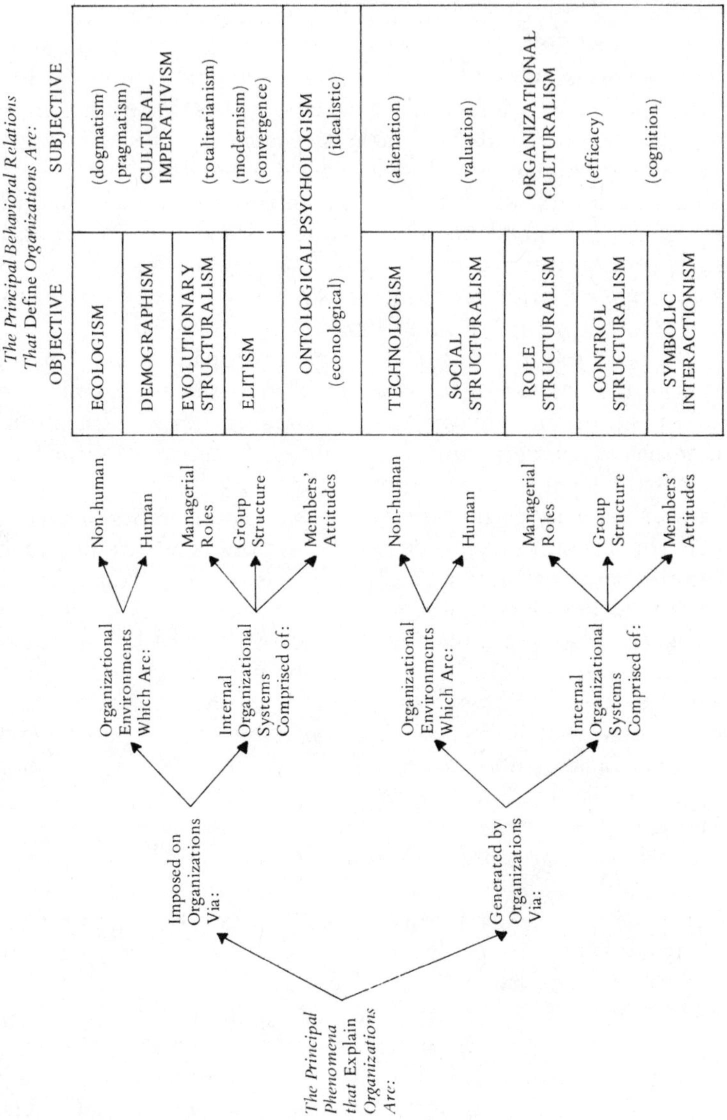

trialization, and urbanization, promotes the secularization of ideology, contributes to the emergence of performance (versus ascription) as an orientation toward action, and creates an increasingly "rational" culture supportive of modern science and technology.[44] (5) Convergence, which is a methodological superimposition of modernism on a conventional legal typology of socialist versus capitalist systems, maintains that trends in both objective and subjective behavioral relations are increasingly similar.[45] Lastly, (6) ontological psychologism in its idealistic form involves assumptions about the inherent perfectibility of organizational members. Idealistic psychologism offers explanations of behavioral changes which will occur once material incentives and hierarchical authority structures are made subordinate to humanistic organizational goals and the moral values of socialism.[46] Econological (assumptions about economic man) and idealistic psychologism both treat subjective behavior relations as constants imposed on organizations via the inherent nature of members.

*Subjective* definitions of organizational behavior are also connected with explanations based on classes of phenomena *generated* by organizations and environments. "Organizational culturalism" denotes a theoretical concern with explaining changes in attitudes, beliefs, and values of members of complex adaptive organizations.[47] There are various efforts designed to explain variations in organizational cultures. (1) Alienation, denoting subjective attitudes of personal inefficacy with regard to the performance of tasks, has been explained by the complexity of technology, the degree of competition and differentiation in markets, and the scope of hierarchical roles.[48] (2) Values of egalitarianism and cooperation have been explained by variations in technology, social structure, and social values.[49] (3) Personal efficacy, satisfaction, and motivation have been explained by the scope of participation in decision-making and the structure of wages.[50] (4) The organizational cognition of members, manifested in variations in the acquisition of knowledge of organizational tasks, has been explained by formal participation and group involvement in decisions.[51]

Emphases on *objective* behavior relations are also accompanied by explanations based on conditions *generated* by organizations and their environments. (1) Economic growth and efficiency are functions of technology; multiple technological forms may promote similar or greater levels of economic efficiency with different social consequences (technologism).[52] (2) Social structure and social values, particularly rapid social mobility and egalitarianism, govern variations in the feasibility of establishing and sustaining participative industrial authority structures in different systems (social structuralism).[53] (3) Organizational effectiveness is explained by decentralization of influence, multiple roles, and democratization of authority structures (role structuralism).[54] (4) The structure and content of group communications explains the scope and intensity of participation and organizational control (control structuralism).[55] (5) Authority structure, roles, group interaction, and the attitudes and values of members are in a constant process of change and adaptation (symbolic interactionism).[56] In principle, it is unfeasible to explain or predict objective behavior relations on the basis of imposed conditions of any kind. Preoccupation with constants in the form of evolutionary universals, global tendency statements, and uniform check-lists may serve more to obscure than clarify organizational change. Global predictability and exhaustive explanation are unlikely and methodologically problematic.

*Comparing Socialist Economic Organizations:*
*Conceptual Framework and Propositions*

Socialist economic organizations embody relationships between a social system, a technical system, and organization. The latter includes a managerial system, group structure, and membership. Relationships between these systems and their components, attributes, variables, and processes may be conceptualized as generated and imposed, and as including both subjective and objective behavior relations. Causation, which may be treated as multi-linear, complex, and cumulative, involves patterns of relative salience between technology, environing social structures, and the organization itself. Interrelationships are represented below in a conceptual framework of a potentially self-generating organizational system (Figure 5). This conceptual framework, based on open systems assumptions, provides us with an opportunity to compare socialist economic organizations in Cuba, China, and Yugoslavia along dimensions of adaptiveness and self-guidance.[57]

**Figure 5.**

*Conceptual Framework of a Self-Generating Organizational System*

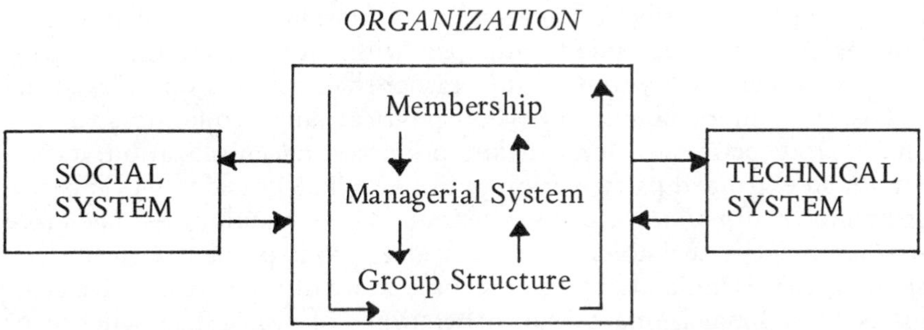


The conceptual framework of a self-generating organizational system permits the exploration of interrelationships between variables in the form of propositions. Propositions express: (1) the relative salience of organizational, technical and social systems influences, considered together; and the separate influence exerted by (2) the social system, (3) the technical system, and (4) the organization itself. Studies of socialist economic organizations from which propositions have been developed are seldom explicitly and systematically comparative.[58] Existing research on China, Cuba, and Yugoslavia is, however, sufficiently demonstrative of organizational interrelationships to permit comparative inferences in the form of propositions and tentative hypotheses.[59]

*Patterns of Relative Salience.* Influences exerted by social and technical systems promote variations in economic organizations within and between enterprises in China, Cuba, and Yugoslavia. Patterns of relative salience are suggested by studies of organizations in the three countries during the Cultural Revolution (1966- ) in China, and during the decade of the 1960s in Yugoslavia and Cuba.

> 1. *The more highly differentiated and/or the more unstable the social system—as manifested primarily in pluralistic patterns of political power, multiple resources necessary to organizational performance, and irregularity and unpredictability of interactions with organized interests—the less salient it is in influence variations in organizations.*
>
> 2. *The more flexible the technical system—as evidenced by technologies which permit the same output by means of multiple technical operations—the less salient it is in influencing variations in organizations.*
>
> 3. *The less salient the social and technical systems, the more salient the organization itself, as evidenced by dominant influences of management, informal groups, and/or individual members.*

Survey research on individuals, groups, and organizational members in Yugoslavia suggests diverse political values and perceptions of low party and trade union influence within organizations.[60] Firms responded increasingly to economic rather than political variables in the 1960s.[61] A more pluralistic social, political, and economic structure and a more permissive legal regime promoted decentralization, autonomy, and expanded participation in firms.[62] The intended participative structure of firms, however, is constrained by technology.[63] The more mechanized the technology, the less effective is participation in decision-making. Handicraft industries share more of the participative attributes of self-management than other types of firms. The salience of self-managed organizations is relatively greater in small, handicraft industries with low technological complexity, high flexibility, and largely self-generated technical operations.

Cuba, with an increasingly complex managerial technology in the form of computerized budgetary finance, particularly since 1971, and simple productive technologies in a predominantly agrarian society, shares characteristics of high and low complexity in a unitary socio-political setting. Dependence on centrally allocated resources, planned targets, and calculated inputs is supplemented with unitary pressures by the party and trade unions to observe production norms.[64] The use of computer-assisted central planning and material incentives has increased considerably since 1971.[65] Import-export firms with comparatively more complex technologies were exempted during 1964-65 from constraints of budgetary finance, although in 1968-70 the entire economy was converted to budgetary finance. In the earlier period forms were subject to a more flexible managerial technology permitting direct contracts with suppliers and producers.[66] Such firms operated in a more fluid, differentiated, and uncertain economic environment, as did industrial and agricultural firms in China during the Cultural Revolution. They were constrained by few fixed targets in the period since 1966. In China, party groups exert pressures to observe norms, although there are differences between organizations in agriculture (Tachai Scale System) and industry (Tach'ing System).[67] The latter manifests greater technological inflexibility. The group basis of Chinese organizations seems to facilitate decision-making and technological design by work groups composed of party cadres, technicians, and production workers, suggesting a technological flexibility shared perhaps only by handicrafts industries in Yugoslavia. The salience of economic organizations in China and Yugoslavia is relatively great. Budgetary finance in Cuba suggests the lowest organizational salience among the three systems, and is more comparable to organizations in the Soviet Union, irrespective of the mix between moral and material incentives. Patterns of relative salience in "typical" Chinese, Cuban, and Yugoslav organizations are represented below (Figure 6).[68]

> 4. *The greater the amount of technological complexity–i.e., the scope of different knowledges required to perform operations effectively–the greater the emphasis on managerial coordination and routinization to maintain given levels of performance.*

Research on Yugoslavia suggests that the higher the level of technological production, the lesser the role of production workers in decision-making, which is transferred to experts, although compensatory participation has been induced by activities of the League of Communists, particularly in the metal and chemical industries.[69] Studies of mechanized firms indicate pre-consultation among managers and technical staff and formalization and routinization of decisions in Workers' Council meetings.[70] In China, the exemption of defense and heavy industry from norms of the Tach'ing System is consistent with posited relationships between technological complexity and managerial co-ordination, a pattern also apparent in import-export industries in Cuba.

Figure 6.

*Patterns of Salience in "Typical" Economic Organizations: China, Cuba, and Yugoslavia*

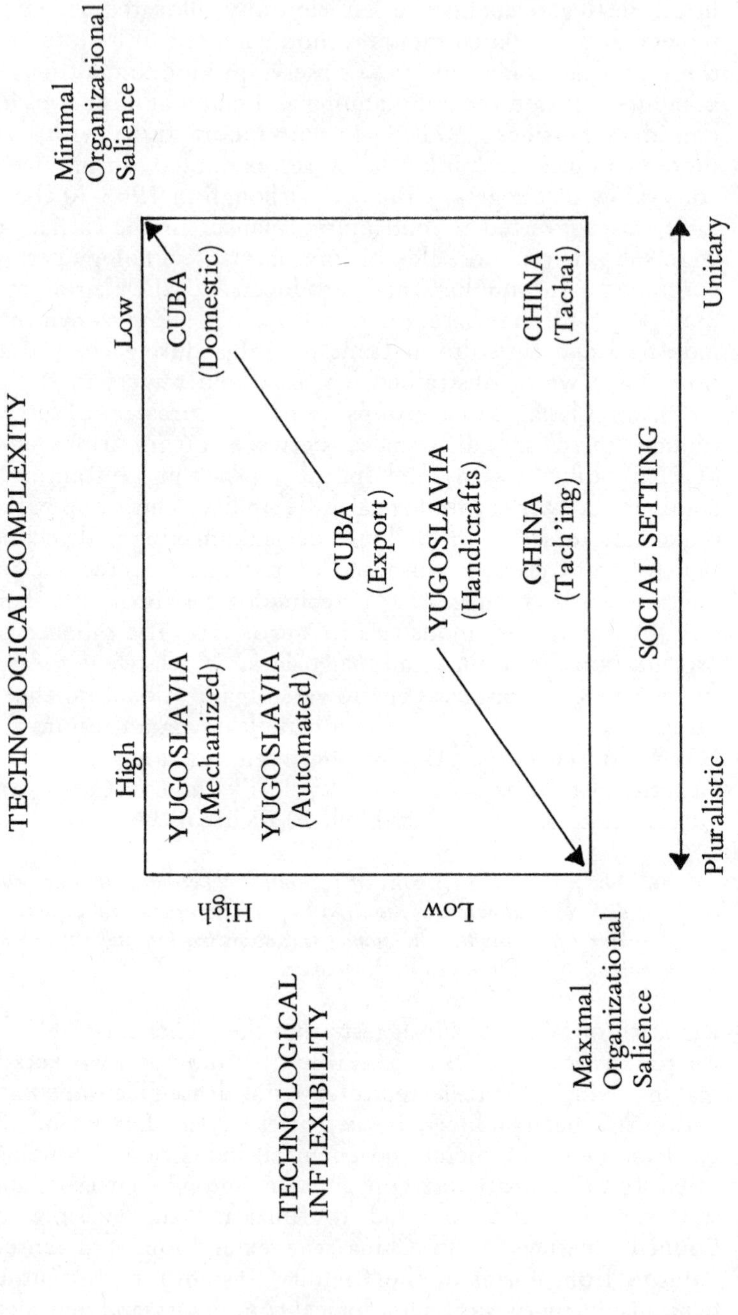

5. *The more permanent the organization, the lower its rate of turnover of personnel, and the less rigid (mechanized) its technology, the greater the salience of its group structure.*

Turnover of personnel in China, Cuba, and Yugoslavia has been comparatively great. The primary source of labor turnover in China and Cuba has been administrative transfer of workers, which lowers the probability that workers will have sufficient time to interact and become socially cohesive. Administrative surveillance in Cuba is facilitated by the workers' identity card (*carnet laboral*),[71] which extends control over attitudinal and behavioral deviance, as does labor mobilization through successive emulation campaigns. Group cohesiveness in China and Cuba involves group socialization into norms and values of the work place. Socialist emulation in Cuban enterprises and cadre socialization in "May 7" Schools in China create more salient group structures in less permanent organizations. In China, flexible technologies, promoted by group structures which involve overlapping membership of cadres, experts, and production workers, are supportive of group cohesiveness. Cuban firms are technologically less flexible, which constrains group cohesiveness and probably lowers the effectiveness of emulation campaigns.

Inflexible technologies in mechanized industries in Yugoslavia combine with high labor turnover to impede interaction and cohesiveness. In 1972 approximately one million workers were registered as employed abroad. Labor turnover is mitigated, however, by two factors: a pregnancy and attrition effect associated with reluctance to hire new workers;[72] and a high proportion of agricultural workers among migrants in a rapidly industrializing society.[73] Given the relative inactivity of political groups in socialization activities, technical groups were highly salient throughout the late 1960s. High labor turnover, technological inflexibility, and low salience of group structure among workers are likely related to the high incidence of strikes and work stoppages in northern republics.[74]

6. *In organizations where technical expertise is most highly valued, because of its indispensability to organizational performance, group influence in the form of experts is more salient.*

Yugoslav and Cuban firms share a basically economistic orientation. Economic goals tend to predominate, although socialist emulation in Cuba contributes both to increased labor inputs and group cohesiveness.[75] Although a large number of "political factories" and successive ideological mobilizations in Yugoslavia suggests high salience of political groups, the increasingly influential role of experts has not until recently been challenged.[76] During the Great Leap Forward and the Cultural Revolution economic and socio-political objectives seem to have been treated as equal in importance, through a dual emphasis on industrialization and socialization of labor.[77] In these periods the relative influence of experts was purposefully down-graded, ideologically and in radical organizational reforms. Experts are highly salient in Yugoslavia, less so in Cuba, and least in China. In Yugoslavia "liberal-technocratic" groups have been challenged since 1972, although demoted directors and technical staff include law violators and the inefficient.

> 7. *Under conditions of extreme external pressures, growing uncertainty, and conflicts over organizational policies and objectives, the more salient are individual participants and the greater the tendency toward inspirational leadership of various kinds.*

Inspirational or charismatic leadership within firms seems to be a characteristic of China only. During the Great Leap Forward and Cultural Revolution a combination of economic pressures and lack of agreement on objectives and policy instruments was associated with inspirational leadership by cadres. Although extreme economic pressures and uncertainty have been present in Cuba (1968-70) and Yugoslavia (1969-72), conflicts over organizational objectives have not been evident. Conflicts have focused, rather, on organizational instruments: "moral" versus "material" stimulation of production in Cuba; and centralized versus decentralized and "depoliticized" productive activity in Yugoslavia.[78] Ideology has served as a constraint on economic objectives, as distinguished from an objective in its own right. Economic values seem frequently to have served as constraints on social and political objectives in China.[79]

*The Social System*. There are two primary means through which the social system influences organizations. Ecological mechanisms limit organizational choice and promote adaptation to material and human factors so as to maintain given levels of performance. Psychological mechanisms, which involve socialization both outside the work place and motivation within firms, create attitudes which affect organizational behavior. Relationships between incentive structures and motivation raise questions concerning the role of ideology in maintaining performance in socialist firms.

> 8. *The greater the breadth and diffusiveness of external pressures, the more decentralized the decision-making process within the firm, the greater the scope of communications and group interaction, and the greater the commitment of participants to organizational objectives.*

In Yugoslavia, the decline of central planning, combined with increased external pressures from suppliers and buyers, has been associated with firm autonomy and decentralization. Expanded participation in decentralized authority structures seems to be positively associated with increased communications, group interaction, and worker commitment.[80] Although positive relationships between participation and effectiveness have been identified in Chinese organizations, organizations seem unable fully to control diverse pressures from the external social setting. A major adaptive response has been formalization of group interaction, cooptation of primary groups, and diffusion of decision-making power vertically and horizontally, which promotes greater involvement.[81] External pressures are neither diffuse nor broad in Cuba. Bureaucratically structured relationships, combined with moral stimulation of production, promotes socially legitimized status competition, but without mitigating effects of overlapping group membership, rotation, and workers' participation.[82]

> 9. *The larger the size of the organization, the greater the number and scope of subgroups and units within it, giving rise to a greater emphasis on formal and impersonal rules and the differentiation of specific roles.*

The design of Cuban firms according to Lenin's model of a "government office" institutionalizes major characteristics of bureaucratic organization. The entire economy, given the system of budgetary finance, may be regarded analytically as one large organization planned from the center.[83] Despite moral stimulation, the relation between size and the control of units (firms) through impersonal rules and role differentiation is evident in the division of responsibilities between management, emulation offices, and the trade unions in enforcing norms of production, quality control, and labor discipline.[84] Similar relationships between size, control, and bureaucratization are also found in other socialist countries, although the basis of organizational control differs due to the widespread use of more stimulation through five successive emulation campaigns in Cuba in the period of 1961-1973. Decentralized organizations in China and Yugoslavia promote patterns of group interaction and participation which render role hierarchy, differentiation, and formalization less necessary to maintain given levels of performance.[85]

> 10. *The more formal and performance-oriented the managerial system, and the less ascriptive the recruitment system, the greater the emphasis on material rewards as opposed to political, moral, and ideological obligations.*

The emphasis on material rewards in Yugoslav firms is related to a managerial system primarily oriented toward performance. A decreasingly ascriptive recruitment system has been paralleled by increasing workers' interest in remuneration, as compared with values of participation.[86] While a large number of party members occupy managerial and technical roles, party membership is primarily a vehicle for social mobility, with little independent influence on decision-making.[87] Moreover, a large proportion of party members share "modernizing" attitudes and values, including achievement motivation and a pragmatic approach to problem-solving.[88] Value attached to material rewards is also evidenced in labor unrest. Strikes and work stoppages tend to be associated with frustrated expectations of higher wages and wage instability, more than dissatisfaction with power structure, bureaucracy, and limits to participation.[89] Moral and political obligations are nonetheless evident in pressures of party units in some enterprises to invest in local development and welfare projects. Similarly, the presence of "political factories" suggests a willingness to depart from cost-efficiency criteria so as to maintain current employment.

Utilitarian values associated with performance tend to be treated co-equally with values of equality, participation, and the socialization of labor in China. Recruitment processes emphasize competence and loyalty, the latter of which has assumed greater salience in mobilization periods when "politics in command" has taken precedence.[90] Material incentives have been employed with social and political rewards both as a basis for compliance and as success indicators.[91] One of the similarities between China and Yugoslavia, irrespective of the mix between remuneration and moral obligation, is the group basis for evaluating performance. In contrast, the evaluation of performance according to economic as well as ideological criteria in Cuba is accomplished by ministries, intermediate associations, and trade unions.[92]

In 1971, the "year of productivity," Cuban firms instituted cost-efficiency analysis, planning was rationalized, computer techniques were more widely applied, and attempts were made to eliminate labor surplus and upgrade the status of remuneration.[93] A departure from ascriptive recruitment criteria was also reflected in an emphasis on technical education in universities and secondary and training schools throughout the 1960s.[94] The average wage differential in Yugoslav firms is about 5:1, compared with estimates of ratios in Cuba which range from 4:1 to 13:1 in the mid-60s.[95] Reports on China suggest differentials between 3-4:1, although ratios have been compressed and then expanded since the Cultural Revolution.[96] Inter-industry, inter-regional, and inter-skill differentials in Yugoslavia are becoming smaller, particularly since the 1972 offensive against social differences, which promises to reduce further the present inequalities in pay and housing opportunities. Increasing use of material incentives and expanding differentials characterize Cuba since 1971.

> 11. *Given greater differentiation of economic activities and technological complexity, work based on material rewards is more efficient than work based on political or moral obligations, unless the latter are supplemented with institutionalized group interaction promoting cohesiveness and morale.*

Elements of this proposition have been advanced as a global tendency toward decline of ideology in social systems.[97] Insufficient attention has been directed toward variations in organizations themselves, particularly group structure. Differentiation and technological complexity in Chinese firms are mitigated by group interaction, participation, and technological flexibility. Although material stimulation of production characterizes the case of Yugoslavia, extensive group interaction in self-managed firms has promoted greater communication and worker commitment. Selected experiments with group decision-making in Yugoslav firms indicate impressive increases in productivity, quality control, and morale.[98] Recent amendments to the Yugoslav Constitution provide that decision processes shall be formalized on a group basis.[99] Group-based Chinese organizations suggest that a predominance of moral stimulation is not inherently inefficient. The Yugoslav experience suggests that the use of material incentives in comparatively participative industrial authority structures can be made more effective through group decision processes. The command structure of Cuban firms seems thus far to have precluded group decision processes.[100]

> 12. *The greater the number and scope of incompatible expectations between social and managerial roles, the greater the probability of role conflict among members.*

Role conflicts among managers of self-managed firms are a function of increased participation by workers, who tend to behave according to socially defined expectations that they are entitled to perform a managerial role in enterprises.[101] Workers' participation produces role strain in directors and technical staff, whose decisions in an uncertain economic environment require greater rapidity than meetings of Workers' Councils permit. Authority has often been separated from responsibility. Adaptive responses to role conflicts among managers include the manipulation of communications flows—which reduces information available to workers and inhibits participation—and prior consultation and informal bargaining before meetings of Councils.[102] Such adaptive responses may partially explain the decline of participation among other values in a cross-section of Yugoslav workers surveyed in recent years.[103] Role conflict is primarily a function of the tensions between socially generated ideological norms and values, and those of productivity and efficiency held principally by managers, technicians, and an increasing number of workers. Chinese organizations manifest similar patterns of role conflict, particularly during the Cultural Revolution. There has been greater turnover of cadres and managers than in Yugoslavia, however, accompanied by cyclical patterns in which ideological goals are recurrently replaced with economic ones as the predominant objectives of organizations. Role conflict in Cuba and Yugoslavia has not involved reorientation of organizational goals; rather modes of control have varied in their emphasis on remunerative versus normative power.

13. *The mode of resolution of social versus managerial role conflicts is a function of the ways that group interaction affects members.*

The salience of managers and technicians in resolving conflicts in Yugoslav firms is a function of the relative lack of influence of other groups, including the party and trade unions. Conflicts tend to be resolved by managers who apply cost-efficiency criteria to decisions, which are subsequently legitimized by managerial and technical personnel, leading members of Workers' Councils, and party and union representatives.[104] Conflict resolution in China assumed a markedly different form during the Cultural Revolution, with fluid overlapping groups asserting norms and values embodied in ideological doctrines. Conflicts between Maoists and Liuists included disagreements concerning appropriate criteria for making decisions, as well as procedures for coping with risks.[105] The Maoist model prescribes criteria of decisions and procedures for resolving conflict which are derived from ideological values and norms. The Liuist approach stresses rational calculation of probabilities attached to alternatives. During the Cultural Revolution risks and uncertainty were dealt with by concurrent or *post facto* estimation procedures, as contrasted with pre-calculation of risks in periods when technicians and managers dominated organizations.

Given highly salient government organizations, the party, trade union bodies, and politically loyal managers in Cuba, there has been less occasion for conflict and uncertainty, although the increasing emphasis on expertise over loyalty in the selection of managers since 1971 may be expected to promote changes. When conflicts occurred they appear to have been resolved largely by coercive means, including transfer of workers, suspensions, and rehabilitation.[106] Thought reform and rehabilitation also characterize China, although these have been employed primarily for control of ideological deviance, and not as a response to absenteeism, inefficiency, lack of discipline, and theft. Chinese organizations tend to be concerned with group processes for resolving "ideological" versus "economic" conflicts. Cuban and Yugoslav firms have emphasized pre-calculation of risks and controls by managers and technicians, as limited by incomplete information at the center and slowness of decisions in Workers' Councils meetings, respectively.

14. *The ideology of management characteristic of a social system engenders the dependency expectations of members, establishes norms of authority, and promotes variations in supervisory style.*

The official ideologies of socialist systems emphasize equality, cooperation, and self-realization. Managerial ideologies differ. Official ideology in Yugoslavia depicts workers as collective managers to whom directors are subordinate. Concrete managerial norms and values, however, emphasize strong leadership, hierarchical authority, and efficiency. Original expectations of active participation in decisions were frustrated and have become less salient, as indicated by the low priority assigned by workers and managers alike to self-management and participation, as compared with values of equality, equity, personal freedom, security, and standard of living.[107] The relative salience of managers and a largely authoritarian supervisory style are associated with the development in the late 1960s of self-management as a managerial ideology stressing control, discipline, and performance.[108]

Dependency expectations in Cuba are generated by a managerial ideology that emphasizes enforced discipline, control through emulation campaigns, and performance, but without widespread institutionalized means for workers' participation. Workers' participation has been generally low, although introduction of workers' councils and workers' assemblies began in late 1973.[109] Relative scarcity, high dependence on central resources, and a managerial structure which centralizes authority reinforce dependency expectations. The ideology of management characteristic of China discourages dependency and is supported structurally by fluid role relationships, egalitarian supervisory styles, group decision-making, and purposeful mitigation of hierarchy through upward and downward rotation. The official ideology of China under Mao seems to be more consistent with managerial norms and values than are official doctrines prevalent in Cuba and Yugoslavia.[110]

*The Technical System.* The technical system operates through ecological and psychological mechanisms and affects managerial structures, group interaction, and the behavior of organizational members. Several propositions are suggested in regard to technological influences on socialist economic organizations:

> 15. *The greater the number of technically possible ways to accomplish work (flexibility), the greater the absolute amount of horizontal communication, and the greater the group cohesiveness. Absolute amounts of vertical communication are a function of the degree of inflexibility of the production process.*

Studies of Chinese industrial organization suggest cumulatively interdependent relationships between technological flexibility, horizontal communication, and group cohesiveness.[111] These relationships are reinforced by managerial and group structures based on heterogeneous work teams in the Tach'ing System of factory management. Few efforts have been made in Yugoslavia to alter technological patterns which limit the effectiveness of self-managed firms. Managerial technologies in Yugoslavia are becoming increasingly complex and inflexible, partly as a result of activities of specialized schools and institutes. This has prompted debates about the creation of a technical elite.[112] The least flexible managerial technology, evidenced in the increasing use since 1971 of computer-assisted planometric techniques, is Cuba. Inflexibility is supplemented by moral stimulation, which promotes a measure of commitment and control within hierarchical authority structures. Flexible technical arrangements and egalitarian work relations characteristic of periodic sugar harvests are exceptions to a general pattern of bureaucratic rigidity and technological inflexibility, despite the relative lack of complexity of machine technology.[113]

16. *The more proximal work activities are spatially, and the more flexible are time schedules, the greater the probability of social interaction, group cohesiveness, and awareness of group structural differences.*

Chinese industrial firms suggest a significant degree of work proximity and temporal flexibility.[114] Cadres, technicians, and production workers are combined in work teams. Cadres and technicians work several days a week at production tasks. Egalitarian interaction is reflected also by dress and language. Research on Yugoslav firms suggests that social interaction, cohesiveness, and commitment are functions of communications patterns between representatives of Workers' Councils and their peer groups.[115] Time schedules are nevertheless rigid and limit social interaction. Workers' Council meetings are convened monthly and attended on the workers' time, not that of the enterprise.

*The Organizational System: Combined Interrelationships and Influences.* Organizations have so far been examined in a context of relative dependency on social and technical systems, which represent imposed conditions to which organizations adapt. Organizations also generate their own conditions and influence social setting and technology, which in turn affect organizations. Causation is therefore mutual, although patterns of relative salience indicate that some types of organizations are more important as sources of variation in an entire organizational system comprised of organization, technology, and social setting. This is particularly critical in the analysis of socialist economic organizations, for we cannot assume that internal organizational variables are constants. Comparisons of Cuba, China, and Yugoslavia suggest pronounced variations which are dependent on combined interrelationships and influences between organizations, their social settings, and technologies.[116]

17. *The greater the scope of disagreement concerning policy objectives (preferred outcomes) and the greater the uncertainty surrounding beliefs about the effects of policy alternatives (causation), the more variation there is in decision strategies and organizational structures.*[117]

Cuban firms seem increasingly to approximate an ideal-typical bureaucracy in which there is little disagreement on policy objectives, which are established at the center, and relatively great certainty regarding the probability that given policy alternatives will yield expected consequences. The predominance of moral stimulation of production from 1966 to 1970 did not alter the essentially bureaucratic structure of organizations, although the use of moral incentives does challenge the view that bureaucratic organization requires monetization and depoliticized behavior. The context of decision-making in Cuban firms seems increasingly to be one of relative agreement and certainty. Computational decision strategies, supported with ideological mobilization and emulation campaigns, are most appropriate for maintaining performance levels within a bureaucratic structure. (Figure 7).

China approximates a pure-type of organizational structure in which group exchange and interaction promote a "dialectical" decision strategy under conditions of relative uncertainty and disagreement.[118] A group exchange structure is one in which: (1) groups are interdependent; (2) collective problem-solving is stressed; (3) there is a multiplicity of preference scales held by opposing groups with approximately equal power; (4) information is routed through multiple communication channels; and (5) each member has access to major channels of communication. The strategy employed in this structure is dialectical decision-making, a process in which major groups press claims and arguments until agreement is reached. Appeals to the authority of the thought of Mao Tse-tung establish broad guidelines for the resolution of conflict by contending groups.[119] During the Cultural Revolution all organizations did not conform to this pure type. Organizations in the period 1961-66 probably approximated a compromise strategy in a representative structure composed of contending political and technical factions which disagreed over goals and objectives, but employed agreed-upon decision procedures directed toward optimization of production. These two pure types reflect major differences between Maoist and Liuist organizational models.[120] The former stresses institutionalized mass participation, heterogeneous membership in revolutionary committees, democratic centralism, and non-rational decision processes in which risks are calculated concurrently or after a policy has been executed. The Liuist model emphasizes rule by elites, functional specificity of roles, self-criticism within the party only, and rational decision processes in which probabilities are assigned to alternatives so as to pre-calculate risks and reduce uncertainty.

Depending on the period being examined, Yugoslav firms approximate either a collegial structure or a representative one. The normative ideal of workers' management prescribes majority judgment in collegial structures in which major policy objectives are widely shared, but uncertainty as to which policy alternatives will promote objectives most effectively. Handicraft industries and a number of small firms in the industrial sector seem to approximate a collegial structure in the period

**Figure 7.**

*Pure Strategies and Structures of Decision: Chinese, Cuban, and Yugoslav Organizations*

| *Beliefs About Policy Alternatives* (Causation) | *Preferences About Policy Objectives* (Outcomes): Agreement | Disagreement |
|---|---|---|
| Certain | COMPUTATION IN BUREAUCRATIC STRUCTURE (CUBA, 1968- ) | COMPROMISE IN REPRESENTATIVE STRUCTURE (YUGOSLAVIA, 1971) |
| Uncertain | MAJORITY JUDGMENT IN COLLEGIAL STRUCTURE (YUGOSLAVIA, 1965) | DIALECTICS IN GROUP EXCHANGE STRUCTURE (CHINA, 1968) |

1965-68, although it seems clear that by 1971 objectives of organizations were in serious question. Disagreements whether firms should maximize profits, or promote social equality within organizations and society generally, characterize recent debates on new constitutional amendments. A veto right for "units of associated labor" in organizations is now guaranteed by law (Amendment 23). A reasonably effective group structure will compel much more informal bargaining and compromise than has existed thus far. The institutionalization of a group bargaining structure is partly a response to the ineffectiveness of a collegial model, which in the 1965-70 period increasingly relied on managers, technical staff, and foremen to generate consensus for decisions. They also engaged in informal bargaining and compromise, often at the expense of workers' perceived interests. In short, the Yugoslav case seems to fall between the two pure types in the period since the 1965 reforms.

> 18. *The greater the horizontal and vertical interaction, the greater the absolute amount of communications, and the greater the morale and commitment among subordinates. The greater the ratio of functions to differentiated organizational roles (de-differentiation), the greater the number of roles performed by each member, and the greater the social learning and clarity of perception of organizational structure, tasks, and operations among members.*

Chinese and Yugoslav firms share two major characteristics. First, organizations evidence a relatively high degree of horizontal and vertical interaction compared with previous periods of centralization and one-man management in both countries. Second, there has been an increase in the number of roles performed by each member, reflected in a higher ratio of functions or work assignments to organizational roles. This ratio is significantly higher in China than in Yugoslavia, and only in the former case does job rotation apply to superiors and subordinates alike. In both systems, subordinates enjoy vertical upward mobiblity through Workers' Councils and the Two-Group Rotation and Triple Combination systems.

Vertical and horizontal interaction through participation in Yugoslav firms is positively associated with worker morale, identification with organizational objectives, and organizational effectiveness.[121] An important study reports that social learning and cognitive apperception of organizational tasks in self-managed firms is strikingly high.[122] A cross-section of active participants scored remarkably high on tests measuring knowledge necessary to manage firms, suggesting that increased formal education and training may be unnecessary or redundant. Yugoslav and Chinese organizations alike are important modes for informal education, social learning, and assimilation in societies making a transition to industrial life. Chinese organizations—which promote more interaction, communication, and participation than those in Yugoslavia—are probably comparatively effective in socializing labor in a predominantly agrarian society. It is also probable that losses in efficiency that derive from power-equalization are compensated by increased efficiency resulting from higher morale and increased involvement, which release productive energy and provide conditions for effective social learning at work.[123]

> 19. *Given permissive or supportive environmental conditions, the greater the dissatisfaction of members, the greater the number of opposing groups and the greater their influence on management. Given restrictive or unsupportive environmental conditions, dissatisfaction tends to assume characteristics of reactive individualism.*

Permissive environmental conditions are more pervasive in Yugoslavia than China, although the restriction of group interaction is less in China than Cuba. Absenteeism is a serious problem in Cuba, while resignations from rural organizations characterized China during the Cultural Revolution.[124] Nevertheless, institutionalized expression of group dissatisfaction is a characteristic of Chinese organizations, and an essential feature of conflicts between party cadres, workers, technicians, and the masses.[125] Yugoslavia has experienced the greatest organized opposition of workers, primarily on grounds of dissatisfaction with wages. In the period 1958-1969 there were more than 1,750 strikes and work stoppages involving at least a hundred thousand workers.[126] In 1968, strikes and collective bargaining were legalized.

> 20. *Perceptions of group structure and social distance govern levels and rates of interaction and participation, irrespective of variations in wage differentials and schemes for worker participation based on indirect representation.*

Wage differentials in Yugoslavia have contracted since 1968, irrespective of increasing marketization of the economy.[127] Concurrently, social distance and status differentials, according to Slovenian reports, seem to have increased significantly.[128] A majority of children of production workers do not attend universities or technical schools and do not acquire positions as managers or technical staff. Social interaction is highly stratified. Organizational members tend in some areas to socialize primarily with others who occupy equivalent or higher status positions in organizations. These patterns, found in Yugoslavia's most developed republic, suggest that *social inequality is not primarily attributable to the market or the incentive system*, but to the social system in which worker-managed firms are embedded. It is unlikely that status differentials would be eliminated or reduced by central planning, further compression of wage differentials, or the use of moral stimulation. In short, the claim that the market and material incentives are principal sources of inequality and alienation is doubtful or incorrect. The Yugoslav case suggests that status competition is unresponsive to compression of wage differentials and participation in Workers' Councils. Only substantial changes in organization structure, group interaction, recruitment patterns, and the educational system seem sufficiently salient to mitigate status competition. Thus far only China has succeeded in partially implementing such changes.

> 21. *The greater the variation in the size, reward structure, and resources between organizations, the greater the tendency toward social stratification based on organizational status differentials.*
>
> 22. *Given an egalitarian goal-culture, the greater the salience of external political groups, the greater the tendency to control organizational status differentials through external political pressures, which promotes internal managerial defenses and creates conflicts between political leadership and experts.*
>
> 23. *Given a tendency toward uneven organizational growth, conflicts between managerial groups and political bodies are recurrent phenomena which create unstable and irregular patterns of organizational change in socialist systems.*

In the three systems under consideration there has been recurrent commitment to dual objectives of revolution and modernization. Organizational dualism in China has tended to assume the form of a simultaneous commitment to the socialization of labor and industrial growth. The latter has sometimes been incrementally reduced through commitments to socialist values of equality and humanization of work processes. Dualism in Cuba has been manifested in concurrent efforts to achieve rapid economic growth and create a new socialist man through moral stimulation. In Yugoslavia, workers' participation has been pursued as an egalitarian alternative to centralized state bureaucracy in a context of concern with rapid social and economic development. Recently workers' participation has sometimes been treated as a primary value, subject to economic constraints. New constitutional amendments, for example, seek in various ways to alter economically effective but essentially elitist managerial structures, although limited participation may be associated with increased organizational effectiveness up to a point, suggesting curvilinear relationships between participation and effectiveness.[129] This poses critical problems of adjusting to various group demands when participative-egalitarian values are sacrificed for economic objectives. Given complex variations between firms—in terms of external pressures, technological complexity, socio-cultural values, and the scope of members' involvement—it is impossible to arrive at a uniform "optimization schedule" for all firms. The possibility that different optimization procedures will satisfy all major groups, from national and local party leaders to trade union and managerial groups, is remote indeed. Conflict is therefore an essential feature of the system, and this is largely attributable to dualistic properties of organizations in a basically egalitarian goal-culture.

Patterns of organizational compliance in the three systems manifest distinct differences (Figure 8). Markedly different organizational designs have been implemented for purposes both of reducing inequality and alienation, and pursuing national programs of modernization. In China, dual organizations seem to have manifested, at successive stages, a predominance of one set of objectives versus another. In contrast, Cuban and Yugoslav firms evidence a predominant concern with economic objectives of modernization, although modes of compliance (material versus moral incentives) differ markedly. Structures and strategies of decision and procedures for conflict resolution also differ markedly. Although patterns of change in all systems are complex and non-linear, only China appears to manifest identifiable cyclical regularities.[130]

Organizational change in Cuba and Yugoslavia may be represented as an irregular series of fluctuations involving shifts in the degree to which party mobilization and the incentive systems emphasize material rewards or political and moral obligations as a basis of compliance. Socio-cultural goals have not predominated, however, as is the case with compliance succession in China. Several tentative hypotheses help to explain differences in goals, power, and involvement, which are set forth in Figure 9. Cuba and Yugoslavia are comparatively open to changes in an uncertain and unstable product market. In Cuba, international market pressures are particularly salient, while Yugoslav organizations are subject to international and domestic pressures from external suppliers and consumers. External pressures account for the markedly "economistic" orientation evident in both countries.

The relative intensity of conflict with the social setting is much less in Cuba and Yugoslavia than in China. In Cuban firms, leadership exercised by central administrative officials and party cadres, to whom experts and technicians are subordinated, facilitates co-alignment of centrally established goals, targets, and values with those of the enterprise, as does the use of planometric procedures and socialist emulation for purposes of control. In Yugoslavia, a "deinstitutionalized" party, confined in the 1960s to a role as educator and ideological persuader, contributed in past years to a relative absence of conflict, as did informal cooptation of party members to managerial and technical roles and a recruitment system increasingly based on performance as the sufficient condition for organizational leadership. Fluctuations in party mobilization and enterprise management nevertheless occurred in 1954, 1961, 1966, and 1971, years in which ideological offensives sought to strengthen the leading role of the party. Sanctions–including reprimand, expulsion, dismissal, and demotion–were applied in each period.

Figure 8.

*Preferred Outcomes and Compliance Processes in Dual Organizations*

| *Compliance Process (Power/ Involvement)* | *Preferred Outcomes (Goals)* Economic | Socio-cultural |
|---|---|---|
| Utilitarian/ Calculative | ONE-MAN MANAGEMENT IN CHINA (1950-1955) | IDEOLOGICAL OFFENSIVE IN YUGOSLAVIA (1971) |
| Normative/Moral | REVOLUTIONARY OFFENSIVE IN CUBA (1968) | CULTURAL REVOLUTION IN CHINA (1966) |

**Figure 9.**

*Patterns of Change in Socialist Organizations*

| | | *Patterns of Change* | |
|---|---|---|---|
| | | Cyclical | Fluctuating |
| *Mode of Conflict Resolution* | Sequential Attention (Time) | CHINA: CULTURAL REVOLUTION (1966- ) | CUBA (1961, 1963, 1966, 1970) |
| | Functional Differentiation (Space) | CHINA: GREAT LEAP FORWARD (1956-58) | YUGOSLAVIA (1954, 1961, 1966, 1971) |

Nevertheless, organizational change did not depart from predominant goals of productivity and economic efficiency. Fluctuations in Cuba, represented by a series of mobilization campaigns and a recurrent stress on moral incentives in the period 1966-1970, are now marked by an emphasis on material incentives as a means toward more effective realization of economic goals.

The pursuit of dualistic goals through different modes of compliance has created conflicts in each of the three systems, raising the problem of devising a satisfactory means of optimization acceptable to major groups. During the Great Leap Forward and the Cultural Revolution, socio-cultural goals appear to have prominated. Conflicts between goals and compliance modes were resolved through sequential attention over time in 1966-1969. Functional differentiation of problem-solving activities and compartmentalization in space seem to have been the major means of conflict resolution in 1956-1958, although this rapidly broke down.[131] Sequential attention over time involves a purposeful search for optimal returns likely to result from the application of one mode of compliance (normative power) or another (utilitarian power). Chinese leaders committed to Maoism have nevertheless seen no "antagonistic contradiction" in conflicting requirements of different goal-compliance structures. Under conditions of imperfect socialization and an inability to control social system influences on organizational members in a predominantly agrarian society, shifts in goal-compliance structures have been an adaptive response to conflict. Organizational leaders "will often have to leave persuasion and invoke hierarchical authority or threaten sanctions if they are to satisfy the demands of their own superiors. In so doing they presumably make it less likely that a store of positive orientations and social cohesion will be built up for future use."[132] Disagreements over objectives and policy alternatives, together with comparatively intense conflicts with mass political organizations, promote sequential treatment of issues in fused political-economic structures. Compliance cycles seem essentially to be a function of these combined factors.

The environments of Cuban and Yugoslav organizations also include social system influences which are not fully controllable. Responses have nevertheless differed. The interlocking party-managerial structure of the Cuban firms promotes sequential attention as a mode of conflict resolution, but with far less conflict with external political groups and little institutionalized direct participation. In Yugoslavia, conflicts between goals and compliance modes have been resolved by functional differentiation and specialization (compartmentalization in space) of party and managerial activities. Special units treat separate problems arising from shortfalls in realizing socio-cultural and economic goals. In China, during the Great Leap Forward, organizations also tended to embody elements of functional differentiation, although this experiment was short-lived and culminated in a system in which party and managerial functions were blurred. One consequence of such role ambiguity was an inability of party units to perform tasks of political guidance. Compartmentalization of space proves particularly infeasible in a tightly organized territorial system with heterogeneous revolutionary committees, pressures from mass organizations, fluid organizations with a group exchange structure, and dialectical decision strategies which emphasize emergent solutions and the post-calculation of risk.

*Conclusions*

Economic organizations in China, Cuba, and Yugoslavia are not simply socialist variants of complex organizations which everywhere confront problems of goal conflict and demands for optimization. Cyclical and fluctuating patterns of organizational change reflect different patterns of institutionalized conflict in societies committed to dual objectives of revolution and modernization. The capacity of organizations to respond to such conflicts may well constitute a comparative advantage over capitalist systems in meeting demands for social responsibility.[133] Critical variables governing patterns of change in socialist systems are the intensity of conflict with the social setting, the mode of conflict resolution employed, and the characteristic goals and values of leaders, as constrained by factors of risk, uncertainty, and competition. Patterns of organizational change are less dependent on variations in modes of compliance—represented in this case by the composition of moral and material stimulation—than on variations in social setting, technology, and the structures of organizations themselves. Interrelationships between variables expressed in propositions above should serve as an admonition that organizations in socialist systems vary significantly in terms of complexity, adaptiveness, and self-guiding properties. A persuasive case can be made that until organizational change can be explained or otherwise accounted for, generalizations, taxonomies, and ideal-types employed for the comparative analysis of entire socialist systems will remain methodologically problematic.

The comparative analysis of socialist economic organizations as complex-adaptive systems suggests that the search for co-linearity among ideological, political, economic, and socio-cultural variables may obscure more than clarify variations within and between systems. While the methodological properties of categories and derived attributes employed in the construction of comparative frameworks have a critical bearing on questions of change and continuity, the exploratory analysis of interrelationships between variables calls into question the adequacy of major classification schemes. Variations between organizations in Cuba, China, and Yugoslavia are less satisfactorily explained by wage differentials and the scope of market relations—factors typically proposed as major explanatory variables—than by the structure of managerial roles, group interaction, technology, and social system influences.

Conclusions reached above suggest that reconstructed typologies which use organizational variables as a basis for comparison might require placing Yugoslavia and China in a similar "category," and Cuba in another.

An analysis of interrelationships between variables in special cases of socialist organization raises serious questions about the utility of contemporary approaches. These approaches often fail to identify important similarities between control processes, communications patterns, and authority structures in China and Yugoslavia, cases ostensibly best placed at opposite ends of a continuum. There appear to be more similarities between Chinese and Yugoslav organizations than between Chinese and Cuban ones. Similarities become significant, however, only when formal characteristics of ideological doctrines are rejected as principal criteria of inclusion and exclusion in comparative categories. In short, a complex-adaptive systems approach to comparative organizational analysis provides us with tools for questioning current categories and developing new ones which are more related to concrete similarities and differences between structures, processes, and behavior in socialist organizations.

For that growing number of social scientists who combine theoretical, empirical, and applied research out of a commitment to social science and an active concern with the humanization of organizational life, the comparative analysis of socialist systems with the tools of organization theory promises organizational futures which are more understandable and more amenable to the creation of conditions for the humanization of work. One way to proceed toward this future at a more satisfactory pace is to recognize the conceptual inadequacies of forms of misplaced abstraction which are largely unrelated to organized complexity, adaptiveness, conflict, and variation. Comparative organizational analysis, a major vehicle for the construction of middle-range theories of change, recognizes patterned deviation, diversity, and self-guided adaptation and sensitizes us to the critical role of organizations in socialist development: "The organization is the form of the mediation between theory and practice."[134]

## NOTES

1. The concept of dual organization is adapted from Amitai Etzioni, *A Comparative Analysis of Complex Organizations* (New York: Free Press, 1961), pp. 55-56. For applications of Etzioni's framework to China and Yugoslavia see G. William Skinner and Edwin Winckler, "Compliance Succession in Rural Communist China: A Cyclical Theory," in *Complex Organizations: A Sociological Reader*, ed. Amitai Etzioni (New York: Holt, Rinehart and Winston, 1969), pp. 410-438; Martin King Whyte, "Mao Tse-tung Versus Max Weber: Organization and Modernization in China" (forthcoming); and W. N. Dunn, "Ideology and Organization in

Socialist Yugoslavia: Modernization and the Obsolescence of Praxis," *Newsletter on Comparative Studies of Communism* 4 (August 1972):21-56.

2. On humanistic and economistic dimensions of socialist economic organizations see John Gurley, "Capitalist and Maoist Economic Development," in *America's Asia*, ed. Edward Friedman and Mark Selden (New York: Vintage Books, 1969), pp. 324-356; Paul C. Roberts, *Alienation and the Soviet Economy* (Albuquerque, N.M.: University of New Mexico Press, 1971); Frederick J. and Lou Jean Fleron, "Administration Theory as Repressive Political Theory: The Communist Experience," *Newsletter on Comparative Studies of Communism* 6 (December 1972); and Carmelo Mesa-Lago, "Ideological, Political, and Economic Factors in the Cuban Controversy on Material Versus Moral Incentives," *Journal of Interamerican Studies and World Affairs* 14 (February 1972):49-111.

3. Economic organizations in socialist systems share other characteristics which distinguish them from organizations in capitalist countries: (a) relative salience of environing political organizations; (b) presence of coherent ideological doctrines and programs enforced for purposes of organizational guidance; (c) relative scope and pervasiveness of organizational norms; and (d) perceptions of relative equivalence of socio-cultural values (cooperation, equality, self-realization) and more strictly economic ones (growth, productivity, efficiency).

4. Established socialist doctrines in China, Cuba, and Yugoslavia have sometimes tended to dismiss or minimize conflicts between economic, socio-cultural, and political goals. Similar tendencies are also evident in recent academic accounts of organizational change in these countries. See Stephen Andors, "Revolution and Modernization: Man and Machine in Industrializing Societies: The Chinese Case," in Friedman and Selden, *America's Asia*, pp. 393-444; Robert M. Bernardo, *The Theory of Moral Incentives in Cuba* (University, Ala.: University of Alabama Press, 1971); and Carole Pateman, *Participation and Democratic Theory* (Cambridge, England: The University Press, 1970), pp. 85-103.

5. Three models of organizational change in socialist economic organizations with dual compliance structures may be identified: (a) stable equilibrium with circular causation between variables; (b) unstable equilibrium with cumulative causation and linear relationships between variables; and (c) multiple stable and unstable equilibria with complex causation and non-linear relationships between variables. See W.N. Dunn, "The Economics of Organizational Ideology: The Problem of Compliance in the Worker-Managed Socialist Firm," *Journal of Comparative Administration* 5 (February 1974):395-441.

6. Methodological guidelines for comparative organizational analysis may be found in Stanley H. Udy, Jr., "The Comparative Analysis of Organizations," in *Handbook of Organizations*, ed. James C. March (Chicago: Rand-McNally, 1965), pp. 678-710; James D. Thompson and Arthur Tuden, eds., *Comparative Studies in Administration* (Pittsburgh: University of Pittsburgh Press, 1959); Todd La Porte, "The Recovery of Relevance in the Study of Public Organizations," in *Toward a New Public Administration*, ed. Frank Marini (Scranton, London, and Toronto: Chandler, 1971), pp. 17-47; and Warren F. Ilchman, *Comparative Wisdom and Conventional Administration* (Beverly Hills, Calif.: Sage Publications, 1973).

7. Methodological problems of comparative analysis expressed in alleged incompatibilities between nomothetic and ideographic approaches are discussed and resolved in Adam Przeworski and Henry Teune, *The Logic of Comparative Social Inquiry* (New York: Wiley, 1970).

8. See Ilchman, *Comparative Wisdom*.

9. See residual comparisons of China, Cuba, and North Korea in Robert Bernardo, *The Theory of Moral Incentives in Cuba*, pp. 30-31, 49-51, 84-88. Bernardo does speculate (119-140) that future differences between systems may be influenced by variations in social setting, including natural resources, population, domestic demand, and foreign trade.

10. On the use of various social setting categories see Chalmers Johnson, ed., *Change in Communist Systems* (Stanford, Calif.: Stanford University Press, 1970); and Alexander Eckstein, ed., *Comparison of Economic Systems* (Berkeley, Calif.: University of California Press, 1971). See also contributions to this volume by Carmelo Mesa-Lago and John M. Montias.

11. See, e.g., Alexander Eckstein, "Economic Development and Political Change in Communist Systems," *World Politics* 22 (1970):475-495.

12. See E. Furobotn and Svetozar Pejovich, "Property Rights and the Behavior of a Firm in a Socialist State: The Example of Yugoslavia," *Zeitschrift für Nationalokonomie* 30 (1970):431-454; and Richard Carson's contribution to this volume.

13. See Ilchman's *Comparative Wisdom*, pp. 7-8 distinctions between "existentialist" and "essentialist" strategies for comparative analysis; and Norman T. Uphoff and Warren F. Ilchman, *The Political Economy of Development* (Berkeley, Calif.: University of California Press, 1972), pp. 14-17. Significantly "essentialist" classification schemes employed to compare Yugoslav market socialism with other socialist systems are shared by ideological opponents. Writers for *Fortune* and *Business Week* reach similar conclusions about Yugoslavia's "capitalist" status as do contributors to *Monthly Review Press*.

14. See Udy, "Comparative Analysis of Organizations," pp. 679-687.

15. For a review of academic controversies concerning the relevant maximizing principle of the worker-managed firm in the works of Ward, Domar, and Horvat see Deborah D. Milenkovitch, *Plan and Market in Yugoslav Economic Thought* (New Haven, Conn.: Yale University Press, 1971), pp. 187-227.

16. Ichak Adizes, *Industrial Democracy: Yugoslav Style* (New York: Free Press, 1971). Adizes' hypotheses concerning the impact of leadership style, deduced from organization theory, do not conform to observations and conclusions, which derive from exploratory analysis. This inconsistency is not evident in his formal research design.

17. See Carmelo Mesa-Lago, "Ideological, Political and Economic Factors in the Cuban Controversy on Material Versus Moral Incentives"; and *The Labor Sector and Socialist Distribution in Cuba* (New York: Praeger, 1968). See also Bernardo, *Theory of Moral Incentives in Cuba*, pp. 80-118.

18. See Charles Hoffman, *Work Incentive Practices and Policies in the People's Republic of China, 1953-1965* (New York: State University of New York Press, 1967); and references to Andors and Eckstein above.

19. Branko Horvat, *Privredni Sistem i Ekonomska Politika Jugoslavije* [The Industrial System and Economic Policy of Yugoslavia] (Belgrade: Institute of Economic Research, 1970), pp. 41-52.

20. Branko Horvat, "Self-Management, Centralism and Planning," Institute for Economic Research, Monograph No. 7 (Belgrade, 1964). Reports of research in 1962 are not typical of investment behavior in subsequent periods.

21. See Milenkovitch, *Plan and Market in Yugoslav Economic Thought*, pp. 196-210.

22. See Furobotn and Pejovich "Property Rights and the Behavior of a Firm

in a Socialist State"; Richard Carson, *Comparative Economic Systems* (New York: MacMillan, 1973), chapters 5 and 7; and Carson's contribution to this volume.

23. Jaroslav Vanek, *The Participatory Economy* (Ithaca,N.Y.: Cornell University Press, 1971).

24. See research reported in Eugen Pusić,ed., *Participation and Self-Management*, 6 Vols. (Zagreb: Institute for Social Research, University of Zagreb, 1972, 1973, 1974). Vanek's assumptions, which are not borne out by empirical research, include: (a) self-managed firms manifest cohesiveness, not conflict; (b) firms behave as collective entrepreneurs; and (c) firms seek to maximize collective income. See also G. David Garson, *On Democratic Administration and Socialist Self-Management* (Beverly Hills, Calif.: Sage Publications, 1974).

25. Skinner and Winckler, "Compliance Succession in Rural Communist China." See also Edwin Winckler, "Political Management of the Development Process: Assessing the Chinese Development Experience," *China Quarterly* (July-September 1973), pp. 560-566. In effect, Winckler proposes both hypothesis-testing and exploratory analysis of interrelationships between variables, criticizing the "essentialist" strategy employed by Thomas G. Hart, *The Dynamics of Revolution: A Cybernetic Theory of the Dynamics of Modern Social Revolution with a Study of Ideological Change and Organizational Dynamics in the Chinese Revolution* (Stockholm: Stockholm University, 1971).

26. See Josip Obradović, "Participation and Work Attitudes in Yugoslavia," *Industrial Relations* 6, no. 2 (1970):161-169. This is a report of parts of a larger study of the effects of technology on workers' participation and motivation published in Serbo-Croatian in 1967.

27. E.g.,Bernardo, *Theory of Moral Incentives in Cuba, passim*, which compares other socialist systems residually and by means of two categories: "Libermanism" versus "moral incentives."

28. Such decisions include:(a) the adoption of Workers' Councils and economic decentralization in Yugoslavia, which was not rational from an economic perspective in 1951; (b) the periodic sacrifice of industrial production for increased equality and socialization of labor during the Cultural Revolution in China; and (c) the preference in Cuba for budgetary finance rather than economic decentralization, on grounds of increased equality and dealienation.

29. The validity of "collective entrepreneurship" as a behavioral attribute of workers' management has been challenged by Josip Županov, "Employees' Participation and Social Power in Industry," *Participation and Self-Management* 1:36-37.

30. Work incentives (moral versus material stimulation) are often assumed to be logically connected with the movement of wage differentials (equality versus inequality). Recent reports raise serious doubts about this relationship between categories (market and material incentives) and attributes (inequality). See Bodgan Denitch, "Notes on the Relevance of Yugoslav Self-Management," in *Participation and Self-Management*, Vol. 3. and Howard Wachtel, *Workers' Management and Wage Differentials in Yugoslavia* (Ithaca, N.Y.: Cornell University Press, 1973).

31. A number of empirical sociologists in Yugoslavia are oriented toward general organization theory. Veljko Rus, "The Limits of Organized Participation," *Participation and Self-Management* 2:165-189, reports higher levels of worker alienation in Yugoslav than U.S. firms, a conclusion which should be interpreted with extreme caution because of the inadequacy of methodological controls for differences in levels of expectation.

32. Parts of the following discussion are adapted from Walter L. Wallace, *Sociological Theory* (Chicago: Aldine, 1969), pp. 5-64.

33. See, e.g., Walter Buckley, *Sociology and Modern Systems Theory* (Englewood Cliffs,N.J.: Prentice-Hall, 1967).

34. Works by Vanek, Bernardo, Adizes, Andors, and Whyte are cited above. The relevant work by Horvat is *Towards a Theory of Planned Economy* (Belgrade: Institute of Economic Research, 1964).

35. See, e.g., Karl Wittfogel, *Oriental Despotism: A Comparative Study in Total Power* (New Haven, Conn.: Yale University Press, 1957).

36. See, e.g., demographic explanations employed in various contributions to Eckstein, *Comparison of Economic Systems*.

37. See, e.g., Vanek, *The Participatory Economy*; and Horvat, *Towards a Theory of Planned Economy*.

38. See, e.g., M. George Zaninovich, *The Development of Socialist Yugoslavia* (Baltimore: Johns Hopkins Press, 1968).

39. The best treatment of this methodological problem in the analysis of socialist systems is Fleron and Fleron, "Administration Theory as Repressive Political Theory."

40. Cultural imperativism refers to the view that it is somehow necessary or inevitable that certain cultural requisites be fulfilled in order to adapt effectively to increasingly differentiated, specialized, and complex societies. This theoretical viewpoint follows functional requisite analysis as developed by Parsons, Levy, and Inkeles.

41. See, e.g., Eckstein, "Economic Development and Political Change in Communist Systems."

42. See, e.g., Zaninovich, *The Development of Socialist Yugoslavia*.

43. See, e.g., Carl J. Friedrich and Zbigniew K. Brzezinski, *Totalitarian Dictatorship and Autocracy* (Cambridge, Mass.: Harvard University Press, 1956).

44. See, e.g., Gary K. Bertsch, "A Cross-National Analysis of the Community-Building Process in Yugoslavia," *Comparative Political Studies* 4 (1972):438-460.

45. See recent discussions of convergence in *Newsletter on Comparative Studies of Communism* 4, no. 2 (February 1971) and 4, no. 3 (May 1971).

46. Studies of China and Cuba seem implicitly to express, or acquiesce in, this viewpoint. See references to Gurley, Andors, and Bernardo above. The latter suggests (*Theory of Moral Incentives in Cuba*, pp. 155-156) that a choice must be made between mutually exclusive ontological assumptions about the nature of man allegedly expressed in Marxian and Maslowian psychology.

47. Organizational culturalism differs from cultural imperativism primarily in its emphasis on variables, but also in its tendency to focus on organizational change and conflict. Although terminology differs, a useful methodological analysis is contained in Buckley, *Sociology and Modern Systems Theory*, chapters 1 and 2.

48. See, e.g., Obradović, "Participation and Work Attitudes in Yugoslavia"; and Rudi Supek, "Some Contradictions and Insufficiencies of Yugoslav Self-Managing Socialism, *Praxis* 8 (1971):375-398.

49. See, e.g., Charles Hoffman, "The Maoist Economic Model," *Journal of Economic Issues* 5, no. 3 (September 1971):12-27.

50. See, e.g., the analysis of Yugoslavia by Pateman, *Participation and Democratic Theory*, pp. 85-103.

51. See, e.g., Živan Tanić, "Dimensions and Factors of the Apperception of Self-Management," *Participation and Self-Management* 1:139-50.

52. See the analysis of technological substitutability by Andors, "Revolution and Modernization."

53. See, e.g., Solomon J. Rawin, "Social Values and the Managerial Structure: The Cases of Yugoslavia and Poland," *Journal of Comparative Administration* 2, no. 2 (August 1970):131-159.

54. See, e.g., Bogdan Kavcić, Veljko Rus,and Arnold Tannenbaum, "Control Participation and Effectiveness in Four Yugoslav Industrial Organizations," *Administrative Science Quarterly* 16, no. 1 (1971):74-86.

55. See, e.g., Pavao Novosel, "Self-Managerial Participation and the Great China Wall of Communication," in *Participation and Self-Management*, Vol. 3.

56. An illustration of this viewpoint, although not designated as such, is Eugen Pusić, "Participation and the Multidimensional Development of Complexity," *Participation and Self-Management* 2:174-199. Explicit treatments of symbolic interactionism by East European sociologists may be found in Peter Berger, ed., *Marxism and Sociology: Views from Eastern Europe* (New York: Appleton-Century-Crofts, 1970).

57. Comparisons of socialist economic organizations along these dimensions would result in the placement of the USSR and Cuba at one pole of a continuum, and China and Yugoslavia at the other, notwithstanding the important methodological assumption that all socialist organizations share some capacity for self-guidance. This assumption is consistent with an open systems strategy for understanding complex organizations. See J.D. Thompson, *Organizations in Action* (New York: McGraw-Hill, 1967), pp. 3-14.

58. The absence of explicit and systematic comparisons derives from a predominance of case or country studies which are linked together, if at all, by *ceteris paribus* assumptions. The absence of a spatio-temporal dimension in cross-sectional research means also that causal relationships must be inferred. The analysis which follows abstracts and generalizes characteristics of: (a) one type of organization in one country (e.g., the Tachai Scale System); (b) several types of organizations (e.g., self-managed handicrafts and mechanized industries in Yugoslavia) in one country; and (c) several types of organizations or structures (e.g., compliance) in two or more countries. This is a methodological convenience only, prompted by an insufficiency of empirical research on organizations in all countries except Yugoslavia.

59. Propositions have been adapted from Udy, "Comparative Analysis of Organizations," unless otherwise noted. Source materials on organizational change in China, Cuba, and Yugoslavia are uneven and fragmentary, frequently requiring extensive interpretation in accordance with our conceptual framework.

60. See, e.g., Yugoslav sections of ISVIP, *Values and the Active Community* (New York: Free Press, 1971); Mitja Kamušić, "Economic Efficiency and Workers' Self-Management," in *Yugoslav Workers' Self-Management*, ed. J.B. Broekmeyer (Dordrecht, Holland: D. Reidel, 1970), pp. 76-117; and V. Rus, "Influence Structure in Yugoslav Enterprises," *Industrial Relations* 9, no. 2 (1970):148-160.

61. See Howard Wachtel, *Workers' Management and Wage Differentials in Yugoslavia*.

62. In addition to references above to Adizes (1971), Horvat (1970), Kamušić (1970), and Milenkovitch (1970), see Zdravko Mlinar and Henry Teune, "Development and Participation," in *Participation and Self-Management* 2:114-136.

63. Josip Obradović, "Participation and Work Attitudes in Yugoslavia."

64. See Bernardo, *The Theory of Moral Incentives in Cuba*, *passim*; and Bernardo, "Managing and Financing the Cuban Firm Like a Government Office," in *Revolutionary Change in Cuba*, ed. Carmelo Mesa-Lago (Pittsburgh: University of Pittsburgh Press, 1971).

65. See Carmelo Mesa-Lago, "Conversion of the Cuban Economy to Soviet Orthodoxy," *Journal of Economic Issues* 8, no. 1 (March 1974):41-66.

66. Bernardo, *The Theory of Moral Incentives in Cuba*, pp. 130-134.

67. See Jan S. Prybyla, "The Economics of Maoism: China's Economy since the Great Proletarian Cultural Revolution," Unpublished Manuscript, 1971; and Hoffman, "The Maoist Economic Model," pp. 24-25. Under the Tachai Scale System agricultural workers receive work points based on periodic self and group evaluations. While personal and civic qualities have taken precedence over productivity, evaluations are made according to five criteria: high skills; enthusiasm and motivation for work; support by the masses; honesty; and class consciousness. The Tach'ing System in industry, set forth in the Constitution of the Anshan Iron and Steel Company, is based on several principles: (a) "grasp revolution and spur production"; (b) "politics in command" (versus "production in command"); (c) "strengthen party leadership"; (d) "launch vigorous mass movements"; (e) "cadre participation in productive labor and worker participation in management" (the "two participations" or "two-group rotation" system); (f) "reform of irrational and outdated rules and regulations;" (g) "close cooperation among cadres, workers, and technicians" (the "three-thirds" or "triple-combination"system); and (h) "go full steam ahead with the technical revolution."

68. The assumption that there are "typical" organizations is a methodological convenience only. Whyte observes that some organizations in China approximate the Maoist ideal, "while others diverge in various ways: toward a more traditional bureaucratic pattern, toward a personal despotism or a more totalitarian pattern, toward a more decentralized pattern, and so forth." See Whyte, "Mao Tse-tung Versus Max Weber."

69. See Rudi Supek, "Two Types of Self-Managing Organizations and Technological Progress," *Participation and Self-Management* 1:150-173.

70. See Josip Golčić, *Analiza Struktura Utjecaja u Samoupravnom Odlučivanju u Brodogralištu "3 Maj" Rijeka* [An Analysis of the Structure of Influence in Self-Managed Decision-Making in the "May Third" Shipyards in Rijeka] (Zagreb: Institute for Social Research, 1970). Other studies which reach similar conclusions have been published by the Institute for Social Research in Zagreb.

71. See Bernardo, *The Theory of Moral Incentives in Cuba*, pp. 64-65. Since 1971, labor allocation has increasingly operated through wages and economic incentives.

72. See Milenkovitch, *Plan and Market in Yugoslav Economic Thought*, pp. 270-271.

73. See *Neki Pokazatelji Razvoja Jugoslavije, Socijalističkih Republika i Autonomnih Pokrajina, 1950-1970* (Belgrade: Savezni Zavod za Statistiku, 1971), pp. 19-22.

74. Milenkovitch (*Plan and Market in Yugoslav Economic Thought*, p. 260) notes that labor migration is closely correlated with job availability and rates of pay, which are considerably higher in northern republics. The greatest proportion of labor migrants abroad (approximately 60%) comes from Slovenia, Croatia, and Central Serbia.

75. The predominance of economic goals in Cuban organizations does not affect the thesis that sub-goals include equality and de-alienation, and that an exclusive focus on economic objectives would not have required moral stimulation and budgetary finance. See Bernardo, *The Theory of Moral Incentives in Cuba*, pp. 3-25.

76. See, e.g., M. George Zaninovich, "Yugoslav Party Evolution: Moving Beyond Institutionalization," in *Authoritarian Politics in Modern Society*, ed. S.P. Huntington and C.H. Moore (New York: Basic Books, 1970).

77. See Hoffman, "The Maoist Economic Model"; and Jack Gray, "The Chinese Model: Some Characteristics of Maoist Policies for Social Change and Economic Growth," in *Socialist Economics*, ed. Alec Nove and D.M. Nuti (Baltimore: Penguine Books, 1972), pp. 491-510.

78. Conflicts over the extent of "politicization" of economic decisions were basic to the events surrounding the expulsion of Aleksandar Ranković from party and government posts in July 1966. Leaders from northern republics, notably Edvard Kardelj, were spokesmen for "depoliticized" decision-making. See Richard P. Farkas, "The Politics of Economic Decision-Making in Yugoslavia," Unpublished Manuscript (State University of New York at Geneseo, 1970).

79. See John G. Gurley, "Capitalist and Maoist Economic Development," pp. 324-356.

80. See studies by Adizes; Rus; and Kavčić, Rus, and Tannenbaum, cited above. See also Bogdan Kavčić, "Some Trends in the Development of Self-Management," in *Participation and Self-Management*.

81. Whyte, "Mao Tse-tung Versus Max Weber," pp. 18-23.

82. See Bernardo, *Theory of Moral Incentives in Cuba*, pp. 25-47. To argue, as does Bernardo (88), that moral incentives are "a way of tapping competitive and status urges in a socially approved manner," simply begs the question of inequality which the Cuban system is purportedly designed to resolve. Competition for status can be as repressive and alienating as competition for material gain, as the sociological study of modern managerial elites has shown. On balance the competition for moral prizes seems to be primarily individual, not collective.

83. For a conceptualization of the Soviet economy as one large hierarchical organization, see David Granick, "Managerial Incentives in the USSR and in Western Firms: Implications for Behavior," *Journal of Comparative Administration* 5, no. 2 (August 1973):169-199.

84. Bernardo, *Theory of Moral Incentives in Cuba*, pp. 59-60. While success indicators employed in the Tachai and Tach'ing systems are social, political, and personal, Emulation Offices apply such impersonal economistic criteria of success as the following: (a) "Control of each worker's tasks, including quality control; (b) Monthly control of basic materials cost for such items as metal, wood, fuel, cotton, auxiliary materials. . .; (c) Daily control of attendance and punctuality. . . . In case management fails in complying with these measures, the labor union section is obliged to denounce it so that superior bodies may take the appropriate disciplinary measures." (p. 60) Labor discipline in China is enforced by enterprise groups themselves. In Yugoslav firms, special committees perform disciplinary functions, as do informal groups which exercise pressures to produce for the collective so as to share benefits in the form of higher average wages.

85. Variations in the size and modernity of Chinese firms nevertheless influence the scope of participation in management. A 1972 article warned that "Particularly in large enterprises it is imperative to guard against the tendency to stress unduly management by the masses, while ignoring management by specialized personnel." See Christopher Howe, "Labour Organization and Incentives in Industry, Before and After the Cultural Revolution," in *Authority, Participation and Cultural Change in China*, ed. Stuart R. Schram (Cambridge, England: The University Press, 1973), p. 254.

86. See M.D. Jezernik, "Changes in the Hierarchy of Motivational Values in Slovenian Industry," *Journal of Social Issues* 24 (1968):103-114.

87. See references to Rus, Supek, and Kamušić above. A recent study presents highly interesting findings concerning the role of the League of Communists. While decisions involving strictly economic activities were made by managers and technicians, decisions involving socio-cultural goals were heavily influenced by party members. Two issue areas, both of which are directly related to social obligations of the collective, were particularly important: (a) cooperation, joint ventures, and integration with other enterprises; and (b) distribution of personal incomes. See Josip Obradović, "Distribution of Participation in the Process of Decision-Making on Problems Related to the Economic Activity of the Company," in *Participation and Self-Management* 2:137-164.

88. See Zaninovich, *The Development of Socialist Yugoslavia*, pp. 106-107, 113.

89. See Neca Jovanov, "Le rapport entre le grève comme conflit social et l'autogestion comme systeme social," *Participation and Self-Management* 1:62-96; and Ichak Adizes, "Economic Change in Yugoslavia," *East Europe* 21, no. 10 (October 1972):16.

90. See Ezra Vogel, "Politicized Bureaucracy: Communist China," *Newsletter on Comparative Studies of Communism* 4, no. 3 (May 1971):23-33.

91. See note 66, above.

92. See Richard Carson's discussion of success indicators in his contribution to this volume; and Bernardo, *Theory of Moral Incentives in Cuba*, pp. 59-60.

93. Carmelo Mesa-Lago, "The Conversion of the Cuban Economy to Soviet Orthodoxy."

94. Bernardo (*Theory of Moral Incentives in Cuba*, pp. 71) notes that a major principle of wage differentials is "the long-run material encouragement of the formation of badly needed technical skills. This can be regarded . . .as a future allocative function since its purpose is to attract students to enter the technical professions and encourage workers to upgrade their skills by enrolling in technical courses."

95. See Yugoslav National Report, XVI International Conference on Social Welfare, *Developing Social Policy in Conditions of Rapid Change* (The Hague, Netherlands, August 13-19, 1972), pp. 9-10. Wachtel's (*Worker's Management and Wage Differentials in Yugoslavia*) estimates for the 1965-1968 period range as high as 6.5:1. On wage differentials in Cuba see Bernardo, *Theory of Moral Incentives in Cuba*, pp. 70-71; and Mesa-Lago, *The Labor Sector and Socialist Distribution in Cuba*. In Cuba, leading government officials are exempted from the generally applied wage scheme.

96. See Howe, "Labour Organization and Incentives in Industry," pp. 241-254. Complexities of the wage system are discussed in detail in Howe, *Wage Patterns and Wage Policy in Modern China, 1919-1972* (Cambridge, England: The University Press, 1973).

97. See, e.g., Eckstein, "Economic Development and Political Change in Communist Systems," pp. 494-495.

98. See, e.g., Stane Možina, "T-Grupe—Uspešan Vid Obrazovanja Rukovodećih Radnik," *Moderna Organizacija* 1 (1970):23-34; and Ernest Vršec, "Grupno Nagradjivanje u Alatnici," *Moderna Organizacija* 1 (1970):35-50.

99. Amendments 21-23, concerning "basic units of associated labor." See Jovan Djordjević et al., *Teorija i Praksa Samoupravljanja u Jugoslaviji* (Belgrade:

Radnička Štampa, 1972), pp. 1127-1131, for texts of Amendments 21 and 22.

100. Bernardo, *Theory of Moral Incentives in Cuba*, p. 55, does refer to "task-oriented groups" and "emulation assemblies," although their overall significance in enterprises seems marginal.

101. See Adizes, *Industrial Democracy*, pp. 251-254.

102. See Golčić, *Analiza Struktura*; and Novosel, "Self-Managerial Participation and the Great China Wall of Communication."

103. Silvano Bolčić, "The Value System of a Participatory Economy," in *Participation and Self-Management* 1:111, Tables 10 and 11.

104. Adizes, *Industrial Democracy*, p. 147.

105. See Harry Harding, "Maoist Theories of Policy-Making and Organization: Lessons from the Cultural Revolution," Publication R-487-PR, RAND Corporation (Santa Monica, 1969), pp. 4-13.

106. Bernardo (*Theory of Moral Incentives in Cuba*, p. 51) suggests that "informal bargaining between administrators and workers and their various organizations, blunts the bias towards coercive administrative direction."

107. See Bolcić, in "The Value System of a Participatory Economy." Self-management as a value ranked eighth in a scale of nine items, according to this 1971-72 survey.

108. See Dunn, "The Economics of Organizational Ideology."

109. See chapter 3: "Government and Society: Towards Institutionalization" in Carmelo Mesa-Lago, *Cuba in the 1970's: Pragmatism and Institutionalization* (Albuquerque, N.M.: University of New Mexico Press, 1974).

110. Whyte, "Mao Tse-tung Versus Max Weber," concludes that organizational processes approximate the Maoist ideal-type, notwithstanding organizational diversity and exceptions to general practices.

111. The best source here is Andors, "Revolution and Modernization," who compares Chinese organizations to Scanlon Plan companies in the United States.

112. This issue has been widely debated in Yugoslav journals and in the press. A 1970 issue of *Moderna Organizacija*, published by the Advanced School for the Organization of Work in Kranj, expressed concern with the growth of elitism in schools of industrial management, modelled largely after the Carnegie Institute of Technology in Pittsburgh and the Sloane School of Industrial Management at M.I.T. The article ended with a commitment to the need for a small elite of experts, as well as a large mass of skilled workers. See *Moderna Organizacija* 4 (1970):242-243.

113. Bernardo, *Theory of Moral Incentives in Cuba* (pp. 44-45), notes that moral incentives have been largely ineffective as a managerial tool, except in cases involving massive labor mobilization, as during the 1970 Sugar Harvest.

114. See Andors, "Revolution and Modernization."

115. Rus, "Influence Structure in Yugoslav Enterprises;" and Kavčić, Rus, and Tannenbaum, "Control, Participation and Effectiveness in Four Yugoslav Industrial Organizations."

116. See Udy, "Comparative Analysis of Organizations," pp. 687-688, 702-704.

117. This proposition is adapted from J. D. Thompson, *Organization in Action* (New York: McGraw-Hill, 1968), pp. 132-144. For an application of this proposition to organizational change in Yugoslavia see Dunn, "Ideology and Organization in Socialist Yugoslavia."

118. Group exchange structure and dialectical decision strategy, as a pure type, have been adapted with changes of language from J.D. Thompson and Arthur

Tuden, "Strategies, Structures and Processes of Organizational Decision," in *Readings in Managerial Psychology*, ed. H.J. Leavitt and L.R. Pondy (Englewood Cliffs, N.J.: Prentice-Hall, 1966), pp. 203-204.

119. Harding, "Maoist Theories of Policy-making and Organization," pp. 7-8.

120. Andors, "Revolution and Modernization," pp. 418-419, observes that by 1963 the primacy of politics had been undercut. Firms concentrated largely on policy and operations in a context of conflicts within the party over its proper role in setting goals, or implementing them.

121. Kavčić, Rus, and Tannenbaum, "Control, Participation and Effectiveness in Four Yugoslav Industrial Organizations."

122. Tanić, "Dimensions and Factors of the Apperception of Self-Management," p. 149, concludes: "The claims that our working class is not yet politically mature and able to manage directly the development of the society are groundless."

123. This is one conclusion of Paul Blumberg, *Industrial Democracy: The Sociology of Participation* (London: Constable, 1968).

124. See Bernardo, *Theory of Moral Incentives in Cuba*, pp. 45-47; and Prybyla, "The Economics of Maoism."

125. As Hoffman, in "The Maoist Economic Model," p. 17, observes, the operation of the principle of democratic centralism as a means for achieving direct mass participation "calls for three guidelines: (a) allowing everyone to have his say; (b) consulting repeatedly on important matters; and (c) paying attention to the view of the few since they are sometimes correct."

126. See Jovanov, "Le rapport entre le grève. . . , " p. 79.

127. See Wachtel, *Worker's Management and Wage Differentials in Yugoslavia*, chapters 2 and 3.

128. See Drago Tović, "Walls Between People," *Vjesnik u Srijedu* (27 October 1971), pp. 23-26.

129. See Jan Tinbergen, "On the Optimum Social Order," in Broekmeyer, *Yugoslav Workers' Self-Management*.

130. See Skinner and Winckler, "Compliance Succession in Rural Communist China"; and Mesa-Lago, "A Continuum Model for Global Comparison," elsewhere in this volume. Although this author does not agree in all respects with the conceptualization of cycles by Mesa-Lago and Skinner and Winkler, these contributions mark a basic advance over conventional linear approaches to change in socialist systems. Mesa-Lago's piece, in particular, gave rise to a series of questions which the following approach seeks partially to answer.

131. Skinner and Winckler, "Compliance Succession in Rural Communist China," p. 414, regard sequential attention over time as the "basic cause" of cycles in China. For the original formulation of the two modes of conflict resolution see R. M. Cyert and J. G. March, *A Behavioral Theory of the Firm* (Englewood Cliffs, N. J.: Prentice-Hall, 1963), chapter 6.

132. Whyte, "Mao Tse-tung Versus Max Weber," p. 25.

133. See Ichak Andizes and J. Fred Weston, "Comparative Models of Social Responsibility," *Academy of Management Journal* 16, no. 1 (March 1973):112-128.

134. George Lukàcs, *History and Class Consciousness* (Cambridge, Mass.: Harvard University Press, 1971), p. 299. Cited in Jurgen Habermas, *Theory and Practice* (Boston: Beacon Press, 1973), p. 34.

# 7

# Liberalization Processes

Andrzej Korbonski

The relatively recent concern of political scientists with the problem of change in communist societies can only be applauded. After years of sticking rather stubbornly to the notion that only systems other than communist can "change," "develop," or "modernize," scholars who over the years had made a name for themselves by analyzing various aspects of the "totalitarian," "mobilization," or "command" syndromes concluded that their professional credibility was at stake unless they mended their ways and acknowledged if not the bankruptcy then at least the disutility of their models as analytical tools to be used for explanatory and predictive purposes with regard to the post-Stalinist communist systems.

Space does not permit a discussion of the reasons for the disenchantment with the old models, or the parentage of this particular development: they are by now too well known to be repeated once again even if they still remain somewhat controversial. Clearly, they stemmed from two sources: the general intellectual ferment in Western social sciences under the loose heading of "behaviorism," and a growing belief among the more articulate practitioners in the field that the demise of the totalitarian model, accompanied by a growing availability of political, economic and social data, made the traditional distinction between "communist" and "non-communist" systems obsolete and redundant. This meant, in turn, that the whole galaxy of analytical tools developed in the "Western" (non-communist) setting should (and could) from now on be applied in the communist context.

This is roughly the situation at the present time. The challenge issued to political scientists concerned with communist Europe did not remain unheeded and was followed by the appearance of a number of books and monographs which either advocated or utilized a variety of approaches hitherto confined almost exclusively to the study of advanced industrial societies and, somewhat paradoxically, the less developed countries.[1] In addition to the synthetic and individual country studies there was born also a new scholarly field—"comparative communism"—which reflected on the one hand the continuing fragmentation and differentiation within the communist systems in Europe and Asia, and on the other hand the overwhelming urge of Western social scientists to compare, to quantify, and to operationalize.

The results of this attempt to "modernize" communist studies appear to be mixed. The new emphasis on the application of rigorous and sophisticated methodology and research techniques was responsible for the emergence of several interesting and valuable studies analyzing various systemic components and processes such as party elites, recruitment patterns, socialization policies, group behavior, and the like.[2]

At the same time, however, the new developments in the Soviet and East European field—in both comparative politics and international relations—reached the stage where superficially elaborate frameworks and schemes tended to produce often trivial and inconsequential results. Thus some of the East European specialists seemed to "have returned to the ancient art of scholasticism, armed to be sure with new terminology, but not any more successful than were the ancients in narrowing the gap between abstract formulations and theoretical realities."[3] It appeared that some of them were almost eager to repeat the errors committed by their opposite numbers in other geographic areas who in their zeal to be more "scientific" tended to lose sight of the one thing they were supposed to be concerned with—politics. Moreover, as it was suggested recently, "one could ask whether the behavioral approach is not as culture-bound as the older legal-institutional or traditional approach it is meant to supplant."[4]

The purpose of this paper is to take the middle road between the "traditionalists" and the "behaviorists" in an effort to throw some light on one particular aspect of the process of political change in Eastern Europe which I shall call "liberalization." Some nine years ago Allen Kassof made the astute observation that "to say that the system is being liberalized is like walking away backwards from a receding reference point, a procedure that gives too little information about what lies on the road ahead."[5] More recently I tried in a somewhat unsystematic fashion to scan "the road ahead" with the aid of a checklist of conditions which in my opinion accompanied the process of liberalization in Eastern Europe and which were assumed to determine its outcome.[6] "Liberalization" was chosen as a dependent variable while the dozen or so conditions were perceived, at least implicitly, as independent variables. The paradigm was applied to three countries—Czechoslovakia, Hungary, and Poland—in an attempt to predict the chances of liberalization in the individual countries becoming more or less permanent.

It must be emphasized that the analysis was highly preliminary and as such it was frequently conceptually weak and methodologically ambiguous. Moreover, it not only left out a number of variables but the various judgments regarding the range of changes in the variables were often impressionistic and not buttressed by concrete evidence. The present study will address itself to some of the above issues in the hope of advancing the discussion of liberalization in Eastern Europe a step further.

There are some problems that are not specifically discussed in the paper. For example, no attempt is made to define the concept of "change." This has been done by others and in the context of this article there is no need to summarize the various arguments.[7] The same applies to the concept of a system, "political" or otherwise: for the purpose of this particular discussion any one of the available definitions will do.[8] Finally, in comparing the political systems and patterns of liberalization, the paper does not pretend to postulate any far-reaching hypotheses or to engage in theory-building. To borrow two of Tucker's terms, its scope falls between the "empirical" and "generalizing" comparisons.[9] It is primarily confined to the task of identifying, defining, and classifying conditions and variables associated with the process of liberalization which result in the emergence of a "liberalized" system.

*The Concept of Liberalization*

The concept of liberalization is not easy to define and its meaning lies in the eye of the beholder. It can be viewed as both a state and a process. A "liberalized" communist political system is postulated to be the ultimate result of a process of change in a number of variables and can be defined in a variety of ways. While it is true that "general agreement on a precise definition of 'liberalization' would probably be impossible to achieve,"[10] all available definitions seem to contain at least one common concept, that of "pluralism." One might possibly include here also "freedom of expression" and/or "decentralization" in political and economic decision-making although it can be argued that the concept of pluralism implies the existence of more than one center or level of decision-making which in turn carries with it the possibility for each decision-making body or an interest group to articulate its views in a relatively unrestricted fashion. Since the concept of pluralism itself is not unambiguous, it was felt that a broader rather than a narrower definition might reduce that ambiguity, and for the purpose of this discussion a "liberalized" system was defined as one containing a measure of pluralism, a degree of political and economic decentralization, and an opportunity for free expression by the participants.[11]

Since the value of a definition lies primarily in its utility for research and theory-building, there are several advantages associated with this particular definition. It is, above all, a "parsimonious" definition which avoids the necessity of using such ambiguous concepts and terms as "assertoric" versus "problematic," "rationalization," and "self-fulfillment," all of which are subject to controversy and are impossible to operationalize.[12] The definition also seems to be "neutral" in the geographic and systemic sense, which permits us to compare liberalization in various countries and systems regardless of their respective levels of political and economic development. By being "low-key" it enables us to conduct meaningful research in the absence of a fully satisfactory data base. Hence, as mentioned earlier, liberalization as a dependent variable is defined broadly rather than narrowly; it is not culture-bound, and although it may not be conceptually watertight, its drawbacks are more than offset by its simplicity and its empirical verifiability. In the final analysis, however, Inkeles' well-known admonition still holds true.[13]

The most controversial component of liberalization in its static sense is clearly the notion of pluralism. On the one hand, it is felt that the concept makes little if any sense in the communist context for the simple reason that a non-democratic system, however defined, makes the idea of pluralism or "group politics" essentially meaningless.[14] On the other hand, the proponents of the group approach claim that the concepts of pluralism and interest groups have been interpreted too narrowly and that they were guilty of the perennial sin of "ethnocentrism."[15]

There is little doubt that both sides in the controversy are correct to some extent. It is obvious that articulation of interest in communist societies is not perfectly "free" and that the groups are not autonomous and are at the mercy of the ruling party which restricts the scope of their activities to narrowly defined non-political and largely technical issues, and which can lift its imprimatur at any time. Thus in the strictly formal sense, pluralism has no place in communist polities. It can be argued, however, that the above view is too restrictive to be of much value for research purposes. To quote a recent suggestion: "In order to push on with serious studies of interest group politics in the Soviet Union we must first rid ourselves of the constricting belief that group theory applies only to groups which operate openly and straightforwardly within a political culture which not only tolerates, but celebrates, pluralism."[16] What is true for the USSR is obviously even truer for the majority of East European countries. Enough empirical evidence has been accumulated over the past few years to indicate that there is considerable group activity going on in communist systems, including even the Soviet Union, and that interest articulation has become (or is in the process of becoming) legitimized by the ruling party.[17]

In a recent article Jerry Hough suggested a possible way out of the dilemma by introducing the concept of "institutional pluralism."[18] While Hough found it useful for the purpose of analyzing the post-Khrushchevian Soviet political system, it seems that it is even more applicable to Eastern Europe.

The "model" consists of six characteristic features: the existence of multiple interests that are presumably freely articulated; the presence of conflicts among alliances whose membership tends to vary in accordance with shifting interests; the resolution of conflicts that takes place through negotiation and bargaining among interested parties; political leaders who perform the function of brokers or mediators; decision-making processes which involve the participation of both experts as well as those to be affected by the outcome; and the political process that is characterized by incrementalism.

One of the major advantages of Hough's model is that it does not focus on any specific variable in the political system such as, for example, the ruling party despite the obvious temptation to do so. Not only did the classic definition of totalitarianism postulate the presence of a monolithic party as a *sine qua non* of the totalitarian system, but there is also a tendency to focus on the change in the character of the ruling party as the necessary and sufficient condition of liberalization or democratization emphasizing the appearance of "collective leadership," "full intra-party democracy," and open party membership. The concept of "institutional pluralism" implicitly puts the party on a more or less the same footing as other elites and groups, which is particularly useful for the purpose of this investigation which is not intended to analyze in detail changes in the individual variables, but is more interested in their outcome.

The question to be faced next is: how does one measure pluralism? The simplest, albeit the most primitive, way would be to count the number of political parties, interest groups, and other associations of various hues operating within a given system. This would obviously be a poor and misleading yardstick, since what we are after are not "transmission belts" but organizations that articulate and aggregate their interests *vis-à-vis* the ruling elite and which participate in a genuine fashion in the political process. It can also be argued in theory that even in a one-party state totally devoid of any other associational groups we may still witness the existence of pluralistic tendencies in the ruling party unless the latter happens to be of the orthodox totalitarian character.

In view of the limitations imposed by the still often paranoiac communist systems, the only way to validate empirically the presence or absence of pluralism is to engage in a rather painstaking task of assembling a collection of case studies showing the interaction between the various categories of elites in different countries. While this type of research would have been difficult if not impossible less than a decade ago, the gradual loosening of several of the East European political systems provides an opportunity for the study of institutionalized group activities. Such research could also be supplemented by content analysis of mass media and by the study of elections and decision-making processes at various levels. While the accumulated evidence may not fully satisfy the purists, it is likely to show that even in such hitherto orthodox countries as Czechoslovakia and East Germany "nothing is monolithic about society or the political system, and no single interest dominates either. The political process revolves around conflict among a complex set of cross-cutting and shifting alliances of persons with divergent interests."[19]

It was suggested earlier that "freedom of expression" ought possibly to be considered as a necessary prerequisite of a "liberalized" communist system. The reason for it is that control over means of expression appears to be the most cherished and jealously guarded prerogative of a repressive ruling elite, and a decision to reduce or relinquish that control usually marks the critical breakthrough in the process of liberalization. Thus the abandonment of mass media censorship in the spring of 1968 not only accelerated the process of liberalization in Czechoslovakia, but also made it into a truly popular mass movement. The same was largely true for Hungary in 1956, and for Poland in 1956-1957 and since 1971. There is some evidence to suggest that a similar process is currently taking place in East Germany and Rumania as part of a gradual political relaxation observed in both countries. Conversely, re-imposition or tightening of media controls is usually the first sign that re-compression is about to take place.

As was the case with pluralism, the notion of "freedom of expression" has also to be qualified. What is meant here is not the Western concept of legally guaranteed freedom to criticize and challenge the established system, but the official imprimatur granted to groups and individuals to voice their views. The permission can be withdrawn at any time and it usually concerns a carefully circumscribed area of technical expertise and/or cultural and artistic endeavor; within the imposed limits (which are by no means inflexible) there is a good deal of argumentation, advocacy, criticism, and debate. The concept of free expression is not easily measurable. Legal-constitutional guarantees tend to be largely meaningless and here, once again, we have to rely on case studies and content analysis.

The final component of a "liberalized" system—"decentralization"—implies both the participation of groups and individuals other than the ruling elite in the decision-making process and the devolution of authority from the center on down to lower-level governmental institutions and economic enterprises. It was suggested earlier that both freedom of expression and decentralization stem directly from the presence of pluralism and that both are not really independent conditions. Still, decentralization frequently goes hand in hand with the abolition of censorship as the two most identifiable variables in the process of liberalization, and singling them out for special attention was motivated by the desire to make the concept of a "liberalized" system easier to understand and to operationalize.

Decentralization in this particular context refers mainly to the economic sphere and is usually tied in to a series of economic reforms aimed at reducing the extent of central planning and at introducing elements of market mechanism into the economy. The final "model" of the economic system tends to stress increased authority of government agencies below the ministerial level and growing autonomy of enterprises. It is more often than not the outcome of prolonged discussions and preparations which involve the participation of specialized elites called upon to provide expert advice which take advantage of the enlarged scope of free discussion to articulate their demands and resolve their conflicts. Economic decentralization is usually accompanied or followed by an administrative decentralization which gives greater responsibility to local government bodies.

In contrast to the other two conditions, decentralization is relatively easy to measure. In the economic sphere the share of GNP produced by the "reformed" or "decentralized" sectors can be taken as an indicator. In the absence of reliable GNP statistics, gross output figures, employment data, or other economic data can be used (e.g., capital assets). In the area of public administration the situation is less clear; apart from institutional arrangements, which often do not mean much, one might again look at the relationship between central and local governments in such sectors as education, public health, planning, and others.

The concept of a "liberalized" system is next applied to three East European countries (Czechoslovakia, Hungary, and Poland) at four different points of time. The reasons for selecting these particular countries were simple. All of them have gone through a "liberalized" stage at least once in the last twenty years which afforded a base for a meaningful comparison. Moreover, a fairly impressive data base has been accumulated over the years for each of them, permitting the making of judgments grounded for the most part in some empirical evidence. Except for Yugoslavia, which can be said to belong to a hybrid category all by itself, no other country in Eastern Europe has so far come close to the above three with regard to the depth of systemic transformation and availability of data.

Each component in the "liberalization" syndrome was assigned a ranking of "high," "mixed," and "low," indicating the intuitive judgment reflecting the relative magnitude of pluralism, freedom of expression, and decentralization. The final judgment denotes the relative level of "liberalization" of the political system at different intervals. It is derived as the sum of the three variables all of which are assumed to carry identical weights. The result appears in Table 1.

The Table 1 comparison must be taken with a considerable amount of salt. To begin with, the four points in time were not randomly selected but they corresponded to major "liberal" upheavals in the three countries: the "Hungarian Revolution" of October-November 1956; the "Polish October" of 1956; the "Prague Spring" of 1968; and the "December Events" of 1970 in Poland. This was done mainly for illustrative purposes since these particular dates represented conven-

**Table 1**

*"Liberalized" Systems in Eastern Europe*

| | *CZECHOSLOVAKIA* | | | | *HUNGARY* | | | | *POLAND* | | | |
|---|---|---|---|---|---|---|---|---|---|---|---|---|
| | *1953-54* | *1955-56* | *1967-68* | *1970-71* | *1953-54* | *1955-56* | *1967-68* | *1970-71* | *1953-54* | *1955-56* | *1967-68* | *1970-71* |
| Pluralism | low | low | high | low | mixed | high | mixed | high | low | high | low | mixed-high |
| Freedom of expression | low | low | high | low | low | high | mixed | mixed | low | high | low | high |
| Decentralization | low | low | high | mixed | low | low | mixed | high | low | low | low | mixed |
| Level of Liberalization | low | low | high | low-mixed | low-mixed | high-mixed | mixed | high | low | high-mixed | low | mixed-high |

ient sign-posts on the path of change away from the Stalinist model of 1953.

The judgments or rankings of "high," "mixed," and "low" are largely intuitive and impressionistic and are not based on any solid empirical evidence. This means that they do not fully reflect the situation in each country at a particular point in time. They are intended to describe approximately the degree of "liberalization" relative to the other countries in the sample, as well as the degree of "liberalization" in the given country over time. Even then the rankings can be quite misleading: thus Czechoslovakia in 1955-56 was more "liberal" than in 1953-54 although the judgment does not reflect it. Hungary in 1970-71 did not resemble Hungary on the eve of the 1956 revolt, and yet the rankings for both periods are roughly similar. Apart from the sheer vagueness of the three components defining the concept of "liberalization" there is, as always, the problem of their relative weights which, for the sake of simplicity, were assumed to be equal.

The above result can also be represented diagrammatically, as in Figure 1. Figure 1 shows the imaginary movement from one level of "liberalization" to another as a straight line. This was done for illustrative purposes and it is not a true reflection of the actual progression or

**Figure 1**

*Level of "Liberalization"*

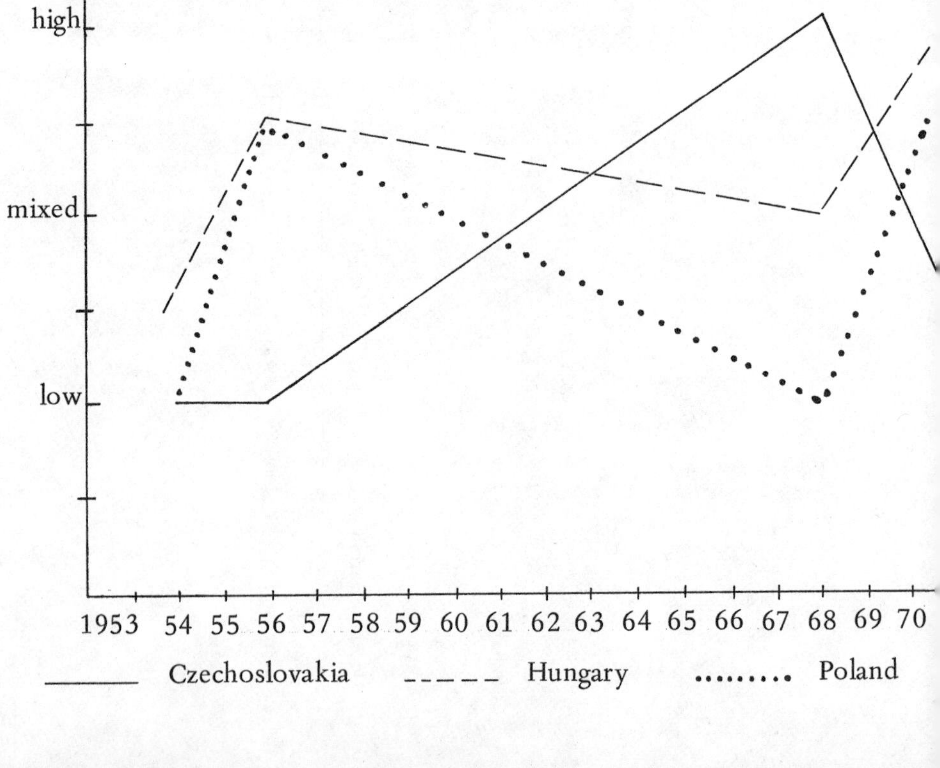

regression, which has seldom been incremental. With some exceptions, the process of change in each country tended to be exponential rather than gradual, discrete rather than continuous. In Hungary, for example, the interval between 1953 and 1956 witnessed the relatively liberal period associated with the premiership of Imre Nagy (1953-1955), followed by the return to power of Rakosi and the resulting tightening of the screw. In Poland, the period after Gomulka's assumption of leadership in October 1956 did not show an instantaneous demise of the "liberalized" system, which persisted with relatively minor changes until the early 1960s before being dismantled. The process of liberalization in Czechoslovakia began several years prior to the "Prague Spring" of 1968. Thus instead of a straight line the movement from one level of "liberalization" to another ought really to be represented by a ratchet or zig-zag curve showing the ups and downs in the process of change.[20]

The results of the comparison are not particularly interesting. Even an unsophisticated observer is likely to notice without great difficulty that in the early 1970s Hungary and Poland were more "liberal" or "liberalized" than Czechoslovakia. The question still remains, however, how the three countries reached the respective stages they happen to be at at different points in time. Thus the time has come to take a look at "liberalization" in its dynamic sense.

*The Dynamics of "Liberalization"*

In the article referred to earlier I attempted to compare the process of liberalization in Czechoslovakia, Hungary, and Poland with the aid of a paradigm composed of twelve variables.[21] The preliminary analysis was intended to accomplish the following:

(1) to identify and categorize conditions accompanying the process of liberalization in each country;

(2) to single out variables responsible for the transition from one stage in the process to the next one;

(3) to postulate a functional-causal relationship between the dependent variable (the "liberalized" system) and the twelve independent variables.

In addition to addressing itself to the above issues this study hopes to accomplish the following tasks:

(1) to tighten the definition of the operative variables;

(2) to suggest methods of operationalizing the variables;

(3) to test the preliminary paradigm on the example of Poland in the period before and after December 1970.

The first six variables in the original "liberalization paradigm" grouped together under the heading of "background conditions" were thought to be responsible for setting the stage for the process of liberalization to get under way. They were: (a) alienation of intellectuals and youth; (b) political reforms; (c) economic difficulties; (d) divisions within the party; (e) contacts with the West; and (f) anti-Soviet attitudes. All these variables were assumed to have been independent of each other and to carry the same relative weight as causal factors.

On second thought, however, it became obvious that these assumptions were highly unrealistic and not especially helpful in explaining the situation in each country on the eve of a major quantum jump in the direction of liberalization. This was particularly true with regard to the notions of "alienation," "contacts with the West," and "anti-Soviet attitudes." There is little doubt that if the intellectuals and the youth felt alienated from the system it was more often than not the result of their contacts with the West and/or of their hostile feelings toward the Soviet Union, compounded further by their perception of the economic difficulties which they interpreted as having been caused by the inefficient performance of the centrally planned economic system. Thus it can be argued that while alienation as an independent phenomenon played a major role in generating demands for a change, the same was not necessarily true for the attitudes to, and contacts with, both the USSR and the West.

Parenthetically it may be noted that while there existed strong anti-Soviet feelings in both Hungary and Poland prior to the upheavals of 1956, the Sovet Union enjoyed considerable popularity in Czechoslovakia almost until the eve of the August 1968 intervention. Furthermore, the December 1970 riots in Poland which brought down Gomulka and initiated the second round of liberalization in that country were, as far as it can be ascertained, largely devoid of anti-Soviet overtones and were the outcome of purely domestic policies. In a somewhat different vein, the changeover in all three countries was accomplished with the Western influence either non-existent or confined to very narrow areas. With minor exceptions the "iron curtain" was still hanging in Poland and Hungary throughout most of 1956, and although Czechoslovakia became a favorite vacation target for West European tourists beginning in the mid-1960s, there is no evidence of the seemingly close contacts with the West having any appreciable impact on the process of liberalization in that country.

Between 1957 and 1962, cultural and economic relations between Poland and the West were expanding at a rapid pace. Several hundred young Polish scholars studied in Western Europe and the United States, many of them in the field of social sciences. Since most of them were actual or prospective members of the political and other elites, it could have been speculated that upon their return to Poland they would join the group of disaffected intellectuals and maintain, if not increase, the pressure in favor of continuing liberalization. For reasons which are still somewhat obscure, the Western-educated intellectuals played a relatively minor role throughout the 1960s which witnessed the retreat from the relatively liberal late 1950s. In contrast, the cultural relations between Czechoslovakia and the West, especially the United States, were practically nil prior to 1968, and yet it was the young scholars, journalists, artists, writers, and students, untouched by personal contacts with the West, who were in the forefront of liberalization. The Hungarian students who refused to listen to Erno Gerö in the crucial days of October 1956 were also untainted by Western influences.

Hence it appears that, on closer look, neither the pro-Western attitudes nor the anti-Soviet feelings had a major independent impact on initiating the process of change in the countries under discussion, and that their influence was mainly confined to the brewing of intellectual ferment among fairly narrow, albeit important, groups and individuals. Thus in the revised paradigm these two variables are eliminated and subsumed implicitly under the heading of "alienation."

The remaining three variables in the first category are felt to be important and relevant, although not equally so. Both "divisions within the party" as well as "economic difficulties" are clearly strategic in the sense of being probably both the necessary and sufficient conditions of liberalization. Intra-party conflict tends to be a *sine qua non* of change, at least in its early stages, in two different ways: lack of consensus within the top elite means, *ceteris paribus*, that the "old" system cannot be maintained in the long or even middle run, while the presence of two or more competing groups within the party oligarchy indicates the potential availability of alternative leadership(s) which may be called upon to take over. The latter may perhaps be truer in theory than in practice but its significance should not be overlooked.

It must be added that while the existence of an intra-party split is a strategic variable largely responsible for the take off of the process of change, the absence of such a conflict may play a dual role: on the one hand, it may well be an important condition guaranteeing the maintenance of *status quo*, and on the other hand, it may also propel the system in the direction of a major change. This can be illustrated with reference to Hungary and Rumania in the late 1960s and early 1970s. There is evidence that both Kadar and Ceausescu have succeeded in creating a united party seemingly loyal to them personally. The apparent absence of factionalism in either party makes it possible for the respective leaders to pursue their policies—maintenance of a largely "liberalized" system in Hungary and continuation of an independent stance in foreign affairs in Rumania. Thus, here again the concept of "division within the party" is not entirely unambiguous.

The variable "economic difficulties" performs a major function in stimulating change in more ways than one. To start with, the performance of the economic system is generally recognized as probably the most important yardstick measuring the success or failure of the existing regime. The presence of high rates of growth and improvement in living standards makes the initiation of the process of change difficult if not impossible, and vice versa. Intra-party conflicts may be due to a variety of causes, but poor economic record is likely to be an important catalyst in destroying or weakening consensus. Moreover, economic stagnation is bound to increase the alienation of intellectuals and especially of youth, whose future is largely dependent on continued rapid economic development.

It may be noted that often it is the relative rather than absolute, perceived rather than actual, change in the economic performance that counts. Neither the economic difficulties in Czechoslovakia in the early 1960s nor the comprehensive price reform in Poland in December 1970 represented major crises in absolute terms, and yet both were seen as such and both gave rise to major upheavals. On the other hand, the East German economic system, at least since the construction of the Berlin Wall in August 1961, has performed rather well if not spectacularly, resulting in a slow but steady improvement in the standard of living, greatly appreciated by the population which, as in all communist countries, tended to be highly sensitive to the ups and downs in the economic performance. The same has largely been true for Rumania, and neither country has shown any signs of a forthcoming systemic change until recently.

The final "background" condition—the "political reforms"—is to a large extent a derivative of the former three variables. Discord within the party is often the source of various kinds of reforms such as amnesty for political prisoners, rehabilitation, upgrading of popularly elected bodies, administrative decentralization, and the like. Economic difficulties tend to be alleviated by resorting to economic reforms aimed at the elimination of the worst features of the traditional command system. Both types of reforms are implicitly intended also to reduce the alienation of key groups in society and to bring them back into the polity.

So much for the "background conditions." The category of "changeover conditions" ("changes in the party," "changes in the government," and "changes in the economy"), which were assumed to cause the appearance of the third stage in the liberalization process, seems unambiguous enough and does not need to be revised.

The same is largely true for the final category, that of "liberalization conditions," with one significant exception. The three original variables in that category—"emergence of pluralism," "abolition of censorship" (now called "freedom of expression"), and "changes in the economy" (to be re-named "economic reforms")—were seen as the necessary conditions for the appearance of a "liberalized" political system. All of them were described earlier and need not be discussed again. However, to make this particular category correspond more closely to reality, an additional variable needs to be introduced—that of "tolerance by other communist countries." It was omitted from the original paradigm which included only the endogenous variables and which treated the reaction of the other members of the bloc as a parameter. This may have simplified the presentation and explication of the paradigm, but it was not very helpful from the explanatory point of view. It is well-established that the opposition of the Soviet Union, Poland, and East Germany was, in the final analysis, responsible for the destruction of the "liberalized" system in Czechoslovakia in 1968, and that the fears of several neighboring countries contributed to the defeat of the Hungarian Revolution of 1956. Conversely, the benign neglect of the Hungarian developments since the early 1960s and the apparent toleration of the current changes in Poland may well spell the difference between the success and failure of the liberal experiment in both countries.

The revised paradigm is, then, as follows:

I. *Background Conditions*
(1) Economic difficulties
(2) Divisions within the party
(3) Alienation of intellectuals and youth
(4) Political reforms

II. *Changeover Conditions*
(5) Changes in the party
(6) Changes in the government
(7) Changes in the economy

III. *Liberalization Conditions*
(8) Emergence of pluralism
(9) Freedom of expression
(10) Economic reforms
(11) Tolerance by other communist countries

One of the more interesting aspects of Figure 2 concerns the transition from stage II to stage III, which determines the direction of the change. Throughout the discussion it was assumed at least implicitly that the process of change in Eastern Europe was uni-directional, resulting in the emergence of a "liberalized" or "modernized" system. However, as Huntington tells us, next to modernization and political development we also have political decay, and the same conditions that may give rise to liberalization can also induce an opposite reaction aimed at reestablishing the "old" system. The direction of the change cannot be determined from the paradigm without having additional information about the country in question. In other words, even if a country scores high in both the "background" and "changeover" categories, it does not mean that liberalization will follow automatically. Unless we know something about the background of the top political elite which assumed authority during the "changeover" stage, and about the character of changes in the party and the economy, it is difficult to predict the direction of the change. Just to make the situation even more unpredictable, the background and political history of the new leadership may be misleading—in either direction. Gomulka, the victim of Stalinism, accused of harboring nationalist sentiments,

# Figure 2

*Liberalization Paradigm*

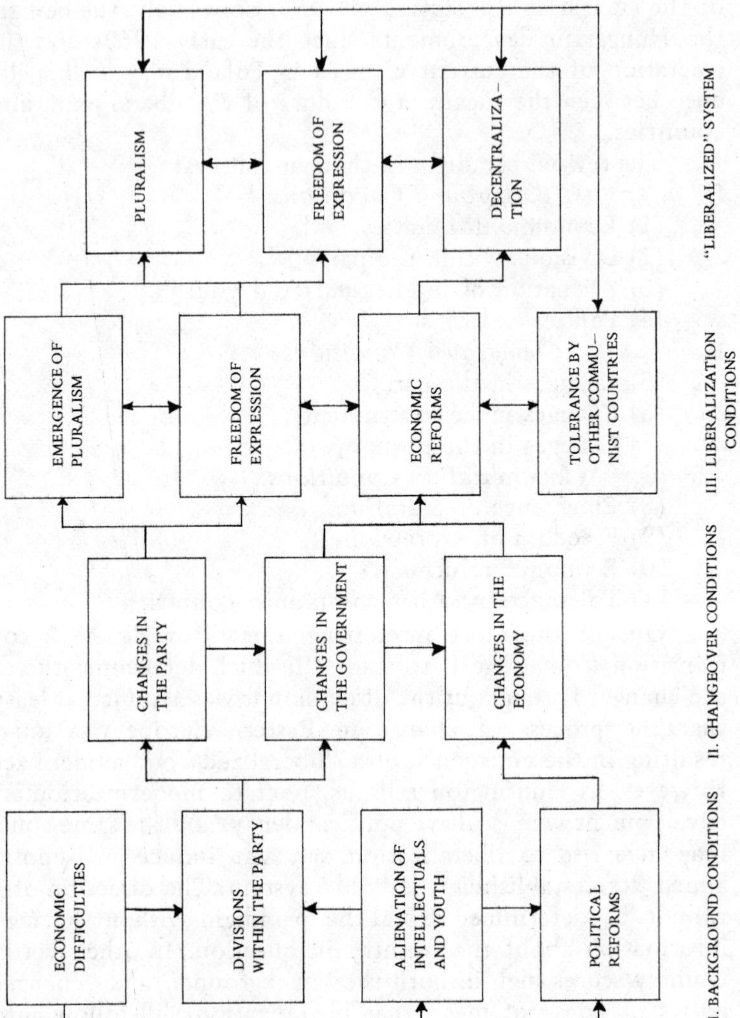

was hailed by one and all in 1956 as the savior of People's Poland who would keep it on a liberal course indefinitely. Five years later it became obvious that the hopes were largely misplaced. In contrast, Kadar, probably the most hated Hungarian communist in late 1956, who was imposed on the country by courtesy of the Soviet army, in a relatively short time turned out to be one of the most popular Hungarian leaders in this century. All of this means that additional factual evidence is often necessary in order to determine that liberalization rather than re-compression will ensue.

It is a truism that a "model" or a "paradigm" can be made particularly useful for explanatory and predictive purposes if its variables can be operationalized or, to put it more crudely, quantified. What follows are some suggestions as to the ways and means of making the "liberalization paradigm" more operational.

Starting with the "background conditions," empirical evidence can be gathered with relative ease only with respect to "economic difficulties." By now it can be taken for granted that East European economic statistics may be more or less trusted to present a true picture of the economy. Hence, it should not be too hard to construct an index reflecting the changes in variables such as GNP, industrial and agricultural output (both absolutely and per capita), retail price and wage levels, housing construction, and others. "Division within the party" is sometimes not easy to demonstrate: here one would have to study the changes in the top party bodies—the Politburo and the Central Committee—and the turnover at the middle and low levels of the apparat, purges and "verification campaigns," and also search the party central and local press for clues of an actual or impending conflict. "Alienation of intellectuals and youth" is also not easily documented: one could possibly look at the numbers of political trials involving both groups (e.g., Poland in 1968-1969), at membership in various voluntary associations, purges of universities, research institutes, editorial boards, youth organizations, etc. Information is not easily accessible but it can be obtained and a quantitative measure arrived at. The final "background" condition—"political reforms"—may perhaps be represented by an index showing the number of released political prisoners, the number of non-communist candidates in various elections, the share of non-party members in the government service and other bureaucracies, and so on.

Moving to the category of "changeover" conditions, information regarding turnover among top party, government, military, and economic elites is generally available. The same is true with respect to the changes at the provincial and local levels, and an appropriate index should not be difficult to construct. The background of delegates to party congresses and conferences, of deputies to the national assemblies and other collective bodies, should provide a clue to the changes in those sub-variables. "Changes in the economy" can be measured with reference to the share of industrial and agricultural output produced by enterprises and farms operating under the "reformed" system. Alternatively, employment or wage bill data can be used.

Among the "liberalization" conditions, "emergence of pluralism" manifested in the numerical growth and increased activity of satellite parties, political clubs, labor unions, and youth and religious organizations can be operationalized with the help of indices showing changes in membership of the various organizations and growth of their participation in the political process at various levels (central and local administration; elections; "National Front" activities; discussions of planned major political, economic, and social reforms, and the like). The variable "freedom of expression" is one of the hardest to measure. One possible indicator may be used showing the variations in the number of citizens traveling to the non-communist countries and the number of Westerners entering the country in question. Both tend to be related to the presence or absence of restrictions and freedom of movement and expression. Another measure may be derived from data on publication and circulation of new journals and books (or closing down and withdrawal of old ones). "Economic reforms" can be operationalized in the same way as the variable "changes in the economy" discussed in the preceding paragraph. Finally, the "tolerance" (or lack of it) of the liberalization process on the part of the other communist countries can best be measured with reference to the frequency and depth of attacks on, or criticism of, the process appearing in the mass media of the hostile countries, or praise and support emanating from the friendly ones. Alternatively, one could also look at the frequency of visits by representatives of the ruling parties of the other countries, which often reflects the lack of happiness with the character and direction of the changes.

While it is clear that the paradigm cannot be easily operationalized, the above discussion shows that the process of change can be measured to some extent, thus making the comparison and prediction more meaningful. It ought to be emphasized, however, that whatever ultimate measures of liberalization emerge from the paradigm, they will still be heavily influenced by the implicit equal weights assigned to the individual variables and aggregate categories. It goes without saying that this is a highly unsatisfactory arrangement, but the alternatives are not much better and equally arbitrary. Thus no one is likely to argue that the importance (weight) of such variables as "economic difficulties" or "division within the party" is greater than those of the other two "background" conditions—but the question still remains: how much greater? Similarly, are the "background" conditions more or less significant than either the "changeover" or "liberalization" conditions? All this means that the final weighted synthetic indicator showing the chance (likelihood? probability?) of a lasting "liberalized" system emerging from the process of change described in the paradigm must be accepted as a first approximation, subject to subsequent revision in the event that new data and/or methodology become available.

There remains the question of periodization or time-span of the liberalization process. In its early version, the paradigm involved the three chosen countries at two different points of time (Hungary and Poland in 1956; Czechoslovakia in 1968). In the paradigm shown in Table 2, the periods preceding the emergence of the "liberalized" system in each country varied in length from three to twelve years. This is not very satisfactory, since the longer the time span, the greater the opportunity for the different variables to unfold and change. The alternative would be to compare the different countries at a single point in time, or to use identical time periods for each stage.[22] The former approach has some advantages, but it is static and the purpose of this paper is to investigate the dynamics of liberalization.

The paradigm was "tested" on the example of Poland in the period 1968-71 and the "fit" appeared surprisingly close. Thus the economic conditions in the country in the second half of the 1960s were deteriorating, and the price reform of December 1970 represented the official acknowledgement of failure. The party was divided at least three ways among the "Partisans" led by Moczar, the "technocrats" headed by Gierek, and the *status quo*-oriented faction under Gomulka. Alienation of intellectuals and youth reached its peak in March 1968 when both the writers and students openly (and unsuccessfully) challenged the Gomulka regime. The widespread purge of Jews and liberals represented a political reform in the negative sense.

Following the Baltic Coast riots, there was an almost complete turnover in the top party and government hierarchy with Gierek assuming the post of First Secretary. Only the top military command remained unscathed while the middle- and low-level party apparat was also largely purged. Changes in the economy were reflected in the rollback of the notorious price reform, the retail price freeze, wage increases, and other changes.

Satellite parties (the Peasant and Democratic parties) showed relatively little activity, probably because they became mostly demoralized during the stagnant sixties. By 1970 the political clubs for all practical purposes disappeared from the scene. In contrast, the labor unions, both formal and informal, having tasted success in December 1970, began to articulate their demands with unprecedented force. The youth organizations which carried the banner of resistance in the spring of 1968 tended to sit on the fence while the Catholic Church, as usual, took advantage of the new configuration of political forces to press anew its traditional desiderata. Freedom of expression, largely dormant during the latter stage of Gomulka's reign, expanded relatively rapidly after Gierek's accession to power. Major agricultural and industrial reforms were announced in 1971, although they were not to be implemented until later. Finally, the whole process was watched carefully by the Soviet Union and its allies without any sign of criticism of the changeover. Hence the chances of a lasting "liberalized" system being established in Poland during the seventies appears to be good.

The revised "liberalization paradigm" applied to Hungary, Czechoslovakia and Poland is shown in Table 2. The different rankings assigned to individual categories and variables for each country and period are based on factual information derived from the literature, mass media, and personal interviews. Space does not permit detailed discussion of every single variable but most of them can be easily documented and verified and only some involve impressionistic and/or intuitive judgments. By and large, the overall verdict regarding the direction of change and the probability of "liberalization" appears reasonable.

A word of caution is required at this stage. Throughout the entire exercise it was implicitly postulated that the three chosen countries had a similar if not identical "national profile." To put it differently, it was tacitly assumed that there were no significant discrepancies among the countries with regard to the conventional measures of "modernization" or "development" (industrialization, urbanization, education, etc.) and no major differences with respect to the types of political culture, patterns of socialization, circulation of elites, bureaucratization, and the like. Needless to say, there were significant national differences in all these categories which were more than likely to supply the extra ingredient that affected both the direction and depth of change in each country. It is also clear, however, that a thorough investigation of all these factors deserves a separate treatment which is obviously impossible within the confines of this study and which should form an important part of the agenda for future research.

*Conclusion and Agenda for Future Research*

It is hoped that the entire discussion will make a contribution, however small, to the understanding of the process of change in Eastern Europe. The purpose of the paper was a modest one: it was intended among other things to bridge the gap between the "traditionalists" and the "behaviorists" by suggesting ways and means of synthesizing factual and historical knowledge with conventional social science analysis which had been hitherto largely neglected and even scorned by scholars in the field of East European studies. The final product is not likely to appeal either to the area specialists or to the "modernizers" but it is hoped that the idea of a "liberalization paradigm" may have some heuristic value, if only by showing the complexity of the process of political change in Eastern Europe and by providing an incentive to delve deeper into the problem.

Throughout the study there were several suggestions regarding the empty boxes that needed to be filled. To begin with, the sample of

# Table 2

## *Liberalization Paradigm*

| | *CZECHOSLOVAKIA* | | | *HUNGARY* | | | *POLAND* | | |
|---|---|---|---|---|---|---|---|---|---|
| | *1953-56* | *1956-68* | *1968-71* | *1953-56* | *1956-68* | *1968-71* | *1953-56* | *1956-68* | *1968-71* |
| I. *Background conditions* | | | | | | | | | |
| 1. Economic difficulties | mixed | mixed | mixed | high | mixed | low | high | mixed | high |
| 2. Divisions within the party | low | high | low | high | low | low | high | mixed | high |
| 3. Alienation of intellectuals and youth | low | high | high | high | high | low | high | mixed | high |
| 4. Political reforms | low | mixed | low | mixed | mixed | mixed | mixed | mixed | mixed |
| *Total judgment* | *low* | *high-mixed* | *mixed-low* | *high* | *mixed* | *low* | *high* | *mixed* | *high-mixed* |
| III. *Liberalization conditions* | | | | | | | | | |
| 5. Changes in the party | high-mixed | high | high | high-mixed | high | low | high-mixed | low | high |
| a. First Secretary | high | high | high | high | high | low | high | low | high |
| b. Presidium (Politburo) | high | high | high | high | high | low | high | low | high |
| c. Central Committee | low | mixed | high | low | high | low | low | low | high |
| d. Other (Congress; lower organs) | low | high | high | low | high | low | low | low | high |
| 6. Changes in the government | mixed | high | mixed-low | mixed | mixed | low | mixed | low | high |
| a. Head of state | high | high | low | low | mixed | low | mixed | low | high |
| b. Council of Ministers | mixed | high | high | high | mixed | low | mixed | low | high |
| c. Armed forces command | low | high | low | high | low | low | high | low | high-mixed |
| d. National assembly (Parliament) | low | mixed | low | low | high | low | mixed | low | mixed |
| 7. Changes in the economy | low | high | mixed | low | mixed | high | mixed | low | mixed |
| *Total judgment* | *mixed-low* | *high* | *mixed* | *mixed* | *high-mixed* | *low* | *mixed* | *low* | *high* |
| II. *Changeover conditions* | | | | | | | | | |
| 8. Emergence of pluralism | low | high | low | high | low-mixed | low | high-mixed | low | high-mixed |
| a. Satellite parties | low | high | low | high | mixed | low | high | low | mixed |
| b. Political clubs | low | high | low | high | mixed | low | mixed | low | low |
| c. Labor unions | low | high | low | high | mixed | low | mixed | low | high |
| d. Youth organizations | low | high | low | high | low | low | high | low | mixed |
| e. Religious organizations | low | mixed | low | mixed | low | low | high | mixed | mixed |
| 9. Freedom of expression | low | high | low | high | mixed | mixed | high-mixed | mixed | high-mixed |
| 10. Economic reforms | low | high | mixed | mixed | mixed | high | mixed | low | high-mixed |
| 11. Toleration by other communist countries | high | low-mixed | high-mixed | low | high | high | mixed | high | high |
| *Total judgment* | *low* | *high-mixed* | *low* | *high-mixed* | *mixed* | *high-mixed* | *high-mixed* | *low* | *high-mixed* |
| *Chances of lasting "liberalized" system* | *low* | *high-mixed* | *low* | *high-mixed* | *mixed* | *high-mixed* | *high-mixed* | *low* | *high-mixed* |

countries ought to be expanded through the addition of other communist countries, above all in Europe, but also elsewhere. The absence of meaningful data bases may make it difficult, but it is my belief that such countries as East Germany and Romania, and even the Soviet Union, could and should be included in future comparative investigations.

The second urgent task has to do with the operationalization of the existing variables and with the possible addition of new ones. The selection of a certain number of variables is, in the final analysis, a matter of personal judgment of the selector which betrays his own biases. While the ultimate choice is arbitrary, the measurement of the change in the variables must be grounded in some empirical evidence if it is to be taken seriously. Thus it is hoped that the steadily growing research opportunities in Eastern Europe will encourage Western (and Eastern) scholars to explore in a more systematic fashion some of the key processes and phenomena which so far have been largely (and surprisingly) neglected. I have in mind here in the first place the research on communist elites, parties, bureaucracies, and pressure groups. Not enough is known about their inner workings, their leaders, and memberships. Sophisticated analytical techniques can now be used, for example, to prove or disprove conventional wisdoms regarding turnover of leaders and mobility of followers. Furthermore, there are gaps in our knowledge of the interaction between the political and other sectors in East European societies. Finally, it would be useful to develop some additional measures showing the range of variations in individual categories and variables. All of these are bound to yield fresh and rewarding insights into the highly complex, and yet also highly interesting, problem of political change in Eastern Europe.

## NOTES

1. Among the better known are Frederic J. Fleron, Jr., ed., *Communist Studies and the Social Sciences: Essays on Methodology and Empirical Theory* (Chicago: Rand McNally, 1971); Chalmers Johnson, ed., *Change in Communist Systems* (Palo Alto, Calif.: Stanford University Press, 1970); and Roger E. Kanet, ed., *The Behavioral Revolution and Communist Studies* (New York: Free Press, 1971), pp. 125-149.

2. For example, R. Barry Farrell, ed., *Political Leadership in Eastern Europe and the Soviet Union* (Chicago: Aldine, 1970); Kenneth Jowitt, *Revolutionary Breakthroughs and National Development: The Case of Romania 1944-1965* (Berkeley and Los Angeles, Calif.: University of California Press, 1971); Joseph R. Fiszman, *Revolution and Tradition in People's Poland* (Princeton, N.J.: Princeton University Press, 1972); Carl Beck *et al.*, *Comparative Communist Political Leadership* (New York: D. McKay Co., 1973); David Lane and George Kolankiewicz, eds., *Social Groups in Polish Society* (New York: Columbia University Press, 1973).

3. Joseph LaPalombara, "Macrotheories and Microapplications in Comparative Politics: A Widening Chasm," *Comparative Politics* (October 1968), p. 54.

4. Karl W. Ryavec, "Kremlinology or Behavioralism"? *Problems of Communism* (January-February 1973), pp. 84-85.

5. Allen Kassof, "The Administered Society: Totalitarianism without Terror," *World Politics* (July 1964), p. 561.

6. "Comparing Liberalization Processes in Eastern Europe: A Preliminary Analysis," *Comparative Politics* (January 1972), pp. 231-249.

7. For an interesting discussion of the definitional and conceptual problems in this particular area, see Samuel P. Huntington, "The Change to Change," *Comparative Politics* (April 1971), pp. 283 ff. See also Chalmers Johnson, "Comparing Communist Nations," and H. Gordon Skilling, "Group Conflict and Political Change," in *Change in Communist Systems*, ed. Chalmers Johnson.

8. For example, the definition of a "system" suggested by Tjalling C. Koopmans and John Michael Montias, "On the Description and Comparison of Economic Systems," in *Comparison of Economic Systems*, ed. Alexander Eckstein (Berkeley, Calif.: University of California Press, 1971), pp. 31-32.

9. Robert C. Tucker, "On the Comparative Study of Communism," *World Politics* (January 1967), pp. 246-247.

10. D. Richard Little, ed., *Liberalization in the USSR: Facade or Reality* (Lexington, Mass.: D. C. Heath, 1968), Introduction, p. 5.

11. "Pluralism" or "group conflict" alone is used by Skilling as a classificatory criterion to arrive at a taxonomy of East European communist systems. My "liberalized" model seems to fit between his "quasi-pluralistic authoritarianism" and "democratizing and pluralistic authoritarianism." H. Gordon Skilling, "Group Conflict and Political Change," pp. 224-225.

12. Kenneth Jowitt, "The Concepts of Liberalization, Integration, and Rationalization in the Context of East European Development," *Studies in Comparative Communism* (April 1971), pp. 81ff.

13. "In my opinion there is no such thing as a right or wrong sociological model. There are richer and poorer ones. There are more sensitive and less sensitive. There are those which are more appropriate to one time or place than another. All have a piece of the truth, but it is rare that any *one* model is really adequate to the analysis of a richly complex concrete historical case." Alex Inkeles, "Models and Issues in the Analysis of Soviet Society," *Survey* (July 1966), p. 3.

14. Andrew C. Janos, "Group Politics in Communist Society: A Second Look at the Pluralistic Model," in *Authoritarian Politics in Modern Society*, ed. Samuel P. Huntington and Clement H. Moore (New York Basic Books, 1970), pp. 441-448.

15. Andrzej Korbonski, "Bureaucracy and Interest Groups in Communist Societies: The Case of Czechoslovakia," *Studies in Comparative Communism* (January 1971), pp. 68-71.

16. David E. Langsam and David W. Paul, "Soviet Politics and the Group Approach: A Conceptual Note," *Slavic Review* (March 1972), pp. 136-137.

17. H. Gordon Skilling, "Interest Groups and Communist Politics: An Introduction," in *Interest Groups in Soviet Politics*, ed. H. Gordon Skilling and Franklyn Griffiths (Princeton, N.J.: Princeton University Press, 1971), pp. 3-18. See also

Francis G. Castles, "Interest Articulation: A Totalitarian Paradox," *Survey* (Autumn 96 ), pp. 116-132.

18. Jerry F. Hough, "The Soviet System: Petrification or Pluralism," *Problems of Communism* (March-April 1972), pp. 27-29.

19. Ibid., p. 28.

20. A possible solution has been suggested by Carmelo Mesa-Lago who utilized a "continuum model" to compare five communist countries (see his study elsewhere in this volume). His ingenious approach avoids a number of pitfalls connected with the above presentation.

21. "Comparing Liberalization Processes in Eastern Europe," pp. 235-236.

22. For example, Mesa-Lago took mid-1968 as the basis for his five-country comparison. Mesa-Lago, "Continuum Model for Global Comparison," elsewhere in this volume.

# 8

# Bureaucracy and Party Control

Paul Cocks

A general phenomenon throughout the communist world since Stalin's death has been the need for his successors to come to terms, in some fashion or other, with their past. In the most fundamental sense, this has entailed attempts to explain, if only to excuse, the abuses of Stalinism. Inevitably, abuse of power or bureaucratism becomes the leitmotif not only of Khrushchev's Secret Speech in 1956, as Robert Tucker notes, but indeed of all reappraisals and denunciations of Stalinism in its various national manifestations.[1]

Not surprisingly, those who have sought to probe deeply the conditions and causes that facilitated the rise of Stalin and of his system of terrorist totalitarian rule have all singled out and decried the absence of any viable restraints against the misuse of power as the fundamental defect of the Soviet system (and Soviet-type systems).* This was the underlying conclusion, for example, of the reform-minded Commission of Inquiry that was set up in Czechoslovakia in 1968 under the Dubcek regime to investigate the political trials and terrorist practices of the fifties. Deploring the unbridled concentration of power that was amassed in the hands of a small elite and the pervasive attitude among the Communist Party membership of uncritical faith and infallibility toward the use of that power, the Commission, in concluding its report, insisted most adamantly, "The Party itself has to find ways and means of controlling power."[2] Similarly, Roy Medvedev, the dissident Russian historian, comes to the same inescapable conclusion in his recent monumental study of Stalinism. "The weakness was in the guarantees and barriers that should have been set up in our Party and

*For purposes of this discussion, the term "totalitarian" is used simply to mean the totalist *aspirations and claims* on society by a political elite that seeks to remake society according to its own preconceived image. The emphasis is on the desire and determination of the elite to amass and maintain in its own hands and to use the totality of power in order to achieve and control political change and social engineering.

state against the rise of leaders like Stalin. It was not the struggle with the autocracy, not jail or exile, that were the real tests for revolutionaries," he says, looking back upon the Bolsheviks. "Much harder was the test of power at a time when the Party acquired almost unlimited power." It was a test, moreover, which Lenin's followers failed miserably, Medvedev claims, by not erecting any effective barriers against bureaucratic decay and the misuse of boundless power.[3]

What are the reasons behind the reluctance and failure of the men who made the October Revolution, and of their successors at home and abroad, to build a viable system of restraints against arbitrary and absolute power? Why is the history of intra-party control organs a melancholy illustration of the inability of communist authoritarian elites to control their own abuses? It is to these questions of intra-party and intra-elite controls that the present study addresses itself. While it takes as its main focus the Russian experience, it seeks at the same time to provide a broad conceptual construct from which to view the problem of controlling communist bureaucracy not only in the CPSU but in a comparative context as well.

### *The Functional Focus of Control: Ethics, Rationality, and Terror*

Generally speaking, it is possible to discern in the history of the Soviet regime the use of fundamentally three kinds of controls and restraints against communist bureaucratism—ethics, rationality, and terror. Which particular form of control is applied depends largely upon whether the phenomenon is perceived to be primarily a moral, technical, or political problem. Within each category of control, moreover, there is both a populist and elitist dimension as well as a Party and non-party dichotomy. A study of the nature and function of Party control, therefore, necessarily entails an examination of the following variables and processes: (a) the changing character of the mix of controls over time; (b) the dynamics of interaction and conflict between ethics, rationality, and terror; (c) the dynamics of interaction and tension between populist and elitist strands within each form of control; and (d) the blurring and breakdown of Party and non-party boundaries among the forms of control and the subsequent disintegration of separate Party and state control systems. Placing the problem of control within a broad historical perspective, one also observes cyclical patterns of development and change. It is almost as if a form of dialectic of success and failure were at work. Forms of control, such as administrative rationalization, which fail or are abandoned at early stages of revolutionary-totalitarian system-building sometimes reemerge later as more appropriate and necessary means for purposes of post-revolutionary and post-totalitarian system change. Similarly, what succeeds or is considered necessary at one time—for example, political terror—may be seen at another time to be ineffective and undesirable.

New conditions and different needs open up new possibilities and foreclose old options. One is reminded of E. H. Carr's observation about the wheels of history: "The apparent failure of today may turn out to have made a vital contribution to the achievement of tomorrow."[4] Men inspired by a particular set of ideas or strategems, such as a Trotsky of the New Course, a Djilas of the New Class, or a Dubcek of the New Face, may be prophets born before their time.

Finally, the breakdown of restraints on the arbitrary use of power in the formative stages of communist rule needs to be viewed from two perspectives: the perceived imperatives of revolutionary-totalitarian system-building and the power needs, interests, and personality of the communist supreme leader who typically dominates this phase of communist political development.[5] In like manner, the effort to rebuild limited restraints back into the system at more advanced stages of communist rule when "collective leadership" becomes more the dominant form of executive command should also be seen to have a dual focus. On the one hand, the increasingly post-revolutionary nature and thrust of communist development ("socialist construction") requires less arbitrary use of power and policies of imposed change from above. On the other hand, it becomes in the interest of the ruling oligarchy itself to impose restraints and mutual controls on arbitrary power which can also be turned against the elite as in the past by a supreme leader. Hence, the developmental needs of post-revolutionary, still more post-totalitarian, system-building and system-maintenance, as well as the power interests of the entrenched ruling elite, coalesce and push for the creation of controls on the excessive abuse of power. These are directed, above all, against the rise again of arbitrary one-man rule and originate first within the Party itself. But the resurrection of intra-party controls is designed principally to protect the ruling elite from the possibility of tyrannical power by one of its own members, while at the same time preserving its monopoly of power. It does not necessarily involve or presage the appearance of broader constraints devised for the purpose of protecting society from arbitrary power and breaking the monopolistic control of its use and abuse by the Communist Party. Indeed, the extent to which a communist regime allows these restraints to emanate from without as well as from within the Party and ruling elite, and permits them to be directed more generally against abuses not only in the Party but on the part of the Party in society as well, may be taken to be a measure of the degree of its "post-totalitarianization" or "de-totalitarianization."[6]

Such, in very skeletal form, is a theoretical construct of the problem of controlling communist abuses that is suggested by the Russian experience. However, as a conceptual tool, the triad of ethics, rationality, and terror may also be useful for comparative study of the communist bureaucratic phenomenon and Party control. It provides at least one analytical handle by which we can try to explore the variety of experience and variability of communist political systems and to explain such divergent remedies to curb bureaucratism as Dubcek's effort to give socialism a human face in Czechoslovakia, the attempt by the post-Stalin and particularly post-Khrushchev leadership to build a more rational and technocratic authoritarian control edifice in the Soviet Union, and Mao's resort to more coercive controls in the Cultural Revolution in China.[7]

*Party Ethics*

At first glance, it may appear incongruous with the communist experience to speak of ethical principles and moral restraints on power. Communists are often described as amoral, even immoral, power-seekers and heartless manipulators whose operational code subordinates ethics to political expediency. The sinister, inhuman, and tyrannical face of Stalinism tends merely to confirm this image. Needless to say, the idea that the practitioners of communism could have ever been men with convictions and consciences has not been given much voice. Perhaps because of this, Djilas himself, fifteen years after his break with Stalinist-deformed communism, still felt a deep need to remind his Western readers, "My past has not been all taken up with revolution and violence; idealism and humanity are part of it, too."[8] Earlier, in *The New Class*, he had described the nature and scope of the moral world of communists largely in terms of a comradely code of ethics among Party members. And it is in this more narrow sense of Party ethics that the term is used in our analytical construct.

What is the nature of Party ethics? Above all, they are conceived to be revolutionary ethics, to denote a moral code among communist revolutionaries which defines and prescribes for Party members proper and improper kinds of relations, modes of behavior, and methods of struggle both inside and outside their ranks. In a sense, Party ethics resemble what Michael Walzer has called the "obligations of oppressed minorities." Communist revolutionary elites are very representative of such minorities, which act typically in relation to two groups: first, within the group that they themselves constitute; secondly, within the larger community and against their oppressors. In depicting the moral life of the oppressed, Walzer notes:

> Not their rights as individuals but their connection to the mass of the oppressed is their reference point in explaining to themselves and to each other what they can and cannot do. . . . Oppressed individuals rarely experience their oppression as individuals. Their suffering is shared, and they come to know one another in a special way.
>
> They have an understanding among themselves which no one outside the circle of oppression can readily share and which no one inside the circle can easily escape.

> From this understanding obligations follow, obligations which they owe one another. . . .
>
> It is the fate of the oppressed that the whole of their moral lives be mediated by their common situation.[9]

This mirrors closely the moral world of communist revolutionaries. Djilas, for example, relates how the latter become attached to each other "not only by ideas and suffering but also by selfless love, comradeship, solidarity, and that warm and direct sincerity that can be produced only by battles in which men are doomed either to win or die." Such relations give rise to a "psychic and moral unity, for which no statutes or laws have been written, but which occurs spontaneously, to become a custom and a conscious habit." "True, these are the morals of a sect," Djilas admits, "but they are morals on a high plane."[10] While they forge the bonds of brotherhood among communist revolutionaries, the principles of comradeship, mutual trust, and confidence also create moral obligations which are supposedly to regulate intraparty human relations. They above all set boundaries against abusive actions and arbitrary behavior on the part of one comrade against another. The roots for such a code of conduct may be traced more generally to the origins of radical politics at the dawn of the modern era with the puritan revolution in England.[11] They are also deeply embedded in the Marxian revolutionary tradition. Indeed, the Party statutes adopted by the First International laid down early the rule that "truth, justice, and morality" were to be the basis of comradely relations and conduct among its members.

Needless to say, this beautiful image of the fraternal world of communist revolutionaries diverges sharply from reality. Just as Walzer notes more generally of solidarity among activists, so among communists there has always been a gaping discrepancy, between actual and ideal coworkers, of belonging to a real organization and a community only dreamed of.[12] Perhaps nowhere was this gap so great as in the Russian revolutionary movement. The Bolsheviks particularly distinguished themselves by their notorious intrigue, ruthless infighting, and embittered polemics. Obviously, such an atmosphere was no soil for a cult of comradeship to implant deep roots. The very acrimony of intra-party struggle among the Russian revolutionaries, however, makes it difficult to imagine that any comradeship ever existed at all. Yet Trotsky, later recalling the times, observed that the movement did live substantially on "its faith in the future and on its spirit of self-sacrifice." "The same ideas, the same struggle, the same danger, and a common isolation from the rest of the world," he stressed, "wielded strong bonds."[13] Furthermore, early in the development of Bolshevism Lenin himself saw comradely influence and trust–Party ethics–as the only viable checks against arbitrary and absolute power within the Party. That he continued to view the problem of communist bureaucratism in part as a personal malady and ethical question is evident from his final "testament," in which he made Stalin's rudeness and capriciousness adequate cause for his removal from the post of Party General Secretary.

While communist ethics impose minimal moral obligations on a Party member in his relations with fellow comrades, they virtually free him of any moral restraints in his actions outside the Party circle in pursuit of revolutionary goals. In fact, the ethical code demands that he "buckle on the armor of revolutionary hardness," to use any means available, no matter how oppressive and unscrupulous, if it serves the mission of the Revolution. As Lenin made plain in 1920, "Morality for us is subordinated to the interests of the class struggle of the proletariat." He had early rejected for the Party a moral tone "approved in schools for daughters of the nobility," which turns revolutionary fighters into "wet hens."[14] Adamantly rejecting the "morality of priests" and any "transcendental knout," he attacked mercilessly all those who tried to drown the problems of the Party and the Revolution in "moralizing vomit." The Russian leader was also willing to overlook excesses and misdemeanors in the personal lives of communists even though they were at variance with a strict moral code which prescribed an almost Spartan and puritan existence. As long as he considered a comrade a useful man, devoted to the Revolution and the Party, he said flatly about misconduct in his private life, "I don't care a damn about the rest."[15] The aims he pursued were supra-personal and he subordinated his moral criteria to them. Revolutionary struggle was above all, Lenin constantly reiterated, "struggle without kid gloves."

What underlies, indeed justifies, this ethical code with its double standard of conduct inside and outside the Party, toward comrades and non-comrades? Again Walzer's more general observation about the moral world of political radicals is germane to communist revolutionaries. The activist, he says, "is not bound to the masses whose consciousness he rejects. He is bound only to himself, if that is possible, and to the small band of militants who share his commitments."[16] Trotsky described the revolutionary movement in Russia in similar terms. "The Bolshevik Party created not only a political but a moral medium of its own, independent of bourgeois social opinion and implacably opposed to it."[17] Indeed, the dichotomy between consciousness and spontaneity lay at the core of Bolshevism. Because the masses in Lenin's mind were capable of developing only false consciousness, they required a conscious vanguard to direct and lead them. In a sense, communist revolutionaries are the twentieth century secular variant of the puritan revolutionaries in seventeenth-century England. Both cast themselves in the role of selfless saints aspiring to create a beautiful, ideal society. While the puritans saw themselves as divine instruments of God, communists conceive of themselves as agents of the Dialectic of History. The politics of both, however, are the politics of wreckers, architects, and builders.[18] As with all militant creeds, their devotion to pure utopia and revolt against a polluted society feed the communist revolutionarites' self-image of being "the only righteous men in a crooked world."[19] Communist Revolution itself, willed by history and divined by Party infallibility, becomes for its practitioner the moral imperative, the end that justifies all means and at the same time leaves him with a blissfully clean conscience as he wreaks havoc upon man and the world.

At the same time, it is this double morality and the idea that "all is permitted" in the name of historical necessity that make possible the transformation of communist revolutionaries into "defective saints," to borrow a phrase of Rubashov, the fictional veteran Bolshevik in Arthur Koestler's *Darkness at Noon*. The result, of course, is diseased revolution, a yawning gap between supposedly right principles but wrong results. As Rubashov agonizingly says, "We brought you truth, and in our mouths it sounded a lie. We brought you freedom, and it looks in our hands like a whip."[20] Or in the equally eloquent words of the Polish poet Adam Wazyk:

> They lived off the dawn
> and brought the night.
> They lived off the idea
> and lost the language of men.
> They lived off the dream
> and the lie became their daily bread.[21]

When viewed from the perspective of the above moral code with both its egalitarian comradely ethic and its vision of a selfless vanguard devoted to remaking society in its own saintly image and according to its own ideological dream of a classless and virtuous order, the phenomenon of bureaucratism is seen to be primarily an ethical question. It is a problem of the corruptibility of revolutionaries who, upon becoming officials, abuse their power and privileges for purposes of private self-interest. This refers to communist functionaries both in a revolutionary movement and later in a ruling establishment after the seizure of power.

### *Administrative Rationality*

Bureaucratism, however, has also been approached as essentially a technical problem involving not so much a corrupt as an incompetent revolutionary or official and an inefficient organizational machine. From this perspective, the remedy for preventing bureaucratic decay and misuse of power lies not in the realm of Party morality but in the area of administrative rationality.

Use of the term "rationalization" in Western organization theory dates back to Max Weber, who associated the word with the general process of adaptation and adjustment within bureaucratic structures. It is also the term used in the Russian dictionary of administration and Soviet history to refer to the process of retooling faulty and archaic administrative machinery and methods. Although at times he used the word very ambiguously and broadly, Weber essentially distinguished two meanings of the term. In one sense, rationalization refers to the appropriateness and adaptation of means to ends. In the other more abstract sense, it is identified with the de-mystification of the world in man's thinking and with what Weber called the "routinization of charisma." Given the nature of communist political systems which, during their more formative phases, bear the heavy stamp–indeed the cult of personality–of a supreme leader and typically their founding fathers, their rationalization at advanced stages of development necessarily acquires overtones of Weber's second meaning. It is important to stress, however, that in Russian *ratsionalizatsiia* has a much more limited usage and meaning. Defined as the process of improving the organization of activity, rationalization is applied generally to administration and economic production. Concerned narrowly with techniques, not politics, and making a cult of efficiency, it is geared to perfecting, not to liquidating, existing machinery. Its focus is strictly on modifying administrative means, not political ends. As in Western organization theory, then, rationality in its Russian context is a virtual synonym for efficiency and economy.

While communist ethics is concerned with the human composition of the machinery of power and the socialist transformation of the "soul" of communist officialdom, rationalization focuses primarily upon the function of administration and remodeling the structure and technical operation of the bureaucratic machine along rational and efficient lines. The premise that society should and can be consciously organized and rationally directed is a central element of Marxism. Such a notion is deeply rooted in the intellectual heritage out of which the Marxist tradition grew. Similarly, the conception of administration as essentially a technical process, both de-politicized and de-humanized, also derives from Marxist theory with its economic determinism and mechanistic views of nature, history, and above all administration. Taken together, these various intellectual frames of reference make for a strongly manipulative and mechanistic approach to building socialism.

It is only with Lenin, however, that Marxist social engineering gains its truly technocratic twist. Marx did not really foresee the threat of technocracy under socialism, partly because he tended to underestimate the importance of expertise required for economic and societal management. In fact, he believed that technological progress would so simplify and de-mystify the administrative process that the masses would be able to administer themselves. It is primarily this perspective that provides the populist and democratic strand of communist administrative doctrine. Rather it was the anarchists, as Leon Smolinski has pointed out, who were the more perceptive in their prognostications about the future applications of Marx's teachings.[22] Already in 1873, for example, Bakunin warned of the possibility that Marxist socialism might lead to a situation where "the bulk of the people would be divided into two armies: one industrial and one agricultural, under the direct command of state engineers who will constitute a new privileged class."[23] Ironically, it was in Bakunin's own native Russia that socialism acquired its most distinctive technocratic face. With its characteristic elitism, fetishization of technique, and distrust of human spontaneity, Leninism sows the seeds not for a humanistic utopia but for a technocratic computopia.

While Lenin certainly expected that his vanguard of professional revolutionaries would and should embody all the right proletarian virtues, he dwelled, as Benjamin Schwartz says, "not so much on their virtues as on their professionalism, their organizational expertise."[24] For him the secret of success in both making revolution and then building socialism lay ultimately in the efficacy of organization. Efficiency, not morality, was the chief yardstick by which he judged a man's worth. Consequently, he had little use for the virtuous but incompetent communist. And he labeled him flatly, "a nice man and good comrade but a good-for-nothing daydreamer and preposterous fumblefist."[25] After coming to power and coping with the problems of political rule, Lenin harped even more incessantly on the need for expertise rather than simply "redness" among communist officialdom. He insisted most firmly, "We shall punish for such delays the most saintly but negligent dunderheads, because we . . . do not need saintliness but efficient management."[26]

Toward the end of his life, even though he continued to see bureaucratism in part as an ethical problem, Lenin moved more and more to a technical conception of and technocratic solution to the communist bureaucratic phenomenon. It is here, moreover, that he contrasts most markedly with Mao's last strategy and struggle against bureaucracy. While both leaders preface their anti-bureaucratic assaults with the call for a cultural revolution, they attach diametrically opposite meanings to "culture." To Lenin it meant primarily managerial ability while to Mao it connotes revolutionary virtue. Consequently, the latter's effort to establish through the Cultural Revolution a "reign of virtue" contrasts with the former's last prescription of a "reign of rationality" for the bureaucratic machine. Whereas in the end Lenin saw the key to communist progress in administrative rationalization and peaceful evolution, Mao abhors them as the evil harbingers of revisionist decay and of ultimately capitalist restoration. Seeing the solution to Russia's bureaucratic ills to be a technocratic revolution from above, Lenin sought to make his primary agents of change none other than the Party controllers, who, according to his final plan, were to be transformed from being largely judges of Party virtue into administrative rationalizers, efficiency experts, and organization specialists. To Mao, however, the anti-bureaucratic revolution meant *sui generis* revolution from without and below, led not by cold rationalizers and technocrats but by spirited revolutionary saints. Involving inherently an organic relationship between the Party and the people, bureaucratism could not be generically dispelled by institutional and technical means but only by human action, mass action, ethically inspired or emotionally fired. Bureaucracy could be gutted completely only by the torch and fire of a super mass revolutionary movement, not by the cutting edge of a finely-tooled, super-control agency. Lenin's almost magical faith in the creative and healing power of technique and organization is matched by Mao's almost mystical faith in human will and mass movements.

As for the kinds of restraints imposed by administrative rationality on the arbitrary use of power, they take more the form of impersonal rules, technical functions, and institutional structures. By their very nature they differ substantially from ethical restraints. The latter derive primarily from comradely personal relations, informal trust, and spontaneous revolutionary activity. Rational restraints emanate, on the contrary, principally from regularized machinery, formalized procedures, and routinized bureaucratic behavior. One set of restraints has its roots in the past in a code of conduct among revolutionaries. The other is designed more appropriately for officials in a post-revolutionary society. Since he expected communist revolution to occur at an advanced stage of capitalist development and high level of economic and technological progress, Marx did not foresee any extensive gap between the revolutionary seizure of power and post-revolutionary communist institutionalization. Consequently, Marxist doctrine does not provide for any additional or different kinds of restraints on arbitrary power during a long transitional period of socialist construction required as a result of premature communist seizures of power in backward and underdeveloped countries. For purposes of revolutionary-totalitarian system-building, moreover, the former ethical restraints become *obsolete* while the projected rational-technical ones are seen to be *premature*, especially in the eyes of the existing or aspiring communist supreme leader. It is in this void, then, that intra-party terror begins to turn as the inevitable consequence and most distinctive instrument of the revolutionary program.[27]

## *Political Terror*

Wherever communist elites come to power, the old revolutionary code of camaraderie tends to break down, is itself bureaucratized, and gives way more and more to a moral vacuum which prepares the soil for the growth of intra-party terror. This process has been described cogently by Djilas. As he notes, the moral world of communist revolutionaries "slowly fades, disintegrates, and drowns during the course of the climb to complete power." Revolutionary ethics are ultimately transformed into "the intolerant and Pharisaical morals of a privileged caste." If, prior to the seizure of power, "wonderful human features were the criterion for creating and attracting power for the movement," then afterwards, "exclusive caste spirit and complete lack of ethical principles and virtues become the conditions for the power and maintenance of the movement." In the process, communist revolutionaries are turned into "self-centered cowards without ideas or comrades, willing to renounce everything—honor, name, truth, and morals—in order to keep their place in the ruling class and the hierarchical circle."[28] It is precisely this phenomenon of moral decay and revolutionary betrayal that provokes the outcry from Koestler, "When and where in history had there ever been such defective saints? Whenever had a good cause been worse represented?"[29]

Simultaneously, as this comradely code breaks down from within the elite, the boundaries between Party and non-party elements become increasingly blurred. The floodgates are then opened for the application within the Party and against "comrades" of the same moral license and methods of struggle that were previously sanctioned for use against "enemies" outside the Party ranks. This is not to deny that the process of moral erosion may proceed faster and further among some communist revolutionary elites than others. Obviously, the intensity and cohesiveness of the bonds of brotherhood and links between Party and society will vary with the nature and duration of the revolutionary struggle, with the path, pace, and program of building socialism after the seizure of power, with the homogeneity and degree of ideological commitment of the elite, and with the peculiar historical and cultural legacy of the national setting. But everywhere in practice communist comradely ethics have ultimately withered. Even Mao Tse-tung, though he espouses the primacy of the revolutionary virtue, was forced to abandon the old code of Party ethics with its restraints and limits governing intra-party struggle and the resolution of intra-party conflicts. In the Cultural Revolution ideological rectification, long the hallmark of CCP organizational doctrine, gave way to violent and massive organizational purge.

The purposive use of terror inside the Party against the communist elite as a form of negative restraint tends to arise predominantly from a *political* conception of bureaucratism. Significantly, neither Party ethics nor administrative rationality take into account the problem of power. Concern with administrative efficiency generally puts all policy considerations affecting the use of power outside the pale of bureaucratic competence. As Reinhard Bendix observes, "Bureaucracy is therefore all powerful and at the same time incapable of determining how its power should be used."[30] This was particularly the case with communist rationalization policy in the Soviet Union during the 1920s, which by its very nature and focus was apolitical, strongly mechanistic, and overly abstract. Similarly, the old code of comradely ethics pertains to a set of human relations and relationships of a rapidly disappearing era and does not provide for a system of power relations among a ruling communist elite. Equally germane to communist polities in this regard is Samuel Huntington's observation about the effects on political development more generally of "traditional" and "modern" values. As he notes, both the ethical values emanating from fanatical puritanism and an anti-corruption mentality and the technical values associated with industrialization and modernity challenge the autonomy of politics.[31] Preserving the autonomy of politics, however, is the fundamental political prerequisite for any program aiming at revolutionary-totalitarian change.

The resort to terror arises, therefore, in part, it seems, because of the failure of ethics and rationality, first, to foresee the possibility of fundamental political differences emerging ultimately within the leadership and elite over the proper use of power and appropriate direction and pace of building socialism; and, secondly, to provide viable means of resolving such political conflicts. It also emerges by way of deliberate and personal design on the part of the Party leader, be it a Stalin or Mao, for the purposes of settling the factional struggle and growing polarization within the elite decisively in favor of his own power position and plans for revolutionary-totalitarian system-building.

In regard to the nature and role of terror as a negative restraint, it is important to differentiate between its punitive and prophylactic functions, between "physical" and "psychic" terror. Quite apart from the actual application of violence and the physical liquidation of enemies, real and imagined, the mere threat of terror produces a pervasive atmosphere of anxiety which can also be manipulated and used for purposes of preserving political control and facilitating socio-economic change.[32] With regard to the actual role and extent of physical terror in communist systems, there is considerable diversity. Besides important differences in the value complex and cohesiveness of communist elites, here, it seems, the personality of the leader can be most crucial in providing an additional and typically critical dimension that influences heavily "the scope, the virulence, the frequency, the methods, and the victims of terror."[33]

When we speak of terror more generally, however, as a method of rule and system of power, we have in mind not so much its actual punitive use as its prophylactic function of creating a condition of diffuse anxiety and insecurity. Psychic rather than physical terror, the threat rather than the actual use of arbitrary coercion, is the more basic dimension, the more generic form of terror in communist systems. Long ago Alex Inkeles singled out "nagging uncertainty" and the institutionalization of anxiety as the characteristic features of the "totalitarian mystique."[34] Similarly, Fainsod described an atmosphere of institutionalized mutual suspicion that spreads a pall of anxiety as the underlying condition of terror as a "system of power."[35]

While it is certainly true that terror serves many functions and purposes in communist systems and has numerous causes and consequences, its primary effect—if not its principal aim—is to impede and check institutionalization of the Revolution and its concomitant bureaucratization. If ethics and rationality denote positive restraints and seek to institutionalize two key elements of communist society, terror is negative both as a punitive instrument and as a prophylactic condition with respect to change and political institutionalization. On the one hand, it seeks to check the rationalizing influences and forces that are spawned in and required for industrial development. On the other hand, it is also directed at keeping in check the human feelings and idealistic values growing out of communist ethics that may oppose and resist both the costs and consequences of industrialization in terms of the social stratification that it instills, the emphasis on technical and achievement-based norms that it inculcates, not to mention the loss in human lives that it entails. That is, terror is used to curb and negate both ethical considerations and rational constraints on the uses and abuses of political power for purposes of achieving the revolutionary transformation of society and the economy. It serves as the most effective instrument by which to maintain the autonomy of politics, to preserve a domain of independent action for political power, and, above all, to impede and prevent institutionalization in the political superstructure until the unfinished revolution is completed in the socio-economic base.

It is primarily this role of a great de-stabilizer, of a disrupter of and retarding force on political institutionalization, therefore, that makes terror a functionally rational instrument for promoting revolutionary change. In essence, fear becomes the organizing principle of permanent revolution. By creating an atmosphere of lingering anxiety, terror maintains a condition of what has been aptly called "abnormal normalcy" in which both individuals and institutions alike are deprived of security and stability.[36] During this stage of revolutionary-totalitarian system-building in which both destruction and construction are concurrent processes, any restraints on the uses of political power become fetters on the forces of revolutionary progress. Hence, organizational structures are necessarily denied permanence, regularity, and functional autonomy. Such attributes, if not stringently checked, could lead easily to a premature institutionalization of a system that is seen, especially by the leader, to be still in the process of "becoming." Organizations, like the men that run them, are considered simply technical means to serve revolutionary ends and are not to be ends in themselves, infused with value. What is institutionalized, therefore, is anxiety, not political structures and functions *per se*.

The purposive use of intra-party terror to prevent institutionalization of the revolution becomes integrally intertwined with its use to preserve the power and position of the supreme leader. Needless to say, intent and purpose are among the most indeterminate factors in any calculus of power. Whether a leader is motivated to use terror by his own self-interest and power needs or by desire for the interests of the revolution is exceedingly difficult, if not impossible, to determine fully. The important point is that it is virtually impossible to separate the question of the institutionalization of the revolution from the issue of the preservation of power of the leader. In communist systems, particularly of the indigenous variety, the revolution and the leader become synonymous and are perceived to be so, above all, by the leader. It is simply impossible to distinguish between the movement and its leader, between the work and its master. Thus, it is not without substance that we tend to describe "communism" as a political phenomenon and model largely in terms of a personal "ism" of its national leader. Like the communist statesman in Mnacko's *The Taste of Power*, the communist supreme leader, be it Lenin, Stalin, Mao, Tito, or Castro, is led by the maxim, "I am the revolution and the revolution is myself."[37] What is ultimately involved in the institutionalization of the revolution is the bureaucratization of power. This phenomenon represents not only a betrayal of the revolution but also a fundamental threat to the personal authority of the leader. It is precisely in regard to the need to check the growth of bureaucratic institutionalization in the political sector, therefore, that the interests of the revolution and the leader converge.

If the use of physical terror is strongly influenced by the *personality* of the leader, then the use of psychic terror as a destabilizing, debureaucratizing condition among the communist elite is integrally connected with not only his personality but also his *role* as supreme leader. Since his power is personal, not institutional, the leader necessarily opposes the development of organizations into institutions, infused with value and with a corporate life and power of their own, that could both restrain and rival his supreme authority. This pertains first and foremost to the Party itself.[38] But how a leader chooses to use terror as a check and restraint on bureaucratization will vary to some extent according to his political orientation and value complex, to the importance he ascribes to technical and human factors, and to populist and elitist forces in building socialism as well as in preserving his power.[39] While the character and instruments of terror may be slightly different, the thrust is to surround the official in an atmosphere of suspicion and anxiety in order to prevent the crystallization of autonomous islands of countervailing force.

As practiced by Mao and Stalin respectively, then, terror can be used largely in the service of either ethics or technique. Resorting to terror ultimately in order to keep "politics in command," the leader denies, however, both ethical and technical restraints on political power irrespective of his stance in regard to Party ethics and administrative rationality more generally. For example, while Mao prior to the Cultural Revolution certainly had a deeper sense of and commitment to comradely ethics than Stalin, still like the latter he was forced to break with the Party's ethical code with its restraints and limits regulating intra-party struggle. Similarly, even though Stalin was himself preeminently a "technician of power" and intrinsically much more taken with administrative technique than Mao, he like the Chinese leader came to oppose rationalization as a means and strategy for communist political development. With its inherent emphasis on routine, regularity, and harmony, rationalization harbors its own set of constraints on power and revolution-making.

In conjunction with terror, communist leaders also rely typically on a personality cult, genuine or synthetic, to impede institutionalization of the revolutionary process as well as to maintain their power. As a result, the basis of communist rule in both indigenous and imposed regimes, at least of the Stalinist variety as in East Europe, becomes not only highly coercive but also essentially personal. Arbitrary personal rule based upon charismatic or pseudo-charismatic authority rather than rule through institutions based upon routinized, bureaucratic authority is made the axis of political power. The supreme leader becomes the pivot of the system. To speak of the power elite in this situation as a "bureaucracy" is inaccurate, as Leonard Schapiro notes. It is more like a "body of retainers."[40]

This transformation of the political system to serve the power, personality, and plans of the supreme leader represents from the point of view of communist ethics an extreme form of self-interest and corruption. Terror is likewise a negation and perversion of rationality. In a broader context, however, personalization of power and political terror in communist regimes become twisted analogs of "corruption" and "coercion," phenomena that Huntington notes are typically symptomatic of the absence of effective political institutionalization in modernizing non-communist societies.[41] They perform some of the same functions which corruption and coercion serve in developing societies. For example, "both are means by which individuals and groups relate themselves to the political system and, indeed, participate in the system in ways which violate the mores of the system."[42] In communist polities this involves, above all, the refashioning of the Party purge into a terroristic and personal instrument of the supreme leader. Through the purge he is then able to change the composition of the ruling elite according to his own liking and will, turning it essentially into his own subordinate personal entourage. Not only are enemies and opponents real and imagined, removed, but those loyal to him personally who combine what in his eyes is the proper mix of redness and/or expertise are promoted into the inner circle. This is as true for Mao in the Cultural Revolution as for Stalin in the thirties. For both leaders, personalization of power and intra-party terror were irregular but necessary means of making demands on a political system that was deemed to be going dangerously astray.

### *The Decline of Terror and Creeping Rationalization*

Since terror has long occupied a central place in Western theories of totalitarianism, there has been a tendency to see in the general decline of terror in the Soviet Union and East Europe since Stalin's death *ipso facto* a demise of communist totalitarianism. Increasingly dissatisfied with the efficacy of the "totalitarian syndrome" as a model of communist reality as well as a mode for its analysis, some scholars have been all too willing to throw out, so to speak, the baby (totalitarianism) with the bathwater (terror). By the same token, there has been too simplistic a tendency to explain the decline of terror primarily in terms of its growing economic "dysfunctionality" at higher stages of socialist development. The planning and administration of an increasingly complex economy requires, it is argued, more sophisticated methods of control than crude terror. Consequently, terror tends simply but necessarily to wither away as the rational imperatives and impersonal laws of socio-economic modernization inexorably assert themselves. The "cunning of history" and Marxian dialectic are vindicated as terror and totalitarianism are shown to be merely infantile features of communist development, much like bureaucratism was naively believed to be a sign of the immaturity of socialism and residual of capitalism. Such explanations for the decline of terror generally give little place to politics and human will. Thus violating communism's most sacred law of politics in command, they have, to use another worn cliche, essentially the tail (economics) wagging the dog (politics).

The relegation of terror to a less prominent place in the arsenal of controls results, we hold, predominantly from changes in the political structure and ethos of communist systems. These involve, above all, a change in the dominant form of executive command from arbitrary one-man rule to increasingly stronger oligarchical rule and a change in the basic thrust of communist system-building from being revolutionary to essentially post-revolutionary in character. In a sense, the decline of intra-party, intra-elite terror entails a mixture of default and design that is the reverse of the one which accounts for its rise. That is, terror subsides in part because of the failure of terror to maintain itself as a system of power in the absence of a supreme leader, occasioned by the latter's death (e.g., Stalin), and/or his or, more typically, his successor's inability to preserve the substance of absolute personal power in the presence of growing elite consensus about the desirability, even necessity, of abandoning not only arbitrary personal rule but also revolutionary system-building. It also subsides in part because of *deliberate and collective* design on the part of the ruling oligarchy to renounce out of desire for its own self-interest and self-preservation the use of terror as the chief means of controlling the elite as well as changing the system or, more appropriately, impeding its bureaucratic institutionalization. The decline of terror involves, therefore, not the demise of totalitarianism but rather change and evolution within totalitarianism along the lines suggested most perceptively by Brzezinski more than fifteen years ago. That is, "terrorist" totalitarianism tends to give way to "rationalist" totalitarianism.[43]

The rationalization of totalitarianism occurs, moreover, in both senses of Weber's use of the term: de-mystification in man's thinking about the world and the adaptation of means to ends. In the communist context, the former phenomenon relates not only to the routinization of charisma and explicit denunciation of the cult of personality but equally important the severe tempering, if not implicit renunciation, of revolutionary aspirations (and methods) with regard to system change and building socialism. As we have already noted, during the revolutionary-totalitarian or, to use Brzezinski's terminology, the terrorist-totalitarian stage of communist development the image and interest of the revolution and the leader tend to converge. The latter becomes both the primary agent and the personification of the revolution. In post-revolutionary, rationalist totalitarianism the ruling oligarchy displaces the supreme leader as the fulcrum and main perceptual node of the system and signifies the institutionalization of the revolution. If previously incipient bureaucratic institutionalization represented a threat to both the revolution and the leader, then its rise to dominance in rationalist totalitarianism denotes the victory of bureaucracy over both the leader and the revolution. And conversely, in the eyes of the oligarchy, absolute one-man rule and arbitrary, potentially destructive system change pose now as the greatest threats to both their power and the system which they have come to embody and to command. No longer is the revolution their life and their life the revolution. Like the masses, the ruling stratum, as Amalrik says of the present Soviet elite, yearns more and more for "a quiet life and for comfort," even chases after a "comfort cult."[44]

This basically post-revolutionary character of elite perceptions and priorities regarding both their power interests and system needs, moreover, affects directly the nature and process of administrative reform and retooling the organizational machinery of communist power. Indeed, it is in this area that a deliberate policy of rationalization is increasingly pursued at higher stages of communist development. Underlying this phenomenon is the fact that the political system itself is considered by the elite to be no longer "becoming," but, in fact, it is seen as "in being." In the eyes of the elite—though not necessarily the masses—the system has acquired value, legitimacy, and institutionalized status. Organizations are no longer viewed as simply means but have become ends in themselves. "Every government institution and position," writes Amalrik of the Soviet system, "is sustained by no other force than the realization that it is an essential part of the existing system."[45] The Party, above all, is identified as an inviolable institution and corporate body in and for itself. In a word, the system is essentially built and now needs only to be maintained. The latter task demands particularly "no rocking of the system by dangerous and unfamiliar reforms."[46] On the contrary, the main imperative is to provide and ensure the conditions necessary for maintaining what is now called a developed socialist society. These include, first and foremost, greater security and stability to individuals and organizational structures within the bureaucracy, attributes that have been deliberately denied them in the past by extreme personalization of power and terror.

It is most appropriate, therefore, that as communist regimes move steadily into a stage of post-revolutionary totalitarian development, rationalization should replace terror as the primary means of controlling bureaucratism and preserving system stability. Rationalization has long been the traditional means of adjustment and adaptation within bureaucratic structures. The distinctive feature of revolutionary-totalitarianism, as Lowenthal stresses, is system growth through politically forced development. Change and control are imposed not only from above but also from without through recurrent and forceful wrenchings of the system, typically by a supreme leader. Terror is the instrument by which he promotes revolutionary change and at the same time impedes political institutionalization.[47] In post-revolutionary totalitarianism, however, both the hopes and fears of the ruling oligarchy lead it to rely more and more on administrative rationality and technocracy to cope with problems of control, change, and stability. Intra-elite controls assume more the form of mutual self-imposed restraints of bureaucratic rationality. Revolutionary change initiated from without gives way to gradual and piecemeal reform of the system from *within* the existing institutional structures. Change, however, is still basically imposed and managed from above, not by a supreme and arbitrary ruler but by the ruling oligarchy, through more sophisticated techniques of social engineering and control, including computers and modern managerial technologies as well as more limited and selected forms of terror on a much less massive scale than under Stalin but not necessarily less crude. In the words of Brzezinski, "The revolutionary torch and the unending quest are accordingly displaced by the swivel chair and the time clock."[48] Although this was not yet the dominant motif of the Soviet system in 1956 when he made the above statement, it certainly captures the spirit and thrust of Soviet Russia and much of East Europe as they move into the 1970s attempting to give socialism not a more human but a more technocratic face.

Interestingly, the first organ in the Soviet government that began to concern itself with the tasks of administrative rationalization four years after the October Revolution was initially called the Bureau of Normalization *(biuro normalizatsii).*[49] The idea of normalizing administration in what was taken to be essentially a post-revolutionary period expresses well, in fact, the spirit of the rationalization movement as it developed in the Soviet Union during the 1920s and the era of NEP.

With its inherent emphasis upon efficiency, stability, and peaceful evolution as well as its overly mechanistic focus on regularized machinery, formalized procedures, and routinized behavior, rationalization was geared more properly for the demands of post-revolutionary institutionalization. As such, however, it came to be viewed increasingly as premature for the Soviet system—though not necessarily for economic production—in light of the political imperatives of forced industrialization. According to Valerian Kuibyshev, who headed the Party control establishment from 1923 to 1926, the bureaucratic apparatus of the young Soviet state was still more like a rough and gnarled stump. Scientific rationalization was "too weak a medicine" to cure the immediate ills of the communist regime. The rationalizers, he held, were trying to shave this stump with a plane, an instrument that is used to polish an already workable surface, whereas in fact it was necessary first to lay in with an axe to get rid of the rough protrusions.[50] Consequently, the rationalist plane was abandoned by the early 1930s for the terrorist axe. If the latter is the more appropriate tool for revolutionary-totalitarianism, then the demands of post-revolutionary totalitarian development require the resurrection of the rationalizer's plane to polish and perfect what is conceived now to be a fully developed and workable system. Rationalization is needed to normalize the "abnormal normalcy" associated with terroristic and highly personalized political rule. The pressures for greater rationality, regularity, and efficiency—always present in the economy but never predominant in politics—increasingly find support in the political sector and ruling strata. Communism enters into a new stage of political evolution.

The transition to this more mature stage and face of communist totalitarianism, however, has been neither abrupt nor easy. Rather it has taken much more the form of "creeping" rationality. Resistance and reluctance have followed constantly in its path. This has been so partly because change of any kind is always a painful process, especially for bureaucracies. But, in addition, rationalization is itself seen as a double-edged sword that can be used to destroy as well as to preserve the existing system. It instills both deep fear and high hope in the ruling oligarchs: fear that it will have potentially broader rationalizing, even liberalizing, effects on the system and hope that its more sophisticated techiques of social engineering and control can preserve the substance and structure of totalitarian power essentially intact. Not Stalin's death but Khrushchev's removal signifies the real benchmark of its emerging dominance. Indeed, only since the mid-sixties has administrative rationalization been recognized officially in the Soviet Union and Eastern Europe to have increasingly a "political relevance" in the age of the so-called "scientific and technological revolution."

Even though terror, personality cults, and subjectivism have been denounced and leaders of the old totalitarian mold (Khrushchev, Novotny, Gomulka, and Ulbricht) removed, still little progress has been actually made in any communist regime in regularizing the essentially coercive and personalistic basis of rule. While perhaps somewhat exaggerated, Mel Croan's description of the Soviet regime as being essentially "post-revolutionary but pre-institutional" captures well the still highly problematical character and primitiveness of political institutions in communist systems.[51] Efforts at formalizing powers, rights, and responsibilities and delineating lines of authority and jurisdictional competence both within and among organizations that have always been left deliberately vague and blurred are still very recent and meager. To a certain extent the political void which originally contributed to the rise of intra-party terror still exists, partly because the task of terror was not to fill the void but to maintain it, to keep politics in command and free from ethical and rational restraints.

*From Rationalization to Democratization: The Return to Ethics*

It also needs to be stressed that rationalization is not to be confused with democratization. As Brzezinski noted long ago, rationalist totalitarianism tends to accentuate rationalist features present from the start and to minimize some of the irrational outbursts of the terrorist past.[52] The purpose of rationalization is to perfect, not to liquidate, the existing system, to eliminate or mollify some of the abuses and aberrations of terroristic and highly personalized rule but to maintain the substance of totalitarian power. This is precisely why it is a more appropriate tool for reforming and polishing a developed system than for revolutionary system-building and, similarly, why it tends to be abandoned as premature at one stage of communist development but brought back as timely and necessary for the needs of a less turbulent era.

To seek not simply perfection of the administrative machinery but indeed qualitative change of the system in a post-totalitarian, more democratic direction requires going beyond rationalization. On the one hand, it entails explicit renunciation of the revolutionary class struggle, discarding once and for all the "dogma of the immaculate proletarian conception." Democratization involves abandoning not only the revolutionary assault on society but also the whole notion of comprehensive social engineering, planned change, and monopolistic control of society from above by the Communist Party. Most of all, it means bringing back ethics, not just rationality, giving priority to the general interests of society over the special interests of its ruling class, and asserting the primacy of human development over strictly technico-economic progress. The individual citizen becomes not simply an object of politics and political care but a political agent, not merely a means but an end with political identity and status, valued in and for itself.

Democratization involves, therefore, giving socialism "a human face" and efforts akin to what the Czech communist reformers attempted, or at least contemplated, in 1968. For the latter rationalization was a necessary but clearly insufficient condition for democratization. According to Zdenek Mlynar, who headed the Party's special team of investigators working on the Czech Political Model,

> Scientific rational direction cannot be implemented in a political system without specific political preconditions. Otherwise we might come up with an efficiently working, rational 'machine,' without being able to recognize or control the social and human effects of its operation.[53]

In a similar vein, Milan Huebl, who was removed by Novotny from the Higher Party School in 1964, stressed, "This cannot be a model built on a mechanism of administrative levers alone." On the contrary, man, not the apparat, had to be made the basis of the system and the focus of concern." As he explained,

> A society in which democratic guarantees for every individual citizen are lacking is in a situation which resembles that of a mountaineer who attempts to climb to great heights with an oxygen mask. As the air rarefies, his limbs become sluggish and his movements slower. To prevent this, the mountaineer uses an oxygen mask. Society cannot permanently employ aids of this type but must create an atmosphere sufficiently dense to allow normal breathing and a normal pulse.[54]

If the Dubcek reformers aimed at normalizing and democratizing the political system in order to save socialism and give it a human face, the Soviet leaders have continually sought basically to rationalize and perfect the instruments of control—the oxygen mask—in order to save and preserve the existing system. Mao, on the other hand, continues to pursue a third path. Like the Czechs he has tried to keep the ethical and human dimension dominant, "to treat the illness in order to save the patient." But unlike the Prague Spring reformers, he also continues to pursue the revolutionary dream and struggle by totalitarian means, including terror.

From a comparative perspective, what is important is the peculiar "mix" of ethics, rationality, and terror and how it varies over time both within a particular country and between different communist regimes. In the Soviet experience it has been a mix which has always stressed heavily rational-technical and terrorist controls. This fundamental emphasis on political authoritarianism and scientific technique and lack of a strong ethical dimension, however, derives not only from distinctively Bolshevik principles and preferences. It is also deeply rooted in Russian history and political culture. For example, already in 1857 Alexander Herzen forecasted the possible coming of an unprecedented system "of slavery and brute force upheld by every achievement of science: a Genghis Khan equipped with telegraph, steamships, and railways."[55] Painfully aware of what Lenin cursed as the "damned Russian past,"

Andrei Amalrik more than a hundred years after Herzen similarly predicts pessimistically, "It is possible that we will indeed have a 'socialism' with bare knees someday, but not likely one with a human face." "As a people," he emphasizes, "we have not benefited from Europe's humanist tradition. In Russian history man has always been a means and never in any sense an end."[56]

In Mao's China, on the other hand, a different set of historical and political factors, both Chinese and communist, has tended to produce a different mix of controls. A strong emphasis on human ethics and populism linking society and the Party is rooted in part in the nature of the Chinese communist revolutionary movement as a mass guerrilla type movement but also in part in China's cultural past with its Confucian ethic and emphasis on the moral quality of political leadership. Similarly, a traditional Chinese hostility to administration and bureaucratic mentality is reinforced by Mao's own glorification of struggle as a state of "happiness," his suspicion of organizational structures and technical functions, and his aversion to office routine and rationalization. The latter can produce at best in his eyes only "hothouse flowers" and not true revolutionary fighters. In order to understand, therefore, not only the shape of the problem of bureaucracy but also the nature of the remedy chosen to control it in any communist regime, we must ultimately try to place its communist experience into a perspective that takes into account its non-communist past and national culture.

### *The Institutional Focus of Control: The Party Control Commission*

In addition to the functional controls of ethics, rationality, and terror, communist regimes have also always relied primarily upon special institutional machinery inside the Party to preserve its revolutionary purity and to cope with the problems and abuses of bureaucratic power. Every communist party, ruling and non-ruling, has a special agency that is charged with combating bureaucratic tendencies and misconduct within its ranks. While the official designation of this body may vary slightly from one party to another, it is generally called, like in the CPSU, simply the party control commission or committee. Given the dominant role of the Russian party—indeed the history of bolshevization—in the international communist movement, it is not surprising to find that the Soviet model has had its most lasting influence in the area of Communist Party organization.

Thus, one of the leading authorities on communist China writes that the Party control committee in the CCP, which was abolished by Mao in the Cultural Revolution, had functioned "more or less the same" as its Russian counterpart.[57] Similarly, with the forceful imposition of the Soviet model on the people's democracies in Eastern Europe after World War II, each party was ordered by Moscow to establish a control commission along Russian lines to deal with communist bureaucratic abuses and problems of intra-party control.[58] Because the control commission in the CPSU has served as a universal model for much of the communist world, it is important to examine the role and record of this party institution in order to enhance our understanding not only of Soviet history but of the communist experience in comparative perspective as well.

There is no communist institution, except perhaps the secret police, however, that is more difficult to study, especially for an outsider, than the Party control commission. It functions as essentially the police establishment within the Party and has always maintained a very close and interlocking relationship with the state security organs. Under Stalin it became, in fact, largely an annex of the secret police. Since it concerns itself with the most unsavory aspects of Party life, with misconduct in both the public careers and so-called "private corners" of Party members, the operations of the commission have always been highly secretive and sensitive. Indeed, no Communist Party has ever liked to disclose its inner failings and problems, to wash its dirty linen in public. With the control commission, then, we necessarily find ourselves very much in an area that is generally and sometimes contemptuously called "backstairs history."

It is not surprising, therefore, that a thorough study of intra-party control in the CPSU has not yet appeared in Moscow. Particularly lacking has been any study of the Central Control Commission (CCC), which served as the organizational center of the party control establishment from 1920 to 1934. As late as 1963, a young Russian historian at Moscow State University acknowledged, "In the historical file of works on party and state control, it is, in fact, impossible to name even *one* investigation of the history of the CCC, although V. I. Lenin in his last works attached tremendous importance to it and in the history of our Party it by no means played a secondary role." He then urged Soviet historians to fill this gap in developing the history of the CPSU and "to render the Central Control Commission its proper due."[59] Although a considerable amount of material and documentation regarding the CCC has appeared by Soviet scholars since the early 1960s when the institution once again became a legitimate subject of inquiry, the politics of Soviet historiography have prevented, nevertheless, a balanced and objective account of this important party body.

Western scholars, on the other hand, have long recognized the significance of the control commission, but they have always been unable to penetrate the aura of mystery in which it remains shrouded. Although the commission originally emerged as a device to arrest and check bureaucratic power, its transformation by Stalin's hand into an instrument of bureaucratic control has received our dominant attention. Indeed, the control commission has been remembered almost solely as the ruthless purging arm of the Party apparat and the club by which Stalin personally browbeat Trotsky, Bukharin, and others into submission and forged his totalitarian order. The original mission and heritage of the control commission as an agency designed to struggle against the evils of bureaucracy have been virtually forgotten in our accounts of this important institution. With communism, then, we have the same kind of dismal institutional failure that has characterized other movements in the past which have been haunted by the vision of incorruptibility. The attempt to organize great moral insights always seems to turn out badly. Thus, the Christian Church produced the Inquisitor. The French Revolution produced the Committee of Public Safety and the Reign of Terror. Similarly, communism created the control commission and secret police.[60]

For the most part, however, we have taken an oversimplified and one-sided view of the Party control establishment. We have overpainted the punitive dimension of the institution, even though it was clearly the dominant one, and we have sorely neglected other aspects of its activity and posture. We have concentrated too much on its use as the sword of the Party bureaucracy and too little on its role as the shield–though always ineffective and increasingly impotent–designed to protect the Party from abuses by its bureaucratic machine. The picture that emerges from a close examination of the history of the Central Control Commission is that of a much more complex organization which wore a number of faces and performed a variety of important and conflicting functions. Party ethics, administrative rationality, and political terror were all integral threads interlacing the organizational edifice and impinging upon the institutional image of the control commission. In the end, the control machinery broke down under the burden of its multiple and contradictory functional roles. Instead of serving as Stalin's reliable and ruthless purging arm, the CCC by the early 1930s was becoming more and more a brake on and barrier to the consolidation of his personal autocracy and terrorist rule. Its dismantlement in 1934 marked a significant turning point in the history of the Soviet regime and was a prerequisite for the final march to full-fledged Stalinism.[61]

To be sure, the one-sided and distorted image that we have traditionally had of the control commission has obscured our interpretation of the role of this institution in Soviet party development. In addition to the inaccuracy of our perception of the Russian example, however, we have also tended to project all too readily and unquestioningly a universality of its emulation throughout the communist world. Both factors have impeded our understanding of the differences in the function and instrumentalities of party control in other communist parties and polities. Indeed, more generally, the tyranny of the Soviet model and the dominant tendency to view communist problems and phenomena largely with Russian eyes have caused us to lose sight of important variations or, at least, of the vagaries of comparative communism.

Unfortunately, the descriptive formula "more or less the same as its Russian counterpart" conceals as much as it reveals about the Party control commission in a comparative context, particularly in the case of China. In the East European communist regimes, the control commission was virtually imposed by Moscow, structured closely along Russian lines, and even acquired quickly a typically Stalinist face and sinister role. Indeed, its institutional growth became integrally connected with Stalin's efforts to purge both from above and from without the East European parties of "Titoists" and other recalcitrant elements and to subordinate them fully to his own will and control. Consequently, before long the intra-party control machinery everywhere was working in collusion not only with its own respective secret police establishment but also with Russian security officials and advisers. In Czechoslovakia, for example, an investigation in 1968 of the Party archives for this initial period of communist rule described the role of the control commission in the CPCS as follows:

> In time it became one of the executors of unlawful measures, the initiator of a number of accusations and unauthorized secret police interventions. From it grew, to put it figuratively, "a security corps" in the Party. It adopted state security methods, gave information to the security apparatus and received its information from it. The jurisdiction of the control commission was widespread. It decided the fates of people and made agreements with the security apparatus about the preparation of cases against "enemies and agents". . . .[62]

"The idea that behind everything was the hand of an enemy," noted the 1968 archival study, "pervaded the minds and activities of the investigatory organs of the Party control commission as well as those of the state security. . .and became an integral part of the Party subconscious.[63] The control commission not only reflected but contributed directly to the suffocating atmosphere of terror which quickly enveloped political life in Czechoslovakia and the rest of communist East Europe. From the beginning, then, the commission in Eastern Europe functioned essentially as an instrument of political terror.

In China, on the contrary, the "Russian odor" of the Party control committee, which was established only in 1955 at the height of the Chinese emulation of the Soviet model and in the aftermath of the Kao Kang-Jao Shu-shih purge, impeded its growth as a powerful and, above all, terroristic instituion in the CCP. The lessons of Soviet experience seem to have been prominently in the minds of the Chinese leadership. Unlike the CCC in the CPSU, which was an important institution in the 1920s with broad functional scope though ambiguous autonomy, the Central Control Committee in China was created as simply an investigatory agency with extremely limited disciplinary powers—like the stunted body to which Stalin reduced the control commission in the

CPSU after the mid-thirties. The Chinese Party leaders asserted early and most emphatically, "Control personnel must not think that those correcting the errors of others will not themselves commit errors or that those who exercise supervision over others may not be controlled by others . . . . Therefore, in this respect we shall never permit the idea of special rights. Our principle must, like any other work of the Party, be placed under the leadership of the Party center and the Party committees."[64] Among the Russian party membership, various "exaggerated notions" existed about the CCC and continued to exist, especially among its dissident and anti-Stalin factions, throughout the 1920s. Some imagined that it was "something that stands above all institutions, that this is the Supreme Court over the whole party, higher than the Central Committee." Some members even dared to suggest that the CCC should control the Central Committee.[65] Nor did this image die quickly. Even as late as 1930 there were still a few Russian Communists who believed, "The CCC must be higher than everyone and everything."[66] Such ideas have been prominently absent from the theoretical underpinnings and history of the control committee in China. Similarly, in China—and for that matter in Eastern Europe as well—administrative rationalization was never a prominent activity of the control committee as it was for the CCC in the first decade of Soviet power. Indeed, the technocratic zeal characteristic of the Soviet twenties has been largely absent in China or at least always much more tempered by a strong accent on moral zeal.

Some Chinese also had not forgotten how Stalin had used the CCC in the CPSU as his own personal club with which he sought to terrorize the entire party into submission to his own will. These men sought consciously to prevent the development of such a weapon in the Chinese party. Long ago in 1940 in his "On Inner-Party Struggle," Liu Shao-ch'i had observed that the CCP had had its "100 percent Bolsheviks," its "struggle specialists" who had no regard for principle, and its "brawl experts" who were given to fighting. Liu's solution was to propose what became for more than two decades the sacred law of intra-party relations—that intra-party struggle ought to be struggle over principle among comrades. This law relied for a remedy far more on ideological education and rectification than on arbitrary and physical terror, though rectification itself often became an intense form of "coercive persuasion" and psychic terror. To allay any fears about the newly created control committee, Teng Hsiao-p'ing, the Party General Secretary, reaffirmed at the Eighth CCP Congress in 1956, "The crucial thing about control, whether coming from inside or outside the Party, is to develop our Party's traditional style of work."[67]

Before the Cultural Revolution, severe and arbitrary terror had been regarded by the Chinese leaders not only as ineffective but harmful, for it generated its own evils which imperiled party unity and harmony and stifled party vitality and initiative. Extreme terror was conceived as going against Party traditions and the sanctity of Yen-an-rooted techniques in inner-party relations. The so-called "leftist period of ruthless struggle and merciless blow" (i.e., 1929-1934) was always contrasted with the period since Mao assumed leadership after 1935. Any expansion of intra-party terror was viewed as a threat to the success of rectification methods of struggle. All these factors—apprehension over the lessons of Soviet experience as well as strong elite (and leader) commitment to traditional methods of intra-party struggle and a conscious desire to avoid a Stalinist type of intra-party terror—constituted great obstacles to the development of the control committee as an agency of terror in the CCP. Indeed, until the early 1960s, the committee remained a relatively insignificant and limited organ.

With the deepening polarization within the Party leadership after the abortive Great Leap Forward, however, it became increasingly more difficult to conduct Party rectification and resolve disputes according to the prescribed practices and formulas inherited from a rapidly disappearing era. Attempts to apply Yenan texts in a completely changed context merely exposed the outdated image and ineffective methods of intra-party struggle supplied by the Yenan experience. Suffice it to say that on the level of bureaucratic politics as well as Party policy the control committee became inevitably and inextricably embroiled in the growing conflict among the top leadership which eventually erupted in the Cultural Revolution. In this developing struggle the control committee faced ever more sharply the question of what should be its proper face and function. That is, was its primary role and responsibility that of a purging arm or restraining hand on excesses of the purge and abuses of power? Significantly, this was the same dilemma that the Party controllers faced in Soviet Russia in the late twenties and early thirties as polarization grew among the political elite over the proper pace and direction of Soviet development and as Stalin sought to step up the scope and terroristic bite of the purge in pursuit of forced industrialization and collectivization as well as the consolidation of his own personal power. Like their Russian counterparts the exercisers of party control in China, it seems, found themselves increasingly caught in a whirling spiral of forces and web of pressures that made it more and more difficult for them to choose between and reconcile their conflicting functional roles and competing loyalties to the Party, the Party bureaucracy, and the Party leader. Significantly, in both cases, the Party control organs acted more and more as an instrument of restraint rather than as an instrument of terror and came to oppose the policy and position of the Party supreme leader. As a result, both Stalin and Mao were forced ultimately to circumvent the regular control machinery and to go outside the Party for the means to purge the organization and reduce it to their personal will. That Stalin resorted to the secret police and Mao to the Red Guards and the Army for this purpose reflected more their own divergent styles, priorities, available alternatives, and preferences. But in the eyes of both leaders, the control commission had become clearly an insufficient and unreliable purging weapon to serve their own personal plans, power needs, and political designs.[68]

Turning once again to Czechoslovakia, but this time in 1968, we encounter a different set of circumstances and political choices affecting the issue and instrumentalities of Party control. In China, Mao was forced to resort to ever more terroristic means in order to preserve the revolutionary-totalitarian thrust of China's development and his own absolute power. In Czechoslovakia, on the contrary, the desire of the Dubcek reformers to move the political system out of its basically Stalinist-terroristic mold in a post-revolutionary and post-totalitarian direction led them to emphasize more rational and ethical means of political change and control. While Mao's hardening preoccupation with revolutionary goals led him to obscure more and more the question of means, the Czech reformers, having realized (and experienced) fully the results and legacy of revolutionary-totalitarian terror, came to appreciate the importance of means. In a sense, they acquired or regained a conscience. They, too, seem to have come to the same conclusion that Djilas had reached a decade before: "The power of reality and the power of life have always been stronger than any kind of brutal force and more real than any theory."[69] And they took as their cue one of the closing lines of *The New Class*, "Certainly if the communists interpreted the world realistically, they might lose but they would gain as human beings, as part of the human race."[70] Precisely the desire to gain as human beings motivated them to abandon the revolutionary struggle and to try to give socialism a human and ethical face.

The role that the planners of the Prague Spring projected for the Party control commission was fully in accord with the path of democratization that they envisaged for the political system more generally. Basically, they aimed at returning the control organs to their original judicial and ethical function of serving as the Party's institutionalized conscience, the overseer of the norms of Party life and its comradely court where members could seek redress against injustices and abuses. Instead of acting as it had in the past as the arbitrary, indeed, terroristic sword of the Party bureaucracy and, above all, of its leader, the control commission was to be refashioned into an ethical shield to protect the Party from bureaucratic abuses. In order for it to exercise effectively this role of a guarantee of intra-party democracy and the morality of power, the Czech communist reformers proposed a number of measures in the new draft party statutes issued shortly before the Soviet invasion that were designed to transform the commission into an independent organ.[71]

Fundamentally, these proposals of the Czech communists in 1968 resemble very closely Lenin's last ideas and plans for transforming the Central Control Commission in the CPSU into a viable agency to check abuses by the Party machine. In their effort to give socialism a human face, then, the Dubcek reformers were in a sense going back to Lenin. At the same time, however, their proposals revealed deep communist biases and a strong reluctance to go beyond Lenin in seeking ways to bridle communist bureaucracy. Like the founder of Bolshevism, the Czech Communists remained basically unwilling to check power with power and sought instead to check it only with conscience. In addition, they still rejected adamantly the idea that any agency outside the Party should be allowed to check and restrain effectively the leading force of society and conscious vanguard of history.[72]

Just as Lenin's final plans for a super-control agency to combat bureaucratic abuses miscarried dismally in Soviet Russia, the plans of the Prague Spring reformers to humanize and democratize not only the control commission but the Czech political system more generally were also aborted by the Soviet-led invasion in August 1968. Moreover, in the subsequent "normalization" achieved by the Husak regime, the Party control machinery again played a prominent role as the punitive arm of the apparat, purging nearly 30 percent of the membership of the CPCS by the spring of 1971.

Finally, it is necessary to note that the Soviet leadership, especially in the post-Khrushchev period, has pursued yet a third path of development with respect to its machinery of control and the political system generally. Suffice it to say at this point that it has sought fundamentally to rely less on massive and arbitrary terror of the Stalinist type and more on rational-technical means to move and manage the system in an increasingly post-revolutionary direction, but at the same time to preserve the structure and substance of authoritarian, if not totalitarian, power. The thrust of development of the Soviet system has been, then, not towards socialism with a human face but more towards an "automated Stalinism" and rationalist and technocratic totalitarianism.[73]

Much like the mix of functional controls more broadly, the functional scope and face of the Party control commission have tended to vary and change over time both within and among different communist regimes. By the mid-1960s the divergent faces and directions of development of intra-party control organs reflected an increasingly diverse and changing communist world. In a sense, then, the functional role(s) that the Party control machinery plays and the political profile it assumes at any one time reflect the basic thrust and path of development of the political system more generally. The control commission is both a microcosm and mirror of the larger system of which it is an integral part. As such, it is necessarily subject to the same pressures and cross pressures, the same changing and conflicting forces that impinge upon and ultimately shape communist political development more broadly. It is, therefore, not always just the villain that it is sometimes made out to be but also is frequently a victim of circumstances and forces not of its own making and beyond its control.

Merely because they may have suffered a similar fate, possess the same name, and are entrusted with the same anti-bureaucratic mission, however, does not necessarily mean that Party control organs in different Communist parties have shared the same historical experience, have worn identical faces, and have performed similar functional roles in their respective national parties and political systems. Indeed, just as each Communist Party has traveled its own road, so has its control commission its own distinct history. Each has its own story to tell about its political struggles, failures, and fate.

## NOTES

1. Robert C. Tucker, *The Soviet Political Mind*, rev. ed. (New York: Norton, 1971), p. 114.

2. Jiri Pelikan, ed., *The Czechoslovak Political Trials 1950-1954: The Suppressed Report of the Dubcek Government's Commission of Inquiry, 1968* (Stanford, Calif: Stanford University Press, 1971), p. 283. Accordingly, a set of effective safeguards against arbitrary and absolute power came to be regarded by the leaders of the Prague Spring as both an integral part of and essential condition for their projected model of a reformed and democratic socialist political system. To quote from the report by the Commission of Inquiry: "The Party leadership and the Government in its programs have more than once proclaimed that a return to similar conditions [as in the fifties] will never be permitted. Yet these honorable intentions cannot be dependent on the goodwill or the wishes of politicians–they require the backing of built-in guarantees in the political system, in the mechanism that initiates, exercises and controls policy, and in the mode of exercising the Party's leading role. . . . The Party sees the creation of a system of guarantees against any repetition of the political trials as an inseparable part of its post-January [1968] policy, and part of its endeavor to eliminate the bureaucratic distortions of the political system." Ibid., p. 277.

3. Roy Medvedev, *Let History Judge* (New York: Knopf, 1971), pp. 315, 415.

4. E. H. Carr, *What Is History* (New York: Vintage Books, 1962), p. 171.

5. For a general discussion of this theme, see Leonard Schapiro and John W. Lewis, "The Roles of the Monolithic Party under the Totalitarian Leader," *The China Quarterly*, no. 40 (October-December 1969): 39-64.

6. Earlier Brzezinski and Friedrich had described a similar relationship in reverse between restraints and totalitarianism. Indeed, the extent to which a regime succeeds in minimizing and destroying constraints on its power was taken to be a major yardstick by which to gauge "the degree of its totalitarianization." Carl J. Friedrich and Zbigniew K. Brzezinski, *Totalitarian Dictatorship and Autocracy* (Cambridge, Mass.: Harvard University Press, 1956), pp. 3-13. The dominant tendency has been, however, to conceive of these restraints as emanating principally from outside the political sector in society, such as in the family and church.

7. The triad of ethics, rationality, and terror may be conceived as essentially the communist analogs of normative, remunerative, and coercive power, categories used by Amitai Etzioni in his *A Comparative Analysis of Complex Organizations*

(New York: Free Press, 1961), esp. pp. 3-27. An attempt to apply an Etzioni scheme to communist systems and specifically to the problem of terror is the recent study by Alexander Dallin and George W. Breslauer, *Political Terror in Communist Systems* (Stanford, Calif.: Stanford University Press, 1970).

8. Milovan Djilas, *The Unperfect Society: Beyond the New Class* (New York: Harcourt, Brace and World, 1969), pp. 253-254.

9. Michael Walzer, *Obligations: Essays on Disobedience, War, and Citizenship* (Cambridge, Mass.: Harvard University Press, 1970), pp. 50-51.

10. Milovan Djilas, *The New Class* (New York: Praeger, 1957), pp. 153-154.

11. See Michael Walzer, *The Revolution of the Saints: A Study in the Origins of Radical Politics* (Cambridge, Mass.: Harvard University Press, 1965).

12. Walzer, *Obligations*, p. 191. With regard to communism, see, for example, André Gide, Richard Wright, *et al.*, *The God that Failed* (New York: Harper, 1949).

13. Trotsky, *Stalin: An Appraisal of the Man and His Influence* (London: Harper and Brothers, 1947), pp. 51, 55.

14. Quoted in Nikolay Valentinov (N. V. Volsky), *Encounters with Lenin* (London: Oxford University Press, 1968), p. 243.

15. Ibid., pp. 241-242.

16. Walzer, *Obligations*, p. 52.

17. Leon Trotsky, *The History of the Russian Revolution* (New York: Simon and Schuster, 1936), 3:166.

18. See Walzer, *The Revolution of the Saints.*

19. Remark by Arthur Koestler in Gide *et al.*, *The God that Failed*, p. 12.

20. Arthur Koestler, *Darkness at Noon* (London: Hutchinson and Company, 1973), p. 47.

21. From his poem, "Two Fragments," in Edmund Stillman, ed., *Bitter Harvest: The Intellectual Revolt behind the Iron Curtain* (New York: Praeger, 1959), p. 137.

22. See his paper, "Technocratic Elements in Soviet Socialism" (presented at the McMaster University Conference on Current Problems of Socialist Economics, October 23, 1970).

23. Quoted in Ibid., p. 8.

24. Benjamin I. Schwartz, "The Reign of Virtue: Some Broad Perspectives on Leader and Party in the Cultural Revolution," *The China Quarterly*, no. 35 (July/September 1968): 12.

25. V. I. Lenin, *Polnoe Sobranie Sochinenii* (Moscow) 43: 387.

26. Ibid., p. 557.

27. See the essay by Zbigniew Brzezinski, "Totalitarianism and Rationality," in his *Ideology and Power in Soviet Politics* (New York: Praeger, 1962), p. 18.

28. Djilas, *The New Class*, p. 155.

29. Koestler, *Darkness at Noon*, p. 46.

30. Reinhard Bendix, "Bureaucracy and the Problem of Power," in Robert K. Merton *et al.*, *Reader in Bureaucracy* (Glencoe, Ill.: Free Press, 1952), p. 129.

31. Samuel P. Huntington, *Political Order in Changing Societies* (New Haven, Conn.: Yale University Press, 1968), p. 63.

32. See Dallin and Breslauer, *Political Terror in Communist Systems*, p. 5.

33. Ibid., p. 42.

34. Alex Inkeles, "The Totalitarian Mystique," in *Totalitarianism*, ed. Carl J. Friedlich (Cambridge, Mass.: Harvard University Press, 1954), esp. pp. 105-107.

35. Merle Fainsod, *How Russia Is Ruled* (Cambridge, Mass.: Harvard University Press, 1953), pp. 354-389.

36. Otto Ulc, "Koestler Revisited," *Survey* no. 72 (Summer 1969): 118.

37. Ladislav Mnacko, *The Taste of Power* (New York: Praeger, 1967), p. 61.

38. See Leonard Schapiro, "Reflections on the Changing Role of the Party in the Totalitarian Polity," *Studies in Comparative Communism* 2, no. 2 (April 1969): 1-13, and Schapiro and Lewis, "The Roles of the Monolithic Party under the Totalitarian Leader."

39. For example, if Stalin sought to check institutionalization by devitalizing organizations from within and by duplicating parallel structures from without which have overlapping jurisdictions and blurred lines of authority, Mao has pursued a somewhat different approach reflecting his more intrinsic distrust of technical structures and administration. Instead of, or perhaps more appropriately in addition to, having organizations checking organizations in an atmosphere of institutionalized mutual suspicion, he has tried also to check bureaucratization by stimulating and simulating an atmosphere of struggle both from within and from without organizations in which the checking force is predominantly non-organizational, non-technical, populist activism, human spontaneity, and periodic mass movements.

40. Schapiro, "Reflections on the Changing Role of the Party," pp. 6-7.

41. See the discussion by Huntington, *Political Order in Changing Societies*, pp. 39-71.

42. Ibid., p. 63.

43. See his "Totalitarianism and Rationality."

44. Andrei Amalrik, *Will the USSR Survive Until 1984?* (New York: Harper and Row, 1970), p. 31. Self-preservation has become clearly their dominant drive. If in an earlier era the dynamism of revolutionary dreams facilitated the rise of political terror, then the dynamics of post-revolutionary reality push increasingly for its decline.

45. Ibid., p. 22.

46. Ibid.

47. See Richard Lowenthal, "Development vs. Utopia in Communist Policy," in Chalmers Johnson, ed., *Change in Communist Systems* (Stanford, Calif.: Stanford University Press, 1970), pp. 33-116. See also his essay, "The Model of the Totalitarian State," in Royal Institute of International Affairs, *The Impact of the Russian Revolution, 1917-1967* (London: Oxford University Press, 1967).

48. Brzezinski, "Totalitarianism and Rationality," p. 26.

49. This bureau was created within the Workers' and Peasants' Inspectorate in the summer of 1922, and it was soon changed to the Department of Rationalization. In his letter to V. A. Avanesov, the Deputy Commissar of WPI, on September 1, 1922, Lenin wrote that he attached "the greatest significance" to this department.

50. V. V. Kuibyshev, "Prevyi god raboty," *Voprosy sovetskogo khoziaistva i uprvaleniia* nos. 4-5 (April/May 1924):8.

51. *Survey* no. 72 (Summer 1969):42.

52. Brzezinski, "Totalitarianism and Rationality," pp. 32-33.

53. Zdenek Mlynar, "Our Political System and the Division of Power," *Rude Pravo*, 13 February 1968, in Robin Remington, ed., *Winter in Prague: Documents on Czechoslovak Communism in Crisis* (Cambridge, Mass.: MIT Press, 1969), p. 47.

54. Milan Huebl, "Socialism for Us," *Kulturny Zivot*, 5 January 1968, in RFE, Czechoslovak Press Survey, no. 1996 (16 January 1968).

55. Cited in Tibor Szamuely in *Survey* no. 72 (Summer 1969): 66.

56. Amalrik, *Will the USSR Survive Until 1984?*, pp. 29, 34.

57. Franz Schurmann, *Ideology and Organization in Communist China* (Berkeley, Calif.: University of California Press, 1968), p. 314.

58. In Czechoslovakia, for example, after the February 1948 coup the phenomenon of abuses of power by communist officials, who began acting more and more like arrogant "kings and princelings," raised its head. For a time there was some diversity among the Czech Party leaders about how to cope with this problem. Premier Klement Gottwald apparently thought in terms of having groups of opposition parties exercise a controlling function in this area. Antonin Zapotocky, the future president of Czechoslovakia, suggested that such a responsibility should perhaps be assigned to the National Front or the Revolutionary Trade Union Movement. These ideas, however, were quickly rejected by Moscow and condemned by the Cominform as non-Marxist. Consequently in September 1948, Gottwald announced that the function of defending society against the misuse of communist power was being taken over by the Party control commission. See A. Kaplan, "Thoughts about the Political Trials," *Nova Mysl* no. 6, 1968, in RFE, Czechoslovak Press Survey, no. 2147 (9 December 1968).

59. I. M. Moskalen'ko, "Bor'ba TsKK-RKI za razvitie partiinoi i sovetskoi demokratii (1923-1925gg)" (Unpublished diss., Moscow State University, 1963), p. xvi.

60. See Kenneth E. Boulding, *The Organizational Revolution: A Study in the Ethics of Economic Organization* (Chicago: Quadrangle Books, 1968), p. 69.

61. See my *Controlling Communist Bureaucracy: Ethics, Rationality, and Terror* (forthcoming). Some of my ideas can be found in my "The Rationalization of Party Control," in Johnson, *Change in Communist Systems*, pp. 153-190.

62. Kaplan, "Thoughts about the Political Trials," p. 6.

63. Ibid., in RFE, Czechoslovak Press Survey, no. 2147 (9 December 1968), p. 19.

64. *Jen Min Jih Pao*, 29 September 1956, in *Survey of the China Mainland Press*, no. 1435, p. 15.

65. *Desiatyi S'ezdd RKP(b): Stenograficheskii Otchet* (Moscow, 1963), p. 62.

66. *XVI S'ezd Vsesoiuznoi Kommunisticheskoi Partii (b): Stenograficheskii Otchet* (Moscow, 1961), p. 326.

67. Cited in *Current Background* (Hong Kong), no. 417:2. Italics added.

68. For a more detailed discussion, see Paul Cocks, "The Role of the Party Control Committee in Communist China," in *Papers on China*, Harvard University, East Asian Center, vol. 22B (December 1969), pp. 49-95.

69. Djilas, *The New Class*, p. 214.

70. Ibid.

71. First of all, it was made responsible only to the body which elected it. Thus, for example, the Central Control Commission was to answer only to the Party Congress. The previous requirement that the Central Committee endorse the selection of the chairman and vice chairman of the CCC was withdrawn. To ensure the independence of the control machinery from the regular Party apparatus, the CCC was allowed to name its own staff and to control its activity. The draft statutes also stipulated explicitly that an important part of the mandate of the control commission was to ensure that the rights of party members and party minorities are protected and that the Party observes democratic principles in its activity. Furthermore, all Party administrative and executive functions were to be taken away from the control organs so that they could concentrate fully on their

essentially judicial tasks. To enhance their independence in this regard, they received the right to call a congress or conference of the Party organization to which they were responsible or a plenary session of the executive control in the new draft statutes, published in *Rude Pravo*, 10 August 1968, in Remington, *Winter in Prague*, pp. 283-284.

72. Again one is reminded of Djilas' remark in 1956 when he noted that "the return to Leninism is the result of the inability of communist leaders to develop a theory sufficiently realistic for the modern world." *INS Bulletin*, no. 1199 (October 1, 1956), cited in RFE, Yugoslav Research Report (11 July 1968), pp. 5-6. Similarly, he reiterated the idea in his *The Unperfect Society* (p. 211), saying "the return to Lenin and his Party 'rules'. . .is no more than the usual communist flight into mythology, and in this instance a spectral and anachronistic mythology."

73. See Cocks, "The Rationalization of Party Control," pp. 165-190.

# 9

# Political Development and Political Change

Jan F. Triska and Paul M. Johnson

This study represents an examination of political change—in time and in space—in Eastern Europe. We approach the problem in two separate ways: First, relying on selected political development literature, via a synchronous cross-national "political development" analysis, and second, following some recent shifts of emphasis in the literature, via political change analysis. We then evaluate the usefulness of both approaches in terms of our concern, namely the study of political change in Eastern Europe.

*Political Development: Cross-National Comparison*

The polemic concerning the meaning of "political development"[1] and its utility as an organizing or unifying theoretical concept has been both interesting and important in sharpening the conceptual tools with which we approach the study of change in political systems.[2] In the long run, however, the value of any theoretical concept will be judged by the quality of the research which it stimulates and by the breadth of the findings which it enables us to subsume under limited and verified generalizations about phenomena in the real world. It is still too early to come to any comprehensive judgment as to which, if any, of the various processes identified with "political development" by one or another theorist is the most fundamental or the most broadly useful in explaining political change. We prefer not to identify "political development" with any one particular process, but rather to use it as an umbrella concept to cover a number of specific but theoretically distinct concepts which seem promising, but whose empirical interrelationships remain to be determined by research.

What follows is, first, an empirically-based comparison of the nine European Communist Party states according to operational measures of alternative theoretical criteria of political development—measures which are gauged finely enough to permit isolating differences as well as similarities among them. Second, we ask whether any relationships among the various kinds of "political development" in these states can be discerned and, if so, whether we can account for the differences.

*Selecting Concepts of Political Development for Investigation.* While it would be desirable from a theoretical standpoint to apply as many and as diverse political development concepts as possible, practical considerations of time, space, availability of information, and personal interest dictate that we limit our considerations to only a relative handful. To compensate for this, we have tried to make our selection as catholic and as representative of the literature as possible. Lucian Pye has suggested that there is substantial, if diffuse, consensus in the literature that "political development" is about one or all of three things: increased *equality* among individuals in relation to the political system; increased *differentiation* of political institutions and structures; and increased *capacity* of the political system in regard to its performance in its environment.[3] An earlier and overlapping formulation emanating from the Social Science Research Council's Committee on Comparative Politics specified somewhat more concretely the spread of political *participation* (subsumed by Pye under "equality"), *national integration* or nation-building, and the growth of governmental authority or *state-building* (the latter two being largely included under "capacity" by Pye). Almond and Powell[4] lay great emphasis on separating analytically the degree of effective *autonomy* exercised by political/social structures ("subsystem autonomy") from the degree of differentiation of political structures.[5] In addition, there has been increasing interest in coming to grips with the phenomenon of foreign participation in national political processes leading to assertions by "radical" (and not-so-radical) analysts that *national autonomy* is a crucial dimension of political development.

"Political development" might thus be broken down into five dimensions: *national integration, participation, functional differentiation of political structures, subsystem autonomy* (or, in more value-laden terms, "liberalization" or "decentralization of power"), and *national autonomy* (or, obversely, penetration or dependency). In this paper we do not deal with comparisons of the degrees of functional differentiation exhibited by the various political systems of Eastern Europe, mainly because this dimension is valuable in differentiating the obviously rudimentary political systems from the vast majority of contemporary nation-states. We also exclude consideration of the problem of national integration from this paper; this problem is so crucial and has received so much lucid discussion by East European single-country specialists that any attempt to place it in comparative perspective cries out for treatment far more extended than could be given here involving, at a minimum, analysis of the political effects of persistent nationality cleavages in the USSR, Czechoslovakia, and Yugoslavia, the existence of alternative governments for various nationality groups such as the "East" Germans and the Albanians, and the threats to territorial integrity posed by possible revanchist claims of other nations such as Germany. That leaves us with *subsystem autonomy, participation*, and *national autonomy*, and it is with these that the bulk of this part of the study is concerned.

### *Operationalizing the Theoretical Variables*

*Subsystem Autonomy or Liberalization.* One crucial distinction between more and less developed polities is that the former display a higher degree of structural differentiation. As used here, the subsystem autonomy concept assumes the existence of a substantial number of specialized structures—such as different governmental bureaucracies, mass media of communications, courts, legislatures, public schools, trade unions, associations, and so forth—and it refers to the quality of their interactions rather than the quantity which exist. Specifically, the concept denotes the degree to which structures and institutions are subordinated to and controlled by another political structure or structures. A social, economic, or political structure which is substantially free to generate and pursue its own politically relevant goals is highly autonomous, while one which serves merely as an instrument or "transmission belt" for the policies and goals of another (such as the central political "high command") has low autonomy.

While political, social, and economic structures in all the European Communist Party states exhibit a rather low degree of autonomy, there are variations in autonomy from structure to structure and from country to country. Indeed, it is the degree and rapidity of the expansion of such autonomy (liberalization) in various countries which has constituted the principal subject for commentary on political change in Eastern Europe over the past fifteen years.

The indicators of "subsystem autonomy" (or, more conventionally, "degree of liberalization") which we employ are displayed in Table 1, and are as follows: (a) ECOREF66, a ten-item Guttman scale designed by Johnson to indicate the degree of decentralizing *economic reforms* which had been formally approved by the Central Committee of the Communist Parties of the respective countries as of January 1966, though the reforms were not necessarily implemented by that time; (b) PRESS64, an index of the degree of *press censorship* exercised in 1964 as assessed by a panel of journalistic experts[6] ("1" = completely free, "9" = completely controlled); (c) SRVRES66, a four-point scale measuring the degree of autonomy permitted to *empirical social research* as of 1965-66, coded by John S. Shippee[7] ("0" = not allowed, "1" = instrumental, "2" = semi-autonomous, "3" = autonomous); (d) INTSEC62, estimates of total *internal security forces* as a percentage of adult population about 1962-63[8]; (e) PRIVAG65, computed as the percentage of total *agricultural land which was privately tilled* (excluding the land held in personal plots of collective and state farm workers) circa 1965[9]; and (f) ELECCON, a dichotomous measure denoting the presence or absence of the custom of presenting *more candidates for national office than the number of seats* to be filled (thus permitting the electorate at least a degree of choice), circa 1965.

**Table 1**

*Some Indicators Measuring Relative Degrees of Subsystem Autonomy in Eastern European Communist Party States in the Mid-1960s*

| *COUNTRY* | *ECOREF66* | *PRESS64* | *SRVRES66* | *INTSEC62* | *PRIVAG65* | *ELECC* |
|---|---|---|---|---|---|---|
| Albania | 0 | 9 | 0 | 10.7% | 9.6% | 0 |
| Bulgaria | 6 | 8 | 1 | 7.5% | 0.6% | 0 |
| Czechoslovakia | 9 | 8 | 2 | 4.0% | 11.0% | 0 |
| German Democratic Republic | 4 | 8 | 1 | 5.7% | 6.5% | 0 |
| Hungary | 9 | 7 | 1 | 5.3% | 3.0% | 0 |
| Poland | 3 | 7 | 3 | 2.4% | 87.0% | 1 |
| Romania | 1 | 8 | 1 | 4.9% | 8.2% | 0 |
| USSR | 5 | 8 | 2 | 2.7% | 0.0% | 0 |
| Yugoslavia | 10 | 6 | 3 | 3.7% | 90.0% | 1 |

Our reasons for choosing these particular types of subsystem autonomy to measure are several. First, most of the measures deal with what a wide consensus of political analysts would regard as key aspects of the traditional ideal type of the communist regime: the subjugation of the economy to centralized political control (ECOREF66 and PRIVAG65); manipulation of the mass media to monopolize political communication and control public opinion (PRESS64); the control of recruitment to political roles by the central authority to the virtual exclusion of popular elections of the Western type (ELECCON); and the maintenance of a high capability for the physical repression of mass resistance to regime policies (INTSEC62). SRVRES66 (empirical social research) is included because it not only represents in itself a particular aspect of subsystem autonomy (the "academic freedom" enjoyed by the rather small social category of professional sociologists) but also may plausibly be seen as an indication that the goals, or at least the concrete instrumental forms of social organization, are no longer regarded as entirely "given" in the official ideology of Marxism-Leninism as interpreted by the Party leadership. Insofar as empirical sociological inquiry involves survey research and attitude polls, it represents the creation of a potential capability for the leadership to become more "responsive," in that they thereby provide themselves with information as to what public demands actually are and institutionalize the means of acquiring such information on a regular basis.

The common tendency to speak about "liberalization" as a generalized process or tendency in various East European countries reflects a belief that the degree of autonomy allowed to each political structure is apt to be closely consonant with that allowed most other structures in the same system. Our data confirm that this was indeed the case in the Eastern Europe of the mid-1960s. Table 2 displays the matrix of Pearson Correlation Coefficients among our indicators of subsystem autonomy. The high degree of intercorrelation exhibited indicates that a country scoring relatively high on any one indicator of subsystem autonomy is very likely to score relatively high on the other indicators as well (and vice versa). The diversity of the indicators in substance, sources, and coding personnel, coupled with the very high intercorrelations constitute persuasive evidence that we are dealing with a genuine property of these political systems rather than with the idiosyncratic variations or artifacts of the coding system. We can empirically identify a "liberalization syndrome," and we can therefore compare the East European Communist Party states by ordering them according to the degree of liberalization they display in the given time-frame. Such a rank ordering, based on a composite index (LIBINDEX) calculated from the summed z-scores of our six subsystem autonomy indicators, appears in Table three.

*Participation.* In the very broadest sense, political participation might subsume virtually any behavior oriented in any way to the local or national political system—including not only efforts to influence the government or its agents (or fellow citizens), but also supportive behavior such as compulsory attendance at regime-sponsored rallies or involuntary military service. Myron Weiner offers such a broad, yet still theoretically interesting, definition which would have it that political participation refers to

> any voluntary action, successful or unsuccessful, organized or unorganized, episodic or continuous, employing legitimate or illegitimate methods intended to influence the choice of public policies, the administration of public affairs, or the choice of political leaders at any level of government, local or national.[10]

The study of political participation in this broad sense as applied to the European Communist Party states would be an extremely interesting project in its own right, involving, as it would, distinguishing between

## Table 2

### *Correlation Matrix for Measures of Liberalization*

| | ECOREF66 | PRESS64 | SRVRES66 | INTSEC62 | PRIVAG65 | ELECCON | LIBINDEX |
|---|---|---|---|---|---|---|---|
| ECOREF66 | 1.0000 | –0.6553 | 0.4760 | –0.4134 | 0.1864 | 0.2014 | 0.5948 |
| | ( 0) | ( 9) | ( 9) | ( 9) | ( 9) | ( 9) | ( 9) |
| | S= 0.001 | S= 0.028 | S= 0.098 | S= 0.134 | S= 0.316 | S= 0.302 | S= 0.046 |
| PRESS64 | –0.6553 | 1.0000 | –0.7593 | 0.6260 | –0.7395 | –0.7638 | –0.9202 |
| | ( 9) | ( 0) | ( 9) | ( 9) | ( 9) | ( 9) | ( 9) |
| | S= 0.028 | S= 0.001 | S= 0.009 | S= 0.036 | S= 0.011 | S= 0.008 | S= 0.001 |
| SRVRES66 | 0.4760 | –0.7593 | 1.0000 | –0.8500 | 0.7893 | 0.8078 | 0.9491 |
| | ( 9) | ( 9) | ( 0) | ( 9) | ( 9) | ( 9) | ( 9) |
| | S= 0.098 | S= 0.009 | S= 0.001 | S= 0.002 | S= 0.006 | S= 0.004 | S= 0.001 |
| INTSEC62 | –0.4134 | 0.6260 | –0.8500 | 1.0000 | –0.4447 | –0.4730 | –0.7723 |
| | ( 9) | ( 9) | ( 9) | ( 0) | ( 9) | ( 9) | ( 9) |
| | S= 0.134 | S= 0.036 | S= 0.002 | S= 0.001 | S= 0.115 | S= 0.099 | S= 0.007 |
| PRIVAG65 | 0.1864 | –0.7395 | 0.7893 | –0.4447 | 1.0000 | 0.9944 | 0.8408 |
| | ( 9) | ( 9) | ( 9) | ( 9) | ( 0) | ( 9) | ( 9) |
| | S= 0.316 | S= 0.011 | S= 0.006 | S= 0.115 | S= 0.001 | S= 0.001 | S= 0.002 |
| ELECCON | 0.2014 | –0.7639 | 0.8078 | –0.4730 | 0.9944 | 1.0000 | 0.8583 |
| | ( 9) | ( 9) | ( 9) | ( 9) | ( 9) | ( 0) | ( 9) |
| | S= 0.302 | S= 0.008 | S= 0.004 | S= 0.099 | S= 0.001 | S= 0.001 | S= 0.002 |
| LIBINDEX | 0.5948 | –0.9202 | 0.9491 | –0.7723 | 0.8408 | 0.8583 | 1.0000 |
| | ( 9) | ( 9) | ( 9) | ( 9) | ( 9) | ( 9) | ( 0) |
| | S= 0.046 | S= 0.001 | S= 0.001 | S= 0.007 | S= 0.002 | S= 0.002 | S= 0.001 |

(COEFFICIENT/(CASES) / SIGNIFICANCE)

ECOREF66: Guttman scale of degree of economic decentralization approved by Party Central Committee as of 1966.

PRESS64: R.B. Nixon's scale of degree of press censorship, 1964.

SRVRES66: Shippee's ratings of degree of autonomy of social science research circa 1966.

INTSEC62: Gurr's estimate of internal security forces per thousand adult population in 1962.

PRIVAG65: Privately farmed land as a percentage of all agricultural land circa 1965 (excludes garden plots of state and collective farmers).

ELECCON: 2-point scale indicating whether or not the number of candidates in parliament elections exceeded the number of seats to be filled in mid-1960s.

LIBINDEX: Sum of Z-scores of the above six (PRESS64 and INTSEC62 given negative signs).

Table 3

*East European Communist States Ranked in Order of Decreasing Liberalization As of the Mid-1960s*

| *Country* | *LIBINDEX Score** |
|---|---|
| Yugoslavia | 8.81 |
| Poland | 6.13 |
| Czechoslovakia | .73 |
| Hungary | .17 |
| USSR | –.17 |
| German Democratic Republic | –2.44 |
| Bulgaria | –2.73 |
| Romania | –2.91 |
| Albania | –7.54 |

* The composite LIBINDEX score was calculated by first normalizing the raw scores on each indicator by dividing (score-mean score) by standard deviations for the respective variables, then summing each country's normalized scores. This procedure ensures that each component of the Index is given equal weight, despite differences in the original units of measurement. Because we had no theoretical grounds for weighting any of the indicators more heavily than others, equal weighting seemed the most logical approach; because the indicators were so highly intercorrelated, however, it is unlikely that any plausible alternative weighting system would have made any very significant different in the final rank-ordering.

the types of participation indicated in the definition and trying to ascertain their relative frequencies and impact under varying conditions and in varying national settings.

For this reason, and because the problem of participation is so crucial and so central to the study of political development in Eastern Europe, we attempted to go into it as deeply as we could. In 1969, we invited Czechoslovak and Hungarian social scientists to a conference in Yugoslavia for which the Ljubljana social scientists prepared a sample questionnaire which they had pre-tested in Slovenia (320 interviews in four local communities within two communes). At the conference, we discussed the questionnaire with a view to applying it in Czechoslovakia and Hungary, and possibly in other Eastern European Communist Party states as well. How should we go about finding ways in which citizens take part in political activity, the processes that bring them to activity in politics, the problems on which they focus that activity, and the response of leaders to citizen initiatives? We wanted to know the conditions under which one issue rather than some other issue is chosen by citizens; the process by which citizens come to be aware of these problems and to participate *vis-à-vis* them; and the impact of their activity on the degree to which leaders are responsive to these activities. The interviews with local leaders should enable us, we thought, to deal with both citizen activity and the response to it.

Unfortunately, we found in 1970 that the project could be carried out neither in Czechoslovakia nor in Hungary. The comparative aspect of the study was lost. The Ljubljana social scientists did go ahead, however, and formed an all-Yugoslav team, developed the study for the whole country, interviewed cross-samples of 3,000 citizens and 500 local leaders, coped with the data, and processed them for analysis. Before long we should be able to describe political participation in Yugoslavia in terms of the amount and the types of activity, the structure of participation and the relationship among political acts, and the relationships between demographic and ecological (community) characteristics and participation. Unfortunately, although comparative in terms of the Yugoslav republics, and the multi-national aspects of Yugoslavia, the outcome will not be comparative in terms of Eastern Europe. It will show that, while in a number of major ways participation in Yugoslavia is similar to that in other countries, there are a number of differences in the ways in which political acts cluster—differences deriving from two main features of the Yugoslav political system: the absence of competition among political parties and the presence of innovative participatory mechanisms and self-management bodies such as the workers' councils.

Because of our focus in this paper on the broad problem of political development and because of limitations of time and space, it will be necessary for the present to take a more restricted view of participation in East Europe. It seems most expedient for the purposes of this paper simply to direct our attention toward the incidence of legitimate, institutionalized, organized, and more or less continuous participation as a criterion of political development.

The most readily available and cross-nationally comparable measure of this sort of participation is the size of the Communist parties, each of which is, in its own country, normatively and legally sanctioned as the chief source of initiative and guiding supervision for all political, social, economic, and cultural institutions. While the hierarchical and disciplined character of the Party in most communist countries considerably dilutes its suitability as a vehicle for "real" mass participation in the Western sense ("liberal" *or* "radical"), nevertheless one may reasonably argue (a) that in the broader perspectives of comparative political development theory Western style participation is not the only relevant type, and (b) that even in the context of concern with genuinely efficacious individual participation (to the extent it occurs in communist countries), the Party is the most likely vehicle, relative to alternative legitimate organized means of exerting influence. While it would be a vast overstatement to assert that the lower echelon Party member "participates" effectively in the making of decisions of broad scope at the national level, one may nevertheless provisionally accept the probability that he has the opportunity to participate somewhat more meaningfully in lower-level decisions involving his enterprise or his bureau or his apartment building or his town council, and that those who are not Party members generally have less opportunity for participation at even this modest level.

Data on recent trends in the inclusiveness of the various East European Communist Parties are shown in Table 4. Several generalizations emerge rather strikingly from inspection of the data. First of all, there is great variation from country to country in the size of the Party, ranging from slightly over 3 percent of population in Albania to almost five times that percentage in Rumania. It is evident that while the Leninist prescription for a small, highly disciplined Party may command uniform approval as theory in all communist states, nevertheless there is considerable divergence when it comes to translating the general precept into actual numbers in the concrete national situation. Secondly, just as the first half of the 1960s was generally a period of relative liberalization, so also during this period we can discern a clear trend throughout Eastern Europe toward the expansion of participation as measured by incidence of Party membership. From 1960 to 1966, seven of these Parties registered an increase in party membership as a percentage of total population, while two (Yugoslavia and Albania) maintained a constant level—none suffered a decline. The average increase was two percentage points (although if we elimiinate the single spectacular case of Rumania, the average is closer to one percentage point gain). Measured in terms of proportional increase, the average East European Communist Party state increased the proportion of Party members in the population by 41 percent from 1960 to 1966, or by an average of 17 percent if we again exclude Rumania (which increased its Party size by more than 230 percent). Clearly, at least in quantitative terms, we are dealing with rather high rates of change here.

*National Autonomy/Penetration.* The notion of national autonomy (or, obversely, penetration by external powers) is a complicated one, and the difficulties of operationalization are compounded by the fact that, until very recently, theorists in the field of comparative politics have not considered the issue in much depth. (The exception has been the vocal minority of Latin Americanists who have produced the "dependency theory" literature, based principally on elaboration of the Hobson-Lenin theory of imperialism as the inevitable outgrowth of capitalism—a body of theory which expressly excludes the foreign policies of socialist states from its domain.[11]) More recently, political scientists working in the vacuum between comparative politics and international relations have begun to emphasize the interaction between

Table 4

*Party Membership as a Percentage of Population 1960 and 1966, and Change in Membership Rate, 1960 to 1966*

| *Country* | *Party 60* | *Party 66* | *Party GRO* |
|---|---|---|---|
| Romania | 4.5% | 14.9% | 10.4% |
| Czechoslovakia | 11.4% | 12.0% | 0.6% |
| German Democratic Republic | 8.7% | 10.3% | 1.6% |
| Bulgaria | 6.2% | 7.4% | 1.2% |
| Poland | 3.9% | 5.8% | 1.9% |
| Hungary | 4.6% | 5.7% | 1.1% |
| USSR | 4.1% | 5.3% | 1.2% |
| Yugoslavia | 5.3% | 5.3% | 0.0% |
| Albania | 3.3% | 3.3% | 0.0% |

Sources: Party membership figures from U.S. State Department Bureau of Intelligence and Research, World Strength of Communist Party Organizations, various years; population from U.N. Demographic Yearbook.

national and international political processes and to formulate theoretical concepts to deal with this interaction in systematic fashion.[12] At the root of the notion of a highly penetrated or dependent polity is the idea that the decisions of actors or organizations formally external to the polity dominate or set fairly narrow limits to the functioning of important aspects of the social, economic, cultural, and political systems of the dependent country. The dependent country is manipulated in the interests of these external forces, often to its own detriment, as non-members of the national society participate directly and authoritatively (through the cooperation of allied domestic political elites) in the allocation of the society's values and/or the determination of its goals.

Probably the most theoretically satisfactory way to operationalize the penetration concept would be to determine the frequency with which identifiable foreign initiatives (in the East European case, principally from the USSR) have led the "dependent" Party-states to take actions which the leaders would otherwise have judged prejudicial to their national interests or to refrain from taking actions which they otherwise would have considered beneficial, aggregating incidents with some weighting system reflecting the "degree of sacrifice" involved in each instance. This approach has not been undertaken here, mainly because of the complexity of the judgments as to "interests" and "real but concealed desires" which would be involved. We have opted for an approach based on assessment of less direct measures of penetration which are more readily observable by virtue of being large-scale public phenomena. First, it is relatively easy for anyone familiar with East European affairs in the 1960s to provide at least a loose categorization of the Party states according to the degree of overt assertion of national sovereignty exhibited by the leadership in their relations with the USSR. We have done this in Table 5 under the heading RUSLEAD. Secondly, one may supplement this subjective ranking with more concrete measures that are intended to assess the USSR's readily available means for exerting influence in each country, which are also displayed in Table 5.

**Table 5**

*Some Indicators of Penetration in Eastern Europe*

| *Country* | RUSLEAD | RMILPN65 | RTRAN65 | RUSTRD65 | ENERGY65 |
|---|---|---|---|---|---|
| Albania | 0 | 0 | 26% | 0% | + |
| Yugoslavia | 0 | 0 | 13% | 12% | + |
| Romania | 1 | 1 | 20% | 39% | = |
| Poland | 2 | 2 | 23% | 30% | + |
| Czechoslovakia | 3 | 1 | 16% | 37% | = |
| Bulgaria | 3 | 1 | 43% | 51% | = |
| Hungary | 3 | 2 | 16% | 36% | – |
| German Democratic Republic | 3 | 2 | n.a. | 43% | – |

RUSLEAD: We had little difficulty in ranking Albania and Yugoslavia as essentially independent in their relations with the USSR (not only because the leaders of both have vociferously defended the recognition of national sovereignty as a keystone to socialist internationalism, but also because their "outgroup" status has been formalized through public "excommunication" (Yugoslavia in 1948 and Albania in 1960). We ranked Romania next on the basis of the much publicized opposition within Comecon to Soviet plans for economic integration, pressures for reform of the decisional structure in the Warsaw Pact, refusal to make an unqualified condemnation of the Chinese line in the Sino-Soviet polemic, and general rhetorical assertion of the principle of national sovereignty and self-determination in intra-bloc relations—all of which still stopped short of an open break or rejection of special obligations to the USSR and the socialist bloc. We had little hesitation in classifying Czechoslovakia, Bulgaria, Hungary, and East Germany as the most highly penetrated in the early 1960s but felt that it would probably be counterproductive to attempt to discriminate a more precise rank-ordering within this subgroup: accordingly, they were scored identically. We decided to differentiate Poland from this group and rank it after Rumania, despite a visible tendency for Gomulka to withdraw somewhat from the relatively self-assertive posture he had taken in the later 1950s.

Our remaining penetration indicators break down the notion of means for exerting influence into *military, economic,* and *cultural* components, corresponding roughly to the notions of coercive sanctions, remunerative sanctions, and psychological manipulation as generic types of influence. RMILPN65 assesses the extent of *Russian military penetration* circa 1965 and was coded as follows: 2 = one or more divisions of Soviet troops stationed permanently within the country; 1 = no permanent Soviet garrison, but country is active member and participant in the Warsaw Pact and engages in extensive military liaison, exchange of information, and coordination of planning and maneuvers with the Soviet army; 0 = non-participant in Warsaw Pact activities or joint military planning or maneuvers. RTRAN65 is simply *translations of Russian language books* as a percentage of total translations published in 1965 as computed from UNESCO figures. The potential of foreign troops for exerting direct influence upon internal politics is fairly obvious and needs no further discussion here in the light of the experiences of East Germany in 1953, Hungary in 1956, and Czechoslovakia in 1968. RTRAN65 is conceived as a measure of the extent to which Russian cultural influence is fostered in the dependent country. The idea is that, even when elites are not consciously striving to please the Soviets by their policies, there is nonetheless the possibility that Soviet models will be emulated due to the prestige of the USSR as the model for socialist development, or due to a lack of knowledge of reasonable alternatives, or due to an unconscious internalization of Soviet modes of analysis and basic assumptions. Of course, frequent translation of Soviet books may also indicate a conscious policy of the national political elite to emulate the USSR in preference to implementing innovative political, social, economic, or cultural policies based upon the unique circumstances of their own country, thus further emphasizing the dependency of the elite and their probable manipulability.

The variables RUSTRD65 and ENERGY65 are conceived as measures of the extent to which the country is dependent upon the *USSR as a source of economic goods* and as a market for domestic production. RUSTRD65 is *total trade with the USSR* (exports plus imports) as a percentage of the country's total foreign trade. Sudden embargoes or delays in deliveries of key materials have the capacity to cause severe economic dislocations in the dependent country, particularly under the ultra-taut materials balance conditions typical of East European socialist economics, and hence have an obvious coercive potential which is apt to be most extreme where the extent of Soviet dominance of the country's foreign trade is most pronounced. Moreover, if it is true, as is sometimes asserted by Western economic analysts,[13] that the USSR in the 1960s still used its other political resources to extract more than ordinarily favorable terms of trade from its East European trading partners, the indicator may also be a measure of the degree of "exploitation" to which the country submits. The ENERGY65 variable assesses need for a special case of a particularly *crucial type of import for which the USSR is the principal* (and in the short term, virtually the only possible) supplier–imports of energy sources (electricity, coal, petroleum, etc.). Following Nicolas Spulber, we classified these Party states according to their endowment of energy resources, so vital to virtually all modern economic activity. They can be divided into three basic energy groups: *the energy deficient* (Hungary and East Germany); *the energy sufficient*, either in solid and liquid fuels or in hydroelectric resources (Albania, Bulgaria, Czechoslovakia, and Romania); and *the energy surplus countries* (Yugoslavia and Poland).[14] We reason that the energy deficient countries are particularly vulnerable to a potential cutoff of their energy imports and hence are apt to be particularly dependent upon their supplier.

It is perhaps worth noting a few descriptive generalizations suggested by our data. The fact that our indicators, based upon potential means of influence, are not highly intercorrelated among themselves but generally do correlate with RUSLEAD (the single measure based on overt acts and attitudes oriented toward political relations with the USSR) suggests that the mechanisms of Soviet influence in East Europe may often be specialized and tailored to the particular country rather than overlapping and mutually reinforcing. The northern tier of economically more developed socialist states seems to be the most penetrated, with only Czechoslovakia lacking military occupation in 1965 (a deficiency that was to be remedied three years later). Hungary and East Germany are also energy-deficient, but Czechoslovakia is energy sufficient and Poland even shows an energy surplus. But, on the other hand, the inclination to import Russian translations seems to be rather minimal. Bulgaria shows the most lopsidedly Soviet orientation in both trade and translations, but is not host to Soviet troops and is energy sufficient. The other southern socialist states (Albania, Yugoslavia, and Rumania) are the least penetrated, only Rumania being even nominally within the Warsaw Pact by this time, all being energy sufficient or surplus, and only Rumania still engaging in really substantial trade with the USSR (although at a much lower rate than even a few years previously). Interestingly enough, violently anti-Soviet Albania was the second largest translator of Russian books after Bulgaria, perhaps reflecting either a taste for the Stalinist literary debris of the 1930s or a recognition that not even revisionists could do much to spoil textbooks on sanitary engineering.

*Relating the Dimensions of Development.* We indicated at the outset that we regarded "political development" as a multi-dimensional umbrella concept covering a number of different secular trends that theorists have discerned in the study of long-term structural changes in political systems (often as a sort of sidelight to the study of economic development and social-cultural "modernization"), and that the precise nature of the interrelationships between the different theoretical concepts was itself a particularly important matter for empirical research. Therefore, let us now confront the problem, what is the relation, if any, between participation and liberalization and national autonomy.

Table 6 displays correlation coefficients for our three main indicators of political development. It indicates that our three major political development indicators are essentially uncorrelated. It would be easy to conclude that (for Eastern Europe in the mid-1960s at least) liberalization, participation, and penetration are unrelated. It would be *easy*, but it would be *wrong*. The correlation coefficient used here indicates only that there is not a simple *linear* relationship between the indicators. But there is no reason, common social science practice to the contrary notwithstanding, to suppose that all regularities in the real world take the form of linear relationships. In this case, examination of a graphic representation of the variables in a simple scattergram reveals a striking but non-linear relationship. (See Figure 1.) Relatively high inclusiveness of the Party tends to go along with a relatively low degree of liberalization[15] and a relatively high degree of liberalization tends to go along with a relatively small Party, but the array is not linear because of the existence of a number of countries with *both* low liberalization and small parties.

**Table 6**

*Correlation Matrix of Political Development Indicators*

| | *LIBINDEX* | *PARTY66* |
|---|---|---|
| PARTY66 | R= –.153<br>Sig .347 | R = 1.000<br>Sig .001 |
| RUSLEAD | R =–.073<br>Sig .432 | R = .140<br>Sig .371 |

The L-shaped configuration of the scattergram becomes readily comprehensible if we consider it in a dynamic rather than a static context. It is very much what we might expect to find if the Party states had initially begun with rather similar degrees of liberalization and Party inclusiveness (both rather low) imposed by an external power with a taste for uniformity (the USSR), followed by a period in which

## Figure 1

*Scattergram on Relationship Between Degree of Liberalization and Party Membership in Eastern Europe in the Mid-1960s*

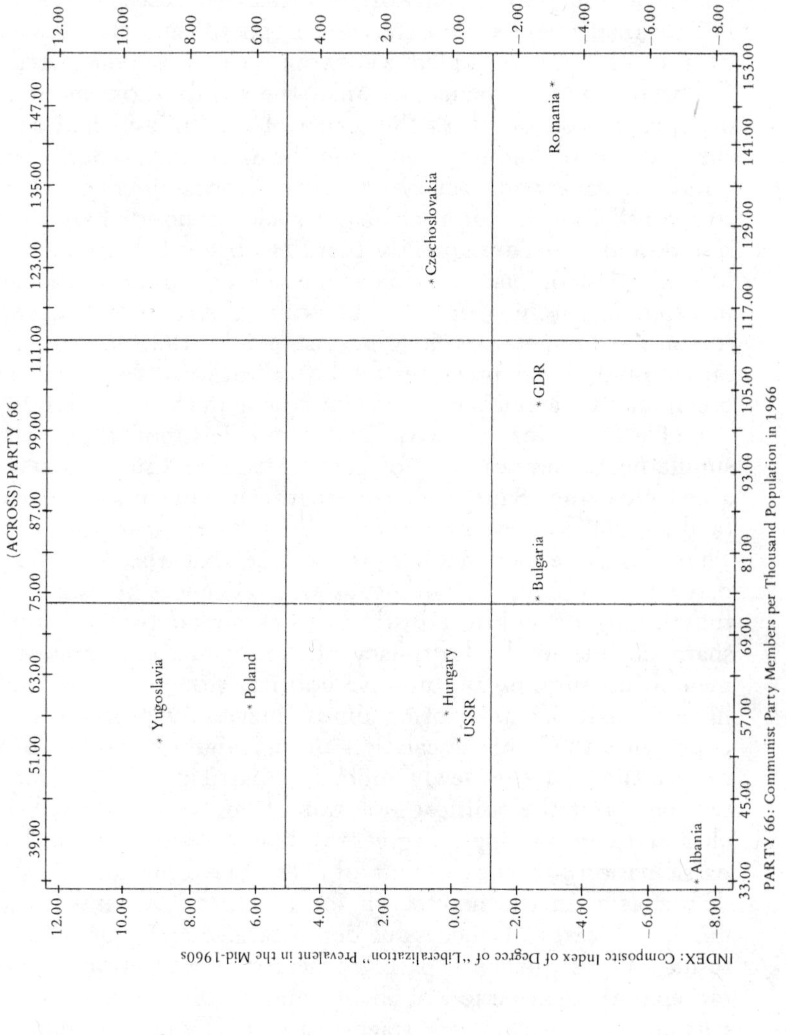

the Party states were somewhat more free to adapt themselves to their differing national environments. This adaptation tended to take the form of either liberalization or expansion of participatory opportunities, but for some reason(s) not both. This interpretation is given further plausability when we notice that the USSR is still rather close to the origin of the graph, located in the angle of the "L" (as the original model, presumably the USSR would require less change to remain adapted to its environment than those countries on which its institutional forms were externally imposed) and that the extreme tips of the "L" are occupied by two of the less penetrated countries, Yugoslavia and Rumania. Albania, the third autonomous Party state, occupies a position below the corner of the "L": we may speculate that the Stalinist regime imposed upon the extremely underdeveloped economy and backward society of Albania represented a political "superstructure" more modern than the socio-economic base upon which it rested, and that consequently there has been little pressure for greater liberalization or participation while the economy and society are still involved in catching up with the political structure. Indeed, according to some commentators, it was resistance by the Albanian leadership to rather mild Soviet pressures for liberalization ("de-Stalinization") that precipitated Albania's independent course in the early 1960s.

The question of why adaptation has not taken the form of simultaneous development of participation and subsystem autonomy is a complex one. Samuel P. Huntington has made a complex argument (and supported it with an array of data drawn from both European and Third World experience) to the effect that the rapid expansion of participation coupled with substantial changes in the structure and functioning of political institutions is an almost sure formula for a sharp decline in the legitimacy of the regime, the paralysis of governmental institutions, and massive political violence, since the process of institutionalizing new forms almost inevitably proceeds too slowly to cope with the rapid escalation of demands generated by the rising expectations of the newly mobilized participants.[16] Robert A. Dahl, writing about the political evolution of "polyarchies" (political systems characterized by high degrees of liberalization and inclusiveness of participation) in the context of West European and Anglo-American democracies in the nineteenth and twentieth centuries, suggested that nearly all cases of successful democratic development have been the result of a sequence ("path") wherein liberalization occurred over a rather prolonged period of elitist politics, followed by the expansion of participation in the later stages; cases of rapid simultaneous development or of participation preceding liberalization have usually led to chaos followed by reassertion of authoritarian rule or the establishment of closed hegemony through suppression of competing elites respectively. (Dahl's explanation parallels Huntington's, but emphasizes the difficulty of working out a system of "mutual security" among the contestants for power and influence when they are not drawn from a small and homogeneous elite with a strong commitment to a set of shared political values.[17]) Dahl and Huntington concur that simultaneous development tends to be seriously destabilizing to the social and political order to a much greater degree than is the case when either participation or liberalization is expanded separately. One can then explain the East European pattern in part by the assumption that the East European Party elites are aware of these dangers and act accordingly in their attempts to adapt their regimes to the exigencies of their countries' domestic environments.

The picture is further complicated, however, when one attempts to consider the impact of the international environment on political development.[18] On at least two occasions, East European communist leaders have attempted simultaneous liberalization and expansion of political participation in which only minimal amounts of popular disorder resulted; but this small degree of disorder was enough to trigger military intervention by the USSR to reverse the developmental process (and, incidentally, to cause massive, if short-lived, popular disorder and rebellion against the foreign occupation plus lingering problems of legitimacy for the domestic communist elites). Although the Polish autumn of 1956 did not generate a Soviet military invasion like that of Hungary 1956 or Czechoslovakia 1968, nevertheless it is also likely that Soviet pressure and the example of Hungary coincided with domestic concerns for stability in Gomulka's partial retreat from liberalization that became most noticeable about 1958 and in the purge that shrunk the Party by about 20 percent in the period 1957-1959.

Whether domestic or international factors are dominant in determining the course of East European political development is a question that is, of course, not fully answerable on the basis of these data. And perhaps it is incorrect to seek a general answer for all the East European Party states. It is clear that for the foreseeable future, the degree and rate of political development in the USSR is going to set some limits to the developmental strategies of East European leaders, but those limits may not necessarily be more restrictive than the fears and unimaginativeness of national communist elites (thinking here particularly of Bulgaria). And the degree of latitude may well vary from country to country. For example, the heavy penetration of the northern tier of Party states may indicate that the Soviet leaders regard these countries as more important than the southern ones, since the north is both militarily strategic in the event of an East-West confrontation in Europe and economically more valuable because more developed. This inference is also supported by the fact that the two successful "break-ways" (Yugoslavia and Albania) are both located in this region, as is Rumania, which so far seems to be a successful "bendaway."

If this interpretation is accurate, then we may have the beginnings of a theoretical explanation for an anomaly that appears in our data when we attempt to relate political development in Eastern Europe with broader processes of economic development and social modernization in which comparative political theorists customarily embed it.

*Political Development, Economic Development, and Social Modernization.* The literature of "political development" includes a large number of studies which successfully link level of economic and social development to level of political development, with the latter usually defined in terms that come close to equating political development with liberal pluralist democracy. Cutright, Lipset, Shannon, Neubauer, Adelman and Morris, Coleman, and Dahl, among others, have published papers concluding that there is indeed a positive relationship between level of economic development and "chances for democracy" based on synchronic cross-national comparisons of various samples of twentieth century polities using slightly different but roughly comparable indices of "democracy" and economic development. Moreover, Dahl suggests that this relationship is strongest in the very economic range in which most of the East European Party states find themselves, between $200 and $800 GNP per capita.[19] These findings are also representative of a more generalized and pervasive notion throughout the literature that political development (in a wider sense than democratic development) is part of a development syndrome, that political development somehow semi-automatically "goes along with" social and economic development in the normal course of (domestically determined) events.

To test the hypothesis in the East European context, a number of alternative measures of level of social-economic development were employed (displayed in Table 7) although all of them are very highly intercorrelated for the European Party states as for the world as a whole. The measures employed are: (1) PRIM64: percentage of economically active *population employed in agriculture and forestry*, 1964; (2) LITRCY63: *literate population* as a percentage of total population, 1963; (3) INCOME66: World Bank estimates of *GNP per capita* in U.S. dollars, 1966; (4) CITY65: proportion of total population resident in *cities over 100,000 population*, 1965; (5) MEAT6466: per capita daily average *consumption of animal protein*, 1964-66; (6) INFANT65: *infant mortality rate* (per thousand), 1965; (7) RADIO64: *radios* per one thousand population, 1964; (8) POWER66: per capita *consumption of energy* in kilograms of coal-equivalent, 1966.

Correlation coefficients between social-economic development indicators and political development indicators are shown in Table 8. In a nutshell, practically no correlations significant at the .05 level appear. We cannot with confidence reject the null hypothesis that there is no positive relationship between level of socio-economic development and the level of political development, at least not so long as we omit penetration/national autonomy from our definition of political development. The figures in Table 8 do indicate, however, a rather strong

Table 7

*Indicators of Level of Socio-Economic Development*

| *Country* | (1) | (2) | (3) | (4) | (5) | (6) | (7) | (8) |
|---|---|---|---|---|---|---|---|---|
| German Democratic Republic | 17% | 99% | 1260 | 16.7% | .407 | 248 | 337 | 5493 |
| Czechoslovakia | 22% | 99% | 960 | 15.0% | .387 | 255 | 263 | 5641 |
| USSR | 33% | 99% | 1000 | 27.5% | .358 | 267 | .315 | 3789 |
| Hungary | 32% | 98% | 870 | 24.7% | .397 | 388 | 245 | 2825 |
| Poland | 45% | 96% | 790 | 21.4% | .426 | 417 | 186 | 3608 |
| Bulgaria | 48% | 93% | 480 | 17.5% | .250 | 308 | 241 | 2726 |
| Yugoslavia | 57% | 82% | 470 | 9.0% | .211 | 718 | 140 | 1202 |
| Romania | 58% | 94% | 440 | 14.7% | .262 | 441 | 142 | 2072 |
| Albania | 68% | 75% | 290 | 8.6% | .212 | 868 | 42 | 331 |

(1) = PRIM64
(2) = LITRCY63
(3) = INCOME66
(4) = CITY65
(5) = MEAT6466
(6) = INFANT65
(7) = RADIO64
(8) = POWER66

*negative relationship between level of socio-economic development and degree of national autonomy.* That is, the more economically developed Party states are also the more penetrated ones. We may speculate that the reason for the absence of strong correlations between socio-economic development indicators, on the one hand, and indicators of participation and liberalization, on the other hand, may be the confounding influence of Soviet penetration. Less developed Party states seem to have more freedom to adapt to pressures generated by the development process but, because of their lower levels of development, less need to do so; while the more economically developed Party states presumably have more pressing needs for political adaptation, but less freedom to do so, particularly insofar as adaptation involves liberalization rather than simple expansion of participation. The very large parties of Czechoslovakia and the GDR, two of the most developed and most penetrated Party states, may indicate an attempt by the leaders to deal with the political pressures of advanced industrial societies through broad inclusiveness of the Party without much development along the more suspect dimension of liberalization.

In attempting to forecast the future of East European political development, we are forced to confront a paradox of conflicting forces. There is a great deal of social theory to suggest that, *while the relationship of participation and liberalization in the short run is antagonistic, in the long run they tend to be complementary*. That is, states which have successfully liberalized tend over the long run to encounter strong pressures for greater inclusiveness of participation, and (though this is less certain) those which extend participation to a broader and broader array of social strata are apt to develop a need for greater liberalization in order to permit efficient and effective coordination of political, social, and economic institutions. For the northern tier of Party states (GDR, Poland, Czechoslovakia, and Hungary) which are in advanced stages of economic development and which are also highly penetrated by the USSR, we may project intensification of social and economic pressures for liberalization and participation, but we must recognize that adaptation by the political elite is apt to be retarded if not frozen altogether by the Soviets and their domestic allies. It seems likely that the degree to which the Soviet elite is able to come to terms with the contingencies of more advanced economies and societies than their own will be crucial in determining the extent to which the northern tier Party states follow a successful adaptive path or to which they succumb to political alienation, economic inefficiency, and cultural escapism and their twin political correlates—apathy and protest.

For the southern tier of Party states, the outlook would seem to be different, though not necessarily more favorable. Here we encounter states whose leaders possess (actually or potentially—the test case will have to be Bulgaria, *Bozhe moi*!) more autonomy for developmental adaptation by virtue of their lesser degree of Soviet penetration. Yet here also we encounter a very different sort of domestic environment as well, due in part to the lower degree of social mobilization, and in part to unique situation factors in each country. Rumania has thus far taken a developmental path involving extremely rapid expansion of participation but little or no liberalization—a decision which probably owes something to the personal tastes and proclivities of the leadership as well as to the need for "unity and strength" in the face of a possible threat of Soviet intervention. Over the long haul, this may build barriers to liberalization which may be difficult to overcome in the future, even if the Soviet threat diminishes considerably (though the still highly underdeveloped state of the Romanian economy may also increase the chances for future success in liberalization by removing much of the pressure for rapid decompression and facilitating a long, slow liberalization process). Here the attitude of Rumanian leaders in the future seems likely to be the crucial variable, a generalization which probably

## Table 8

*Correlation Coefficients–Socio-economic and Political Development Indicators*

| | PRIM64 | LITRCY63 | INCOME66 | CITY65 | MEAT6466 | INFANT65 | RADIO64 | POWER66 |
|---|---|---|---|---|---|---|---|---|
| ECOREF66 | –.4295 | .2572 | .2632 | .1376 | .1681 | .2533 | .3930 | .2687 |
| PRESS64 | .0305 | –.0786 | –.0649 | –.0851 | –.1030 | –.0442 | –.0492 | .0585 |
| SRVRES66 | –.1429 | .2174 | .2007 | .1632 | .2658 | –.1384 | .1660 | .2307 |
| INTSEC62 | .4286 | *–.6188* | –.4973 | –.5085 | –.5441 | .4942 | –.4729 | –.4859 |
| PRIVAG65 | .3007 | –.2878 | –.1867 | –.2570 | –.0511 | .3842 | –.3452 | –.2173 |
| ELECCON | .2869 | –.2499 | –.1640 | –.1788 | –.0310 | .3440 | –.2981 | –.2134 |
| LIBINDEX | –.0909 | .1297 | .1376 | .0942 | .2030 | –.0243 | .0899 | .1015 |
| | | | | | | | | |
| PARTY66 | –.2886 | .4767 | .1670 | –.0972 | .1510 | –.4916 | .2412 | .4525 |
| PARTYGRO | .2274 | .2086 | –.1992 | .0014 | –.1039 | –.1396 | –.1483 | –.0843 |
| | | | | | | | | |
| RMILPN65* | *–.7006* | *.8544* | *.7825* | *.9055* | *.8947* | *–.7563* | *.7233* | *.6724* |
| RTRAN65** | .2390 | –.0585 | –.3755 | .0751 | –.2690 | –.1692 | .0595 | –.1100 |
| RUSTRD65* | *–.6132* | *.8694* | .5069 | *.6471* | .4789 | *–.9400* | *.8013* | *.6660* |
| ENERGY65* | .4035 | –.2384 | –.2970 | –.0182 | –.2396 | .2495 | –.2613 | –.2506 |
| RUSLEAD* | *–.8441* | *.8723* | *.7317* | *.7610* | *.7356* | *–.9222* | *.8977* | *.8120* |

Note: Italicized coefficients are significant at the .05 level (single-tail test). Correlations for variables marked * are based on eight cases (omitting the USSR). Correlations for the one marked ** are based on seven cases (omitting the USSR and the German Democratic Republic).

also applies to the Albanians, who remain essentially uncommitted as to the path of development they may take in the future (if any) and who seem unlikely to be forced into choosing for quite some time.

In the case of Yugoslavia, development in the past has taken the form of increased subsystem autonomy without very much expansion of participation in the affairs of the Party. Here, a dimension of political development not treated systematically in this paper seems likely to be a crucial variable—that of national integration. In the present context of hostility between Yugoslavia's constituent nationality groups, large-scale expansion of participation in an already relatively liberalized situation is apt to be hazardous in the extreme due to the likelihood of decisional paralysis at the federal level and possible exacerbation of secessionist pressures exerted upon regional political leaders. The problem of national integration seems likely to reach crisis proportions soon, and the strategy chosen for resolving this crisis is likely to determine the course of Yugoslav political development for some time to come.

*Political Change: Cross-Time Comparison*

In spite of the data shortcomings, the above analysis is a useful tool for comparative spatial analysis. The problem is that it does not tell us much about political changes in individual countries over time. With better access to data, we could supply a series of developmental time snapshots, the more the better, which would provide a sequential film that would contain an accordion-type data base sufficient for meaningful tracing of political changes. Unfortunately, we have no such access to data. For that reason, we focus our attention now on actual sequences of political change in Eastern Europe, concentrating particularly on the interaction of intrabloc relations with domestic liberalization and participation. We will analyze the changes in terms of sources, types, rates, scopes, directions, intensities, trade-offs, etc., as suggested by Samuel Huntington's theoretical (but not empirical) writing on the subject.[20]

Our basic assumption is that while everything changes all the time, some political changes differ from others in their magnitude, intensity, and rate to such an extent that they may be readily identified as major political changes. To these specified historical episodes we now turn.

*Major Political Changes.* Since World War II, at least twelve major sequences of political change may be identified in East Europe.

*1. Coalition formation.* During and after World War II a foundation for a security community was laid out in East Europe by the USSR, the strongest power in the area, to fill the post-war vacuum. This security community, when it emerged, consisted of eight relatively small countries: East Germany, Poland, Czechoslovakia, Hungary, Romania, Yugoslavia, Bulgaria, and Albania—some hundred and twenty million people living on about a half million square miles, or about one-fourth of the population of Europe living on almost one-fourth of Europe's territory—a group of quite heterogeneous peoples who differed considerably among themselves and from the Soviet Union.

Upon Soviet insistence and under their respective Communist Party leaders, the eight political systems changed their political structures and institutions, their values relevant to politics, their social and economic formations, and their policies. The change was profound—constituting no less than a multiple revolutionary transformation of the area. It was at least in part based on the acknowledged and shared recognition that the Soviet Union was here to stay, that it was the leading power in the area, that it had a legitimate security interest in Eastern Europe, and that there was a need for unified strategy against the capitalist world and against the nuclear diplomacy of the U.S., at least during the incipient Cold War. And so the coalition was formed, by consent when possible and by force when necessary.

The change was fairly rapid and, before long, all-encompassing. The foundation of a Soviet-dominant alliance structure was laid. The new leaders in Eastern Europe acquired power at home by subordinating the needs of components of their respective political systems—policies, culture, institutions and groups—to the Soviet power. The macro trade-off was for the Soviet protection of their regimes against external danger.

*2. Yugoslavia:* Tito's defection from the coalition—a consequence of Stalin's clumsiness in actually forcing the break on the Yugoslavs in 1948—was a Yugoslav reaction to abrupt Soviet policy change. From a loyal coalition member, Yugoslavia moved in the direction of national autonomy. There was at first relatively little change in content of the Yugoslav system components. But the separation brought new power to the leadership which, in forging autonomy at home, traded off Soviet protection for greater internal stability by increasingly sharing the new power with certain domestic groups and institutions. Supported by national and patriotic sentiments, Tito's stature increased correspondingly at home as well as abroad.

*3. Coalition consolidation.* Following the defection of Yugoslavia, a huge, savage offensive against "Titoism," "reformism," and "nationalist tendencies" was launched in the majority of the East European countries. This was the period often referred to as the "Stalinization" or "satellization" of Eastern Europe—when more people (mostly communists) were imprisoned and executed than ever before or after. Repression and terror were the order of the day.

The major reason for this process—though many side- and sub-reasons may be identified—was preventive: namely, preventing the respective East European political systems, and especially those perceived as most strategically important and/or as least integrated into the regional system, from seceding as Yugoslavia did. New and greater Soviet control of the leaderships, policies, cultures, structures, and groups in the East European countries was held imperative. The goal was consolidation of the East European coalition, and the means, creation of as high a degree of cultural, social, economic, and political uniformity as possible. The result was achieved but the price—universal fear, apathy, mistrust—was high. The trade-off of content for power—the local Communist Party leaders trading local purposes, interests, and values for power from the USSR—was almost total. The embrace of Soviet power in Eastern Europe brought modification of content in all components of the respective East European political systems. The local leaders' price of staying in office was an almost total subordination of local purposes, interests, and values; institutions; groups; and policies to the Soviet Union.

*4. Coalition Maintenance.* After Stalin's death, Soviet policies in Eastern Europe again began to change. First, Stalin's successors—chiefly Malenkov and Khrushchev—let it be known that collective leaderships should replace the single dictators in Eastern Europe. But this did not mean much. In fact, it was leadership's sturdy resistance to depersonalization of power in several East European countries that later led to violent attempts at complete breaks with the past. Thus the June 1953 uprising in East Germany, the Rakosi-Nagy conflict in Hungary, the Pilsen workers' demonstrations in Czechoslovakia, the acts of self-criticism and the jockeying back and forth of Gheorgia Dej in Romania and Chervenkov in Bulgaria, the state-party separation in Albania, and the Swiatlo scandal in Poland (which did lead to subsequent reforms) meant little at the time in terms of political change.

The precedent-setting Sino-Soviet agreement of 1954 established cooperation between the two countries "in accordance with the principles of equality of rights, reciprocal advantages, mutual respect, national sovereignty and teritorial integrity." Mao Tse-tung agreed with Khrushchev that to strengthen the East European coalition and the cohesion of all Communist Party states, greater autonomy and independence should be granted to them. In May 1955, Khrushchev, Bulganin, and Mikoyan were reported to have admitted in Belgrade that "grave errors" had been committed. In July, Mikoyan was said to have accused the Soviet ambassador in Warsaw of behaving like a colonial governor. In February 1956, the Twentieth Congress of the CPSU proclaimed the right of each socialist country to work out its own methods of building socialism with reference to its own historical, economic, and social conditions, to build "its own road to socialism." And in October 1956, the Soviet government admitted that "violations and errors [of Stalin] have devalued the principles of legal equality between the socialist states in their relations with each other."[21]

The change in Soviet leadership led to change in Soviet policy. To strengthen the coalition, Khrushchev, supported by Mao Tse-tung and Tito, was ready to give more autonomy to the respective political systems by granting greater control to the East European Communist Party leaders over the content of their own political systems' components.

*5. Poland and 6. Hungary.* The direct but unforeseen consequences of the new Soviet policy of relaxation were the Polish uprising and the Hungarian revolution. If Khrushchev's concept of coalition maintenance differed from that of Stalin, then it differed from that of Gomulka in Poland and Nagy in Hungary. The Polish and the Hungarian crises were reactions to Khrushchev's de-Stalinization, stimulated by anti-Soviet sentiments and nationalist feelings. But while the Polish events were skillfully controlled, the Hungarian events were not. While Gomulka permitted some freedoms, namely development of "socialist democracy" and mild economic reforms, he stood firmly for socialism of the Soviet type, party leadership, and unimpeded total alignment with the Soviet Union. Moreover, Gomulka managed to convince the Poles of the absolute necessity of not overstepping the boundaries, especially of not threatening Soviet interests in Poland. And he did manage to convince Khrushchev that he had convinced the Poles. This Nagy in Hungary was unable to do. Here the party leadership was weak and out of step with popular feelings, which it followed rather than led. And in trying to make his country like Austria or Finland, Nagy violated Soviet strategic interests in Hungary. The Hungarian revolution deteriorated into a nationalist, anti-Soviet, and anti-coalition uprising. While Polish de-Stalinization was compatible with that of Khrushchev, the Hungarian was not. And while nationalism and anti-Sovietism were challenged through and transformed by the party in Poland, in Hungary they were not. Hence the tragedy of Soviet-suppressed revolution in Hungary.

And yet, ironically, the outcome of the crises in both countries—rapid but short-lived in Poland, slow but more lasting in Hungary—was indeed greater diversity than before. The new regimes aimed at new futures different from their pasts, became less oppressive than their neighbors, and achieved a greater degree of autonomy within the coalition than others.

The upcoming Sino-Soviet dispute could have helped the cause of East European members of the coalition. All in all, and in spite of Hungary, however, they preferred the softer touch of Khrushchev to the purer but harsher doctrines of Mao. As it was, only Albania and Romania benefited from the new tensions.

7. *Albania.* Just as Stalin forced the break on the Yugoslavs, so Khrushchev pushed the split on the Albanians. Instead of obtaining Albanian surrender, Khrushchev managed by his clumsy, humiliating methods to move them into the Chinese camp. For the Chinese, this was a matter of prestige; for the Albanians, the opposition to the USSR and Yugoslavia meant little danger, but—as later in the case of Romania—plenty of patriotism and national goodwill for the party leader, Enver Hoxha. In any case, the only change that took place was in the policy content—Soviet-Albanian and Albanian-Chinese. For Albania, the price of autonomy was loss of Soviet trade and assistance and excommunication from the East European alliance.

8. *Romania.* While the Albanian defection was based on allegedly ideological grounds, the Romanian dissent was not. It started as opposition to East European economic integration. Gheorghiu Dej objected to Romania's playing permanent vegetable garden to Comecon—and he did so on the basis of cooperation founded "on the principles of national sovereignty and independence, equality of rights, fraternal aid and mutual interests," just as the Declaration of the Moscow Conference of 81 Parties did in 1960. By 1963, with the now open disruption of Sino-Soviet party relations, Gheorghiu Dej won his case. Khrushchev was too busy elsewhere and Soviet strategic interests were unaffected. Comecon did not become a supernational authority in East Europe after all. In fact, economic development became more of an autonomous domestic, rather than a coalition, issue. The Romanian opposition to the new role of Comecon made for an important precedent. Individual East European countries by and large were left more in charge of their own economic organizations and developments. The outcome was modification of Soviet policy *vis-à-vis* the alliance, and enhancement of Romania's position in the coalition. The increasingly more autonomous Romanian foreign policy was built on this 1963 precedent.

9. *Coalition Members' Development.* Left to their own devices and impressed by the officially tolerated and partially adopted economic proposals of Professor Liberman in the Soviet Union, the East European leaders in the early sixties turned to the problems of their own economic development. This concern was given additional impetus by Khrushchev's departure from power in 1964.

Thus the early sixties witnessed a beginning of a curious new process in Eastern Europe: an increasing sense of their own responsibility for domestic economic problems pervaded the six remaining coalition members. The closed regional system, it seemed, no longer protected their socialistic economies. They were being opened to all kinds of new, extra-coalition competition for which they were ill-prepared—the more dependent on the outside world, the greater the incentive to innovate and to raise their own technological standards. But it was foreign trade, rather than domestic consumption, which was felt to be the compelling issue here. The central question was not whether autonomous economic innovation and development were desirable; there was little quarrel on that issue. All six countries adopted some sort of overall reform format between 1963 and 1968. Given the facts of life in Eastern Europe, the crucial concern was the climate for the reforms—what kind of social, cultural, and political conditions would best guarantee the optimum outcome of the economic innovations? And here men—and their political systems—differed. But the major gap ultimately developed between Poland, East Germany, and Bulgaria on the one hand and the new regime in Czechoslovakia on the other. The former stood for very little further political liberalization, while the latter was determined to go all the way, changing the dominant culture, structures, groups, leadership, and policies almost beyond Yugoslavia. Hungary, under the undisputed authority of the Party, moved gradually and quietly but with determination in the direction of making cultural, social, and political conditions more compatible with the spirit of its economic reform. Romania, with its highly emancipated foreign policy, experimented much more cautiously with reforms at home.

*10. Czechoslovakia.* The Soviet occupation of Czechoslovakia in 1968 ended the dilemma but did not answer the question. It only postponed it. But it raised anew the issue of compatibility of coalition maintenance with members' own political development and advancement.

The lesson of Czechoslovakia, just as the lesson of Hungary in 1956, was not lost on East Europe. There was a difference between Hungary in '56 and Czechoslovakia in '68. As we pointed out above, in Hungary the Party was not in control and things got out of hand. Values and beliefs changed, but institutions and many leaders remained the same; and policies were changed only after pressures from below were exerted. The change was nationalist, anti-Soviet, anti-communist—and toward a neutral Hungary.

In Czechoslovakia, on the other hand, the Party was in control. The leadership became responsive, representative, and "serving the society," unifying the developmental process. It was the Party which changed its leadership, from which emanated new policies, which encouraged cultural development, and which permitted groups—trade unions, youth organizations, peasant cooperatives, cultural organizations, and others—to influence policies. And it was the Party which changed or was about to change its formal structures to accommodate the process. Thus in Czechoslovakia the change was carried out by the Party, not as an anti-communist or anti-Soviet demonstration, but as an authentically socialist transformation in accord with popular feelings and on behalf of the society. In fact, the Party has never been so popular—before or after—as during the 1968 spring and summer.

In that sense, Czechoslovakia in 1968 resembled more the Polish situation in 1956: Both changes were channeled through the Party and both Gomulka and Dubcek managed to convince their respective publics of the absolute necessity of not overstepping the boundaries and especially of not threatening Soviet strategic interests. True, the scope and intensity of the Czechoslovak change was greater and went deeper than in the Polish case; also, the coincidence of Soviet-Polish interests was more significant than in the Soviet Czech situation (which was similar in this respect to the Hungarian case). The crucial difference, however, was Dubcek's inability to convince Brezhnev and the Russians (and the Germans and the Poles), as Gomulka did Khrushchev in 1956, that he had convinced the Czechs and the Slovaks. This was his failure.

After the initial shock and uncertainty, the Soviet invasion of Czechoslovakia was interpreted in Eastern Europe as a *status quo ante* operation—as Soviet intervention coping with a specific national, rather than a general East European, situation. It was also perceived as a warning to the individual East European leaders not to follow the Czechoslovak example; as long as they remained as they were, there would be no repercussions. This was confirmed by the July 1970 Soviet-Romanian Treaty of Friendship and Mutual Aid. There was only minimal ideological content in the Treaty; the heart of the agreement was Article 5, where the two parties promised each other full assistance, including military aid, in case of an armed attack on the other party. Still, Ceaucescu got the message; he has streamlined Romanian domestic politics considerably since that time. In spite of the foreign policy emancipation, and perhaps because of it, Romania is today among the most centralized and authoritarian East European countries.

*11. Poland.* In Poland, a renewed effort to rationalize the economy has continued as it has in East Germany. But unlike in East Germany, the Poles mismanaged the task. As a consequence of December 1970 strikes and riots of workers in Gdansk, Gdynia, and Szczecin (over prices and wages) which spread through Polish cities, the Gomulka government was removed, his stern measures repealed, and a new government with new policies installed. Moreover, arrested persons were released, local labor unions were freed from much of Party control, and some Party-state separation took place. With the Soviet blessing, Edward Gierek, the skillful manager-politician, took over. And there has been no Soviet intervention. The change in leaders, policies, and some structures was autonomous and Party-controlled. Gierek and Brezhnev saw eye to eye.

*12. Hungary.* The economic reform in Hungary, introduced in 1968, represents an important economic system change in that it shifted the Hungarian economy toward economic decentralization. Apart from the question of the actual result of the reform to date, which different economists assess quite differently, there is no doubt that the circumstances associated with the reform ushered in a general improvement in the consumer market and the standard of living. Moreover, there appears greater economic and social stratification based on differentiated salaries and wages, greater cultural freedom, and a somewhat more relaxed political atmosphere. The Hungarian leadership seems to be more responsive to and more supportive of the new, more acquisitive society—in economics, culture, and even in politics—than was the case before the reform. True, some economists argue that there is no or only weak causal nexus between the reform and the other changes, and that these changes cannot be traced back to the economic reform itself. But all indications suggest that there is in fact a somewhat greater freedom from constraints in Hungary today, that officials and institutions are more responsive to demands from below, and that policies are designed to accommodate domestic views broadly associated with citizens' well-being more than anywhere else in Eastern Europe. It appears that the leadership, within limits, trades off more openness for more support; that this is not just a short-term tactic but an integrated, widely understood, sustained policy which had originated in the climate of the economic reform; and that, if all goes well and all cooperate, the future would bring improvement, rather than deterioration, in this trend.

### *Analysis of the Major Political Changes*

What does this collection of twelve brief synopses of major cases of political change tell us about political dynamics in Eastern Europe? What valid generalizations can we make about these changes? And how do they relate to the literature on political change?

To start with, the majority of important political changes which have taken place in Eastern Europe since World War II stem from foreign rather than domestic causes. Although the conflictual tendencies in the relations between the coalition leader, the USSR, and the coalition members have been decreasing somewhat in intensity and distinctly in scope, the single major location of domestic political change-producing conflicts must indeed be traced to the members' relations with the USSR. This is where the principal stress and the tension line may be found. The constellation of *ad hoc* sub-coalitions—the USSR plus one or several members of the coalition (East Germany and Poland in the case of Czechoslovakia in '68, for example)—may change from case to case but the USSR remains the major impact-source.

Political change literature, with the single recent exception of the Almond, Flanagan, and Mundt study,[22] ignores the issue completely. It posits political systems as sovereign masters of their own destiny. Earlier Almond,[23] Dankwart Rustow,[24] David Apter,[25] Samuel Huntington,[26] and Ronald Brunner, and Gary Brewer[27] are all concerned with political change in political systems as if they had no foreign environment. Other political systems, for the purposes of their theories, do not exist. International politics have no effects. States are enveloped by sheer nothingness.

Almond, Flanagan, and Mundt do treat the impact of the external environment on the political system. They distinguish between foreign impacts which have security-military, economic, and political-psychological "infringements." Basing their study on eight historical case studies of political crises—France in 1871, Germany in 1918, Japan in 1931 and 1968, Britain in 1832 and 1931, Mexico in 1936, and India in 1967—they conclude that the security-military variable is "*the* most powerful exogeneous variable in explaining system stability and change."[28]

But Almond, Flanagan, and Mundt's security-military factor is explicitly war or threat of war, not the more subtle, sustained external control and interference with internal matters of coalition members. The cases they have examined are different from the East European cases cited here. The authors rightly identify the international security issue as the most important external system destabilizer (or stabilizer) but do not venture into the gray area of sustained control and threat climate.

Coalition theory is not very helpful in explaining the leader-members relationship nor its tendency to produce internal political changes.[29] But several epexegetical observations can be offered here. In spite of the existence of the Council of Mutual Economic Assistance, the Warsaw Pact, and other lesser all-regional arrangements, the Soviet multilateral approach to its East European allies has been decreasing over time. This trend may be interpreted as reflecting an increasingly felt Soviet need to deal with its allies from a position of strength, one by one, after the defection of Yugoslavia and Albania and the initiation of the more troublesome foreign policy in Romania; but it may also reflect Soviet recognition of varieties in the East European coalition and the need to differentiate among the members' separate identities. After all, with the possible single exception of Bulgaria, all of the East European countries have shown at different times some relational strains with the USSR.

Second, the demands for greater rate, scope, and intensity of innovation and change have been much more voluminous in East European countries in this time period than in the USSR. As we pointed out elsewhere, although the East European countries differ a great deal among themselves, collectively they differ even more from the Soviet Union: their party bureaucracies are less firmly established and are less autonomous and less pressure-resistant than the strong Soviet party bureaucracy; memories of multi-party rule in at least some of the East European countries in the not-too-distant past are still alive;

traditions of at least a certain amount of political freedom have not been forgotten; the longing to rejoin the West is considerable; and while changes in the USSR (de-Stalinization, economic reforms, new harshness against writers) tend to influence its East European neighbors, changes in East Europe do not tend to influence the USSR. As a consequence, the demands for change—and the elites' potential political responsiveness—are considerably greater in the small East European countries than in the Soviet Union. Since these demands are not really understood in the Soviet Union, they tend to produce strains in the East European-Soviet relations which in turn cause Soviet-induced internal political changes in Eastern Europe.[30]

Third, the Soviet position on coalition maintenance in East Europe has been, to say the least, ambivalent. It oscillated between desire for total integration (Stalin) to some kind of relative national autonomy (Khrushchev before the Hungarian revolution) to no-trouble-*status quo* (Brezhnev). The Soviet leadership has not been uniformly hostile to East European aspirations, and the hostility curve has been going down, not up. In the six instances where Soviet leadership felt itself to be challenged—Yugoslavia in '48, Poland in '56, Hungary in '56, Albania in '61, Romania in '64, and Czechoslovakia in '68—it reacted on an *ad hoc* basis, and not always successfully. The learning mechanism has been working on both sides, though only partially. There has been too much to learn and the signals proved often to be misleading. Although a distinction has to be made between short-term and long-term impacts on political change, it has been the short-term impact which has been most visible. The cumulative effect of long-term impacts is there, but it is less obvious.

Fourth, personalization of politics has continued to be one of the major distinguishing characteristics in Eastern Europe. The differences in roles and styles of leaders have been of crucial importance. Men like Stalin, Tito, Khrushchev, Dej, Hoxha, and others left lasting marks on their polities and on the coalition. But interestingly enough, while Stalin acted alone, neither Khrushchev nor Brezhnev did. Khrushchev felt that he needed the approval of Mao or Tito or both for his actions in Eastern Europe. Brezhnev felt that he needed not only the approval but the participation of other East European leaders and systems in his action in Czechoslovakia. This is an important change in the coalition-maintenance strategy. It seems that legitimacy for instigation of political change in coalition maintenance is no longer given; it must be sought and secured.

Parallel with this innovation, the original goal of total coalition integration gave way to coalition members' own controlled development and change—social, economic, cultural, and even political—as long as two conditions were met: (a) the process was approved and controlled by their respective Communist Party leaderships, and (b) the leadership was fully trusted by Soviet leaders. In other words, the

Communist Party's full control has been necessary but not sufficient; Soviet approval of the change had to be secured.

In practice, this important change in coalition maintenance has meant that the scope of permissible domestic change has been relatively increasing, that areas of change not subject to Soviet supervision have been relatively enlarging, and that, to use Huntington's language, the price of power for coalition members has been getting relatively cheaper, i.e., that trade-offs of content for power have tended to be relatively more pragmatic and the bargaining areas have been getting relatively larger.

Thus, change in coalition maintenance strategy together with change in coalition maintenance goals has tended to increase somewhat the scope and rate of domestically induced political change. It remains to be seen whether and how much this potential will be explored by the respective East European leaders.

Fifth, East European politics do not operate in a vacuum. World politics—the Cold War, the 1955 detente, the Sino-Soviet split—have intruded here in full force. At present China, West European countries, the U.S., Japan, and others show varying degrees of interest in East Europe. No analysis of East European political change can dispense with these interests and involvements. And on this level of analysis, East Europe is an anomaly. In the world of disintegrating bipolar rigidity and in the political flux of triangles and pentagonal relations—where salience of security issues decreases, where alliances and coalitions are being loosened rather than strengthened, where small countries seek more independence for more maneuverability, where changes in military technology have reduced the value of forward bases, where coalition leaders tend to be increasingly reluctant to meet costs of maintaining alliances under all conditions, and where changing issues and needs determine relationships among all kinds of pairs of countries for all kinds of trade-offs—the Soviet coalition maintenance in Eastern Europe is becoming obsolete and even unrealistic. It may be even more difficult to sustain in its present shape in the future.

And finally, like that of all politicians, the East European leaders' major goal is to stay in office. As long as their staying in office depends on Soviet leaders alone, all they have to do is to trade content—national values, interests, policies, populations' well-being—for power. They act in fact as Soviet representatives in their own countries.

But with limited domestic economic, social, political, and cultural development things begin to change. East European leaders' responsibilities at home increase. Their staying in office now depends on Soviet leaders as well as on those who help them discharge their growing domestic tasks. And this domestic support group increases in scope and importance with their increasing responsibilities. The individual leader's position becomes precarious. The sustained balancing of the two constituents of their own power grows heavy. What is the way out? At various times different East European leaders decided the question differently: Ulbricht and Gomulka in the '60s, Ceaucescu in the '70s, and Bulgarian leaders from the beginning chose the easy way out and relied on the Soviet leaders. Dubcek tried the balancing act and failed. Kadar, on the other hand, is moderately succeeding, as Gomulka was at first in the late fifties. And this may constitute the test of the future in Eastern Europe—balancing the two major interests, domestic and foreign. It will demand skill, sophistication, practice, and wisdom. Soviet leaders will have to face the fact that the stability of the coalition depends on the stability of its members, and the East European leaders will have to learn how to dance the tightrope between the two major interests; both are here to stay. The question is how to achieve coalition stability compatible with inevitable national political change. And to this problem we now turn.

*Stability, Choice, and Change*

Stability of a political system depends on political changes taking place in an orderly manner to sustain that stability. As a consequence, institutionalization of political changes is the surest way of guaranteeing stability. In a communist system, this guarantor of stability is the institutionalized Communist Party. According to Huntington, the Communist Party is the basis of political order because of its "supremacy . . . . over all social forces." It is "the summum bonum, an end in itself." Everything is subordinated to it—Party members, social groups, leaders, the class, the nation; and everything must be sacrificed ". . .to insure the survival and success of the Party."[31]

Huntington wrote about the original Leninist Party, and made an important contribution to the distinctiveness of that Party which differentiates it from other political parties. He was not concerned with differentiating among several Communist parties. But we are. To put it bluntly, what happens if one Communist Party encroaches upon the "supremacy," "the end in itself," "the summum bonum" of another Communist Party?

At the core of the political change literature is the notion of rational choice—individual choice made with a view of maximizing benefits and affecting resources allocation.[32] But choice must be free, not dictated; as Apter put it, "Choices are illusory if people are victimized by them or afraid to utilize them, and dangerous if they are victimized by them or afraid to utilize them, and dangerous if they are manifestly incapable of directing them."[33] In such a situation, choice ceases to have meaning; political change becomes a response to something else.

Members of the Soviet coalition may be viewed as systems within a system's political systems within a coalition system.[34] This treatment makes it possible to pinpoint relationships among the coalition components. If one of the member-states is system-dominant, and the other member-states are system-subordinate, and if the system-dominant member has a monopoly over both common purposes and individual choice in member-states, then political change in system-subordinate member-states is but a response to systemic change. This line of reasoning suggests the hypothesis that *there is a direct relationship between freedom of choice and coalition stability: the more limited the choice, the more unstable the members and hence the greater the coalition instability, and vice versa.* Political change ceases to be institutionalized, depends on whimsical choice, and, if completely suppressed, tends to have a long-run cumulative effect as in the explosive cases of Hungary in '56 or Czechoslovakia in '68.

In Eastern Europe, the interchange between the coalition leader and the member-states has been the most significant variable in explaining political system stability and change. Of the twelve cases cited above, eight important sets of political changes were either triggered or suppressed in that way (the coalition formation after World War II, the defection of Yugoslavia in '48, the coalition consolidation period of Stalin, the coalition maintenance [de-Stalinization] of Khrushchev, the defection of Albania in '61, Poland in '56, Hungary in '56, and Czechoslovakia in '68). In the four remaining cases (Rumania from '63 on, East European economic reforms in the sixties, Hungary from '68 on, and Poland in '70), this exogenous variable operated only indirectly but was distinctly present. The most frequent issue area within which these impacts took place was security: only in four of the twelve cases was the impact issue economic (Rumania since '63, East European economic reform, Hungary in '68, and Poland in '70) and in all four cases the members, laboring under Soviet supervision, initiated the change. Only one case where a security issue was involved was initiated by a member-state sans an entirely effective Soviet response: Romania's more independent foreign policy initiatives since '63. But there is enough evidence to suggest that this initiative was kept within tolerable bounds by sustained Soviet pressure. The case of Khrushchev's coalition maintenance policy in '55 and '56 was a calculated reaction to the Stalin excesses: by offering more autonomy to the East European countries, Khrushchev meant to give them greater freedom of choice and stability and thus to stabilize the coalition (which, he had hoped, might include Yugoslavia again as well). Unfortunately, the half-hearted execution of this policy had backfired in Poland and in Hungary.

The most significant variable in explaining political system stability and change in East Europe is thus Soviet security. It is the most important of all causal sequences of change, the most persistent political system destabilizer, and the most reliable predictor of the trend of system change. Behind the Soviet security concept and strategy, it follows from our case synopses, is the fear of members' secession from the coalition and their defection. In that sense, the Soviet-East European coalition differs from other traditional coalitions in that the coalition leader insists not only on fidelity of member-states' Communist Party leaders to the alliance but on fidelity of the respective societies as well. Leaders, after all, can be overthrown. Coalition maintenance comes close to community maintenance. This is why tight, sustained Soviet control is required whenever Soviet confidence is not absolute.

With this kind of Soviet insistence on the security issue, domestic political change-producing conflicts—such as the generational change, national integration (nationalities and minorities), party vs. state, bureaucrats vs. technocrats, politicians vs. managers, etc.—are pushed into the background. These conflictual dichotomies do not—and cannot—have the explanatory power that Soviet security has. But there is one endogenous variable which, in four of the twelve cases, has had limited impact on political change: economic innovation. Low-profile, gradual economic system change strategy on the part of the members has been perceived by the coalition leader as compatible with coalition security, proving that economic innovation does not necessarily need to be sacrificed for security. It is an empirical question; it does require some risk-taking on the part of the initiator. But it can lead to limited political system change.

*Conclusion*

In this study we have approached political change in East Europe from two alternative vantage points: cross-national and cross-time comparison. Both proved to be useful in some ways and not in others. The cross-national approach represents a good way to study East European political systems on a comparative basis. The model we constructed is concise, parsimonious, and hypothesis-productive. The study is empirical and, although the data on which it is based are less than ideal, reasonably enlightening. But it is weak in zeroing in on political change, though it explains its environment.

The cross-time approach, on the other hand, although much softer than the cross-national approach, enhances our capacity to pinpoint political change, stability, and choice in Eastern Europe over time. Synopses of cases of major political change coupled with political change literature enable us to explain and, within limits, to predict political change in Eastern Europe. But we can do this only with reference to systemic change at the macro-level. Should the Soviet coalition maintenance strategy change to the point that individual choice in member-states could be freely exercised, the situation would change drastically, and our analysis would no longer apply, or would apply only partially. Although there seems little likelihood that such a change would take place within the foreseeable future, limited changes in the Soviet coalition maintenance strategy have taken place in the past. And that would make the analysis so much more difficult.

## NOTES

1. Lucian Pye, *Aspects of Political Development* (Boston: Little, Brown & Co., 1966), pp. 31-48.

2. For a survey and a critique of this literature, see Samuel P. Huntington's "The Change to Change," *Comparative Politics* (April 1971).

3. Pye, *Aspects of Political Development*, pp. 45-48.

4. Gabriel Almond and Bingham Powell, *Comparative Politics: A Developmental Approach* (Boston: Little, Brown & Co., 1966), passim.

5. Robert A. Dahl, *Polyarchy: Participation and Opposition* (New Haven, Conn.: Yale University Press, 1971).

6. Raymond B. Nixon, "Freedom in the World's Press," *Journalism Quarterly* 42, no. 1 (Winter 1965).

7. See John S. Shippee, "Empirical Sociology in the Eastern European Communist Party-States," in *Communist Party-States: Comparative and International Studies*, ed. Jan F. Triska (New York: Bobbs-Merrill Co., 1969).

8. See Ted Robert Gurr, *New Error-Compensated Measures for Comparing Nations* (Princeton, N.J.: Center of International Studies, Princeton University, 1966), pp. 118-120.

9. Computed from data presented in Nicolas Spulber, *Socialist Management and Planning* (Bloomington, Ind.: Indiana University Press), p. 96; and Richard P. Staar, *The Communist Regimes in Eastern Europe*, rev. ed. (Stanford, Calif.: Hoover Institution, 1970).

10. Myron Weiner, "Political Participation: Crisis of the Political Process," in *Crises and Sequences in Political Development*, ed. Leonard Binder *et al.* (Princeton, N.J.: Princeton University Press, 1971), p. 164.

11. For a clear and relatively concise (but somewhat oversimplified) synthetic exposition in English of the "dependency theory" position, along with a selective but representative bibliography of some principal theorists in the field, see Susanne J. Bodenheimer, "Dependency and Imperialism: Roots of Latin American Underdevelopment," *NACIA Newsletter* (May-June 1970).

12. See, for example, James N. Rosenau, "Pre-Theories and Theories of Foreign Policy," in *Approaches to Comparative and International Politics*, ed. R. Barry Farrell (Evanston, Ill.: Northwestern University Press, 1966).

13. U.S. Congress, Joint Economic Committee, *Economic Developments in Countries of Eastern Europe–A Compendium of Papers* (Washington, D.C.: U.S. Government Printing Office, 1970).

14. See Spulber, *Socialist Management and Planning*, p. 128.

15. This relationship is not a mere artifact of employing the composite LIBINDEX as the vertical axis. Very similar L-shaped configurations result if one substitutes any of the subsystem autonomy indicators employed in this study.

16. See Samuel P. Huntington, *Political Order in Changing Societies* (New Haven, Conn.: Yale University Press, 1968).

17. Dahl, *Polyarchy*, especially chapter 3, "Historical Sequences."

18. And, one might add, in very many of the Western and Third World cases as well. Consider the impact of foreign intervention on the French Revolution or of the Holy Alliance in the early nineteenth century. And while you are at it, consider also the events in the Dominican Republic following the death of Trujillo.

19. Robert A. Dahl, *Modern Political Analysis*, 2nd ed. (New York: Prentice-Hall, 1970), pp. 67-68.

20. See in particular the latter portion of Huntington's "Change to Change."

21. François Fejtő, *A History of the People's Democracies: Eastern Europe Since Stalin* (New York: Praeger, 1971), pp. 31ff.

22. Gabriel A. Almond, Scott C. Flanagan, and Robert J. Mundt, *Crisis, Choice and Change: Historical Studies of Political Development* (Boston: Little, Brown, 1973).

23. "Toward a Comparative Politics of East Europe," *Studies in Comparative Communism* 4, no. 2 (April 1971):71-76. See also Gabriel A. Almond and G. Bingham Powell, *Comparative Politics: A Developmental Approach* (Boston: Little, Brown), p. 41.

24. Brookings Institution, *A World of Nations* (Washington, D.C., 1967). See also "Communism and Change" in *Change in Communist Systems*, ed. Chalmers Johnson (Stanford, Calif.: Stanford University Press, 1970).

25. *Choice and the Politics of Allocation* (New Haven, Conn.: Yale University Press, 1971).

26. *Political Order in Changing Societies* (New Haven, Conn.: Yale University Press, 1968). See also Huntington, "Change to Change."

27. *Organized Complexity: Empirical Theories of Political Development* (New York, 1971).

28. Almond, Flanagan and Mundt, *Crisis, Choice and Change*, p. 628.

29. William H. Riker, *The Theory of Political Coalitions* (New Haven, Conn.: Yale University Press, 1962); Martin Shubik, ed., *Game Theory and Related Approaches to Social Behavior: Selections* (New York: Wiley, 1964); William A. Gamson, "Experimental Studies of Coalition Formation," in *Advances in Experimental Social Psychology*, ed. Leonard Bekowitz (New York: Academic Press, 1964).

30. Jan F. Triska, "Czechoslovakia, A Case Study in Social and Political Development," in *The Changing Face of Communism in Eastern Europe*, ed. Peter A. Tome (Tucson, Ariz.: University of Arizona Press, 1970), p. 190.

31. *Political Order in Changing Societies,* Yale University Press, p. 339.

32. Almond, Flanagan and Mundt, *Crisis, Choice and Change*; Rustow, "Communism and Change," p. 356; Apter, *Choice and the Politics of Allocation*, p. 10.

33. "Premises of Parliamentary Planning," p. 6.

34. George Modelski, "Communist International System," *International Encyclopedia of the Social Sciences* (New York: Macmillan and Free Press, 1970); Jan F. Triska and David D. Finley, *Soviet Foreign Policy* (New York: Macmillan, 1968), chapter 5; P. Terrence Hopmann, "International Conflict and Detente and the Communist System," in *The Behavioral Revolution and Communist Studies*, ed. Roger Kanet (New York: Free Press, 1971).

# 10

# Technology and Communist Culture: Dimensions of Cultural Diffusion*

Frederic J. Fleron, Jr.

Communist revolutions are much more than political revolutions; they are cultural revolutions in the broadest sense. They seek not only to seize and to wield power in societies as they are presently constituted but also to transform the basic relationships among people, and thereby to create the new "communist man." For this reason, as Robert Tucker has argued, it should prove useful to view modern communism as a culture-transforming movement.[1] The participants in the 1971 Arden House Conference on Communist Studies and Political Culture agreed that such an orientation might well open up new possibilities for the comparative study of communist societies.

It is quite clear, as Gabriel Almond suggested in his memorandum to the Arden House Conference, that, "while there has been an assumption in the communist movement that the model of 'communist man' would be the same regardless of differences in culture in the various parts of the world in which the movement acquires a foothold, in fact the content of 'communist man' varies from one communist party to the next, from one communist society to the next." These differences can be explained by the fact that "communism in practice tends to be an amalgam of an innovated cultural system and elements of a national cultural ethos."[2] But there is also a third, crucial element in the amalgam—imported culture. So, when we examine the culture of any particular communist society, we must identify three analytically distinct elements: (1) the innovated cultural system (the indigenous progressive movement; (2) the national cultural ethos (the traditions of

*I should like to take this opportunity to express thanks to members of the Graduate School of Public and International Affairs and the Russian and East European Studies Program at the University of Pittsburgh, who discussed these ideas with me during a colloquium, and to other friends and colleagues who responded to the call for criticism and comments.

society); and (3) aspects of imported foreign culture (the objects of a cultural diffusion). The fact that these basic elements may be fruitfully isolated analytically must not obscure the equally important fact that they are, in reality, highly and very complexly interrelated and interdependent.

Of course, cultural diffusion has been an important and increasingly powerful (or perhaps one should say increasingly possible) mode of historical change in many societies, either with or without the approval of the societies in change. Technology appears to be one of the more easily diffused of all elements of culture; indeed, its spread from the more to the less technologically complex societies has been a hallmark of the modern age. Obviously, that process was in operation long before the communist regimes came to power. For example, in early eighteenth-century Russia, Peter the Great's borrowings from Western culture included not only Western technology but also Western administrative practice, leading to the famous Table of Ranks, or *chin*.[3] Peter was also greatly concerned with appearances and insisted that Russians become clean-shaven and adopt Western styles of dress. Apparently he thought that, in order to do what Westerners did, Russians had to look like Westerners looked. Again, in the latter part of the nineteenth century, Russia borrowed extensively from Western technology. This is discussed in greater detail below.

In the cases of China and Cuba, the presence of Western culture was not so much a matter of conscious choice as it was the product of Western imperialism and economic exploitation. Regardless of the circumstances under which technology was transferred, by the time communist revolution took place in these countries, those technological and other forms of borrowed culture had, to some degree, become part of the national cultural ethos which the innovated cultural system of communism had to confront.

The nature of the communist culture-transforming process depends largely on the state of the society's development at the time of the communist acquisition of power. As Tucker has suggested, a dominant theme of Marx and Engels was that "industrialization, urbanization, machine technology, the concept of nature, the breakdown of traditional society in the backward countries, and the internationalization of society were all the work of the bourgeois era. The bourgeois revolution of modernization was the preparation of society for communism. The mission of the communist revolution was not to modernize society further, but to humanize it, to reintegrate man with himself and nature and make him, collectively, the 'sovereign of circumstances.' "[4] But what, then, happens to communism as a culture-transforming process when these aspects of bourgeois society are not present at the time of the communist revolution, as indeed they have not been in most instances?

This question is obviously related to the development of socialism in a single country. Had history marched along the exact path Marx expected, the world socialist revolution would have confronted the bourgeois world only as tradition, not as a coexisting and competing society. Mondialization would have created circumstances in which socialism could flower upon the base of this materially highly developed world culture—and socialism would not be in any position to "borrow" from bourgeois society in any meaningful sense of the word. In the absence of that development, however, one of the main culture transformations undertaken immediately after the isolated revolution is modernization itself—a bourgeois process which was frequently modeled explicitly on capitalist forms. In those circumstances, then, it is perhaps not surprising that this aspect of the innovative culture necessarily has bourgeois limitations, illustrated most clearly by the Soviet determinist application of Marxism.

In the Soviet case, industrialization and machine technology were not present prior to 1917 to an extent sufficient to have conquered nature and broken down traditional society. Certainly there were the beginnings of these processes in small pockets of Russia,[5] but one could not describe Russian society generally in those terms. So, for Lenin and the Bolsheviks, a central part of the complete cultural revolution was full-scale industrialization and expansion of production capacity, accomplished (and rationally planned because it was state owned and directed) by importing foreign technology and factory organization systems to increase worker productivity.

The "advantages of backwardness" (to borrow Thorstein Veblen's notion) which accrue to "late modernizers" are a mixed blessing. On the one hand, the highly developed and sophisticated technology of the West (i.e., of Western Europe and the United States) can be imported in order to change greatly the shape of a "backward" economic system and to increase productive capacity in a relatively short period of time. On the other hand, the recipient society frequently lacks the cultural infrastructure present in the donor society to support such advanced technology. As Peter Solomon reminds us, "Tsarist Russia had neither the manpower resources of trained workers and engineers nor the entrepreneurial talent and capital to proceed according to previously established patterns of industrial development. To compensate for these deficiencies, the State acted as substitute for private initiative and solicited from abroad capital, machines, and technological know-how."[6] (The resulting new pattern of industrialization has been described by Alexander Gerschenkron in *Economic Backwardness in Historical Perspective*.) This is further complicated when the post-revolutionary regime eschews (at least to some degree) those social forms of the cultural infrastructure of the donor society.

This historical form of state capitalism in Tsarist Russia, the post-revolutionary aim to confine or limit the bourgeois cultural effects of modernization, and the growth-maximizing objectives of the Soviet

Union in competition with capitalism led to capital-intensive techniques and "gigantomania" in the industrial sector. In the more advanced science-based technologies of the West, capital-intensive techniques were highly developed and it was natural that the Russian leaders again turned to the West as a source of technological innovation. Antony Sutton has documented in detail the great extent of Western technical transfer to the Soviet Union.[7]

But machine technology was not the only aspect of technical transfer. Frederick W. Taylor's "Scientific Management" served as the basis for Soviet factory organization in an effort to increase worker productivity.[8] John Armstrong has observed that "the persistent impact of Taylorism in the Soviet Union is remarkable. . . . While some of the early Bolshevik industrial directors distrusted Taylorism because of its capitalist origins, like Alexander I a century earlier *most believed Russia had to borrow any advanced techniques available.*"[9] Armstrong goes on to point out that, given Soviet emphasis on engineering approaches and "the ruthless social control by other agencies, a certain portion of the administrative apparatus (chiefly industrial ministries and enterprises) could virtually disregard human factors."[10] This appears to be in sharp contrast to aspects of the Chinese and Cuban experiences.

In her summary of discussions at the Sussex Study Group on Science and Technology in China's Development, Genevieve Dean emphasized that "the relative success or failure of the strategies chosen for technological modernization in China must. . .be judged, not only in terms of economic 'development,' but also in terms of the broader economic, social, and political objectives associated with particular technological choices."[11]

An example of these broader objectives is the elimination of the "three big differences"—that is, differences between industry and agriculture, city and countryside, and mental and manual labor. Realization of these objectives cannot be accomplished through the development of concentrated capital-intensive technology, but requires a technology of smaller-scale capital development and perhaps even a more labor-intensive technology, which would be more consistent with the decentralization of enterprise administration, the growth of local "self-reliance," and more equitably distributed employment opportunities for the entire population of working age. It is quite clear how concern for social and political objectives would lead to the choice of technological alternatives quite different from those chosen primarily on the basis of growth-maximizing objectives. The latter choice would lead to extensive borrowing from the more advanced science-based technologies of the West and would resemble the Soviet path of technological development. The former choice would require a more "nativist" path of technical development—a point well developed by Rensselaer Lee in an important article on technological nativism in China.[12]

If there are differences within the transferred technology in the sense that some aspects are in conflict with goals in communist culture and others are not, then which ones are chosen? The communist response has been varied. The Soviets apparently have not made this distinction clear and have borrowed almost any advanced techniques available in the areas of machine technology, management forms, and patterns of technical rationality. The Chinese record is mixed: While using labor-intensive techniques in the consumer goods sector, they have tended to utilize capital-intensive and skill-intensive techniques in the producers' goods sector.[13] Even in the latter, however, the Chinese have rejected some elements of technical rationality and sought to develop new organizational forms, such as the Two Participation and the Triple Combination, which are more consonant with their political and social goals. Yugoslav experiments with worker self-management are also techniques designed to overcome elements of technical rationality and organization as developed in the context of capitalist industrialism.

It would be interesting to examine one aspect of this problem by looking at the effects of multi-national corporations based in capitalist countries which have built plants in communist countries, such as the Ford and Fiat automobile plants in the USSR. Such effects might include impacts on patterns of work organization, plant management, and commodity consumption. The question must be asked: Are the organizational and administrative forms in these industries merely transplanted into those enterprises in recipient communist societies, or have there developed "nativist" forms of management and the organization of work?

In the case of Cuba, Richard Fagen has referred to the Cuban view of "technology as the motor of abundance and a component of the new man," and Castro has pointed to the crucial role of modern science and technology in the creation of wealth. In Fagen's view, "this commitment to bringing technology to bear on production is manifested in . . . a series of programs designed to increase productivity by borrowing, modifying or developing an appropriate scientific style of labor."[14] While interested in the process of technical transfer, however, the Cubans have been very much aware of the cultural consequences of their ability to create abundance through science and technology while building a new communist culture and creating the "new Cuban man." From an analysis of Castro's speeches, Fagen has pieced together the Cubans' conception of their dilemma as follows:

> (1) The ideal communist society is defined as a cultural system in which every man acts as a true brother to every other man. (2) It is not possible to achieve such a cultural system until abundance replaces want as the collective situation of the citizenry. (3) The very process of creating abundance, however, can easily destroy the potential of the

> abundant society for being a truly communist society. (4) Thus a society must strive to achieve abundance by creating and nourishing those values and motivations—shared feelings about collective responsibility and gain, and an ethic of societal service—that will one day become internalized as the general character structure of communist man. Above all, abundance achieved by appealing to individual aggrandizement, by rewarding *egoismo* (self-centeredness), leads inexorably not to communism but to increased exploitation of man by man, increased individual alienation, and rising levels of social disorganization.[15]

This suggests that it is not merely technological "methods" which may be in conflict with communist goals, but also that some originally bourgeois goals which remain in communism, especially the notion of material wealth in the form of "abundant" individual consumption, may themselves be in conflict or contradiction with other communist goals. (This may be a problem which can be traced to Marx, who stressed "abundance" right alongside his keen insights into commodity fetishism.)

Ends and means are never more than analytically separable, but for certain analyses that distinction may be quite useful. Here it seems appropriate to apply Anthony Wallace's important distinction between two elements of culture to the innovated cultural system of communism: goal culture and transfer culture. The goal culture is the idealized image of future communist society in which the new communist man lives in harmony with nature and in cooperation with his fellow man. The transfer culture is the system of techniques and procedures for achieving the goal culture.[16] This distinction has found its way into recent discussions of communist political culture.[17] The focus of our interest is on one of several elements of communist culture: the ways in which technology and technical rationality have been incorporated into the transfer culture of several communist societies and how those elements of transfer culture make an impact on the goal culture. This focus includes a concern for both transferred and nativist-innovated elements of technology and technical rationality.

One of the major problems in the study of science and technology is that there is no unified body of theory upon which one can draw. What theory exists has been developed in the various disciplinary compartments of the social sciences. One result of such insulation is that the process commonly referred to as "technical transfer" has been viewed in the very narrow sense of transfer of specific technical innovations from a donor to a recipient society. The study of the impact of that particular technical transfer takes the form of how particular aspects of the *economic* system were affected, that is, the extent to which technical advances have widened the area of effective technical choice and reduced the objective constraints on central planners, or the effect of continuing and extensive technical transfer on the level of native technological innovation within the recipient society. These questions are important indeed, but they focus on only one dimension of the process of technical transfer.[18]

A much broader perspective on the implications of technical transfer could be obtained by viewing this process as one dimension of *cultural diffusion.* More than a decade ago, in an introductory article to the new journal *Technology and Culture*, Melvin Kranzberg quoted Edward B. Tylor's century-old definition of culture as "that complex whole which includes knowledge, belief, art, morals, laws, customs, and any other capabilities and habits acquired by man as a member of society."[19] As an artifact of human experience, technology must be viewed as an element of culture. The process of technological transfer, therefore, can be viewed as an aspect of the more general process of cultural diffusion. Placing the problem of technical transfer in the broader context of cultural diffusion would permit us to adopt a more appropriate use of the term "technology," not in its narrow sense as industrial science, but in its broader sense as technique. William Leiss has expressed this broader meaning of technology as "the authoritative mode of the organization of human labor for the purpose of satisfying needs."[20] A. Zvorikine of the USSR Academy of Sciences Institute of Philosophy has defined technology as "the means of work, the means of human activity developing within a system of social production and social life," a definition which he feels correctly reckons with both the material and social aspects of technology. [21]

In his study of technological transfer in Eastern Europe, Alexander Woroniak has suggested that "technology can be and has been conceptualized in a number of ways, each of which suggests different theoretical and operational approaches. The simplest version views technology as involving only changes in artifacts. A more sophisticated approach adds to the physical objects the labor and the managerial know-how. Finally, technology can be viewed as a 'socio-technological' phenomenon, by adding to the material and artifact changes the cultural, social, and psychological factors as well."[22]

In this study, we start from the assumption of this broadest definition of technology as a "socio-technical" phenomenon and an integral part of the basic values of every culture. Thus, technological change in any culture has direct consequences for other cultural values. In the words of Margaret Mead, "a change in any one part of the culture will be accompanied by changes in other parts, and. . .only by relating any planned detail of change to the central values of the culture is it possible to provide for the repercussions which will occur in other aspects of life."[23] Some of the more basic and interesting questions related to technological change concern the impact of technology on other cultural values, and vice versa.

In order to be in a position really to understand the impact of technology on culture, we must know more than we do now about the impact of culture on technology and its development. For only by coming to grips with the question of the extent to which technology, in its formative stages, is a reflection, embodiment, or reification of dominant cultural values will we be able to progress to solving the problems of the impact of technology on culture and the possibility of developing radically alternative technologies. In the past decade or two, many fashionable volumes have been written concerning the impact of technology on culture—including, among the most popular and widely read, the works of Jacques Ellul, Emmanuel Mesthene, John Kenneth Galbraith, R. J. Forbes, Daniel Bell, and Z. K. Brzezinski—but precious little has been written about the other side of the question: the impact of culture on the formative stages of technology at each of its successive stages of development—industrialization, mechanization, and automation and technotronics.

The important result of this decidedly one-sided approach has been the proliferation of theories which must be characterized as representing one form or another of technological determinism. In an important recent analysis, William Leiss suggested that "the confusions prevalent in the recent literature arise from a failure to treat the particular question (namely, the social consequences of technological progress) within the context of a more general phenomenon (namely, the attempt to shape social behavior according to rational standards and freely chosen goals)."[24] What Leiss suggests is that "if technology is the organization of knowledge for practical purposes, what we need to know is: *Who* organizes it? and how is it organized? Or, if we look at Forbes' definition [of technology as 'the product of interaction between man and environment, based on the wide range of real or imagined needs and desires which guided man in his conquest of Nature'], we must ask: *Who* guided the conquest of nature? and for what purposes? Lasswell's conception, accepted by Ellul [technology as 'the ensemble of practices by which one uses available resources in order to achieve certain valued ends'], prompts us to inquire: *What* ends? and how are they selected?"[25]

But technological determinist theories do not raise such questions and, hence, do not permit us to evaluate the two-way dialectical interaction between technology and cultural milieu. Instead, these theories "mark a retreat in the realm of social theory by isolating the rationality of technology from the rationality of the whole" cultural milieu.[26] Leiss contends that "the essential error in these theories is to isolate one aspect of this totality (technology) and then to relate it back to the totality in a mechanical fashion; accordingly, the cause-and-effect network is resolved upon analysis into a set of circular propositions. The result is that a 'technological veil' (to use Marcuse's term) is cast over the social process which obscures both the general dynamic of advanced societies and the specific role of technology in that dynamic."[27]

One theory which is the exception is the work of Steve Marglin who has been centrally concerned with the cultural sources of technology and technological innovation.[28] Stanley Aronowitz succinctly summarized Marglin's argument to explain the emergence of technologies that relied on the minute division of labor for accelerating output:

> Contrary to most opinion, he denies the determining role of either efficiency or the drive to maximize profit in the choice of production methods. Instead, specialization of tasks is seen as a product of the recognition by capitalists of the importance of devising technologies that maintain the crucial role of management in organizing production. With the reduction of artisan skills to relatively simple tasks, no individual worker or group of workers is able to master the intricacies of either the production process or the market, and the capitalist's centrality to the process of production and distribution of commodities, which consists in his ability to coordinate the relationship between the producers and the market, remains secure.[29]

In effect, what Marglin has attempted to do is "to demonstrate that the organization of production according to this premise *historically precedes* the appearance of complex machinery and was transferred to the machines socially."[30]

This argument can be linked with that of Avineri to provide a more complete picture of the historical evolution of the factory system and production methods. It was, as Gorz and Marglin point out, the tradesmen who organized the artisans and craftsmen into factory-type units for purposes of control.[31] Once organized in that fashion and given the increase in demand for goods brought about by the discovery of new trade routes, it followed that ways would be developed to increase productive capacity. Hence, the beginnings of industrialization. "The industrial revolution for Marx is not the beginning of the capitalist process, but rather its culmination. Capitalism *precedes* industrialization,"[32] writes Avineri. This, of course, is precisely the same point argued by Lukacs in his famous 1925 review of Bukharin's *Historical Materialism*:

> The *social* preconditions of modern mechanized techniques thus arose first, they were the product of a hundred-year social revolution. The technique is the consummation of modern capitalism, not its initial cause. It only appeared after the establishment of its social prerequisites; when the dialectical contradictions of the primitive forms of manufacture had been resolved—when "At a given stage of its development, the narrow technical base on which manufacture rested, came into conflict with requirements of production that were created by manufacture itself" (*Capital I*). It goes without saying that technical development is thereby extraordinarily accelerated. But this *reciprocal interaction* by no means surpasses the real historical and methodological primacy of the economy over technique.[33]

The core of this argument is that (1) the organization of production precedes the development of complex machinery; (2) this organization of production was accomplished for purposes of control of the workers; and (3) this social control was *socially transferred* to the machines which were developed soon afterward. The industrial revolution of the eighteenth and nineteenth centuries is the source of the substantiation. Julian M. Cooper comments:

> In England after the bourgeois revolution in the second half of the seventeenth century capitalist manufacture became the dominant form of production but the system of technology remained as before in the feudal formation, i.e., hand tools remained the basic instruments of labor. In manufacture, however, a progressive breaking down of the labor process into a series of distinct operations took place; a process which led to the specialization of workers and to the differentiation and specialization of hand tools: "Differentiation, specialization and simplification of instruments of labor, brought about by the division of labor in manufacture, founded in its turn on this division of labor. . .are one of the technological, material pre-conditions for the development of machine production as one of the elements revolutionizing the mode of production and production relations." [Marx, *Critique of Political Economy.*] Manufacture, by breaking down the labor process into relatively simple, repetitive elements, created the conditions facilitating the transfer of the specialized hand tool from the human hand to a working mechanism, thereby forming what Marx termed the "working machine." It was the working machine, in Marx's view, which served as the starting point of the Industrial Revolution. This step did not occur simply as a result of the action of purely technical forces, *but was promoted by motive forces of a social nature. . . .*[34]

Most interestingly, it seems that a similar process occurred in the early twentieth century just prior to the introduction of mechanization.[35] Aronowitz suggests that "the substance of the professional engineer's job at the turn of the century was to organize the labor process in a way that yielded the highest possible profit. In many cases, his efforts were directed at finding ways to break down traditional skills into their components and to describe the limits of these discrete components as new jobs.[36] (It remains to be thoroughly explored, but it would seem not unlikely that a similar abstract dissection of thought patterns played an important part in the development of cybernetics.)

This is very much a part of the thinking of F. W. Taylor's "Scientific Management," and flows from a dominant spirit of the times so nicely described by Siegfried Giedion: "The position is clear. Competition is growing. Wage-cutting has proved impractical as a means of lowering production costs. The machine tools are at hand. They will become continually further differentiated and more specialized, but few real improvements seem likely to raise productivity."[37] So the focus shifted from new inventions to methods of organization within the plant which could lower costs and increase productivity. Our primary point here can be made by briefly examining the main contributions of two of the most outstanding contributors to the movement for rationalizing operations within the factory: Frederick Winslow Taylor and Frank B. Gilbreth.

Probably the best place to start with Taylor is to recognize that he viewed the factory as a completely closed organism; it was a goal in itself. Taylor was only concerned with mechanical efficiency and *how* things were manufactured, not with questions of *what* was produced and *why*. It is common knowledge that Taylor was preoccupied with matters of human efficiency—how the human body can increase its productive capacity with a maximum of ease and a minimum of fatigue. What this meant in reality, Giedion suggests, is that "the human body is studied to discover how far it can be transformed into a mechanism."[38] This study involved the minute scrutiny of the physical movements of the worker in performing his tasks. After numerous experiments with time and motion studies of workers, *the* most efficient way to perform each task was discovered and recorded as the job description for each worker. When it came to deciding *which* task would be performed *when* by each worker, Taylor insisted on the "military type of organization. . . . One of the cardinal principles of the military type of management is that every man in the organization shall receive his orders directly through the one superior who is over him. The general superintendent of the works transmits his orders on tickets or written cardboards through the various officers to the workmen in the same way that orders through a general in command of a division are transmitted."[39] The net result, Giedion suggests, is the automatization of the mass of the workers whereby "human movements become levers in the machine."

Taylor's methods of time/motion study are greatly refined by Gilbreth's cyclograph (or "motion recorder") which could photographically capture the forms of the worker's movement invisible to the naked eye. "The light patterns reveal all hesitation or habits interfering with the worker's dexterity and automaticity. In a word, they embrace the sources of error as well as the perfect performance."[40] On the basis of these refined methods, Gilbreth could be much more precise in the contents of the Taylor-type "military dispatches" to the workers. His *Concrete System* (1908) sets forth some four hundred rules for the process of ferro-concrete building, and Gilbreth describes the book as "almost a stenographic report of what a successful contractor said to his workmen."[41]

The foregoing suggests that the process of the "mechanization of man" involved breaking down traditional skills into component parts, each of which was described as a new job (in effect, increased division of labor), and the observation and recording of the minutiae of motions required to perform each task, with these descriptions becoming the only acceptable ways to perform the task. All of this having been accomplished, the next logical step was to replace the "human mechanism" by an inanimate mechanism. This step was taken by Henry Ford's introduction of the assembly line which was in full operation at his Highland Park plant in 1915—the year of Taylor's death.[42]

If similar motive forces of a social nature (that is, requirements for control) stand behind the development of the next highest stage of technological development—automation and cybernetics, the quaternary level—then one must seriously question the ability of automation to perform the human liberatory function which many Western and socialist theorists attribute to it. Automation is clearly liberating in certain respects. Drudgerous, monotonous, and physically dangerous human labor can be reduced, and has been to some extent. Theoretically at least, the reduction of unrewarding human toil can result in the opportunity for more creative and satisfying human activities, although the substance and range of those opportunities are, of course, socially determined.

Yet automation is not without its drawbacks and its own potential and real hazards, not all of which can be anticipated. One highly visible drawback at present is automation's requirements for inanimate energy. Many sources of energy in the world are virtually without limit (wind energy, solar energy, tidal energy), but the sources which have been utilized and most of those immediately projected for harnessing to fill the rapidly escalating demands are either quantitatively limited (fossil fuels), ecologically disastrous (some forms of extraction and transportation of fossil fuels, nuclear energy, some hydropower), and/or decidedly incompatible in their development with a free society (nuclear power). The case of choice of power sources is an excellent example of the social choices behind technological development, and they are beginning to be painted in rather stark relief in the West, with research indicating, for a crucial example, that workers in nuclear power generators are subjected to strict regimentation and hierarchical controls because of safety factors, that a highly trained special military unit would be required to guard such installations (called "nuclear parks" in the U.S.), that potential for blackmail would be so high as to necessitate the elimination of civil liberties in the search for alleged thieves of materials such as plutonium which would be used in the production of nuclear energy.[43]

Automation raises other, somewhat more subtle threats to human liberation—most of which have been bantied about wildly in the West in forms ranging from highly speculative popular treatments (Theodore Roszak, *Where the Wasteland Ends*) to serious inquiry, such as the work of Jacques Ellul. In substance, they generally raise the specter of human automatons—physically inferior from a sedentary life, psychologically damaged by the time-oriented precision and compulsion of daily existence, mentally crippled by the transfer of creative and productive power to the machine, and socially-politically thwarted by the inability to influence one's own life world.

Yet for socialist theorists, and not without good reason, automation is a key component of the scientific and technological revolution. Of course, only under socialism can the revolutionary and liberatory potential of automation be fully realized. Under capitalism, suggests one Russian, the "synthesis of revolutionary science and technology meets insurmountable obstacles."[44] Or, as another Soviet source has put it, "the new scientific and technical revolution is beyond the capabilities of modern rotting capitalism. As the CPSU program notes, socialism alone is capable of fully implementing its potential and utilizing it in the interest of the whole of society."[45]

But there is an important element of this question of the liberatory role of automation which Soviet theorists have apparently continued to underplay. The capitalist industrial system is dependent upon the capitalist mode of purposeful rational action, i.e., the particular form of technical rationality which had developed through the last two hundred years of the industrial revolution in the capitalist West. (Although this concept of capitalist technological rationality is quite an illusive one, it nevertheless seems to have some usefulness in referring to a broad set of basic social attitudes, and as such would include the dichotomization of means and ends, of work activity and product; the compartmentalization of knowledge; the separation of manual and mental labor; the human domination of nature; efficiency defined in non-human terms; the hierarchical control of production; and, underlying it all, the assumption of the priority and insatiability of human material wants.) It is this aspect of technology, perhaps more than the technological hardware itself, which has the greater impact as cultural diffusion. To the extent that the communist countries, especially the USSR, have accepted capitalist technical rationality as well as hardware, serious questions have been raised concerning the extent to which this process of cultural diffusion will inhibit the qualitative transcending of capitalist industrial technology in the form of automation. That is, if automation is developed within the framework of a capitalist technological rationality, it may merely deepen the potential contradiction between automation and liberation. So directed, the transfer culture of communism may come to acquire a degree of cultural autonomy which proves subversive of communist goal culture and, as in capitalist states, prevents the realization of the human liberatory potential of automation. Such a development would not surprise the founders of the Frankfurt School of Critical Social Theory, who argued that as technology develops, it becomes an almost autonomous and mystical force in society.[46]

## NOTES

1. See, for example, Robert C. Tucker, "Culture, Political Culture, and Communist Society," *Political Science Quarterly* 88 (June 1973):173-190.

2. Ibid., p. 190.

3. Marc Raeff, "The Russian Autocracy and Its Officials," in *Russian Thought and Politics*, ed. Hugh McLean, Martin E. Maila, and George Fischer, Harvard Russian Studies, vol. 4 (Cambridge, Mass.: Harvard University Press, 1957), pp. 78-79.

4. Robert C. Tucker, *The Marxian Revolutionary Idea: Essays on Marxist Thought and Its Impact on Radical Movements* (New York: Norton, 1969), p. 106.

5. Theodore H. Von Laue, *Sergei Witte and the Industrialization of Russia* (New York: Atheneum, 1969).

6. Peter Solomon, "Technological Innovation and Soviet Industrialization," in *The Social Consequences of Modernization in Communist Societies*, ed. Mark G. Field (Cambridge, Mass.: Harvard University Press, forthcoming).

7. Antony C. Sutton, *Western Technology and Soviet Economic Development, 1917-1945*, 2 vols. (Stanford, Calif.: Hoover Institution Press, 1968 and 1971).

8. Referred to in Frederic J. Fleron, Jr., and Lou Jean Fleron, "Administration Theory as Repressive Political Theory: The Communist Experience," *Newsletter on Comparative Studies in Communism* 6 (November 1972).

9. John A. Armstrong, *The European Administrative Elite* (Princeton, N.J.: Princeton University Press, 1973), p. 189. Emphasis added.

10. Ibid., p. 190.

11. Genevieve Dean, "Science, Technology and Development: China as a 'Case Study,' " *The China Quarterly* 51 (1972):521.

12. Rensselaer W. Lee III, "The Politics of Technology in Communist China," *Comparative Politics* 5, no. 2 (January 1973):237-260.

13. Dean, "Science, Technology and Development," p. 528.

14. Richard R. Fagen, *The Transformation of Political Culture in Cuba* (Stanford, Calif.: Stanford University Press, 1969), p. 141.

15. Ibid., p. 140.

16. Anthony F. C. Wallace, *Culture and Personality*, 2nd ed. (New York, 1970), p. 27.

17. Tucker, "Communist Society," p. 186; and Chalmers Johnson, "Comparing Communist Nations," in *Change in Communist Systems*, ed. Chalmers Johnson (Stanford, Calif.: Stanford University Press, 1969), p. 141.

18. See, for example, Sutton, *Soviet Economic Development;* Solomon, "Soviet Industrialization"; and R. V. Burks, "Technology and Political Change in Eastern Europe," in *Change in Communist Systems*.

19. *Technology and Culture* 1, no. 1 (Winter 1960):1.

20. William Leiss, *The Domination of Nature*, Postscript to the French edition (Paris: Le Seuil, 1974).

21. A. Zvorikine, "Technology and the Laws of Its Development," *Technology and Culture* 3, no. 4 (1962):443.

22. Alexander Woroniak, "Technological Transfer in Eastern Europe: Receiving Countries," in *East-West Trade and the Technology Gap: A Political and Economic Appraisal*, ed. Stanislaw Wasowski (New York: Praeger, 1970), p. 87.

23. Margaret Mead (ed.), *Cultural Patterns and Technical Change* (New York: Mentor, 1955), p. 13.

24. William Leiss, "The Social Consequences of Technological Progress: Critical Comments on Recent Theories," *Canadian Public Administration* 13, no. 3 (1970):247.

25. Ibid., p. 250.

26. Ibid., p. 261.

27. Ibid., p. 253.

28. Stephen A. Marglin, "What Do Bosses Do? The Origins and Functions of Hierarchy in Capitalist Production," Mimeographed (Cambridge, Mass.: Harvard University, 1971).

29. Stanley Aronowitz, *False Promises: The Shaping of American Working Class Consciousness* (New York: McGraw-Hill, 1973), p. 155.

30. Ibid., p. 155. Emphasis added.

31. See, for example, Andre Gorz, "Technical Intelligence and the Capitalist Division of Labor," *Telos* 12 (1972):27-41; and Marglin, "What Do Bosses Do?"

32. Shlomo Avineri, *The Social and Political Thought of Karl Marx* (Cambridge, England: Cambridge University Press, 1970), p. 1954. Emphasis author's.

33. Georg Lukacs, *Marxism and Human Liberation* (New York: Dell, 1973), p. 56. Emphasis author's.

34. Julian M. Cooper, "The Concept of the Scientific and Technical Revolution in Soviet Theory," CREES Discussion Paper No. 9, Centre for Russian and East European Studies, University of Birmingham, England, 1973, p. 17. Emphasis mine.

35. See, for example, Aronowitz, *False Promises*, p. 156; and Siegfried Giedion, *Mechanization Takes Command* (New York: Norton, 1969), pp. 96ff. for details.

36. Aronowitz, *False Promises*, p. 156.

37. Giedion, *Mechanization Takes Command*, p. 96.

38. Ibid., p. 98.

39. Ibid., p. 99.

40. Ibid., p. 103.

41. Ibid., p. 102.

42. Ibid., p. 115.

43. See Alvin M. Weinberg, "Social Institutions and Nuclear Energy," *Science* 177 (July 7, 1972):27-34, for a discussion of these possibilities.

44. B. Kuznetsov, *Kommunizm i Tekhnika Budushchego* (Moscow: 1940), p. 15.

45. V. I. Gromeka and V. S. Vasil'yev, "Bourgeois Theorists on the Scientific and Technical Revolution," *USA: Economics, Politics, and Ideology* (Moscow) 1 (January 1971):73.

46. See Max Horkheimer and T. W. Adorno, *Dialectic of Enlightenment.*

# PART THREE

# ECONOMICS

# 11

# Testing the Realism of Plans

Stanislaw Gomulka and Peter J. F. Wiles

The medium-range plan is by far the most important basis of Sovietological prediction, since it is binding not merely on the enterprise but even largely on the government.

At the very worst, the useful tautology holds that a five-year plan (FYP) is binding until altered. Therefore, if it is coherent and feasible it will be fulfilled if it is not altered; and if we find that it is not, we automatically predict that it will be altered. It may also, however, be altered in the case of some exogenous cause, such as a new government or a diplomatic crisis. These exogenous causes are, of course, no easier to predict than in any other case, and we are on a par with all other specialists in being forced explicitly to assume them away.

Experience tells us two things about these plans. First, Kyril FritzLyon[1] has shown that plans for large aggregates like the national income or industrial production are better fulfilled than plans for small aggregates like tractor output. This is one of those extremely valuable and practical propositions that turn out to be tautologies. But they are none the worse for that. The intuitively obvious can be rigorously demonstrated, even without algebra, as follows. We restate the proposition thus: *bad predictions are commoner among small categories than among the large ones of which they are parts, provided that the parts are exhaustively enumerated.* Then the error of the prediction of the large category is simply the weighted average of the errors of the predictions of its sub-categories. But for the former error to be equal to the largest of the latter errors it would be necessary that all the other errors be of equal magnitude and sign. This is the limiting case: in all others at least one sub-category has a greater error than the total, and in most cases more than one. So bad predictions are commoner among sub-categories.

It is therefore not surprising that the same *pattern* of errors shows itself in French planning. But it is surprising that the *size* of the errors is the same in France as in the USSR (and smaller in agriculture!).[2] It has been shown by Stanislaw Wellisz that econometrical models are not better predictors of the evolution of the French economy than the four-year plans. But the realism of these plans is a great deal more easy to check.[3]

*Aggregation*

The opening dilemma which everyone attempting to assess the realism of a national plan faces concerns aggregation. Should we look at the plan as expressed in its most synthetic variables, with a small number of relatively stable technical parameters? Or, alternatively, at a detailed plan, offering a valuable insight into the internal structure of the economy, but requiring a critical evaluation of a great number of usually highly unstable technical coefficients? A plan may be termed realistic if all the technical coefficients assumed in it are realistic. Socially, a plan is the outcome of a game, a compromise reflecting various and frequently contradictory interests of planners, producers, and consumers. Therefore, these detailed technical coefficients must be and are the most essential part of the game. They may easily be unrealistic because they are deliberately fudged in order to obtain agreement, or because they are never fully known to the individual producers, still less to the central planners. As always in economics, the actual choice thus not only is a matter of the actual technical possibilities, but also depends heavily on the amount and quality of knowledge about them and on the relative bargaining power of the game's participants, the latter affecting the "direction of error."

The exact detection of the production possibilities, and then the accurate prediction of the final outcome of the game is clearly an impossible task for any planning body. Of course, it is far less possible for us, and we are under some obligation to make a pronouncement on a plan *quickly*: say, at least within the first two years of its five-year currency.

Nor is a detailed analysis of a part of a plan very useful for estimating the realism of the national plan as a whole. Such a partial analysis could indeed easily be misleading. Let these points serve as an excuse for our intention to choose in this paper the most aggregated level of national planning. We believe, however, that one could at least investigate the three main sectors: industry, services, and agriculture, using the same technique which we will apply to the economy as a whole.

An analysis of the sectoral plans would in fact be a welcome supplement to this discussion by adding to it a significant segment of the structural dimension.

The purpose of the paper is to find how far we can go in evaluating the realism of a new plan without commitment to the highly uncertain *absolute* values of the aggregated technical parameters. We intend instead to postulate something about the time *changes* in those values. It is well known that there are good reasons to expect the aggregated parameters to change rather slowly over time. Therefore, well-chosen assumptions about the changes over the plan period seem to be much less risky than a commitment to the absolute average values during the plan. We start with the assumption that there will be no such changes. This initial assumption is then modified to permit some changes to occur.

*The Statement of the Problem*

By national plan, we mean the aggregated volumes of planned employment L, capital K, and output Y. Employment is expressed in men, or in man-years, whenever possible. Capital and output are aggregated at the fixed prices of a given year. Both K and L are engaged in activities producing Y. As a period of reference we are forced to take a five-year plan, but this is not regrettable, for five years is a period in which the short-term fluctuations (e.g., those caused by weather) already cease to act as a major disturbing factor, and in which the impact of uncertainty as to the long-term change in technology is yet relatively minor. The income and employment equations derived by using the vintage approach would be most useful for our purpose. But this approach is ruled out by the lack of data on the age structure of the capital stock and the corresponding structure of employment and output. Therefore we estimate the production effect of the planned inputs using instead an aggregate production function:

$$Y = F(K, L; t) \tag{1}$$

As usual, time t in (1) signifies the influence of all factors other than K and L. By writing this equation we implicitly assume that this influence does not depend on changes in the age and product distribution of K, or on the age, sex, and skill distribution of L. This assumption is no doubt highly unrealistic. To justify (1) we must thus assume that over any five-year plan all the structural changes are relatively minor. The realism of this particular assumption depends in turn on the level of aggregation, that is, on what is meant by "product" and "skill." It is clear that the assumption in question is far less acceptable at a lower level of aggregation, but is not so restrictive at a higher one, for example, at the branch or industry level.

Let

$$Y/Y = g_Y, \; K/K = g_K, \; L/L - g_L \tag{2}$$

By the Euler theorem, $\mu Y = F_K K + F_L L$, and from (1) it follows that:

$$g_Y = a g_K + (\mu - a)\, g_L + \lambda \tag{3}$$

where $\mu$ and a are, respectively, elasticity of Y with respect to scale of production and with respect to capital. The term $\lambda = \frac{1}{Y}\frac{\partial Y}{\partial t}$ is the contribution of factors other than K and L. These factors are, of course, the capital and labor employed in activities producing "qualitative" changes in the economy. The activities in question are above all those which produce and diffuse, from abroad and within the economy, the technological and organizational changes, and those which upgrade skills to the level required by these changes. We follow others in calling $\lambda$ the Factor Productivity Residual (FPR); residual, since it is usually, and in this paper also, left unexplained by those extra inputs. But most frequently we will refer to $\lambda$ as an index of the rate of technical change. Though generally well known, it seems worth repeating that the value of $\lambda$ gives only the direct contribution of technical change to $g_Y$. From (1) it is obvious that a 1 percent increase in $\lambda$ will directly increase $g_Y$ by the same rate. But this is not the end of the story. Indeed, at any given $g_L$ and at any given and positive savings-investment rate s, greater $g_Y$ will inevitably increase $g_K$, giving rise to an additional increase in $g_Y$. This additional increase in $g_Y$ will increase $g_K$ still further, and so on. It is thus clear that a change in $\lambda$ is capable of generating something which may be termed a growth propagation effect. This effect comprises both the direct and the indirect contribution of $\lambda$ to $g_Y$.[4]

To see both contributions together, we rearrange (3) to read:

$$g_Y = \frac{a}{1-a}(g_K - g_Y) + \frac{\mu - a}{1-a} g_L + \frac{\lambda}{1-a} \qquad (4)$$

From K = sY it follows that at s constant $g_K = g_K (g_Y - g_K)$, that is $g_K$ increases (decreases) as long as $g_Y$ is greater (less) than $g_K$. Given s, $g_L$, a, and $\mu$, the propagation process acts to increase $g_Y$ and, therefore, to increase $g_K$. Each additional round of the process adds a small amount, which itself diminishes with the number of the round. Assuming $a < 1$, the newly emerging $g_K$ must be a finite number. Therefore, by the end of the process $g_Y = g_K$, irrespective of the value of $\lambda$. Since the difference $g_K - g_Y$ in (4), as it emerges when the process ends, is "insensitive" to changes in $\lambda$, the total direct and indirect contribution of technical progress to $g_Y$ is given by $\frac{\lambda}{1-a}$. Changes in $\lambda$ have thus a multiplier effect on the growth rate of output, with $\frac{1}{1-a}$ as the multiplier.

We make this comment on $\lambda$ for two reasons. First, we feel that in the debate on the so-called Soviet strategy or Soviet model of growth, the indirect contribution of $\lambda$ to $g_Y$ has not been exposed strongly enough. An elaboration of this point requires, however, a separate paper. Second, the existence of this indirect contribution underlines the extreme importance we must attach to the proper estimation of $\lambda$ if a plan is to be realistic. It reminds us also how essential it is for the planners to know the relative strengths of the factors by which $\lambda$ could be changed if they are to be able to improve the growth performance.

Most estimated $\lambda$'s are positive.[5] They are estimated either simultaneously with other parameters (a and $\mu$ in 3) or at some given values of a and $\mu$. In the latter case the estimated value of $\lambda$ very much depends on the weights used, a and ($\mu$ - a in [3]), and virtually any weights are defensible.

For instance, we may take the view that agricultural labor in overpopulated countries (USSR until recently, India still) has zero or nearly zero marginal productivity, and so deserves a lower weight than that indicated by the living wage it must *ex hypothesi* receive. And if the labor market is not too imperfect, that weight must apply to the whole economy. Note that this has nothing to do with a Soviet-type economy as such. Indeed the labor market must be assumed there to be highly imperfect, so that near-zero marginal productivity is or was confined to agriculture. But nobody knows exactly how imperfect it is, i.e., what the marginal-value-product-to-wage ratio actually is in each sector. Or we may argue that even in overpopulated countries there is seldom surplus labor at the harvest peak, and this will involve us in complicated readjustments. Finally, the Soviet planners used to allow no capital charge, and its present tax arrangements for the use of capital are extremely remote from a productivity-related charge.

For these three reasons, to name no others, we cannot approach a and $\mu$ - a via the paid-out income shares. The attempt to estimate $\lambda$ simultaneously with other parameters from the time series itself is hindered by multi-collinearity, and unduly sensitive to minor changes in the basic data. Nevertheless, since Cobb and Douglas first proposed their production function in the twenties, there have been undertaken countless attempts of that kind. The experience accumulated thus far seems to indicate that this method is fairly reliable if data are of good quality and assembled for long periods of time, say fifty years—that is, for countries such as the United Kingdom or U.S. However, the USSR and the East European countries can hardly be said to meet these requirements. The data are available for not much more than fifteen recent years, and their quality deteriorates quickly when one goes back into the past. The recent extensive study by Rychetnik supports strongly our view that the *absolute* values of $\lambda$, a, $\mu$, and other technical parameters (see below) found for these countries by applying that method are wholly untrustworthy.[6] Below we will try to estimate the realism of a new plan without commitment to such values.

*Macro-Tests of Realism of a Five-Year Plan*

Equation (3) may be rearranged to read:

$$g_Y = ag_K + (1 - a)\, g_L + \lambda^B \tag{5}$$

where $\lambda^B = \lambda + (\mu - 1)\, g_L$ contains also the direct influence of non-constant returns to scale. We call $\lambda^B$ biased FPR, in short BFPR. Because $\mu$ probably does not differ much from 1, and $g_L$ is usually is a slowly changing small amount, the term $(\mu - 1)\, g_L$ may be expected to be minor relative to $\lambda$, and thus $\lambda^B$ will change as slowly as $\lambda$.

*Hypothesis 1.* We expect $\lambda^{\bar{B}}$ and a to continue, and input targets to be fulfilled. That is to say, we do not expect any significant change in the rate of technical progress, for instance neither vast-scale diffusion of American technology nor Khrushchev-type mistakes, nor a change in the returns to scale. But we do expect, on the basis of previous experience, that the input targets will be fulfilled or overfulfilled. We do not have, however, any good excuse for assuming a to be a constant. This assumption will be partly relaxed later.

Let $g_{0Y}$, $g_{0K}$, $g_{0L}$, and $\lambda_0^B$ be the performance figures of the last five-year plan. By (5):

$$\lambda_0^B = g_{0Y} - a\, g_{0K} - (1 - a)\, g_{0L} = \lambda_0^B\ (a) \tag{6}$$

It is thus a linear function of a. But we do not know the exact value of a. It can be said only, since we assume positive marginal products of labor and capital, that $0 < a < \mu$.

Let the figures for the new plan be: $g_{1Y}$, $g_{1K}$, and $g_{1L}$. They imply that:

$$\lambda_1^B = g_{1Y} - a\, g_{1K} - (1 - a)\, g_{1L} = \lambda_1^B\ (a) \tag{7}$$

The possibly crudest test of realism thus would be as follows:

*Test 1.* A plan $(g_{1Y}, g_{1K}, g_{1L})$ is realistic if:

$$\lambda_1^B\ (a) \leqq \lambda_0^B\ (a) \text{ for all } a \in (0, \mu) \tag{8}$$

The trouble with this test is that we do not know $\mu$, the upper limit to a. Sometimes we may not need to know it, as in the example below. But situations when the answer supplied by this test depends on $\mu$ may unfortunately occur, and rather frequently.

*Two examples, USSR and Poland*

Let us first examine the realism of the 1971-1975 Soviet five-year plan using the test above. The performance and the plan figures are given in Table 1. These are official data; all figures are percentage growth rates per annum. Y = NMP, K is "productive" capital stock, L stands for the total employment; we do not know $g_L$ for the "material" sphere of the Soviet economy.

Table 1:
*Soviet Growth Rates:*
*Actual Performance in 1966-1970 and Planned for 1971-1975*

| *Growth rate* | *Actual in 1966-1970* | *Planned for 1971-1975* |
|---|---|---|
| $g_Y$ | 7.2 | 6.8 |
| $g_K$ | 8.0 | 8.5 |
| $g_L$ | 1.9 | 1.5 (?) |

Substituting these figures into (6) and (7) we have that $\lambda_0^B$=5.3-6.1a and $\lambda_1^B$=5.3-7.0a. Hence $\lambda_1^B$-$\lambda_0^B$=0.9a; the new plan does not assume any increase in the residual, whatever the actual absolute value of a in the range (0, $\mu$). Therefore the plan meets our test of realism. However, the figure 1.5 percent for $g_L$ is only our guess. If the actually planned $g_L$ for the material-goods sector is lower than 1.5 percent, as the data given by G. Grossman would suggest,[7] the answer could be different. If, for instance, $g_L$ = 1.0 percent, then $\lambda^B$=5.8-7.5a. The latter implies that $\lambda_1^B \leqq \lambda_0^B$ only if a$\geqq$0.36.

The corresponding figures for Poland are given in Table 2. The growth rates $g_Y$ and $g_K$ planned for 1971-75 are those of the original plan. The plan is now (1973) substantially revised, a result of markedly better economic performance in 1971-72, but the new plan is yet not known.

Table 2:
*Polish Growth Rates:*
*Actual Performance in 1966-1970 and Planned for 1971-1975*

| *Growth rate* | *Actual in 1966-1970* | *Planned for 1971-1975* |
|---|---|---|
| $g_Y$ | 6.1, 6.7 (1) | 6.8, 6.4 1 |
| $g_K$ | 6.2 | 6.8 2 |
| $g_L$ | 1.5 (3) | 2.1 3 |

1 This growth rate of Y is derived if the highly under-trend actual value for agriculture and the food industry in 1970 is replaced by the respective trend values.

2 Our own estimation.

3 Growth of population in the following age brackets: 18-59 for male, 18-54 for female.

Again from (6) and (7) we can find that $\lambda_0^B = 4.6\text{-}4.7a$ and $\lambda_1^B = 4.7\text{-}4.7a$. Hence $\lambda_0^B = \lambda_1^B = 0.1$ ; the new plan assumes a slight increase in the residual. But the last two years of the 1966-70 plan were very bad for the Polish agricultural sector. If we replace the actual figures for agriculture and the food industry by their trend values, then $\lambda^B = 4.3 - 4.7a$. That is to say, the original five-year plan for Poland implies a decrease in $\lambda^B$ by 0.9, whatever the actual value of a, and therefore was realistic. In Hypothesis 1 we expect a to be a constant, irrespective of the form of technical changes the economy is facing, and irrespective of the changes in capital labor or capital/output ratio. We shall now relax this restrictive requirement. But in order to keep the complexity of the problem at a manageable level, constant returns to scale will be assumed. We know that on this assumption a may depend only on the capital/output ratio v and time t, that is, a = a(v,t). Note that $\frac{v}{a}\frac{\partial a}{\partial v} = (1 - \frac{1}{\sigma})$, an implication of the definition of the elasticity of substitution $\sigma$. The rate of change in a over time is as follows:

$$\frac{\dot{a}}{a} = (1 - \frac{1}{\sigma})\frac{\dot{v}}{v} + b \qquad (9)$$

where $b = \frac{1}{a}\frac{\partial a}{\partial t}$. When labor can be easily substituted by capital ($\sigma > 1$), the planners may increase a and, assuming $\lambda$ does not decrease, the growth rate of output, simply by increasing v. For $\sigma < 1$ they could do the same by decreasing v.

Parameter b in (9) is either positive (technical change capital-using in the Harrod sense), zero (neutral), or negative (capital-saving). Its absolute value may therefore be regarded as a measure of the intensity of the corresponding form of technical change. Do we know anything about this very important technical parameter? Econometric studies are helpless in the short run. In the long run they seem to indicate, for the U.S. and the U.K. at least, that both v and a change relatively slowly over time, with no evident long-run trend. This would indicate that b is either fluctuating around zero or of definite sign, but of very small absolute value. According to Robert M. Solow[8], for instance, "The empirical evidence is not very convincing, but such as it is it seems to indicate the presence of a small component of capital-augmenting technical change" (with the labor-augmenting or Harrod neutral forms being the main component). If this now widely shared view is correct, b would indeed be of a small value, positive (whenever $\sigma > 1$), and negative otherwise.

Of course we do not know whether or not a non-neutral component of technical progress is present in the Soviet Union, nor whether if present it is of the capital-augmenting form. It seems, however, reasonable to expect b to be at least of a small absolute value.

*Hypothesis 2.* We expect $\lambda$, $\sigma$, and b to have the same value as in the past five years, and input targets to be fulfilled.

We do not know the absolute values of $\lambda$, $\sigma$, and b, but whatever they have been in the last plan, we expect them to continue over the next five-year period. Note that previously we expected $\sigma$ and b in (9) to be such that the resulting a is constant, irrespective of changes in v. This could always be fulfilled only if $\sigma = 1$, $b = 0$ during the current and new five-year periods, that is, by the economy satisfying over that time a standard Cobb-Douglas production function. Now we approximate F(K, L, t) by a CES (constant elasticity of substitution) production function.

To make it clear, we do expect $\sigma$ to vary markedly from one industry to another, still more from one factory to another. At the micro-level it may also change significantly over time. Assume we know the distribution of production according to the value of $\sigma$. We may then interpret it as a probability distribution, and our aggregated $\sigma$ as a weighted mean value associated with this distribution. It is quite probable that a given production unit may shift from one place in the distribution to another. Due to offsetting shifts it is less probable, though still quite possible, that the shape of the distribution may change over time. But a significant movement of the weighted mean value itself is much less likely. It is thus the high level of aggregation which we believe supports the assumption of the constancy of $\sigma$. The constancy of b is assumed on similar grounds.

From (9) we have that:

$$a_1/a/_0 = 1 + (1 - \tfrac{1}{\sigma}) \frac{v_1 - v_0}{v_0} + b \tag{10}$$

where a five-year period is taken as the time unit. The performance figures imply that

$$\lambda_0 = g_{0Y} - a_0\, g_{0K} - (1 - a_0)\, g_{0L} = \lambda_0\,(a_0)$$

The planned value of $\lambda_1$ depends upon $a_1$, hence by (10), upon $a_0$, and b.

$$\lambda_1 = g_{1Y} - a_1\, g_{1K} - (1 - a_1)\, g_{1L} = \lambda_1\,(a_1) = \lambda_1\,(a_0; \sigma, b)$$

Our somewhat less crude test of realism would thus be as follows:

*Test 2.* A plan $(g_{1Y}, g_{1K}, g_{1L})$ is realistic if

$$\lambda_1\,(a_0; \sigma, b) < \lambda_0\,(a_0) \tag{11}$$

for all admissible values of $a_0$, $\sigma$, and b, that is for $a_0 \in (0, 1)$ $\sigma \in (0, \infty)$, and $b \in (-\infty, +\infty)$.

It is very likely, however, that no plan ever prepared would have passed this test. It may, therefore, be practically useless. The test has only the virtue of its unconditioned non-commitment to the uncertain absolute values of $a_0$, $\sigma$, and b. But as we mentioned earlier it is highly improbable for b to take on values much different than zero, or for $\sigma$ to assume values much greater than one. So it could not be very risky to make a commitment to some *ranges* in which we expect $a_0$, $\sigma$, and b to be found. Hence the following test of realism.

*Test 3.* A plan $(g_{1Y}, g_{1K}, g_{1L})$ is realistic if (11) is satisfied for all $a_0 \in (\underline{a}_0, \bar{a}_0)$, $\sigma \in (\underline{\sigma}, \bar{\sigma})$, and $b \in (\underline{b}, \bar{b})$, where the symbols in the parentheses refer, respectively, to the lower and upper limit to the value of the corresponding technical parameter. This test requires us to state explicitly the ranges for $a_0$, $\sigma$, and b to which the term "realistic" applies. Let us return to our example of the current Soviet five-year plan. According to the official data, the average capital/output ratio will increase during 1971-75 by 8 percent. By substituting the performance and planned figures given in Table 1 into (11), we eventually obtain

$$1.5 - g_{1L} - a_0 \left[ (8.5 - g_{1L}) (2.08 + b - \frac{1.08}{\sigma}) - 6.1 \right] \leqq 0$$

Assume $g_{1L}$ = 1.5 percent. In this case b and $\sigma$ for which the plan is realistic should satisfy the following inequality: $\sigma \geqq \frac{1.08}{b + 1.21}$

**Figure 1.**
*Area of Plan Unreality*

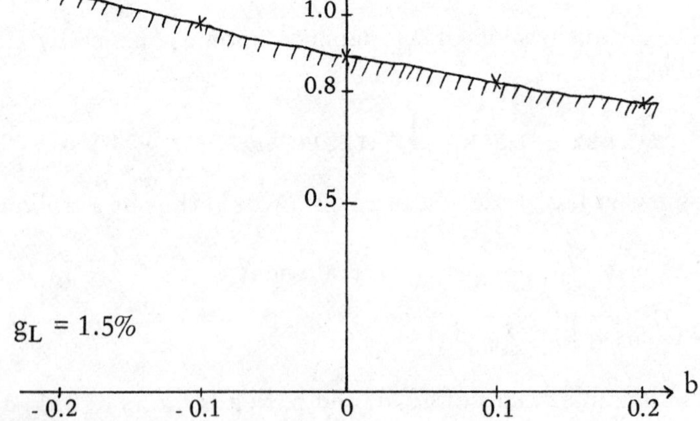

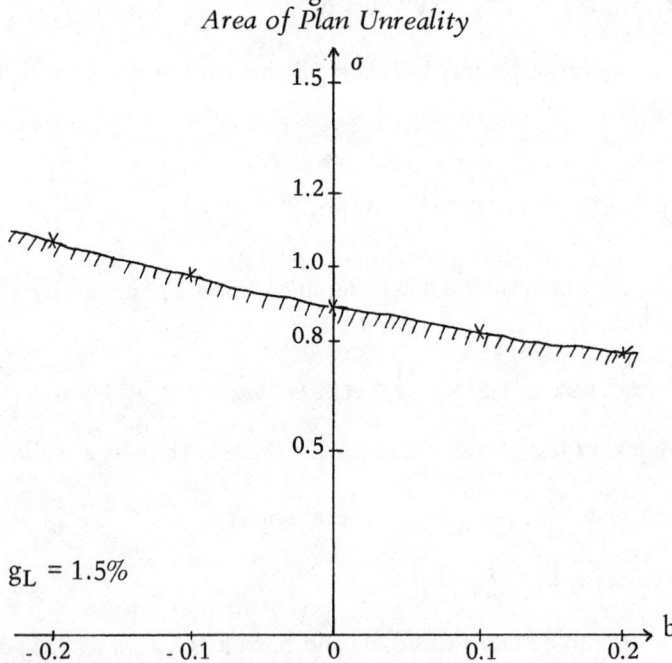

The current five-year plan is unrealistic for b and $\sigma$ in the shadowed area.

The shaded area in Figure 1 refers to the pairs (b, $\sigma$) for which the inequality does not hold. It is clear from it that in the sense of Test 2 the plan is not realistic. It may, however, be realistic in the sense of Test 3, provided $\sigma$ does not deviate much from unity and b from zero. Its realism appears not to be affected by the value of $a_0$.

This picture changes significantly if $g_{1L}$ = 1 percent. The plan is now realistic for $a_0$, b and $\sigma$ satisfying

$$\frac{1}{a_0} \leqq 1.98 + 15b - \frac{1.08}{\sigma}$$

The shaded area in Figure 2 refers to the pairs (b, $\sigma$) for which the plan is not realistic at $a_0$ equal to: 0.3, 0.4, 0.6 and 0.8. The difference with the corresponding area in Figure 1 shows the decline in "realism."

**Figure 2.**
*Area of Plan Reality*

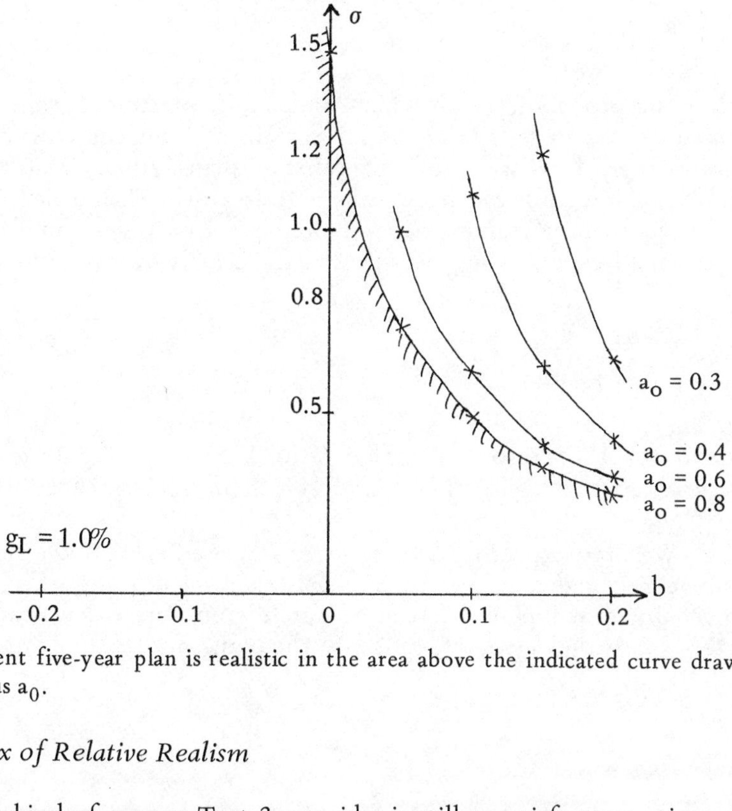


The current five-year plan is realistic in the area above the indicated curve drawn for various $a_0$.

*An Index of Relative Realism*

The kind of answer Test 3 provides is still unsatisfactory since it very much depends on the limit values of $a_0$, $\sigma$, and b, beyond which the plan is *not* expected to pass the test. To be sure that the actual (and unknown) $a_0$, $\sigma$ and b fall within the specified ranges, the lower limits have to be chosen low enough and the upper ones high enough. But if the ranges are too great, then hardly any actual plan could be expected to pass the test. It is thus clear that we need to develop a more "realistic" test of realism which should be less sensitive to changes in the limit values.

In the three-dimensional space $a_0$ $\sigma$ b the permissible values of the parameters pack a cube of the volume

$$V^* = (\bar{a}_0 - \underline{a}_0)\,(\bar{\sigma} - \underline{\sigma})\,(\bar{b} - \underline{b}) \tag{12}$$

A part of the cube comprises points which satisfy condition (11). Let its volume be denoted by V. We shall assume now that all combinations of values over the whole cube are equally probable. Under this assumption the ratio

$$r = V/V^* \tag{13}$$

gives the probability with which the plan in question is realistic. This is an index of, so to speak, "relative realism." Indeed, now we do not have simply "realistic" and "unrealistic" plans. All are realistic (or not realistic), but some are more realistic (unrealistic) than others.

Now the usefulness of r for prediction purposes could be greatly increased by employing past information on five-year plans. Let

$$a = \frac{g_{Y\ \text{actual}}}{g_{Y\ \text{planned}}}$$

stand for the performance/plan ratio. We may compute $a$ and r for several past five-year plans and set them against each other in an $ar$-plane.

We may expect $a$ to be positively related to r. If the relationship between r and $a$ proves to be statistically significant, then once r is given for a new plan, by reading out $a$ from Figure 3 we can immediately assess the *degree* of realism of the plan.

**Figure 3.**
*Degree of Realism of the Plan*

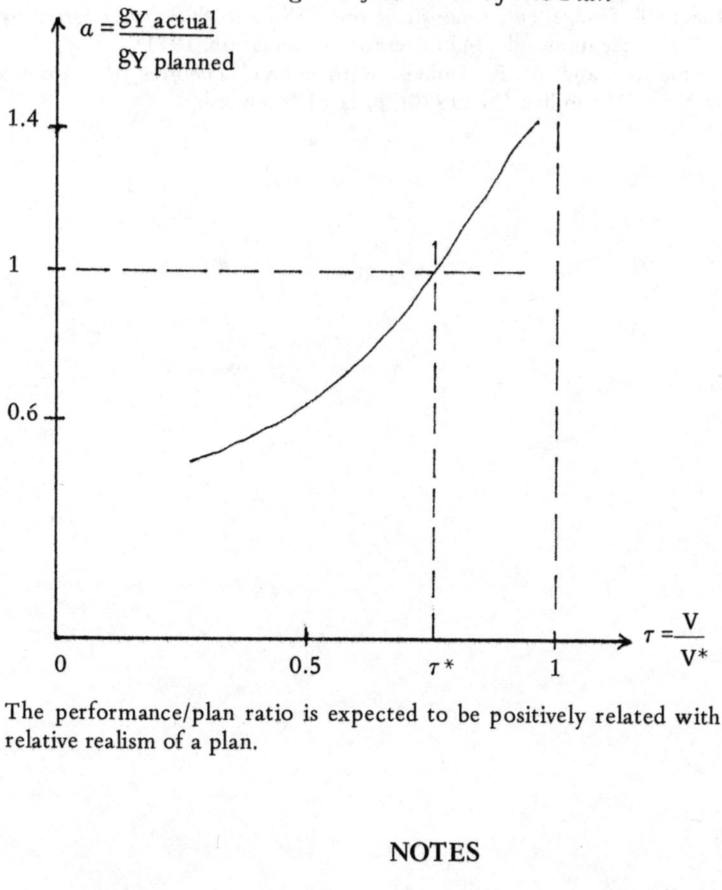


The performance/plan ratio is expected to be positively related with the index of relative realism of a plan.

## NOTES

1. FritzLyon, Kyril, "Plan and Prediction," *Soviet Studies* 21 (October 1969):164-192.

2. Review by Mark Wasserman and Peter J. F. Wiles of Vera Lutz, "Central Planning for the Market Economy: An Analysis of the French Theory and Experience," *Economica* 36 (November 1969):444-447.

3. "Comment" in Max F. Millikan, ed., *National Economic Planning* (New York: National Bureau of Economic Research, 1967), pp. 300-304.

4. Note that it may be looked at as the total effect of a change in $\lambda$ from zero to $\lambda$. More rapid growth would also increase the novelty of the capital stock, but we have excluded this from our presentation here.

5. $\lambda < 0$ implies heavy subsidization and/or a command economy. Instances are Soviet agriculture (Peter J. F. Wiles, *The Prediction of Communist Economic Performance* [Cambridge, England: Cambridge University Press, 1971], chapter 26) and the national income of Bosnia, Macedonia, and Montenegro (Emile Primorac and Peter J. F. Wiles, *Location Criteria in Countries with Different Economic Systems* [Vienna: UNIDO, 1968] –the zero residuals in this document should be negative).

6. L. Rychetnik, "The Production Function in Postwar Eastern Europe," mimeographed (Oxford: St. Antony's College, 1971).

7. In Norton T. Dodge, ed., *Analysis of the USSR's 24th Party Congress and 9th Five Year Plan* (Mechumrsville, Md.: Cremona Foundation, 1971).

8. E. Burmeister and A. R. Dobell, *Mathematical Theories of Economic Growth* (New York: Macmillan Co., 1970), p. ix of foreword.

# 12

# Property Rights

Richard Carson

It has been the vogue since before Marx to place existing economic systems into two broad categories labeled "capitalist" and "socialist" respectively. Although there are many exceptions, the usual basis for classification rests on legal ownership of most of the material means of production. Under capitalism these are principally private and under socialism mainly state or publicly owned.[1] To the economist who wishes to study socialist (or, more generally, comparative) economic systems, however, such a classification is both very broad and, on occasion, misleading. It is possible to name two socialist economies—Yugoslavia and the USSR—which are in many ways further apart in terms of structure and functioning than a socialist economy, on the one hand, and a capitalist system, on the other—for example, Yugoslavia and West Germany.

The problem essentially is that legal ownership means one thing under one set of circumstances and something else under another. Public ownership, for example, does not distinguish between the Renault works in France and the Togliatti plant producing modified Fiats in the Soviet Union. Consequently, even when we know something of a society's resource endowment and level of technology, we cannot necessarily infer much that is useful about its structure and functioning or its performance characteristics purely from knowing whether it is capitalist or socialist from a legal standpoint. This has led economists to search for a more detailed classifier of systems that will also shed more clues on how the economic problem in a given society is being solved.

Recently, the focus of this search has been on what are called property *rights*. These refer to the rights of particular individuals or organizations to use goods and services (or property) in particular ways, to exclude other individuals and organizations from using them, and to receive all or part of the income (or surplus value) that they generate. Property rights are really relations between individuals and groups in society that find expression in its laws, rules, edicts, customs, mores, and traditions and, on that account, are often called property *relations*.

These relations, it is argued, form the basis for production, consumption, and exchange and, hence, for a more detailed and useful classification of economic systems. The present paper will explore this claim by focusing on differences in property rights between various economies, all of which are "socialist" in terms of legal ownership.

If we take an identifiable governed area (such as a country, a province, or a city) or organization as our basic unit and frame of reference, we may identify three kinds of property within it from a property-rights standpoint. In their pure forms, these types are as follows:[2]

1. Private Property: An individual or group, designated the "owner," has the right to determine how a piece of private property shall be used, subject to the owner remaining within the bounds of "good citizenship." (This is defined by society's political decision-making processes and should be viewed as a set of constraints in practice rather than in principle.) Equally important, he can exclude others from using it, and he has a right to its income. Finally, he may also transfer the rights to use that property and to receive the income which it generates to another owner through gift or sale.

2. State Property: The government has the right to use state property and to distribute the income generated by this property as it wishes, subject to accepted political procedures. The government may also exclude any particular use of state property by any given individual or group. Thus, it decides who shall manage (or act as custodian over) it and what rules he must obey.

3. Communal Property: Individuals and groups in society have the right to freely use communal property as they wish and are able, again subject to good citizenship. The government does *not* exclude anyone from using it nor may one group exclude another. This nonexclusion principle is the most important feature of communal property.

We may then define private, state, and communal property rights in the same vein. Thus, a private property right is a right of a particular individual or group to use a specific piece of property in a specific way, to receive all or part of its income, to exclude others from using it, or to transfer these rights. The rights to consume a given good, to produce it in a specific way, and to decide how much of it to buy or sell are private property rights, as is the right to enter into a specific type of contract. We may also add a time dimension to most private property rights, covering the duration before the right is expected by its owner to expire. We may thereby distinguish between stock and flow rights (or between leases of different durations), although we shall not emphasize this aspect in the present study.

A state property right is a right of a government executive or administrative agency to exclude a specific use of a specific piece of property, to distribute all or part of the income generated by it, or to make some or all decisions about its management. Taxation rights are usually state property rights, as often are the rights to grant specific subsidies. The constraints that define good citizenship in any given society may be viewed as state property rights. (Once again, we may add a time dimension.)

Finally, a communal property right is a right of all citizens to make a specific unconstrained use of a given piece of property—for example, to stroll through a public park, to fish or to make use of the waters of a stream. While communal rights in the material means of production exist in every economy, they do not predominate except in some primitive societies. The reason is that communally "owned" resources (in a property rights sense) tend to be overexploited. Either they will be used up or else used to the point where their marginal product or marginal utility to each potential user is zero. (Thus, the problem of pollution may often be viewed as one arising from free access to air and water resources.) Moreover, the incentive to invest or to maintain property is diluted by the fact that the benefits resulting from this activity must be shared.

Many organizations which are communal in nature, such as religious orders or what are popularly known as "communes," will have property that is nominally common to all members. But upon closer examination, access to this property will turn out to be restricted—so that its use is governed by a combination of state and communal rights within the organization—although the distribution of rights to its use and to the income which it generates may be quite equal among its various members. The tendency to overexploit communal resources may thereby by attenuated, although *private* incentives to work and to accumulate would still be reduced by a need to share the benefits. Presumably, the most important investment decisions will have to be made collectively.[3]

It is more generally true that we can rarely, if ever, find pure forms of property in practice, and the way in which we classify a given piece of property will depend upon the relative importance that we assign to the bundles—that is, the private, state, and communal property rights attached to it. For example, private property rights are eroded in almost every society by taxation, despite loopholes, and by the provisions of civil and criminal law. By the same token, most managers are able to gain some freedom to produce as they like, even in the most highly centralized command economies.

Nevertheless, if we can decide whether private, state, or communal property rights *vis-à-vis* the material means of production are dominant in some sense, within a particular economy, we can classify it as capitalist, socialist, or communist on that basis. Such a categorization would inevitably be subject to dispute, and it would not always correspond to one based on legal ownership.

Regardless of whether it did, moreover, there would continue to be considerable variations in property rights within each category that will cause marked differences in performance. For example, we may say that moral incentives prevail to the extent that the pay and promotion possibilities of managers and workers are uncorrelated with their contributions to achieving the production goals of the state. In the extreme, a worker or manager who raised his productive contribution would gain no increase in material rewards of any kind. It appears that a heavier reliance on moral incentives in China and Cuba (until 1970) than in the USSR and Eastern Europe has stunted the growth performance of the former, while, at the same time, giving them more equal income distributions.[4]

Under the "capitalist" umbrella (in terms of legal ownership), the Swedish central government has more extensive powers to tax and to subsidize than do the federal governments of Canada and the United States. The result is a more equal distribution of (post-tax and post-subsidy) income in Sweden. Indeed, after distribution, Swedish income inequities are probably less than those in several legally socialist countries, even though more than 90 percent of the material means of production in Sweden are legally in private hands. Because the distribution of property incomes, and especially income from dividends, is much less equal in capitalist countries than the distribution of income from wages and salaries, it has been argued that a removal of the right to pass on large estates to heirs would, by itself, considerably reduce income inequities. Finally, a greater willingness of the French and Japanese governments to act like insurance agents in removing part of the risk associated with investment from the shoulders of enterprise management has probably speeded up growth in these two countries during the post-World War II era in comparison with other economies where legal private ownership of the material means of production predominates.

In the final analysis, perhaps the only certain result is that we would find no genuinely communist nations today above a primitive level of economic development. From an economic standpoint, the notion of utopia is often identified as a situation where the problem of scarcity has been solved. Even in the absence of all restrictions, the demand for every resource is less than the supply at each positive price. In particular, there is no need to restrict access to resources on the basis of price, or the ability to pay for their use. Thus, zero price levels and communal property rights can prevail without interfering with efficiency. We can generate a spectrum of utopias of this nature, each of which is some combination of two polar cases. In the first polar case, suggested by Thoreau's *Walden*, the excess supply of resources results from extreme voluntary want restriction. The second is Marx's full communism based upon superabundance.

In this context, full communism is also an utopic aspiration of most economies that are currently socialist in the sense of legal ownership. It will not arrive until all problems relating to natural resource exhaustibility have been solved, and the economy has become so super-productive that, in the words of Peter Wiles, "Leisure increases to almost intolerable proportions, money falls out of use, and we can all go and help ourselves in the shops."[5] In these conditions, more than adequate saving, investment, and work efforts are forthcoming out of an inner need to create, a desire to serve the community, as a means of self-expression, and last of all, to relieve the boredom of too much leisure.

*Rights of Managers*

In part, an economic system is a distribution of property rights or relations among the various firms, households, government administrators, and other decision-making bodies which inhabit it. We may also think of this distribution as the property-rights structure of an economy, and we now wish to briefly examine variations in property-rights structures among three economies, all of which are socialist in terms of legal ownership of the means of production. These are Yugoslavia, Hungary, and the USSR. For the most part, we shall compare the roles of enterprise management in each system, confining ourselves largely to industry.[6]

Of the three, the range of freedoms granted Yugoslav management comes closest to that customarily found in a North American firm. That is, the Yugoslav enterprise has the most latitude to decide what and how to produce, including the introduction of new products and technologies and the founding of new enterprises. On balance, Yugoslavia probably has higher industrial entry barriers than does Canada or the United States, partly because the market is smaller and effective barriers to international trade are even higher.

In this context, Yugoslav firms apparently enjoy even greater freedom from anti-monopoly prosecution. Local governments condone and even encourage market-sharing and price-fixing agreements. While such cartel-like arrangements may sometimes contribute to the realization of scale economies, they are probably damaging, on balance, from the standpoint of economy-wide efficiency. A possible check on monopoly abuse comes in the form of widespread price controls, however, and profit-sharing among all of the employees of a firm is widespread in Yugoslavia as a part of the broader phenomenon known as workers' management. This probably mitigates the income-distribution effects of monopoly power, and these are likely to be reduced still further over the long run by the inability to inherit executive management positions or extremely large amounts of wealth.

In addition, restrictions on the mobility of investment funds across regional boundaries in Yugoslavia reduce the average yield on all investment projects. These restrictions are much greater than in North America, Japan, or Western Europe. There is, of course, no stock market in Yugoslavia (where stock ownership includes voting rights *vis-à-vis* managerial performance) and virtually no bond market. The behavior of banks and of the various levels of government is such that savings often do not flow to the highest-yielding investment projects, even within the same region. One firm can lend money or rent or sell capital equipment to another, but only subject to the requirement that interest earnings are not paid out as wages and that the book value of any equipment sold will be reinvested.

We can view the latter requirement as the state's way of asserting its claim to ownership of the enterprise's material means of production. The current management may use the firm's capital stock to a large extent as it wishes, and alter the physical composition of assets. But it may not reduce the value of the stock without explicit permission from the government. The state also asserts its property rights in the enterprise through a very low tax on the undepreciated value of its capital and by having a voice in the selection of the professional director or manager. However, the latter right must be shared with the employees of the firm.

In addition, the fact that workers lose all claim to the earnings of the firm currently employing them when they leave it tends to make enterprises prefer outside financing of investment. (Internal financing tends to come at the expense of additions of the fund from which current wages are paid, and most of the benefits of investments made today accrue in the form of higher future profits for the enterprise.) This has combined with low interest rates and the practice of extending especially easy credit in various circumstances to produce an excess of planned investment over planned saving. The savings-investment gap has, in turn, been filled by rapid increases in the money supply which have fueled rapid inflation. (The official cost-of-living index rose by nearly 40 percent between 1971 and 1973.)

Finally, workers' management may well increase the internal operating efficiency of the firm in some instances and, at the same time, give the employees a chance to vote for a more humane workplace, as its advocates claim. But the worker-managed firm may also be more reluctant to expand than a conventionally managed profit-maximizing enterprise in both the long and short run, in the absence of offsetting government subsidies. This is because workers' management is, among other things, an enforced internal risk-sharing agreement (regarding investment, research, and innovation) among all of the employees of a firm, even those who are most risk-averse. Moreover, both the control over the enterprise and any additional profits from expansion will have to be shared with new employees. Implicit and explicit subsidies, including loans at interest rates below the rate of inflation, have, however, been forthcoming, and have probably more than offset these factors.[7] These subsidies have undoubtedly raised the level of entrepreneurship in Yugoslavia, at some cost of encouraging inefficient firms, along with excessive capital intensity which, in turn, helps to keep up the rate of unemployment. (Currently, registered unemployment in Yugoslavia is more than 4 percent of the domestic labor force, and probably more than one million Yugoslavs are working abroad.)

The Hungarian manager faces a number of additional constraints on his freedom to choose product mixes and production methods, especially where long-run investment decisions are concerned. Hungary is at least a semi-market economy, following the reform aimed at decentralizing economic decision-making begun in 1968 and now stalled short of its original goals. Nevertheless, for the most part, firms cannot rent or sell capital equipment or lend money to one another. There is no bond market, and most long-term loans cost far less than an equilibrium rate of interest (as in Yugoslavia), giving the Central Investment Bank and the state budget considerable authority to channel funds directly to those users which they (or the plan) wish to favor. There has also been considerable repressed inflation in the form of unfinished construction.

In addition, an enterprise cannot normally tool up to produce a good that is significantly different from one it has produced before without permission from higher-level authorities. A would-be manager usually cannot start his own firm. The decision and the initiative for such a venture would have to come from the ministerial level or above. Thus, firms are largely constrained to plowing back their retained earnings into traditional lines of production.[8] (In addition, industrial ministries still hire and fire enterprise managers, just as they did before the reform, and set managerial pay. In contrast with Yugoslavia, this right has been entirely retained by the state.)

Consequently, barriers to new competition are extremely high. One estimate is that new firms are not started more often than approximately once per year. The industrial structure is strongly monopolistic to oligopolistic: "Including industrial cooperatives, 291 enterprises employed 74 percent of the country's labor force [in late 1970]."[9] Import competition remains low, a factor which tends to mean that, in many industries, the small size of the Hungarian market will only permit a very few firms that are large enough to realize their scale economies. Once again, however, the effects of this highly concentrated structure diverge from what we would expect in North America. There is some redistribution of profit within the firm, although to a far lesser extent than in Yugoslavia. More importantly, because of the small number of firms, the government can more easily use moral suasion and direct price controls to prevent managers from raising prices.[10]

These controls are backed up by an extremely harsh incomes policy designed to shift the Phillips curve down. Memories of runaway inflations after both World Wars are still fresh in Hungary. Thus for political reasons, Hungary cannot tolerate more than a tiny amount of unemployment and a low rate of inflation without jeopardizing the reform. In sharp contrast to Yugoslavia, price controls backed by the incomes policy have kept open inflation to an average of less than 3 percent annually since 1968.

Additional political constraints make it difficult to remove inefficient managers or to transfer workers to new jobs against their will, even when the goods they are helping to produce would not sell in the absence of a sellers' market, and more productive occupations in the same area are going begging. Indeed, if a change of skills is required, such an involuntary transfer often cannot occur within a given factory. This is consistent with the increased emphasis on conditions of work rather than goods consumed as a source of welfare by Marxist *vis-à-vis* "bourgeois" economists, and explains a portion of the emphasis in (legally) socialist nations on job security rights at the expense of the consumer's right to quality and service. However, the state's reduced ability to transfer or dismiss managers who have failed to adapt to the switch from command to market planning and the managers' inability to dismiss or to transfer workers involuntarily become sources of inefficiency. In particular, the state must subsidize many inefficient firms and maintain the traditional sellers' market to keep down the size of inventories that can only be sold at a heavy loss.[11]

One consequence of a high job security for managers and workers and a high propensity by the government to bail out inefficient enterprises is that material incentives must be slanted away from penalties for failure and toward bonuses for success. Again, however, political factors have asserted themselves. A manager faces a stiff reduction in his salary if he raises the average wage of all the employees in his enterprise by more than some designated amount, which depends upon tolerable inflation plus desired labor mobility. This constant average wage control is a principal managerial success indicator and the form taken by the incomes policy mentioned above.[12] In addition, efforts to tie managerial incomes to enterprise profitability through large bonuses have led to sharp worker protests because of the visibility of these awards. Consequently, since 1968 these bonuses have tended to become part of managerial salaries, less visible, but also tied to position rather than to performance. The tendency to tax profitable enterprises, while subsidizing unprofitable ones, has worked in the same direction.

Thus, income differentials have come increasingly to depend upon occupation rather than job performance and do not operate very efficiently as work incentives. In particular, the weakened incentive to cut costs and raise profits has led to waste and has also helped to make Hungarian managers extremely risk-averse. A compensating benefit, given the avowed aims of Hungary's rulers, may occur in the form of reduced income inequalities, but a high productivity price was paid for extreme job security and the need to shift the Phillips curve down over the first four years of the reform (1968-1971). In addition, the foreign trade deficit grew worse and the volume of unfinished construction rose during this period. The year 1972 saw an improvement in the balance of payments, but also creeping recentralization, notably in investment decision-making. By 1973, the state's right to ration funds to enterprises directly from the budget and the ministries' rights to supervise the use of such funds and the progress of investment projects, were being increasingly reasserted. During the same year, 50 of the largest industrial enterprises employing about two-thirds of all industrial workers and producing half of all industrial output came under especially close central supervision, and the high-water mark of the reform had clearly passed.

Nevertheless, within their restricted freedoms to change product mixes, Hungarian managers still have an important voice in determining their overall investment programs. On balance, nearly half of all gross fixed investment in manufacturing appears to have resulted from managerial, as opposed to higher-level decision-making in 1970, although the percentage has fallen since then.[13] Thus, the reduction in managerial decision-making freedom as we go from Yugoslavia to Hungary involves the choice of what goods to produce to a greater extent than the choice of how (or of what production methods to use). Both reductions go hand-in-hand with a greater decision-making role for higher-level government authorities. From another standpoint, the government contracts out fewer property rights to managers and delegates them instead to higher-level authorities in a chain of command. With some oversimplification, we may compare Hungarian managers to divisional or branch-plant managers in North America. When we switch to the USSR, the autonomy of an enterprise manager closes in toward an orbit that we associate more closely with a North American plant foreman.

Thus, the most important feature of Soviet industrial planning is a collection of legally binding physical targets. To back these up, raw materials and intermediate goods are physically rationed among user firms. An enterprise will also receive a budget constraint for wages and salaries, combined with directives for the skill and the white-collar/blue-collar mixes of its labor force. Like his Hungarian counterpart, a Soviet manager faces major restrictions on dismissal and transfer of personnel between jobs.

This does not mean that managers in the USSR have no room in which to make their own decisions. They can reorganize production to get more output from given inputs if they are able, and Soviet planners are constantly trying to pressure them into doing this. They have some freedom to vary product assortment and production methods. Particularly since the mini-reforms of the late 1960s, they have some freedom to determine their investment programs.[14] Occasionally they are allowed to market their goods. Considerable evidence has accumulated to indicate that they have more freedom to do all of the above things in practice than they have on paper.

Nevertheless, basic production decisions in the USSR are taken above the level of the firm by central planners who communicate their choices to managers in the form of input and output targets. This is why we have compared managers there to foremen in North America. An American foreman does not have to worry about the financing of the firm or too much about the selling of the product, beyond the fact that it must meet certain specifications. He has limited freedom to change the mix of inputs that he uses or of outputs that he produces. His major problems are physical. He must put his allotted labor to work in a productive manner. He must see that the equipment is in good operating order and make sure that the production process functions more or less smoothly.

The Soviet manager's decision-making orbit is larger than this, but closer to it than to the role of a Western corporate manager. The decisions which occupy most of the latter's time are made higher up a chain of command or planning hierarchy, and in this sense the decisions that solve the economic problem (or implement socio-economic goals) are more centralized in the USSR than in Hungary, Yugoslavia, or any developed Western country. They are probably more centralized still in Rumania, Bulgaria, and Cuba. China, on the other hand, is much less centralized than the USSR, although it would not classify as a predominantly market economy.[15] Indeed, the only preponderantly socialist market economies are Yugoslavia and Hungary, and the latter is a borderline case, a fact that becomes more evident when we turn to what may be called the "problem of correspondence."

Over the period 1962-64, prior to the reform, the Hungarian planners promulgated a major merger movement in a drive to realize scale economies under the then-existing command mechanism. The number of centrally directed firms fell from 840 at the end of 1962 to 435 by the middle of 1964. The percentage reduction in some industries—for example, construction—was much greater, and a simultaneous effort was made to increase the specialization of the newly created firms. After the reorganization, the planning chain of command ran from the National Planning Office to the ministries (who supervised different branches of industry) to the new enterprises and thence to the various divisions of each firm. The reform did not reverse the 1962-64 reorganization. Marketization and its associated increase in decision-making autonomy therefore applied mainly to management at the enlarged enterprise level. Lower-level divisional and plant managers often continued to receive plan targets and to be assessed on their performances in meeting these.

Elsewhere in Eastern Europe, the reform movements begun in the 1960s and early 1970s have now turned to a large extent toward strengthening intermediate links in the planning chain of command between ministries and firms. These intermediate organizations are usually known as industrial or production associations, and it is to their managements that the most important increases in autonomy have gone or are intended to go. Basically, industrial associations are giant trusts, embracing a number of firms which collectively produce a significant percentage (in some cases, all) of the output of given product lines. For example, one production association is eventually to account for all of the rubber-tire output in the USSR and a few associations for all of the steel production.

In many industries in East Germany, Poland, Romania, or the USSR, it is the production or industrial association rather than the enterprise which is most comparable to the average Hungarian enterprise in terms of share of output or wages bill. An additional analogy is that the industrial association is also supposed to concern itself largely with current operating decisions, while the ministry looks after long-run investment decisions.

Consequently, we can only continue to maintain that production decision-making is less centralized in Hungary if we can show that Hungarian enterprise managers have greater autonomy than managers of industrial associations elsewhere in Eastern Europe. The crux of such an argument is that the most important production decisions are still made above the level of the industrial associations and communicated as binding physical targets to association managements. While production plans at the industry level continue to be drawn up in Hungary and a firm cannot ignore these, it does not receive physical output targets, nor is it subject to physical rationing of materials inputs, except in a few instances.[16] The prevalence of tied budgetary grants *vis-à-vis* loans as a means of investment financing also appears to be greater in most other East European countries.

In the final analysis, a major difficulty confronting any property-rights comparison of two economies is the fact that what is called an "enterprise," a "ministry," or a "household" in one system may not correspond to something bearing a similar title in the other. Yet, until some sort of correspondence at least partly based on the physical acts of production and consumption is established, a useful comparison is generally not possible.

### *Other Property Right Variations*

Let us define the "state" in a socialist economy to consist of industrial ministries, along with all planning, government, and Communist Party policy-making bodies, with their staffs, including national and regional banks, to the extent that the latter help to consciously form or implement government policies. Thus, the "state" consists of primarily administrative organs, above the level of the enterprise and largely divorced from actual production.

As a first approximation, we have associated greater centralization of production decision-making with a greater preponderance of state *vis-à-vis* enterprise management rights in directly determining how the material means of production shall be allocated and used. We can further divide the category of state property rights into sub-categories for each agency in the planning chain of command above the level of the firm. Assuming that we can order these agencies according to rank or degree of authority, we may say that an *administrative decentralization* occurs when a higher agency, such as a ministry, passes some of its rights to determine how the material means of production shall be allocated and used down the hierarchy to a lower agency, such as a production association, which is still above the level of the firm. (If we think of a *market* exchange as taking place between independent decision-makers, an administrative decentralization is less likely to result in increased marketization than one in which the rights in question devolve upon enterprise managements.)[17]

The other kinds of property rights *vis-à-vis* the material means of production are mainly state rights in all legally socialist economies except Yugoslavia. The latter economy is unique in the amount of freedom given enterprise managements to distribute the income from capital and to prevent reorganization of their firms. In the long run, they probably have substantial collective power to prevent a recentralization of production decision-making. Finally, as noted earlier, the professional director of the enterprise must be chosen jointly by the state and by the elected representatives of all of the employees. Thus viewed as a group within the economy as a whole, the employees of each enterprise have more private property rights *vis-à-vis* the means of production than any similar group would have (except in very small firms) in any other country normally said to be in the "socialist bloc."[18]

This does not mean that aspects of property-right variations beyond those dealing with the use of capital are not interesting or helpful in throwing light on the structure and functioning of different kinds of socialist economies. We shall explore three examples in this section, dealing with variations in managerial incentives, the political side of property rights, and changes in property rights as part of a theory of systemic change.

The Marx-Engels economic view of history is the most famous of the latter theories. In it, autonomous technological progress, broadly defined, is the prime moving force behind the evolution of one kind of system into another. After a lag, property relations adjust to accommodate major improvements in technology in such a way that an economy is able to return to a point close to its production or production-cum-international-trade-possibility frontier. (It is assumed that no set of property relations is strong enough to permanently impede the emergence and subsequent spreading of the optimal technology.) The lag occurs because autonomous changes in technology breed class conflict by making a previously optimal set of property relations, from the standpoint of accommodating efficiency in production and exchange, no longer optimal. That socio-economic class which had elite status under the old property relations tries to prolong them and collides with another class whose vested interests lie in the new.

In the end, nearly the whole of a given society acquires a vested interest in bursting the bonds of laissez faire capitalism and in establishing the property relations of "state socialism" (which, however, were not precisely specified). Subsequently, a classless dictatorship of the proletariat emerges. Modern theories of systemic change often depart from Marx in permitting other kinds of autonomous prime movers, such as changes in taste, and in not accepting Marx's specific historical cycle, or, in some cases, any deterministic view of history. As Professor Pejovich has pointed out, the latter permits us to view the state as an active instrument for promoting or facilitating property-rights changes, something Marx did not do.[19]

This, in turn, leads us to the political side of property rights. Again, speaking loosely, we may say that a society's *political* decision-making processes collectively formulate its socio-economic goals, including implicit or explicit decisions to extend the status quo, and also create its distribution of property rights—that is, determine the nature of its economic system. Society's *economic* decision processes implement these goals.[20] While economic decisions directly specify what, how, or for whom, political decisions help to establish the context within which economic decisions are made. For example, decisions by the manager of an enterprise or an industrial ministry that set specific output targets or determine specific production methods are economic decisions, as are wage contracts or unemployment insurance payments for specific individuals. However, a law defining a general policy on taxes and subsidies is the result of a political decision, as is a five-year plan, whose targets are normally expressions of intent rather than specific orders, and monopoly positions for firms and trade unions. (These positions notably help to create and to sustain the vested interests which Marx identified with laissez faire capitalism.) When one of the latter takes advantage of its monopoly position, it is making an economic decision. For the most part, any society's political decisions comprise those taken by the legislative, executive, and judicial branches of its government, along with voting and lobbying. They include the greater part of its laws, notably those assigning liability or fault.

Clearly, economic and political decisions are always interdependent, and it is never possible to analyze economic behavior except in some context of actual, anticipated, or hoped-for outcomes of political processes. Nevertheless, our discussion above dealt primarily with (de)-centralization of economic decisions as mirrored by the distribution of rights over the use of capital. That is, it focused on the *loci* of decisions about what and how to produce—more specifically, on which decisions were made at the managerial level and which above.

More decentralized political decision-making, on the other hand, implies wider or more equal participation in goal formation or in electing the representatives who directly determine society's economic priorities. More centralized political decision-making is more dictatorial, in the sense that a small group more successfully imposes its will upon the rest of society. In particular, this group is able to determine a distribution of property rights that it believes will maximize its own welfare as a function of its chosen socio-economic priorities. By examining any specific distribution of property rights, therefore, we can often discover where many of the seats of (monopoly and bureaucratic) power lie.[21]

Political and economic (de)centralization need not go together, although they often do. Within a command economy it is at least conceivable that representatives elected by many segments of society would participate in decisions about broad policy matters and delegate, subject to periodic recall, the authority to implement these policies to professional bureaucrats. The combination of dictatorial goal formation and marketization is often observed in practice. "A market economy does not necessarily lead to a retreat from authoritarianism."[22]

In this context, most East European reforms initiated since the mid-1960s stand out as efforts to make the economy function more efficiently by decentralizing production decision-making without expanding the political power base. Hungarian tracts on the reform, for example, stress continuing Communist Party control.[23] By implication, the (partial) substitution of market for command planning results primarily from efforts to find a more effective way to implement the goals chosen by the party elite. (Under favorable circumstances, the substitution of indirect for direct controls over production and distribution would be more than compensated for by gains in efficiency of operation.) The major exception was the Czech reform of 1966-68 which sought to combine marketization with increased democratization. In particular, Communist Party membership was expanded beyond the 3-7 percent of the population characteristic of most socialist countries.[24]

Since the reversal of this movement, only in Yugoslavia and, perhaps, China can one assume that goal formation is broadly participatory, even at intermediate levels of importance. As we have seen, the unique feature of the Yugoslav system, in addition to a federal parliament and local and regional governments with genuine power, is workers' management—that is, profit sharing plus formulation of the basic goals of the firm by the elected representatives of all of the employees. On an economy-wide level, this may be viewed as an income redistribution scheme which can partly replace more conventional fiscal redistribution through taxes and subsidies.

But we may also view the worker-managed firms as a system in itself within a larger system. The predominant property-rights features of this smaller system are a collective claim on net property income, plus automatic abandonment of this claim when an employee leaves the enterprise, and greater participation in goal formation. (Hence, the term "industrial democracy," which is often applied to workers' management.) It does not *automatically* imply greater decentralization in goal implementation (this would be a matter to be decided between the professional director and the workers' council) and most theoretical models of workers' management as well as nearly all Yugoslav firms provide for professional management of the enterprise's day-to-day affairs and of the technical aspects of long-run decision-making. Nevertheless, in Yugoslavia, workers' management has passed through an efficiency crisis (which may not be over) because "a rather naive ideology contained in legislation and political propaganda advocated direct participation in administrative work as indispensable to safeguarding the interests of workers."[25]

Lastly, let us examine variations in incentives. We may think of these as variations in the way the state uses its right to distribute the income or surplus value generated by capital, and our earlier discussion of the Hungarian reform has indicated that the use of incentives can influence an economy's functioning in an important way. If we wish, we may also view this as a third dimension of a property-rights spectrum of socialist economies whose first two dimensions are (de)centralization of production and of political decision-making.

Normally, the state (or, more precisely, the top leadership) will try to distribute property income in such a way as to maximize the attainment of its socio-economic objectives. In most socialist countries, there are two broad goals whose separate pursuit would suggest different incentive policies. These objectives are rapid growth or development, notably of defense and other heavy industries, on the one hand, and approximate equality of incomes on the other hand. In practice, these goals generally conflict to some extent because growth usually requires the incomes of managers and workers to be correlated with their marginal productivities in helping to produce growth.

We can, however, imagine at least two instances—aside from reliance on promises of future rewards, which cannot be postponed indefinitely—when the need for such a correlation may be greatly reduced. The two cases will coincide to some extent, but what we shall call case A arises when there is sufficient enthusiasm for the basic goals of the regime or loyalty to its leaders that individuals are automatically rewarded by aligning their work efforts with the wishes of their superiors. In the extreme, managers and workers would require no right to material compensation for their efforts, and all incomes above a subsistence level would be rent. In less extreme and more likely circumstances, mass meetings and rallies and other kinds of mobilization efforts by Party cadres, who are either dedicated or eager to advance through Party ranks, may help to whip up the necessary enthusiasm. When the accent is on egalitarianism, work rotation may also play a role.

It has been argued that the "mobilization phase" of a socialist economy is likely to come soon after the overthrow of the old capitalist or feudal order, when optimism and idealism run highest. (This may also be the time when the tasks to be accomplished are simplest and most obvious and therefore most readily lend themselves to incentives associated with exhortation.) As the initial fervor accompanying the transformation to socialism dies down, it becomes increasingly necessary to rely upon material incentives and, in the case of a command economy, a greater degree of formal planning and organization.[26] However, both the Great Leap Forward and its aftermath (1958-1961) and the Cultural Revolution (1966-1969) in China saw efforts to rekindle a revolutionary consciousness, at considerable cost in terms of lost output, and the nominal long-range goal is to rely primarily on moral incentives, even if the material abundance of full communism is not achieved.[27]

Indeed, the Mao-Guévarist "road to communism" places much more emphasis on a transmutation of human nature so that man is no longer self-seeking. A "true" communist, by this view, is altruistic and absolutely selfless, and success in attaining such a transmutation gives us a second case (case B) in which reliance on material incentives may be unnecessary.[28] As above, we must also require that most managers and workers are won over to the regime's goals—presumably because they identify these goals with the welfares of their neighbors, families, or fellow workers, or whoever may become the focus of their altruism. Finally, we must again assume that a mechanism exists—either a market or a physical plan, or some combination of the two—that provides enough information to each decision-maker to translate the regime's objectives into suitable concrete directives for action.

To deviate somewhat from case A, let us now suppose that efforts to further the regime's goals entail a positive net cost to at least some managers and workers—for example, in the form of long hours of rapid, grueling, repetitive, risky, or otherwise unpleasant work. In this sense, work is no longer its own reward, or at least not sufficiently so, but, given selflessness, the individual might still be sufficiently motivated if he could see his own effort rewarded in progress toward the regime's goals or in the increased welfare of his neighbors or fellow workers. Unfortunately, by himself, an individual worker cannot do much to further the achievement of national goals or even of the production goals of his own firm (unless it is a small one) by raising his own productivity. In effect, the fruits of his efforts are dissipated over a number of other individuals, in sharp contrast to a good material-incentive program that concentrates them on one individual, namely himself.[29]

A manager can do much more than an ordinary worker to achieve a given set of production targets for his firm, but not much to achieve national goals, unless the enterprise happens to be an extremely important one. For the worker, the achievement of either kind of objective is largely a public good, outside of his control as an individual (although not outside of the collective control of many workers). For the manager, a high degree of publicity will normally attach to the achievement of national or of regional goals. In the absence of material stimulators, this factor serves as a work disincentive that may be exacerbated by (presumed) unfair work assignments, poor administration by superiors, doubts about the regime's intentions, and a host of similar matters.

To mitigate the public good disincentive, the state will probably have to adopt some combination of three types of measures. First, it must focus each individual's attention on a sphere of productive effort whose success he can influence, while convincing him that this sphere is important. This effort is aided, in turn, by development of a mass social consciousness in which each individual is able to link his own effort to those of many others. (Collectively, they can overcome the public good problem.) Finally, in an era when the desired transformation of human nature is admittedly not complete, the state can mix material with moral incentives, raising the emphasis on the latter as the individual's decision-making responsibilities and sphere of influence expand and also as the salary attached to his position rises. An example combining all three approaches occurs when the authorities place a small work unit, such as a production brigade or team on a collective farm, on material incentives, while constraining the differentiation of earnings within the work unit. From the standpoint of equality, a danger here is that an unequal distribution of income between different work units may then develop.

In China, which has experimented the most with various moral incentive schemes—and with the allied problem of reducing work alienation—all of the above measures are receiving a continuing trial. Space limitations prohibit a discussion in detail, but we would note that most of the moral stimuli employed in China may also be viewed as types of material incentives or disincentives—the ambiguity perhaps once again reflecting persistent "bourgeois" selfish attitudes that must still be reckoned with.[30] For example, in the drive to develop mass social consciousness, Chinese society is often portrayed as a giant "family" in which rights to full membership are only granted to the efficient, disciplined worker who sacrifices his personal aspirations to state goals. In practice, however, "denial of full membership rights" means a variety of social and psychological pressures on the inefficient or poorly motivated worker, including visits to his home by model workers or Party cadres.

The same thing is true of the suppression of prestige symbols for managers and upper-echelon bureaucrats and also of such practices as the "sending-down" movement and work rotation. In principle, not only does a general in the Chinese army wear little evidence of his status on his uniform, but he is also supposed to take his turn at cleaning latrines. Most managers (or "most responsible persons," as they are now called), wear clothing quite similar to that of an ordinary worker and are now nominally required to spend at least one day a week in physical labor. Apparently many do, and most bureaucrats must spend a month or more at periodic intervals performing menial farm chores. The point is that this policy also reminds the upper socio-economic strata of how the lower strata live, particularly since a common type of punishment for the former is a prolonged or even permanent period of unskilled labor.

In fact, most socialist nations have chosen material over moral incentives as primary work motivators, despite the egalitarian appeal of the latter. The ultimate reason is greater urgency of the growth priority mentioned above. Consequently, we are best advised to view material incentives as part of the overall problem of enforcing the state's production priority. Under command planning, material incentives will ideally make it in the manager's interest to conform to plan targets, both in letter and in spirit. Under market planning, the aim is to use indicators and non-quantitative commands—taxes, subsidies, manipulation of managerial goals, information about future market conditions, etc.—to induce managers to choose a combination of outputs in production space that ranks high according to the state's priorities.

Space prohibits a discussion of the contrasting information properties of different kinds of economic systems.[31] However, the conventional trade-off between markets and commands as coordinators of a nation's industrial sector is said to be that markets have a greater efficiency potential, while commands give a strong planning authority greater potential leverage to steer the economy along lines deemed to be of national advantage.[32]

The emphasis here must be on potential. The efficiency advantages of markets may depend upon the government's ability to check monopoly power by promoting competition or a substitute for it, just as the advantages of command planning will depend upon the government's enforcement ability. To the extent that a good is communal or "public," in the sense that once it is available to a single individual, it automatically becomes available at no cost to others, it cannot normally be efficiently marketed, even in the best of conditions. If the role of competition as a generator of new products and efficient resource allocation is not understood, such a country could forego both the efficiency advantages of markets and the steering power of command planning. It is not inconceivable that Hungary has been having problems of this nature.[33]

One efficiency advantage claimed for markets over commands is that the former tend, under "workably" competitive conditions, to be self-enforcing in the following sense. Suppose that the incomes of an enterprise's top management are highly correlated with the firm's success in cutting costs for any given assortment (and quality) of output. This may be because salaries are geared to the enterprise's long-run profitability or to its sales or growth, subject to a firm constraint that the enterprise cover its social opportunity cost. Then, it is argued, the market itself will discipline management by encouraging it to bring about efficient organization and to otherwise enforce cost controls within the enterprise.[34]

This conclusion is subject to a number of qualifications. If management finds it either impossible or too easy to increase profits, sales, or whatever its success criteria may be, it is likely to choose some nonpecuniary benefits, in the form of padded expense accounts, pretty secretaries, excessive leisure, etc., in preference to maximizing its income. The role of competition or of effective competition substitutes is, therefore, to make large profits achievable, but not too easy to come by. Several of the desirable aspects of the self-enforcement property of markets also presuppose that the revenues of a firm must cover its social costs. Even in the absence of environmental disruption, this is often not the case in socialist countries because of the proliferation of subsidies and also because of the short time-horizon to which the bonuses of most managers are tied, at least in Eastern Europe.

There (to paraphrase Joseph Bower), most directors are likely to find that the consequences of their decisions cover a longer time span than the measures of their performances. Thus, they have an incentive to ignore and even to resist many kinds of innovations, which may disrupt current production, as well as any investments which do not pay off rapidly. They have also been known to slight maintenance, replacement, and repair expenditures. Under workers' management, the latter effect may be less strong, but there is still a shortened time-horizon resulting from the earlier-noted fact that workers have no claim on the enterprise's profits after they leave the firm.[35]

Furthermore, even if the socialist market does discipline enterprise management, the benefits from this do not necessarily go beyond improvements in the internal operating efficiency (or "X-efficiency") of the firm. Irrational pricing, subsidies, or managerial success criteria may still cause a misallocation of resources between enterprises, given the central planners' social welfare function. On the other hand, there is no reason why a sufficient emphasis on such managerial success criteria as profits or cost control, combined with acceptability of goods produced to users, could not lead to substantial improvements in X-efficiency under command planning. (Sufficient managerial autonomy to implement many cost controls would not force the planners to relinquish control of the "main levers" of economic performance.) Indeed, the design of such a system appears to have been the central concern of the reforms proposed for the Soviet economy by Liberman in 1962.[36]

Next, let us examine the reverse hypothesis—namely, that when top management's incomes do not correlate with its success in keeping down costs, the firm will operate with a high degree of X-inefficiency. We have indicated that the conditions of this hypothesis apply to Hungary, and what (admittedly scanty) evidence we have suggests that X-inefficiency is a serious problem there. (The inexperience of managers in dealing with a market economy is, however, an additional reason for this.)[37] In the case of Yugoslavia, this reverse hypothesis rests on the collective right of all of the employees to the enterprise's profit residual. Such a claim automatically dilutes that of top management, which we take to comprise the professional director of the firm and his staff plus the management board of the workers' council.

Nevertheless, at least three factors operate in the other direction, with the consequence that proponents of workers' management usually claim that it is the *most* X-efficient managerial form.[38] We may think of X-inefficiency as some combination of bad organization of the firm, bad feedback to management, and employee shirking. With regard to the second of these, successful workers' management should be the best form of labor relations, since it minimizes conflicts between workers and management. Thereby, it should reduce time lost due to strikes, featherbedding, and slowdowns, and encourage workers on the job to help management find ways of raising productivity, since employees would normally benefit directly from the latter.

Regarding the first and third components of X-inefficiency, the main potential disadvantage of workers' management would appear to lie in a greater incentive for both management and non-managerial employees to shirk. Yet, it is in the collective interest of all of the employees to prevent managers from shirking which, in turn, involves greater control by management over employee shirking.[39] If the management board of the workers' council is behaving in the collective interests of all of its electors, it will have a strong incentive to exercise this supervision over managerial behavior.

Moreover, suppose that an employee of a worker-managed firm decides to shirk and is observed by other employees. The shirker's motivation is likely to stem largely from the fact that, except in small firms, he cannot as an individual raise or reduce profits per employee and thus the profit share of his wage by very much. Likewise, the pecuniary gains to the observers from preventing this particular act of shirking will be low. However, let us assume that the co-op in question alleviates work alienation, gives its employees a sense of pride, creativity, and fulfillment in their work, and makes them feel like their own bosses—in short, all that is claimed for workers' management by its proponents. Then the cost to the observers of preventing the shirking will also be low and, indeed, shirkers will be ostracized. Such a co-op would be internally self-enforcing to a large degree.

When we turn to enforcement of command planning, we encounter a completely different conventional model which, for the most part, stems from Western observations of Soviet and East European experience. It begins by posing a need for enforcement based on a natural, virtually inevitable conflict of interest between upper and lower levels in any chain of command. Because the goals of the two levels are bound to diverge, according to the argument, a command economy is not self-enforcing, and this requires the upper echelons to build specific means of enforcement into the system. Beyond direct supervision and control over subordinates, there are at least three such means: supervision of financial flows by the state banking system; enforcement of specific targets and of the spirit of the plan by local Communist Party and trade union representatives; and bonuses that tie managerial salaries to meeting specific current production targets.[40]

The conventional view has been that the last means of enforcement tends to dominate the others, both because of the strong output orientation of East European central planners and because the relevant party representatives are judged to a large extent by the abilities of the firms to which they are assigned to meet their most important production targets. The purpose of bonus payments is to compensate managers for doing what the state wants them to do instead of what they want to do. In practice, bonus payments have achieved their objectives in part, but they have also shifted the hierarchical conflict of interest to another dimension. Managers have tended to concentrate on production for its own sake and also to prefer output targets that are easy to meet (and, in the process, to conceal some production capacity). Together, these factors have led to the "problem of success indicators."

Because it is impossible for the planners to break down input and output targets in complete detail, they must rely upon common denominators. In effect, these tie managerial bonuses to such current targets as the weight, length, volume, surface area, or gross or net value of a firm's output. The trouble is that neither a good's physical characteristics nor its price in a command economy is likely to represent its value to the planners. The result, enshrined in stories about furniture that is too heavy to get up the stairs, pipeline that is too short, and equipment for which spare parts are unavailable, is production to meet (composite) plan targets in the easiest and quickest way, rather than to serve the needs of users.

In this sense, the success-indicator method leads managers to use their powers of substitution to violate the spirit of the plan, thereby causing waste and resource misallocation. Because firms, as users of inputs, must accustom themselves to a defective supply network, they tend to integrate backwards, and the same is true of intermediate planning authorities, who are judged in the same way. The result is too little specialization at the enterprise level and too much autarchy within sub-hierarchies (e.g., ministries) in the overall planning chain of command. Finally, firms and intermediate planners will tend to hoard inventories of the scarcest (and, therefore, in many instances, of the most valuable) inputs. This artificially increases scarcities, reduces the productivity of capital, and thereby works against the intentions of the central planners.

Not all socialist economies have relied upon the conventional success-indicator method, however. China, Romania, and perhaps, East Germany are cases in point. At least in the former two countries, the judgment of a manager's performance based on specific plan targets has been almost completely subordinated to efforts to judge his total contribution (including ideological factors), viewed as an entity. In Romania, judgment is by superior authorities, at least up through the ministerial level, a reflection of the highly centralized nature of that country's producing sector.[41] In China, judgment is also made by workers, by local Communist Party representatives, and even by users of the firm's products. Ideology and loyalty to the regime have played a major, although variable, role in this assessment.[42]

Managerial bonuses appear to have played a small to non-existent role as motivators in both Romania and China.[43] Instead, these countries have relied upon career advancement, based on the subjective evaluations just noted, plus the achievement drive, and, in China, the various incentives discussed earlier, including altruism. The Chinese have probably made the greatest effort to blunt the "natural" hierarchical conflict of interest by utilizing the charisma of their leaders (largely Mao Tse-tung) and by promoting loyalty from below, along with a sharing of common ideology and broad goals.

To an extent, the Chinese leadership has sought to recreate in Chinese society, again viewed as a giant "family," conditions similar to those which make for mutual self-enforcement in the "ideal" worker-managed firm. These conditions include a sense of mutual need and understanding, a feeling of comradeship or brotherhood and common heritage, and also ostracism for shirkers plus eulogy for, and emulation of, achievers. In order to maintain this mentality over very long periods of time, the state may have to tailor its social priorities more closely to some sort of synthesized "will" of the people than it otherwise would. Consequently, this entire approach may also turn out to be at least a partial substitute for the Western concept of democracy.

In the limit, a chain of command could conceivably be completely self-enforcing, for the above reasons, provided lower-level decision-makers have enough information to behave rationally, and moral incentives could play a major role in such a limiting case. This would probably not be a highly centralized command economy. Indeed, plan targets could be quite aggregated, since it could be taken for granted that managers would not use their resulting autonomy to violate the spirit of the plan. Promotion of horizontal, market, or quasi-market links between producers and users would be a feature of such a system, as it is in China, and there should be an information cost-saving in comparison with the Soviet model.[44]

This is not meant to imply that China yet approximates the

limiting case. Conflicts of interest between different echelons in the planning hierarchy have not been fully resolved and have occasionally been severe. The form taken by this conflict, however, has sometimes been much the reverse of the Soviet case described above. For example, as the Chinese First Five-Year Plan progressed, and especially from late 1955 on, Communist Party cadres were progressively supplanting professional managers within most enterprises and also on collective farms. (The collectivization drive, for the most part, was carried out in 1955 and 1956.) These cadres were anxious to please their party superiors, partly because they wanted to advance within the party's ranks, and were also extremely unsophisticated and inexperienced in their management roles.

Consequently, when they got the opportunity, these cadres tended to maximize output, largely ignoring costs and prices. Professional managers—that is, the experts who remained with their firms, albeit with reduced authority—tended to adopt a similar goal as a defensive posture, and the same influence penetrated the banks, which relaxed credit controls. Restraints were imposed on the cadres' zeal during this era, however, by intermediate-level planning authorities. Thus, the alleged conflict of interest between Soviet managers and their superiors, in which the former seek easy and the latter ambitious output targets, was reversed to an extent, although the enterprise cadres received their share of sympathy from within the ranks of the planning authorities.

After the administrative decentralization of 1957-58, the restraints from above were largely removed, and there was a definite shift in the attitude of the top party leadership toward "guerrilla" campaigns of output maximization. The result was that firms and collective farms engaged in an orgy of target-raising, often losing all touch with reality. Later, their production claims were tinged with the same optimism. The consequence was a virtual breakdown of planning which helped to cause the chaos of the Great Leap Forward aftermath. Decentralization did not become compatible with economic efficiency until the influence of professional managers increased, financial goals replaced output targets, and much tighter financial controls were imposed during 1961-62.

## NOTES

1. This example is suggested by Professor Clayton. See Elizabeth Clayton, "Property Rights Under Socialism" (University of Missouri, Columbia, Mo., 1971).

To illustrate the ambiguity with which the terms "capitalism" and "socialism" are used, some economists would claim that Sweden is a "socialist" country, even though more than 90 percent of the material means of production are privately owned there. Others would claim that China or the USSR, Cuba, Yugoslavia, etc., has the only "true" brand of socialism, and some would maintain that the USSR, for example, is a form of "state capitalism."

The difference between socialism and state capitalism, to those who use the latter term, often revolves around some notion of exploitation or alienation in the Marxian sense and also around rights to a given job or type of work. For example, a "truly" socialist state is constrained in forcing workers to switch jobs involuntarily, even when a higher level of efficiency would result.

2. The discussion below expands and elaborates on a classification scheme used by Demsetz. See Harold Demsetz, "Toward a Theory of Property Rights," *American Economic Review* (May 1967). See, as well, R. Carson, *Comparative Economic Systems* (New York: Macmillan, 1973), chapters 1 and 5; and Aleksander Bajt, "Property in Capital and in the Means of Production in Socialist Economies," *Journal of Law and Economics* (April 1968).

3. Let us say that *transactions costs* are the costs of carrying through an exchange to the mutual satisfaction of all the parties involved. These comprise the costs of arriving at and enforcing such an agreement. Market failures, or departures from efficiency in a market context, result from transactions costs that are high enough to prevent certain exchanges from being carried out, and the principle of nonexclusion usually enters as an element making such costs higher than they would otherwise be. For example, see R. Carson, *Comparative Economic Systems*, Section 2-3 and chapter 15.

4. Regarding moral incentives in Cuba and China, respectively, see Carmelo Mesa-Lago, "Ideological, Political and Economic Factors in the Cuban Controversy on Material vs. Moral Incentives," *Journal of Interamerican Studies and World Affairs* (February 1972); and Barry Richman, "Ideology and Management: The Chinese Oscillate," *Columbia Journal of World Business* (January-February 1971).

At least one socialist economist has argued that the essence of socialism from an economic standpoint is the right of the state to the income (or surplus value) generated by capital. See Bajt, "Property in Capital." This is consistent with Marx, but because it does not automatically imply anything about rights of transferability or use, the governments of most socialist economies would not agree.

5. P. J. D. Wiles, "Growth vs. Choice," *Economic Journal* (June 1956):245.

6. Most Yugoslav firms with more than five employees are nominally managed by the elected representatives of all the employees (who comprise a workers' council), together with a professional director and his staff. References to "management" in the Yugoslav context will comprise both of these elements, unless otherwise stated.

7. The Yugoslav government also encourages the establishment of new enterprises through external risk-sharing arrangements. Stephen Sacks notes that "Included as participants in the risk-bearing associated with entrepreneurship in Yugoslavia are the new enterprise, its founder, the bank, and three levels of government." (An added consequence of this is some encouragement to found inefficient firms.)

However, to the extent that workers' management is genuine, it will tend to discourage expansion and risk-bearing in comparison with the textbook model of a profit-maximization firm, for reasons outlined below in the text. On balance, at least one author concludes that "Yugoslavia. . . suffers from recklessness" rather than overcautiousness insofar as entrepreneurship is concerned. See Stephen R. Sacks, *Entry of New Competitors in Yugoslav Market Socialism*, University of California, Institute of International Studies, Research Series No. 19 (Berkeley, Calif.: University of California–Berkeley, 1973), p. 134.

Rather than expand on this and other complex issues in workers' management, theory, and practice, we shall cite the following additional works: Benjamin Ward, "The Firm in Illyria: Market Syndicalism," *American Economic Review* (September 1958); Jaroslov Vanek, "Decentralization Under Workers' Management: A Theoretical Appraisal," *American Economic Review* (December 1969); Eirik Furobotn and Svetozar Pejovich, "Property Rights, Economic Decentralization, and the Evolution of the Yugoslav Firm, 1965-1972: From Labor-Management to the Social Contract," *Journal of Law and Economics* (forthcoming); Werner Sichel, "The Threat to Market Socialism: The Case of Yugoslavia," *Antitrust Bulletin* (Summer 1971); Joel Dirlam, "Problems of Market Power and Public Policy in Yugoslavia," in *Comparative Economic Systems: Models and Cases*, ed. Morris Bornstein (Homewood, Ill.: Irwin, 1969).

8. In principle, enterprises can pool their investment funds and establish a kind of consortium which founds a new enterprise. Each of the founding firms would hold shares in the new one. However, this device has been little used so far. The information about more conventional foundings comes from Professor David Granick in a personal communication to the author.

9. See David Granick, "The Hungarian Economic Reform," *World Politics* (April 1973). Other sources on these reforms are Richard Portes, "Economic Reforms in Hungary," *American Economic Review* (May 1970), and Bela Balassa, "The Economic Reform in Hungary," *Economica* (February 1970).

10. Granick, "Hungarian Economic Reform." Although many prices are nominally free to vary in response to supply and demand forces, permission to raise them must be obtained from the national price board whenever the average price of a firm's entire product line would go up in consequence. The primary justification would be cost increases. Price hikes must also be justified to local Communist Party officials. Price decreases need not be negotiated in this way unless there is a formal floor on the price in question.

In theory, prices fall into three categories—those free to fluctuate in response to supply and demand, those which are fixed, and those allowed to fluctuate subject to upper and/or lower bounds. In practice, one suspects that these categories are not so sharply delineated, with the accent falling on price rigidity.

11. Granick, "Hungarian Economic Reform." We would also refer the reader to the second paragraph of note one. The rights of one individual to a job at which the value of his marginal social product is less than his wage will often directly or indirectly deny other individuals access to the same or to different jobs which they would like to take at wages equal to their marginal social productivities. Thus, the welfare advantages of extreme job security are partly illusory. Indeed, this is a form of featherbedding.

12. Constant average wage control encourages the hiring of unskilled and semiskilled (i.e., low-wage) labor, and in this way can be a deterrent to unemployment. It can likewise exacerbate labor shortages and labor turnover, however, while keeping productivity low, in the face of a strong aggregate demand. (In effect, it encourages disguised unemployment, regardless of whether there would be an excess supply of labor without it.)

Labor shortages in some sectors of the Hungarian economy, coupled with a high rate of labor turnover and continued low productivity, caused a change in the practice of constant average wage control as of January 1, 1970. From then on, the wages of recently hired workers were deducted from the enterprise's profit-sharing fund in an effort to reduce turnover. Apparently, this did not work well enough because direct restrictions on voluntary labor mobility were introduced over the course of 1970. These came on top of the job security measures described above.

13. Granick, "Hungarian Economic Reform." For statistical comparisons of performance between the periods before (1964-67) and after (1968-71) the reform, utilizing Hungarian sources, see Barnabas Büky, "Hungary's NEM on a Treadmill," *Problems of Communism* (September-October 1972).

14. The present intention of Soviet leaders, however, is to shift most freedoms that were to have been delegated to enterprise managements, according to the reforms begun in 1965 (including some actually granted), one step up the chain of command to the production or industrial associations, about which we shall have a bit more to say below.

15. Marketization is the most complete form that decentralization can take, *vis-à-vis* what has come to be known as a Soviet-type command economy, but it is not the only form. In China, for example, since 1957-58 all firms but those of utmost importance have been under the control of provincial and lower-level government authorities. The central planners and the ministries concentrate on directing key enterprises; on setting aggregate targets relating to such matters as (a) the outputs of the most important industrial and agricultural goods, (b) investment, (c) manpower and wages, and (d) imports and exports; on research and development; and on coordinating and supervising interprovincial transfers of goods and services. (The last is partly to countervail "built-in" autarchic tendencies of the provincial authorities.)

In addition, except where the most important commodities are concerned, and subject to a relatively few major priorities of the central planners, planning tends to be "bottom up" rather than "top down." That is, national plans are aggregated from provincial plans which, in turn, are aggregated from the plans of lower-level units, and so on down to the level of production. This is in contrast to the customary East European approach, where centrally set aggregate targets are progressively disaggregated down to the enterprise level. (In practice, the latter procedure is accompanied by provisions for enterprise feedback in the form of responses to proposed or expected plan targets, requests for additional supplies, etc., so that the difference between the two methods, while important, is one of degree.)

We would add that since the Cultural Revolution, the supervisory and coordinating roles of the ministries appear to have declined, accentuating regional autarchic tendencies. See Audrey M. Donnithorne, "China's Cellular Economy: Some Economic Trends Since the Cultural Revolution," *China Quarterly* (October-December 1972).

Basic references for Cuba, China, and Romania are: Carmelo Mesa-Lago, ed., *Revolutionary Change in Cuba* (Pittsburgh: University of Pittsburgh Press, 1971), especially parts II and III; Audrey Donnithorne, *China's Economic System* (London: George Allen and Unwin, 1966); John M. Montias, *Economic Development in Communist Rumania* (Cambridge, Mass.: M.I.T. Press, 1967). See also, David Granick, "The Orthodox Model of the Soviet-type Firm Versus Romanian Experience," Indiana University Development Research Center Working Paper No. 18 (September 1972).

16. We may wish to think of the physical targets in Hungary as being more indicative—that is, more in the nature of forecasts—than the physical targets in the Soviet Union, although the difference is one of degree. To properly distinguish between commands and indicators, however, we would have to develop a model of the economy as an information system, which space does not permit. For such a

discussion see R. Carson, *Comparative Economic Systems*; Leonid Hurwicz, "Centralization and Decentralization in Economic Processes," in *Comparison of Economic Systems*, ed. Alexander Eckstein (Berkeley, Calif.: University of California Press, 1971); and references cited by Hurwicz.

We would also note that, owing to the existence of the sellers' market in Hungary, there is often unofficial physical rationing through queuing or some sort of priority designation.

17. The notion of a chain of command, however, is quite different to develop rigorously. For an example, see Hurwicz, "Centralization and Decentralization."

18. We would specifically not apply this statement to all of the various Arab and African countries which describe themselves as socialist or to Israel.

There are no industrial ministries in Yugoslavia. Consequently, the "state" there consists of federal, republican, and communal government bodies, along with the various organs of the Communist Party and the National Bank of Yugoslavia. The rights of enterprise managements (that is, professional directors *cum* workers' councils) have significantly expanded in the past decade *vis-à-vis* the government and the Communist Party. Hence, the current emphasis on strengthening party influence. At present, the government's powers to tax enterprises and to indirectly motivate them to conform to national economic priorities through fiscal and monetary policy tools are less than in most capitalist countries. Dennison Rusinow has coined the term "laissez faire socialism" to describe this inability to plan effectively, even through the market. See Dennison I. Rusinow, "Laissez-Faire Socialism in Yugoslavia," American Universities Field Staff, South-East Europe Series, Vol. 14, No. 2.

19. Svetozar Pejovich, "Toward an Economic Theory of the Creation and Specification of Property Rights," *Review of Social Economy* (September 1972), and the references cited there. For a survey of the Marx-Engels economic theory of history, see M. M. Bober, *Karl Marx's Interpretation of History* (Cambridge, Mass.: Harvard University Press, 1962).

20. That is, society's political decisions collectively formulate its social welfare or social preference function, while its economic decisions choose the best achievable points in welfare and production space, given the goals and trade-offs which this function embodies. See Abram Bergson, "A Reformulation of Certain Aspects of Welfare Economics," *Quarterly Journal of Economics* (February 1938); and Paul Samuelson, *The Foundations of Economic Analysis* (Cambridge, Mass.: Harvard University Press, 1961), chapter 8.

For a discussion of democracy and political decision-making, see Anthony Downs, *An Economic Theory of Democracy* (New York: Harper and Row, 1957).

21. For example, most market power is embodied in artificial (or man-made) industrial and occupational entry barriers, such as the license needed to grow tobacco in Ontario, the medallion required to drive a taxi in New York City, and in the various market-sharing agreements whose proliferation is said to pose a long-run threat to the survival of market socialism in Yugoslavia. Generally speaking, these are legal barriers or understandings which fill gaps in the law or even (as appears to be the case in Yugoslavia) openly defy it. See the references in note 7.

22. Rusinow, "Laissez-Faire Socialism," p. 3.

23. See, for example, Reszo Nyers, *Twenty Questions and Answers* (Budapest: Paunonia Press, 1970). Also Istvan Friss, *Reform of the Economic Mechanism in Hungary* (Budapest: Akademiai Kiado, 1969).

The Hungarian reform coincides with a political decision to place more emphasis on satisfying consumer wants at the expense of investment. However, the latter also appears to be explicable entirely on efficiency grounds—arising from a need to pacify the consumer and to make him as productive a worker as possible, subject to the constraints outlined earlier.

24. In fact, both North Korea and the German Democratic Republic have Communist Party memberships in excess of 11 percent of their respective populations, while Cuba is under 1 percent. During the Czech reform, the corresponding percentage reached over 12 percent, and even at this level, party control was far less absolute than it is now in either East Germany or North Korea. Moreover, goal formation within the ranks of the party under Dubcek was less centralized—in the sense that lower-level cadres had more influence—than is currently true in either Korea or Germany. (Indeed, the latter two parties appear to be more autocratic than in most socialist countries.)

It is generally the case that the upper ranks of Communist parties have far more power in goal formation than the lower echelons. In addition, both party membership and advancement within its ranks are by cooptation. Democracy would suggest that individual party members should be evaluated by nonmembers as well as by their "peers" within the organization. That is, party cadres should be judged by their contributions to serving the needs of those affected by party policies. The latter, of course, comprise the entire population.

25. Branko Horvat, "The Labor-Managed Enterprise" (Paper presented to the Workshop on Economic Organization and Development, Ottawa, Carleton University, March, 1972), p. 7.

26. We would add that the period following the overthrow of the old order may be a time when promises of future benefits have their greatest incentive effects. J. M. Montias has developed a classification of socialist economic systems in which mobilization plays a role. See his "Types of Communist Economic Systems," in *Change in Communist Systems*, ed. Chalmers Johnson (Stanford, Calif.: Stanford University Press, 1970).

27. Each of these periods stressing moral motivators has eventually given way to a return to material incentives as the development priority became more urgent with neglect. Since 1956, however, when income differentials reached their highest level, there has been an irregular long-run de-emphasis of material incentives in the sense that, with each return, the differentials have been less than formerly.

On balance, of all socialist nations, Cuba and China appear to have relied most heavily on moral incentives, and these nations also appear to have the lowest growth rates of per-capita income and output, although any estimate of the latter invariably involves considerable guesswork. While reliance on moral incentives is by no means the only cause of low growth, the leaders of these nations have been more willing to sacrifice growth for greater equality than have most of the East European countries. Regarding growth in Cuba and China, see Carmelo Mesa-Lago, "Economic Policies and Growth," in *Revolutionary Change in Cuba*; and Arthur Ashbrook, Jr., "China: Economic Policy and Economic Results, 1949-1971," in *People's Republic of China: An Economic Assessment*, U.S. Congress, Joint Economic Committee (Washington, D.C.: U.S. Government Printing Office, 1972).

28. The most concise description of a "true" communist by this standard may be found in Mao Tse-tung's essay, "In Memory of Norman Bethune," *Selected Works of Mao Tse-tung*, vol. 3 (London: Lawrence and Wishart, 1954).

29. The basic reference for this paragraph and the one to follow is Mancur Olson, Jr., *The Logic of Collective Action* (New York: Schocken, 1971).

30. As evidence of the inadequacy of purely moral incentives, a recent broadcast from Kwangsi Province noted that "Farm tasks such as manure collection and odd jobs that peasants were formerly expected to do mainly out of concern for the communal good and with little or no award of work points should now receive adequate work points," on which collective farmers' pay is based. See Tillman Durdin, "China Links Pay to Productivity," *New York Times*, 7 May 1972, p. 17.

31. In effect, the organization of production within an economy may be viewed either from the standpoint of the distribution of property rights or from that of its network of information flows. The two views are opposite sides of the same coin in the sense that the rights of an individual or organization to use property, to exclude others from using it, or to capture its income will determine the types of signals they send to other individuals and organizations (insofar as the latter are genuinely relevant to production and consumption decision-making). See the references in note 16.

32. One hypothesized efficiency advantage of the market mechanism is a superior ability to break up the overall economic problem facing society as a whole into many smaller sub-problems. One aspect of this is the self-enforcing property discussed below. (However, for an exception see further discussion below.)

For an exploration of the trade-offs between markets and commands, see John C. McManus, "The Organization of Production," Carleton University, Department of Economics, Working Paper No. 71-05 (Ottawa: Carleton University, June, 1971), and Hajime Oniki, "Communications Costs of Operating Economic Organizations," (unpublished paper, Boston: Harvard University, 1971). There is also a great deal of "casual" empirical evidence to suggest the trade-off given in the text.

33. See the earlier references to Hungary in note 9.

34. The idea that management's claim to the firm's profit residual after all explicit costs have been met motivates it to control costs and to innovate under appropriate market conditions has a long tradition in the Western economic literature. Perhaps the best logical development of the idea is to be found in A. A. Alchian and Harold Demsetz, "Production, Information Costs, and Economic Organization," *American Economic Review* (December 1972).

Marx, of course, disagreed emphatically with this view. In his opinion, a manager could be induced to perform his duties efficiently for modest "wages of superintendence" that did not have to be correlated with the firm's profit residual.

In the words of a modern Marxian economist advising nationalization, "What one fool can do, another fool can do." (This statement comes from the convocation address delivered by Joan Robinson at Carleton University, Ottawa, Canada, June 1, 1973.)

35. On this point, see E. G. Furubotn and Svetozar Pejovich, "Property Rights and the Behavior of the Firm in a Socialist State," *Zeitschrift Für Nationalökonomie*, nos. 3-4 (1970):431-454. See, as well, Joseph L. Bower, "Planning Within the Firm" (paper delivered to the I.R.R.A. Conference in New York, December 1969), esp. pp. 9-10.

36. Most of Liberman's proposals have not been adopted and apparently will not be, at least at the enterprise level (see note 14). See chapters 18-21 of Morris Bornstein and Daniel R. Fusfeld, eds., *The Soviet Economy* (Homewood, Ill.: Irwin, 1970). (The first of these is the 1962 Pravda article by Liberman.)

Regarding X-inefficiency, see Harvey Leibenstein, "Allocative Efficiency vs. 'X-efficiency,'" *American Economic Review* (June 1966).

37. See the references to Hungary in notes 9 and 13.

38. See, for example, Jaroslav Vanek, "Decentralization Under Workers' Management: A Theoretical Appraisal," *American Economic Review* (December 1969), and the references cited there. There is also a vast sociological literature on this subject. See, for example, F. J. Roethlisberger and W. J. Dickson, *Management and the Worker* (Cambridge, Mass.: Harvard University Press, 1939); Paul Blumberg, *Industrial Democracy: The Sociology of Participation* (London: Constable, 1968); and P. McGregor, *The Human Side of Enterprise* (New York: McGraw-Hill, 1960).

39. This apparent paradox is explained by the fact that it is in the collective interest of all employees to prevent shirking—or, at any rate, much of it—as a means of raising the enterprise's profits, whereas it may still be in the interest of an individual worker to shirk.

40. Users may also complain about poor quality, wrong assortment, late arrival, etc., of goods. When such complaints reach the supplier firm, however, they usually do so through the chain of command. Thus, we include them in the supervisory powers of the planning authorities. More often than not, the pressure of command planning has tended to favor the supplier over the user firm in such instances. In addition, suppliers within the state sector rarely compete for customers.

41. According to Granick, ministries are, in some ways, analogous to firms or industrial associations elsewhere in Eastern Europe. See David Granick, "The Orthodox Model of the Soviet-type Firm Versus Romanian Experience," Indiana University, Working Paper No. 18, International Development Research Center (Bloomington, Ind.: Indiana University, 1972).

42. See Barry Richman's articles, "Ideology and Management: The Chinese Oscillate"; "Capitalists and Managers in Communist China," *Harvard Business Review* (January-February 1967); and "A Firsthand Study of Marketing in Communist China," *Journal of Retailing* (Summer 1970).

43. Workers and technical personnel, however, have been eligible for bonuses in China and also able to exert some pressure should these not be paid because of poor management.

44. In this way, Chinese leaders relied to some extent on the self-enforcing property of markets described earlier, and, indeed, the conditions under which markets and hierarchies will tend to be self-enforcing are not mutually exclusive.

# 13

# Industrial Organization*

Frederic L. Pryor

Most comprehensive studies of socialist economies cover the principal features of the organization of industry in one major socialist country. However, there has been little attention paid to the similarities and differences of the industrial organization in different socialist economies; nor have the similarities and differences with capitalist nations been systematically discussed in detail, except with regard to planning and material allocations. The purpose of this study is to provide such a comparative perspective and to investigate in a quantitative fashion a number of features of the industrial organization in a sample of nations with different economic systems.

I first focus on the nature of the units in which production is actually carried out, namely the establishments and enterprises. Then I turn to an examination of the administrative units between the top decision-making organs (state planning bureaus and ministries) and the productive units. Finally, I briefly outline the impact of the economic reforms of the sixties on the overall organization of industry.

In order to avoid duplication with the analyses of other studies in this volume, I confine my attention primarily to the formal aspects of industrial organization. Although the quantitative data come primarily from Eastern Europe, several particular features of industrial organization in China and Cuba are also briefly discussed.

*The Nature of the Productive Units*

In all economically developed or semi-developed nations—regardless of economic system—the primary industrial production units are establishments and enterprises. (The putting-out system or backyard blast furnaces do not seem suited for twentieth-century industrial technology.) An "establishment" is an industrial unit at a single physical location; it can consist of several "plants," "workshops," or "fac-

*This essay was written while I was a Visiting Fellow at the Institute of International Studies, University of California, at Berkeley.

tories," as long as these are located together and under a single management. An "enterprise" (or "firm") is a business organization consisting of one or more establishments under common ownership and control. It is a consolidated decision-making unit because wholly owned subsidiaries are included as part of the parent enterprise, even though for tax and other purposes such units may report on an unconsolidated basis. The nature of industrial establishments and enterprises is separately and briefly discussed below.

*Establishments.*[1] Two kinds of issues concern us about industrial establishments. First, what features of industrial establishments in East and West are affected by technological-economic forces that operate in a similar manner in both economic systems? Second, what features of industrial establishments are different in the two systems?

Similar aspects of industrial establishments in various nations often arise directly from certain features of the production process. For instance, in both East and West the ranking of industrial branches according to capital intensity of production (the ratio of capital to labor) is similar; this means that in any given nation industrial establishments in particular industries (e.g., petroleum production, paper products, primary metals, chemicals, and mining) are more capital-intensive than establishments in other industries (e.g., lumber products, leather products, furniture, and clothing). Another example of such similarities arising from the production process concerns the relative sizes of enterprises. In all nations in both East and West the ranking of industrial branches according to average establishment size (measured by employment; all establishments with less than twenty workers and employees are excluded) is similar. Thus, in any given country, establishments in certain industries (e.g., primary metals, tobacco products, rubber products, and transport equipment) are larger than establishments in other industries (e.g., clothing, leather products, lumber products, and furniture and fixtures.)[2]

Other similar aspects of industrial establishments seem to arise from general economic-technological forces that act in the same manner in the economically developed or semi-developed countries. For instance, in both East and West the ranking of industrial branches according to the ratio of white- to blue-collar workers is similar. Thus in the various nations, establishments in the same industries have a relatively high or low percentage of white-collar workers. A more surprising similarity is that the spatial distribution of establishments between the more and less developed regions of a given nation does not depend on the economic system. Although the spatial distribution of manufacturing varies considerably among nations, due to different historic and geographical patterns of growth, the economic system (defined in terms of capitalism and socialism, or in terms of market and planned economies) does not seem a significant causal variable either at a single point in time or in the change of spatial distribution of manufacturing over time. Another East-West similarity is that the pattern of relative wages among industries seems roughly similar; thus high-wage establishments are found in the same industries in all nations.

One very important difference in industrial establishments in economically developed or semi-developed nations is their average size (defined in terms of employment). Generally speaking the larger the domestic market, the larger the average size industrial establishment, a generalization strongly confirmed with data from West European nations. In East Europe scattered data suggest that industrial establishments in the Soviet Union are, on the average, larger than in the East European countries. If we wish to examine these matters in detail, adequate data for detailed comparisons are unfortunately not available for most socialist nations. Therefore, we must base our conclusions on data from only three nations (Hungary, Poland, and Yugoslavia) and use as a base of comparison a large sample of Western nations. The following generalizations are obtained:

1. The average employment size of establishments (excluding those with less than 20 workers and employees) in the three East European nations is roughly 2.5 to 4 times larger than in the West, holding market size and other factors influencing establishment size constant.

2. The size distribution of establishments in various industries is quite different, the range of variation being much less in the East than in the West. The lack of very many industrial establishments with less than 100 workers and employees in the East is one important reason for their greater average size industrial establishment.

3. The greatest differences in average employment size of establishments in East and West occur in those industries in which the range of variation in average establishment size is greatest in the West. That is, decision-makers in the East appear to have chosen the largest establishment sizes within the technological-economic constraints operating in the particular industry. This is a second important reason why average employment size of establishment is greater in the East than in the West, other factors remaining the same.

Although the last three generalizations are based only on three East European nations, scattered data and qualitative remarks in the economic literature of other East European nations suggest that these conclusions would hold if data from all other socialist nations were included in the comparisons.

*Enterprises.* Enterprises are the key decision-making units of production in both East and West and, fortunately, considerable comparable data are available, at least until the mid-sixties. After this time different types of enterprise consolidations were carried out in many of the socialist nations and it is difficult to know exactly what industrial units the published data on "enterprises" actually refer to.

Again there are many similarities among enterprises that arise from the production process.[3] For instance, the ranking of industries according to average employment size of enterprise is quite similar in both East and West. And as we might suspect from the establishment data, the range of enterprise size is very much greater in the West than in the East. In particular, there are considerably fewer enterprises with less than 100 workers and employees in the East.

The major differences in enterprises between East and West, as well as among the various socialist nations, lie in the realm of average enterprise size. In the size comparisons below I exclude all enterprises with less than 20 workers and employees. Size is measured by total employment using three different measurements: an arithmetic average, a Niehans index (which is a weighted average with the greatest weights placed on the largest enterprises),[4] and the percentage of the labor force in enterprises employing over 1000 workers and employees (all enterprises are included in this statistic).

Two types of comparisons of enterprise size are useful to make. The first is a comparison of enterprise size in East and West, holding constant factors such as market size which influence enterprise size. Such calculations (which are labeled "predicted" size) are based on a formula that was estimated from a regression analysis of a sample of Western capitalist nations and are presented in Table 1. The second is a comparison of changes in enterprise size over time, for which data are presented in Table 2. Both sets of data cover only East Europe.

Four major conclusions can be drawn from the data in the tables.

First, it is clear that in all countries except the Soviet Union, the actual employment size of enterprises is very much larger than predicted using the formula derived from the West.[7] Indeed, two relatively small nations—Hungary and Czechoslovakia—show the largest average enterprise sizes in all Europe. This greater employment size in the East seems due to the fact that the constituent establishment sizes are greater and that in some (but not all) socialist nations, the relative importance of multi-establishment enterprises is greater than in the West.

Second, there is no discernible pattern of enterprise size among the socialist nations and the economic influence most important in determining average employment size in the West—namely, the relative size of the domestic market—seems to be overshadowed by other factors. The decisive factor in the lack of pattern among socialist nations appears to be that there is no consistent quantitative rule that is followed in all of the various socialist nations about the number of establishments that are combined in one enterprise. In some countries such as East Germany, the Soviet Union, and Yugoslavia, the importance of multi-establishment enterprises appears relatively low; in other countries such as Czechoslovakia and Hungary, multi-establishment

## Table 1

*Average Employment Sizes of Enterprises in Manufacturing and Mining in East Europe with Predictions Made From a Regression Formula Calculated From Data of Capitalist Nations*[5]

| Country | Date | Arithmetic Average | | Niehans Index | | Percentage of Labor Force in Enterprises Over 1000 | |
|---|---|---|---|---|---|---|---|
| | | Actual | Predicted | Actual | Predicted | Actual | Predicted |
| Soviet Union | 1964 | | | | | | |
| State Enterprises | | 610 | – | 5909 | – | 59.6% | – |
| All Enterprises | | – | 178 | – | 10546 | – | 40.8% |
| Bulgaria | 1965 | | | | | | |
| State Enterprises | | 533 | – | 1779 | – | 47.0 | – |
| All Enterprises | | 420 | 104 | 1566 | 781 | 41.6 | 16.7 |
| Czechoslovakia | 1966 | | | | | | |
| State Enterprises | | 2590 | – | 5967 | – | 89.1 | – |
| All Enterprises | | 1981 | 123 | 5733 | 1756 | 84.9 | 27.0 |
| East Germany | 1965 | | | | | | |
| State Enterprises | | 605 | – | 2929 | – | 64.3 | – |
| All Enterprises | | 236 | 127 | 2418 | 2024 | 47.2 | 28.4 |
| Hungary | 1966 | | | | | | |
| State Enterprises | | 1595 | – | 6176 | – | 82.5 | – |
| All Enterprises | | 917 | 113 | 5325 | 1147 | 66.2 | 21.4 |
| Poland | 1966 | | | | | | |
| State Enterprises | | 1016 | – | 3137 | – | 71.1 | – |
| All Enterprises | | 612 | 130 | 2720 | 2286 | 60.4 | 24.4 |
| Romania | 1966 | | | | | | |
| State Enterprises | | 1244 | – | 3095 | – | 70.3 | – |
| All Enterprises | | 1077 | 120 | 2924 | 1538 | 61.7 | 21.3 |
| Yugoslavia | 1965 | | | | | | |
| State Enterprises | | 574 | – | 1874 | – | 57.2 | – |
| All Enterprises | | 402 | 113 | 1777 | 1143 | 50.4 | 16.4 |

## Table 2

*Changes in Employment Size of State Enterprises in East Europe*[6]

| Country | Years | Averages Arithmetic | Averages Niehans Index | Percentage of labor force in enterprises over 1000 persons |
|---|---|---|---|---|
| Soviet Union | 1960 | 481 | 3982 | 54.3 |
| | 1964 | 610 | 5909 | 59.6 |
| Bulgaria | 1961 | 518 | 1700 | 43.2 |
| | 1965 | 533 | 1779 | 47.0 |
| Czechoslovakia | 1960 | 2000 | 4319 | 84.6 |
| | 1966 | 2590 | 5967 | 89.1 |
| East Germany | 1960 | 503 | 2678 | 60.9 |
| | 1965 | 605 | 2929 | 64.3 |
| Hungary | 1960 | 818 | 3929 | 58.8 |
| | 1966 | 1596 | 6176 | 82.5 |
| Poland | 1960 | 719 | 2555 | 64.9 |
| | 1966 | 1016 | 3137 | 71.1 |
| Romania | 1960 | 869 | 2660 | 57.6 |
| | 1966 | 1244 | 3095 | 70.3 |
| Yugoslavia | 1960 | 457 | 1544 | 50.3 |
| | 1965 | 574 | 1874 | 57.2 |

enterprises are very frequent and many establishments are combined in a single enterprise. Further, the decision-making rule for combining establishments seems to vary qualitatively among socialist nations. For instance, in Hungary a variety of different size establishments appear to be combined in a single enterprise; in Poland, the largest industrial establishments operate as single-establishment enterprises, while the smallest establishments are combined together in a single enterprise. It should be added that the diversity of decision-making rules about combining establishments probably lies partly in the fact that Marxist theory—as far as I have been able to determine—says nothing about the matter and there are also almost no discussions of such matters in the economic literature of these nations.

Third, Table 1 shows state enterprises larger than all enterprises, which include not only state enterprises but cooperatives, private handicraft, and, in East Germany, half-state enterprises as well. That is to say, the enterprises that are not owned completely by the state are smaller and, as I later show, are primarily in the light industries where enterprise size is generally also smaller.

Fourth, the picture of enterprise size shown in Table 1 is a changing one. The data in Table 2 show that there was a rapid increase in average employment size of state enterprises in the early 1960s. This wave of growth was brought about primarily by the consolidation of single-establishment enterprises into multi-establishment enterprises and the consolidation of multi-establishment enterprises into enterprises of even larger size. The experience among various East European nations was quite different since the mid-1960s. In Hungary and Czechoslovakia such enterprise consolidations appeared to have greatly slowed down. In East Germany consolidation continued, albeit primarily in a special form, the creation of combines (which are discussed below). In Romania enterprises appeared to lose their autonomy to intermediate administrative units, which may be considered as a consolidation of enterprises. During the late sixties the Soviet Union experimented with various types of enterprise consolidations, which represented different forms of *ob'edin'eiye* or *firmi*. In April 1973 the Soviet Union announced that "all" enterprises (at the present time it is not clear whether only centrally directed enterprises are involved) will be combined into 200 or so super-enterprises of mammoth size in the next three years.

Since Marxist economic theory is quite inadequate about problems dealing with the size of enterprises, it should not be surprising that the public justifications of these enterprise consolidations were mixed and, for the most part, quite inadequate. The Czechoslovaks and the Hungarians had important waves of enterprise consolidations which markedly increased the degree to which a single producer dominated sales of particular goods; this occurred only a short time prior to their introducing measures allegedly designed to introduce market elements into the management of their economies. That is, they made changes in their organization of industry that subverted the purpose of the subsequent reforms in the economy; this suggests either total confusion on the part of economic policy-makers or considerable conflicts between policy-makers of different persuasions, with ascendancy gained by different groups at different times. The latter explanation appears more plausible.

Let us turn now from questions of enterprise size to the composition of enterprise production. An enterprise of a given size can devote its productive facilities toward producing a large amount of a very narrow product range (a "horizontal" organization); or a small amount of a very large product range (a "conglomerate" organization); or a small final amount of a narrow product range, but all the intermediate products that are used to produce the final product as well (a "vertical" organization). Conglomerate organization was not a very usual form of enterprise organization in any of the socialist nations; decision-makers seemed to consider only horizontal and vertical organization (the latter enterprises are called "combines").

The advantage of a horizontal organization is that economies of scale can be achieved. The advantage of the combine form of enterprise is that coordination of intermediate inputs is handled much more by the enterprise managers than by the central planners and fewer supply bottlenecks arise. The horizontal form of organization requires the planners to worry constantly about coordination of production between enterprises; the vertical form of organization places less strain on the planners, but at the cost of less overall efficiency because economies of scale are not utilized.

It has generally been believed that vertical elements in socialist enterprises were much greater than in Western enterprises. For instance, we know that in the Soviet Union only 20 percent of total instrument production was carried out in factories designated for this purpose, while in the United States, this ratio was 70 percent. We know that in Soviet machine-building plants, 99 percent produced their own cog wheels; 84 percent, their own diecastings; 71 percent, their own iron castings; and 57 percent, their own nonferrous castings.[8] In evaluating such scattered evidence, it is difficult to decide whether these results are due to some special feature of the Soviet Union (such as its vast geographical expanse and communications problem) or to some feature of central planning.

One method of examining this matter more systematically is to start with data on the value of production by industrial branch (where industrial branch is defined in terms of establishments whose most important products are classified as belonging to this branch). We then determine the value of the various products that are produced outside these branches and calculate the ratios of these to the total value of production of the major branches. For instance, if establishments whose major products are machines produce 1000 rubles of goods and if other establishments outside this branch produce 150 rubles of machines, then the calculated ratio (which I call the extra-branch production ratio, or the E.B.P. ratio) is 15 percent. Proper data on these matters are available only for East Germany and Hungary, but the results warrant brief examination. By classifying the data according to the two-digit categories of the International Standard Industrial Classification (ISIC), comparisons can also be made with selected Western nations. Relevant data are presented in Table 3.

In East Germany and Hungary the aggregate E.B.P. ratios were respectively 10 and 14 percent. The somewhat higher ratio in Hungary was probably due to the larger-size enterprises in the latter nation. From remarks in the Soviet economic literature, it appears that the aggregate E.B.P. ratio was probably much greater in the USSR than in

## Table 3

*Extra-branch Production Ratios in East Germany and Hungary*[9]

| *Industry and Approximate ISIC Numbers* | | *Extra-branch Production Ratios* Hungary 1959 | *Extra-branch Production Ratios* East Germany 1965 |
|---|---|---|---|
| 10-19 | Mining | 2% | 12% |
| 20, 21, 22 | Food processing, beverages, tobacco | 1 | 8 |
| 23 | Textiles | 7 | 2 |
| 24 | Clothing | 5 | 9 |
| 25, 26 | Lumber and wood working | 8 | 7 |
| 27 | Paper and paper products | 4 | 13 |
| 28 | Printing and publishing | 0 | 10 |
| 29 | Leather and fur products | 5 | 6 |
| 30 | Rubber products | 7 | } 4 (30–32 combined) |
| 31, 32 | Chemicals, petroleum, and coal products | 8 | |
| 33 | Nonmetalic mineral products | 5 | 9 |
| 34 | Primary metals | 7 | 13 |
| 35 | Metal products except machines | 72 | 36 |
| 36 | Machinery except electrical and transport | 8 } (36, 38 combined) | 16 |
| 38 | Transport equipment | | 6 |
| 37 | Electrical machinery | 6 | 14 |
| 39 | Other and miscellaneous | 2 | 8 |
| All manufacturing and mining | | 14 | 10 |

these two East European nations, but without adequate data, we cannot draw any definite conclusions.

To place these results in perspective, it is useful to note that in the early 1960s the E.B.P. ratio was 7 percent in West Germany and 13 percent in the United States (where conglomerate enterprises were relatively more important).[10] Even allowing for certain noncomparabilities of the data, these results suggest that the two East European nations did not feature greatly different vertical elements in their enterprises than in the West. It is also worthy of note that the rank orderings of E.B.P. ratios by industry for West Germany, the United States, and East Germany were significantly correlated with each other, but that the rank ordering of industries according to E.B.P. ratio in Hungary was not correlated with any of the other three nations. This result may have been due either to a helter-skelter enterprise consolidation in Hungary during the late 1950s and early 1960s or to the fact that there is no "natural" ranking of industries by E.B.P. ratios.

Several pieces of evidence suggest that the importance of vertical elements in enterprises will increase in a number of socialist nations. Cuba began creating vertically integrated combines in the mid-sixties in order to solve critical problems of coordination of intermediate and final goods production, and the experiment was sufficiently successful that combines now produce a significant percentage of total Cuban industrial production.[11] East Germany also began to create a number of combines in the late sixties, even though coordination problems were not as severe. The projected Soviet enterprise consolidation will combine enterprises producing roughly the same assortment of goods. The creation of superenterprises may increase vertical elements by making it easier for the directors of such enterprises to hid such extra-branch production from the planners. Of course, the actual results of the Soviet moves in this respect cannot be judged until the proposed policy is actually implemented, a process that may take years. The projected Soviet changes parallel changes that occurred in Romania after the creation of Industrial Centers (very large horizontally organized units that have taken over decision-making powers of enterprises in particular fields) after 1968. Unfortunately, the Romanian data do not permit us to evaluate whether vertical elements of enterprise production have increased.

### *The Nature of Intermediate Organs*

If the planned economies had only a two-tiered industrial hierarchy (central planning and administration organs, and enterprises), then we could comprehend most of the system by focusing on decision-making of enterprise managers. However, the introduction of an intermediate decision-making organ between these hierarchical levels considerably complicates the picture. The degree of centralization of this system is less apparent; and prediction of the course of the economy by focusing on managerial actions becomes more problematic.

Although the intermediate administrative organs may play a crucial role in the operation of the economy, they are seldom clearly described or analyzed in the East European economic press. Therefore, my remarks about these organs must be more qualitative and less precise than in the analysis of enterprises.

*Lines of Communication between Higher and Lower Organs.* At the most general level the problem of intermediate organs concerns the ways in which communications are structured between the central economic administrators and the enterprises. It should be clear that as the level of economic development rises, such communications become more complex and the structuring of such communications becomes more important. The general theoretical issues of such communication structuring are discussed in any competent text on the organization of the large capitalist business organization. In the East European literature, the following major alternatives have received most attention:

1. The "production principle." Using this principle of organization, the higher organs are arranged according to ministries administering the production of a related line of goods (e.g., machines, clothing, transport equipment, chemicals) and the communication lines (carrying orders, plans, and data) extend from production ministries to intermediate organs concerned with the same products and thence to the enterprises which produce the particular goods. This was the major organizational principle of the Soviet Union in 1973, as well as most of the other socialist nations in the world.

2. The "territorial principle." Using this principle of organization, the higher administrative organs communicate with territorial units which, in turn, communicate with the different enterprises. Such territorial units may include not only "natural" governmental units (e.g., districts) but artificially created units (e.g., the *Sovnarkhozi* of the USSR between 1958 and 1965) or even nongovernmental territorial units such as associations of cooperatives. This was the major organizational principle of Soviet industry during the last years of the Khrushchev era (1958-1965) and, as I show below, plays an important secondary role in a number of East European nations as well.

3. The "functional principle." Using this principle of organization, ministries are organized according to industrial "function" (e.g., production, domestic sales, finance, research and development, foreign trade) and communication lines go to similarly arranged intermediate organs and thence to all enterprises in which the function is relevant. This was the major organizational principle employed in the Soviet Union in the early 1930s before it was superseded by the production principle.

4. Other principles. Communication between the highest organs of government and the enterprises can take place through "subsidiary" channels (e.g., communication through the party apparatus; communication through the secret police; communication through the mass media). In various countries at various times, these have played important secondary roles. Other patterns of communication are also imaginable but are not relevant to our discussion below.

In the East European nations, all of these patterns of communication occur together. All countries have production ministries; all have certain "functional" ministries such as ministries of finance or ministries of foreign trade; all have certain enterprises directed by territorial units; and all have communication through subsidiary channels. It is difficult to determine quantitatively the relative importance of functional and subsidiary communication channels. An interesting comparison can be made, however, of the relative importance of the territorial and production lines of communication. This arises from the fact that data are available on the extent to which production is administered by central and by territorial organs.

Let us first turn to the degree to which particular industries are connected to the center by territorial or production lines of communication. In Table 4, I present data for East Germany and Poland on the percentage of workers and employees who work in enterprises not administered by the central government. Such enterprises include those controlled by various territorial governments, producer cooperatives, half-state industries (only in East Germany), and the few private industries (primarily private industrial handicrafts). Several conclusions can be drawn from the data.

First, the percentage of workers and employees in non-central industries varies enormously in both countries in different industries.

Second, the pattern of variation is quite similar in both nations. High percentages of non-central enterprises appear in food processing, clothing, lumber and wood products, and the leather and fur products industries. Low percentages of non-central enterprises (i.e., a high percentage of centrally administered enterprises) appear in mining, primary metals, transport equipment, electrical machinery, and chemical and rubber products industries.

Third, the pattern of non-centrally administered industries is inversely related to the pattern of nationalization of industries by industrial branch in the West (i.e., the pattern of centrally administered industries is directly related to the Western pattern of nationalization by industry).[13] In the West the greatest degree of nationalization is found in the mining, transport equipment, and primary metals industries and the lowest degree of nationalization is found in the food processing, clothing, lumber and wood products, and the leather and fur products industries; these are respectively the industries with the highest and lowest degrees of central administration in Eastern Europe. The causal factors leading to nationalization in the West and central state administration in Eastern Europe are undoubtedly the same.

On an aggregated basis we can also examine the degree to which industry is centrally and territorially administered in the other countries. Wide variations can be observed. The share of workers and employees in non-centrally administered enterprises in manufacturing, mining, and certain utilities during the mid-1960s was quite high in East Germany (36 percent), Poland (30 percent), and (pre-reform) Hungary (27 percent), and was relatively low in Romania (16 percent) and Czechoslovakia (8 percent).[14] Although comparable data are not available for the remaining countries in Eastern Europe, scattered evidence suggests that such ratios for Bulgaria and the Soviet Union were closer to the first than the second group. Of all socialist nations, China has most dramatically organized industry according to territorial lines by administering all but a small fraction of its manufacturing on provincial,

## Table 4

*Percentage of Workers and Employees in Enterprises not Administered by Central Administrative Organs*[12]

| Industry and Approximate ISIC Number | | Percentage of employed in non-central enterprises: East Germany 1965 | Poland 1967 |
|---|---|---|---|
| 10-19 | Mining | 15% | 0% |
| 20, 21, 22 | Food processing, beverages, tobacco | 71 | 74 |
| 23 | Textiles | 41 | 12 |
| 24 | Clothing | 82 | 91 |
| 25, 26 | Lumber and wood working | 73 | 55 |
| 27 | Paper and paper products | 40 | 31 |
| 28 | Printing and publishing | 42 | 49 |
| 29 | Leather and fur products | 64 | 67 |
| 30 | Rubber products | 16 (30, 31, 32 combined) | 26 |
| 31, 32 | Chemicals, petroleum, and coal products | | 24 |
| 33 | Nonmetalic mineral products | 37 | 36 |
| 34 | Primary metals | 4 | 0 |
| 35 | Metal products except machines | 49 | 42 |
| 36 | Machinery except elec. and trans. | 29 | 8 |
| 38 | Transport equipment | 18 | 10 |
| 37 | Electrical machinery | 25 | 14 |
| 39 | Other | 22 | 92 |
| All manufacturing and mining | | 37 | 31 |

regional, district, commune, and city levels; unfortunately, comparable data to those in Eastern Europe on these matters could not be located.

Part of the differences between socialist nations with regard to the relative balance of territorial and central administration of industry—reflecting production and territorial lines of communication—can be explained by reference to the economic size of the nation. Other things being equal, we would expect to find greater territorial administration of industry in centrally planned nations with large gross national products. But other factors including national administration traditions, strength of cooperatives, and relative political power of central and local factions must be examined before the differential pattern observed in Eastern Europe begins to make sense.

In all socialist nations except China, post-reform Hungary, and

Yugoslavia, communication organized according to the production principle appears to predominate over communication according to the territorial principle, although the degree of domination varies according to country. In China, the reverse appears to be true. In post-reform Hungary and Yugoslavia, where detailed planning of current production has been abandoned and market forces admitted, market communication appears to dominate over vertical communication from the highest organs to the enterprises so that a comparison of production and territorial control does not seem meaningful.

*Possible and Actual Roles of Intermediate Organs.* After such consideration of general problems of communications patterns, we can now turn to the more concrete problems of the role of administrative organs between the central agencies and the centrally directed enterprises. Before analyzing the different actual roles that such intermediate organs play in the various nations, it is useful to consider briefly the spectrum of roles which such organs could play.

1. First, such intermediate organs could be simply agents of the central government, acting as "transmission belts" of orders going down and data going up between the center and the enterprises. These intermediate organs would interfere in the operations of the enterprises only with regard to, and not independently of, the orders received from above. More specifically, they could divide up the plan goals between the enterprises below them, but they could not impose new plan goals nor shift capital equipment, funds, or labor between enterprises under their aegis. This is the classical role of the intermediate organs under the Stalinist organization of industry following World War II.

2. Second, they could serve the role of an "administrative cartel" (for lack of a better term), receiving orders from the center and transmitting them but also participating in the administration of enterprises under their control independently of orders from above. They could, for instance, set up additional plan goals or shift capital equipment, funds, or labor between their subordinate enterprises. As I explain below, this role appears to have been played by intermediate organs in East Germany after 1963. The logical extreme of such an expansion in the power of these intermediate organs would occur when all independent powers of decision-making would be removed from the enterprises below them so that the enterprises would act as establishments in the multi-establishment enterprise that is the intermediate organ. This appeared to be happening to a certain extent in Romania after the reform in 1968.

3. Third, the intermediate organs could receive almost no orders from the center and act as agents of the enterprises in the manner of American trade associations. As noted below, this is the role of the Yugoslav intermediate organs. The logical extreme would be where intermediate organs become their own agents, not receiving any orders

from above and treating the enterprises below them as divisions in a multi-establishment enterprise, a situation that did not occur in any of the socialist nations.

One might suspect that the more the intermediate organs serve as a transmission belt, the more advantageous it would be for the central planners if the enterprises were very large, since the planners would have to take particular characteristics of individual units into account. On the other hand, the more the intermediate organ serves as an "administrative cartel," the less the central planners need to concern themselves with the individual enterprises and the smaller the enterprises can be. Unfortunately, the empirical data do not support this supposition since no inverse relation between enterprise size (see Table 1) and relative independent power of the intermediate organs (see below) can be observed in looking at the experiences of the various East European nations.

It should be clear that the role played by the intermediate organs is a key element in the distribution of decision-making power in the industrial hierarchy and, as such, is an integral part of the economic system. It is impossible to summarize the roles of the intermediate organs in the various East European nations, since the economic reforms have been so very different; therefore, we must examine the role of these organs country by country.

As noted above, administrative organs between the center and the enterprises in the Soviet Union played primarily a transmission belt role during Stalin's later years and, indeed, were parts of the ministries. After the experiment in territorial administration of industry during the latter half of Khrushchev's reign, the intermediate organs were reestablished and continued to play their former role. The planned creation of 200 or so superenterprises appears to be the extreme expansion of the "administrative cartel" role and suggests that monopoly communism may be the highest stage of socialism.

In Poland in the early 1970s the intermediate organs were separate organizational units from the ministries, but with only a small range of independent powers so that they served primarily a transmission belt role. In the discussions centering on the economic reforms of the mid-seventies, various economists have argued that such administrative organs should either be eliminated, since their function seems largely mechanical, or given much more decision-making power so that they can play a positive role.

The "administrative cartel" role of the intermediate organs was more prominent in the East German and Romanian post-reform economies. In East Germany the decision-making power of the intermediate organs was gained primarily at the expense of the center. In Romania the decision-making power of these organs was gained primarily at the expense of the enterprises so that in many cases such intermediate organs have begun to act as superenterprises with the former enterprises as divisions.

Only in Hungary and Yugoslavia, the two nations which have been moving toward market socialism, have the intermediate organs acted as agents of the enterprises with few independent powers. In Yugoslavia, one type of intermediate organ (the Chambers) distributed scarce foreign currency to the enterprises it represented, but such a function is certainly not necessary if the foreign exchange rate were pegged at the equilibrium rate.

In the remaining two East European nations—Czechoslovakia and Bulgaria—determination of the role of the intermediate organs is the most difficult. These two nations had the most inconsistent economic reform programs and the roles of the intermediate organs were not well defined. In Czechoslovakia in the mid-sixties the associations were primarily agents of the center (first as transmission belts until about 1966, then as "administrative cartels") until 1968 when the potential conflicts between enterprises and intermediate organs in decision-making in the transition stages toward a guided market socialism became apparent. During 1968 the intermediate organs began to be stripped of their powers over the enterprises so that they would become more agents of the latter, but such measures were apparently reversed after the partial scuttling of the economic reforms following the Soviet invasion. In the early seventies it was impossible to determine the relative degree of decision-making power of these administrative units. In Bulgaria the economic literature describing the intermediate organs is extremely confusing since most of the issues about the role of these units were not forthrightly faced. During the mid-sixties the intermediate organs appeared to be moving from a transmission belt to an administrative cartel role, but with the reversal of the reforms in 1961 this movement appears to have been halted and the exact role of these organs in the industrial hierarchy does not seem at all clear.

The role of the intermediate organs thus rests on the conceptions of the major policy-makers of the ways in which decision-making is to be carried out and the economy is to be administered. A desire for considerable centralization leads to the transmission belt model; a desire for decentralization—at least partway down the hierarchy—leads to the administrative cartel model; and a desire for a type of market socialism has led to the enterprise agent model of intermediate administrative organs. Confusion in the original administrative conception also leads to confusion in the role of the intermediate organs as exemplified by the Bulgarian case.

### *Industrial Organization and the Economic Reforms*

The economic reforms generally affected the entire industrial sphere and it is useful to see how these changes affected the organization in industry in terms of the entire system.

In most of the East European nations the reform cycle began with discussions in the early sixties, continued with the implementation of the reforms in the mid-sixties, and finished with a partial reversal of the reform measures in the late sixties or early seventies. In several countries, notably the Soviet Union and Poland, a new reform cycle has begun with renewed reform discussions in 1972-73. Hungary and Romania are exceptions to the above generalization since their reforms were not implemented until the late sixties and, at the time of writing, the momentum of their reform drives has not yet abated. In East Germany and Yugoslavia the reform measures do not appear to have been significantly reversed, at least by the early seventies.[15]

*Impact of the Reforms on the Industrial Organization.* In all East European countries with the exception of Romania the economic reforms of the sixties represented a decentralization of decision-making power. However the type of decentralization varied greatly among nations, as did the changes in the formal organization of industry.

In one group of countries—East Germany, Poland, and the Soviet Union—this decentralization represented releasing the enterprises from the "petty tutelage" of higher authorities, allowing the enterprise manager greater scope for decision-making within a relatively narrowly defined decision-set, and involving the manager more directly in the planning process. Particular emphasis was placed on changing the incentive structure facing the enterprise managers so as to bring closer into alignment managerial goals (i.e., those actions bringing the largest bonuses) and the goals of the planners. Thus in these nations the reforms represented an administrative streamlining in which the basic features of the planning and administrative system (the material balance system) remained intact. In these nations the reforms affected the administrative rules rather than the formal organizational structure of industry; as a result, little outward change of the industrial organization could be observed except for the strengthening of intermediate organs (the V.V.B.) in East Germany.

In Bulgaria, Czechoslovakia, Hungary, and Yugoslavia the reforms were originated toward the introduction of market socialism. Yugoslavia already had a type of functioning market socialism and the thrust of the reforms focused on changing the role of foreign trade and the rules for price setting, rather than on changes in the planning and administrative system or the organization of industry. In Hungary and Czechoslovakia the material-balance systems of planning and administration were dismantled (although in the latter country the system was partially reintroduced after the Soviet invasion) and enterprise decision-making rules were drastically changed. In these two nations little change occurred in the formal organization of industry which, as noted above, was unfortunate since enterprises were very large and strong monopolistic elements existed.[16] In Bulgaria the motives underlying the reform were quite mixed and, although greater decision-making powers were given to the enterprises, the planning and administrative systems were not dismantled. Intermediate administrative organs with an ill-defined nature were created, but before the reformed system had a time to properly function (and before the crucial but often delayed reform of wholesale prices was implemented), the reforms were reversed and a modified version of the previous system was instituted.

Only in Romania did the economic reforms of the sixties represent a centralization in that enterprises lost decision-making powers to newly created intermediate organs called Industrial Centrals. As I have suggested above, this new organ actually represented an important form of enterprise consolidation.

In few of the East European nations did the reforms change the formal organization of industry in any major manner. Indeed, the lack of consideration of formal industrial organization in the reform plans may have been an important source of weakness. It should be added that the partial reversal of the reform measures in a number of countries has not been tied to any major changes in the formal organization of industry either.

*Competitive Elements.* Except for Hungary and Yugoslavia, the two nations which have successfully implemented types of market socialist systems, all the other East European nations, China, and Cuba now have in a formal sense centrally planned and administered economies. There are, however, certain sources of competition which deserve brief examination.

1. Competition between domestic producers and imported goods. Since most of the socialist nations feel that they have balance-of-payment difficulties and, as a consequence, have strongly regulated foreign trade, the competitive potential of imports is not great. In most East European nations, however, the economic reforms brought greater direct contact between domestic producers (or intermediate organs) and foreign markets (through granting permission to those units to engage directly in foreign trade) so that certain alternative sources of supply are more available than before.

2. Competition between centrally and non-centrally administered enterprises. As I showed above, the relative importance of non-centrally administered enterprises varied considerably among nations. If the non-centrally directed enterprises produced the same commodities as the centrally administered enterprises, if the former could obtain needed material inputs (as well as capital equipment and skilled labor) as easily as the latter, then a certain competition could arise. However, in Eastern Europe at the present time these conditions—especially the second—are probably not fulfilled so that the competitive force of the non-centrally administered enterprise is probably slight.

3. Competition between enterprises in different branches producing the same commodity. As shown above there is a certain extra-

branch production, but it does not appear very great for those countries for which we have adequate data. I doubt that such competition should represent a very important economic influence in the socialist economies.

In brief, we must conclude that although the organization of industry in the socialist nations admits of a certain competition, at present such competitive influences are probably slight.

*Summary*

This essay began with an examination of the productive units in the socialist nations. Although their industrial establishments have many resemblances to those in the West, their average size is much greater and their size distribution is different. A similar conclusion was reached concerning the industrial enterprises of the socialist nations. It was noted that although the vertical aspects of enterprises in the East appear to have been overrated, such aspects may be increasing over time with the increasing importance of the combine form of enterprise.

The administrative organs between the enterprise and the highest administrative organs can and do play a variety of roles in the different socialist nations. A key element of their role is the degree of administrative centralization of the system, with the intermediate organs acting as transmission belts in highly centralized systems, as administrative cartels in less centralized systems, and as relatively powerless agents of the enterprises in market socialist systems.

The economic reforms of the sixties did not result in important changes in the formal organization of industry; the most important changes occurred in the redistribution of power and in decision-making roles of various hierarchical levels. For those nations that maintained the framework of the centrally planned and administered industrial systems, the potential sources of competition that existed within the organization of industry have not been developed.

## NOTES

1. The data on which the following generalizations are based are presented in my book, *Property and Industrial Organization in Communist and Capitalist Nations* (Bloomington, Ind.: Indiana University Press, 1973), chapters 5, 8, 9, and appendices.

2. This generalization for the socialist nations is based on data for only three nations.

3. These generalizations are based on data presented in Pryor, *Property and Industrial Organization*, chapter 6.

4. More precisely the formula for the index is: $N = \Sigma s_i L_i$, where $s_i$ is the share of the labor force in enterprise i and $L_i$ is the labor force employed in that unit. This measure is analyzed in detail by Jurg Niehans, "An Index of the Size of

Industrial Establishments," *International Economic Papers* 8 (London: Macmillan, 1958), and can be used for enterprises as well.

5. The data come from Pryor, *Property and Industrial Organization*, chapter 6. The predicted values are based on the use of a formula derived by a regression analysis of Western enterprise size.

6. The data come from Pryor, *Property and Industrial Organization*, chapter 7.

7. The strange results for the Soviet Union (in which the predicted enterprise size is smaller for two measures of size and larger for one measure of size than actual enterprise size) stem from the size distribution of enterprises there. There are very few enterprises with less than 100 workers and employees, which raises the arithmetic average in comparison with the predicted value. However, there are also relatively few multi-establishment enterprises or very large enterprises, which lowers the Niehans index (which places great weight on extremely large enterprises) in comparison with the predicted value.

8. These and other data are cited by Alexander Woroniak, "Industrial Concentration in Eastern Europe: The Search for Optimum Size and Efficiency," in a forthcoming volume of essays published by the List Gesellschaft.

9. The sources of these data and their method of calculation, as well as certain warnings about non-comparabilities, are presented in Pryor, *Property and Industrial Organization*, chapter 7.

10. Western data come from ibid.

11. Much research needs to be carried out before we have a very clear quantitative picture of Cuban industrial organization. The remarks in the text are based on a discussion of Roberto M. Bernardo, "Managing and Financing the Firm," in *Revolutionary Change in Cuba*, ed. Carmelo Mesa-Lago (Pittsburgh: University of Pittsburgh Press, 1971), pp. 187-190.

12. These data come from Pryor, *Property and Industrial Organization*, chapter 8. The ratio totals in the table are slightly higher than the aggregate data presented in the text because electricity production (which was completely centrally controlled) is omitted from the table.

13. Data on nationalization by industrial branch for many Western nations can be found in Pryor, *Property and Industrial Organization*, chapter 2.

14. These data come from Pryor, *Property and Industrial Organization*, chapter 8. Please note the caveat in footnote 11.

15. The extent to which the reforms in East Germany were reversed is quite controversial. The strongest case for this argument has been made by Michael Keren, "A Postmortem on the East German Reforms" (forthcoming).

16. The situation is different in Yugoslavia, where the average degree of industrial concentration is roughly the same as in Sweden. (Data to support this point are presented in Pryor, *Property and Industrial Organization*, chapter 7.)

# 14

# Foreign Trade*

Paul Marer

Foreign trade statistics are important in any study of a country's economy, since nations are related to the rest of the world primarily through their commodity exports and imports. From data pertaining to the foreign sector, important conclusions are drawn which become the bases for judgments by economists, actions by policy-makers, and decisions by businessmen.

Balance-of-payments statistics in particular are watched closely as manifestations of an economy's strength or weakness. For the seven socialist countries of Eastern Europe which are the subject of this study—the USSR, Bulgaria, Czechoslovakia, East Germany, Hungary, Poland, and Romania (the European members of the Council for Mutual Economic Assistance, or CEMA)—trade statistics assume particular importance because these countries do not publish comprehensive balance-of-payments information and because their international service and credit transactions are relatively less important than they are for most Western countries.

The first part of this chapter deals with the difficulties of ascertaining the quality of foreign trade statistics of the seven CEMA countries as they relate to East-West transactions. We have reconstructed the annual and cumulative 1960-72 balance of trade of individual CEMA countries with individual countries of the Organization for Economic Cooperation and Development (OECD), first on the basis of CEMA and then on the basis of Western statistics. We find that the cumulative balance of trade for 1960-72 of the seven CEMA countries combined, obtained on the basis of East European statistics, shows a $7.2 billion deficit; on the basis of OECD sources, a $200 million surplus. The difference is about $7.5 billion, or over 12 percent of cumulative 1960-72 CEMA exports to the OECD group. The discrepancy is not

*The author gratefully acknowledges support and facilities from the International Development Research Center of Indiana University, where he is a resident scholar. He is indebted to Akbar Nafari for help with the calculations. The sole responsibility for errors and opinions remains with the author.

accounted for by transport costs, as will be shown below.

Most Western analysts make use of data from East European sources to calculate these countries' balance of trade, with a view toward estimating their balance of payments. However, in analyzing the trends and the geographic and commodity composition of East-West trade flows, most analysts rely on the statistics of Western countries, which are available in more comprehensive and standardized form. But uncritical acceptance of either set of statistics, unless they are reconciled, might lead to unwarranted conclusions about important issues, such as the credit-worthiness of a CEMA country. More generally, such discrepancies present an interesting problem in the relation between data and theory. As Oscar Morgenstern observed: "Economic theory has unquestionably postulated a fine structure in the international field; yet we cannot describe this structure adequately by relying on data with which we are confronted."[1]

The first part of this study attempts a reconciliation between sets of Eastern and Western trade partner ("mirror") statistics which purport to quantify the same flow of trade. The purpose of this exercise is to call attention to this important problem in a comparative setting, to identify the approximate orders of magnitudes involved, and to offer tentative conclusions about the causes and implications of the problem.

The second section focuses on the issue of bilateralism versus multilateralism in East-West trade. There seems to be some disagreement among experts as to what the facts are: Franklyn Holzman suggests that East-West trade is largely multilateral,[2] whereas Samuel Pisar concludes that bilateralism has been a permanent feature of East-West trade.[3] One reason why the clarification of the facts is important is to determine prospects that the Soviet Union and Eastern Europe might be able to finance large prospective trade deficits with the United States by the use of hard currency earned through exporting to other Western countries. Since this would require the existence of multilateral trading and clearing patterns, we want to know more about such patterns in the recent past. After discussing some conceptual issues, we turn to a critical review of standard statistical measures of multilateralism. We find reasons to introduce a simple alternative methodology of measuring multilateralism, which we proceed to apply to East-West trade, covering the 1960-72 period. This in turn provides an opportunity to explore some of the implications of our findings about discrepant "mirror" statistics.

The third section of this study examines the possibility that CEMA countries might use the relatively large surpluses they generate in trade with less developed countries (LDCs) as a means of financing imports from the West. It has been argued that CEMA countries are doing just that:

> The policy pursued by the Soviets and the other countries in the Soviet

> bloc [is] to earn foreign exchange by sales of capital equipment to the under-developed countries, then purchase with that exchange other capital equipment in the industrial countries which are members of the OECD. The countries in the Soviet bloc have succeeded in introducing this triangular trade system on a large scale in the world market.[4]

There are numerous formal and informal arrangements, to be sure, which enable CEMA countries to transform some of their surpluses with LDCs into imports from OECD countries.[5] But since CEMA sources have given little indication that LDCs have been or could be a significant source of convertible currency for CEMA, and there also appear to be independent reasons to subject the cited conclusion to empirical verification, in the third and final section we attempt to do that. In the case of CEMA-LDC trade, we do not try to measure the degree of multilateralism because in LDC trade there are even more serious data problems than in OECD trade and because large, aid-type credit transactions, tied to purchases in the grantor CEMA country, would make it especially doubtful that one should be permitted to deduce "multilateralism" from "trade irreciprocity." The approach instead is to divide LDCs into "clearing-currency" and "convertible-currency" groups, and to calculate CEMA's cumulative 1960-71 trade balance with each group separately. We interpret the quote above as a hypothesis and test it by examining whether CEMA countries have succeeded in obtaining trade surpluses with the convertible-currency LDC group.

*"Mirror" Statistics in East-West Trade*

We cited above a nearly $7.5 billion trade balance discrepancy in cumulative 1960-72 CEMA-OECD trade, depending upon whether East European or OECD statistics are used to calculate the trade balance. Differences between the two sets of balance-of-trade estimates can be divided into differences between estimates of East European imports (OECD exports) and East European exports (OECD imports). Table 1 compares cumulative 1960-72 East European imports with corresponding OECD exports for individual and groups of OECD countries; Table 2, East European exports with corresponding OECD imports; and Table 3 the two sets of balance-of-trade figures. In each table the East Europe total excludes the USSR, to avoid the smothering effect of the large Soviet numbers. OECD countries are ranged according to percentage differences between total East Europe and trade partner estimates (i.e., how much larger are East European exports, imports, or the trade surplus than the corresponding mirror estimates?). Thus in Table 1, row 1, column 1 shows that the combined imports of the six East European countries from Switzerland during 1960-72 exceed reported Swiss exports to East Europe by almost $1.3 billion, an amount which represents 49 percent of East Europe's total imports from Switzerland during the period. The second number in parentheses shows the number of country-years in which East Europe's figures show a larger positive (in the case of trade balance, also a smaller negative) amount than those of their trade partner. For an individual East European country the maximum number is 78 (six East European countries X 13). Thus, we find that in trade with Switzerland, East Europe's imports exceed Swiss exports for *each* East European country and for *each* year, and on the average by amounts which range from a low of 41 percent for Czechoslovakia to a high of 85 percent by Bulgaria. In this case this statistic highlights the perfect regularity of the pattern, both across East Europe and over time. In other cases this statistic calls attention to irregularities, as in the case of USSR exports to the United Kingdom (Table 2); in this case it is revealed that although the USSR's cumulative 1960-72 exports approximately correspond to cumulative British imports (the difference is 1 percent), it was in only 2 out of 13 years that Soviet exports were larger than British imports.[6]

The separation of factors causing disparities in "mirror" statistics is exceedingly difficult; in addition to recording time lags, which should not be significant over a 13-year period, these are some of the most important elements: (1) valuation problems, including conversion of statistics to a common dollar unit; (2) treatment of transport and related expenses (f.o.b. vs. c.i.f.); (3) method of showing "provenance" of imports and destination of exports; (4) systems of recording trade, which differ chiefly in their treatment of re-exports; and (5) coverage of merchandise trade.

1. Differences in valuation due to inconsistent exchange rates should not be a prime source of trouble before the December 1971 dollar devaluation because East-West transactions were conducted in Western currencies, in many cases the dollar, with contract values converted to national ("devisa") currency units at the official exchange rates and here reconverted to dollars at the same official rates.[7] For 1972 data we continued to use the pre-1971 official exchange rates, so that 1972 Eastern European data are shown in terms of International Monetary Fund special drawing rights. If East European countries used the new exchange rates which reflect the dollar devaluation of December 1971, then our procedure biases downward the value of East Europe's export and import flows (and to a very small extent also the trade balance) for the last year of this 13-year period.[8]

2. All East European countries and the USSR, except Hungary, record both imports and exports f.o.b. border of supplying country; Hungary shows imports c.i.f. All OECD countries except Canada and the U.S. report imports c.i.f. and exports f.o.b. at their own border. Thus East European imports (except Hungary) should match OECD exports, but Table 1 shows that in most cases they do not. East European exports should be smaller than OECD imports by the amount of transport and related expenses, of which a customary rough estimate

is 10 percent of the value of goods being shipped.[9] Table 2 shows, however, that on the average Eastern Europe reports larger exports than OECD shows imports, with a comparison of mirror statistics by pairs of countries revealing such large fluctuations around the average that the role of transport costs in explaining the discrepancies is doubtful.

3. All East European countries record statistics according to country of *purchase* or *sale*, i.e., origin and destination being determined by the residence of seller and buyer.[10] Twelve of the seventeen OECD countries listed in the tables use the same definition, while five countries (the U.K., Netherlands, Belgium-Luxembourg, Canada, and Finland) report according to consignment, defined for imports as the country from which goods are directly received, and for exports the country to which goods are directly sent.

*East European Imports.* Only in trade with the five OECD countries mentioned above could differences in the method of showing "provenance" of East European imports and destination of OECD exports account for some of the discrepancies noted. We find that for four of the five countries (except Finland), East Europe shows larger imports than they report exports, which suggests that the final destination of some East Europe purchases from these countries might be other than Eastern Europe. This finding for the total for East Europe is consistent with what we observe across the board for the six East European countries, with one exception.[11]

All in all, it is not clear, however, how much confidence can be placed in this explanation, among other reasons because the two OECD countries for which the "mirror" discrepancies are the largest, Switzerland (very much larger East European imports) and West Germany (much smaller East European imports) have the same origin-destination reporting system as Eastern Europe.

*East European Exports.* We find that for the same four OECD countries East Europe shows larger exports than the OECD countries show imports, although in general the reverse would be expected because of the c.i.f.-f.o.b. differential. This implies that while these countries were the purchasers, some of the goods were shipped by Eastern Europe to other destinations. But once again, this pattern is not fully convincing because there are even larger differences in favor of Eastern Europe for some other countries (Switzerland, Austria, and Greece) for which differences in the origin-destination reporting system provide no explanation.

4. Closely related to the question of "provenance" of imports and destination of exports is the treatment of re-exports. All East European countries report *general trade*, which in imports is the combined total of purchases for domestic consumption plus imports for re-exports, and in exports the combined total of national exports plus re-exports. Seven OECD countries employ the *general trade* system; nine others (West

Germany, Italy, France, Belgium, Netherlands, Austria, Switzerland, Spain, and Greece) report *special trade*, excluding re-exports from both flows; the U.K. reports *general imports* and *special exports.*

If the treatment of re-exports were an important factor, then East Europe should report systematically larger imports from, and exports to, countries which report *special trade* only. On the import side (Table 1), this is indeed the case for seven of the ten (U.K. included) *special trade* countries. On the other hand, the one OECD country which reports substantially larger exports to all East European countries as well as to the USSR than CEMA shows as importing from it–West Germany–is also a *special trade* country.

On the export side (Table 2), six of the eight countries for which East Europe shows a larger figure are *special trade* countries, so re-exports probably represent an important component of the "mirror" discrepancy.

5. It is beyond the scope of our effort to establish how much of the discrepancy might be accounted for by differences in what commodities are included by the respective countries in merchandise trade.[12]

Let us call attention to some of the most significant findings and attempt to suggest, whenever possible, an explanation.

In Table 1, East Europe's Imports, the overall pattern is that Eastern Europe and the USSR report very substantially larger imports from OECD than what these countries show as exports to CEMA. Transport cost is not a factor, as both sides report f.o.b. border of supplying country. There are good reasons to believe that re-exports are involved because seven of the eight OECD countries with which the CEMA countries' "surplus" is the largest, both absolutely and relative to the volume of imports, report *special exports* which exclude re-exports. If we exclude West Germany, which is a most unusual special case (see below), we find that assumed re-exports are very large: during 1960-72 about \$5.4 billion for the six East European countries and over \$2 billion for the USSR, for a total of \$7.5 billion for the CEMA group! This brings to mind one striking question: how much is it that we don't know about OECD exports to the Soviet bloc if over a 13-year period \$7.5 billion's worth of exports (12 percent of the total actually reported) are not revealed by published OECD statistics?

It is not possible to determine from these summary tables which might be the countries of origin of these assumed re-exports. Some undoubtedly are the OECD countries themselves (could goods originating in the U.S. play a significant role?); some, assuredly, are LDCs, since we know from CEMA sources that they are frequently relying on West European intermediaries.

One important reason for suggesting further research into this matter is to understand the balance-of-payments implications of these findings for CEMA. For example, to whom and in what currency do CEMA countries pay for goods that originate in LDCs?

# Table 1

*Amount and Percent by Which East European Countries' Imports from OECD Countries Exceed OECD Countries' Exports to East European Countries, and Number of Years It Does So, Cumulative 1960-1972*
(In Millions of Current Dollars, Percent, and Number of Years)

| OECD Country | Total East Europe* | | Bulgaria | | Czechoslovakia | | East Germany | | Hungary | | Poland | | Romania | | USSR | |
|---|---|---|---|---|---|---|---|---|---|---|---|---|---|---|---|---|
| | *Imports of East Europe Less Exports of OECD Country* | | | | | | | | | | | | | | | |
| Switzerland | 1268 | ( 49%, 76) | 84 | ( 44%, 11) | 415 | ( 56%, 13) | 324 | ( 64%, 13) | 162 | ( 48%, 13) | 164 | ( 39%, 13) | 118 | ( 34%, 13) | 149 | ( 31%, 10) |
| U. K. | 2148 | ( 39%, 78) | 111 | ( 39%, 13) | 533 | ( 51%, 13) | 327 | ( 47%, 13) | 316 | ( 45%, 13) | 558 | ( 29%, 13) | 303 | ( 34%, 13) | 109 | ( 5%, 9) |
| Netherlands | 557 | ( 28%, 72) | 0 | ( 0%, 9) | 186 | ( 38%, 13) | 114 | ( 23%, 13) | 52 | ( 18%, 11) | 125 | ( 31%, 13) | 80 | ( 34%, 13) | 265 | ( 36%, 13) |
| Austria | 704 | ( 20%, 75) | 87 | ( 24%, 13) | 230 | ( 28%, 13) | 53 | (-13%, 12) | 117 | ( 11%, 12) | 135 | ( 22%, 13) | 81 | ( 17%, 12) | 227 | ( 22%, 12) |
| Belgium | 259 | ( 18%, 53) | 16 | ( 16%, 8) | -3 | ( -1%, 7) | 114 | ( 35%, 12) | 52 | ( 24%, 11) | 6 | ( 2%, 6) | 73 | ( 28%, 9) | 160 | ( 24%, 12) |
| Italy | 319 | ( 8%, 62) | 40 | ( 8%, 10) | -2 | ( 0%, 6) | 80 | ( 25%, 13) | 84 | ( 11%, 12) | -4 | ( -1%, 9) | 122 | ( 14%, 12) | 132 | ( 6%, 10) |
| Japan | 59 | ( 6%, 51) | 8 | ( 5%, 10) | 21 | ( 18%, 11) | 37 | ( 25%, 12) | 21 | ( 25%, 12) | -23 | (-13%, 0) | -5 | ( -2%, 6) | 47 | ( 2%, 11) |
| France | 150 | ( 4%, 52) | 9 | ( 2%, 8) | -25 | ( -5%, 8) | -5 | ( -1%, 7) | 71 | ( 13%, 12) | 6 | ( 1%, 8) | 95 | ( 11%, 9) | 466 | ( 17%, 13) |
| Canada | 31 | ( 4%, 37) | 4 | ( 8%, 5) | 73 | ( 30%, 13) | 25 | ( 30%, 11) | 12 | ( 20%, 6) | -69 | (-24%, 1) | -15 | (-69%, 1) | 382 | ( 19%, 12) |
| U.S.A. | -11 | ( -1%, 39) | -24 | (-97%, 5) | 14 | ( 5%, 10) | 61 | ( 21%, 5) | 83 | ( 34%, 11) | -150 | (-16%, 1) | 6 | ( 2%, 7) | 54 | ( 2%, 9) |
| Greece | -9 | ( -1%, 33) | 6 | ( 6%, 8) | 2 | ( 1%, 7) | -3 | ( -3%, 4) | 4 | ( 3%, 8) | -9 | ( -7%, 3) | -9 | (-14%, 3) | -2 | ( 0%, 7) |
| Finland | -9 | ( -1%, 38) | -3 | (-12%, 2) | 3 | ( 2%, 10) | -15 | ( -9%, 2) | 11 | ( 11%, 12) | -3 | ( -1%, 6) | -2 | ( -3%, 6) | 43 | ( 1%, 9) |
| Sweden | -20 | ( -1%, 33) | 5 | ( 6%, 7) | 12 | ( 4%, 7) | -55 | (-12%, 1) | 7 | ( 4%, 7) | 3 | ( 1%, 4) | 9 | ( 5%, 7) | 105 | ( 10%, 12) |
| Norway | -13 | ( -3%, 30) | 0 | ( -1%, 0) | 15 | ( 13%, 13) | -27 | (-29%, 1) | 6 | ( 11%, 12) | -4 | ( -3%, 3) | -2 | (-15%, 1) | 34 | ( 14%, 11) |
| Spain | -21 | ( -5%, 23) | -15 | (-31%, 2) | 0 | ( 0%, 4) | --- | --- | 6 | ( 8%, 9) | -10 | ( -7%, 4) | -3 | ( -3%, 4) | -12 | (-13%, 7) |
| Denmark | -54 | ( -6%, 28) | -3 | (-13%, 3) | 2 | ( 1%, 7) | -44 | (-19%, 1) | 10 | ( 11%, 10) | -14 | ( -4%, 5) | -5 | (-11%, 2) | 3 | ( 1%, 7) |
| West Germany | -2218 | (-20%, 18) | -21 | ( -3%, 6) | -648 | (-43%, 0) | -1062 | (-24%, 0) | -72 | ( -6%, 5) | -294 | (-19%, 0) | -121 | ( -7%, 7) | -326 | (-10%, 3) |
| OECD Total** | 3156 | ( 7%, 66) | 304 | ( 11%, 12) | 834 | ( 11%, 13) | -77 | ( -1%, 6) | 942 | ( 16%, 12) | 426 | ( 4%, 10) | 726 | ( 11%, 13) | 1838 | ( 7%, 12) |
| EFTA | 4042 | ( 26%, 78) | 281 | ( 27%, 13) | 1214 | ( 37%, 13) | 5631 | ( 22%, 13) | 629 | ( 27%, 13) | 854 | ( 20%, 13) | 502 | ( 25%, 13) | 670 | ( 8%, 12) |
| EEC | -932 | ( -4%, 39) | 44 | ( 2%, 9) | -492 | (-15%, 1) | -758 | (-12%, 2) | 187 | ( 6%, 12) | -162 | ( -4%, 3) | 249 | ( 6%, 12) | 696 | ( 7%, 12) |

* Excludes USSR.

** Sum of countries listed differs slightly from OECD total because the latter also includes Iceland, Ireland, and Portugal, not listed in this table, and because of rounding.

Source: Indiana University, International Development Research Center, *International Trade Information Management System* (based on official East European and OECD sources).

A most curious case is the "mirror" discrepancy of CEMA imports from West Germany, a country which in every case reports substantially larger exports to Eastern Europe and the USSR than those countries show as purchasing from West Germany, even though CEMA imports include imports for re-exports, while West German exports exclude re-exports. Method of showing "provenance" of imports and destination of exports is now known to be a factor. About half of the more than $2 billion cumulative discrepancy with East Europe is in trade between the two Germanies. Does East Germany under-report what it buys? But why would also Czechoslovakia (by 43 percent), Poland (by 19 percent) and the rest of CEMA, too?

In Table 2, East Europe's Exports, we would expect to exceed East Europe's exports to OECD on account of the c.i.f.-f.o.b. differential. The entries should thus be negative, with the negative percentage difference generally rising as the distance between pairs of countries increases. However, Table 2 generally does not look like this.

A comparison of total East European exports to OECD with total OECD imports from Eastern Europe shows figures that are almost the same: the only difference is about 1 percent of the trade flow, in favor of East Europe. Therefore, perhaps the most important implicit finding is that the amount by which East Europe's exports exceed OECD imports is so small that (after a downward adjustment for the c.i.f. differential which does not represent earnings for Eastern Europe) there appears to be no compensating differential against the large "excess" imports we found in Table 1.

Unexpected, however, are the large positive and negative "mirror" differences by country pairs. For example, all East European countries report substantially larger sales to Switzerland each year than the Swiss show as purchases from East Europe; in fact for every East European country, the largest positive difference by far is to this destination.

Six of the eight OECD countries to which East Europe's exports exceed the corresponding imports are *special trade* countries (imports for re-export are excluded), which suggests that substantial re-exports are a prime cause of the discrepancy. Why do countries like Switzerland, the Netherlands, Austria, and Greece play an apparently important intermediary role? One might speculate that re-exports are ways of getting around bilateralism and that some countries, like Switzerland, the Netherlands, and Greece, which are big *entrepot* centers, are convenient for this purpose, as is Austria, located next door to Eastern Europe and long nurturing its trade relations with it.[13] In other cases East European countries might be forced to transact business through third countries because of barriers their direct exports face in some OECD countries. Even if the OECD countries which are purchasing goods from Eastern Europe tend to be those which report *special trade* and the ultimate destination of these goods is those OECD countries which report *general trade*, as appears to be the case, these shipments

# Table 2

## *Amount and Percent by Which East European Countries' Exports to OECD Countries Exceed OECD Countries' Imports from East European Countries, and Number of Years It Does So, Cumulative 1960-1972*

(In Millions of Current Dollars, Percent, and Number of Years)

| OECD Country | *Exports of East Europe Less Imports of OECD Country* Total East Europe* | Bulgaria | Czechoslovakia | East Germany | Hungary | Poland | Romania | USSR |
|---|---|---|---|---|---|---|---|---|
| Switzerland | 1217 ( 55%, 78) | 214 ( 85%, 13) | 227 ( 41%, 13) | 191 ( 62%, 13) | 262 ( 51%, 13) | 158 ( 48%, 13) | 165 ( 62%, 13) | 31 ( 14%, 9) |
| Netherlands | 239 ( 14%, 68) | 38 ( 43%, 13) | 36 ( 9%, 11) | 51 ( 10%, 10) | 31 ( 12%, 11) | 34 ( 12%, 11) | 49 ( 28%, 12) | 550 ( 45%, 12) |
| Austria | 349 ( 13%, 59) | 75 ( 35%, 13) | 96 ( 14%, 13) | 0 ( 0%, 5) | 83 ( 13%, 13) | 20 ( -4%, 2) | 114 ( 30%, 13) | -40 ( -5%, 4) |
| Greece | 100 ( 12%, 44) | 9 ( 6%, 7) | -14 ( -9%, 0) | 21 ( 20%, 12) | 10 ( 9%, 8) | 30 ( 20%, 8) | 45 ( 27%, 9) | -18 ( -5%, 5) |
| U. K. | 368 ( 9%, 53) | 57 ( 23%, 10) | 180 ( 21%, 13) | 21 ( 5%, 7) | 142 ( 35%, 11) | -26 ( -1%, 6) | -7 ( -1%, 6) | -39 ( -1%, 2) |
| France | 116 ( 5%, 48) | 46 ( 22%, 11) | 57 ( 13%, 11) | 3 ( 1%, 7) | 6 ( 2%, 8) | -59 (-11%, 2) | 62 ( 11%, 9) | -548 (-33%, 0) |
| Belgium | 53 ( 5%, 43) | 16 ( 25%, 9) | 4 ( 2%, 8) | -7 ( -2%, 4) | 14 ( 11%, 9) | -19 ( -9%, 2) | 45 ( 32%, 11) | 87 ( 10%, 10) |
| Canada | 12 ( 2%, 45) | 0 ( 3%, 3) | 2 ( 1%, 10) | 1 ( 3%, 9) | 7 ( 11%, 12) | 7 ( 5%, 10) | -4 (-13%, 11) | 24 ( 17%, 11) |
| U. S. A. | -15 ( -1%, 49) | 2 ( 9%, 9) | 0 ( 0%, 6) | 5 ( 6%, 10) | 27 ( 34%, 13) | -67 ( -7%, 2) | 18 ( 17%, 9). | -28 ( -5%, 0) |
| Italy | -206 ( -4%, 29) | 23 ( 4%, 7) | -23 ( -4%, 3) | 0 ( 0%, 8) | 18 ( 2%, 9) | -141 (-14%, 0) | -83 ( -8%, 2) | -493 (-21%, 0) |
| West Germany | -838 ( -8%, 34) | -22 ( -4%, 6) | 45 ( 3%, 11) | -675 (-16%, 1) | 18 ( 2%, 10) | 169 (-11%, 0) | -34 ( 3%, 6) | -810 (-34%, 0) |
| Sweden | -140 (-10%, 6) | -7 (-29%, 0) | -36 (-14%, 0) | -14 ( -4%, 3) | -9 ( -5%, 2) | -61 (-13%, 0) | -14 (-17%, 1) | -262 (-25%, 0) |
| Norway | -60 (-10%, 12) | 2 ( 7%, 3) | -20 (-14%, 1) | 6 ( 4%, 3) | -9 (-16%, 4) | -35 (-19%, 0) | -4 (-27%, 1) | -63 (-21%, 0) |
| Spain | -55 (-11%, 19) | -2 ( -3%, 6) | -11 (-15%, 0) | 2 ( 5%, 1) | 4 ( 7%, 9) | -37 (-24%, 1) | -12 (-13%, 2) | -9 ( -6%, 4) |
| Denmark | -155 (-17%, 7) | -4 (-28%, 0) | -31 (-17%, 0) | 0 ( 0%, 4) | -5 ( -6%, 3) | -110 (-31%, 0) | -6 (-28%, 0) | -80 (-24%, 0) |
| Finland | -156 (-19%, 8) | -3 (-12%, 3) | -16 (-12%, 1) | -22 (-11%, 1) | -7 ( -8%, 3) | -90 (-26%, 0) | -17 (-30%, 0) | -318 (-10%, 3) |
| Japan | -193 (-31%, 20) | -5 ( -6%, 3) | -39 (-43%, 0) | -31 (-23%, 7) | 1 ( 3%, 7) | -83 (-55%, 0) | -36 (-30%, 3) | -921 (-28%, 0) |
| OECD Total** | 525 ( 1%, 47) | 440 ( 17%, 12) | 445 ( 6%, 13) | -454 ( -5%, 2) | 594 ( 12%, 11) | -764 ( -8%, 0) | 264 ( 5%, 9) | 2960 ( 13%, 0) |
| EFTA | 1387 ( 11%, 62) | 336 ( 42%, 13) | 398 ( 14%, 13) | 182 ( 9%, 11) | 458 ( 23%, 12) | -202 ( -5%, 0) | 216 ( 16%, 13) | -770 ( -8%, 2) |
| EEC | -637 ( -3%, 39) | 100 ( 7%, 9) | 119 ( 4%, 11) | -628 (-11%, 1) | 87 ( 3%, 11) | -354 (-10%, 0) | 39 ( 1%, 7) | -1213 (-14%, 0) |

* Excludes USSR.

** Sum of countries listed differs slightly from OECD total because the total includes Iceland, Ireland, and Portugal, not listed in this table, and because of rounding.

Source: Indiana University, International Development Research Center, *International Trade Information Management System* (based on official East European and OECD sources).

will not be reported in Western statistics because the recipient countries will show them as imports from another OECD country. All East European countries appear to be participating in this triangular trade, but Bulgaria and Hungary perhaps to a greater extent than the others.

Relatively small differences in "mirror" exports or imports will be magnified in the "balance-of-trade mirror," expressed in Table 3, East Europe's Trade Balance, as percentage of the actual trade balance reported by East Europe, because the denominator is often small.

We find that with only two exceptions, West Germany and Greece, East European sources show either a smaller positive or (in most cases) a larger negative trade balance than their OECD counterparts. The difference for combined East Europe with OECD as a group during 1960-72 was $2.6 billion, i.e., East Europe sources showing a trade deficit approximately 50 percent larger than that obtained from Western statistics. The comparable discrepancy for the USSR is $4.8 billion. The combined trade balance discrepancy for CEMA during 1960-72 was close to $7.5 billion.

The importance of this finding and the preceding analysis lies in pointing out that much of this discrepancy cannot be attributed to the c.i.f.-f.o.b. differential but comes from East Europe reporting larger imports than OECD shows exports (both are shown f.o.b. border of supplying country), rather than OECD reporting larger imports (c.i.f.) than East Europe shows exports (f.o.b.). One implication of this finding is that East European statistics, which are generally less favorable from the point of view of their own balance of payments, appear to be a better approximation of the true situation than are OECD statistics.

Table 3 also shows that the pattern we just described for all of East Europe also holds for five of the six East European countries individually, as well as for the USSR. The single exception is Bulgaria which shows a cumulative trade balance with OECD more favorable than that calculated from OECD sources, and this because Bulgaria is the only CEMA country whose positive export differential (sales to OECD less OECD purchases) is larger than its positive import differential, with Switzerland being an important destination of shipments by Bulgaria, apparently destined for re-exports.

One practical use of all this tedious information is that the findings suggest some potentially interesting cases for analyzing the "mirror" problem. A prime candidate would be trade with West Germany, particularly imports from it, as no obvious explanation appears for the large discrepancy. Other interesting cases would be Switzerland and the U.K.

### *How "Multilateral" Is East-West Trade?*

*Conceptual Issues*. Multilateralism usually refers to the convertibility of trade and other balances that result from transactions between

# Table 3

*Amount and Percent by Which East European Countries' Trade Balance with OECD Countries Based on East European Sources Exceeds Trade Balance Based on OECD Sources, and Number of Years It Does So, Cumulative 1960-1972*
(In Millions of Current Dollars, Percent, and Number of Years)

| | | | *Trade Balance Based on East European Source Less Trade Balance Based on OECD Source* | | | | | | |
|---|---|---|---|---|---|---|---|---|---|
| *OECD Country* | *Total* | *East Europe** | *Bulgaria* | *Czechoslovakia* | *East Germany* | *Hungary* | *Poland* | *Romania* | *USSR* |
| Finland | -147 | (-692%, 11) | 0 ( 7%, 3) | -20 ( -563%, 2) | -7 ( -33%, 5) | -18 (-113%, 1) | -88 (-328%, 0) | -15 (-531%, 0) | -361 (-1776%, 0) |
| Denmark | -101 | (-330%, 24) | 0 ( -2%, 5) | -33 ( -78%, 0) | 45 ( 230%, 11) | -16 (-403%, 0) | -96 (-824%, 1) | -1 ( -2%, 7) | -83 (- 250%, 0) |
| U. K. | -1781 | (-133%, 3) | -54 ( -140%, 3) | -353 ( -170%, 0) | -308 ( -119%, 0) | -173 ( -58%, 0) | -584 (-340%, 0) | -310 ( -84%, 0) | -148 ( -8%, 2) |
| Spain | -34 | (-125%, 21) | 13 ( 1015%, 7) | -11 ( -108%, 2) | 2 ( 8%, 1) | -2 ( -13%, 7) | -27 (-155%, 1) | -9 ( -74%, 3) | 3 ( 4%, 4) |
| Netherlands | -318 | (-113%, 19) | 38 ( -318%, 11) | -150 ( -210%, 0) | -64 ( -579%, 1) | -22 ( -57%, 4) | -90 ( -85%, 0) | -31 ( -49%, 3) | 286 ( 60%, 7) |
| Italy | -526 | ( -95%, 13) | -18 ( -101%, 5) | -21 ( -97%, 4) | -80 (-2667%, 1) | -66 ( -27%, 3) | -136 ( -73%, 0) | -205 (-236%, 0) | -625 ( -640%, 0) |
| Japan | -254 | ( -78%, 14) | -13 ( -16%, 3) | -60 ( -249%, 0) | -68 ( -357%, 6) | -20 ( -40%, 2) | -60 (-257%, 0) | -32 ( -25%, 3) | -968 ( -280%, 0) |
| Belgium | -206 | ( -59%, 32) | 0 ( 0%, 6) | 7 ( 14%, 10) | -121 (-2521%, 1) | -38 ( -42%, 2) | -26 ( -56%, 4) | -28 ( -23%, 9) | -72 ( -33%, 1) |
| Austria | -355 | ( -51%, 18) | -12 ( -8%, 6) | -134 ( -105%, 1) | -52 ( -66%, 2) | -34 ( -21%, 2) | -155 (-214%, 0) | 33 ( 34%, 7) | -267 ( -98%, 0) |
| Sweden | -120 | ( -42%, 18) | -12 ( -18%, 2) | -48 ( -136%, 1) | 41 ( 41%, 9) | -15 (-150%, 2) | -64 (-217%, 1) | -22 ( -21%, 3) | -366 (-2510%, 0) |
| Norway | -46 | ( -40%, 16) | 2 ( 32%, 4) | -35 ( - 165%, 1) | 33 ( -47%, 6) | -15 (-635%, 0) | -30 ( -93%, 1) | -2 ( -79%, 4) | -97 ( -160%, 0) |
| Switzerland | -50 | ( -14%, 47) | 130 ( 221%, 13) | -188 ( -105%, 7) | -133 ( 66%, 2) | 100 ( 71%, 10) | -6 ( -6%, 6) | 47 ( 57%, 9) | -118 ( -45%, 3) |
| Canada | -19 | ( -9%, 34) | -3 ( -10%, 1) | -72 (-1233%, 0) | -25 ( -46%, 2) | -6 (-380%, 8) | 76 ( 54%, 12) | 10 ( 96%, 11) | -358 ( -19%, 2) |
| France | -35 | ( -3%, 39) | 37 ( 23%, 8) | 82 ( 149%, 13) | 8 ( 4%, 5) | -65 ( -24%, 3) | -64 ( -26%, 4) | -32 ( -11%, 6) | -1014 ( -105%, 0) |
| U. S. A. | -4 | ( -1%, 46) | 26 ( 746%, 10) | -14 ( -51%, 3) | -56 ( -27%, 9) | -55 ( -34%, 7) | 83 ( 655%, 9) | 12 ( 6%, 8) | -81 ( -9%, 1) |
| West Germany | 1380 | ( 208%, 53) | -2 ( -1%, 6) | 693 ( 484%, 13) | 387 ( 289%, 10) | 90 ( 86%, 10) | 125 ( 254%, 9) | 87 ( 20%, 5) | -484 ( -50%, 1) |
| Greece | 107 | ( 61%, 49) | 2 ( 9%, 7) | -16 ( -86%, 4) | 24 ( 5950%, 12) | 5 ( 87%, 7) | 39 ( 144%, 10) | 54 ( 53%, 9) | -17 ( -33%, 2) |
| OECD Total** | -2631 | ( -49%, 15) | 136 ( 19%, 7) | -389 ( -75%, 2) | -377 ( -33%, 4) | -347 ( -41%, 0) | -1190 (-260%, 0) | -462 ( -27%, 2) | -4799 ( -252%, 0) |
| EFTA | -2655 | (-106%, 10) | 54 ( 24%, 7) | -816 ( -166%, 0) | -381 ( -72%, 1) | -170 ( -48%, 2) | -1057 (-474%, 0) | -286 ( -42%, 1) | -1440 ( -102%, 2) |
| EEC | 295 | ( 15%, 33) | 57 ( 14%, 6) | 611 ( 4773%, 13) | 130 ( 40%, 8) | -101 ( -38%, 2) | -192 (-118%, 2) | -210 ( -26%, 2) | -1909 ( -170%, 0) |

* Excludes USSR.
** Sum of countries listed differs slightly from OECD total because the total also includes Iceland, Ireland, and Portugal, not listed in this table, and because of rounding.
Source: Indiana University, International Development Research Center, *International Trade Information Management System* (based on official East European and OECD sources).

countries. Bilateralism, on the other hand, may refer to a variety of arrangements, from explicit barter deals to trade agreements which seek to foster mutual trade. In the present context, bilateralism is defined as the opposite of multilateralism: inconvertibility of trade balances, which is assumed to be reflected in trade reciprocity.

Before turning to the empirical measurement of multilateralism, let us catalogue some of the forces for and against multilateral trading and clearing in the East and in the West.

A strong force for multilateralism in any country is the need for efficiency. Strict bilateralism imposes severe constraints on the pattern of trade by preventing countries from buying on the lowest-priced and selling on the highest-priced market. In the Eastern countries, this pressure for multilateralism is less strong than in Western countries because ideology and institutional set-up hinder the understanding of economic gains to be derived from multilateral trade based on comparative advantage. (Trading patterns within the Soviet bloc have remained largely bilateral since CEMA was formed in 1949.) Another pressure in the East for bilateralism is the strong concern for plan fulfillment. Bilateral contracts not only help to ensure plan fulfillment; they also inhibit responding to unplanned but profitable trading opportunities which would result in greater multilateralism. Bilateral agreements help Eastern countries to balance exports and imports; the agreements facilitate Eastern exports by reducing Western trade barriers. Finally, bilateral agreements enhance the monopolistic/monopsonistic power of state trading agencies, thus providing an inducement to pursue bilateralist trade policies.[14]

In the West, the expected surpluses which Western countries wish to see settled in hard currency, are a strong pressure for multilateralism. But there are opposing pressures also. Bilateral agreements enable Western governments to specify the exact quantity of "sensitive" commodities in those industries where the state wishes to afford protection to domestic producers or fears market disruption.[15] Another such pressure is the reluctance to accumulate inconvertible rubles and other East European currencies.[16]

Multilateralism flourishes in an environment of assured equality of trading opportunity which Eastern countries cannot guarantee, at least not to the full satisfaction of Western governments. Bilateral trading methods, which secure a certain volume of exports or a certain ratio of exports to imports, are thus viewed by Western governments as substitutes for guaranteed equality of trading opportunity. Obtaining a bilateral commitment from an Eastern country to increase its imports as a *quid pro quo* for granting most-favored-nation (MFN) status is a case in point.

Bilateralist trading policies are infectious. A trade agreement providing for bilateral balancing prevents the Eastern country from using all (some) of its earnings multilaterally. Thus, in the interest of earning "free" convertible currency, it might be forced to buy as little as possible from countries which do *not* insist on bilateral balancing, in effect discriminating against their exports. These Western countries in turn might feel impelled to promote bilateral trading practices to provide for reciprocity.

*Standard Statistical Measures of Multilateralism.* To shed light on the viability of the option for CEMA to finance prospective large import surpluses with the U.S. or with other OECD countries with hard-currency surpluses earned elsewhere, one would like to know what has been the actual degree of multilateralism in East-West trade. But multilateralism cannot be measured directly, only trade reciprocity can. Perfectly reciprocal trade (*j*'s exports to country *s* equal *j*'s imports from country *s*), however, is consistent with multilateralism *or* bilateralism. In the long run, continued irreciprocity usually implies multilateralism, unless there are offsetting service or credit transactions. In the absence of comprehensive balance-of-payments data for CEMA countries, one must rely on trade data alone.

The most frequently used index of irreciprocity ($T_j$) is that of Michaely[17]; other standard measures have been employed by the League of Nations[18] and Pryor.[19] The algebraic definitions of the three standard indices are:

Michaely

$$T_j = 100 \frac{\sum_s \left| \frac{X_{sj}}{X_{\cdot j}} - \frac{M_{sj}}{M_{\cdot j}} \right|}{2}$$

League of Nations (LN)

$$T_j = 100 \frac{\sum_s \left| X_{sj} - M_{sj} \right|}{X_{\cdot j} + M_{\cdot j} - \left| X_{\cdot j} - M_{\cdot j} \right|}$$

Pryor

$$T_j = 100 \frac{\sum_s \left| X_{sj} - M_{sj} \right|}{X_{\cdot j} + M_{\cdot j}}$$

where

$T_j$ = degree of irreciprocity in a given year;
$X_{sj}$, $M_{sj}$ = country *j*'s exports to or imports from country *s*;
$X_{\cdot j}$, $M_{\cdot j}$ = country *j*'s total exports or total imports.

Each measure ranges from zero, indicating reciprocity, to 100, defined as perfect irreciprocity (i.e., multilateral balancing).

The three indices will yield different $T_j$s if $X_{\cdot j} \neq M_{\cdot j}$. To illustrate, assume that country *j* trades with three trade partners in a given year as shown in the tabulation below.

| Trade Partner | j's exports | j's imports |
|---|---|---|
| A | 30 | 45 |
| B | 50 | 75 |
| C | 30 | 45 |
| Total | 110 | 165 |

| | League of Nations | Pryor | Michaely |
|---|---|---|---|
| $T_j$ = | .25 | .20 | 0 |

The largest $T_j$ is shown by the League of Nations index because it takes into account the difference between total exports and imports, implicitly in the numerator (if $X_{.j} \neq M_{.j}$, some $X_{sj}$ must also differ from the corresponding $M_{sj}$), and explicitly in the denominator (where the difference is subtracted, thereby increasing $T_j$). At the other extreme, Michaely's index disregards the difference between total exports and imports; the value of $T_j$ depends only on how the share of exports to a given country in total exports differs from the share of imports from the same country relative to total imports. In between the League of Nations and Michaely measures is Pryor's index, in which the difference between total exports and imports is accounted for (implicitly) only in the numerator. Thus, the larger the difference between total exports and imports, the greater the tendency for the Michaely measure to show a lower $T_j$ than shown by the other measures.

Which index is a more accurate measure of $T_j$? That differences between a country's total exports and imports affect the $T_j$ suggests that it is not possible to abstract from the question of medium- and long-term capital transfers, since many countries tend to be persistent debtors or creditors, at least over a certain period.[20] Michaely recognizes this problem. He excludes from coverage countries which maintain consistently large import or export surpluses, which he defines as those where exports differ from imports by over 50 percent. In the example above, imports exceed exports by just 50 percent, so the country would be included by Michaely, with his measure showing the country to be perfectly bilateral, the other measures as relatively multilateral; in fact, the $T_j$ is about the same as the weighted average of the $T_j$s of all non-communist countries in 1954 and 1958, according to Michaely's own calculations. We would thus prefer to use the League of Nations or Pryor indices over the Michaely index.

All three indices use annual data to calculate $T_j$. But since even under strict bilateralism, a balance at the end of a year may be offset by a balance with the opposite sign in subsequent years, $T_j$s based on annual data will tend to impart an upward bias to the index. We prefer, therefore, to base calculations on trade balances for longer periods, a method that is here followed.

Still another issue concerns the appropriate method of weighting an individual country's bilateral trade balances. Which country is more "multilateral": country A, which has a large imbalance with one or a few of its largest trade partners and close to perfect reciprocity with all others, or country B, which trades multilaterally with many of its smaller trade partners but is reciprocal with its largest partner(s)? If the choice is country A, then the principal criterion is the absolute size of the imbalance; if it is country B, then the criterion also incorporates the *number* of countries with which trade is conducted multilaterally. The standard $T_j$ measures above use trade values as weights; hence, the assumption is implicit that only the absolute size of the imbalance matters.

*An Alternative Measure of Trade Reciprocity.* To provide an alternative $T_j$ which gives potentially equal weight to all trade partners, we introduce the unweighted average absolute deviation of the bilateral balance-of-trade ratios from 1, expressed in percentage terms so that the resulting statistic can be compared with those obtained on the basis of the standard measures.

$$T_j = 100 \frac{\sum_s \left| \frac{X_{sj}}{M_{sj}} - 1) \right|}{N},$$

Still another issue is the appropriate method of averaging $T_j$s for groups of countries, such as CEMA. Since in this instance a weighted average would be dominated by the performance of the USSR, we prefer the unweighted average.[21]

Perhaps the most thorny issue of all is the interpretation of results. If trade is shown to be highly reciprocal, can one unerringly infer bilateralism? Surely not, since even the most perfectly multilateral framework need not result in much irreciprocity. In East-West trade we also need to be concerned about the reverse possibility: if trade is shown to be irreciprocal, can one infer that it is also multilateral? Even abstracting from the problem of service transactions (a trade balance may compensate for a balance on the services account with the opposite sign), and taking into account severe doubts about the accuracy of trade data, long-term capital flows might influence the results. If the flow of credits is largely in one direction, as is the case in East-West trade, and if the loans granted can be used exclusively or largely for purchases from the credit country only, as is the case at least to some degree in East-West trade, then a relatively high degree of irreciprocity might be consistent with bilateral trading practices. We shall attempt to entertain this possibility by partitioning the $T_j$s into positive and negative components. The positive component reflects irreciprocity accounted for by East European surpluses, the negative component by East European deficits. We then speculate that the more nearly the positive and negative components are equal, the more likely that a large

$T_j$ might reflect actual multilateral balancing rather than a one-way flow of long term credit. Conversely, the larger the negative component, the more reason to suspect that increasing indebtedness has played a role in shaping the results.

There are other problems of interpretation, too. There is always the possibility that triangular or "switch" arrangements have been used to settle outstanding balances. While trilateral deals are more efficient
to settle outstanding balances. While trilateral deals are more efficient
than strict bilateral balancing, it is still a somewhat constraining procedure, and the $T_j$ index cannot distinguish such transactions from genuinely multilateral ones.

Finally, what value of $T_j$ should be considered relatively multilateral or bilateral? Results can only be interpreted relative to the $T_j$s of other countries or country groups, or by comparisons over time. But much work remains to determine the expected influence of country size, geographic location, resource endowment, the level of development, and other possible variables on the expected degree of a multilateral balancing, so one interpretation should pay heed to the appropriateness of the standard.

*Empirical Results.* Two sets of $T_j$ indices are calculated, one according to the League of Nations formula, the other on the basis of our formula, for trade among (a) eight Eastern countries (comprised of the seven CEMA countries plus Yugoslavia); (b) eight West European countries;[22] and (c) between the eight Eastern and all OECD countries, except Iceland, Ireland, Turkey, and Portugal.[23] For each group of countries and each $T_j$ index, calculations were made for cumulative four-year subperiods: 1960-63 (subperiod A), 1964-67 (subperiod B), and 1968-71 (subperiod C). The East-West indices were computed both according to OECD and according to East European sources, to determine the influence of the statistical problem discussed earlier.

The $T_j$ indices are presented in Appendix Tables A-1 and A-2 (League of Nations index) and Appendix Tables B-1 and B-2 (our index), with countries ranked from highest to lowest $T_j$ values. Because of differences in the $T_j$ formulas, the absolute values of the indices are not directly comparable. But the broad interrelationship of East-East, East-West, and West-West indices, averaged for each group of countries, is shown in Table 4, which takes the unweighted average of East-East indices in each subperiod as the base. Also included in the tabulation are the results obtained by Wilczynski.[24] Table 4 shows that East-East trade, as expected, is the most reciprocal and, we can safely conclude, the most bilateral. We also find that during the 1964-67 and 1968-71 periods, West-West trade is measured to be more reciprocal than East-West trade; during 1960-63 there appears no significant difference between West-West and East-West trade. Without bringing additional evidence to bear on these findings, the results would seem to be consistent with Holzman's statement that East-West trade is largely multilateral.

Evidence presented in Table 4 establishes that East-West trade appears to be about as "multilateral" as West-West trade regardless of the formula used, or whether annual or cumulative data are employed, or the number of countries included in the respective country groups, weighted or unweighted averages of country indices are considered, and Western or Eastern trade data are used for the calculations. To be sure, we find that the degree of irreciprocity based on East European data sources is consistently and significantly lower than that obtained on the basis of OECD data sources. How about the influence of Western credits on measured $T_j$s? To ascertain whether the observed relatively large trade irreciprocity in East-West trade might be due to persistent Eastern Europe import surpluses being financed by Western credits, $T_j$ indices are partitioned into positive and negative components. Their ratios, averaged for the three groups of countries and subperiods, are shown in the tabulation below:

| Period | East-East | East-West | | West-West |
|---|---|---|---|---|
| | | OECD Source | E. Europe Source | |
| 1960-63 | 1.0: 0.7 | 1.0: 1.1 | 1.0: 2.4 | 1.0: 0.6 |
| 1964-67 | 1.0: 0.8 | 1.0: 1.0 | 1.0: 2.1 | 1.0: 0.7 |
| 1968-71 | 1.0: 0.7 | 1.0: 0.8 | 1.0: 1.4 | 1.0: 0.8 |

We find that the positive and negative components are in relatively close balance in East-East and West-West trade, but for East-West trade, the results depend upon which set of statistics is used. Based on OECD sources, the number of positive and negative deviations is closely matched; based on East-European sources, import of surpluses occurs anywhere from 40 to 140 percent more often than export surpluses, depending upon the subperiod. Since early in this study we tentatively concluded that the use of East European sources is preferable, these results suggest that the increasing indebtedness of East European countries plays a role in yielding $T_j$s which correspond more closely to those calculated for West-West than for East-East trade. Thus, using East European statistics and assuming that the extent to which negative imbalances exceed positive ones reflects a flow of long-term credits, the $T_j$s are adjusted, obtaining the following results:

| Year | East-East | East-West | West-West |
|---|---|---|---|
| 1960-63 | 1.0 | 1.2 | 2.4 |
| 1964-67 | 1.0 | 1.8 | 2.7 |
| 1968-71 | 1.0 | 2.5 | 2.4 |

## Table 4

*Indices of Trade Irreciprocity ($T_j$) in East-East, East-West and West-West Trade, 1960-1971 by Subperiods*
(East-East = 1.0)

| *$T_j$ Measure* | *East-East* | *East-West* | *West-West* |
|---|---|---|---|
| *1960-1963* | | | |
| LN | | | |
| OECD-Based | 1.0 | 2.9 | 3.4 |
| EE-Based | 1.0 | | –– |
| Our | | | |
| OECD-Based | 1.0 | 2.3 | 2.4 |
| EE-Based | 1.0 | 2.1 | –– |
| Wilczynski | 1.0 | 2.7 | 2.1 |
| *1964-1967* | | | |
| LN | | | |
| OECD-Based | 1.0 | 5.2 | 4.2 |
| EE-Based | 1.0 | | –– |
| Our | | | |
| OECD-Based | 1.0 | 3.7 | 2.7 |
| EE-Based | 1.0 | 2.8 | –– |
| Wilczynski | 1.0 | 4.2 | 2.7 |
| *1968-1971* | | | |
| LN | | | |
| OECD-Based | 1.0 | 4.7 | 4.1 |
| EE-Based | 1.0 | | –– |
| Our | | | |
| OECD-Based | 1.0 | 3.7 | 2.4 |
| EE-Based | 1.0 | 3.0 | –– |
| Wilczynski | n.a. | n.a. | n.a. |

Source: Appendix Tables A and B.

We find that during 1960-63 and 1964-67, East-West trade was not as reciprocal as East-East and not as multilateral as West-West trade. During 1968-71, however, East-West trade appears to be about as "multilateral" as West-West trade.[25]

We have not been able to answer conclusively the original question: how multilateral is East-West trade? As Wiles pointed out, the extent of bilateral balancing is a question of government policy or central banking arrangement, so the only way to find out for sure is to ask the central banks.[26]

*Sources and Amounts of East Europe's Hard-Currency Earnings.* Perhaps the simplest and most direct approach to the question: can Eastern Europe finance some of its prospective deficit with the U.S. by the use of hard currency earned by exporting to other countries? is to look at the sources and amounts of hard currency it has been able to generate through exports up to now. Appendix Tables C and D show individual East European countries' cumulative 1960-72 trade surplus with individual OECD countries: Table C based on OECD, Table D on East European sources. The USSR is included in the last column of each table for comparison, but is not included in the East Europe total. Also shown is the percent of the trade surplus relative to the volume of East European exports to (OECD imports from) the respective trade partner, which serves as the basis for ranking the OECD countries.

Appendix Table C, row 1, column 1 shows that the combined exports of the six East European countries during 1960-72 to Ireland exceed Eastern Europe's imports from Ireland by $173 million, an amount which represents 81 percent of Ireland's cumulative imports from Eastern Europe. The second number in the parentheses shows the number of country-years in which a trade balance in favor of East Europe occurred. We find that in trade with Ireland, Eastern Europe's exports exceed Irish exports in each East European country (also the USSR) for most years, and on the average by amounts which range from a low of 26 percent of exports for Hungary to a high of about 90 percent of exports for East Germany, Romania, and the USSR. That these results are not a quirk of Ireland's statistics is confirmed by East European sources (Appendix Table D), according to which Ireland also ranks as the country with which Eastern Europe accumulates the largest surplus relative to the volume of its exports to that country.

Other OECD countries where East Europe regularly earns substantial trade surpluses include Italy ($1.1 billion according to Italian and about half that amount according to East European sources) and Norway ($175 or $127 million, depending upon sources). It is interesting to note that according to Italian sources, during 1960-72 the USSR accumulated a $722 million surplus (25 percent of Italian purchases from the USSR), while according to Soviet sources, which record exports according to final destination, the trade surplus with Italy was only about $100 million (4 percent of exports to Italy). In trade with Ireland, Italy, and Norway, practically all East European countries regularly cumulate trade surpluses according to both sets of trade statistics.

There are other OECD countries which appear to be important hard-currency sources for individual CEMA countries, although the two sets of statistics often lead to opposite conclusions. For example, the U.K. shows that Eastern Europe has had a cumulative 1960-72 surplus of $622 million; in contrast, no East European country shows the U.K. as a country with which they had earned a trade surplus.[27]

The last row of Appendix Tables C and D shows the combined cumulative trade surpluses of Eastern Europe with all OECD countries, total and annual average. If the past is a prologue, then we do not find evidence that the volume of trade surplus East Europe has been able to generate would indicate a strong possibility that this could be an important source of revenue to finance imports from the U.S. Based on CEMA statistics, East Europe's average annual hard-currency trade surplus with OECD countries (where surpluses were apparently earned regularly during 1960-72) was only $125 million ($263 million based on OECD sources), the USSR's $226 million ($455 million based on OECD sources). Even if we make the admittedly extreme assumption that all these funds could be transferred entirely to the U.S., this amount would not enable CEMA countries to increase their purchases from the U.S. substantially—since that amount represents only one-fifth of East Europe's and the USSR's 1973 imports of $600 million and $1.3 billion, respectively, from this country.

*CEMA Trade With Less Developed Countries*

How about the possibility of converting East Europe's export surplus with LDCs to finance imports from the West? Table 5 shows that the cumulative 1960-70 trade surplus of the CEMA group with LDCs was about $5.7 billion, an amount whose rough order of magnitude is about the same as the area's deficit with more developed countries (MDCs) during the period. Since there is an important group of LDCs with whom, in the absence of bilateral payments agreements, CEMA countries finance trade in convertible currencies (a group comprised of much of Latin America and selected countries in Asia and Africa), there is a possibility that a certain portion of the surplus with LDCs might be convertible into hard-currency earnings and used to finance imports from MDCs. This, in fact, is one of the main conclusions of a study sponsored by the OECD and cited earlier.

We calculated individual East European countries' 1960-70 trade balance separately with the so-called "convertible-currency" and "clearing-house" LDCs, using trade partner data to supplement East Europe's statistics. Convertible-currency LDCs are identified as those with which

## Table 5

*Cumulative 1960-1970 Trade Surplus (Deficit) with Clearing-Currency and Convertible-Currency LDCs*
(Millions of Current Dollars)

Cumulative 1960-1970 Trade Surplus (Deficit) with LDCs

Cumulative 1960-1970 Trade Surplus (Deficit) with LDCs

| Country | All LDCs | Clearing-Currency LDCs | Convertible Currency LDCs |
|---|---|---|---|
| USSR | 3,938 | 5,700 | (1,762) |
| Bulgaria | 169 | 141 | 28 |
| Czechoslovakia | 716 | 720 | (5) |
| East Germany | 196 | 266 | (70) |
| Hungary | 123 | 173 | (50) |
| Poland | 157 | 220 | (63) |
| Romania | 387 | 320 | 67 |
| CEMA | 5,686 | 7,540 | deficit |

Source: Indiana University, International Development Research Center, *International Trade Information Management System* (based on official East European sources, supplemented by LDC "mirror" statistics). Partition of clearing- vs. convertible-currency LDCs as explained in the text.

CEMA countries and Yugoslavia have no bilateral payments agreements because trade with these countries is financed in practically all cases in convertible currencies. The country list has been compiled on the basis of information published in the International Monetary Fund's *Annual Report on Exchange Restrictions*, which tabulates the bilateral payments agreements of IMF members. Since practically all LDCs are members, we were able to classify most LDCs, except a few, generally small ones, with which East Europe's trade is known to be insignificant and whose status was, therefore, not investigated.

We find that East European countries tend to have deficits rather than surpluses with convertible-currency LDCs. The cumulative 1960-70 deficit with convertible-currency LDCs of the six East European countries and the USSR combined amounted to over $2 billion (of which almost $1.8 billion is accounted for by the USSR). Hence the trade surplus with "clearing-currency" LDCs alone was greater than with all LDCs combined and amounted cumulatively to about $7.5 billion during the 1960-70 period. Only Bulgaria and Romania earned small cumulative surpluses with convertible-currency LDCs during this period, but in each case the amounts involved represented less than one-fifth of the country's cumulative trade surplus with all LDCs combined.

To be sure, it is known that some bilateral payments agreements with clearing-currency LDCs provide that any excess balance over the swing credit be settled in convertible currency. This then, would provide some hard currency to Eastern Europe. Furthermore, there are reasons to believe that arms sales to LDCs by countries such as Czechoslovakia (which may or may not be included in its trade statistics) are frequently made for convertible currency—another source of hard currency with which to finance Western imports. But even so, our conclusion is that only a relatively small share of the large trade surplus with LDCs yields hard currency to Eastern Europe, and thus trade with LDCs is not a significant option to finance an expansion of Western, including U.S., imports.

# Appendix

## Table A-1.

*Index of Irreciprocity ($T_j$) by the League of Nations Formula in East-East, East-West and West-West Trade, 1960-1971, by Subperiods*
(Percent)

| *East-East* | | *East-West* | | *West-West* | |
|---|---|---|---|---|---|
| *1960-1963* | | *1960-1963* | | *1960-1963* | |
| Poland | 9.1 | Yugoslavia | 33.4 | Switzerland | 42.2 |
| Yugoslavia | 8.2 | Poland | 22.3 | Austria | 32.5 |
| East Germany | 6.4 | USSR | 18.1 | West Germany | 19.1 |
| Czechoslovakia | 5.1 | Hungary | 13.9 | Sweden | 16.3 |
| Romania | 5.1 | Czechoslovakia | 11.9 | Italy | 15.0 |
| Bulgaria | 4.6 | Romania | 11.8 | France | 12.7 |
| Hungary | 3.6 | East Germany | 9.2 | U.K. | 7.8 |
| Average (unwtd.) | 6.0 | | 17.2 | | 20.4 |
| *1964-1967* | | *1964-1967* | | *1964-1967* | |
| | | | 31.5 | Switzerland | |
| Yugoslavia | 12.5 | Bulgaria | 35.9 | Austria | 32.2 |
| Poland | 6.0 | USSR | 31.5 | Switzerland | 30.0 |
| East Germany | 4.4 | Yugoslavia | 27.1 | Denmark | 18.3 |
| Czechoslovakia | 3.3 | Romania | 26.9 | West Germany | 18.2 |
| Hungary | 2.0 | Hungary | 14.8 | Sweden | 15.9 |
| Romania | 1.8 | Poland | 14.3 | France | 9.0 |
| Bulgaria | 1.8 | Czechoslovakia | 12.9 | U.K. | 8.9 |
| USSR | 1.7 | East Germany | 11.4 | Italy | 5.8 |
| Average (unwtd.) | 4.2 | | 21.9 | | 17.3 |
| *1968-1971* | | *1968-1971* | | *1968-1971* | |
| Yugoslavia | 10.8 | Yugoslavia | 43.7 | Switzerland | 33.5 |
| Poland | 4.1 | Romania | 24.4 | Austria | 30.6 |
| East Germany | 4.0 | Bulgaria | 21.8 | Denmark | 18.7 |
| Romania | 3.5 | USSR | 15.5 | West Germany | 17.6 |
| Hungary | 2.8 | Hungary | 13.5 | Sweden | 12.2 |
| Bulgaria | 2.7 | Czechoslovakia | 12.1 | France | 8.9 |
| Czechoslovakia | 2.4 | East Germany | 11.7 | U.K. | 8.4 |
| USSR | 2.2 | Poland | 11.1 | Italy | 3.8 |
| Average (unwtd.) | 4.1 | | 19.2 | | 16.7 |

Source: Data for East-East: International Development Research Center, Indiana University, *International Trade Management Information System* (based on official East Europe sources). Data for East-West and West-West: OECD, *Statistics of Foreign Trade.* Annual.

## Table A-2

*Index of Irreciprocity ($T_j$) by the League of Nations Formula in East-West Trade, 1960-1971, by Subperiods, Based on East European Sources*

*1960-63*

| | | |
|---|---|---|
| Yugoslavia | 36 | (0, 36) |
| Bulgaria | 20 | (6, 14) |
| Hungary | 17 | (2, 15) |
| USSR | 16 | (7, 9) |
| Poland | 15 | (5, 10) |
| Romania | 14 | (2, 12) |
| Czechoslovakia | 14 | (6, 8) |
| East Germany | 9 | (2, 7) |
| Average (unwtd.) | 18 | (4, 14) |

*1964-67*

| | | |
|---|---|---|
| Yugoslavia | 30 | (1, 29) |
| Bulgaria | 30 | (3, 27) |
| Romania | 27 | (3, 24) |
| USSR | 20 | (9, 11) |
| Hungary | 16 | (4, 12) |
| Poland | 10 | (5, 5) |
| Czechoslovakia | 9 | (3, 6) |
| East Germany | 8 | (1, 6) |
| Average (unwtd.) | 19 | (4, 15) |

*1968-71*

| | | |
|---|---|---|
| Yugoslavia | 48 | (0, 48) |
| Romania | 22 | (2, 20) |
| USSR | 19 | (8, 11) |
| Hungary | 15 | (4, 11) |
| Bulgaria | 14 | (2, 12) |
| East Germany | 12 | (2, 10) |
| Poland | 11 | (5, 6) |
| Czechoslovakia | 11 | (2, 9) |
| Average (unwtd.) | 19 | (3, 16) |

Source: Indiana University, International Development Research Center, *International Trade Information Management System* (based on official East European sources).

## Table B-1

*Index of Irreciprocity ($T_j$) by Our Formula in East-East, East-West and West-West Trade, 1960-1971 by Subperiods*
(Percent)

| *East-East* | | *East-West* | | *West-West* | |
|---|---|---|---|---|---|
| *1960-1963* | | *1960-1963* | | *1960-1963* | |
| East Germany | 24 (24, 0) | Yugoslavia | 48 ( 3, 45) | France | 63 (60, 3) |
| Czechoslovakia | 16 (15, 1) | USSR | 46 (35, 11) | West Germany | 52 (52, 0) |
| Hungary | 16 (12, 4) | Bulgaria | 40 (20, 20) | Austria | 40 (18, 22) |
| Yugoslavia | 15 ( 2, 13) | Romania | 34 (17, 17) | Italy | 32 (12, 20) |
| Romania | 14 ( 2, 12) | Poland | 33 (21, 12) | Denmark | 31 ( 9, 21) |
| Bulgaria | 13 (10, 3) | Czechoslovakia | 28 (20, 8) | Switzerland | 29 ( 4, 25) |
| Poland | 12 ( 1, 11) | Hungary | 28 ( 6, 22) | Sweden | 21 ( 7, 14) |
| USSR | 9 ( 7, 2) | East Germany | 21 ( 9, 12) | U.K. | 21 (13, 8) |
| Avg. (unwtd.) | 15 ( 9, 6) | | 35 (16, 18) | | 36 (22, 14) |
| *1964-1967* | | *1964-1967* | | *1964-1967* | |
| Yugoslavia | 21 ( 5, 16) | USSR | 63 (52, 11) | West Germany | 61 (60, 1) |
| East Germany | 14 (14, 0) | Bulgaria | 50 ( 7, 43) | France | 48 (43, 5) |
| Czechoslovakia | 11 ( 8, 3) | Yugoslavia | 44 (10, 34) | Austria | 28 ( 7, 21) |
| Poland | 11 ( 3, 8) | Poland | 40 (32, 8) | Switzerland | 28 ( 4, 24) |
| Bulgaria | 9 ( 8, 2) | East Germany | 37 (21, 16) | Denmark | 22 ( 4, 18) |
| Hungary | 8 ( 4, 4) | Romania | 36 (13, 23) | Sweden | 21 ( 5, 16) |
| Romania | 8 ( 4, 4) | Hungary | 31 ( 9, 22) | Italy | 19 (16, 3) |
| USSR | 3 ( 2, 1) | Czechoslovakia | 29 (22, 7) | U. K. | 15 ( 3, 12) |
| Avg. (unwtd.) | 11 ( 6, 5) | | 41 (21, 20) | | 30 (18, 12) |
| *1968-1971* | | *1968-1971* | | *1968-1971* | |
| East Germany | 18 (18, 0) | Romania | 56 (27, 29) | West Germany | 66 (65, 1) |
| Yugoslavia | 18 ( 2, 16) | Poland | 55 (50, 5) | France | 44 (35, 9) |
| Bulgaria | 16 (14, 2) | Yugoslavia | 52 (10, 42) | Austria | 28 (10, 18) |
| Romania | 12 ( 6, 6) | East Germany | 49 (32, 17) | Switzerland | 26 ( 3, 23) |
| Czechoslovakia | 10 ( 9, 1) | Bulgaria | 40 ( 9, 31) | Denmark | 25 ( 1, 24) |
| Poland | 8 ( 3, 5) | USSR | 38 (26, 12) | Italy | 17 (13, 4) |
| Hungary | 7 ( 1, 6) | Czechoslovakia | 34 (29, 5) | Sweden | 16 ( 6, 10) |
| USSR | 6 ( 5, 1) | Hungary | 25 ( 6, 19) | U. K. | 13 ( 1, 12) |
| Avg. (unwtd.) | 12 ( 7, 5) | | 44 (24, 20) | | 29 (17, 13) |

Source: Data for East-East and East-West: International Development Research Center, Indiana University, *International Trade Information Management System* (based on official East European sources). Data for West-West: OECD, *Statistics of Foreign Trade.* Annual.

**Table B-2**

*Index of Irreciprocity ($T_j$) by our Formula in East-West Trade, 1960-1971, by Subperiods*
(Percent)

*1960-63*

| | | |
|---|---|---|
| Bulgaria | 51 | (22, 29) |
| Yugoslavia | 48 | ( 0, 48) |
| USSR | 33 | (17, 16) |
| Romania | 29 | ( 8, 21) |
| Hungary | 26 | ( 2, 24) |
| Czechoslovakia | 23 | (10, 13) |
| Poland | 22 | ( 7, 15) |
| East Germany | 18 | ( 5, 13) |
| Average | 31 | ( 9, 22) |

*1964-67*

| | | |
|---|---|---|
| Bulgaria | 48 | (13, 34) |
| USSR | 41 | (28, 13) |
| Yugoslavia | 37 | ( 1, 36) |
| Romania | 34 | ( 7, 27) |
| Hungary | 28 | ( 5, 23) |
| East Germany | 27 | (10, 27) |
| Poland | 19 | ( 9, 10) |
| Czechoslovakia | 13 | ( 8, 5) |
| Average | 31 | (10, 21) |

*1968-71*

| | | |
|---|---|---|
| Romania | 54 | (26, 28) |
| Yugoslavia | 47 | ( 8, 39) |
| USSR | 40 | (21, 19) |
| East Germany | 37 | (15, 22) |
| Bulgaria | 35 | (15, 20) |
| Poland | 27 | (19, 8) |
| Czechoslovakia | 27 | (13, 14) |
| Hungary | 25 | ( 4, 21) |
| Average | 36 | (15, 21) |

Source: International Development Research Center, Indiana University, *International Trade Information Management System* (based on official East European sources).

# Table C

*Amount and Percent of East European Countries' Trade Surplus with OECD Countries, and Number of Surplus Years, Cumulative 1960-1972, Based on OECD Sources*
(Millions of Dollars, Percent, and Number of Years)

| *OECD Country* | *Total** | *Bulgaria* | *Czechoslovakia* | *East Germany* | *Hungary* | *Poland* | *Romania* | *USSR* |
|---|---|---|---|---|---|---|---|---|
| Ireland | 173 ( 31%, 64) | 1 ( 50%, 6) | 24 ( 75%, 12) | 29 ( 89%, 13) | 2 ( 26%, 10) | 109 ( 84%, 13) | 9 ( 89%, 10) | 54 ( 91%, 13) |
| Portugal | 69 ( 33%, 35) | 0 ( 5%, 3) | 2 ( 6%, 9) | – ( —, 2) | – ( —, —) | 52 ( 75%, 12) | 15 ( 41%, 9) | 8 ( 73%, 9) |
| Iceland | 27 ( 28%, 41) | – ( —, 1) | 12 ( 37%, 13) | 9 ( 42%, 10) | – ( —, 4) | 6 ( 17%, 9) | 1 ( 12%, 4) | 21 ( 14%, 10) |
| Norway | 175 ( 27%, 56) | – ( —, 3) | 57 ( 35%, 13) | 37 ( 24%, 10) | 12 ( 20%, 10) | 63 ( 29%, 9) | 5 ( 27%, 11) | 157 ( 43%, 13) |
| Italy | 1081 ( 23%, 63) | 36 ( 7%, 9) | 42 ( 6%, 10) | 83 ( 25%, 11) | 305 ( 31%, 10) | 324 ( 29%, 12) | 292 ( 27%, 11) | 722 ( 25%, 11) |
| Denmark | 195 ( 18%, 37) | – ( —, 2) | 75 ( 35%, 12) | – ( 25%, 11) | 12 ( 12%, 9) | 108 ( 23%, 12) | – ( —, —) | 117 ( 28%, 11) |
| Finland | 174 ( 17%, 54) | – ( —, 8) | 16 ( 10%, 9) | 29 ( 14%, 11) | 2 ( 2%, 6) | 114 ( 26%, 11) | 13 ( 17%, 9) | 381 ( 11%, 10) |
| Canada | 85 ( 16%, 31) | – ( —, 6) | 77 ( 31%, 8) | – ( —, 5) | 7 ( 13%, 7) | – ( —, 1) | 0 ( 1%, 4) | – ( —, 1) |
| U. K. | 622 ( 16%, 44) | 15 ( 8%, 8) | 146 ( 22%, 13) | 50 ( 12%, 7) | – ( —, —) | 412 ( 23%, 11) | – ( —, 5) | 1985 ( 48%, 13) |
| Japan | 122 ( 15%, 33) | – ( —, 2) | 36 ( 28%, 9) | 49 ( 30%, 11) | – ( —, —) | 37 ( 16%, 6) | – ( —, 5) | 1434 ( 34%, 12) |
| Greece | 104 ( 14%, 44) | 21 ( 17%, 8) | 35 ( 21%, 12) | – ( —, 3) | – ( —, 7) | – ( —, 2) | 48 ( 39%, 12) | 70 ( 17%, 13) |
| Spain | 68 ( 12%, 35) | – ( —, 3) | 1 ( 1%, 7) | – ( —, 3) | – ( —, 3) | 47 ( 23%, 9) | 22 ( 21%, 10) | 59 ( 36%, 10) |
| Belgium | 126 ( 12%, 22) | – ( —, 1) | – ( —, —) | 126 ( 37%, 12) | – ( —, 2) | – ( —, 3) | – ( —, 4) | 291 ( 37%, 13) |
| Netherlands | 153 ( 10%, 44) | – ( —, 3) | 76 ( 21%, 11) | 75 ( 17%, 11) | – ( —, 6) | – ( —, 7) | – ( —, 6) | 216 ( 32%, 12) |
| Sweden | 111 ( 7%, 28) | – ( —, 1) | 13 ( 4%, 7) | – ( —, —) | 5 ( 3%, 9) | 93 ( 17%, 11) | – ( —, —) | 352 ( 27%, 11) |
| Switzerland | 50 ( 5%, 24) | – ( —, —) | 9 ( 3%, 9) | – ( —, 2) | 41 ( 13%, 10) | – ( —, 3) | – ( —, —) | – ( —, —) |
| Austria | 89 ( 4%, 26) | – ( —, —) | 6 ( 1%, 7) | – ( —, 5) | – ( —, 1) | 82 ( 15%, 11) | – ( —, 2) | – ( —, 4) |
| W. Germany | – ( —, 20) | – ( —, 3) | – ( —, 1) | – ( —, 6) | – ( —, 1) | – ( —, 8) | – ( —, 2) | – ( —, 4) |
| U.S.A. | – ( —, 26) | – ( —, 4) | – ( —, 9) | – ( —, 11) | – ( —, 3) | – ( —, 8) | – ( —, 1) | – ( —, 2) |
| France | – ( —, 7) | – ( —, —) | – ( —, 1) | – ( —, 2) | – ( —, 1) | – ( —, 1) | – ( —, 2) | 51 ( 2%, 6) |
| Total** | 3424 | 73 | 627 | 487 | 386 | 1447 | 405 | 5918 |
| Annual Average | 263 | 6 | 48 | 37 | 30 | 111 | 31 | 455 |

* Excludes USSR.
**Small discrepancies due to rounding.

Source: OECD, *Statistics of Foreign Trade.* Annual

# Table D

*Amount and Percent of East European Countries' Trade Surplus with OECD Countries, and Number of Surplus Years, Cumulative 1960-1972, Based on East European Sources*
(Millions of Dollars, Percent, and Number of Years)

| OECD Country | Total* | Bulgaria | Czechoslovakia | East Germany | Hungary | Poland | Romania | USSR |
|---|---|---|---|---|---|---|---|---|
| Ireland | 116 (77%, 63) | 1 (50%, 6) | 20 (71%, 11) | 23 (90%, 13) | 2 (26%, 10) | 61 (79%, 13) | 9 (89%, 10) | 51 (90%, 13) |
| Norway | 127 (22%, 46) | 0 ( 0%, 4) | 21 (15%, 11) | 70 (43%, 9) | – ( —, 6) | 33 (18%, 8) | 3 (18%, 8) | 60 (20%, 12) |
| Greece | 177 (21%, 56) | 23 (17%, 10) | 19 (12%, 9) | – ( —, 9) | 6 ( 5%, 8) | 27 (18%, 7) | 102 (60%, 13) | 53 (14%, 10) |
| Iceland | 15 (17%, 29) | – ( —, 1) | 4 (16%, 8) | 10 (48%, 10) | – ( —, 4) | 0 ( 0%, 5) | – ( —, 1) | – ( —, 2) |
| Portugal | 18 (16%, 24) | 0 ( 3%, 3) | 0 ( 0%, 4) | – ( —, 3) | – ( —, —) | 18 (35%, 8) | – ( —, 6) | 8 (73%, 9) |
| Italy | 556 (12%, 51) | 18 ( 3%, 7) | 21 ( 3%, 8) | 3 ( 1%, 6) | 239 (24%, 10) | 187 (19%, 10) | 87 ( 9%, 10) | 98 ( 4%, 9) |
| Switzerland | 200 ( 9%, 40) | 59 (23%, 12) | 0 ( 0%, 8) | – ( —, 1) | 141 (27%, 13) | – ( —, 2) | – ( —, 4) | – ( —, 2) |
| Denmark | 74 ( 8%, 37) | – ( —, —) | 42 (23%, 12) | 20 ( 8%, 10) | – ( —, 6) | 12 ( 3%, 9) | – ( —, —) | 33 (10%, 8) |
| Spain | 30 ( 6%, 33) | – ( —, 4) | – ( —, 5) | – ( —, 3) | – ( —, 5) | 18 (11%, 8) | 13 (13%, 8) | 62 (40%, 7) |
| Finland | 48 ( 6%, 37) | – ( —, 7) | – ( —, 7) | 21 (11%, 11) | – ( —, 2) | 27 ( 8%, 7) | – ( —, 3) | 20 ( 1%, 5) |
| Canada | 18 ( 3%, 31) | – ( —, 6) | 6 ( 2%, 8) | – ( —, —) | – ( —, —) | – ( —, 4) | 11 (34%, 6) | – ( —, —) |
| Sweden | 29 ( 2%, 22) | – ( —, —) | – ( —, 4) | – ( —, 4) | – ( —, 7) | 29 ( 6%, 10) | – ( —, —) | – ( —, 5) |
| West Germany | 193 ( 2%, 41) | – ( —, 3) | 143 ( 9%, 11) | – ( —, 7) | – ( —, 4) | 49 ( 3%, 11) | – ( —, 3) | – ( —, 3) |
| Netherlands | 11 ( 1%, 23) | – ( —, 3) | – ( —, 5) | 11 ( 2%, 8) | – ( —, 3) | – ( —, 1) | – ( —, 3) | 502 (41%, 11) |
| Belgium | 5 ( 0%, 21) | – ( —, 1) | – ( —, 6) | 5 ( 1%, 6) | 5 ( 1%, 1) | – ( —, 5) | – ( —, 2) | 219 (25%, 10) |
| U. S. A. | 4 ( 0%, 31) | 4 (13%, 9) | – ( —, 8) | – ( —, 4) | – ( —, 2) | – ( —, 8) | – ( —, —) | – ( —, —) |
| Japan | – ( —, 24) | – ( —, 3) | – ( —, 4) | – ( —, 10) | – ( —, —) | – ( —, 6) | – ( —, 1) | – ( —, —) |
| France | – ( —, 9) | – ( —, 1) | – ( —, 3) | – ( —, 2) | – ( —, —) | – ( —, 1) | – ( —, 2) | – ( —, 2) |
| Austria | – ( —, 14) | – ( —, 1) | – ( —, 1) | – ( —, 2) | – ( —, 1) | – ( —, 5) | – ( —, 4) | – ( —, 2) |
| U. K. | – ( —, 12) | – ( —, 4) | – ( —, 1) | – ( —, 1) | – ( —, —) | – ( —, 5) | – ( —, 1) | 1837 (44%, 13) |
| Total** | 1621 | 105 | 276 | 163 | 393 | 461 | 225 | 2943 |
| Annual Average | 125 | 8 | 21 | 13 | 30 | 35 | 17 | 226 |

* Excludes USSR.

** Small discrepancies due to rounding.

Source: International Development Research Center, Indiana University, *International Trade Information Management System* (based on official East European sources).

## NOTES

1. Oscar Morgenstern, *On the Accuracy of Economic Observations* (Princeton, N.J.: Princeton University Press, 1963), pp. 138-139.

2. Franklyn Holzman, "East-West Trade and Investment Policy Issues: Past and Future," in Joint Economic Committee, U.S. Congress, *Soviet Economic Prospects for the Seventies* (Washington, D.C.: U.S. Government Printing Office, 1973), p. 684.

3. Samuel Pisar, *Coexistence and Commerce* (New York: McGraw-Hill, 1970), p. 169.

4. Vassil Vassilev, *Policy in the Soviet Bloc on Aid to Developing Countries* (Paris: OECD, 1969), p. 54.

5. These arrangements include *switch trading*, i.e., the diversion of cargoes from stated destinations, and *trilateral compensation procedures*.

6. The two years were 1970-71, for which the USSR reported exports $374 million larger than U.K. imports, a discrepancy so great that it counterbalanced the effect of the other eleven years during which British imports exceed Soviet exports.

7. Discrepancies in valuation might occur in the case of countries with floating exchange rates, such as Canada.

8. To be sure, even when there are no doubts about exchange rates, invoices accompanying commodities may not be properly made out or might be falsified; in still other cases, valuation in a Western country may be based not on contract value but on estimates of customs experts, with valuation practices varying from country to country. See Morgenstern, *Accuracy of Economic Observations*, p. 166.

9. There are very large transport cost variations, of course, depending upon distance, type of commodity, and means of transport.

10. This is documented in Paul Marer (with Gary J. Eubanks), *Soviet and East European Foreign Trade 1946-1969: Statistical Compendium and Guide* (Bloomington, Ind.: Indiana University Press, 1972), pp. 358-359. The USSR records imports according to country of production (origin) and exports by country of consumption (final destination).

11. Canada consistently shows larger exports to Poland and Romania than these countries report as imports from that country, implying that the goods were purchased somewhere else or by someone else, but shipped from Canada.

12. Based on official statements, we have determined elsewhere the merchandise coverage of the East European series. See Peter Wiles, *Communist International Economics* (New York: Praeger, 1969), pp. 353-357.

13. "A strict application of bilateralism would have impinged on the development of Austrian exports. Due to switch and swap transactions, the Austrian clearing balances could be kept much lower than the trade balances. . .exports [were] hardly burdened by the bilateral clearing system." Egon Matzner, *Trade Between East and West: The Case of Austria* (Stockholm: Almqvist and Wicksell, 1970), p. 142.

14. C. H. McMillan, "The Bilateral Character of Soviet and East European Foreign Trade" (unpublished study, Ottawa: Carleton University, 1973), pp. 8-9.

15. Pisar, *Coexistence and Commerce*, p. 171.

16. Not only are East European currencies "soft" in the sense that they are not convertible into other financial assets, but they are not freely convertible into the goods and services of the Eastern countries ("commodity-inconvertibility").

17. Michael Michaely, "Multilateral Balancing in International Trade," *The American Economic Review* 52 (September 1962).

18. League of Nations, *Review of World Trade* (Geneva, 1933).

19. Frederic L. Pryor, *The Communist Foreign Trade System* (Cambridge, Mass.: The M.I.T. Press, 1963).

20. Short-term credits bilaterally extended and repaid will "cancel out" by measuring $T_j$ not on annual data but on cumulative balances over several years, as discussed below.

21. Joseph Wilczynski, in *The Economics and Politics of East-West Trade* (New York: Praeger, 1969), p. 209, calculates $T_j$ for East-West trade, using Pryor's index, and obtains the weighted averages for all CPEs as follows:

| | 1960 | 1961 | 1962 | 1963 | 1964 | 1965 | 1966 | 1967 |
|---|---|---|---|---|---|---|---|---|
| $T_j$ | 20 | 23 | 18 | 36(!) | 29 | 21 | 26 | 23 |

The 1963-64 results surely reflect the extraordinary USSR grain purchases (entirely, largely, to some extent?). Wilczynski does call attention to the weighting problem.

22. East Europe's principal trade partners in West Europe.

23. Trade with omitted OECD countries has been very small or highly imbalanced due to the miniscule volume either of imports or exports.

24. Wilczynski used a weighted average of country indices, and a formula practically the same as Pryor's, which he applied to annual data. His country coverage is greater than ours: the East is comprised of CEMA plus Albania and the five Asian CPEs; the West, the 25 developed countries of West Europe, North America, Japan, South Africa, and Oceania. Wilczynski, *Economics and Politics of East-West Trade.*

25. There are some interesting differences among individual East European countries (Appendix, Tables A and B), but space limitations do not allow a discussion of results.

26. Wiles, *Communist International Economics*, p. 255.

27. The discrepancy between U.K. and Polish statistics is particularly intriguing. No such discrepancy exists, however, in U.K.-USSR comparison-both sides show that the USSR had a surplus approaching $2 billion during 1960-72.

# 15

# Cybernetics, Automation and the Transition to Communism

Jozef Wilczynski

Cybernetics is the field of science concerned with communication and control in living organisms and machines. It represents the best example of an interdisciplinary area of knowledge, based on modern achievements in mathematics, logic, physiology, mechanics, electronics, economics, and other sciences. In its modern sense, cybernetics originated in the U.S. during World War II, and since the publication of N. Wiener's pioneering study in 1948,[1] it has witnessed remarkable developments in both theory and practice, not only in the U.S. but also in other advanced countries.

The main branches of the theory of cybernetics are information, statistical prediction, games, programming, and steering mechanisms. Its practical applications can be found in automatic machines, computers, rocketry, military "troop control," economic planning, translation into other languages, musical composition, medical diagnosis, teaching and learning, and many others. Western interest in cybernetics has been mainly limited to technical fields and focused primarily on feedback control systems.[2] On the other hand, in the socialist countries[3] cybernetics has been viewed more broadly, as extending its competence into social and philosophical spheres as well.

Automation can be regarded as a special aspect of cybernetics in its application to the operation of technical equipment, particularly of the advanced and complex type. Advanced automation consists of the consolidation of discrete mechanical operations into a continuous, self-regulating process by means of a servomechanism[4] in accordance with programmed instructions and without direct human participation. Although automation has a much longer ancestry than cybernetics, going back to at least the Industrial Revolution, in the modern sense its development has been radically enhanced by cybernetics, and both of them have become the most characteristic features of the scientific and technical revolution (or the "Second Industrial Revolution").

In Marxist ideology, two stages of communism are envisaged—the lower phase, commonly known as "socialism," and the higher phase designated "communism," or more explicitly "full communism." Socialism essentially represents a transitional stage, during which several characteristic features of capitalism are still retained. These may include such capitalist "survivals" as some private ownership of the means of production, selective operation of the market mechanism ("commodity-money relations"), the utilization of financial instruments and material incentives, distribution according to work, and a persistence of social differences according to the type of work performed.

On the other hand, full communism—as vaguely conceived in the writings of Marx, Engels, and Lenin—is to be marked by the following features: the complete socialization of the means of production, the abolition of money, the elimination of market relations, all-round affluence, distribution according to needs, a classless society, and the "withering away" of the state.[5] All the Comecon countries are still in the lower phase and describe themselves as "socialist" (not "communist").

A proposition could be advanced that the ideas pioneered by N. Wiener may do more toward the realization of Marxian ideals than those of I. P. Pavlov and T. D. Lysenko combined, and that the scientific and technical revolution can do more than the Bolshevik Revolution and those in other socialist countries following World War II put together. The purpose of this paper is to consider this proposition in a detached manner by testing the capacity of the European Comecon countries for cybernation and automation, and examining the extent to which such developments can contribute to the evolution of the "communist cornucopia" and the "communist man."

### *From Dogmatic Prejudice to Pragmatic Opportunism*

One of the most intriguing features of the officially accepted attitude in the socialist countries was the early rejection of cybernetics, and in some respects, automation, as capitalist creations incompatible with Marxian philosophy and directed against the interests of the working masses. In the 1954 edition of the *Concise Dictionary of Philosophy*, published in Moscow by the State Publishing House for Political Literature, cybernetics was described as:

> a reactionary, pseudo-scientific field of knowledge concocted in the U.S.A. after the Second World War and widely peddled in other capitalist countries as well. . . . Cybernetics in its essence is directed against dialectical materialism, against the contemporary scientific physiology based on I. P. Pavlov's work and the scientific Marxist interpretation of society's life. . . . In cybernetics one of the basic features of the bourgeois outlook is patently obvious, viz., its anti-humanitarian predisposition to transform the worker into an appendage

> of the machine, a tool of production and war. . .a dream to substitute a machine for a thinking human being fighting for his interests. Warmongers working towards another world war utilize cybernetics for their own dirty schemings.[6]

The official hostility to cybernetics was conditioned by the conviction that it was a threat to dialectical and historical materialism because like the latter, it sought to provide a system of thinking which explains universal laws and relationships, but unlike the latter, it belittled the role of "social consciousness" and "class struggle" as the most general explanations for social processes. The antagonism was further exacerbated by suspicion of mathematical methods and econometrics which involved marginal analysis in application to planning and management. Furthermore, economic optimization necessitated the scarcity valuation of non-labor resources, which was in conflict with the labor theory of value.

These views prevailed up to the late 1950s, but then a most astonishing reversal of the previous attitude occurred. The communist parties began to look at cybernetics from another angle, and soon they perceived its great potential use under socialism. In 1957 N. Wiener's book was published in a Russian translation and since that time, in the theoretical organ of the Communist Party of the Soviet Union (CPSU), Wiener has been elevated to the rank of "one of the greatest mathematicians of our time."[7] In 1959 the Scientific Council on Cybernetics was established under the patronage of the Academy of Sciences of the USSR. Cybernetic societies soon appeared in other Comecon countries as well, and in 1970 the International Laboratory for Cybernetic Problems was set up in Moscow under Comecon auspices. The 22nd Congress of the CPSU, held in 1961 and described by N. S. Khrushchev as "a milestone in the history of Soviet society,"[8] laid down that, "Cybernetics, electronic computers and control systems will be widely applied in production processes in industry, building and transport, in scientific research, planning, designing, accounting, statistics and management."[9]

The new official party line on the role of cybernetics was recently explained by G. Klaus of the German Democratic Republic, one of the leading philosophers and cyberneticians in Comecon, as follows:

> The mission of cybernetics is to supplement, strengthen and elaborate upon the Marxist-Leninist philosophy. . . . The basic application of cybernetics in the political economy of socialism does not derive merely from this or that economic need, but from the *necessity* of shaping the whole social system of socialism. One of the main tasks of the application of cybernetics in a socialist society is precisely the optimum development of the interrelations of all the elements of the entire social system. . . . A consistent application of this discipline increasingly enhances the utilization of the overwhelming potential of the socialist camp.[10]

It is now generally accepted in socialist thought that machine, man, and society are very similar in structure and that society can be viewed as a complex mechanism consisting of a network of direct and feedback communication channels. These links can be employed on a scientific basis for shaping social processes towards ideologically optimal goals, so that cybernetics provides the key to the scientific and dynamic management of society.

Although automation has never been sweepingly condemned in socialist pronouncements, some of its aspects have been the object of criticism, particularly in its capitalist setting. Ever since the first assembly line (1913) and then the transfer line (1947) were introduced at the Ford Motor Co. in the U.S., automation has been identified by many socialist writers and speakers as a symbol of dehumanized and sweated labor inevitably leading to psychological stresses, exploitation, unemployment, colonialism, and a further concentration of wealth and power.[11] However, although with some hesitation at first, automation has been wholeheartedly embraced in application to a socialist society. Its acceptance has been rationalized by the leadership on the grounds that the usual harmful effects of automation cannot occur under socialism, or they can be prevented by the state which represents the interests of the working masses.

Automation under socialism is viewed as a powerful lever of technological, economic, and social progress, because not only does it involve the production and importing of automated equipment, but it also leads to the diffusion of new methods of production, the introduction of mass-produced articles, and a higher level of skills.[12] In the program of the 24th Congress of the CPSU, adopted in March 1971, it was stated that, "Automation and comprehensive mechanization are the solid foundations for a gradual development of socialist labor into communist labor."[13]

*Computers and the Information Network*

The cybernation of scientific, technical, economic, and social processes necessitates a systematic flow and processing of information. Crucial to meeting such needs is computerization and the development of nationwide information networks. The Comecon countries had a later start in the production of computers than the leading Western nations. The USSR, the most advanced socialist country in this field, began producing experimental computers in 1949 (the U.S. in 1942). The first commercially available computers of the first generation—based on electronic lamps—were produced by the Soviets in 1955 (by the U.S. in 1951); of the second generation—based on transistors—in 1964 (in 1957 by the U.S.); and of the third generation—based on integrated circuits—in 1969 (in 1964 in the U.S., 1966-67 in Britain, France, the Federal Republic of Germany and Japan).

Today all the socialist countries under consideration produce computers of some sort, including third-generation units. The number of important series of computers produced in recent years is about 30 (with more than 130 models). The total number of computers produced up to 1972 is estimated to have been 7,500 (compared with about 120,000 in the capitalist world), almost all of which were small and of the first or second generation.

Since the late 1960s the Comecon countries have cooperated closely in the development of computer technology and production. It has been decided to produce a standardized series of third-generation computers designated *RYAD*.[14] The agreed program envisages at least seven basic models, geared to mass data processing and to be mutually compatible not only with each other but also with some of the most up-to-date Western computers used in Comecon (such as the *IBM-360*).[15] In the interest of the highest possible technical standards and the economies of scale, national specialization has been agreed to. Bulgaria and Hungary are specializing in smaller models (*R-10, R-20*), the German Democratic Republic and Poland in medium ones (*R-21, R-30*), while the USSR concentrates on the largest units (*R-40, R-50, R-60*). The first model in the series entered serial production in 1972; it is the *R-20* computer, produced jointly by Bulgaria and the USSR at the largest computer factory in Comecon—the Ordzhonikidze Computer Works in Minsk (in all, employing 80,000 persons). This cooperation also covers the production of and specialization in certain computer components, peripheral equipment, and software—numbering more than 100 items.

The total number of computers in use in the socialist countries in question in 1970 is estimated to have been 6,450, or less than 6 percent of the world total (it may be mentioned that these countries' share in the world's industrial output is nearly 33 percent). The average number of computers per one million of population in the region was 19, compared with the world average of 31. Further details can be found in Table 1. For the sake of comparison with the leading Western countries, it may be mentioned here that in the same year the total number of computers and the number per one million of population (in that order) were: the United States—70,480 and 344; in the Federal Republic of Germany—6,710 and 109; in Japan—5,790 and 56; in Great Britain—5,070 and 91; in France—4,570 and 90; in Canada—2,280 and 107; and in the Netherlands—1,220 and 94.[16] The extent of computerization in Comecon is in fact lower than the figures in Table 1 suggest. Compared with the capitalist world, the computers in use in Comecon are mostly small and medium and of the first and second generation, noted for low speeds and small memory capacities, and supported with inadequate and inferior peripheral equipment and software.

According to the national plans announced in the late 1960s and early 1970s, by 1976 the total number of computers in the Comecon

**Table 1**

*Digital Computers in the European Comecon Countries in 1970*

| *Country* | *Total Number* | *Number per 1 million of population* |
|---|---|---|
| USSR | 5,500 | 23 |
| German Democratic Republic | 360 | 21 |
| Czechoslovakia | 235 | 16 |
| Hungary | 85 | 8 |
| Poland | 180 | 6 |
| Bulgaria | 40 | 5 |
| Romania | 50 | 2 |
| Comecon | 6,450 | 19 |
| World | 113,000 | 31 |

Sources: Estimates based on daily and periodical literature published in the Comecon countries, and on *Electronic Data Processing in the Soviet Union and Other East European Countries* (Brussels: East-West, 1972), pp. 10, 29.

countries will be about 28,000 (the USSR–25,000; the German Democratic Republic–950; Czechoslovakia–800; Poland–700; Hungary–400).[17] Judging by the performance so far, however, it is most unlikely that this target will be reached–half this figure is more feasible.

The need to develop comprehensive networks of information in the socialist countries became evident to the leadership long ago as a necessary aid to central economic planning. But this need has assumed new magnitude in the context of cybernation and automation. In fact, as N. Fedorenko (the Director of the Central Economic and Mathematical Institute of the USSR) put it, "The management of any process consists in the collection and processing of information and the resulting decisions provide new data for guiding management."[18] As is well known, one of the effects of the scientific and technical revolution has been what some Soviet scientists call the "information explosion,"[19] and this trend toward the proliferation of data is likely to continue. Two Polish economists recently estimated that the number of documents produced in the sphere of knowledge which may be considered useful to a country such as Poland was 2.5 million in 1960, but by 1975 the figure will rise to 9 million and 20 million by 1985.[20] Thus, according to V. Glushkov (the Director of the well-known Cybernetics Institute of the Ukrainian Academy of Sciences), the USSR needs some

10,000 computing stations grouped into 40-50 nodal centers with the latter linked to the national headquarters in Moscow.[21]

It must be realized that the social ownership of the means of production, the mono-party system of government, and central economic planning under socialism provide an advantageous basis (compared with capitalism) for developing a uniform nationwide system of information. In each socialist country there is one (or more) central organization responsible for the development of the information system or of some of its elements. The practical approach differs in each country. On the one hand, development in the German Democratic Republic is essentially proceeding from the center to lower administrative levels and regions and to lower individual operational units. On the other hand, Romania is endeavoring to establish data banks first in major enterprises and in industrial centers (intermediate levels of economic management), and then in regional centers, and all these are gradually to be linked to the national center. In the remaining Comecon countries a compromise approach is evident, with one or the other being dominant.

The work on developing national systems of information has been in process since about the mid-1960s, but little had been achieved in practical results before 1970 as the main effort had been directed toward planning and the introduction of computers. The 1971-75 plans in all these countries embody generous provisions for the development of local and regional data banks equipped with computers and transmission systems to be linked to central bodies. Thus, in Bulgaria 20 regional centers are to be set up by the end of 1975 (there were 3 such centers in 1971).[22] In Poland, the automatic network of information in operation in 1975 is to include 4 centers for central administration, 5 at the disposal of ministries, 10 embracing economic organizations, and 17 for the processing of technical information. These subsystems are to be subsequently expanded and linked to a unified "National System of Information" (KSI).[23] In Romania by the end of the current 1971-75 plan, 80 computing centers (compared with 13 in 1972) are to be developed covering about 400 enterprises.[24]

The task is of course much greater in the USSR owing to the vastness of the country and regional differences. According to D. Gvishiani (the Deputy Chairman of the State Committee for Science and Technology), in 1971 the USSR had 82 information centers based on the branches of the economy, plus 60 republican and territorial centers, together with over 8,000 information units existing in larger combines, plants, research establishments, and design bureaus, all employing more than 130,000 persons.[25] The large data bank which has been established in the State Supply Agency (*Gossnab*) is directly fed with data by 60,000 enterprises. The current five-year plan provides for the establishment of more than 2,700 automated information centers (there were about 420 in 1970) in the country.[26]

Effort in the Comecon countries in the second half of the 1970s will be directed toward the standardization of documents, the automatic transmission of data, and the integration of the subsystems, so that central agencies, ministries, and regional authorities, as well as most industrial branch associations and major enterprises, will be linked to computer centers. If the announced plans are fulfilled, the Comecon countries may have automatic and unified nationwide networks of information by the early or mid-1980s.

The socialist countries under consideration have embarked on far-reaching cooperation with a view to the rationalization and integration of the system of information on a Comecon scale. This cooperation is based on inter-governmental agreements, the implementation of which proceeds on a planned basis through some forty specialized agencies of the Comecon organization. Considerable success has been achieved in the standardization of classification, data, and documents since 1962, when the Institute for Standardization and the permanent commissions for standardization and for statistics were established. In 1971, the member countries set up the International Center for Scientific and Technical Information with headquarters in Moscow.

Another important step taken by the member countries in 1971 was the establishment of the Permanent Commission for Communications (also Moscow-based). Since that time, efforts have been renewed to develop a unified automatic system of telegraphic, photo-telegraphic, and other types of communication to provide "instant" information on weather (in the form of photo-telegraphic weather charts), transport, and the data required for joint economic planning and for coordinated research and development. A means of communication which is revolutionizing the transmission of information is represented by artificial satellites (in which field Soviet pioneering achievements are well known). Satellites are increasingly employed for the transmission of telegraphic and telephone messages, radio and television programs, and weather information, as well as data on inner and outer space. In 1971 the Comecon countries established *Intersputnik* (the International System and Organization of Cosmic Communications), responsible for planning, designing, establishing, and operating space communication facilities for the benefit of the member countries.

*Progress to Automation*

As in the case of the information system, in several ways the socialist countries have an institutional advantage in the pursuit of automation. Under socialism, automation is viewed in a broad social setting, and once sufficient priority is assigned to it the socialist state has the power and means to implement various automation projects—even if they are not immediately commercial propositions in the narrow, short-run sense. Socialism is also in a better position than capitalism in planning and implementing long-run programs of education, vocational training, and retraining in anticipation of such needs associated with automation.

Although the stages of economic and technological development attained by the socialist countries are, so far, well below Western levels, a good deal of attention has been given to automation with some remarkable results. Automation has up to now mostly been introduced in power generation, metallurgy, machine-building, vehicle-construction, the chemical industry, and food processing (roughly in this order of incidence). The cases of automation introduced in the past mostly represented earlier, simpler forms such as automation on-off switches, assembly lines, and automatic machines handling limited segments of production processes. But in recent years increasing importance has been attached to the introduction of advanced ("complex") automation—automatic transfer lines and automated sets of equipment steered by servomechanisms with the aid of electronic computers storing information and capable of choosing appropriate programs. There are also some cases of completely automated factories.

Bulgaria is one of the industrially least-developed Comecon countries and it has embarked on automation rather late. As reported in 1971, the proportion of labor in different branches of the manufacturing industry using automated machines and equipment ranged from 0.5 percent in the building materials industry and 0.6 percent in non-ferrous metallurgy, to 4.8 percent in electric and thermal power and 5.5 percent in the textile industry.[27] A major automation project was begun in the enterprise "Metal," in the machine-building industry in the early 1970s. Bulgaria now produces semi-automatic turret lathes with a kinematic program-controlled mechanism, modular automatic milling machines for bevelling, automatic flotation-reagent metering systems, automatic production lines, etc. It is claimed that 55 percent of the equipment needed for automation in Bulgaria is now locally produced.[28]

A considerable degree of automation has been achieved in Czechoslovakia and the German Democratic Republic, which is not surprising considering that these countries are the most industrially developed in the region. In Czechoslovakia the automatic management of railways with a computer was begun in 1959, and since the mid-1960s work has been directed toward a comprehensive automation and optimization of the management of the operations and technological processes in the railway system. Czechoslovakia also administers the interconnected and partly automated electric power grid, "Peace," linking all the Eastern European countries and the European part of the USSR. In the German Democratic Republic the percentage of automated equipment found in the socialized sector in industry was 25.8 percent in 1968, and the proportion rose to 34.6 percent in 1971; the percentage of equipment which was classified in the "advance automation" category was 4.7 in

1968 and 8.3 in 1971.[29] In 1971, twice as much automated equipment was installed in industry as in 1965, and mostly of the advanced type.[30]

In Hungary, in the state sector of industry in 1972, the proportion represented by partly and fully automated machines was 33.6 percent and that represented by fully automated and advanced units was 1.3 percent.[31] In Poland, the industrial census carried out in 1965 revealed that 2 percent of industrial workers were employed in work involving automated equipment.[32] By 1967, the proportion of industry's needs for automated equipment satisfied from domestic sources rose to 70 percent.[33] In the late 1960s it was reported that automation was being introduced in sixty to seventy plants a year.[34] So far, automation has been mostly introduced in the chemical industry, hydroelectric and thermal power stations, cotton, woolen, and footwear industries, sugar refineries, food processing, shipbuilding, and in some foundries and metalworking plants.

Of all the European socialist countries, Romania has the least developed economy, yet it has demonstrated considerable interest and dynamism in automation since 1960 when the "Automatica" enterprise was established (to design, produce, and install automatic devices and equipment), followed (in 1962) by the Institute for Automation (to conduct research and development in the field). The proportion of investment devoted to automation has been steadily increasing, having doubled in the last decade.[35] By 1980, automatic steering is planned to be introduced in one form or another in more than 1,400 enterprises.[36]

On the whole, most progress in automation in the Comecon region has been made in the USSR. This is not surprising considering the large size of its domestic market and the consequent potential economies of scale, its desire to shine as the technological leader of the socialist camp, and its determination not to be outdistanced by the U.S. and other leading industrial capitalist powers. In 1960, the Central Statistical Office of the USSR carried out a sample study of 1,236 industrial enterprises in the country. The investigation showed that in 58 percent of the enterprises, automation work of one sort or another had been, or was being, carried out, involving 11,072 automatic devices, machines, or processes–*viz.*, 126 automatic assembly lines, 533 automatic steering units, 1,242 automatic and semi-automatic transport mechanisms, 3,588 various automatic instruments, 4,966 automatic and semi-automatic metalworking machines, other machines and presses, and 617 other automatic and semi-automatic devices.[37] One of the best known cases of advanced automation in the USSR (and Comecon as a whole) is that of the State Ball-Bearings Factory in Moscow, completed before the mid-1960s.[38]

The approach to automation in the USSR has been placed on a more systematic basis since the establishment of the Ministry of Instrument-Making Automation and Control Systems in 1965. Of the 9,000 production lines set up in 1971, 1,000 were automated and a further 4,000 existing plants were "mechanized and automated."[39] The 1971-75 plan calls for the introduction of automatic production in 930 large enterprises and of an additional 708 automatic installations in other production entities, so that every fifth enterprise in the USSR in 1975 will be automated in one way or another.[40]

*From Socialism to Communism?*

Although ever since the Bolshevik Revolution the socialist leadership has always been committed to the advancement of society to the communist phase, no specific timetable was officially announced to this effect until the early 1960s. The first concrete plan was put forward in the USSR—the country which has always regarded itself as ideologically and socially the most mature socialist society—in 1961 at the 22nd Congress of the CPSU. According to the program adopted at the Congress, the USSR was scheduled to begin entering the communist phase in about 1980.[41] No date was officially announced in other Comecon countries, but it was implicitly understood that the changeover would begin at about the same time or soon after.[42]

However, that forecast was based on the extrapolated high rates of economic growth which had prevailed in the preceding decade, while in reality a period of stagnation followed.[43] According to the prediction made at the Congress, the USSR was to overtake the U.S. in total national income and in per capita income by the year 1970.[44] But the actual performance was far from those targets.[45] At the East-West economic symposium held in Vienna in 1962 a Soviet spokesman, K. Plotnikov, told the International Economic Association that to enter full communism the USSR needed an increase in the volume of industrial output by six times and in agricultural output by three-and a-half times.[46] Between 1961 and 1970, according to official Soviet statistics, industrial output increased by two-thirds and agricultural output by only a quarter.[47] By this writer's estimates, it appears that the USSR may reach the 1970 level of the U.S. national income per capita in the last decade of this century, and catch up with the U.S. current figure perhaps early next century. Czechoslovakia and the German Democratic Republic are likely to reach such levels earlier, and Bulgaria and Romania later than the USSR.[48]

It is now widely agreed among socialist leaders that the transitional phase ("socialism") to full communism will be much longer than was commonly assumed before.[49] This conclusion in fact emerged from the conference held in Prague in October 1970 on the "Place of Socialism in History and the Stages and Criteria of its Development," attended by delegates from all the European Comecon countries.[50]

The time of the changeover to communism is now uncertain and no specific dates have been officially announced. By the writer's estimate, the closing decade of this century will probably see the necessary material and technical preconditions for the changeover, in the sense predicted for 1980 at the 22nd Congress of the CPSU. By that time, according to socialist sources, the scientific and technical revolution will reach its highest stage of development in Comecon.[51] We shall now briefly consider the extent to which cybernation and automation can contribute to the achievement of Marxian communist ideals.

*The Complete Socialization of the Means of Production.* So far, a complete socialization of the means of production (land and capital) has been achieved only in the USSR. In the other socialist countries under consideration, the proportion of farming land in the socialized sector (i.e., occupied by collective and state farms) ranges from 17 to nearly 100 percent. The extent of the social ownership of productive capital is generally greater, the lowest proportion being 83 percent (in Poland). It may be mentioned that the proportion of national income (Net Material Product) produced in the socialized sector in 1971 ranged from 83.4 percent in Poland and 85.6 percent in the German Democratic Republic to 99.8 percent in Bulgaria and 100.0 percent in the USSR. For further details see Table 2.

**Table 2**

*Percentage Share of the Socialized Sector in the European Comecon Countries in 1971*

| *Country* | *Gross Farming Land* | *Gross Agricultural Output* | *Total Industrial Output* | *Capital Investment* | *National Income* |
|---|---|---|---|---|---|
| Bulgaria | 99.6 | 99.8 | 99.7 | 99.9 | 99.8 |
| Czechoslovakia | 91.1 | 95.1 | 100.0 | 98.7 | 99.2 |
| German Democratic Republic | 94.3 | 92.4 | 85.2 | 95.4 | 86.6 |
| Hungary | 97.2 | 96.9 | 99.1 | 99.0 | 98.0 |
| Poland | 17.0 | 15.6 | 98.3 | 83.4 | 83.4 |
| Romania | 90.7 | 90.2 | 99.9 | 98.9 | 96.6 |
| USSR | 100.0 | 100.0 | 100.0 | 100.0 | 100.0 |

Source: Based on: *Statisticheskii ezhegodnik stran-chlenov Soveta Ekonomicheskoi Vzaimpomoshchi 1972* [Statistical yearbook of the Comecon countries for 1972](Moscow: Comecon Secretariat, 1972), pp. 39-40.

Private farms, where they still exist, are usually small and in most cases backward.[52] The extension of mechanization and automation and the application of industrial methods in farming require very large farms. This process, which has recently assumed its highest form of development in the so-called agro-industrial complexes, is certain to continue.[53] At the same time, better employment (and entertainment) opportunities in nonagricultural occupations will continue making young successors to private farms increasingly reluctant to retain such farms and work on them,[54] and land without private successors is taken over by the state.

Privately owned enterprises will also be less and less attractive, particularly in those types of production where there is a need for modern technology, costly capital equipment, and large-scale production. It is well known that the young generation in socialist countries is not much interested in running private businesses, even when they can be inherited from their parents. However, the private ownership of the means of consumption—durables in particular—will be retained, and is in fact likely to increase with the rising levels of per capita income.

*The Abolition of Money.* It is difficult to see how money can be abolished in a progressive industrial society, but a reduction in its physical handling is feasible. Settlements among socialized enterprises are already largely made by non-cash adjustments by the state bank in their bank accounts. The perfection of the information network, especially the automation of the collection, processing, teletransmission, and storing of data can further improve this system and extend it to payments between enterprises and perhaps even among private persons. Wages can be paid into personal bank accounts, and shopping and payment settlements can be effected by various telecommunication devices (which are likely to be in wide use in the 1980s). There will be little need for hoarding money in a society with generous social security and with a limited scope and need for private transactions in property. However, these developments may lead to a largely cashless but not necessarily a moneyless society—unless economic common sense and efficiency are sacrificed to utopian dreams.[55]

*The Elimination of Market Relations.* The perfection of economic planning is theoretically possible to such an extent as to allow the elimination of the market mechanism. The improvement of mathematical methods and the saturation of the economy with high-memory computers may enable easier and more accurate anticipation of demand and supply on macro as well as micro scales. Oskar Lange's idea of "shadow markets," first put forward in the 1930s but never applied in practice in any Comecon country, may yet become a reality and in a vastly improved scientific form and setting.[56]

The economic reforms since the early 1960s, however, have rather extended the role of the market through the reactivation of such market instruments as interest rates, capital charges, depreciation rates, trade margins, quality and novelty price mark-ups, profit, and material incentives to the management and workers based on enterprise profits.

*All-Round Affluence.* The cybernation of the economy may reduce the extent of voluntarism and the economically arbitrary decision-making which often prevailed in the past and led to the misallocation of resources and widespread waste. The application of advanced mathematical methods and a highly developed network of information and automatic data processing may enable optimal pricing and the optimal allocation of resources.

The extension of automation in production will further promote production and may lead to a radical expansion of total output. Cooperation in Comecon will facilitate the extension of the market, further stimulating large-scale production, automation, and growth of productivity. According to some socialist cyberneticians, the application of automatic steering increases the effectiveness of production in enterprises by 10-15 percent, in large combines and branch associations by 50-60 percent, and on the macroeconomic scale by at least 100 percent.[57]

These developments will continue to release labor from material production, so that the service sector can be radically improved to provide large amounts of services and of a wider range and better quality. The socialist economy may reach such levels of per capita national income that the problem of scarcity of consumer goods and services will be overcome, and the socialist society will enter the era of mass consumption.

*"From Each According to His Ability, to Each According to His Needs."* The information network on a macrosocial scale will facilitate the "scientific" management of society in accordance with communist ideals. There is considerable scope for the application of cybernetics in physiological development and programmed learning. Cybernetic machines can be used on a mass scale to aid teaching, training, and the cultivation of "communist consciousness" in order to condition workers to contribute their utmost to society without having to be prodded by material incentives.[58]

If high levels of per capita national income are reached, the distribution of personal income "according to needs" is feasible. In fact even now what is known as "social consumption" (provided by society free or at nominal charges, below cost) represents at least 15-30 percent of total consumption in the different Comecon countries.[59] These proportions may rise to more than 50 percent in the future. Higher levels of consumption and shorter hours of work may improve social attitudes to work. Work itself is likely to become more interesting and satisfying so that workers may become more responsive to moral motivation.

*A Classless Society.* The complete socialization of the means of production and distribution "according to needs" (and not "according to work") may eliminate the economic basis for social stratification. The rehabilitation and industrialization of agriculture may reduce the differences between rural and urban workers with regard to skills, income, and social prestige. The rising levels of general and vocational education on the one hand, and the disappearance of heavy manual work due to widespread mechanization and automation on the other hand, will contribute to the elimination of social differences between physical and mental labor. In some respects, automation is likely to lead to a new, more egalitarian structure of occupations—from the present conventional pyramid-shaped pattern (with a relatively large number of unskilled and semi-skilled workers at the bottom) to an onion-shaped structure, more closely corresponding to the distribution of abilities in the population.[60]

A new type of occupational stratification may emerge, however—a highly skilled elite of scientists, engineers, and technocrats on the one hand, and the common push-button operators on the other hand. Moreover, some forms of production will lend themselves better to automation, and some not at all—so that the stratification may be further accentuated on an industrial basis. Such developments may lead to new sources of social tension, which is recognized by some socialist writers.[61]

*The "Withering Away" of the State.* The extent to which technological progress can contribute to the phasing out of the state is not clear, but at any rate this question can arise only in the distant future (a precondition for which would be the disappearance of capitalist states). On the one hand, it appears that to accelerate or sustain technological progress in the higher states of economic development it is highly desirable for the state to shed some of its powers (exercised by the State Planning Commission) in favor of decentralization and considerable freedom of initiative at the operational level. The departures from the directive and centralized system of planning and management in favor of a greater independence and responsibility of enterprises, as a result of the economic reforms since the early 1960s, may be looked upon as a move toward the "withering away" of the state. Similarly, cooperation under Comecon and the Warsaw Pact may also be viewed as steps which in effect reduce the power of national states in favor of collective authority.[62]

On the other hand, it is difficult to envisage the elimination of the market mechanism without the retention of central economic planning. The successes being chalked up by the German Democratic Republic suggest that directive centralized planning and management is compatible with a technologically advanced economy. Indeed, it may be argued that central planning, to produce its best results, is more suited to the higher stages of economic development with a well-developed, competent administrative apparatus and system of information. In fact, cybernation and automation may not only facilitate centralized planning and management but in turn the latter may be necessary to maintain a unified nationwide system of information, to promote automation along socially optimal lines, and to take responsibility for the "scientific management of society" in general.

In conclusion, it may also be added that the extent to which the cybernation and automation of the socialist economies can be advanced is far from clear at present. The Comecon countries have been lagging in computerization and the lag behind the leading capitalist countries is in some respects increasing.[63] The advantages of socialism for planned, orderly, nationwide cybernation and automation belong more to theory than practice. Past experience provided evidence of the amazing lack of forward planning, coordination, and clear overall responsibility in these fields where central planning could be expected to demonstrate its superiority. Thus in the USSR bitter struggles behind the scenes are known to have raged between the *Gosplan*, the Central Statistical Office, and various ministries and research institutes, concerning the basis of development and control of the information system and automation—with some deplorable results.[64]

It now appears doubtful if a complete centralized system of information is either feasible or desirable. V. Glushkov himself pointed out in 1971: "Contrary to what some people believe, there is no centralized organ [in the USSR] commanding the totality of economic information, and in fact it will never exist."[65] The actual extent of automation achieved in the socialist countries so far is small, and its progress is likely to be slow in the future. Surprisingly large proportions of labor are still employed in work which is not even mechanized. A visitor to these countries is struck by the large number of workers on building sites still using pick and shovel, and in some cases even women performing manual labor. The proportion of labor working without mechanical means—as recently reported in socialist sources—is 34 percent in the East German industry,[66] 45 percent in Polish industry,[67] 55 percent in the Soviet machine-building and metalworking industries,[68] and as high as 86 percent in the loading and unloading of coal in Bulgarian mines.[69] Automation will continue in many cases to be uneconomic considering the relatively low level of wages and abundant labor.

The rise of the standard of living in the Comecon countries has been slow and the capacity for a rapid growth of efficiency of the socialist economy remains yet to be demonstrated. Although the economic reforms have arrested the decline in the rates of economic growth, they amount to "creeping capitalism," and ideologically they represent a retreat on the road to full communism. Several "birthmarks of capitalism," instead of fading away, have reappeared and have been officially embraced in the interest of economic progress. If they are eliminated in the higher phase of communism, one wonders if it will be possible to sustain high levels of productivity to enable all-round affluence, and avoid stagnation of the type that prevailed in the early 1960s. If, on the other hand, capitalist devices are retained as permanent features, then the system will not be in the image of Marxian full communism.

The author has recently widely discussed the question of the transition to communism with workers, technocrats, and intellectuals in all the European socialist countries. It was surprising to find that most workers either did not know what it was all about, or otherwise cared little. A Hungarian technocrat told the author: "I do not think full communism would ever work in a country like Hungary," and a Soviet intellectual commented: "Examining developments in the West, in particular in such countries as Sweden and New Zealand, I wonder if you [in the West] will not unwittingly arrive at several Marxian ideals earlier than we will—via the back door, quietly, without fuss and in a more humane way."

## NOTES

1. N. Wiener, *Cybernetics or Control and Communication in the Animal and the Machine* (Cambridge, Mass.: M.I.T. Press, 1948).

2. Feedback plays a basic role in automatic steering and it consists in sending signals from the "exit" (output) of the equipment to its "entry" (input), designed to regulate the process according to the required standards of output. A positive feedback is meant to maintain the continuity of operation, while a negative one is concerned with "intervention" in the case of irregularity in order to prevent or remove its effects.

3. This paper is specifically concerned with the European socialist countries which belong to the Council for Mutual Economic Assistance (Comecon) and have embarked on far-reaching economic reforms since the early 1960s, *viz.*, Bulgaria, Czechoslovakia, the German Democratic Republic, Hungary, Poland, Romania, and the USSR.

4. A servomechanism is a type of steering mechanism operating on the basis of integrated circuits and thus it can be self-regulating; it contrasts with an open circuits control, where steering amounts to merely switching on and off, and it is unable to correct irregularities automatically. A servomechanism embodies three essential elements: (a) instruments for the measurement of what is required to be performed and what is being accomplished; (b) an apparatus for transmitting these measurements between the remotely located command (the "low-power" device) and the control (the "high-power" device) and for establishing their difference; and (c) a means of amplifying the difference signals and using them to control a large

amount of power (with the aid of electrical, electronic, hydraulic, mechanical, optical, pneumatic, thermal, or similar devices).

5. K. Marx, *Critique of the Gotha Program;* K. Marx and F. Engels, *The Communist Manifesto;* V. I. Lenin, *The State and Revolution.*

6. M. Rozental and P. Yudin, eds., *Kratkii filosofskii slovar* [A concise dictionary of philosophy](Moscow: GIPL, 1954), pp. 236-237.

7. I. Akchurin, ["Mathematization of Knowledge and Dialectical Materialism"] *Kommunist* (Moscow) no. 2 (1968):48.

8. *The Road to Communism*, Documents of the 22nd Congress of the CPSU (Moscow: FLPH, 1961), p. 187.

9. Ibid., p. 518. For some of the earlier Western discussions of the socialist attitudes to cybernetics which focused on philosophical questions, see L. Kerschner, "Cybernetics: Key to the Future?" *Problems of Communism* (November-December 1965):56-66; also, C. Olgin, "Soviet Ideology and Cybernetics," *Bulletin* (Munich) no. 2 (1962):3-19 and no. 6 (1962):3-19; and his other articles: "Science, Ideology and Cybernetics in the USSR," *Bulletin* no. 7 (1966):3-18, "Speculative Cybernetics," *Bulletin* no. 8 (1966):3-17, and Cybernetics and the Political Economy of Communism," *Bulletin* no. 10 (1966):3-21.

10. G. Klaus, ["Cybernetics and the Class Struggle"], *Einheit* [Unity] (East Berlin) no. 9 (1970):1180, 1187.

11. B. Kedrov, S. Mikulinskii, and I. Frolov, ["Philosophical and Sociological Problems of the Scientific and Technical Revolution"], *Kommunist* no. 4 (1971):75; I. Sokolov, ["The Scientific and Technical Upheaval and the Revolutionary Process"], *Voprosy filosofii* [Problems of Philosophy] (Moscow) no. 4 (1971):23.

12. R. Chwieduk, *Warunki efektywnego zastosowania automatyzacji w przemyśle* [Conditions of the effective application of automation in industry] (Warsaw: PWE, 1970), p. 87.

13. *Tekhnologiya i organizatsiya proizvodstva* [Technology and organization of production] (Kiev) no. 3 (1971), p. 1.

14. It is an abbreviation for the Russian "Unified System of Data Processing." The names of different models in this series are prefixed with *R* (or sometimes with *ES*).

15. *Magyarország* (Budapest, December 3, 1972):9-10.

16. *Electronic Data Processing in the Soviet Union and Other East European Countries* (Brussels: East-West, 1972), pp. 10, 29.

17. *Problemy nauki i techniki a rozwój gospodarczy* [Problems of science and technology and economic development] (Warsaw, May 1972), p. 50; *Rynki zagraniczne* [Foreign markets] (Warsaw, September 30, 1971), p. 1; *Svět hospodárství* [World economy](Prague, August 7, 1970), p. 2; *Współpraca ekonomiczna z zagranica* [Economic cooperation with foreign countries](Warsaw, October 15-21, 1972), pp. AV-AVI.

18. N. Fedorenko, ["Scientific and Technical Revolution and Management"], *Novyi mir* [New world](Moscow) no. 10 (1970), p. 159.

19. S. M. Yampolskii, F. M. Khilnik, and V. A. Lisichkin, *Problemy nauchno-tekhnicheskogo prognozirovaniya* [Problems of scientific and technical projections](Moscow: Ekonomika, 1969), p. 116.

20. A. Bodnar and B. Zahn, *Rewolucja naukowo-techniczna a socjalizm* [Scientific and technical revolution and socialism](Warsaw: KiW, 1971), p. 57.

21. *Izvestiya* (Moscow), July 10, 1966, p. 5.

22. *Vecherni noviny* [Evening news](Sofia), May 13, 1972, pp. 1, 2; *Życie gospodarcze* [Economic life](Warsaw), April 25, 1971, p. 10.

23. *Życie gospodarcze*, May 28, 1972, p. 9.

24. *Muncă* [Work] (Bucharest); April 22, 1972, p. 5; *Probleme economice* [Problems of economics](Bucharest) no. 12 (1972):53.

25. *Soviet News Bulletin*, Soviet Embassy in Canberra, January 31, 1972, p. 6.

26. *Trybuna ludu* [People's tribune](Warsaw), Sept. 11, 1972, p. 2.

27. *Novo vreme* [New Times](Sofia) no. 7 (1971), p. 21.

28. *Planovo stopanstvo* [Planned economy](Sofia) no. 3 (1972), p. 22.

29. The highest degree of automation in 1971 was found in metallurgy–41.2 percent (the percentage represented by advanced automation was 4.5); light industry–39.6 (5.8) percent; the chemical industry–39.2 (8.0) percent; electrical engineering–39.1 (12.5) percent; the textile industry–37.4 (7.7) percent; and fuel and power–36.3 (11.9) percent. *Statistische Praxis* [Statistical practice](East Berlin) no. 1 (1973):38.

30. Ibid., p. 39.

31. The proportions were highest in the following branches: printing–67.5 percent (the percentage represented by advanced automation was 2.4); the paper industry–59.9 (0.1) percent; the chemical industry–48.2 (0.5) percent; and metallurgy–39.4 (1.3) percent. *Figyelö* [Economic observer] (Budapest), January 17, 1973, p. 6.

32. H. Król, *Postep techniczny a kwalifikacje* [Technical progress and skills] (Warsaw: KiW, 1970), p. 46.

33. R. Chwieduk, *Warunki efektywnego zastosowania*, p. 57.

34. *Życie gospodarcze*, July 27, 1969, p. 3.

35. The proportions in the following branches of industry in 1965, 1970, and 1975 (planned), in this order, were: the chemical industry–10, 13, and 15 percent; ferrous metallurgy–7, 11, and 15 percent; the cement industry–5, 8, and 11 percent; and electric power–4, 6, and 8 percent. *Viata economica* [Economic life](Bucharest) June 20, 1969, p. 6.

36. *Muncă*, April 22, 1972, p. 5.

37. Chwieduk, *Warunki efektywnego zastosowania*, p. 48.

38. Automation was carried out in two departments where there are four automatic production lines, each consisting of five sections–turning, tempering, polishing, fitting, and packing. All the operations, from metalworking to packing the completed product, are automatically carried out by machines according to set programs. The employees' tasks in the production process are concerned only with supplying the machines with raw materials (steel pipes and steel rods), the preparation of machinery, the changing of tools, repairs, and the supervision of technological processes. Automation led to a reduction of labor costs by 50 percent and the doubling of output. Nevertheless, the overall economic results have proved disappointing. Production costs in the automated part of the factory are 20 percent higher than in the non-automated part, or in other non-automated factories producing the same type of products. R. Chwieduk, *Warunki efekywnego zastosowania*, pp. 272-273.

39. *Życie gospodarcze*, February 27, 1972, p. 11.

40. *Życie gospodarcze*, May 14, 1972, p. 11.

41. *The Road to Communism*, p. 512.

42. One of the declared objectives of Comecon is: "to assist in the industrial-

ization and the gradual evening out of the historically created differences in the economic development of the socialist countries, to aid in constructing the material base so as to enable these countries to enter full communism within one historical period at about the same time." Anna Roslan, ed., *Rada Wzajemnej Pomocy Gospodarczej. Wybór materialów i dokumentów* [Council for mutual economic assistance. Selected reports and documents](Warsaw: KiW, 1964), p. 159.

43. Taking the Comecon region as a whole, the average annual rate of growth of national income, even as conceded in socialist sources, fell from 10 percent in the 1950s to about half that figure in the early 1960s, and in some countries (*viz.*, Czechoslovakia and the German Democratic Republic) to about a quarter. Although the rates have recovered since, they have not generally exceeded three-quarters of the levels in the 1950s. N. V. Faddeiev, *Soviet Ekonomicheskoi Vzaimpomoshchi* [Council for mutual economic assistance](Moscow: Ekonomika, 1969), p. 237; *Rocznik statystycznyy 1971* [Statistical yearbook 1971] (Warsaw: Central Statistical Office of Poland, 1971), p. 659.

44. *The Road to Communism*, p. 512.

45. It was conceded in an official Soviet source that in 1970 the national income of the USSR (brought to a Western basis) was 65 percent of the U.S. total, and the per capita income only 55 percent of the U.S. figure. *Narodnoe khoziaistvo SSSR v 1970 g.* [National economy of the USSR in 1970](Moscow: Statistika, 1971), pp. 82, 85.

46. E. A. G. Robinson, ed., *Problems in Economic Development* (Proceedings of a conference held by the International Economic Association) (London: Macmillan, 1965), p. 68.

47. *Narodnoe khoziaistvo SSSR v 1970 g.*, p. 59.

48. J. Wilczynski, *Socialist Economic Development and Reforms* (New York: Praeger, 1972), p. 338.

49. See, for example, A. Butenko, ["On the Developed Socialist Society"] *Kommunist* no. 6 (1972):48-58.

50. *Peace, Freedom and Socialism* (Prague) no. 12 (1970), p. 25.

51. Jolanta Kulpińska, ["Industrial Enterprise in the Year 2000"], *Życie gospodarcze*, May 27, 1973, p. 8.

52. For example, in Poland, private farms average 5 hectares (12 acres); one-third of the farms are less than 2 hectares (5 acres) in size. *Rocznik statystyczny 1971*, pp. 275, 289.

53. There has been a strong tendency even for socialized farms to increase in size in recent years. Thus in Hungary between 1960 and 1970 the average size of collective farms increased from 574 to 1,144 hectares and of state farms from 1,963 to 3,344 hectares (and the total number of farms fell from 5,500 to 2,980). *Statisticheskii ezhegodnik stran-chlenov Soveta Ekonomicheskoi Vzaimpomoshchi 1971*, pp. 269-275.

54. In Poland in 1969, for example, there were 285,000 private farms (out of the total of 3,400,000) which nobody wanted to inherit and work on. *Rocznik statystyczny 1971*, p. 289; *Życie gospodarcze*, September 21, 1969, p. 11.

55. A Polish economist, analyzing recent trends in the re-activation of money and other financial instruments in the Comecon countries as a result of economic reforms, concluded: "Who knows, if–in the light of these developments–the theoretical assumption of the abolition of money with the transition to full communism is tenable. Perhaps not all paths leading to communism must deviate from money." Z. Grabowski, ["Money Today"], *Życie gospodarcze*, December 4, 1968, p. 2.

56. O. Lange, "On the Economic Theory of Socialism," *Review of Economic Studies* 4 (1936/67):33-71 and 123-142; O. Lange and F. M. Taylor, "Trial and Error in a Socialist Economy," in *On the Economic Theory of Socialism*, ed. B. E. Lippincott (Minneapolis: University of Minnesota Press, 1938), pp. 72-83; O. Lange, ["Computer and the Market"], *Życie gospodarcze*, Oct. 24, 1965, and his book (translated into English), *Optimal Decisions* (Oxford: Pergamon, 1971).

57. K. Kraus, ["Direction Cybernetics"],*Życie gospodarcze*, July 25, 1971, p. 11.

58. By this token, socialist cyberneticians reject the views put forward by some Western thinkers that man today has created such powerful and uncontrollable technical, economic, and social forces that with fatal inevitability they escape his control and can bring mankind to a tragic end. I. Akchurin, [ "Mathematization of Knowledge" ].

59. R. Krzyżewski, *Konsumpcja społeczna w gospodarce socjalistycznej* [Social consumption in a socialist economy] (Warsaw: PWE, 1968), pp. 116-120.

60. A similar development is also anticipated in capitalist countries as a consequence of automation. See, e.g., P. Sadler, "Social Implications of Automation," *Proceedings of The Institution of Mechanical Engineers: Automatic Control Group* (London, 1972) 186 (no. 12):144-145.

61. Jolanta Kulpińska, ["Industrial Enterprise"], p. 8.

62. There have been attempts to establish a supra-national authority under Comecon. As early as 1959 N. S. Khrushchev stated in Leipzig: "As to the future, it appears to me that further progress in the socialist countries will lead to the formation of a single socialist economic system. The barriers which separated our economies under capitalism will gradually disappear. . .making national frontiers pointless." (*Pravda*, March 27, 1959, p. 2.) A move in this direction was made in 1963 when Khrushchev endeavored to vest the Executive Committee of Comecon with supra-national powers. However, owing to the opposition of Romania, supported by other East European countries, this proposal was not accepted. But efforts along these lines are likely to be repeated in the future and may be more successful as closer economic integration could produce several benefits of long-run consequence (greater national specialization, the extension of the scale of production, and a higher productivity of the Comecon community as a whole).

63. See *Electronic Data Processing in the Soviet Union and Other East European Countries*, pp. 10-12.

64. Kathryn M. Bartol, "Soviet Computer Centres: Network or Tangle?" *Soviet Studies* 23 (1972):608-618.

65. V. Glushkov, ["All-Union Automated System of Management"], *Pravda*, Oct. 28, 1971, p. 3.

66. *Statistische Praxis*, no. 1 (1973):219.

67. H. Król, *Postep techniczny*, p. 64.

68. *Voprosy ekonomiki* [Problems of economics] (Moscow) no. 2 (1971), p. 81.

69. *Novo vreme* [New Times] (Sofia) no. 7 (1971), p. 21.

PART FOUR

# SUMMARY

# 16

# Comparing Socialist Systems: Ends and Results*

Paul Hollander

Beginning the last chapter of this book with questions and reminders about the fundamental objectives of the comparative enterprise is not to suggest that an awareness of them was missing from the preceding contributions. Rather, I feel that a more general discussion of this nature is a useful exercise for all of us engaged in comparative ventures and may help to refocus and sharpen our basic concerns, which at times become submerged in the more narrowly defined tasks we assign to ourselves and the preoccupations which follow from our specialized interests and qualifications. The remarks which follow may also fruitfully supplement the contents of a volume which was, after all, designed to present primarily the methodological issues related to the comparison of socialist societies. Thus in these final comments it might be fruitful to ask one more *why* we compare different societies and why socialist ones in particular?

Some of the answers are among those cliches which happen to be true. The most obvious is that comparison is a basic thought process inseparable from both understanding and evaluation. It takes place constantly in our minds whether or not we are engaged in some social scientific endeavor, explicitly as well as by implication, with and without self-conscious intent. No serious social scientific undertaking can proceed without comparing various aspects of social reality—specific institutions, processes, events, or entire societies. Nor can theoretical generalizations and propositions be produced without comparison, and the relationship between the unique and the general be examined

*I am taking here the position that, at least from an ideal typical standpoint, socialist societies are non-pluralistic, or less pluralistic than Western, democratic societies with a mixed or capitalist economy. I am of course aware that many contributors would question this and that of late it has become more widely believed that socialist societies contain many pluralistic elements or tendencies, while Western ones are less pluralistic than it was earlier assumed.

and established. All this is fairly obvious, and comparative studies certainly do not need defense and justification since few social scientists would question their importance. Nevertheless, the actual number of such studies is hardly commensurate with the recognition of their importance.

All these considerations apply to the comparative study of socialist societies but some additional reasons can be found which further enhance their utility.

First of all, we know less about most socialist systems than about non-socialist ones, especially if comparison is made with the capitalist-pluralistic types.* This is so both because the social sciences have developed more recently in socialist societies and because information-gathering remains limited in the socialist countries concerned. Thus the comparative study of socialist societies can be viewed as a part of the more general striving for more information about them and for a better understanding of their major characteristics.

Comparing and thus better understanding socialist societies also offers the additional benefit of a better understanding, appreciation, or more informed criticism, as the case may be, of our own Western societies. Thus, for example, by learning more about the advantages and disadvantages of the economic institutions of socialist societies—which, after all, are the major determinants of their being called "socialist"—we can make more reasoned judgments about the efficiency and inefficiency of Western capitalist and mixed economic systems.

Among the socialist systems the East European ones exercised a particular attraction for American social scientists in the last decade or so, because their development (with some notable exceptions) confirmed to some degree the hopes of the evolution of socialist systems in a direction appealing to Western liberal or social democratic sensibilities. These countries provided examples of welcome forms of deviation from the Soviet model: some experimentation in the economic field, greater freedom of expression, incipient pluralism, and more diversity in domestic policies. Moreover, they also offered a theoretical challenge to Western social scientists since the transformations of their political structures provided evidence of the limited usefulness of the totalitarian model which had prevailed earlier. At the same time much disagreement remains among scholars pursuing new models and theories as to the most appropriate and fruitful classification and conceptualization of such systems. This state of affairs is also reflected in the wide variety of terms used to describe them and found in this volume. Mesa-Lago observed the proliferation of such concepts in his essay, which included the following groups: command, statist, administrative, bureaucratic, centrally planned; mobilization, communal, leftist, orthodox; market socialist, rightist, reformist, decentralized (p. 95). The title of this volume, "Comparative *Socialist* Systems," is a reflection of the persisting difficulties in providing a satisfactory label to such countries, since designating them as "socialist" is open to questioning and contradicts some implications of the term.

A closer scrutiny of the essays in this volume suggests interesting aspects of the current state of scholarship on socialist systems. Although neither the disciplinary affiliation of the authors nor the particular topics included can be taken as necessarily representative of the field as a whole, the patterns revealed by the contents of this volume are not totally accidental and do reflect certain trends in the scholarship concerned with socialist systems. It must be stressed again that the design of the volume encouraged methodological concerns and interests which in turn influenced the selection of the authors, all of whom (except for this writer) are either economists or political scientists. Perhaps it should be no surprise that there were no historians included, given the lesser interest of historians in methodological issues, and that likewise there were no anthropologists, since they generally do not study complex modern societies. Somewhat more surprising, though not altogether startling, is the absence of sociologists (other than this writer), who more often contemplate social systems in toto and occasionally try to compare them. Still, not many of them bring such studies to fruition. In any event, the combination of interest in socialist systems, comparative studies in general, *and* methodology is certainly not widespread among American sociologists. Thus the preponderance of economists and political scientists among the contributors is, on the whole, probably a fair reflection of the degree of interest social scientists in different disciplines evince in socialist systems and particularly in the methodological problems raised by their comparative study. Such a selective representation of the various disciplines in the comparative study of socialist systems has considerable implications for what we know and hope to learn about them, about the topics investigated or left unexplored, and questions raised or neglected. This somewhat uneven development of the field of comparative socialist systems is reflected not only in this volume but elsewhere as well. I will return to this issue later.

The choice of specific topics has of course been determined both by the objectives of the volume and the specific interests and competences of the contributors. Thus it is hardly surprising that four essays (those dealing with indicators, classifications, typology, and continuum model and written by Shoup, Montias, Welsh, and Mesa-Lago respectively) are addressed explicitly to the methodology and strategy of the comparisons. Somewhat less self-evident is the high proportion of chapters focused on economics or economically related topics (seven out of thirteen, excluding the introduction and conclusion). This may be explained in part by the fact that concern with methodological refinements and rigor is more widely found among economists than other groups of social scientists. The net result of such a distribution of specialties and expertise is that many important topics are not covered or even touched upon. This is not to suggest that a single volume such as this (or one of comparable length) could address itself to all important issues pertaining to the comparison of socialist systems.

It is also noteworthy that *outside* the topics related to economics, very few substantive problems or institutions are dealt with. The few included are political liberalization (Korbonski), bureaucracy (Cocks), and political change (Triska and Johnson). The rest of the essays either fall into the group of strictly methodological discussions (mentioned above) or of economics (i.e., five-year plans, property rights, industrial organization, foreign trade, cybernetics, and automation).

The contributors could also be divided, in addition to their discipline and the particular topics, between those who compare (specific institutions or problems) and those who discuss ways of comparing, though in some instances these orientations merge. Perhaps this is a distinction that separates methodologists from those interested in substantive problem areas.

Another difficulty inherent in a volume comparing socialist systems is that there are many of them (thirteen is the figure usually referred to by the contributors) and few scholars can possibly be familiar with all or most of them. This means that in practice actual comparisons will be limited, at any rate in the framework of any single essay. Nobody can discourse knowledgeably on, say, crime, or economic controls, or political institutions in the USSR, North Korea, Albania, Yugoslavia, etc. In most cases experts fall into one of three major groups of specialization on socialist systems. They are either 1) Sovietologists, 2) Sinologists, or 3) students of one (or sometimes more than one) East European country. The handful of scholars who study Albania, North Korea, and North Vietnam or Mongolia hardly merit the designation of "group." Nor is scholarship on Cuba intensively cultivated. Sometimes there is an overlap between specialists on the USSR and some country of East Europe but there are virtually no experts on both the USSR and China, or on China and East Europe, or the five "residual" countries mentioned *and* either the USSR or China. For such (and some other) reasons the comparisons are uneven; some of the contributors compare (or make some reference to) all socialist countries, others only to the USSR and East Europe. Often the length and depth of such references and concerns is, understandably enough, quite asymmetrical.

Since East Europe features most prominently of all the areas discussed in this volume, with four essays explicitly dealing with it and several others devoting large amounts of space to it, it may be appropriate to comment here on what appears a resurgent interest in the types of socialism manifest in East Europe.[1]

First to be noted is that social scientific interest in East Europe has been largely independent of corresponding interest in the Soviet Union. In the heyday of Soviet area studies not much was said and written about East Europe, but it seems that as the interest in the Soviet system waned some of it was transferred to East Europe. The decline in concern with the USSR has been reflected, among other things, in the much lamented decrease in financial support for research in the Soviet area, in falling course enrollments, and fewer research projects undertaken. This is somewhat paradoxical on at least two counts. First, such developments took place when Soviet society has become more accessible and Soviet social scientists themselves began to provide more information about their own society, and secondly, it coincided with Soviet society losing some of its unappealing, repressive characteristics.

One explanation of the new-found interest in East Europe might be that it has coincided with the decline of the total Soviet domination of the area (with the exception of Yugoslavia, which has been free of such domination since 1948). While earlier the tight control of and the attendant wholesale transplantation of Soviet institutions to East Europe might have made the countries concerned look like mere replicas of the Soviet Union, beginning with the late 1950s this was no longer the case. Inasmuch as the East European countries used to be truly satellites of the Soviet Union, their social and political structures closely modelled on the Soviet, they stimulated little interest among researchers who could assume with some justification that whatever they learned about the Soviet Union, its institutions and policies, was readily applicable to East European societies as well, which therefore did not merit independent study.

By the same token, developments in the last two decades explain the resurgent interest in East Europe, and the East European varieties of socialism. Most importantly, it has become clear that East Europe is more than an undifferentiated appendage of the Soviet Union, even though Soviet influence in the area has not come to an end. To the extent that internal changes in the Soviet Union came to be reflected in lesser controls over East Europe, the historical differences between the Soviet Union and the countries of East Europe began to reemerge. A process of limited differentiation began, although the fundamentals of the institutional framework have not become significantly altered. In particular the principle of party control over all aspects of life and a foreign policy subservient to the Soviet[2] remained stable while many economic, social, and cultural policies started to diverge from the Soviet mode. As a result East Europe and its constituent parts have become a more interesting entity providing Western social scientists with new opportunities to observe and study the process of deviation from the Soviet model of socialism and in particular with versions of socialism which were politically and culturally more open and liberal and more experimental in the economic sphere.

Not only have East European systems succeeded in gradually differentiating themselves from their Soviet progenitor to become interesting objects of study in their own right, but their new appeal—as noted before—has much to do with the fact that the changes which took place were of a liberalizing nature. They have made the countries concerned more attractive for American social scientists by holding out once more the promise of the combination of greater social justice through socialist economic arrangements with some degree of political democracy or pluralism.

Last but not least, the degree of liberalization achieved in East Europe had significant enough consequences for the freedom to conduct social scientific research, both for natives and foreigners, although this has varied considerably from country to country and also fluctuated somewhat in time. Many American social scientists interested in studying socialist systems turned their attention to East Europe because they wished to cease being "armchair experts," to be more empirical and gain better access to data—a desire that could be more easily gratified in East Europe than in socialist countries elsewhere. Not only have the governments of most East European countries become more hospitable to social research, encouraging, for the first time in their history, the collection of data rather than defining social realities by ideological fiat; even actual field work for Western social scientists (as well as cooperative ventures between them and their East European colleagues) becomes possible at times.

These considerations applying primarily to the study of East Europe are among the factors conducive to a perspective on socialist systems which might be called optimistic-evolutionary and is much in evidence in this volume. The changes which have taken place in East Europe and to a lesser extent in the Soviet Union are the best-known, most conspicuous, and most promising of a more complex, diversified, and liberal form of socialism. If "socialism with a human face" was a possibility anywhere, East Europe (or some parts of it) might have appeared as its most likely location. The liberalizing changes have also coincided with economic development, that is, further industrialization and urbanization, as well as improvement in the educational attainments of the populations concerned. Such a confluence of economic and political change takes us back to the notion of evolutionary optimism virtually synonymous with modernization theory. The heart of modernization theory, to which most of the contributors seem to subscribe, is economic development. Motivated by the generalizing impulse, the contributors to this volume are looking more for similarities than differences among socialist systems and they are most likely to find them in the framework of modernization theory. Of course in the case of East Europe economic development cannot be treated, even by the most ardent believer in modernization, as the sole or major determinant of the systems concerned. As the contributors are well aware, Soviet policy toward Eastern Europe is another powerful determinant of the shape of the societies concerned, while both Soviet policy and economic development interact with the more unique historically derived qualities of each society.

It is the connections between the generalizing impulse and the evolutionary perspective which help explain the otherwise somewhat startling observation of Professor Korbonski—also illustrative of the major thrust of the current social scientific approach toward socialist systems, and East Europe in particular—according to which "the demise of the totalitarian model, accompanied by the growing availability of political, economic and social data, made the traditional distinction between 'communist' and 'non-communist' systems obsolete and redundant" (p. 192). What is implied here, is that distinctions between various social-political systems reduce to differences between stages of development.

While the viewpoint quoted (shared by some other contributors as well) bespeaks the intention to integrate the study of socialist systems more fully into the study of all political systems, or into what is judged to be the mainstream of Western political science, other authors find the study of socialist systems a useful corrective to the characteristic biases and preconceptions which prevail among many influential American political scientists. Again, East European states in particular provide welcome reminders of the fact that political change frequently has its origins in external rather than indigenous "within-system" sources. Thus Triska and Johnson note:

> Political change literature . . . posits political systems as sovereign masters of their own destiny. Earlier Almond, Dankwart Rustow, David Apter, Samuel Huntington, and Ronald Bruner and Gary Brewer are all concerned with political change in political systems as if they had no foreign environment . . . [whereas] the most significant variable in explaining political systems stability and change in East Europe is . . . Soviet security (pp. 277-278).

It should hardly be surprising that social scientists, such as those represented in this volume, committed to both improvements in methodology (techniques) and the development of ambitious theoretical generalizations, are also interested in prediction—the most hazardous of all intellectual exercises social scientists can undertake.

To the extent that these essays venture in the realm of prediction, their underlying message tends to be optimistic. Interestingly enough, this seems to be a part of a more general tendency among American social scientists who incline to more optimism in regard to the future of other societies than their own. It applies especially to the future of Soviet and East European societies and is warranted to some extent by certain facts of history which cannot be disputed, notably the relaxation of the terror which has gripped these regions for a long time. But such optimistic leanings are also influenced by the perspectives of modernization, which remain permeated by the nineteenth-century belief in progress. The ingredients of this outlook have been familiar enough, especially as applied to the Soviet Union between the late 1950s and the intervention in Czechoslovakia in 1968, which somewhat deflated the hopes of those who envisaged a unilinear progression from repressive to tolerant Soviet policies, foreign and domestic. In the modernization approach change and improvement are inextricably intertwined, change tending to mean change for the better.[3] Economic development creates pressures for political development which translate into democratization and the growth of pluralistic tendencies. The scheme is not far removed from Marxist economic determinism, though more complex, containing several intervening variables between economic development and political democracy. Most importantly, economic development, and industrialization in particular, are seen as a basically rational and benevolent process building on and at the same time multiplying scientific and administrative rationality. They are associated with the spread of education, which is both a precondition and a derivative of successful industrialization. Education, regardless of its substantive content, is further assumed to be a rational, liberating, and liberalizing force—that is to say, a modernizing force. It is suggested that an educated population will press increasingly for greater political participation and freedom. (Unfortunately, at times such participation is also viewed in unidimensional terms, whether it has any impact on political decision-making or not, whether it is a ritual of political mobilization designed to provide symbolic endorsement of elite policies or not.)

Another aspect of industrialization seen as conducive to democratizing trends is found in its contribution to raising the standards of living. People who consume more are more difficult to control, indoctrinate, mobilize, inflame, or misuse, they become more committed to the status quo, more apolitical, more unideological, less susceptible to demagogic manipulation, more aware of their real versus apparent, or officially alleged interests—so the argument runs. They have more to lose, in short. (Again, this line of reasoning fails to take adequate account of the disincentive created by such circumstances to participate in politics or promote social-political change when "rocking the boat" is becoming undesirable, an attitude which in turn can help to perpetuate an oppressive system.) Moreover, the structural complexity of a more advanced industrial society is also said to invite a different and more enlightened political approach. Decentralization in the economy becomes imperative for the achievement of greater efficiency and initiative in decision-making, and is expected to spread to the political sphere. A highly industrialized society is supposed to be under pressure to maintain or increase contacts with the world outside (since all such societies are becoming more and more interdependent) and this too in turn contributes to the erosion of ideological rigidities, blinders, and suspicions which isolation reinforced earlier. New models of consumption as well as of political freedom become more available and censorship over the mass media (e.g., over foreign radio broadcasts), becomes more relaxed. Thus industrialization creates not merely structural but also attitudinal changes and it raises expectations which exert pressures on the leadership to introduce more flexible policies in various realms of life. "Apolitical technocrats" and specialists become increasingly important and their roles and values further dilute the ideological commitments and objectives of such regimes. This may be a brief sketch of the assumptions and reasoning which underlie evolutionary optimism and the types of prediction of the future of socialist societies which seem most congenial to several contributors of this volume.

Having commented on some of the orientations and specific interests displayed in this collection, I will turn to a brief review of those aspects of the socialist societies compared which have been given little attention. This is not meant as a criticism of this volume, which was designed primarily to explore the methodological issues related to the comparison of socialist systems. This discussion is intended to follow the not altogether useless ritual of using available scholarly accomplishments as occasions for pointing to future research that may logically follow from them.

We may begin by noting that not much has been said about the core concept tying these societies (and essays) together, namely, "socialism." Few authors paused to ask what the concept means, or rather, what are its different meanings and usages, in or outside systems which call themselves "socialist." How many transformations has the concept gone through? How many kinds of socialism exist, implemented and imaginary? How far from, or close to, those of Marx and Lenin, are the current usages of the term?

Another major topic that has received hardly any attention is that of legitimacy, the entitlement to rule, the spontaneous popular support enjoyed by or withheld from the systems in question. Likewise little is said about possible measures to assess the degree of legitimacy such systems possess and their potential ranking based on the degree (or kind) of legitimacy.

On the whole it appears that the contributors, or most of them, assume that the regimes in question enjoy substantial legitimacy and therefore the matter needs little discussion or further exploration. But there may be other reasons too, not limited to this volume, which account for the neglect of the topic. First, there is the difficulty of assessing and measuring legitimacy. Even if scholars could agree on its indicators and measures, the research required for applying them could hardly be carried out in socialist societies. There is sufficient evidence to suggest that socialist regimes do not welcome the questioning, social scientific or otherwise, of their legitimacy and are intolerant of the slightest challenge to it. For the same reason Western research into the degree of legitimacy socialist systems possess is avoided because of the criticism it implies. Investigating and thus questioning the legitimacy of such systems by Western social scientists is likely to be seen as an unfriendly gesture equated with the revival of the cold war spirit. Needless to say such a response to the interest in legitimacy would also undercut other opportunities for research in the socialist countries concerned. Finally it is also possible that Alfred Meyer's hesitation to inquire into the legitimacy of East European socialist systems is shared by others. He wrote a few years ago: "At a time when the legitimacy of power in the leading nation of the Western world [the U.S.] appears to be shaken to its very foundation . . . and the country troubled by deepening cleavages—at such a time it somehow does not seem quite appropriate for an American . . . to inquire into the legitimacy of power in Eastern Europe."[4]

Although many students of socialist systems reject this position (as was made clear in rebuttals to Professor Meyer's discussion in the same volume), others may share it without being fully aware of it. In any event the lack of attention given to the question of legitimacy in socialist systems is not peculiar to this volume. While this omission is understandable both in the light of the methodological difficulties involved and the more subtle psychological ones alluded to, it remains one of the major gaps in the comparative study of socialist systems. This is regrettable since the study of legitimacy in socialist systems offers a point of departure for a better understanding, rather than wholesale rejection of the concept in general. I believe that the type of legitimacy socialist systems enjoy has yet to be adequately conceptualized even though it may apply to many non-socialist systems as well and may turn out to be the most widespread form of legitimacy. Such legitimacy is a hybrid comprising elements of acceptance and rejection, born out of the lack of alternatives. It rests on the fact that these systems have endured, that opposition to them has been made institutionally impossible and practically futile, and that traditions of popular participation in government have not been among the historical legacies of the areas and cultures in question. One may propose that socialist regimes (as many others) are legitimate by virtue of resigned acceptance rather than active endorsement on the part of the majorities of the populations involved; that they are neither actively opposed nor supported, either at the attitudinal or behavioral level. It may further be possible that they are sometimes seen as legitimate not for reasons derived from moral-ethical principles but because of a popular acceptance of the notion that might is right, that those who can tenaciously and resourcefully cling to power earned their right to do so—a notion very different from the Western conceptions of what constitutes the legitimation of political power.

Although the investigation and assessment of legitimacy indeed present great difficulties in every society, and especially socialist ones—which cannot even allow the questioning of its degree—I would like to suggest that the problem is not totally intractable, and propose a few general lines of inquiry that might be followed in comparing the legitimacy of socialist systems.

The first precondition for assessing and measuring legitimacy might be found in the presence or absence of institutionalized opportunities for criticizing, modifying, or altering the political system. If, and only when, such opportunities are available can we begin to assess the degree of support or acceptance any political system enjoys. Fearful and intolerant of criticism, a political system, like an individual, reveals its own profound sense of insecurity. But the intolerance of criticism is not in itself a sufficient proof of illegitimacy that should lead one to conclude that if tolerated, the floodgates of popular hostility would burst open and swamp the system.

If a political system allows itself to be criticized and its structures modified without violence, it will probably also allow more direct investigations of its legitimacy through opinion and attitude surveys and the population will less likely be intimidated or discouraged from responding to such attempts.

There are other more indirect though equally telling indicators of legitimacy. Among them is the size and differentiation of the coercive apparatus. Large and highly differentiated coercive institutions (police forces of various kinds concerned with political matters) are suggestive of a flawed sense of legitimacy, of the expectation of dissent, opposition, subversion—in short, of the forceful questioning of legitimacy. The actual and expected (or potential) contact between members of society and coercive agencies can be equally revealing, as are the popular conceptions and awareness of their activities. The freedom to travel abroad (and emigrate)—and thereby have the opportunity to "vote with one's feet"—is another useful indicator of the legitimacy and self-confidence of a political system. Measuring levels of intimidation among the population—especially as connected with free expression—might be another of the devices leading to assessments of legitimacy. Examples here are political jokes; the use of telephones for political conversation; the sharp distinction made between friends, acquaintances, and strangers in regard to such conversations; and the differentiation between public and private places when sensitive topics are broached. Attitudes toward state or public property could provide still further clues of the legitimacy of (and the related sense of identification with) the political system. Mass participation in public affairs and the degree of its voluntary or involuntary nature is yet another obvious indicator, although the difficulties of assessing voluntarism are hard to overestimate. Finally, there are the crises attendant to the obvious breakdown of legitimacy: strikes, riots, sabotage, armed rebellions—the whole gamut of political violence directed against the elites in power or the symbols of their power and legitimacy.[5] Mechanisms of political succession and their functioning supply further indirect information about the legitimacy of elite groups in power.

In concluding this discussion it should also be pointed out that the legitimacy of socialist (and not only socialist) systems is also connected with the degree to which the preservation of their political power depends on, or has been derived from, external sources. Hence at times what may be critical in judging the legitimacy of a political system is not so much its reliance (or potential reliance) on force, but rather the nature and kind of force involved. Calling in the troops to maintain order is one thing, but calling in those of a neighboring power is quite another. For such reasons one may propose that, for example, no matter how Stalinist the Albanian regime might have remained and how ruthlessly its internal security forces might repress any challenge to its legitimacy, it cannot count in a crisis on Soviet or Chinese or any other intervention to ward off threats to its survival—as opposed to most other regimes of East Europe.

Another set of problems which may usefully supplement comparisons in the area of legitimacy are those connected with nationalities and ethnic minorities in socialist systems. It is not hard to discern links between legitimacy and the position of such minorities. The extent to which they are represented, underrepresented, or excluded from the political decision-making process and deprived of the rewards of their society, their ratio in the general population—all these have considerable bearing on the legitimacy of the system involved. In ethnically homogeneous societies there is one threat fewer to legitimacy than in those which are heterogeneous and distribute power and material rewards unequally among different ethnic groups.

Although many socialist systems have made considerable efforts to equalize the position of such minorities, the record of their accomplishments has been mixed. Thus, few reasonably impartial observers could argue that in the USSR, Romania, or Yugoslavia the nationality problem has been solved once and for all. Future research should also be addressed to one of the most critical aspects of the nationality and ethnic problems, namely that of bias and prejudice, and the extent to which socialist systems, as compared with others, have succeeded in eradicating or controlling such sentiments and attitudes.

Another topic that may be included in future comparative research on social systems is the existence of social problems. It is hardly a secret that socialist systems, like capitalist ones, have an abundance of social problems, which include crime, juvenile delinquency, family instability, pollution, various forms of escapist behavior, the position of old people, and many others. Such problems constitute a dimension that can be applied not only to the comparison of socialist societies with one another, but also with non-socialist ones. Though the availability of data varies there is enough for meaningful comparisons, especially between industrially advanced socialist and non-socialist societies, and such comparisons could lead to theoretically significant generalizations. Even preliminary attempts in this direction suggest that the most striking similarities between highly industrialized and urbanized socialist and capitalist societies may well be found in the realm of social problems.[6]

At least two other important areas invite comparison and could throw further light on the nature of socialist systems. They are those of stratification and prevailing official and unofficial or popular beliefs. Concerning social stratification, there has been a steady accumulation of data from East Europe and the USSR (following the emergence of sociology as a legitimate discipline) but much less from the other socialist countries. This is a sensitive area of inquiry insofar as it may lead to findings calling into question the strides made toward the attainment of socio-economic equality. For this reason the available data are far from comprehensive, especially as they pertain to income distribution and access to privilege of a non-monetary nature (e.g., housing, travel, special shops, etc.).

The comparative study of beliefs and values, except those which are official and public, is still more difficult. What people truly believe in is hard to investigate in any society but particularly so in those which adhere to a well-defined and aggressively propagated official belief system, such as the versions of Marxism-Leninism prevailing in socialist societies. Yet a deeper understanding of such systems will be deficient as long as we do not and cannot investigate with some degree of freedom the genuine and privately held beliefs of their citizens and the relationships of these beliefs to those publicly professed.

Although this volume has not addressed itself to the comparison of socialist societies with non-socialist ones, it is hard to avoid some final reflections about the strength and weaknesses of the societies surveyed here compared with others. By "others" I mean those with a capitalist or mixed economy, high levels of pluralism, urbanization, and democratic political institutions, that is, more highly developed mechanisms for controlling the concentration of political power. If we take a look at such societies currently wallowing in a wide variety of crises, the socialist ones present an appearance that is at least superficially appealing. First of all they are, or seem to be, vastly more stable, whatever indicator of stability we take. In the lands of socialism governments rarely change, the police do not have to disperse rioters, workers do not go on strike, heads of states do not get assassinated. Prices of consumer goods and food do not soar (though they may be high to begin with, in relation to earnings). There is no inflation of serious proportions in socialist countries, although it is risky to make such sweeping statements about countries which range from Yugoslavia to the Soviet Union with significantly different economic structures. While in any objective, measurable sense living conditions in most socialist countries are less favorable than in the group of countries with which they are being contrasted here, deprivations are less keenly felt. This is so because conditions have not rapidly deteriorated but have been more or less stable and in many cases improved over time. In Western societies today economic difficulties erupted unexpectedly, sowing the seeds of anger, bewilderment, and frustration. The same could apply to the political sphere at some point in the future. Although in Western societies personal and group freedoms have not declined thus far, should they become more restricted, their absence would be more keenly felt. Again, by contrast, in socialist countries such freedoms have been always more circumscribed; hence their absence has been barely felt, or only by a few. The key factor in regard to all such issues—living standards, personal freedoms, and the variety of deprivations people suffer—lies in the realm of expectations, the mainstay of stability. Of course the relationship between relatively low expectations and stability is circular. Political stability is facilitated by low expectations, but stability in turn reinforces low expectations. When people have little reason to believe that change will be for the better, or that they can bring it about, they will be quiescent and passive. The few who are not, usually the dissident intellectuals, are viewed by the majority either as fools or troublemakers or at best, misguided idealists.

Let us take a closer look at some more specific factors which, interacting with the low level of expectations, are conducive to stability. Most of the socialist countries do not have a tradition of active or widespread popular participation in government, or self-government of local units. The countries in question developed and maintained strong and efficient coercive apparatuses and made a heavy initial investment in "revolutionary" terror, the lessons of which linger on for generations. In many of the countries there is a historical legacy of popular fatalism which has not been dispelled by the mobilization of the population for the performance of economic tasks or crash programs or by the rituals of political participation. In fact the type of participation, or more accurately, pseudo-participation, encouraged and indeed demanded by the leaders of many socialist societies is quite compatible with the traditional passive and fatalistic attitude toward politics present in many of these societies.

The stability of socialist societies is also connected, in more subtle ways, with this tradition of non-participation in politics. Such societies, being highly organized, significantly limit the choices individuals have and create a secure if circumscribed context in which personal responsibility for success and failure is more limited than in Western societies. Fewer choices mean fewer dilemmas, and narrower limits on personal achievement—in politics, money making, or social mobility. They also limit the sense of failure. Small gains in living conditions or personal freedoms are therefore doubly appreciated; any revolutionary rise in expectations is restrained by the determination of the political elite to hang on to power (and the means at its disposal to assure this). In the case of the smaller nations in areas contiguous with either the Soviet

Union or China, the ruling groups, unless they defy significantly the policies of the neighboring big power—can count on such external support should popular discontent emerge forcefully.[7] If expectations are low in the political realm it is not only because the vast majority are currently deprived of meaningful political participation. This state of affairs can also be accounted for by cumulative exclusion from political activities over generations by the unpleasant and at times bloody consequences of the attempts to challenge the powers-that-be, and the resulting pervasive disenchantment with politics that cannot be measured by abstention from voting, as it can in Western societies. This profound disenchantment means that people, including most intellectuals, are not tempted to seek salvation or personal fulfillment through politics, as some significant if small groups do in other parts of the world.

In the final analysis, comparing socialist systems is not fundamentally different from comparing non-socialist ones and doing so presents the scholar with problems and rewards similar to those which are generally encountered in comparative studies. To say this is not to belittle such still-pioneering efforts. Comparing socialist systems is more difficult from a methodological point of view because the study of such systems in general is relatively new (except in regard to the Soviet Union), the data are less abundant, the accumulated theoretical guidance more sparse, and there are few safe assumptions to build on. Yet basically the objectives of the enterprise are the same as those which guide any large-scale comparisons of societies. When we compare socialist systems, we do so because we wish to learn more about the basic patterns and regularities of social systems, find new data for enduring theoretical generalizations, and uncover the ways in which social institutions do or do not hang together and affect (or fail to affect) the lives of people. We also want through such studies to learn more about the sources and varieties of social change and try to build better foundations for the hazardous undertakings of prediction. More fundamental to all such endeavors is the desire to learn more about the ways in which various human collectivities, organizations, and institutions grapple with human frustration, satisfaction, and misery; about the interaction between social order and personal freedom; and the endless attempts to meet or evade the endemic problems of scarcity. As the saying goes, there is room for further research.

## NOTES

1. There are many expressions of such interest outside this volume, including a growing number of publications on East Europe, the increase in scholarly exchanges, the newsletter on sociology in East Europe, etc.

2. Yugoslavia, as always, is an exception to most of these remarks since both

its domestic and foreign policy have been largely free of Soviet control since 1948. Romanian foreign policy is another partial exception in that it has achieved a greater degree of independence than other countries of East Europe. Likewise Albania, allied with China, has excluded herself from the Soviet bloc while retaining rigid Stalinist domestic policies which might not have displeased the "hardliners" in the Soviet leadership.

3. For a recently published empirical study based on extensive survey research, which, by and large, reaffirms this association, see Alex Inkeles, *Becoming Modern: Individual Change in Six Developing Countries* (Cambridge: Harvard University Press, 1974).

4. Alfred Meyer, "Legitimacy of Power in East Central Europe," in S. Sinanian, I. Deak, and P. Ludz, eds., *Eastern Europe in the 1970s* (New York: Praeger, 1972), pp. 67-68.

5. It is worth noting the frequency with which crowds, hostile to a particular political system, burn flags and destroy public buildings, pictures, and statues of political leaders as soon as the opportunity presents itself.

6. For a comparative discussion of Soviet and American social problems see pp. 300-373 in Paul Hollander, *Soviet and American Society: A Comparison* (New York: Oxford University Press, 1973).

7. This would probably even apply to countries which enjoy greater autonomy and lesser satellite status, e.g., North Korea and North Vietnam. In the totally improbable event of such regimes being threatened by "non-socialist" forces, it is hard to imagine that China would stand by idly. The corresponding determination of the Soviet Union has of course been demonstrated on a number of occasions: in 1953 in East Germany, in 1956 in Hungary and Poland, and in 1968 in Czechoslovakia. Only Albania would be unprotected by such assistance should domestic discontent threaten the system, in view of its distance from China and the Soviet hostility toward the present regime.

# ABOUT THE CONTRIBUTORS

CARL BECK is professor of political science and sociology and director of the University Center for International Studies at the University of Pittsburgh. He is also executive director of the International Studies Association, chairman of the Pittsburgh Inter-University Program on Comparative Communism, and director of Pitt's Archive on Political Elites in Eastern Europe. Dr. Beck received his M.A. in political science from Pitt and the Ph.D. from Duke University and has studied at the University of Munich. He is the author of *Aggregate Career Characteristics of Eastern European Political Leaders* (1968); co-author of *Comparative Communist Leadership* (1972) and *Political Elites: A Select and Computerized Bibliography* (1968); editor of three books; and author of numerous chapters in books and of articles in *Comparative Political Studies, Journal of Politics, American Behavioral Scientist*, and *Social Science Information.*

RICHARD CARSON is associate professor of economics at Carleton University. He received an M.A. from the University of Minnesota and the Ph.D. in economics from Indiana University. Professor Carson is the author of *Comparative Economic Systems* (1973) and "The Convergence of Two Systems in Theory and Practice" (1971) and co-author of "Elements for a Theory of Systemic Change" (1971). He has contributed articles to *Western Economic Journal* and *Canadian Perspectives in Economics.*

PAUL COCKS is a research fellow at the Hoover Institution of War, Revolution and Peace and a lecturer at Stanford University. He holds M.A. degrees in both Soviet and East Asian studies and the Ph.D. in political science from Harvard University, where he has also taught. Dr. Cocks is the author of *Controlling Communist Bureaucracy: Ethics, Rationality and Terror* (forthcoming) and is completing a study on "The Scientific-Technological Revolution and Soviet Politics."

WILLIAM N. DUNN is associate professor at the Graduate School of Public and International Affairs, University of Pittsburgh. He received an M.A. and Ph.D. in government and international relations from Claremont Graduate School and University Center. Professor Dunn is the author of *Towards a Critical Administrative Theory* (1975); co-author of *Sociology of Participation: Theoretical and Empirical Contributions from Yugoslavia* (forthcoming); and the author of "The Economics of Organizational Ideology: The Problem of Compliance Structures in Workers' Management" (1973) and of articles in *Journal of Comparative Administration, Social and Economic Studies, Newsletter on Comparative Studies of Communism*, and *Latin American Research Review.*

FREDERIC J. FLERON, JR. is associate professor of political science at the State University of New York–Buffalo. He received his Ph.D. from Indiana University and has taught at the University of Kentucky. The chairman of the American Council of Learned Societies' Conference on Technology and Communist Culture, he was the editor of the *Newsletter on Comparative Studies of Communism*. Professor Fleron is co-author of *Comparative Communist Political Leadership* (1972); co-editor of *The Conduct of Soviet Foreign Policy* (1971); editor of *Communist Studies and the Social Sciences: Essays on Methodology and Empirical Theory* (1969); and has contributed articles to *The American Political Science Review, Polity, Comparative Politics, Soviet Studies,* and *Canadian Slavic Studies.*

STANISLAW GOMULKA is lecturer in economics at the London School of Economics and Political Science. He received an M.S. and the Ph.D. in economics from Warsaw University. Dr. Gomulka has taught at Warsaw University and the Aarkus University, Denmark, and has done research at the Ministry of Building and the Institute of Home Trade, Warsaw. He is the author of *Inventive Activity, Diffusion and the Stages of Economic Growth* (1971), "The Contribution of Labour, Capital and Technical Progress to the Polish Industrial Growth: 1950-1967" (1970), and of articles published in *Ekonomista, Review of Economic Studies, Journal of Economic Theory, Ekonomika i Matematicheskie Metody, Rivista di Politica Economica,* and *Bulletin of the Political Economy Department of Warsaw University.*

PAUL HOLLANDER is professor of sociology at the University of Massachusetts (Amherst) and an associate of the Russian Research Center at Harvard University. He obtained his Ph.D. from Princeton University and also studied at the London School of Economics. Professor Hollander is the author of *Soviet and American Society: A Comparison* (1973) and editor of *American and Soviet Society: A Reader in Comparative Sociology and Perception* (1969). He has in addition authored numerous articles on Soviet society, political sociology, and the sociology of knowledge.

PAUL M. JOHNSON is a Ph.D. candidate in political science at Stanford University where he also received an M.A. A former Woodrow Wilson Fellow and research assistant for Studies of the Communist System, Mr. Johnson has served as lecturer in the University of Maryland Overseas Extension Program.

ANDRZEJ KORBONSKI is a professor of political science, University of California–Los Angeles. He received an M.A. in economics and a Ph.D. in public law and government from Columbia University. Dr. Korbonski has also been a lecturer at City College of New York, a research associate at Columbia University, and a program officer at the Ford Foundation. He is the author of *Politics of Socialist Agriculture in Poland: 1945-1960* (1965) and *Polish National Income and Product: 1954-1956* (1965), of numerous chapters in books, and of articles in *Comparative Politics, Current History, Slavic Review, Journal of International Affairs,* and *Studies in Comparative Communism.*

PAUL MARER is associate professor of economics and director of the East Europe Program at Indiana University. He received both his M.A. and Ph.D. in economics from the University of Pennsylvania, has taught at City University of New York, and done research at Columbia. Professor Marer is the author of *Soviet and East European Foreign Trade, 1946-1969: Statistical Compendium and Guide* (1972), *Postwar Pricing and Price Patterns in Socialist Foreign Trade (1946-1971)* (1972), and *Selected Comparisons of the Financial Systems of the USSR, Czechoslovakia, Hungary and Poland* (1971); the co-editor of *Proceedings of the Conference on East-West Trade and Technology Transfer* (1974); the co-author of *Recent Developments in the Hungarian Financial System* (1971); and the author of numerous chapters in books and of articles in *The American Economic Review, Slavic Review, Soviet Studies, Communist Affairs, Studies in Comparative Communism, ASTE Bulletin,* and *East Europe.*

CARMELO MESA-LAGO is associate professor of economics at the University of Pittsburgh and directed the program "Methodological Comparison of Socialist Systems," which produced this book. He holds law degrees from the Universities of Havana and Madrid, an M.A. in economics from the University of Miami, and a Ph.D. from Cornell. He is the author of *Cuba in the 1970s: Pragmatism and Institutionalization* (1974), "A Continuum Model to Compare Socialist Systems Globally" (1973), "Unemployment in a Socialist Economy: The Case of Yugoslavia" (1971), and *The Labor Sector and Socialist Distribution in Cuba* (1968); and the editor of *Revolutionary Change in Cuba* (1971) and of the journal *Cuban Studies.* He has contributed articles to *Economic Development and Cultural Change, Journal of Economic Issues, Studies in Comparative International Development, El Trimestre Económico, Problems of Communism,* and others.

JOHN M. MONTIAS is professor of economics and chairman of the Council of Russian and East European Studies at Yale University. He received his M.A. and Ph.D. in economics from Columbia University and has worked for the United Nations. Professor Montias is the author of *Economic Development of Communist Rumania* (1967), *Central Planning in Poland* (1967), and "Types of Communist Economic Systems" (1970); co-author of "On the Description and Comparison of Economic Systems" (1971); and the author of articles in *American*

*Economic Review*, *Journal of Political Economy*, *Oxford Economics Papers*, *Review of Economic Studies*, *Foreign Affairs*, *Slavic Review*, and other scholarly journals.

FREDERIC L. PRYOR is professor of economics at Swarthmore College. He received his M.A. and Ph.D. in economics from Yale University, has served on the faculty of the University of Michigan and Yale University, and has had research appointments at the University of California–Berkeley and the University of Indiana. Professor Pryor is the author of *Property and Industrial Organization in Communist and Capitalist Nations* (1973), *Public Expenditures in Communist and Capitalist Nations* (1968), and *The Communist Foreign Trade System* (1963), plus numerous chapters in books and articles in scholarly journals.

PAUL S. SHOUP is associate professor of political science at the University of Virginia. He received his Ph.D. from Columbia University and previous to his current position taught at Kenyon College. Professor Shoup is the author of *Communism and the Yugoslav National Question* (1968), "Eastern Europe and the Soviet Union: Convergence and Divergence in Historical Perspective" (1974), "The National Question in the Political System of Eastern Europe" (1972), and of articles in *The American Political Science Review*, *Problems of Communism*, and *Slavic Review*.

JAN F. TRISKA is professor of political science, director of Studies of the Communist System, and associate chairman of the Institute of Political Studies at Stanford University. He has a J.U.D. from Charles University, LL.M. and J.S.D. degrees from Yale, and a Ph.D. in political science from Harvard. He has taught at Cornell and the University of California–Berkeley and done research at Harvard. Professor Triska is co-author of *Soviet Foreign Policy* (1968) and *The Theory, Law and Policy of Soviet Treaties* (1962); editor of *Communist Party-States: Comparative and International Studies* (1969), *Integration and Community Building Among Fourteen Communist Party-States* (1968), and *Constitutions of the Communist Party-States* (1968); and the author of several chapters in books and of articles in *The American Political Science Review*, *Review of Politics*, *World Politics*, *Journal of Conflict Resolution*, *Studies in Comparative Communism*, and *Problems of Communism*.

WILLIAM A. WELSH is professor of political science and chairman of the Computer Operations Committee at the University of Iowa. He received his Ph.D. from Northwestern University and previous to his current position held teaching or research positions at the Universities of Munich, Istanbul, and Georgia. Professor Welsh is co-author of

*Comparative Communist Political Leadership* (1973) and *A Methodological Primer for Political Scientists* (1969) and author of *Studying Politics* (1973) and *Leaders and Elites* (forthcoming). His articles have appeared in *Comparative Politics, The American Behavioral Scientist, Latin American Research Review,* and *Balkan Studies.* He is also the editor of the Praeger Basic Concepts in Political Science series.

JOZEF WILCZYNSKI is associate professor of economics at the Royal Military College, University of New South Wales, Australia. He holds an M.Ec. degree from Australian National University and a Ph.D. in economics from the University of London, has done research at the Central School of Planning and Statistics of Warsaw, and taught at the University of Pittsburgh. Professor Wilczynski is the author of *Technology in Comecon* (1974), *Profit, Risk and Incentives Under Socialist Economic Planning* (1973), *Socialist Economic Development and Reforms* (1972), *Towards Multilateral Payments in Comecon Foreign Trade* (1971), *The Economics of Socialism* (1970), and *The Economics and Politics of East-West Trade* (1969). His articles have appeared in American, Australian, British, German, Indian, Italian, Japanese, Kenyan, Malayan, and Norwegian journals.

PETER J. F. WILES is professor of Russian social and economic studies at the University of London. He completed his studies of politics and economics in England, has been a fellow at Oxford, a visiting professor at Brandeis University and City College of New York, and a research associate at the Institutet for Internationell Ekonomi of Stockholm. His list of numerous publications includes a classic, *The Political Economy of Communism* (1962), as well as *The Prediction of Communist Economic Performance* (1971) and *Communist International Economics* (1969). Professor Wiles' articles have been published all over the world and reprinted in several compilations.

# INDEX